RISING TO SECOND
FREEDOM

Enlightened Minds and Ignited Spirit

NIXON FERNANDO

INDIA • SINGAPORE • MALAYSIA

Notion Press

Old No. 38, New No. 6
McNichols Road, Chetpet
Chennai - 600 031

First Published by Notion Press 2018
Copyright © Nixon Fernando 2018
All Rights Reserved.

ISBN 978-1-64429-905-0

Contents

PART 1:
RETURN TO AN ANCIENT AND GLORIOUS TRYST

PART 2:
PANCHAYATI SWARAJ: FREEDOM AT THE DOORSTEP

PART 3:
TRANSITION TO REAL FREEDOM: THROUGH INSTITUTIONS BUILT ON RIGHTEOUSNESS

Summary

Filtering the perceptions
Interesting result

1.4 – GENUINE PRACTICAL HINDUISM IS THE GLOBAL ANSWER FOR PEACE
Hindu
Is Hinduism a religion?
Summarizing
A vision of oneness
Practical Hinduism
Some universal indices
Dharma
Motivators for action – the four *Purusharths*
Where it matters
The real fight
The issue of Kashmir
Ayodhya
The concept of Pakistan

SECTION II
THE MAKING OF MODERN INDIA AFTER SLIGHTING INDIGENOUS CONTENT

Can a nation prosper if it does not build on its indigenous strengths?

2.1 – A COLONIAL ADMINISTRATION: NOT DESIGNED TO NURTURE INDIGENOUS WISDOM
An administration subject to business interests
So also the people of the Raj
An alien character
How they went about it
The buffer classes came
Protection for the men of the system
The impact
Questionable legacy
Alternate benchmarks
A corrosive system

2.2 – HOW THE DESIGN OF THE INDIAN EDUCATION SYSTEM MISSED GREAT TREASURES
Education in India
Of degrees and vocational courses
What about values?
Irrelevant to daily life
Education is a business
Lack of indigenous content
A steal over a hereditary-based system
Limitations in terms of personality development

SECTION III
APPLIED SPIRITUALITY: RECONVERTING CASTEISM BACK INTO A BOON

This section deals with how deep the understanding of human nature and spirituality was eventually applied to Indian society...

Hierarchy of the yogas
Ascendency in what one stakes
How this notion got applied
Of Gods, Devas and Asuras
Of gunas, yogas, stakes and ego types
When a spiritualist says high or low
Elevated in spirit

3.7 – MYTHS CONCERNING THE ELEVATION OF THE LOWER CASTES

Myth 1: Wipe out the entre caste system and attempt to replace it with a uniform alternative, and it will solve the problem.
Myth 2: Education will lead to a casteless society.
Myth 3: Professional education and economic development will lead to a classless society.
Myth 4: There is poetic justice in lower castes being given power and authority today.
Myth 5: Reservation will lead to elevating castes.
Myth 6: The so-called lower castes have suffered for centuries, and that is why they are where they are now.
Myth 7: Emancipation of the lower castes is possible only if lower castes represent lower castes.
Myth 8: Intolerant shouting will lead to emancipation.
Myth 9: The constitution essentially calls for showering additional benefits on scheduled classes and tribes in order to treat them as equals in the spirit of the fundamental rights enshrined in the constitution.

3.8 – THIS IS A GREAT TIME TO RISE TOGETHER

The case for perpetuation has weakened
To dilute the impact of the rigidity of caste-consciousness
Know what it takes to rise
Freedom must happen in the mind first
Preserve self-dignity and build on indigenous strength
Am I compelled to be in the varna system?
For the faithful of today

APPENDIX

A: DETRACTORS WILL USE PASSIONATE SHOUTING

Victory will eventually happen on the side of truth.

B: PANDIT DEENDHAYAL UPADHYAYA'S VIEWS ON DHARMA

He speaks out from gut feeling as against reasoning on the basis of core ideals or basic principles. And he is quite on the mark.

C: NEED TO UPHOLD DHARMA (K. Subrahmanyam; as it appeared in The Speaking Tree: Times of India; 3rd Feb 2011)

Dharma is not immutable but is liable to change to be in consonance with changing times.

D: SWAMI VIVEKANANDA'S ADDRESS TO THE WORLD PARLIAMENT OF RELIGIONS: SEPTEMBER 1893

E: EVALUATING THE SPIRITUAL ATTRIBUTES OF A LEADER
Who should be our leader?

F: INTER-CASTE MARRIAGES
Designed in the context of patriarchy and level of wisdom

G: WHO IS WISE?
Some recommended indices

PART 2

**PANCHAYATI SWARAJ: FREEDOM AT THE DOORSTEP
DEDICATED TO
FR. AGNELO PINTO SJ,
FR. PATRICK D'LIMA SJ
AND
MY TEACHERS AT ST PAUL'S HIGH SCHOOL**

CONTENTS IN DETAIL

INTRODUCTION
AN IDEA WHOSE TIME HAS COME

The power of an idea
A simple idea, if it is really good, can achieve wonders
Conceiving a journey back to freedom

SECTION I
THE VISION

1.1 – THE VILLAGES OF INDIA IN THE EYES OF MAHATMA GANDHI
1.2 – MY GANDHIAN EDEN: HOME SWEET HOME
A story about a village that is experiencing freedom

1.3 – THE PURPOSE OF THE VISION AND THE STORY
From individual aims to team aims
Using a mind-science tool to present the vision in an acceptable form
How that story can be used

SECTION II
AN EXPOSE OF THE VISION

2.1 – THE SIX FREEDOMS THAT WILL LEAD TO THE GANDHIAN VISION

2.2 – FREEDOM 1: REVENUE ACCOUNTING
Accounting Freedom 1: Land Records:
Accounting Freedom 2: Taxes (a record of taxation and expenses)
Accounting Freedom 3: Scheme List
Accounting Freedom 4: Census

2.3 – FREEDOM 2: ECONOMIC
Economic Freedom 1: Adaptation and Integration
Economic Freedom 2: Employment
Economic Freedom 3: Financial
Economic Freedom 4: Technological
Economic Freedom 5: Resource Economization

2.4 – FREEDOM 3: CULTURAL
Cultural Freedom 1: Education
Cultural Freedom 2: Skill Sets
Cultural Freedom 3: Traditions
Cultural Freedom 4: Freedom in the Arts
Cultural Freedom 5: Spiritual

2.5 – FREEDOM 4: HEALTH
Health Freedom 1: Sports
Health Freedom 2: Health Care and Wellness
Health Freedom 3: Hygiene
Health Freedom 4: Nutrition
Health Freedom 5: Medical Care

2.6 – FREEDOM 5: GOVERNMENT
Governance Freedom 1: Legislative
Governance Freedom 2: Executive
Governance Freedom 3: Judicial
Governance Freedom 4: Integration

2.7 – FREEDOM 6: VISION
Vision Freedom 1: Environmental
Vision Freedom 2: Developmental
Vision Freedom 3: Contributory

2.8 – USING THE INDICES TO MOVE TOWARD SECOND FREEDOM
'So has my village achieved the six freedoms?'
A vision is the start
What is a project?
The challenges of moving from vision to project implementation
Village freedom mind map

What is the thought behind generating this village freedom mind map?

How to use this mind map and point in the direction of freedom

2.9 – PLAN OF ACTION FOR EACH VILLAGE

Step 1: Swaraj Seedling(s)

Step 2: Freedom Nursery

Step 2a: Freedom Nursery Presentation

Step 3: Village Freedom Council

Step 4: The NRV Meet

Step 5: The Village Swaraj Master Plan

A very critical reform required for the pursuit of swaraj

The important tax reform

A caution for tax reform

Our possessions belong to the brave who put their lives in the line of duty

SECTION III
THE NUANCES OF THE PURSUIT OF FREEDOM

3.1 – IDEA 1: THE CONNECTION BETWEEN DECENTRALIZATION AND SUCCESSFUL KINGDOMS

What is the difference between magisterial duties and judicial duties?

Chanakya's idea of decentralizing judicial power

The indigenous grassroots judicial system

3.2 – IDEA 2: BENEVOLENCE IN CENTRALIZATION IS IGNORANCE PERSONIFIED

…there is no need to rule from above or for kings and politicians to be benevolent from a distance. People can do their own thing. Let the people have the freedom to take care of themselves, and they will, in no time, rise up to the task…

3.3 – IDEA 3: THE ANCIENT INDIAN VILLAGE REPUBLIC

Inscriptions

3.4 – IDEA 4: TWO CARDINAL PRINCIPLES FOR DECENTRALIZATION

The first cardinal principle

The second cardinal principle

3.5 – IDEA 5: A QUESTION TO VILLAGE CITIZENS: WHEN DOES ONE QUALIFY TO BE CALLED FREE?

Index 1 – The irresponsibility dimension of slavery

Index 2 – A feeling of being subjugated

Index 3 – The question of rights

Index 4 – The highest freedom

To summarize

3.6 – IDEA 6: CAN THE INDIAN ADMINISTRATION NURTURED IN SLAVERY NURTURE FREEDOM?

Foreign vs. native

Institution-building by colonial masters

The true colors of the bureaucracy

PART 3
TRANSITION TO REAL FREEDOM: THROUGH INSTITUTIONS BUILT ON RIGHTEOUSNESS

CONTENTS IN DETAIL

SECTION IV
REVOLUTIONARY AUGMENTATION OF THE JUDICIAL LEG OF INDIAN DEMOCRACY

Is the present judicial system dharmic?

Today, money can buy better justice

Dharma of a lawyer is decided by the larger cause

Justice needs to have a public fervor

Should increase in lawlessness should give more bread and butter to men of law?

The existing system is basically reactive

THE IDEALISM OF THE EXISTING JUDICIARY

Ideal judiciary – Two important traditions that gave completeness

The tradition of isolation of judges

The pocket in the lawyer's back

GIVING POWER BACK TO THE PEOPLE THROUGH THE RE-INTRODUCTION OF GRASSROOTS-LEVEL COURTS IN A MODERN SETUP:

Village courts

The next higher level

Protecting the authority of panchayat courts

SECTION V
THE PEOPLES' POLICE FORCE: CONSPICUOUS ARM OF A DHARMIC EXECUTIVE

A colonial character is today's norm

The dharma perspective on policing

It is a citizens' system

When the police take to dharma

Community participation in policing; guarded from the inside and monitored from the outside

A self-policing panchayat

Citizens' policing must also happen in cities

Novel efforts must get the system's patronage:

SECTION VI
ORGANIZE THE SOCIAL SERVICE SECTOR TO BRING COMPLETENESS IN GOVERNANCE

Social work completes dharmic arrangements

Social service results from doing justice to an inner drive

Organizing social work is a challenge, but it has great rewards

How that organization will shape up

To push the system toward dharmic wholeness, social service must cater to some basic grassroots-level goals

INTER-PERSONNEL RELATIONSHIPS IN SOCIAL WORKERS' ORGANIZATIONS NEED SERVICE SPIRIT:

No rigid command structure and yet cooperative

Teaming-up and mutual respect

Loose federation – Enlightened anarchy

There is no duty

Adequate defense against vested interests

A coordinating agency promoting a 'flat' structure

Practical constitution of social workers' councils

Minimal secretarial infrastructure

Fine structure of councils – Customized and flexible

Setting up task forces using volunteers

Maximizing output through planned teamwork and cooperation

Setting benchmarks for society by proper profiling of candidates for the councils

While electing

The council must be non-political and one of its kind for an area

SECTION VII
A HOLISTIC HEALTHCARE SYSTEM MUST CATER TO EVERY INDIAN: THINKING BEYOND THE BOXES OF ALLOPATHY AND CAPITALISM

A radical solution is imminent for healthcare

The present medical institution is a limb of the capitalist system

The current system is predominantly cure-based and reactive

Government support dilutes the impact of hard-core capitalism

Need for an alternative approach

Solutions by virtue of dealing with the dynamics of demand and supply of medical services

Facilitating other institutions for holistic health and medicine

Medical research institutions with the duty of monitoring society

Government and private hospitals

Self-rule is destiny; all planning for systems must be done with that in mind

SECTION VIII
SPORTS AND ART FORMS: FOUNDATION STONE OF LIFE AND CIVILIZATION

There is a valuable spiritual dimension to sports and arts

A group's approach to sports and arts must therefore reflect connoisseurship

Institutional reforms to cater to a sporting and artful nation

Akhadas (and sports/art Gurus) and their funding

Elected bodies for managing sports/art forms

Regional sports centers

Similar solutions for art forms

Patronage for the arts and sports – Celebration of life and service to society:

SECTION IX
EDUCATION MUST ADDRESS CIVILIZATIONAL NEEDS AND NOT JUST ECONOMIC NEEDS

What truly distinguishes a person?

Primacy of wisdom in an individual's pursuit of education

The education system tuned to a higher purpose

Expanding the definition of education to include all learning processes in human interaction

Acknowledgements

Most of all, I thank God for the countless blessings He has showered on me and for giving me the strength and endurance to keep at this task. I thank my Guru who has endowed me with a lot of strength through self-discovery and helped me dispel my doubts.

I am indebted to my teachers in the distinguished institutions in which I have studied for the insights they have offered me on various matters ranging from science and law to the socio-political and economic conditions of the nation and the world.

I am grateful to the many social activists who have given me access to their areas of work from which I could learn first-hand. I also thank the many activists and visionaries who shared with me their knowledge and experience. I am grateful to my relatives in my native place, to members of certain villages in and around Belgaum and to citizens of certain villages in Maharashtra for sharing with me their journeys in life. Their lives may be challenging on the material level, and some regions are truly troubled, but I have always found a lot of richness, peace and joy in these settings.

I am thankful to Mr. T. N. Seshan, to Dr. Lalitha Ramamurthi and to Prof. Bala V. Balachandran for writing the forwards to the various parts of the book. I am deeply honoured that these stalwarts have lent their voice to this mission.

I am also grateful to Mr. Pradeep for his invaluable support in editing this book.

I am grateful to my parents, relatives, friends, critics and colleagues who have helped me in my journey of discovery and/or have participated in various ways in this effort.

I am thankful to Notion Press for accepting to dedicate their talents to getting this book to potential readers.

Nixon Fernando
Chennai

Introduction

Where do we Indians as a nation go from where we stand? Amble along, subject to the pulls and pushes of the world, surviving as we go along, doing our best but uncertain about where we are headed? Or have a plan that will focus our energies on something that promises the release of our highest potentials? The pushes and pulls will not stop, but if our response comes out of a well thought out strategy, the world is our oyster.

A lot of good is possible if we can pick up the pearls of wisdom from our ancient past and string them together with a modern thread.

The challenges are many: to tackle the ills of poverty, to harmonize our relationships across castes and religions, to preserve and protect the thousands of local cultures dotting the length and breadth of the nation and to still meet our economic goals and climb upwards on all the indices that denote a prosperous people so that this nation stands out as an example to follow.

At some time or the other, we need to take the bull by the horns. What is our stand on spirituality? Religions do deal with spirituality; so, in being secular in our public life, are we supposed to abstain from spirituality? And if we do take up spirituality, how do we keep religion out of it? And if we take to spirituality and the secular aspects of religion, how do we keep caste out of it?

All you need to do is raise these questions about spirituality, religion and caste, and there it is! Popping out like a jack-in-the-box, there is a cacophony created by all kinds of representatives shouting themselves hoarse. But that is not going to solve any problem for anybody.

It is inevitable that consciousness must rise. It is inevitable that the truth will be uncovered and the facts will be known about the ideas and ideals that can transform India.

What is wrong if the ideas come from the West? And what if the good ideas come from the East? And then, what is wrong if the ideas come from the ancient wisdom of the seers? Something that will take us, "WE, THE PEOPLE OF INDIA" (from the preamble of our constitution), to a better destiny... all of us together?

Great nations have risen indeed when they have stretched into higher consciousness. The United States rose with the idealism contained in the fight against slavery in the Civil War. The knights of King Arthur provided an idealism that made Britain rise. Closer home, the Mauryas established themselves based on the idealism spawned by Chanakya. Akbar set up a stable nation using the idealism that fired Sher Shah Suri. Hari Hara and Bukka set up Vijayanagara inspired by their teacher Vidyaranya. Shivaji, the Maratha chieftain, made a mark inspired by his mother, his teacher Dadoji Konddeo and his Guru Samarth Swami Ramdas. Today's India too must rise on the basis of ideas that inspire us into a higher level of consciousness. And there are great pointers to this in our ancient heritage.

For setting a direction, clarity of thought is required. Clarity of thought will lead to clarity of purpose and ease in team action. It starts with getting the ideas right. Two areas in which clarity of thought is yet to come are stated below:

1) The destiny of a prosperous togetherness as conceived by the wise men of the past

2) The contours of a constitution of local communities in India which will truly put the destiny of the citizens in their own hands

Digging into the past, one can come up with pointers that give clarity on how we can move ahead as a nation on these two crucial points.

This research of close to twenty-five years is now being presented in three parts. The first part is about the gifts of our ancient heritage, the second is about how true freedom can be experienced in a village and the third part is about how the other aspects of life in the nation can promote the best that the nation has to offer. Overall, in the words of the American Declaration of Independence, it is about a nation which assures 'life, liberty and pursuit of happiness' to its citizens. This comes as a sequel to the book *Towards the Kingdom of Heaven* (Bharatiya Vidya Bhavan, 2000), which questioned the presumption that the wisdom of the ancients can be glossed over by modern thinkers. The present book takes the debate further and digs deep into ancient thought processes for answers to today's problems.

The ideas are profound and need consideration and thought, which, incidentally, the wise men of yore have put into our heads already using their ingenuity. We shall see how they did that as we go along. And taking these and some practical solutions, we can definitely improve the sting in all efforts at the emancipation of the nation.

Even if 10% of the villages of the nation take up to the freedom they are promised, this nation will transform.

This book is for the Indian who needs clarity about his roots, who has been browbeaten to believe that his ancient past consisted of class-based harassment, who thinks that it will take forever for the poor to rise out of poverty, who thinks that liberty is down the path of economic prosperity, who believes that the reality of life is along the lines of 'clash of civilizations' rather than '*vasudaivakutumbakam*' and who thinks that science can progress without spirituality and vice versa.

You will see in this book why Hinduism is the future of the world. Is it a religion in the first place? You will see why we are barking up the wrong tree on issues like Ram Janmabhoomi, Kashmir and Pakistan. You will see how the caste system can never be wished away and instead find in it the opportunity to elevate castes. You will see that emancipation through reservation is a myth.

You will also go on to see that true freedom is yet to touch the lives of the rural poor. You will see that an empowered community has the potential to solve most of the poverty and illiteracy problems facing our nation. Ideas from our ancient past have the potential to tackle the environmental problems that are affecting humanity. And the book offers practical steps that village communities need to take to take charge of their destinies.

Those who have doubts about their ancient heritage, those that are concerned about their nation and their neighborhoods and especially those in public life need to invest time in understanding the concepts presented here. The barest minimum gained will be a better understanding of how the ideas are all linked, and that will help one to be more effective in dealing with issues encountered in life in India. There is no finality about this work, but it surely is an in-depth research. The Indian togetherness has much promise and much to offer to the world. Let us take charge of our inheritance and bring peace to the world.

Feedback is more than welcome. It will only serve to improve the quality of the debate. Please do take the effort to pen down your thoughts and send the same to the author at nixfdo@gmail.com. Only request: please join forces as a problem solver on behalf of the highest.

Return to an Ancient and Glorious Tryst

Part 1

This part deals with what true freedom means in the view of our best traditions and how a togetherness that celebrates that highest freedom is the one that will take us to being world leaders.

Dedicated to
My Guru
Tej Guru Sir Shree Tejparkhiji

Foreword

I have known Nixon for the last few years ever since he came over to intern with me and help with the research leading to my autobiography. He is an alumnus of the MIT School of Government, Pune, which we set up to groom leaders and experts in the government. Nixon's shifting of focus from teaching physics to studying about the government is apparently due to an attempt on his part to understand what ails India in order to offer solutions. Over time, I have come to realize that he has developed strong views on this, and his books on the Vidarbha farmers' suicides and on village self-rule reflect these views. So also this book on Hinduism—A Return to an Ancient and Glorious Tryst—which a reader will find delightfully insightful for a Catholic to write. His perspectives on the various aspects of Hinduism are well-presented, and he makes a convincing case for the reader to pay heed to the intellectual giants of ancient India. In my view, this is an excellent book, and very briefly, it is a great tribute to Hinduism.

I have always held that anyone who calls himself an Indian is a Hindu. In this book, Nixon has thrown light on what that essentially means. I may not agree with the way he has gone about it, but that is merely a matter of a difference in the way we think and approach any subject. He has, with quite clear reasoning in his own way, handled the subject with firm conviction. And by the time the book concludes, a huge question mark appears on the sensibility of our current leaders' approach to (1) the understanding of human nature coming to us from our ancients and (2) the solutions adopted to resolve national issues.

Let me add my vote in favor of what the wise men of ancient India have said. Whenever I was faced with important questions that I had to handle in my life, I have always resorted to the silence of my mind. On the day before I finally signed the August 2nd order of 1993 postponing all elections in India, I spent time reading *Vikram Betal* and the *Bhagavad Gita*. It gives me inner peace and clarity of thought and adds to my conviction that the crucial decisions I make are impersonal and pure. I have always loved the peace and tranquility of temple surroundings, and these give my soul much relief. I have taken important personal decisions at the instructions of the sages from Kanchi, and though I may have felt a tinge of disappointment at times, I have never regretted going by their word. I have full conviction that there is enough and more guidance pertaining to living in a sublime way and staying successful in the works of the ancient sages.

In today's India, the politics of short-sightedness deals essentially with the next electoral victory. It is a cesspool that sustains and amplifies ill-beings like corruption, casteism, communalism and so many other attributes of public life that torment us today. There is obviously a need to rethink and redirect the way we make progress—and no ready-made solution is at hand. But I am sure that India can be led only by a leader who has a true grasp of its indigenous culture. And definitely, despite all the flaws in Hinduism, I remain optimistic that it is in Hinduism's nature to eventually come up with the answers and lead the way to global peace and prosperity.

T. N. Seshan (IAS)
Former Chief Election Commissioner of India
Chennai, February 2013

It will no longer remain to be doubted that
the priests of Egypt and the sages of Greece
have drawn directly from the original well of India,
that it is to the banks of the Ganges and the Indus
that our hearts feel drawn as [if] by some hidden urge.

– Friedrich Mejer

Introduction

Some people compare India to the sleeping Kumbhakarna of the Ramayana. This is right in the context that it is indeed something huge and asleep, but it is wrong in the sense that unlike Kumbhakarna, India is not on the side of Ravana. In truth, India will wake up when it learns to appreciate and respect Lord Rama for what he truly is. In fact, the slumber is the inability of the nation to relate to this essential strength that the scriptures and traditions impart.

The following analogy sums it up well. A farmer had a lorry in which he carried farm produce, and suddenly, one day, the lorry stopped working. He had no help, so he let it stand in his yard and started carrying farm produce on his head or at the most in a hand cart. He eventually resigned himself to his fate. Then, the farm passed on to the son. The son had always seen the lorry standing in the yard, but he knew nothing of it other than that it was a showpiece and a place where children played. He too carried farm produce on his head and in a hand cart—and always thought that this was the way it was supposed to be.

There was this neighbor who purchased a horse-drawn cart. The neighbor would use it to ferry things very fast. It was nothing like anything the farmer had seen before, and he was mightily impressed.

His kind neighbor suggested one day, 'You have four strong bulls in your farm. Why don't you borrow four of my cart wheels and fix them to the showpiece you have in your yard? If you yoke the bulls to the showpiece, then you can get a lot of your work done too.'

Fair enough. It was a good idea; the deed was done. Even though it was not as light and fast as the horse cart, it could be used. He anyway found it better than carrying things little by little in the handcart.

We Indians are just like this son of the farmer. Little do we realize that all we need to do is a little tinkering, fill diesel in the lorry, set the tires back and learn how to drive; we will have something that will quite outdo the horse cart in a great many number of ways. Little do we realize that something that can do immense work lies unused. It lies hidden in our rich diversity of traditions and culture. A bit of tinkering, a bit of patronage, a little cleaning up of the mind to assure ourselves that it is neither a plaything nor a horror piece and a little learning of how to use it and we will have something fantastic working for us—moving us to a glorious tryst.

It is true that within the last two hundred years or so, the leaders of our freedom struggle made a tryst with destiny. Depending on how one saw it, part or whole of that tryst was complete at independence and at the birth of the republic of India… But is that all one can think of? Was the goal/tryst set with a true awareness of the highest thought that was supposed to pervade the thinking process of the land?

Would the wise from ancient India have done differently? Had the wise from ancient India lived today, what would be the destiny that they would have dreamed for us?

On the face of it, what comes to us from our ancient past is pretty maligned. Feminist organizations quote Manu and say that it is abhorrent when someone who made a law about whipping women with a stick could be among the wise. Caste groups quote the same Manu and talk about the atrocity of molten lead being poured into the ears of the Dalits for a crime as simple as listening to certain secret recitals. The atheists have a long list of Indian Gods and Goddesses who can be mocked besides a whole lot of superstitions that they decry as defying common sense and logic. The science enthusiasts treat anything which is metaphysical as a potential hallucination. Socialists see the inequality in a rigid caste system that has been practiced over centuries. The communists see the opium of the masses being used to keep people in a state of perpetual stupor. Modern philosophers and psychologists equate all that is in the ancient texts to be ancient and therefore in the infancy of ideation. Historians record great atrocities committed on the lower castes in a systematic manner. The scholars who represent Indian spirituality conceive of 'spirituality genes' written into the DNA of humans which separate men at birth. And thanks [sic] to the ideas from Samuel Huntington and to some western observers/reporters of Hinduism, the essential spiritualism of this land is seen to be a 'religion' and one that is in conflict with other 'religions' around the world.

Yes, all these are facts. Are they not? There won't be any smoke if there is no fire, right?

NO!

Talk of everything and miss the heart of the matter… Look at all the muck in the bath water and forget the baby sitting in it… It is not only unreasonable, it is also unfair.

The dynamics of a bygone era were different from what they are today. In an age when bows and arrows were used, when the fastest way to move an army was on horseback, when villages lived in reasonable seclusion from one another, when tribes constantly fought with each other and tried to do away with each other's resources… In that age, the rules were different. Pulling facts and figures out of history unholistically and then presenting it in high-pitched political debates where din is more important than reason and where winning political power is more important than finding the truth is how we seem to be missing out on wisdom.

Wisdom distinguished certain people and groups from the average gentry of those times. These special people went on to be icons of mercy, graciousness, inclusiveness, wisdom, delight, integrity and prosperity. The ancient land of ours has learned from these icons. The wealth in its culture, traditions, scriptures and spirituality are gifts from these outstanding people who knew how to raise individuals and nations to peace, prosperity and glory.

The shut-up call to the howlers is contained in the fact that Manu himself, who is often painted to be the villain of the caste system, says, 'All men are born equal.' If everyone is the same, then why so much difference? What is the secret that can make these others (downtrodden) who are actually equals also rise in stature and prosperity?

Indeed, what should that song of the liberation of the lower castes be? The same that we use today? Or then, are we blinding ourselves to the very thing that is capable of raising these marginalized groups to prosperity?

The wisdom of the ancients has the potential of not only raising individuals, caste groups and nations to prosperity. It can even bring peace to the global community that is torn apart by misunderstandings and chauvinistic fears.

Kind of hard to believe this in the light of the ills Hinduism is known to represent. But then, what if it is the truth? We know that there are howlers who don't want to listen and don't want others to speak. What if these howlers are blocking out from their (and our) minds the very thing that can give liberation to the masses of India?

This nation is destined to rise to great glory, and it will rise only on the wings of that wisdom which will bring peace and prosperity to the whole world. Do sit back and travel along this book so that we can take a peek at a very broad-minded way of looking at things and doing them right in the nation and the world.

The treasure from the ancient system is invaluable, and one of the lifetime missions of an Indian should be to dig into it—after all, it is supposed to be the highest treasure known to man. If there is something that can raise individuals, communities and nations to prosperity and if it takes only a few hours of reading to be introduced to it… Then, why not?

The motion of the stars calculated by the Hindus before some 4500 years vary not even a single minute from the tables of Cassine and Meyer (used in the 19ᵗʰ century).

… The Hindu systems of astronomy are by far the oldest and that from which the Egyptians, Greek, Romans and - even the Jews derived from the Hindus their knowledge.

– Jean-Sylvain Bailly
French Astronomer (1736–1793)

Section I

Rediscovering the Genuine Universality of Hinduism

This section deals with what it essentially means to belong to the life and culture of the land that is to the north of the seas and the south of the Himalayan ranges.

India has great geographical diversity, and this influences the lifestyle of the people tremendously. Religious, linguistic and ethnic convictions are expressed in the background of these geographical factors. Followers of almost all the religions in the world reside in India, and with each of these religions come diverse religious practices. Apart from these main religions, there are numerous tribal faiths as well. Then, there are traditions and practices that have emerged out of the socio-political system that existed since the days of the earliest Indian civilizations. For example, casteism, the traditional *nyay panchayats*, the characteristic roles of the sexes, etc. There is also this strong tradition of learning that has existed since millennia, which is indigenous to the land; it has a range of subjects which is quite distinct from the subjects studied in the present age. Ancient learning had its own unique methods as well. Finally, there is this arts and crafts dimension with a kind of philosophical and spiritual support, which is special to this subcontinent.

All this makes the Indian experience a heady cocktail that can confuse the best of thinkers. However, in all this diversity, there is a remarkable core that holds this ethos together. Understanding that core is important.

Is it wise to turn a blind eye to everything ancient or Indian? Of course, the scientific civilization has exerted great domination over India and continues to do so even now. Does that mean what is in India is of no worth?

There surely are facts and incidents in India's long history that could embarrass a proud Indian nationalist and a conscientious Indian human rights activist, but is that enough reason to back off from the ancient philosophies? For all we know, we might only be focused on the failures of the system.

Many Indians in the past have been given the task of shouldering the responsibility of carrying forward Indian traditions and learning. What makes us so sure that they did not bungle to the extent of embarrassment? Those responsible for delivering the goods might have performed half-heartedly—without conviction. Is that not the way of many of today's scholars? What makes us so sure that ignorance and bad implementation of otherwise priceless philosophies didn't lead to its current state?

Without a doubt, instances of *sati*, child marriage and casteism are cited to indicate that all was not well with the Indian society of pre-British times. But then, it is also important to remember that no scientific conclusion should be made based on political rhetoric. Was a balanced study of civilization as it existed in India really made?

India accounted for more than 27% of the global trade and 23% of the global economy before the British took over (today, it is a small fraction of that). Was such a feat possible if there was no prosperity, scholarship or peace in this land?

It is true that the kind of education that was available in Europe did not exist in India at that time, but then, it is also known that there were many Indian kings who were men of letters and many more men, renowned in wisdom, who were patronized by the kings of India in their courts. What was this non-European learning then which created intellectual giants in India? Did all that learning count for nothing?

This alternate learning, which is held by priests in temples, monks in monasteries, uneducated village folk, people of the older generation and people who are deeply religious is generally termed as orthodox and sometimes termed as primitive, narrow-minded and conservative. Is it possible that something substantial exists within it and that we are turning a blind eye to something that can really make a huge difference to India?

The important question is this: have we given our traditions a fair chance?

Breaking free from prejudices: A little reflection shows that the 'educated Indian' is a creation of the European outlook. That is, the educated Indians, those educated in English or in vernacular languages, who hold forth on the basis of their literacy and their degrees and who occupy almost all the important positions of authority in the country have been taught to view India through the western perspective. The educated Indian's appreciation of Indian culture depends on the West's appreciation of India. Put it this way: most Indians will start seeing unmatched scholarship in ancient learning if Valmiki or Veda Vyasa were posthumously given a Nobel Prize!

The reason for this, which we will see in the next section, is that the educated Indian is a child of the William Bentinck initiative of creating 'Indians by blood and British by intellect and mannerism'. However much he may have been impacted by the learning that is indigenous to this land through other means (family, for instance), he finds that this indigenous learning is officially recognized as almost equal to nothing.

The importance of considering these factors lies in the need to guard against all sorts of prejudices while contemplating on the contents of ancient learning. Instead of looking through a prism provided by formal education, there is a need to take up the matter objectively, rationally and with the highest spirit of scientific inquiry, giving a fair chance to the possibility of hidden wisdom in ancient learning. After all, it is the truth that one wants to be aware of. And merely admitting this possibility of hidden wisdom is a logical and natural step in the scientific method.

Why such a raw deal for Indian learning? Now, when one talks of prejudices induced by western actors, two direct causes naturally come to mind. Somewhere at the end of the eighteenth century, some scholars from Europe condemned all the learning in the East to just nothing, stating that all the books of wisdom in all of the East were equal to the knowledge contained in one shelf of a certain library in Europe. The other cause is that of there being an element of deliberateness in the colonial masters to under-write the true contents of ancient Indian learning for political ends.

In other words, an educated Indian may be excused for his lack of faith in the indigenous system since at the outset itself, 'authorities' have told him that there is nothing here to see. But then, this leads to an interesting bottleneck. It is ironic that these formally educated Indians (in the schools, colleges and universities of India) are a hindrance to the free flow of ancient knowledge and wisdom. They take credit for being 'Indian scholars' based on a western standard, but they ignore the scholarship that is indigenous to ancient India. When Indian scholars don't consider Indian wisdom great, why would someone else? In their silence and abstinence from ancient Indian wisdom, they become hindrances in the attempts to unravel the treasures which ancient Indians may have left for us. Ultimately, only a small group of western thinkers and philosophers have truly seen the remarkable scholarship of ancient Indians. Our intellectuals and scholars, the slumbering Kumbhakarna, need to wake up…

Yet another reason for the failure of Indian learning to take center stage is in the difference in the composition of scholarship in the Indian and western world. Consider this. According to the western perception, philosophy and spiritualism are seen differently, almost as having two different identities. This probably stems from there being two sources of authority in the West. Those associated with religion held the right to authority on spiritualism, and scholars in universities staked the claim on philosophy. It is acknowledged that each one would also speak of the other's subject and that this is because there is interdependence between the two fields. While philosophers see spirituality

as a subset of philosophy, spiritualists see philosophy as a derivative of spirituality. Ultimately, a certain distance/ discipline is maintained between the two, and these are generally perceived as two different spheres.

One can engage in a lengthy debate about the origin of this orientation and the merits of the same, but without going into too much depth, we can point out a few things. This perception can be traced back to the developments in Europe ever since the medieval period. It is known from history that traditionally, religious authorities wielded a lot of political clout. Gradually, the principle of separation of state from religion evolved on account of the changing power dynamics. This consolidated into a pattern wherein the government and the religious authority were expected to refrain from meddling in each other's activities. And since education in universities evolved into the government domain and education in monasteries evolved into the religious domain, the two separate streams achieved some kind of consolidation. But then, there is a lot of fraternizing, and there are many examples of philosophers and monks doing each other's work. But whatever be the case, it cannot be denied that stemming from the separation of state from religion, philosophy and spiritual studies are perceived as separate things.

In Indian spiritualism, there is a significant difference. There is a recognition of two important spheres of learning called *param vidya* and *aparam vidya*; the former deals with things concerning the Divine Spirit while the latter deals with all other studies. But such a division is not identical to the division of spiritualism and philosophy as demarcated in the West. On the other hand, in the Indian system, there is a path to 'spiritual wisdom' known as *gyan yoga*, which can be roughly translated to 'yoga of knowledge' (posture of knowledge). This subject has a lot to do with 'understanding' the human nature; such 'understanding' automatically leads the disciple to attaining the highest spiritual goal of transcendence. This would mean that for Indian thinkers, both philosophy and spiritualism are synonymous. There is a bridge connecting the two. In India, philosophers who successfully prosecuted the goal of gyan yoga were considered saints and vice versa. In fact, the *Bhagavad Gita* says, 'A man of self-realization is a source of all wisdom.'

The paradox: So then, are the Indian scriptures 'scriptures' or 'books of philosophy'?

To date, they are considered scriptures—not as books on philosophy or as research outpourings of a scientific analysis of human nature. The truth, though, is that some of them are indeed both.

In the modern world, systems related to education and politics through the principle of separation of state from religion classify religion as a matter of private pursuit by individuals. It follows that 'scriptures' having to do with the 'Hindu religion' cannot be taken for reckoning in secular schools of learning!

The result is that ancient Indian learning is not considered as secular philosophy and is hence largely kept out of (West-inspired) universities.

But then, if it is not going to be the universities that are handling this subject, the other option is that it should be taken up by western religious studies organizations... But then again, why would a Christian or Islamic scholar work on the scriptures of 'another' religion—especially if there is a 'fundamentalist' inclination in such religious researchers? The net result is that the study of ancient Indian scriptures is supposed to be a matter of 'private' studies by 'Hindus', and the spiritual West stays away from it.

So, Indian learning is more or less kept out of both the channels present in western learning—the universities and the religious studies organizations... And the dilemma is that true appreciation of Indian philosophy needs an interpretation that is both scholarly and faith-filled. And when the West does not take it up, West-educated Indians do not take it up either...

It is a strange cycle, and the only way to break it is to endeavor on a scientific exploration of the messages, hypotheses, symbols, theories and models proposed by the learned of ancient India.

A strong case for learning: And there is urgency for it. Indians (and all of humanity) are losing out heavily on account of an apparent indecisiveness about Indian culture. When Indians are faced with a lengthy list of necessities that are essential for the building of a nation, it becomes necessary that they draw in as many constructive influences as possible to chart out a path of progress. And

for this, a deep understanding of the indigenous culture is vital. And one definitely cannot approach nation-building with negatively prejudiced thoughts directed against what is indigenous. Wishing the Indian learning away would be a foolish thing too. It is not going to go away anywhere in a hurry as that would imply the case we reckoned as 'throwing away the baby with the bathwater'. The only way out is to not only give ancient learning a patient hearing but also study it in depth. Or wait for some western scientist, sociologist, psychologist or philosopher to re-discover it...

Humans have a new generation every eighteen to twenty-five years. Working backward, there have been so many generations in India in the last three to four thousand years. This is a time lapse over which the major aspects of today's indigenous culture evolved. Now, a philosophy which has been cherished by men through 150 to 200 generations should surely have at least 'something' of value.

Moreover, the tradition of learning that existed over these generations in India has been pretty serious. In such a long tradition of rigorous learning, the experiences of men, generation after generation, would naturally have accumulated into the associated literature and scriptures. As human nature has it, 'however bad they are, people know how to give good things to their children' (quote: Jesus Christ). So, each generation's discoveries on how to lead a better life would surely have been transferred down through such learning traditions. The same discoveries, accumulated as knowledge, would still be hidden in the living learning traditions of India.

To conclude that these persons, throughout all these generations, were foolish or had only half-baked ideas or that we 'moderns' have seen every nook and corner of their horizons and that their learning consists of nothing other than preservation of selfish class interests is essentially naïve; it is rather unbecoming of people of the scientific era.

And unfortunately, these are the very same conclusions that we are jumping to in scholarly circles today.

Of course, again, there are exceptions; individuals and small scholarly circles do exist who have an inherent belief in the wisdom contained in the knowledge, but these are small exceptions. In intellectual conclusions (which back 'common sense') and in institutions that are meant for any significant purpose in public and private life, Indians fail to give importance to even basic theories or hypotheses offered by ancient learning. Only the faithful of diverse religions seem to hold on to it with some unexplained irrationality. They sometimes don't even have a flicker of doubt; their conviction is total.

So, at the cost of sounding repetitive, we really need to ask this question: is there potential in our indigenous learning and its systems? Is there something in it which can show Indians a way out of the hardships that the nations of today face? Is the contention about ancient Indian learning being primitive, superstitious and redundant really correct?

The pursuit of truth: A counter question can be asked, 'If what the Indians have is indeed good, why has it not yet asserted itself? Why is it that there are so many ills in the basic caste structure? Why is it that religions squabble with each other? Why does India have so many problems in its communities?' Indeed, why?

Whatever it is, if there are answers, then they have to be extracted by this generation of people. The culture is what it is; it is for the users of today to find good or bad in it. It will make a difference only if we as a generation choose to pursue the truth (… in contrast to judgmental shouting).

Indians need to draw from these cultural roots, sieve out the unnecessary discordant aspects and build and reinforce what is left with what is good in the modern world.

The efforts need to be guided by the fact that if an established scientist makes a claim of having in-depth knowledge of the atomic nucleus, then we'd better give him a proper hearing—especially if he has results (a nuclear explosion or a nuclear reactor) to prove his point. This principle should be applied to the stalwarts of yesteryear too: Veda Vyasa, Valmiki and Vashist were no average men in the field they are remembered for. They definitely deserve better attention.

Is there a need to act in total faith? No! It is not necessary, but thoughtful hearing is probably a duty which intellectuals of today owe to them, to themselves and to the coming generations.

It would be too vain to think that among the men who ever existed on this earth, only we, the selfless benevolent intellectuals of the latter half of the twentieth century and the start of the twenty-first, or the latter half of the second millennia AD for that matter, have the ultimate concern for our brethren like none others before us ever had. It is most unscientific to draw a conclusion that since I belong to this latest generation, my knowledge is NATURALLY (?!) superior. We do admit, in our scientific pursuits, that we have not been endowed with magnificent, renowned wisdom that can be equated to the end of knowledge, but to conclude, without proper analysis, that we know better than the ancients is also probably not the right thing to do.

Of course, the Indian of today has the right to take decisions for himself regarding how he wishes to move ahead; the nation too is free to decide for itself. That right cannot be denied. But the best way to go about using that right would probably be to hear out the seers too and only then figure out where to finally go.

It is good to remember here that Japan draws its strength from the strong culture it possesses. There, the western influence was used to build upon what it already had. (The author recommends watching the movie *The Last Samurai* and, if possible, the director's and actor's comments about the roles. It is a wonderful way for two civilizations to look at each other.) This can be applied to India as well. For all we know, the spirit of Indianness could possibly add splendor to what the West has achieved. Maybe India can lead the world into the wisdom of contentment and knowledge of happy living. Taking advantage of science and technology, the world could probably be led into a 'Golden Era'…

After all, it is a standing promise made by the ancients. And it wouldn't be very nice for us to be known as a generation that wasted itself away by sitting on top of a mountain of priceless treasures. All for the want of patience to look, to observe, to study, to know the truth…

I like to think that someone will trace how the deepest thinking of India made its way to Greece and from there to the philosophy of our times.'

– John Archibald Wheeler
Theoretical Physicist who coined 'Black Hole' (1911)

Influx: A look at the history of the Indian subcontinent unravels an interesting list of influences that have played a role here. And the relevant influences date back to thousands of years. An important factor dating back more than four millennia is the question of the Aryans and the Dravidians. The Harappan culture (attributed to the Dravidians) that existed seems to have left behind its impressions on the Indian psyche. The Aryans are said to have been nomadic travelers who later came in with their own elements, and the synthesis of these two streams accounts for a lot of what comes under Hinduism. The Iron Age is also known to have had its influence on India. Tribes expanded, and 'kingdoms' were created; there was surplus production and an expansion of human occupancy. Then, there was an influx of foreigners. The Iranians invaded and ruled parts of the Indus plain, and with the coming of Alexander, it was the Greeks. Through these two contacts, Iranian and Greek influences entered the Indian system.

Under the Mauryans, in the third and second centuries BC, much of the Indian subcontinent was united under one king. King Ashoka can be remembered here. Between second century BC and second century AD, there was an influx of foreigners again. The Shakas, Parthians and Kushanas ruled over domains which covered much of Afghanistan, Pakistan and large parts of northern India. These groups, especially the Shakas and Parthians, got absorbed into the subcontinent. The Rajputs had already begun to make their presence felt by this time. Next came the Gupta period. Hinduism is supposed to have found a golden period under the Guptas. They ruled with sufficient clout for a little more than two centuries. The Huna invasion destabilized the Gupta reign, and even these invaders came to stay. North India found another important ruler in Harsha Vardhana around the sixth century. Meanwhile, South India witnessed the rule of several dynasties. We could list about eight or ten of them who were able to assert themselves at some time

or the other between second century BC and thirteenth century AD. The Cholas, Chalukyas, Pandiyas, Pallavas, Rashtrakutas and Cheras were some of the important players.

The advent of Islam brought in the next set of influences. Islam was first carried in by the Arab traders. Subsequently, it came into India through many sets of rulers. The sultanate, which in due course got established at Delhi, then became a factor that made a few more foreigners settle in India. The Sayyids, Lodis, Khilgies and Tuglaqs who were the major players in this phase ruled from Delhi for about two hundred years. The Mongoloid influence can also be seen in this phase. Then came a phase dominated by two kingdoms in the South: the Bahamani Kingdom and the Vijayanagar Empire. Later, India again found itself united under the Mughals, who came around about the sixteenth century. The reign of Akbar is of tremendous importance during this period.

It was about this time that the Europeans began exerting their influence on the subcontinent with ever-increasing intensity. An important event here is the Hindu nationalism of the Marathas, which peaked on the death bed of the Mughal rule. The others were relatively smaller influences on the political scene of the land, though of much importance where they mattered.

Do note that among those rulers who came to India on conquests, there were very few instances of return without residue. In majority of the cases, people came to stay. Such influxes resulted in the coming of much more than mere faith. The people brought with them a way of life. And that included a depth of culture, which could have possibly sustained groups or tribes for centuries in their respective places of origin. And we are talking of everything, from large things such as 'how to react to death' right up to things as little as, maybe, 'when to have a day's biggest meal'. Such traits get carried down through the numerous families (and castes too) and, as undercurrents, still continue to shape lives today. Invariably, these little nodes of culture contributed to the surroundings, adjusted themselves to the local geographical conditions and took from the society that they finally became a part of. And every such node is a part of what is known today as the Indian nation. As already mentioned, there have been influences from the time of the Aryans, then in around the fourth century BC, then during the Christian era, then again after the advent of Islam, after that in the form of European influence and the latest being the Tibetan culture in modern times. This is after ignoring, for the moment, what mass communication and the internet bring in…

Who is an Indian? It would not be out of place then to ask the following question: if everyone has come in, who is the original inhabitant of this land? Which Indian has the right to claim being the original Indian?

The Indian constitution offers citizenship to any individual who has stayed in India for just five years—with appropriate reasonable restrictions. By birth, people stake a strong claim to be the inhabitants of a particular land. So then, even between these two categories, where does one draw the line between foreigner and Indian?

If one keeps working backward in time, at some time or the other, each group in India would have to leave the 'Indian' camp and enter the 'foreigner' camp. That ultimately would mean that the whole idea of who is Indian and who is not is a non-starter. One can artificially draw a line somewhere in history and claim that anyone that came in before that is Indian and any one after is not. The point is that this becomes an arbitrary exercise at chauvinism and division, where each person chooses a line according to his own whim or political compulsion.

So, indeed, where does one draw the 'authentic' line? At five years? At birth? At independence? At the Muslim invasion? At Alexander's time? Or back when the Aryans came? Taking it a step further, maybe one could draw it at a time when humanity was coming into existence in Africa about a quarter of a million years ago—that would have interesting implications. In fact, the answer probably lies in this question itself. Is Hinduism really interested in where one comes from?

Contrary to Huntington's theory: Islam came into India predominantly through the violence and intolerance of the kings who took advantage of it. Like everything else, even Islam has been used by opportunists to achieve personal ends. But this is no measure of the true content of religion; evaluating Islam on the basis of Ghazni's invasion would be in no way different from evaluating Hinduism on the basis of the orchestrated slaughter of Sikhs in Delhi or Muslims in Gujarat or evaluating Christianity on the basis of Hitler's holocaust or Judaism on the basis of crucifying Jesus Christ. In any case, despite the violence of Islamic kings, it did not take long for the awakening lying under Islam's maligned exterior to stimulate the spiritual resurrection in India. Beginning with the ninth and tenth centuries right up to yesteryear's Sai Baba of Shirdi, Islam in India has aided and has been aided in the search of truth. Is it not too much of a coincidence that the Advaita philosophy reasserted itself in India less than a century after the advent of Islam in Arabia?

The egalitarian philosophy of the Islamic faith too had its impact on the Indian condition. The strength derived from Islamic wisdom of the equality of man and the eligibility of every individual to learning condemned the rigidity of the caste system. Egalitarianism was also the message of Swami Basaveshwara of the twelfth century. The Bhakti saints of Hinduism and the Sufis of the Muslim traditions shared similarities. And finally, there are several instances of saints like Kabir and Sai Baba who preached and practiced the oneness of the Hindu and Muslim goals.

Jainism, Buddhism and the Sikh faith are three religions that have a unique place in the Indian system. Each of these constitutes an independent path behind its respective leader in the pursuit for the final truth. And all three of them arose to reform the degraded state of affairs of their respective times in the subcontinent.

Jainism and Buddhism, in their long history, have been part and parcel of the Indian socio-political system. These faiths too have had their ups and downs—patronage sometimes and persecution sometimes. And they have naturally contributed to the overall ethos. Buddhism, though exported from here, has found ready acceptance in the East. And surely, much has come back too. Buddhism has indeed formed a channel of contact with the East. In the fields of arts, architecture, literature, etc., the contributions of these religions have been tremendous. And most importantly, they have delivered some indelible characteristics close to the core of the Hindu way of life.

Unlike these two faiths, the Sikh faith is recent in its origin. It arose from the divine inspiration attained by Guru Nanak. And later, it also provided a militant reply to the persecution by Delhi rulers. From then on, it has remained as a militant brotherhood. It has, relatively, much more in common with Hinduism than both Jainism and Buddhism. For instance, the Guru Granth Sahib has, seemingly, drawn heavy insights from Vedic literature. The first Sikhs were Hindus, Muslims and others who populated the area at that time and who found solace in following the Guru. And finally, the Sikh culture has opened its doors wide for faithful Hindus. With regard to identity, Sikhs will always remain distinct, as long as they follow the path ignited by their leader, Guru Nanak. They will still be a part of the culture of the Sindu-land, however far away from the nucleus of the Hindu religion they may be.

The Christian influence assumed prominence with the coming of the Europeans from sixteenth century onwards, but there is enough evidence of its arrival even from the first century AD when St. Thomas, an apostle of Jesus Christ, is supposed to have reached India's shores. He was only the first among several influential saints who came here. Judaism has been a part of the Indian system too and for a long time. The Parsees are very much a part of Indian culture as well. The Baha'i faith has its representatives too.

The scientific method and spirit and western education began an onslaught by targeting the evils that existed in the Indian system. The socio-religious reforms of the nineteenth century also left its impression on society. And while all this was happening, the overall traditions carried down through the generations of Hindus continued to work—sometimes very obviously and most of the times subtly.

It is important to see that in this dynamics, there is clear evidence that much has come to stay in India, and the benefit has been mutual. To date, any method of labeling to say that one group belongs and the other does not will sound contradictory to the ethos of this land. In fact, the Indian subcontinent stands for a 'global brotherhood', and

expression of any kind of chauvinism is actually equivalent to being anti-Indian in spirit.

Samuel Huntington, in all his research, has inadvertently been trying to run down a belief which the Indian subcontinent has upheld for ages. In fact, his theories run contrary to the learning that is available to the Indian philosopher and spiritualist, in both practice and theory, for more than 4000 years. The Indian philosopher believes that there is NO essential conflict among religions.

As a matter of fact, even Indian kings have persecuted people of other faiths and sects with purely earthly intentions. And what Huntington speaks about is not 'clash of civilizations' but 'clash of ruling philosophies' or 'clash of chauvinistic manifestoes'. Check out the movie *Dasavataram* where the storytellers expose this strategy rather effectively.

India Special: The truth today is that Islam is at peace with itself and with the world around in very few places in the world, and one of these places is India. In India, the Sufi brand of Islam has evolved into a way forward that is much softer and considerate; in contrast, where the Wahhabi brand of Islam is being propagated, there are problems. Freaks and fundamentalists do exist in India too, but as a society, Islam is definitely at peace and flourishing in India. If Pakistan were to keep its interference, coming out of its ignorance, to itself, the score of Indian Islam would be even better. Probably, if Indian Islam divorces itself from the influences from across the seas, it may become closer to the teachings of the Holy Prophet.

As far as Christianity goes, the Christian religions in India proudly proclaim to their western counterparts that Indian churches are filled with youth and that patrons do not wait until they are old to come to the churches— opposite to what happens in churches in Europe.

One can easily come across people in India who have pictures of a range of saints, from a range of religions, hung on their prayer room walls in their homes. It is not uncommon for a Hindu devotee to go to a mosque or *darga* to pay his respects and then follow that with lighting a candle in a Christian chapel—absolutely at peace with himself. When we look back at all this, it becomes obvious that the socio-politico-cultural-religious methods available in this land had, and has, an innate capacity to absorb diverse religions. Therefore, a Hindu, by character, identifies and respects true worship in any form. A Hindu accommodates the worship of the other, respects the deity of the other, gives space for the other and is not rigidly confined to specific dogmas. In fact, there is probably even more...

Hinduism is not described as a 'boa' that gulps in and digests religions for nothing.

Aryans and Dravidians: Why has the Indian civilization acquired the character of a boa?

It would do us a lot of good here if we analyse the past in reference to the Aryans and Dravidians.

Historical inference (still debated upon) show that the Aryans were not the original inhabitants of this land, and their advent into India brought with them the foundations of the Vedic culture. A fair idea of the history of this incoming culture is found through the correlation of the Vedic texts and linguistic, archaeological and historical evidence. In fact, the Vedas form the rock bed of Hinduism. But there is a problem here. What about the indigenous population that existed before this advent? Outside the geographical boundaries controlled by Vedic societies, which by itself constitutes a rather large part of India, there was in all likelihood a throbbing culture having its own beliefs and ways. Moreover, it is unlikely that one civilization was wiped away clean and the next replaced it. In all probability, the cultures coexisted within a single kingdom.

Getting over the racial difference should have been difficult. But, as human nature has it, just living together facilitates cross-fertilization of cultures. Even between different faiths having distinct identities, an equilibrium or a meeting-point naturally develops. And this results from various causes like passage of time, absorption of one race as the slaves of another or after several instances of reverses in power equations. The developments in the Indian subcontinent seem to suggest that this truth manifested with textbook certainty in the Aryan-Dravidian case.

What better proof of this can be given than the fact that these original locals found reference in the holiest of the holy Vedic works? In fact, there were active participants from the native races in events recorded in the scriptures related to Vedic learning. There is much more. The chronological order of the scriptures inspired by the Vedas displays the increasing influence of indigenous beliefs and methods. In fact, the synthesis is so deep that it is difficult to identify any two separate streams.

A hypothesis can therefore be made that since Hinduism is a culture that has evolved through this synthesis, since it has managed to absorb diversity at its very origin and since it would have taken into reckoning numerous tribal cultures that would have existed at those times, there is every reason for it to have retained this characteristic to this day.

What remains to be seen is whether this is true. Is there something about the Hindu religion and learning that gives it this inherent ability to absorb diverse faiths?

India conquered and dominated China culturally for 20 centuries without ever having to send a single soldier across her border.

Hu Shih
Former Ambassador of China to USA (1891–1962)

… In the morning I bathe my intellect in the stupendous and cosmological philosophy of the Bhagavad-Gita in comparison with which our modern world and its literature seem puny and trivial."

… Whenever I have read any part of the Vedas, I have felt that some unearthly and unknown light illuminated me. In the great teaching of the Vedas, there is no touch of the sectarianism.

It is of ages, climes, and nationalities and is the royal road for the attainment of the Great Knowledge. When I am at it, I feel that I am under the spangled heavens of a summer night.

Henry David Thoreau
American Philosopher (1817–1862)

Is there a 'core idea' in the scriptures? Is there a pattern that makes sense? Is there some point having arrived at which one gains complete grasp of what the scriptures contain (as is the claim with regard to the end of knowledge in param vidya)?

Even if there is one, how does one extract that core idea? How can one scan hundreds of thousands of verses that are contained in the various holy books of the Hindus and try to sieve out from it that knowledge of the core idea it is supposed to contain? There are the Vedas, the puranas, the Upanishads and many more. The question is this: how does a researcher draw wisdom from it?

Here is an interesting example. In the defense of gay and lesbian rights, some activists recently quoted that it is written in the *Ramayana* that the wives of Ravana were known to have shared a lesbian relationship. Using this example, the claim was that gay and lesbian relationships are a part of Indian culture. Take another example. A lot of people are inspired by the narration contained in the Mahabharata, but it is found that some people are inspired by the ideal of Shakuni, the scheming uncle, rather than Lord Krishna, who is supposed to be the hero of the epic. The question, therefore, is this: how does one really figure out what is to be followed and accepted in the scriptures? What is to be taken as an ideal to be accepted and what is to be taken as an example to be shunned?

Consider the following parameters. These can be considered as broad constraints, belief systems, axioms, etc. that give a hint of the direction one may wish to look at.

The Guru: It is said that it takes a master—a Guru, really—to be able to extract knowledge from the contents of the scriptures and deliver it to the student or disciple.

And then again, how does one distinguish a mere lecturer/*Acharya* from a Guru? How does one know that a learned man and teacher has indeed made the transition from being a mere scholar to a wise man?

Again, there are lessons regarding this in the scriptures. And when one gets into studying it with diligence, one ends up finding many passages dealing with it in many sources.

But again, for every passage one finds in the scriptures, there are many interpretations of them given by various scholars. And this leads the layman into a tricky situation. A true Guru will give an interpretation of the passage to mean that he himself is a Guru. Would a student then accept such an interpretation? So, a question mark still lingers, and there is still a debate as to what the truth really is.

Anyway, let us say that the Hindu scriptures say that there is something called 'Guru', who is wisdom itself, in whom there is manifested the attainment of freedom from the duality of joy and sorrow. Such a person is to be followed. (We shall see more of this later.)

The experience: And then again, the truth brought out by the scriptures is not something that someone can pluck from a tree and hand it over to a disciple for him to taste it. It is for the disciple to reach out and take from what is available.

It is said of the 'exalted' experience which the Indian spiritual researchers pursue that it is in one sense similar to the experience of eating a sweet. Let's take a *Jilebi* (an Indian delicacy), for instance. One can write pages and pages about it. One can describe how it is made, what ingredients go into it, how it looks, what shape it has, what color it has, its taste and even how it feels on the tongue. But even if one has read books and books about it, there is no other way for someone to know truly what a Jilebi is unless he himself eats it.

Therefore, there is a claim that there is 'a reality', a truth and that it needs to be experienced for it to be understood. It is supposed to be a journey that one has to make for oneself.

Rigorous pursuit: The search can be maddening. It is said that when the Zen (*Chen/Dhyan/*Meditation) masters wanted to teach their students about the 'Final Truth', they merely give them an idea, a line or a thought. Something to ponder about. When the student diligently follows that, he may finally 'see' what it is all about. There are supposed to be sages, ascetics, monks, priests and philosophers who have tried all kinds of meditations in all kinds of places and scanned scores of scriptural texts for their entire lifetimes in pursuit of that truth and have come out only with mixed luck. In other words, some say that it is just about latching on to an important point, and for others, it is supposed to result from a lifetime of penance, meditation and research.

Pursuit of wisdom: So, that makes an interesting combination. There is a need for a Guru (difficult to define), it consists of an experience (one has to seek and attain it by oneself) and the work toward getting it can be very rigorous. Not too motivating an idea, really... And yet, Hinduism holds this so-called 'knowledge' in extremely high esteem. Critics and scoffers say that all this knowledge is just an 'invention' by scheming persons; others say that it is a truth of nature which has been 'discovered'. The debate does not show signs of getting resolved in the public sphere.

So much for one who thinks he can just pick up a book and know all that is contained in spiritualism... And so much for someone else who thinks he can write a chapter in a book and tell his readers what it is all about...

The conclusion is that it would make no sense to try and compress what is essentially an experience into a chapter of this book.

But it would also be improper to leave it and not make a point at all. Can we work our way around this problem? If not the real deal, can we have a compromise or an alternative or some viable media for it?

Why not leave it to the specialists who deal in the subject?

The author thinks it is both appropriate and opportune that one such specialist, a favorite of the author, is highlighted—someone who can make the relevant point.

Just one will do: It should be remembered here that all scriptures are like pointers to something. For example, let's say that there is a room into which only one person can go at a time. The task given to the person going into the room is to discover a certain place in the room where there is a button to open a premier door. That door is supposed to lead into another room having great wonders and entertainments. If one does not find the button and push it, the premier door does not open. He has to eventually leave through an ordinary door, having failed to see those special wonders that could be accessed through the other door.

Now, a person enters the room, and he finds that the things in the room are arranged in some kind of arrow pattern, and even as he keeps moving around the room, he finds many such patterns. In some places, hairpins are arranged in that fashion. In other places, there are small pebbles. Sometimes, it is woodwork all chipped up and laid down to make an arrow. Apparently, the persons who have been to this room before him have made these arrow marks.

What is important here is that this person needs to recognize that it is an 'arrow' and start wondering where it is pointing. For this, even a single arrow serves the purpose. The alternative task of the person spotting and recognizing hundreds of arrows is not the best thing to occupy his time with. (And neither is it sensible to keep looking at one particular arrow and sing praises of how it is the best arrow ever and so on.)

Scriptural studies are similar; it is not about reading a lot of scriptures. It is about understanding at least one of them, and it is said that once this happens, all others will be easily understood.

Going by this, let us focus on one of the pointers/ arrows. The author's pet reference is Veda Vyasa.

A fascinating work: Let us take up one book from his enormous list of works, the *Mahabharata,* and in this book, one brilliant piece of literature. The reference is to the *Bhagavad Gita*, a discourse given by Lord Krishna to the talented Arjuna on the battlefield just before the commencement of the Kurukshetra War. Before we get to the message the book gives, let us consider a few points about the book itself.

Now, were Lord Krishna and Arjuna historical figures? Or were they a deification of real characters that existed at some point? Or were they a figment of some author's imagination? Irrelevant questions…

What is the point in debating over chaff? Whether the truth was this way or that, there is no denying the fact that there was a tremendous intellect behind the thinking that went into the content in the *Bhagavad Gita*, and knowing this is enough for us. The brilliance in the scripture speaks for itself—the content is outstanding. So, let us get to the substance directly by skipping questions that raise unnecessary controversy.

Tips to unravel the *Bhagavad Gita* jigsaw puzzle: The interesting part is that this lesson is imparted in the context of a war—on a battlefield, to be precise. It is the most appropriate place to come out with such a work for the reason that even a lay reader will be able to fathom the passions that run high before the start of a war. If he is smart enough to relate the lesson to how he felt before he played a cricket match or performed a dance on stage, he can easily place himself in a similar zone of experience and experience what Arjuna might have felt when he was on the battlefield. And we should remember that going through the human feeling and experience is an important aspect of spiritual learning.

There is yet another clue regarding how we could approach the lessons imparted in the Gita. Let us say that there is a football match that is going to start, and the star striker is down and out, saying that he has no motivation to get on to the field and play. So, his coach steps in and tries to bring him around. When he does so,

we cannot expect him to sit there for days and explain verse for verse why the footballer should get up and start playing. Rather, it will be a conversation between two individuals—a conversation between coach and player— and far from the dissecting of verses and phrases that happen in communication, the focus should be on trying to figure out what the points the two adults were making to each other. One of them is totally confident, without a doubt and wise, and the other is shaken and dejected.

Another clue left in this construct is that even as we follow the conversation, as we hear what Lord Krishna has just said, and understand the same, a question might arise in our minds. The same question is brought up by Arjuna! Then, we may understand that we are indeed tracking the conversation in the manner in which it is to be interpreted and followed.

And beyond these things, it is a huge puzzle that one needs to solve. The copy of the Gita that the author has in his hand is a translation, in English, of the original Sanskrit work. It takes all the ingenuity in one's command to decipher what the original author, Veda Vyasa, wanted to say. Check out this sequence:

i)   The original author encountered an idea somewhere in the past.

ii) He decided that he would convert it into a learning that could be transferred.

iii) He composed a huge poem that would convey what he discovered/witnessed.

iv) With whatever hold he had over his language, he put down his ideas in verse.

v)   And then, it is apt to remember that it was an oral tradition of learning at that time. So, the composition was not penned down. It was verbally composed.

vi) The composition was based on the objects that existed at that time—the technology of those days, the style of storytelling of that time, the common sense of those times, the accepted culture of the times, the accepted authority centers in terms of philosophy, the cultural and social preferences of those times, the political constitution of society of that time and most of all, the language of that time…

vii) Then, it was transferred down the ages through an oral tradition of learning, hopefully without any interpolation or extrapolation. It was finally penned down somewhere in the beginning of the first millennium AD.

viii) Somewhere at the end of the second millennium AD, we have a translator working on the same text.

ix) Hopefully, the language Sanskrit that existed ages ago has not changed much through the centuries, and even if it has not, hopefully, the translator really knows what each word stands for... And then, hopefully, the translator also has a good grasp of the English language into which he translates the text...

x) And then, the translator is in the socio-cultural-political setting of the present generation, where the use of bows and arrows, value systems, caste compositions, family values and social roles all have different meanings and where common conventions differs from the common conventions of yesteryears.

xi) And when this work reaches the reader, there is the question of colored spectacles; the final reader of today may have his own limitations in terms of perception, his grasp of the English language and the socio-cultural setting that he grew up in.

The crunch question is this: in this rather long sequence of events/filters, what is the guarantee that the ideas that are formed in the mind of the English reader of the twentieth century are the same that were in the mind of the original poet (Veda Vyasa) who wrote the poem in the first place?

Pretty low, one must say, since there is so much scope for error in the various stages of perception, interpretation, contexts and skill sets of the involved persons through which the ideas have to pass. No wonder then that there are so many interpretations of the verses in the *Bhagavad Gita*. No wonder then that people easily fail to fathom the brilliance of the works of the likes of Veda Vyasa.

Filtering the perceptions: The question that arises is whether it is possible to arrive at a scientific thought process by which we can figure out as to which interpretation can be accepted as correct.

Hopefully, scientists will come up with something soon. But in the meanwhile, we can accept the following two pointers.

First, the poet wrote about 'people' he witnessed during his time, so the truths about 'people' will apply to the 'people' of this age too. Therefore, we can crosscheck every conclusion that we make from the *Bhagavad Gita* with the truth we see in people around us. If the conclusions made in a certain study truly reflect human behavior that we see around us, then the interpretation is on the right track.

Second, there is the idea of the jigsaw puzzle. There is a correct way to put a jigsaw puzzle into place, and the correctness of our progress becomes evident when we see a consistent picture emerging. As the picture grows in its details, and as the consistency grows, confidence in the correctness of the pursuit increases.

As of now, these are the limited pointers to tell us if we are on the right track.

Interesting result: When one goes through this process of deciphering what the author of the Bhagavad Gita had in mind, it becomes evident that it stands for something very important. *The Bhagavad Gita more or less presents an excellent secular picture of all spiritualities and all religions.*

A very tall claim, one may say. But if it is indeed right, then it becomes evident why Hinduism may be considered a boa.

Among the lessons that come out of the Gita is one which says that all pursuits of religion and spiritualism in their purest form essentially involve the shift from ignorance to self-realization, from *samsara* to *nirvana*, from manliness to Godliness, from bondage to freedom and that there is no other way for doing this than giving up one's ego and self-centeredness.

The Gita also contains a general description of the various ways in which an individual may perceive himself, which have consequences on his demeanor. For example, if he thinks he is an exalted animal, his behavior is according to that. If he believes he is essentially spirit, he behaves differently.

There is also a description of various 'exercises' that can be resorted to by the seeker in order to shift from bondage to freedom. Most of all, the *Bhagavad Gita* pays respect to all such 'exercises' that help shift man from one state to the other. The technical term used for this is yoga. It is not the same as the yoga that is taught in yoga classes pertaining to postures of the body. There is a vague similarity by a long shot though. Yoga, in this context, has more to do with a certain mental posture or bearing which an individual needs to take in his pursuit of higher goals.

Then, there are lessons contained in the Gita which explain how to recognize a genuine Guru. Studying the Gita diligently also endows one with the ability to recognize another exercise/yoga taught by someone else, which can help achieve the desired transition to liberation.

Once this recognition happens with respect to a certain self-realized soul, that is, once it has been accepted by a seeker/scholar/wise man of India that this self-realized soul has a genuine means for achieving the final goal, that self-realized person is recognized as a Guru or even an 'avatar'. The method becomes a part of Hinduism. The boa has done its job. This is why when the truth dawned on Hinduism that Saint Mahaveer is a self-realized soul and that he leads the devout to liberation, he was accorded recognition as an avatar of Lord Vishnu.

There is no chauvinism in this. Hinduism recognizes the right of every individual to find his own Guru, to pick up his religion—in fact, Gandhiji argues that there are as many religions as there are individuals. This is because each individual actually travels on a unique path. The Divine speaks to each individual in a unique way. For example, the *Bhagavad Gita* was the lesson that taught Arjuna his religion, and the Gita would have been different had it been directed at another character in the Mahabharata. *The author of the Bhagavad Gita is therefore more interested*

in the fact that one is journeying toward self-realization and is not particular about the Guru that is being followed or the yoga that is being used.

At the very foundation of Hinduism are the Vedas. It may surprise some that in all the Vedas, there is no mention made of any deity. It is based purely on an understanding of the essential nature of the Divine. And it is the lessons contained in the Vedas that are brought out in a substantial measure in the *Bhagavad Gita*. It is said of the *Bhagavad Gita* that if all the Upanishads were a cow, then the *Bhagavad Gita* is the milk. This is a metaphor that suggests that the *Bhagavad Gita* is a digest of all that is contained in the Upanishads and delivers to the reader, in adequate measure, all there is to have from it.

Therefore, from our considerations of the Gita, we see that the Vedas speak about spiritualism in general, not insisting on a particular spiritual practice or a few practices that are propounded under certain Guru-traditions, and the *Bhagavad Gita* faithfully transmits this learning.

As such, Hinduism accords recognition to genuine Guru-traditions, irrespective of the origin or source, and accepts them as legitimate paths. This ability and the Catholicism of Hinduism explains why it distinguishes itself as a 'boa of religions'. Needless to say, it is a just a matter of time before it gulps down Christianity and Islam. Many Indian saints have already firmly stated that these religions are legitimate paths to the highest spiritual goal. Those who know say that this swallowing by the boa is already official.

The (Bhagavad) Gita is one of the clearest and most comprehensive summaries of the perennial philosophy ever to have been done. Hence, its enduring value, not only for the Indians, but also for all mankind. It is perhaps the most systematic spiritual statement of the perennial philosophy.

Aldous Huxley
English Novelist (1894–1963)

1.4 GENUINE PRACTICAL HINDUISM IS THE GLOBAL ANSWER FOR PEACE

With due humility I believe that who calls himself an Indian is a Hindu

T. N. Seshan (29/01/1994)
Former CEC of India

Hindu: An interesting fact about Hinduism is the origin of the term used to define it: Hindu.

A report on the culture and traditions in the land where the river Sindu flows went to Persia through a Persian reporter. The king asked about the religious practices of the people of the land. The reporter could not specify anything in particular and said that they could just call them 'Sindu' or people who lived in the land were the river Sindu flows. Unfortunately, the Persians had trouble pronouncing the 'sin' in the word 'Sindu'. They said 'hin' instead, and so, the 'Sin'dus were called 'Hin'dus. And the name stuck…

But do note that this would also mean that the term 'Hindus' was used to define literally everything about the place this visitor had come across. Hence, it cannot be said that it refers to a religion. Indeed, is Hinduism truly a religion?

But then again, what is a religion?

Is Hinduism a religion? Unfortunately, there is no clear definition of the term, so we need to skirt around it. We could possibly start at the point of acknowledging Christianity as a religion. Let us for the moment ignore the fact that there are a host of sub-groups claiming to be followers of Jesus Christ; clubbing them all together, we could broadly say that a religion should have the following characteristics:

1) An inspirational founder
2) A community or group that follows that leader through inspired faith
3) A system of thought, or a scripture, which carries the inspirational message of the leader
4) A set of dogmas, practices, rituals, traditions and sacraments that have spiritual content, which together give the group an identity and a bouquet of activities with which they occupy themselves

This list of aspects of religion is by no means all-encompassing, but it does cover the essential features of Christianity which could distinguish it from, say, Islam. The point that we need to consider now is whether this allows us to define Hinduism as a religion.

The problem is that there are many inspirational leaders in Hinduism. Each of these Gurus has inspired followers who are blessed with faith. There is a voluminous scriptural foundation for Hinduism, but it has given rise to a whole lot of Gurus who have drawn from these sources. There are a host of Guru-*paramparas* (Guru-traditions) that have resulted from their work, and such traditions take on diverse dogmatic approaches, practices, rituals, sacraments, etc. Therefore, we may ask the question as to how this complete arrangement compares to Christianity as a religion.

The answer to this puzzle comes from an analysis of the definition of a Guru-parampara. If we get back to the core of the Vedas, it becomes clear that true religion is that which a person adopts in his thinking, in his living and in practice which preserves him in the good of righteousness, keeps him focused on the present and makes him constantly endeavor at practices that can take him from ignorance to bliss, from samsara to nirvana, from slavery under *maya* to dominion over it.

These Guru-paramparas also chart, for the faithful, a pattern of life that facilitates their attaining of the final goal in spirituality while they still carry on with their earthly functions.

Therefore, if self-realization/nirvana is the final goal of all spirituality, and if there is nothing higher, then any Guru-tradition which has the potential to facilitate the achievement of that goal in its followers is complete in that sense. We could possibly define this as a religion.

What remains to be seen is whether Christianity is indeed a Guru-parampara, and the answer seems to be in the affirmative.

The only difference between Christianity as a Guru-parampara and the Guru-paramparas of Indian origin is that Christianity is based on a substratum of scriptures that has come from a different source—from the Semitic traditions.

But then, is this difference a significant aspect of practical spirituality?

'Scriptural substrata score far below what is really substantial,' says Hinduism. For it is known to the Hindu scholar that for the final transition from ignorance to bliss, it is important for the practitioner to give up each and everything that associates his 'self-hood' to any 'identity' aspect of an individual. That a person is a Christian, a Hindu, a Muslim or a Buddhist is an association with an identity, which also needs to be given up in the final transition to wisdom. Therefore, association with a different scriptural substratum is of no major consequence when the prime goal of a religion is to achieve the transition from ignorance to understanding.

Therefore, functionally speaking, the Guru-paramparas in Hinduism can be easily equated to religions. In which case, Hinduism cannot be equated to a religion. Hinduism is the compendium of religions!

Summarizing: The literal interpretation of the label 'Hindu' is the best description of it. A Hindu is a person who lives in the land where the river Sindu flows. Hinduism thus stands for the socio-politico-economic-cultural-religious condition in this land. More specifically, it stands for the spiritual aspect of this geographic demographic. The Hinduism that we know as a religion is actually a confluence of sub-religions. Hinduism, as such, is more than a religion. Like Christianity and Islam, the various sects in Hinduism are complete paths in themselves, but there is interdependence among them. The interdependence is small when we concern ourselves with Buddhism, Jainism and the Sikh religion, but in the case of channels like Shaivism, Vaishnavism, Vedic learning, Bhagvathism and a host of other Guru-paramparas, the interdependence runs very deep. And everything together forms that big mosaic called as Hinduism. It has a central

ethos with no marked boundaries, having a dissipating reach extending to all of humanity.

A vision of oneness: So, all that remains is to look into what Hinduism thinks about people following someone like Jesus Christ.

Reckoning the definition of a self-realized soul, if it gets established that the description fits Jesus Christ, then Hinduism encourages a devotee of Jesus Christ to really make all attempts to understand Christ's work in depth and follow him to the extent that one is able to give up, totally, his selfishness. It suggests that there should be a complete surrender to him, *samarpan*. In fact, this is what Jesus Christ asks as well, 'Give up yourself, take up your cross and follow me.'

As for Islam, the Hindu tradition seems to classify the kind of work put in by the Noble Prophet as that of a *Rishi*—Islam is then a Rishi-parampara.

Note that the Bible refers to the source of all wisdom as the 'Word', which was made flesh in Jesus Christ. The Veda also has similar connotations, meaning that there is one eternal feeling/experience. The sages of yore experienced it and penned it down to result in the Vedas. Through equivalence, we could say that for the Hindus, the Word was made into text in the Vedas or something like that. In both cases, the reference is to the manifestation of an eternal truth. In Islam too, the 'experience' of the Divine attained manifestation in the words of the Quran. Hinduism has no conflict with either of these views from the Semitic religions.

Therefore, we can again take note here that the Hindu perspective turns Samuel Huntington's theory of clash of civilizations on its head; *Samuel's theory is an antithesis of Hinduism.* Hinduism claims that there is really no clash at the level of civilizations.

Essential Hinduism—its very existence is proof of the fact that multiple religious traditions (Guru-paramparas) can happily coexist. And this fact clearly places a great responsibility on Indians to take the message of peace across the world.

This also calls to question the approach of some of the so-called faithful of Islam who seem to give more weight to Samuel Huntington than to the Prophet himself. Many others from other religions also react on the same lines.

Samuel Huntington had a field day projecting political opportunism as a clash of civilizations, as if these groups are all fundamentally different. Taken up by it, a few people are into the business of attempting to wipe out 'other' religions from the face of the earth. The truth though is that there is no question of a clash if Yahweh, The Father and Allah are the same as is the claim of the Quran. If there are groups that are truly devoted to the other two faces of the Universal Truth (Yahweh, The Father), then those groups ought not to clash with Islam. The Prophet would want the faithful of Islam to focus on whether they are faithful to the Universal Truth or not (regardless of name) rather than condemn people on the basis of group classifications decided by man at an earthly level on the basis of earthly practices (though, of course, in pursuit of the heavenly truth).

The truth is that any group can truly become a civilization if and only if it learns to appreciate the true worth of the Divine. All such groups which give a central place to that divine experience rise up to become civilizations. Therefore, the theory that is worth studying is not the 'clash' but the 'commonality of civilizations'; the moment a person discovers the commonality in a way that frees and elevates him, he has arrived at the goal of all spiritualities.

We can summarize that *if there is a clash, it is between political ideologies and aims and that the real substance of any civilization is the commonality that it shares with all other civilizations.*

The study of Hinduism opens for us great opportunities that lie in it. The antithesis of Huntington has been the nature of Hinduism for centuries, and it has shown that it is possible for the various Guru-paramparas to live side by side in peace. This means that there are elements in the Hindu culture that facilitate this peaceful co-existence of different faiths. Or, in other words, if the world is looking for a culture of peace that should develop between religions of the world, which should help them understand, accept and respect each other, then one can look into the solutions that have evolved in Hinduism.

Practical Hinduism: Arising from the understanding of the universal truth that is available in the core of the Vedas, Bharat Varsha, or the land of the Bharatas, has adopted in its life blood the principle of *'sarva dharma samabhava'* or in other words 'every dharma on par'. This belief is that all humans are guided by one force and one law; irrespective of what path a seeker takes, it should lead him to realize the same fundamental truth. Therefore, we come to the point that the stress, in Hinduism, is to travel with one's whole heart and soul on whatever path one chooses. It does not insist on traveling on a 'particular' path. And stress is also laid on the description of the culminating point of one's travel. In fact, Hindus are taught to identify those who have realized this final truth so that they may be honored and looked up to for guidance. And we have seen that the Hindu system also describes, broadly, the methods and exercises to be used by individuals in that process of self-discovery. So, we come to that famous saying of Hinduism, 'Each acknowledges that the other path is also a possible route but stresses that his own way is the best to take.' If not for the others, then for himself at least...

It should not be difficult for an individual to note that this is the most refined form of secularism. Not atheistic secularism, but secularism that acknowledges that divinity may be the fundamental nature of humans. It is about a 'believing secularism' or a 'theistic secularism' (Refer to Appendix E on secularism).

Some universal indices: Also, adherence to the fundamental spirit of Hinduism involves mutual respect for people's individuality, conformity with one's dharma and an essential inclination for that which is termed as *puniya*. It defines an association with this land—Bharat Varsha—not on the basis of ethnicity but on the basis of 'action' or *karma*. Clearly, this raises the issue far above the confines of narrow nationalism and enters the sphere of the common brotherhood of man; it raises the issue into the universality that lies beyond the confines of groups.

The greatest of the Indian festivals, Diwali, is a reminder and a celebration of the fact that the biggest of joys in this land is the triumph of good over evil; those that flow contrary to the trust and love under the grace of The One Supreme Being are the enemies. And victory has to be had over them, irrespective of the affiliation they belong to.

In this sphere, the important values treasured by the Hindu system can be reckoned by elaborating on the term Bharat Varsha—*Puniya Bhoomi, Dharma Bhoomi* and *Karma Bhoomi*.

Puniya Bhoomi means a land of the good, where people do what is good and where people are honored for doing so.

Dharma Bhoomi means a land where each person is assigned a duty. He ought to do that duty and find, as he performs that duty selflessly, attainment of the highest spiritual goal and find fulfillment in life through that. And most importantly, that duty is such that the addition of the duties of all individuals leads to the maintenance of a society called *Ram Rajya*, a land ruled by the principles used by Lord Rama or better known to the Christian world as the Kingdom of Heaven, a kingdom that embodies the spirit of heaven. We shall see more of this later.

And finally, Karma Bhoomi means a land where an individual is evaluated on the basis of his karma or his actions. Again, one should note that this also has a parallel Christian principle. Jesus Christ has instructed his followers that they will be able to identify the persons who come from God through their actions—after all, people may hold and profess great notions and ideas but it's only by how they behave that we come to know what substance they are made of.

Anyway, the Hindu system associates great importance to the principle of karma. The doings of man define both his happiness and the rewards that he receives. In some beliefs, it is perceived in terms of rewards and punishments in the next birth. In others, the results are described as instantaneous. However, in the land of dharma, it is hoped that dharma will ensure that an individual gets the appropriate external results of his karma in as much as his doings interfere with the lives of others around him—an evil deed drawing punishment, a good deed approval and sacrifice receiving due respect and appreciation.

So, finally, we have Bharat Varsha, a land where the inspiration is the Kingdom of Heaven, where people strive to do good and where people are valued for the manner in which they serve rather than for 'where' they serve.

Dharma: Let us revert to the term 'dharma'. What is this dharma that is so central to Hinduism?

Before we get to that, we need to understand that the term is used often in the recent past in ways that it was not originally meant to be. In colloquial usage, the term has come to be equated loosely to religion. People commonly say, 'Hindu Dharma', 'Isai Dharma (Christian Dharma)' or 'Jain Dharma'. In truth, such a usage fails on two counts. The first is that Hinduism, Christianity and Jainism cannot be technically equated in one class. Second, even if we exclude Hinduism from the list, the word cannot be used to stand for religion. In fact, the term Hindu Dharma can be used in a sense to indicate that there is more to it than religion and is closer to a way of life. This term is closer to the truth, but it is still not accurate. So then, what is dharma? The way to resolve this is to go back to the academicians of ancient India who used the word authoritatively.

From the fact that it is said in the Mahabharata that Arjuna was asked to 'perform' his Kshatriya dharma, it becomes clear that there is an element of 'duty' in dharma.

Next, it is said that the role of Lord Krishna was to establish dharma in society. This would mean that the word is used to reflect the notion of 'setting up law and order' or, to put it in a more refined way, 'rule of law'.

Yet another aspect of dharma can be understood from the words of Lord Krishna when he says, 'For one that is self-realized, there is no duty.' This needs a small elaboration. As opposed to someone doing his duty, he could be doing what he wants to do—his personal wish. When a person sees his work in society not as a duty to perform but rather as his personal wish, then he has no duty! In other words, the prodding is for people to attain a state of existence in which they see the role they perform in society as something they themselves desire should happen for society—they are happily doing their own thing! Take that one step further. It means that when the self-realized soul wishes that certain functions should be performed in society and when society is constructed according to that, the system that gets established is called as dharma. If there is no self-realized soul to set up systems in society, then a fair substitute is a democratic process where the entire group tries to express the common wish and desire of the entire society. Therefore, it can be said that the third aspect of dharma is the self-realized soul, the Supreme Will. God's Will, if one may… It is common to all humans. When the desire and wish of that highest principle is reflected in a system, then it is said that dharma is established.

And the last is the fact that dharma gets established at certain times. For instance, dharma was set with the work of Manu (Manu Dharma). It has a contextual aspect; dharma is for a place and age. Today, there are no kings in France, for instance. Establishment of dharma does not mean imposition of the four *varnas* in France. Rather, it requires the setting up of a system or order that is inspired by the Highest Principle. The French can look for self-realized souls to set systems for them or they can perfect their democracy to ensure that the highest goals of inner and outer liberty are facilitated in all their decisions. The constitution they so create would form the basis of dharma there. Therefore, we can conclude that the fourth aspect of dharma is that dharma is set up for a certain place, age, context and technological setup.

We can therefore list the aspects of dharma as follows:
1) Sense of duty
2) Rule of law
3) The Divine Will
4) The context (nation and era) in which it is set up

It is therefore important to note that the public life and dialog in India cannot be elevated to greater heights without the use of the concept of dharma. In fact, what is needed is a redefinition of dharma for this age and time.

It must be pointed out that all admired leaders, in all of history, in the whole world will easily reflect these four elements in their work. The best of leaders have a great sense of duty; they do uphold the rule of law (or at least attempt to set up a genuine rule of law); they are inspired to sacrifice their individual aims and are impelled by the highest that is in all of us, thus finding resonance in their followers' hearts, and they do respond to the needs of that particular time and age.

No wonder dharma has such a central place in the works of the ancient Indian sages (*dhammam* in Buddhism essentially is inspired by the same thing).

So then, is dharma an invention, or is it something that has to be discovered for a certain age and time? The argument of the ancients is that it is to be discovered. The following passage makes the statement. Note that Rishis going to Brahma is equivalent to saying Rishis looked into nature and tried to understand what the truth was. Brahma giving them something is equivalent to saying that it was discovered in nature by the Rishis.

Dharma was on the decline and the rule of 'Might is Right' prevailed. The Rishis were perturbed over the developments. They all went to Brahma to seek counsel. Brahma gave them a treatise on 'Law and the Functions of the State,' which he himself had written. At the same time he asked Manu to become the first king…

Pandit Deendhayal Upadhayay
Integral Humanism, 1965

(Refer to the Appendix for Pandit Deendhayal Upadhyay's views on dharma.)

So, it is evident the claim is that when dharma was in decline, they went back to the basics and what emerged is a discovery of rules applied in that context as the Divine Himself wanted. So, dharma is something that is discovered by looking at what God willed, not what man invented.

Motivators for action – the four *Purusharths*: Another important component of practical Hinduism is the idea of the four Purusharths. The root word is *Purusha,* which is considered as the active agent in the universe. Let me elaborate on this. All that is contained in the universe is defined by the term 'Universal Brahman'. Its two components are termed as Purusha and *Prakriti.* Purusha is considered as the active agent, which is in the realm of the Supreme Self. Prakriti, on the other hand, includes everything that comes under the realm of cause and effect. This includes everything that we can perceive with our five senses and imagine with the mind. Further, the theory suggests that every individual is composed of both elements. Therefore, the truly active element in all of us humans is the Purusha, and the rest that we can see, smell, touch, etc. consists of Prakriti. The term Purushartha is used in the sense that what drives us is truly the Purusha that is within all of us (Purusha-*artha* can be thus interpreted as that which has meaning [artha] for the Purusha). Driven by Purusha and reflected onto material nature—Prakriti—which is the reactive part of each creature, there are four motivators for action by creatures (humans). These four motivators or impellors for work are stated here:

1) *Artha*: This pertains to material gains, status, etc. It includes everything that can be considered as attributes that add on to a person as wealth.

2) *Kama*: This stands for everything to do with satisfying the senses. All biological factors that have to do with a living being come under this. Hunger is an example here.

3) *Dharma*: This is a motivator in an individual which makes him work for order in society. It is an expression of a wish that fellow beings may share harmony with the individual and among themselves so that all can live in peace and justice.

4) *Moksha*: This is a motivator that makes individuals yearn for happiness; this manifests as a want to work toward spiritual elevation among those that have been exposed to this link. It is something that makes sensitized ones want to pursue the rigors of religion, music, dance, etc. In the case of one who is not initiated, it impels him to follow desires and pleasures in the hope that there is happiness at the end.

The importance of understanding this is that only after having acknowledged that these are the four motives that impel man to action can one really make a comprehensive analysis of society and its efficient design. Unfortunately, modern theorists have yet to gravitate on the last two motives of action and have an excessive focus on the first two. It is the Indian seers' belief that completeness or fulfillment lies in taking care of all four aspects. One needs to design one's life in a manner such that all four aspects are catered for, and only then can one attain wholeness, contentment, peace, happiness and prosperity in life. This is one area where the thinkers of ancient India can easily be shown to be ahead of the currently acknowledged experts in the field of human behavior.

Where it matters: From these considerations, it is easy to say that there is a need to study and critically assess the character of Hinduism. And this acquires great significance since it has an important role to play in the life blood of our nation and in bringing peace to the world.

There is a need to understand that excellence in public life cannot be generated in the absence of a pursuit of the highest spiritual goals. By saying that we would like to dissociate religion from politics, we unfortunately imply that we wish to delink spiritualism and morality from public life in India. The Indian ethos uses the notion of dharma to enhance outstanding values in public life; this needs to be understood in its secular form and then used to improve public life in India. In fact, dharma is the central theme around which the *Mahabharata* and *Ramayana* are based; all the avatars of Lord Vishnu are also seen as intervening to establish dharma in society. If the value it stands for is not used in the public life of India today, we cannot raise the standards of public life in the manner that we really need to.

The real fight: As always, there are people even today who use religion as yet another marker to divide society—it is politics (of the dirty kind). There is a need to remember that there is no spiritual sanction for something like Hindu fundamentalists countering Muslim fundamentalists. The only difference that should matter should be of the irrational fundamentalists of both Islam and Hinduism on one side and the genuine followers of the Muslim faith and the upholders of Hindu dharma together on the other.

Whether it is the question of Ayodhya or of other disputed temples or of Kashmir or of Pakistan for that matter, if it is not seen in this light of good vs. evil, the basic lesson of Hinduism is lost.

The issue of Kashmir: Clearly, there is a need to raise the debate above the narrow religious context. It is known to the wise men that have lived in Sindu-land that there is tremendous misery wrought from squabbling states, and therefore, there is religious sanction for the expansion of stable kingdoms. The least we can therefore do is to avoid by all means the tendency to create more walls than those that are already there. Spiritual wisdom points out that the whole idea of Kashmiri separatism is an unwarranted move away from one of the stable political structures (despite all its faults) that is known to exist today, Indian democracy.

The whole idea of an Islamic nation is a non-starter because Islam has nothing against a democracy which respects even a kafir's right to the promises made to him. Even a kafir's right to his own thinking and his own ways, provided he intends no harm to the faithful, is acceptable to Islam. And finally, the other person's right to worship the one and only Supreme Being under another name—and in his own way—is respected in the Quran. For we know that it pays respect to the Yahweh of the Jews and the Father of the Christians.

There is no spiritual, moral or religious backing for the idea of dividing a nation on the basis of religion, and it is high time that we jettison, from the political spectrum, all such so-called leaders who ensure their survival by concocting lies about what the Noble Prophet wants. If one has any doubts, all he needs to do is to think of an imaginary meeting between Lord Krishna and The Prophet and check if they would really be thinking along the lines of dividing the nations.

Einstein was right when he said, 'No problem can be solved in the same level of consciousness that created the problem.'

We need to raise our levels and move into the level that both Lord Krishna and Mohammad the Prophet represented. Then and only then can we get the better of the interests that fuel the seemingly unending conflict among us. In fact, Kashmir should be seen as the opportunity and not a problem between the nations of India and Pakistan.

Ayodhya: This is one other issue that indicates how far away from the truth of religion we can really be.

As mentioned earlier, rather central to Hinduism is dharma. Lord Krishna and Lord Ram represent it. All the avatars of Lord Vishnu play this primary role of maintaining dharma in society.

We have seen that dharma represents a sense of duty, a rule of law, Divine Will and that it is applicable differently to different contexts.

When Lord Krishna wants to establish dharma in society, he wishes to ensure that the rule of law is based on the wishes of the Divine Will that is present in all of us; he wishes that each of us, in pursuit of the drive of the Divine Will within us, will play our part in society. So,

the question arises as to whether Lord Rama would wish that we break laws that have been created by a legitimate process that has been in play in a nation—rules that have been put in place through consultations among the 'elders' of the nation.

Would Lord Rama wish for someone to break into what is being held as somebody else's property in the middle of the night and stake claim on it by such fraud—without reference to the law?

Would Lord Rama consider those among his subjects who pay their respects to another Rishi as 'they', as if they were not his own subjects?

Would He be responsible, even by a long shot, for the death of children ripped out of the wombs of living women subjected to rape and torture?

Would Mohammed the Prophet be insensitive and unfair and not hand over to a group of people what they consider a symbol of all that is exalted and beautiful in man?

Would Mohammed the Prophet really see someone like Gandhiji, who lived and died a life of sacrifice, as a kafir? He was a devotee of Lord Rama.

Who have we given ourselves in ransom to? Where have we pickled our brains? The division of society has never been a successful strategy in the land where the Sindu flows. The sooner we wake up, the better.

One should remember that Lord Rama was far more concerned about dharma than possessing all of Ayodhya—let alone a small piece of land. He should not be misrepresented.

The concept of Pakistan: It is an absurd concept: a nation created in the name of Islam, spearheaded by a leader who was born a Muslim, but not a true or a practicing one by a considerable margin.

What happened during partition was more like a fight between brothers who wanted their own share of the cake rather than anything truly holy. It happened out of a feeling of distrust and intolerance between groups rather than out of the love and benevolence of creating a beautiful nation. Indeed, it can be called to serious question whether it was the assertion of the benevolence of the Holy Prophet or the mere use (misuse, rather) of the name of Islam. To credit the massacre of millions to either the basic principles of Islam or Hinduism is utter nonsense—neither of the two propagates that idea. To accept the line of certain individuals who claim that there is not a single one, among those who are not branded Muslims, who is truly devoted to the Supreme Truth is an exercise in naivety. And if it is truly Islam that has inspired the creation of the nation of Pakistan, would it be in the miserable state it is now?

The partition that happened was an error of judgment of the people of that age and time (including the colonial masters). And how disastrous the consequences—and surely, with no understanding of top or bottom or right or wrong, some would credit the creation of the nation to sacrifices made for the furtherance of religions… [sic]

Partition should be seen as no more than an accident in history where leaders failed us, where important players failed in performing their dharma—especially those that held responsibility for the security of individuals and their property.

It should also be seen as a stage wherein human nature was put to severe test, where even as evidence of human brutality was seen, there were countless stories of unsung heroes too.

It is time we stop propagating the failures of an age gone by and chart a new course. We should not hand our peace of mind over to chauvinists who, in any case, will have nests to feather or axes to grind. Maybe it is high time we just accept our mistakes, let go of the past, pick up the spirit of the Gandhi and the Frontier Gandhi and move on as two nations, if it has turned out like that. If the sayings of the wise, including Prophet Mohammed, are right, then we can make progress only if we elevate our consciousness to reflect genuine spirituality. And all are Hindus in any case; how do political boundaries matter?

In conclusion: The oneness that Hinduism represents needs to spread into the thinking process of the global village. Far from trying to assert an identity for Hinduism among other religions, it is important to demonstrate how, as a way of life, it contains the bond that unites the various religions of the world.

When we read the poetical and philosophical monuments of the East –
above all, those of India,
which are beginning to spread in Europe –
we discover there many a truth,
and truths so profound,
and which make such a contrast with the meanness of the results at which European genius has sometimes stopped,
that we are constrained to bend the knee before the philosophy of the East,
and to see in this cradle of the human race the native land of the highest philosophy.

– Victor Cousin
French Philosopher (1792–1867)

Section II

The Making of Modern India After Slighting Indigenous Content

Can a nation prosper if it does not build on its indigenous strengths? And if it has not taken advantage of its strengths, what is the reason? And if it is to benefit from them, what is it supposed to do?

When we ask these questions in the Indian context, it becomes evident that the answers lie in a series of events that date back a few centuries. These developments have led to the way we think and act today, and it makes sense to go back and take a look at the developments so as to explore whether we could do things differently.

As we travel backward, it becomes clear that the merits of an essentially secular value-based system that Hinduism stands for have not found political center stage; there have been many important prejudices leading to this.

The detractors are of immense strength, strong enough to relegate a huge collection of intellectual and spiritual treasures into the background.

In this section, we travel back into India's recent past to see how several influences have shaped the present government/social mechanisms. These were merely mentioned in the first chapter; here, we shall look at them in some detail so as to achieve two things:

a) Understand the impact of these influences on the nation's perception of Hinduism

b) Explore the possibility of making a difference today

And the exploration does show that there are enough reasons for us to set the prevailing uncertainties aside and step on to solid ground on the basis of wisdom.

2.1 A COLONIAL ADMINISTRATION: NOT DESIGNED TO NURTURE INDIGENOUS WISDOM

One needs to consider what happened way back when colonial rule was being established in India.

At the end of the sixteenth century, India was an empire under the Mughals. When the Mughals lost their sheen early in the eighteenth century, the subcontinent was again dotted with many independent kingdoms. The colonial masters meanwhile did a remarkable job of again bringing much of the subcontinent together under one rule. And when they left, despite a half-hearted attempt to leave behind a weak conglomerate of states, the efforts of Sardar Vallabhai Patel ensured that the Indian nation was a reasonably well-knit unit. While the nation was being integrated, a suitable indigenous governance mechanism was also put in place.

But an indigenous government did not imply a complete delinking from the nation's colonial past. The new government carried forward many ideas, attitudes and institutions that were part of the erstwhile system. A look at the attitudes that ruled the roost at the time when the colonial power was being set up is a good indicator of the true nature of the administration that came into existence then. And since that administration has been carried over, it also throws light on the true nature of the administration that we have today.

Is this the administration that one would want for a free India? Is it accommodative of indigenous methods?

An administration subject to business interests: The aims of governments and the aims of businesses are not the same; governments administer and measure their success by the happiness of their subjects while businesses make profits and measure their success by the satisfaction of their stakeholders. Ideally, members of both the groups should perform their respective duties with the motive of serving people, the kings serving in their field and the business men in theirs. By achieving their respective aims, they help in maintaining the dynamics of an overall society, which in turn pays dividends for a better life for all citizens.

Further, these two sections of society must occupy some place in the overall picture of a nation. Based on their assigned duties, it can be said that since the political leadership has a wider zone of responsibilities, it would be assigned higher authority in society while businesses, owing to their having a limited profit motive, would have lesser and subservient authority.

It becomes messy when businesses take over the administration of a nation, and this was played out in the colonies.

In the industrially revolutionized Europe, becoming rich was about the most important thing that a man had to do in his life. The distinction in status between the nobility and the successful entrepreneur had begun to blur on account of increasing material wealth in the hands of entrepreneurs. The same was the story further down in the social ladder; making money had also become a primary goal of life there, having or not having money had become a matter of life and death—a struggle for survival.

As the industrial revolution progressed, institutions named 'companies' came into existence. For 'investors', it was a means to get richer while simultaneously doing material good to society. All and sundry who had money and wished to increase it (that included the nobility) invested in these companies.

So, for investors, the companies existed basically to make profits. And for this, among other things, the companies' chief concerns revolved around cutting costs and maximizing exploitation of company resources. Fair enough. Then, there were trade companies that hoped to earn profits through trade—nothing bad about that either. But when the companies ran over 'native' governments and became rulers of these 'colonies', the problems began.

The colonies became, what can loosely be called, equivalents of factories, and everything in the factories became 'resources'. The 'company' logic descended upon the spirit of governance, and the aim of good governance in these native states became, in a very basic sense, subject to the aims of the company (read East India Company).

A government is supposed to tax its citizens in order that it may bear the cost of the services it renders. It is often compared to the sun scorching the earth to take water, only to pour it back as rain. But here, we finally had a new situation: a sponge to 'soak up from the banks of the Ganges so as to drain on the banks of the Thames' (John Sullivan, President of the Board of Revenue, Madras, late nineteenth century). It was not a government; it was a constitution for exploitation. Even the Monarch, being an investor in the East India Company, was a part of the setup.

In this larger framework, any activity taken up by the administration had to pass the test of 'profit'. Reform was to be done if it was profitable; new projects were taken up so that it produced profit; welfare measures were taken up because the profits were falling drastically; 'modernity' and all that came with it was encouraged so that the Indian venture would be more efficient and 'profitable'.

Further, an ingenious method was adopted in certain areas by the Company in order to dodge the responsibilities of administration while simultaneously profiting from the control over the financial aspect. This method was at the core of the idea of 'dual' government. This came into prominence in the early nineteenth century. The pomp and pageantry of kingship and the responsibilities contained in it were to be the domain of the local ruler while the control over the money and military remained with the Company. So, the Company had its hand in the pie, and the princes could do little for their citizens while being at the receiving end of all the flack. The dual system filled the coffers of the Company while at the same time giving the Company some respite from the burden of the 'ruler's conscience'.

The situation changed when the British parliament took over from the Company after the uprising of 1857. But even here, it has been concluded by experts that it was a change of no great significance. With the coming of the crown's control, the responsibility buck was passed over to the parliament. However, practical realities on the ground ensured that the parliament had almost no control over the day-to-day functioning of the authorities in India. And the vested interests continued to profit from the ventures, although in a changed scenario.

All in all, it can be clearly seen that the system which came up was designed, from its very fundamentals, to avoid the conscience of a true statesman. Rather, its primary aim was to make the investors rich, and that made it alien indeed! So, in other words, the administration of a nation became subject to the goals of business.

When the basics are such, where is the chance of having benevolence in the administration in India? And so, why should we assume that the institutions put up for such a rule were for the good of society? Is it not a classic case of appointing a sales-cat in a fish-stall or a guard-monkey in a banana orchard?

So also the people of the Raj: The persons of foreign origin among the ruling class in the colony were, on an average, visitors to a treasure island. To people like them, the colonies were fair game. They would leave their homeland in Europe, go out on a long journey, work and return rich and prosperous after many years. A stint in India was considered an adventure—a money-spinning and nobility-winning adventure. Here, they dealt not with 'people' or 'fellowmen' but with 'natives'.

But one should not forget that the colonial rulers were not devoid of a conscience. Gandhiji himself appealed to it in his satyagraha, and through their response, it was proved that a conscientious disposition could be elicited. It also goes very well with what the wise say—that humans are basically God-like and that an appeal at the level of the conscience does not go unheeded. Needless to say, there are those in every society who learn to live by excellent principles and who work for the preserving of a system without any taint of selfishness. There should have been many such among the erstwhile rulers too—rendering their services to God or to the queen and contented with taking what came to them along the way. What we are concerned about is something which was a reality over and above this. The policies of the colony that mattered were indeed driven by compulsions of business.

Despite any good intentions, it was this motive that called the shots—the motive of material riches and glory at the expense of the Treasure Island. And any benevolence was built over this substratum, the profit motive.

And there were those up to wickedness too. Quite a few naturally threw all scruples to the wind. Who cared a damn whether the victims were 'natives' or 'fellowmen'? And over and above this, corruption existed; there are examples of officers of the Company amassing great fortunes.

Therefore, it can be concluded that many individuals of the colonial system on the one hand and the system itself on the other were oriented toward the fundamental goal of material profit—at the colony's cost.

An alien character: Apart from the motive of profit, there was another pivotal factor. It is particularly important to note that the rulers of that time, in general, tried to maintain a distance from the Indian population consciously and with zeal. And this superior attitude was reflected in all their dealings with the Indians.

They could have ruled by accepting this land as their own, as if it were an extension of their own wide nation. That is, by accepting this land as the land they wanted to live in after completing their service—by making this land their home much as the Mughals, the Khiljis and so many others who came before did. But this was not to be. Even Nehru shockingly discovered through interactions with the citizens of Britain at his alma mater in England that they would not treat him on par as a citizen of the empire.

Indeed, there was a sense of alienation that was perceptible in the environment. In due course, as the raj grew in strength, an unwritten philosophy of ruler-ship had evolved, which can be represented by the following points (these can either be beliefs of the rulers or broad thrusts adopted by them to achieve the rulers' ends or may be both):

** The natives don't know how to rule themselves; they need to be taught.

** Their traditions have regressive elements in them, and their learning is of no use to the modern system of education and is best avoided.

** They belong to an inferior race.

(Such extremist views were not all-pervasive though. Some believed them; others did not. There were several instances when the locals proved their mettle thus disproving these points. In any case, these were strong psychological tools used effectively in intimidating the local population.)

** Play one against the other; capitalize on greedy ambitions, and profit from it.

** See that the potential for mass uprising is effectively curtailed (nipped in the bud).

** Cultural traditions, technological knowhow, learning, economic might, institutions and practices that are potential threats to the rule should be discouraged or destroyed at all costs.

** The natives can do well enough with just enough for sustenance. Surplus may be appropriated by the government.

(This final point, even though it was not a deliberate policy, was the reality in the final picture; this became evident after the equilibrium had set in. We shall see that presently.)

How they went about it: There were other elements, or emotions, like British nationalism, the thirst for adventure, the authority of science and technology and Christian missionaries' zeal which aided the efforts of the colonial actors in India. But above all these, the two characteristics of profit motive/exploitation and scorn for the natives were the dominating influences that were prevalent during the process of the colonization of India.

The question therefore arises as to why we should not assume that these characteristics were naturally accommodated into the institutions that were built by the colonial masters. Indeed, when it came to the task of actually building a new system, the 'raj' naturally induced an exploitative and alien nature into it.

The European tradesmen took the opportunities that came their way. Trading rights which they obtained from Indian emperors and princes were followed by rights to hold small properties, and that was followed by rights to hold small contingents of security forces. Eventually, they won the Diwani rights in West Bengal and then slowly expanded until almost all of the subcontinent was under their sway.

Even as the foreign rulers extended their sway over most of India, they took up reforms (or deforms) in order to facilitate their interests in India. In order to suit their goals, they readjusted and fine-tuned the systems that had existed prior to their coming in. And over a period of more than 150 years, when they held sway, a lot of institution-building was done.

An efficient system of administration was built, and the proof of this was that the raj could hold sway for such a long period. But even as this system evolved and grew, the alien character which we considered earlier did become an integral part of it. By the time of independence, it had indeed come a long way.

The buffer classes came: There was a significant strategy adopted by the rulers, something which we have already referred to briefly in the first section, which resulted in a major impact on the socio-political system. This is a well-researched topic by many eminent persons; however, we shall repeat some aspects of it here. The rulers needed allies for their continued existence as masters of the colony, and for this, they aimed at, created and fostered buffer classes between them and the Indian masses. On the political front, these were the zamindars and the Indian princes, and on the cultural front, these were the class of Indians who were 'Indian by blood but western by mannerisms and outlook'. Many of them found jobs in the establishment, and most others coveted these opportunities.

Through the creation of such new classes, the bosses had to deal directly with only a limited few. And they shared with these classes the work and the psychological force required to maintain the system as well as the benefits that came to them from the arrangement.

The intelligentsia upheld the cultural might of the British on the basis of the good it could deliver. Scientific temperament and rational approaches made many of them prefer it to the far less straightforward, more troublesome and less understood situation that existed before science came in. Thus, the pro-western lobby consisted of the rationalized Indian elite who understood the significance of the fruits of the scientific civilization.

In political matters, it was more direct. Through small shifts in state policy, the class of zamindars was vested with new powers and authority. Eventually, these zamindars, through the interest of their own sustenance and survival, formed a shield of defense for the British from possible resistance from the grass roots. In due course, even these classes absorbed and adopted the 'natives-are-fair-game' attitude of their bosses. Finally, the harm that was left undone by the imposed law of the land was done by the ruthlessness of the greed of the players in the game, and that made the complete exploitative system.

One interesting aspect needs to be mentioned here. The British officials did know how to take care of the people who worked for them. They hired people from so-called 'martial' races (the others who revolted were not martial). There is a sense of loyalty to the person whose salt you have eaten—that sentiment was used effectively by the British. But they also did 'care' for their men. Once their platoon returned from a long march, young military officers would take each foot of each soldier in their bare hands and check if they had developed blisters. This was religiously done. That should be an index of how diligent the 'masters' were at their work. The British rule cannot be considered as all brute force; there was humility and team work too.

Protection for the men of the system: The most obvious of all the adjustments naturally arose from the need to protect the occupiers and the buffer classes that aided in the occupation. This meant that the law was inclined toward protecting the policemen, the people of the government, the soldiers and all those who constituted the occupying force. A look into the laws made in the British period would therefore reflect this protection to government employees at all levels. It is a natural thing for soldiers and policemen to have rights in any state, but one also needs to consider the extent to which such rights are given. The laws and systems created two hundred years ago in a colonial setup would definitely have elements that are only suitable to that age—over and above their being suitable for an exploitative system. The laws and systems were therefore naturally favorable—and heavily so—to those in power.

The impact: The effect of the colonial rule on the Indian nation was profound. Though a lot of good was done, the negatives were possibly several times more substantial. Among the good things which happened was the notional integration of the country, which undoubtedly reduced the misery to the common citizen wrought from squabbling nation states. Then, a wide range of nationwide services were introduced: codifying of laws, a bureaucracy, a united armed forces, a common judiciary, post and telegraph, a common language and, most important of all, a channel for the coming of scientific rationalism. The strong foundation laid down by scientific rationalism had the strength to counter many irrational, insensitive and inhuman practices that was a part of Indian life then. It provoked thought into the ideals of Hindu philosophy and opened the gates for a better understanding of it. Those that learned to trust the precepts of the indigenous culture within the scope of this incoming rationalism (or those that imbibed its spirit handed down through the traditions) did extract from it a lot of good for their fellowmen.

On the negative side, there was a heavy price that the nation paid. There was a disastrous impact on the economy—the manufacturing sector was stifled. The share of global trade as far as India was concerned dropped from over 27 percent to under 4 percent. As for the political field, the independent-minded ruling class and the masses were emasculated. Many traditional service institutions lost the patronage of the ruling classes. Confidence in basic Hindu values, even where it was well-placed, was considerably eroded. And the progress of the nation did not keep pace with the times.

It was the unsung citizen who finally paid the price. For majority of them, abject poverty, starvation deaths, a torturous life under the weight of exploitation and injustice under the law and order mechanism were stark realities. It left behind a half-starved, exploited mass of people who had little insulation from the evils committed by those with authority; often, they barely survived. They lacked the strength that could arise from education, from community life and from social welfare. And such prosperity, we should remember, is possible even under normal conditions only when surplus production is achieved.

Another important impact was that the grassroots-level administration which existed before that time was changed in a substantial manner. As a new system of administration was introduced, the erstwhile institutions suffered neglect. Patronage for indigenous grassroots-level institutions was considerably reduced. Most of all, the concerns addressed by the earlier system were not effectively taken care of by the new system that was put into place. Land became a commodity like it never used to be before. There was empowerment of the moneylenders' class, i.e. there were advantages for moneyed persons in the corridors of power and in courts of justice—without the usual checks built on morality. Thus, through all this, an ingenious method for advancing the Company's aims came into existence. The system could squeeze out money and stifle any possible means of revolt.

Further, since the cardinal motive for which the rule existed was profit, the colony had to maintain the exploiting structure in place. The British, the Indian princes, the zamindars and the Company's beneficiaries pooled in their resources and persisted with keeping the system running.

In any case, exploitation could not go on unabated. It had to stop when the future prospects of the Company would be harmed. Thus, between the exploitation and this major loss-producing situation, a final equilibrium set in. In this equilibrium, the rights of the landless laborer were confined to the minimum he needed to survive. Anything in excess was free for appropriation by the higher-ups. Infrastructural projects were the 'company's investments'. Reforms were constrained to be survival kits not medicines or nutritious food. One had to be happy to be alive and running. The bench marks for prosperity and good living naturally got scaled down. What else, then, could come out of this but disaster? And disaster it was when hundreds of thousands of people died in famines.

Questionable legacy: In the light of all this, is it desirable for us to accept the basic structure of the inherited administrative system—the judiciary, the enforcement, the village government—just as it was?

Alternate benchmarks: The reality of the countryside is there for us to see. A look at the situation on the ground reveals inbuilt enslaving tendencies and insensitive methods. The system's unsuitability for the freedom contained in self-rule is perceptible. The current system does not work in the spirit of Gandhiji's *gram swarajya*. It does not stand up to the test of a land 'where every individual has control over his own destiny'.

The intolerance that a Mr. Nobody from the Indian hinterland has to face today if he falls out with the local powers that be shows that the system's fitness for today's India is to be seriously doubted. A look into our villages shows that the system still burdens itself on the common man. It is all a matter of habit, tradition, misplaced beliefs and ignorance than of a wanton desire to suppress! If one wants facts, compare the number of deaths that occurred due to police action to the number of deaths due to naxalite menace ever since the naxalites came into existence. One will understand then.

Interestingly, since people do not have an alternative that they have seen or perceived, they think that the way things are run at present is the way it ought to be. The best example is the zamindari system again. It has lost its political teeth after the coming of the constitution, but the remains of the system still maintain a stranglehold on the countryside by surviving in the present political scenario. It is the only alternative which both the exploiter and the exploited perceive—even in the farthest of their horizons of information. This, they feel, is the way it always was and always will be…

In a changed world with vertical mobility, the attitude spills over. Those who rise in society, economically, naturally cultivate an attitude of suppression, and those left behind condemn themselves to submission. They see no alternative. A Dalit who becomes a zamindar will behave like a standard zamindar. An educated villager will settle in the city and look down his nose at those he recognizes as 'village bumpkins'.

A corrosive system: Nothing can corrupt a man who is strong in his ideals and if he is ready to face the consequences. A corrosive system, indeed, is no excuse. However, it may be difficult to function in a system that was created for some other time in history, a time when values and priorities might have been oriented in some other direction. The system we have now is an example. There are many features in the currently used system that do not make it conducive for its members to act in the manner of sensitive, benevolent, welfare-oriented executives. To put it briefly, the system aims at a rule rather than a self-rule. It motivates its officials to display despotism rather than dignified servitude. It encourages a profit-in-service type of attitude rather than a selfless one. And by far, it is unsympathetic to the depth of learning in this land.

Sardar Vallabhai Patel would have had compelling reasons for wanting to introduce changes in the lower levels of administration, which he unfortunately could not execute due to his untimely demise. The politicians who came after independence did have good intentions in their minds when they introduced land ceiling acts. Rajiv Gandhi did have good intentions too when he tried to press the Panchayati Raj act. But do all these efforts go the length to undo what the occupying forces did? Is this the spirit of freedom that was originally conceived for this land?

India was the motherland of our race, and Sanskrit the mother of Europe's languages; she was the mother of our philosophy;
mother, through the Arabs, of much of our mathematics;
mother, through the Buddha, of the ideals embodied in Christianity; mother, through the village community,
of self-government and democracy.
Mother India is in many ways the mother of us all".
'Perhaps in return for conquest, arrogance and spoliation, India will teach us the tolerance and gentleness of the mature mind,
the quiet content of the unacquisitive soul, the calm of the understanding spirit, and a unifying,
a pacifying love for all living things.

– Will Durant
American historian (1885–1981)

Education systems are indispensable parts of any civilization. They are a prerequisite for any society's continued existence, a natural consequence of the fact that new generations of humans replace older ones.

Education itself has great diversity with respect to (a) content, (b) methods used and (c) depth. There can be many types of practical education systems arising out of the admissible combinations of these characteristics. And the type of system adopted for a nation—its orientation, extent and quality—has a telling impact on both the quality of life of its people and on the nation's date with prosperity (refer to *Towards the Kingdom of Heaven*, Bharitiya Vidya Bhavan, 1999).

Similarly, the system of education adopted by India has an orientation and character of its own. This orientation of the education system emerges as a consequence of the 'fundamental ideas' that went into its designing both at the time of its creation and during its subsequent growth. As of today, this orientation directs the nation's destiny. Let us try and see whether the fundamentals that went into it cater for a free nation. Let us find out if there are alternative perspectives that can lead to a 'freer' India.

Before we consider the situation on the ground, it is essential to take note of an important point here. It is true that the prime mover of an education system can definitely be a government. And the government's success at handling education is taken to be another matter in 'current affairs'. Even so, all aspects of education are not necessarily governed by a government. There are aspects of an educational system that have to do with civilizations; it is possible to pick out some representative points about an education system which constitute features beyond the scope of policy decisions by incumbent governments. Truly speaking, education has more to do with currently accepted common sense and with the progress of learning in global circles. This general opinion gets reflected in government decisions.

Besides, there is also the factor of tradition which accounts for carrying forward trends that have a historical origin. Therefore, education is not about arbitrary decisions of governments alone; there is something about education which makes it a phenomenon on which several agencies have influence, to various degrees. The government is just one of them. We shall keep this in mind as we look into the education system as it exists today in India. Let us see the implications of the same on the subject of our study.

Education in India: A bird's-eye look at the main thrust of formal education in India reveals that at the primary level, education aims at a basic learning in a wide spectrum of branches while at the higher level, it is specialized and chiefly aims to be a feeder to the various institutions contained in the political, commercial, industrial, research, literary and other fields. Therefore, from the perspective of the size of manpower engaged, education imparted at the primary level is relatively based on broad criteria—in fact, the aim is to make it universal. At the higher level though, in view of the fact that there are only limited number of opportunities in established service institutions of a particular kind, it gets naturally targeted toward only a selected population—a population which decreases in size as one moves higher up the education ladder.

It can however be pointed out here that despite universal education being the goal at the primary level, in reality, due to many practical reasons and existing attitudes, this is close to impossible at the present date.

We can summarize a few of the features of our present-day education system in the following manner:

Of degrees and vocational courses: Universities predominantly engage themselves in the basic function of producing graduates. Graduate degrees are offered in a range of subjects. The courses guide students toward a broad and general direction that is headed toward making them fit for scholarly studies in the respective fields. There is a basic initiation of the student into each particular subject, and that acts as a foundation on which he can subsequently build himself up.

As of now, there is an increasing trend of universities offering courses that are unconventional and oriented toward diverse specialized careers in society. In accordance with changing priorities in society, with increasing faith being placed in entrepreneurship and industry, there is a very strong leaning toward professional and vocational education.

What about values? At the highest level, education is oriented toward academic excellence and research. Universities are thought to be basic feeders of manpower for research institutions throughout the country and for research programs within a university itself. Some studies are relevant to pure fields and others toward 'application' areas. The industry also benefits marginally from it. In its best idealism, it aims to contribute to the frontier of knowledge which the modern world currently wrestles with.

On the practical side, however, the ground realities show that all is not too good with these institutions. Very often, there seems to be a cloud of disillusionment hanging around, which makes its presence felt from time to time. Personal egos hold sway. Opportunities and responsibilities here are often treated as a part of one's career rather than a vocation. There is opportunism as anywhere else in society. Carving out cocoons in an established system becomes a priority. Yearning for status and power is an overpowering force for individuals. Of course, that is a general reflection of society itself, but it is important to note that owing to these factors, the education system suffers. The pursuit of excellence is of course hampered, but the bigger damage lies elsewhere.

Persons conversant with the laws of human nature, those that hold the wisdom of the ancient seers in high regard and the wise of all races and tribes will vouch for the fact that this is evidence for an ambient vacuum in matters relating to the human spirit and attitude. There is a lacuna in the fabric of moral integrity somewhere.

And taking note of the fact that every individual of the educated world is churned through the same process, we can easily see that all this has a telling influence on vast areas of important human activity. The spiritual health of the nation itself is at stake.

Positions held here are very much relevant with regard to the catering of the spiritual (which does not imply religious) health of students. But ignorance about this subject or aversion to it leaves a vacuum, which in turn takes its toll on both students and society. An institution that is best suited for strengthening the moral fiber of the student is at a loss to impart this all-too-important component of growth. Students pick up the attitudes prevailing instead, and the cycle continues when they assume positions as teachers later on.

If laying foundations for a productive society is the most important factor in a system, then there is no better place for it than in the universities. But there is hardly anything substantial done for we know that very few come out from their alma maters inspired with the conviction to be useful to society at all costs, to rough it out irrespective of what it takes. And fewer still have the stamina to stick to their guns. As the ancient Indian learning puts it, excellence generally lies beyond the self-centered and attached approach of any individual. And realizing, cherishing and living that gracious attitude in (and through) the present educational setup requires a tremendous effort against the conventional flow.

Quite a few do live up to it though. These persons become immune to the problems generally faced here, in the sense that they have the moral strength to see the irrelevance of these little things, and they do produce substantial work. They generally excel in their respective subjects. They are seen to possess a will to do their bit—whatever be the environment—and they typically also find a place in the hearts and minds of people around them. Most others get cowed down by the faults and do not come out with their best output. Some institutions buck the trend too. These are the ones that are greatly inspired by leaders or by the leadership of its top people. But such institutions excel only marginally because of the design of the system and more because of the individual excellence of those involved.

In any case, fortunately, when reckoning the complete system, the picture is not absolutely bleak. Despite all the ills, on an average, there is something that keeps these institutions relevant and respectable. There is a subconscious craving for knowledge and a sincere appreciation of scholarship somewhere hidden in the background. And since this remains, there is a drive. The vocation is still alive, and there is an inherent pride of belonging to the march of the present civilization. But then again, is it too much to expect better?

Irrelevant to daily life: Another important aspect featured throughout the system of education is its irrelevance to the direct day-to-day lives of the people. It aims to prepare people for livelihoods rather than prepare them for living better lives. Those things that matter for a good life outside the considerations of livelihood are usually included as additional pieces of information, maybe a chapter or two pertaining to health and hygiene, community studies, civics and the like. And given the examination process, even the little good of these few chapters is lost upon the students and teachers.

Again, there is a practical need for creating syllabi that is applicable universally as a background to various specialized courses. The system also requires a specific method of classroom teaching and the usual university-style examination process. All these inspire students to reduce the 'process of learning' into a mere ritual of 'memorizing facts'. Students often do not connect the lessons they learn with the reality that is seen around them.

Character building too does not have an established system.

Physical education too has a very shallow link to the health and hygiene of individuals. Only those who enter competitive sports get the required in-depth attention in this matter; the others are all but completely neglected.

This general lack of relevance to actual lives demotivates students from taking recourse to education. The rural dilemma is a case in point. If an education will lead to a better job and if a better job will take an individual away from his home and churn him in the wheels of the cities so that he receives a paltry something as pay for all that effort, that is, after he manages to get a job (if at all), why go for it? Fifteen odd years dedicated to education…

Is it not a costly proposition? While alternatively, as a child laborer, the child could have earned a handful for his family. Moreover, all the lessons he learns in school don't teach him to respect his parents or his culture, nor do they inculcate some basic values to be cherished in society. They do not teach him some simple things about farming, fisheries, chickens or any relevant thing for that matter. Then, why should he be educated?

Well, maybe to make him a distinguished personality in society. But how many parents would care to pursue that dream? After all, there is little space at the top of the existing hierarchy, too little for all and sundry…

The experience of the literacy campaign that was taken up some years back with great vigor is an indicator of how the aims catered to by this system of education is perceived as nothing useful by common man—the campaign just faded away without great success. Who would not want something that betters one's life? And yet, the illiterate do not take up education with conviction.

The aims of the movement are indeed lofty; there is the belief that once literate, they will become relatively immune to oppression of all kinds inherent in the socio-political-economic system. Apart from this, the campaign also hopes to open doors for their gaining of knowledge through literature, both current affairs and classic. It seeks to elevate them from the lowest to the next lowest rung in the education ladder. And finally, it hopes to open doors for the education of future generations. But despite all this, experience has shown that literacy can come only in the form of a craze—everybody is doing it and so will I—or a mass movement, inspired by the commitment of those up above and that too only after they have effectively hurdled over local vested self-interests. It rarely comes from an initiative born within each individual out of a pure love of learning or out of a practical realization that it will help one with one's individual life.

Education is a business: Another feature of the Indian education system is its commercial aspect. And this has a major role to play in the state of affairs of education in the country. The general leaning toward consumerism does not encourage people to take up services in education. The highly educated who settle down in this line are more often than not inclined to be seen by others, and by themselves, as strugglers trying to scrape out a living—not as accomplished people in society (though of course, with the government hiking up salaries in the education field, people are beginning to see things differently). The idea of a good pupil-teacher relationship, in the pattern of what is considered ideal in the ancient Indian system, cannot be easily applied in the present context. And the motivation for successful teachers to work in remote areas is absent.

It can also be seen that there is a tendency to treat educational institutions like 'companies' dealing with profit and loss. Its financing is based on the 'service' it caters to. Indian students 'pay fees'; they do not 'patronize' schools and colleges. And this has not been very encouraging to the interests of widespread education. It serves exclusive elitism. The availability of higher education to those meritorious by finance, coupled with the other features of capitalism, serves to establish a compartmentalized social structure with restricted vertical mobility. This ultimately augments the deprivation down under.

Lack of indigenous content: The secular credentials of the Indian constitution and the lack of a clear vision on religion and culture tend to make education ignore religion and culture completely, except, of course, for a continuous chirping about all the good in the Indian heritage.

People in positions of power and authority tend to shirk from having anything to do with such 'politically incorrect' decisions least they flare up an ammunition dump for there are many intolerant self-interests lying in wait, ready to pounce at the smallest mention of anything that puts ancient learning or any other scriptural learning into center stage.

Even as far as individuals go, on an average, there is a basic feeling of distrust toward indigenous culture. And one cannot be blamed too much for the same since there is a lot that can detract the average school/college-educated Indian from any good that may be available in it.

In any case, the net result is that only lip service is given to 'Indian culture' while education is kept away from it.

A steal over a hereditary-based system: The education system that is used today also caters to a competition. With lesser opportunities available as we move higher in the social and economic ladder, there is a need for filtration. And education provides this in its own way. With lesser chances available for getting a particular degree and with that degree being a prerequisite for a certain status or position or placement in society, an effective filtering mechanism comes into place.

In any case, there is one optimistic angle to this issue. The present system is considerably more merit-oriented than the erstwhile caste system. When the rigid caste system was the only alternative, technology and context was such that it made practical sense to start the selection process from birth and not at a later stage in life. Today, there is some freedom of choice; merit does matter—however imperfectly. The selection process for roles in society seems to have become distributed over factors like admission to various types of schools and most importantly so at the twelfth standard level. And yes, financial muscle does count toward having a greater freedom of choice of profession. Heredity as the sole decider of profession is therefore not a rigid feature of the current system.

Limitations in terms of personality development: Another important feature of the present education system is that it can give knowledge but cannot assure to inspire. It can measure IQ, but it knows no way to increase the same. Or maybe it does not believe that it can be improved significantly.

Today's learning is also sure that happiness cannot be bought, but it is not sure how happiness can be had and how a student can be trained to be happy in life. This matter is in some way left to people who are considered 'mind-science experts' who write 'feel better', 'get better', 'concentrate better' and a host of other such books. But these are not considered serious enough for inclusion in an academic program.

In comparison, we have seen that the ancient Indian system believed it could bring about transformation in people. The ancients went to great lengths to educate those who were to be entrusted with major responsibilities. They believed they had a system which was considerably fool-proof. Whatever the raw material, the education system believed it had the ability to mold the individual to become worthy of the trust placed in him—any prince could be trained to be a good king.

The Indian education system – what it is and what it can be: We have so far considered at length various characteristics of the system of education we have in India. These considerations give us an inkling of an idea as to the direction the present education system is trying to take. Having seen so far, we can say that it is not too different from the main thrust of education that is being pursued the world over. We can safely say that the various governments at the center have more or less taken the process of education forward along the lines of the modern scientific civilization, and there is improvisation and fine-tuning to suit our socio-economic conditions. There is nothing radically different in India in comparison to what there is elsewhere.

So, this is a system which the 'modern, educated Indian' is familiar with. A natural reaction to the observations so far would be to say, 'Yes, indeed. That is the way it is. So what?' One would tend to accept the same as a matter of fact. It is only when one sees alternatives that one can compare and evaluate how good or relevant the present education system is to the Indian context. The question is whether there is an alternative at all with which such a comparison may be made.

Things will get clearer if we go through the logic behind the fundamentals that went into the creation of the present education system in the colonial era.

How the present education system took birth: Its roots are in the basic features of indigenous European education. This European system of education was based on the scientific order that had gradually developed around the learning in schools, colleges, universities and research institutions. It was financed through the usual methods, and it also catered to the education of those who could pay for it—or rather 'patronize' it. The graduates would look for service in the government or in the numerous services or manufacturing industries that came up after the industrial revolution. In the same vein, here in India too, education aimed to cater approximately to the above goals.

The British did have many good intentions in educating the Indians: of removing stagnation, of destroying evils,

of introducing rationalism, of trying to do what they felt was good in providing salvation for the eastern world and maybe even for the pure love of learning. It was very much in line with the concern they had for their own fellowmen. But it is important to note that nothing was more sacred to them than the continuance of British rule over India. So finally, despite the ideals of this 'European' education, the British encouraged it only when it was suitable for them.

This brings us to a point we briefly considered in the previous chapter. Being a foreign power, the government needed friends in India. It also did not have sufficient men to fill up all the lower level offices of political and economic institutions. It also wanted a group of people with whom it could interact and who would form a channel of contact with the masses. It wanted a uniform language throughout the country to reduce its communication problems. It wanted acceptance for its reforms and institutions. It needed a class of Indians who would accept the philosophy of the occupying force as this would bring them lesser direct opposition from the orthodox element in the vast Indian population. And of course, it would always be preferable to work in a land which was not as barbaric as its reputation said it was. It would be better to work in a land that had imbibed the good of that part of the world that was considered rational.

The good promises were many when an enthusiastic Lord Bentinck was given the go-ahead to work on the Indian system. The British had till then avoided, as far as possible, intervention into local cultures. But, with support from the Indian rationalists, many concrete steps were taken in the 1830s and the 1840s. Education was duly imparted in the English language and in the pattern of the western model. It was a new system of education aimed at producing an enlightened class of persons 'Indian in blood and color, but English in tastes, in opinions, in morals and in intellect' (Thomas Babington Macaulay, February 2, 1835, Minutes concurred by William C. Bentinck).

Attributes of the new system: The system expressed a belief in the seeping-down effect. The elite would learn, and the knowledge would gradually spread downwards.

But a gaping hole in this system was the absence of an initiative in it to liberate the general masses from illiteracy and ignorance and to prod them toward health and happy living. Even a casual look would show that this was an improbable or even a scandalous suggestion by the rulers' standards. Apart from the large amount of resources this would require, it would create a need for 'administration' in place of 'exploitation'. Indeed, a careful analysis shows that the education system totally missed out areas of thrust which could have made India a nation of free individuals having their own dignity and self-respect.

On the contrary, the western system of education constantly reminded the average Indian that he was at the bottom of a heap. The Indian was reminded that without literacy in his own mother tongue, let alone in English, he was a 'zero' as far as knowledge was concerned. Just imagine: Ramakrishna Paramahamsa was considered to be a 'zero' since he was illiterate. This, if one carefully notes, is another dimension of the 'safety valve theory'. It was an attempt to assert the superiority of the Englishman. It was an attempt to present the English-educated Indian as above his fellowmen. With the coming of the new system, the Indian had to be classified either as an educated person or an illiterate with 'some skills' for his survival.

In any case, the Indian elite already had a strong traditional obligation to pursue learning; they adopted the new system quickly, too quickly for the rulers' comfort. Once the Indians started asking questions about the relevance of socialism, democracy and other such factors to their conditions, it was a warning that the rulers were getting what they had not bargained for. The awakening of the Indian consciousness to the liberation song of the modern thought process induced a damper of sorts to any enthusiasm for reform on the side of the rulers. And after the mid-nineteenth century, it was largely the initiative of the Indian nationalists who supplemented education with the required thrust.

Therefore, when we take a look at this process of introduction of modern education into India, we may easily summarize that it was a half-hearted and opportunistic introduction of a European ideal, prodded on by an enthusiastic Indian elite and missing out the overwhelming majority of the Indian population.

And more importantly, it was a substitution of a system that existed earlier in India.

What about indigenous learning? Indeed, there is substance in the new knowledge that came in from the West. There is the science dimension; there is the rational approach; there is the larger quantity of information; English gives access to literature from diverse cultures of the world (through translations). But is it final in all its claims? Does it cover everything that was ever known to Indian thinkers? Does it go beyond ancient Indian learning in terms of depth and understanding in all fields of study known to humanity?

Earlier, in the indigenous system, each individual had enough education and training (informally imparted) to take care of his role in society. In as much as the system in the country matters, even kings and ministers were considered adequately educated though they were not groomed in western systems. None of that is contained in today's formal education system. Indeed, when we take into consideration those subjects of learning which represented excellence and scholarship in India and which were held in high esteem for more than forty centuries (by a safe margin), doubts arise about the claims made by western students that they fully understand the length, breadth, height and depth of our indigenous learning…

There is a distinct possibility that Indian scholars had better standards and scales or models for evaluating people. Going by scales, benchmarks and standards pertaining to wisdom, what really matters should not be academic degrees. Rather, it should be the knowledge and skill of living life to the full. This idea was institutionalized in the Indian system. But in the modern system, no heed is paid to this.

The interesting thing is that this subject matter, which has been so meticulously studied by the Indian seers, is cherished as an undercurrent in the cultures of most successful civilizations and societies. And that implies the West too. Shall we say, for instance, that there is more to America than just capitalism, democracy and freedom which makes it work? That there are those other subtle things that subconsciously prod the United States to a position of distinction… For instance, respect for work ethics, patriotism, the American dream, admiration for karma yoga, love of sacrifice.

And such values are not directly addressed in our present system of education, which were incidentally addressed in systems that existed earlier.

Education obviously existed in India before the coming of the British, but the government of that time did not have reasons to encourage the traditional setup. Scholarly studies conducted by the British did not 'convince' them of anything usable in the Indian heritage. The ills in the Indian system probably acted as a marker to reject any claim of wisdom in it, or maybe, the power dynamics lead to a conclusion that the learning of the masters rather than the subjects was the better choice. And it did not suit their purpose too. Moreover, there was neither an obvious uniform pattern throughout the country nor was there willingness on the part of the age-old institutions to sympathize with the West. And there was also the danger of revolt from the natives if the foreigners were found meddling with their culture. Or it could even be the simple reason that William Bentinck was familiar only with the education system that was available in his native land. Whatever the reason, patronage was ultimately given largely or uniquely to westernized education, and importantly, in the English language.

Could there be more today? At independence, the nation accepted the pattern of education which it inherited from the colony but after making changes that happen to be, relatively, rather superficial. There was merely an expansion of the already established structure through the addition of more institutions and wider range of subjects to study. Despite sincere efforts from many quarters at the level of civilizations, the colonial system of education has been perpetuated without any change.

Engrossed in a balancing act over caste and communal issues, the powers that be have not dared to accommodate some potentially good aspects of indigenous Indian education and culture into the mainstream.

There is no consideration or weight given to the param vidya factor. There is no concerted effort aimed at elevating the character of the individual which will enable him to see his highest potential and which will help him thrive in a sphere of peace, contentment and activity (in that order of abstract nouns). And one should know that this rises well above the dividing walls of religious communities and castes.

No significant provisions have been made to inculcate the awareness of personal health and hygiene, which, of course, may be very difficult, especially in poverty. For instance, how sensitive would it be on anyone's part to advise a child to consume a glass of milk and two eggs a day when the child's family is at its wit's ends over how to manage even one meal a day?

Except for lip service, there is hardly any facility in the education system to provide training so that children may learn to see through the designs of persons who divide society on any grounds.

At the primary levels, there are no provisions included to train him in a manner that will give him the confidence to earn his minimum livelihood by making his contribution to society when faced with the prospect of fending for himself.

There are no lessons for him in his formal training to make him realize that the evaluation of work in the eyes of capitalism is one thing and the evaluation of work as a human being is something different. There is no scope to teach him to see the significance of the efforts of a sweeper being equivalent to those of an engineer or a doctor or any other profession if the spirit behind it is right. And why are such good things not learned from peers in the West?

Does not our education tend to inculcate an attitude of snobby elitism, where a person thinks no end of himself just because he can speak, with unblemished brilliance, Her Majesty's tongue?

Does that education teach the student that such an attitude of pride (in anything, including speaking unblemished English) distances people not only from their own countrymen but also from their peers in the West? For, after all, only when someone learns to respect something of value in these simpletons (or village bumpkins, if one may) will they learn to respect themselves in relation to the West.

If one has not learned to appreciate the actual worth of dedication and hard work, will he know what goes into achieving the 'better' things that the West has achieved so far?

Difficult questions! None of which is effectively answered by the present education system…

And when one does not appreciate the actual worth of his peers in the West, he is ultimately only an awed spectator—never a match in spirit and wisdom. Would all this not contribute to a certain sense of loss of dignity and self-worth even if he were an educated Indian?

In the same manner in which he values his village cousins in relation to himself, he values himself in comparison with his peers in the West. This education is definitely not complete.

Whatever be the intentions behind its formation, good or bad, it is irrefutable that the tendencies of colonialism have left their stamp on this education process. What we have is an education fit for the raj, where a few rule over the rest and assert hegemony over them.

Indeed, there is no doubt that so far, with reason and logic as its mainstay, the system of education has played a good role in intimidating wayward aspects of scholarship in the Hindu nation. But it still is, as we have seen, an ideal with inherent defects, applied incompletely by vested interests without a proper evaluation or understanding of the native system. Continuing to swear by this system does not seem a wise choice for the nation. There is a need to expand its scope and change the focus.

There is a need to broaden the definition of education to cover several other major areas of thrust. There is a need to include diverse indigenous methods that were part and parcel of the life in this land. There is a need to use the opportunities of modern technology and expand the base of the education system to enlighten every individual.

If Indian philosophy is right in its claim to reason and logic, then it is bound to assert itself without conflict with the scientific spirit. There might be a need to think along revolutionary terms in order to clearly understand the potential of our ancient heritage and move while guided by reason and courage. Ensuring that it meets the self-rule needs of a nation of scholarly citizens should be the topmost priority.

We have seen that the Hindu system of learning contains secular principles that directly deal with the complete flowering of an individual. Innovation is required so that the system of education may use these principles to extract lessons from various scriptures of various world religions and convert the same into a syllabus that can address the holistic development of individuals. And yes, that will happen if and only if one understands that the benchmarks set for scholarship by the ancients are indeed pretty unconventional and high.

The Indian Navy is breaking new ground in this area. Focusing on case studies extracted from scriptures in available religions, it is able to elevate the level of discussions in its leadership classrooms to deal with matters of morality, personality and leadership. Maybe that is one good way to start.

Man must have an original cradle land whence the peopling of the earth was brought about by migration.
As to man's cradle land, there have been many theories but the weight of evidence is in favour of Indo-Malaysia.'
If there is a country on earth which can justly claim the honour of having been the cradle of the Human race or at least the scene of primitive civilization, the successive developments of which carried into all parts of the ancient world and even beyond, the blessings of knowledge which is the second life of man, that country is assuredly India.

The Encyclopedia Britannica

On Independence Day, the nation realized a goal which had been on the minds of patriots for nearly two centuries. The nation had realized the ultimate aim of many a determined struggle, struggles which dotted the length and breadth of the nation, struggles in which men had staked everything, even their very lives.

But then again, everyone knew that independence was not the end of everything. It was just the beginning of another phase, a phase of construction in the pursuit of realizing an 'Indian dream'. The foreigner left the country handing over 'power' to the representatives of the Indian people. It was now up to the Indian to take the nation forward.

The representatives who took charge at independence had a new role. From being revolutionaries, freedom fighters, political jail-pilgrims and dummy legislators, they changed over to being wielders of power, shapers of policy, captains of the government and nation builders. Through framing the constitution and using the executive authority that was answerable to the parliament and the provincial/state legislatures, they were to take decisions on behalf of the people and provide a vision so as to direct the country to its destiny. Effectively, this meant that Indians could chart their own course of progress, choosing at will from the best of the ideologies accepted in the world.

Having accepted multi-party democracy, Indians had to look for solutions within the democratic framework. Very soon, the leaders/politicians were hard at work; they became busy with the finer points of the system. They, as a class, struggled within the space the system provided, trying to achieve as much as they could—as much as the power dynamics allowed them to.

In the early years, the strong character of freedom struggle was reflected in the functioning of the parliament, and many forceful personalities played useful roles in its functioning. There have been instances of exemplary parliamentary work right through, and it is so even to this day. But this parliament also began involving itself in what is usual in parliaments all over the world. Among other specialties, negative ones like opportunism, lobbyist tendencies, myopic power struggles, favoritism and use of money and muscle power too showed their increasing presence.

Outstanding results: Needless to say, quite a bit was achieved. A comparative study of all the national census reports and other relevant reports spanning the entire twentieth century do show a remarkable change at the point in history marked by independence. The sudden rise in population, the growth of industries and sudden increase in agricultural production… All naturally point to the significance of the transfer of power. It was nothing short of a quantum leap. There were other causes, of course. For instance, the changed scenario after World War II and the rapid improvement in technology in the twentieth century. But still, even after giving allowance for factors such as these, which have contributed to the increased prosperity the world over during that time, a difference that can be attributed exclusively to Indian independence is easily perceptible.

But before we go any further, let us pause for a moment and check. Let us revisit the idea that there could have been possibly much more delivered by our parliament and our leadership.

Picking up a direction: Indeed, the nation had achieved freedom, and so, India was free to progress—but in what direction?

That direction depended on the priorities of the new leadership. The leaders in turn were obliged to shape things using the parliament. India was to go along the direction set by the decisions of the parliament. So, the relevant questions are: What were the parliamentarians looking up to? What was prosperity according to these leaders? That is, what is it that was considered good by these leaders in the parliament?

After all, the team lead by Pandit Nehru did represent Indian leadership, and Nehru himself was Gandhiji's heir apparent. Obviously, the direction Pandit Nehru and his team showed was the best bet for the nation to follow.

Do we question these leaders? When the direction in which India moved was chosen by the truly sacrificing and erudite leadership that emerged from the Indian freedom struggle, is there a need to revisit or rethink the strategies they adopted?

It is important for the Indian citizen to note that the views held by these second-rung leaders—after keeping Gandhiji exclusively in the first rung—define many things that govern individual Indian lives today. It defines the path on which the nation travels. It defines the things that children are made to believe in, say and do. It defines, in very significant terms, what the environment surrounding the citizen will be like. It, in fact, gives to the average Indian the socio-politico-cultural-economic environment that shapes his individuality. For example, businessmen are only too aware of the impact of government decisions. One percentage here or there in the figures in the budget, and it can sink or give wings to one or the other industry. Similarly, one decision here or there in the courts about gays and lesbians, and it can open a Pandora's box in young impressionable minds, and only the legislators can do something about it. These examples only go to show that there is a need to go through the thought process of the decision-making with a fine comb.

What was the leaders' thinking? A strong nation, prosperity and plenty, having a dignified place in the world order... These were surely the dreams for India which the leaders had, and it cannot be said that they did not want the best for the nation, but what we need to question is this: What, according to them, was the best for the nation?

Modern scientific civilization has a list of some fundamentals or priorities, which it believes in, and since this West-driven civilization was then the dominant force—as it is even today—these priorities come naturally to the common 'thinker' of the day. Some basic ones among those assumed fundamentals are the profoundness of the scientific spirit and method, the belief in material prosperity as a priority, the endlessness of human want and greed, scarcity of resources, competition, the 'struggle' to survive, the coming of merit-based systems (as against

hereditary-based systems), human rights, nationalism and sovereignty. Then, attuned to these fundamentals, there is a complete spectrum of possible 'methods'. As far as political systems go, there is a choice among theocracy, democracy, communism and dictatorship. With regard to economic systems, there are options like the capitalist, socialist, feudalistic and mixed economies or a combination. So, one can see that the 'fundamentals' are subtle and hidden whereas the 'methods' are more obvious, and these methods end up being a bone of contention in common political debates. Thereafter, it is an exercise to choose from the spectrum available. And whichever be the system chosen, a suitable education process, a government organization and a host of other factors will get adopted accordingly.

Therefore, the Indian leaders of that time, participating in this (then) contemporary debate, guided by what was the best by world standards, charted a course that would, in their view, lead India to prosperity.

But it is important to note that most of them had been bred and brought up through a formal training process that was West-dominated. They voted on 'common sense' lines which reflected that westernized learning. And as far as indigenous culture was concerned, with the sincerity they had in their disposition, they also tried to do due, adequate and sound justice to it.

So finally, with capitalism on the one hand and socialism on the other, the goods from both were sought to be introduced into the system. This also included, at a subtle level, a notion of 'progress' which they picked up in their 'education', and it was all sought to be achieved within the perimeters of a democratic setup, which in turn was the trump card of the free world.

What is freedom? It is of particular interest to note that the widely-held notions of freedom and independence by the decision-makers too took shape on the basis of the world's opinion. For many of the decision-makers, independence from foreign rule was the indispensable prerequisite; for them, transfer of power restored the right of the Indian. India was 'free' since its citizens were the holders of power. The people were sovereigns for they could choose who would rule over them. So, after such a freedom was achieved, it was only a matter of time before prosperity would set in, justice would be done and all sorts of oppression would be removed. Independence and indigenous rule were the sure-fire precursors to inevitable freedom. And as far as the provision of a 'just' law was concerned, it was to be the concern of the elected government—the people's own government.

The assumption is that the strength of character of the educated Indian (the aim was to educate every Indian) and the character, wisdom and foresight of the elected leaders would pull the nation through. The various religions, the fruits of modern thought and the indigenous culture would somehow contribute to this process of progressively attaining the fruits of freedom. And ever since independence, this is exactly how the nation has perceived (and perceives) a vision of life and freedom in the mainstream of Indian life.

Now, from thought and belief spring action; therefore, it is on the basis of these beliefs about life and freedom that the leaders of society argue and debate in the intellectual circles that matter and take decisions.

So, given the concept of freedom, given the ideas of civilization and given the system chosen, citizens work by either trying to do good or trying to take advantage of the loopholes therein. That is, beyond this choice of philosophies and methods, it is the good old game of either staying within the confines of the law and/or breaking it. Citizens participate in this game as they choose to, in selfless or self-centered ways, and life goes on.

Gandhian difference: Gandhiji, on the other hand, differed radically with the second line of leaders and, consequently, with the way the average Indian thinker thinks today. For him, a practicable freedom did not restrict itself to the expulsion of the British or the establishment of a government. In his opinion, freedom could be achieved even under a rule which might not be voted to power by the people—indeed, even under the British had they been true and conscientious rulers. And there could be freedom even in spite of the absence of a government, that is, when the concept of an enlightened anarchy was realized. Naturally, this implies that Gandhiji's thinking, in questioning the logic of some of the ideas which the other leaders vouched for, questioned the basic precepts of modern civilization itself.

One of the most controversial decisions in his life was the one he took after the Chauri Chaura incident when he suspended a movement sweeping the length and breadth of the nation on account of a single violence-ridden incident. It was a source of much heartburn among his contemporaries, and most leaders had a lot of resentment toward the way he had 'bungled' on this occasion. Indeed, wasn't what he did in contradiction to the accepted notion of attaining freedom? In a nation of a third of a billion, how much should a single incident count? Why did he recommend the stoppage of the protest?

For him, the basic power dynamics, as it manifested, and the extra emphasis on material goods were neither practical nor fulfilling. He did not find any suitable solutions in them for the conditions of our nation. He believed that in this nation of villages, or any nation for that matter, the basis of the strength of the nation should be its people and humanity rather than its economy. For him, real freedom in India meant the freedom of villages. The material condition of the villages was not hidden from anyone. It had to be elevated, indeed; but far more important than that were the social factors: the evils perpetrated in the system, the lack of self-dignity, emasculation and a frightening government mechanism. Unlike the other 'leaders' who believed that the social factors would be gradually taken care of, Gandhiji believed that prosperity was probably impossible without effectively freeing the villages. His freedom was comprehensive, a freedom which would be the foundation of a land of universal justice. It had to be built up from a 'personal' angle on the basis of strong character and fruitful inter-human relationships, with the roots firmly embedded in religion and indigenous cultures.

A little reasoning shows as to why, in his opinion, the Chauri Chaura incident was closing the door to peoples' freedom. Freedom could not be achieved in an atmosphere of violence where one group of people could not tolerate another and, still worse, express it as they had done on that occasion. That was, in his opinion, no way to pursue freedom!

'I have, therefore, ventured to place before India the ancient law of self-sacrifice. For satyagraha and its off-shoots, non-cooperation and civil resistance, are nothing but new names for the law of suffering. The Rishis (seers) who discovered the law of nonviolence in the midst of violence were greater geniuses than Newton. They were themselves greater warriors than Wellington. Having themselves known the use of arms, they realised their uselessness and taught a weary world that its salvation lay not through violence but through nonviolence.' (M. K. Gandhi as quoted by Devi Prasad, WRI International Seminar, Budapest, 1969)

This apart, his insistence on the impossibility of offering the 'modern' dream to every individual is quite well known. Also well known is the fact that he was not in favor of the kind of industrialization that would deprive the underprivileged Indian of his livelihood, even if it was to signify some spectacular development on the other hand. That does not mean that he did not want India to be a powerful nation. Rather, as far as he knew of human nature, super prosperity in the material world was not the be all and end all of a nation. The basic needs in the material plane and, more importantly, in the spiritual plane had to be addressed first, in a very substantial measure. And therein should be laid the foundation of a strong nation economically, emotionally and, if necessary, militarily.

In all probability, there is no other path to super prosperity…

He was not against people having unequal amounts of material resources; this is very clear from his views about 'the rich being trustees on behalf of the poor'. And this was more akin to saying that there are bound to be inequalities and responsibilities in society. But this did not imply that the rich would be any happier than the poor, for he knew that material resources were not bliss in themselves. And neither did it imply that those with lesser responsibilities would be given a raw deal. Rather, he wanted to ensure that the lack of material resources should not be the cause for heaping evils on the poor or for denying them justice or political rights. A scenario where people are made to work toward material prosperity just for the sake of the pleasures it offers was in no way the nation of his dreams. He wanted them to live their lives to their full while these other things were incidental to a fulfilling life.

He also had strong views on the path of progress. His position on the debate on 'means and ends' is quite well known. For him, life was in the 'manner people exist', not in some hypothetical moments of bliss projected into the future. A satyagrahi, even as he lived and practiced his principles in his life, lived to the fullness of his being—even at a moment when he was sacrificing himself at the altar of friendship. The external surroundings and environment were nothing more than a stimulus in which one had to live and work. That work and life were complete in themselves.

If there was a goal for a nation to look forward to, then it lay in providing each individual the right environment to make that 'free' living conducive. If the incurable British rule came in the way, then it had to go. And if consumerism, power-hungry politics, profit economics and mechanizations to deprive are incurable, they surely have to go too. Then again, inequality is not an absolute no-no. 'Trusteeship' is delightful and fulfilling in itself.

To summarize, to Gandhiji, superlative material prosperity did not necessarily mean 'wealth'. He did not believe that man was increasingly happy with the satisfaction of more and more wants. He did not agree with the idea that an economy built on the basis of a culture spawning attachment was healthy for society. He rather preferred people doing their duty, living each moment joyously. He did not think that a nation looking up to a bunch of power seekers or money seekers (since they are projected as the cream of society and honored for being so) would prosper.

Action from the Gandhians: If his was such a profound vision, why did it not assert itself? Why did the nation not take to his ideals even though he was the father of the nation?

Gandhiji was abstemious in his personal life, and yet, he was a man of action, a man who said what he believed in and did what he said. Many times, though it was difficult to comprehend what he said, his actions did make a lot of sense to a great many people. The simple Indian identified with him and followed him. Thus, in due course, he wielded great moral force.

Becoming a unique leader using a unique method, unparalleled in the history of the world, he inspired a generation of people to live without fear of death and to stand up in their spiritual wholeness. And strong as he was, he also commanded immense respect from people of diverse affiliations. He stood tall in comparison to every other leader, and his status as the father of the nation and as the 'Mahatma' is well deserved. And this is borne out in several events of the first half of the twentieth century.

But everything was not a bed of roses for him. Politically, he suffered a setback in the last years of his life. Degradation had set into the idealism of the freedom struggle. Beginning since the late 1930s, the common man, in general, found it difficult to choose between the elected/selected representative and the genuine leader. Then, in the months preceding and following independence, there was no clear classification or demarcation to identify the erstwhile freedom fighter now rapidly changing into a power wielder. A confused government mechanism was hanging in suspension, caught up in the changing loyalties—between the colonial masters and the new rulers. The times were such that there was a great feeling of uncertainty in the people. And apart from these, there were the usual communal and caste problems, uncertainty regarding the question of princely states, uncertainty about the future of diverse ethnic groups and the opportunistic and very negative role of those handing over power. So, by the time India was getting independence, confusion reigned supreme. And in this scenario, the voice of Gandhiji, which was already losing significance, was almost blown into oblivion.

The conflict between the Gandhian and the mainstream view became very decisive probably with Gandhiji asking for the Congress to be dismantled in order to have it replaced by a grassroots-level organization. Gandhiji's reason was that he did not want the Congress to be a power-chasing organization, for that would block the progress of nation. But the Congress found itself constrained to think otherwise, for elections had to be won if the Congress had to rule the country. That could be done only if they fought elections the way elections were fought the world over. Further, he wanted the Congress to split up into two formations: one slightly left of center and the other to the right so as to lay the foundations for a two-party system. This again was found impracticable and unnecessary by the Congress.

His vision of democracy did not restrict itself to casting votes. He wanted each individual to be able to exert control and responsibility over the environment around him, not merely by picking out someone to be made his own boss or servant, but by selecting someone who would help coordinate his efforts with the efforts of his friends—by selecting someone he knew was senior to him in 'service'. So, Gandhiji wanted to showcase some examples of selfless workers who would inspire those around them through their example of work done in the neighborhood, through the very spirit of selflessness or through their contentment in the simple things of life. Indeed, that nation would surely be strong which honors a selfless worker in the manner Gandhiji sought to do. The ideal for everyone would then be to 'give' and not to 'ask' as is the case in a power-asking scenario. But caught in the flux of those times, what could one do? Who had the patience to see what Gandhiji really meant?

So, during the most crucial last years of his life, Gandhiji was all but tied down. The Congress, which he could once rely upon, now had its alternate concerns. It was not all ears to Gandhiji as it had been before. It is said that it was not the Congress but the socialists who helped Gandhiji organize many of his activities during that time.

Caught in the chess board of politics and statesmanship, the representatives were constrained to take their own decisions, and inflamed by caste and communal passions, the masses couldn't hear Gandhiji's voice.

Then, in the critical days after independence was achieved, all his energies were diverted to the calming of passions unleashed by the disaster of partition. And as a result of this, the dreams he had for India remained what they were—merely notes and comments made in the last days of his life. Waiting to see the light of the day, those dreams froze into history, left for scholars and philosophers who came (come) across them to wonder about the man.

The net result is that the man of action did not have the opportunity to put his final thoughts into action!

All the backup action taken up by Gandhians in this regard was unfortunately no match for what Gandhiji was famous for. With his untimely death, the spirit behind the Indian revolution became unfocused, broken up and defused. And the responsibility of carrying the nation forward was taken up by the government through its efforts in the parliamentary framework.

New leaders, new priorities: Now, we can see that Gandhiji's ideas questioned some of the very fundamentals of 'modern, rational civilization'; that is why what he said sounded irrational or was incomprehensible, unacceptable or impractical to most other leaders. Furthermore, the methods suggested by Gandhiji did not have parallels in the known world. So, the new leaders, having no working examples of societies or nations constructed on the basis of these ideas (which they could otherwise have possibly used as models), preferred to play it down because of a lack of faith in something they did not understand—even if at heart, they may have accepted that Gandhiji could possibly be right.

The intricacies of the handing over of power had enough substance in itself to take up one's complete attention. The task of having to build up a 'nation' being on their shoulder, they were obligated to proceed as they thought best.

For them, there were no alternatives. The question of sovereignty and material prosperity were to be tackled on a priority basis in comparison to concerns about environmental sustenance and social stability. Being far-sighted necessarily meant accepting those intellectual building blocks that had been used by the most powerful nations of modern times. And being considerate to Indian culture meant being neutral about it. And all this was done, naturally, by playing down the concerns of the Mahatma.

A tradition of tribute: But it was not easy. Gandhiji's position as the father of the nation remained in the minds of Indians—both the commoner and leader. A reference was made to Gandhiji in every dealing; Gandhian thought became another important variable in the considerations of the power wielders. Lip service was always offered, and portraits of Gandhiji adorned walls throughout the country. But then, in due course, it ended up as a picture warmly cherished by elders and having little or no meaning for the younger generations. The authority represented by the picture was diluted since the voice and the authority

of the new breed of leaders resounded over that of the pure Gandhians (for the wielding of power does make a difference in a population that cannot differentiate between manager and leader).

So, the managers of the Indian state continued on their way. And in an attempt to fulfill Gandhiji's wishes, a network of government-supported village workers was set up, and the results are there for us to see. There were many other attempts made to take care of the Gandhian angle too. In the framing of the constitution, Gandhiji's ideas were given a place in the directive principles of state policy: people were to evaluate how governments performed by comparing their performance with these ideals. A little later, the community development project came up, and the latest has been the Panchayati Raj amendment bill.

Of course, they are brave attempts within the limits of constitution and parliamentary democracy to rectify the ills of the countryside. But however good they may be, it is doubtful whether they will go anywhere near what Gandhiji could possibly have done.

The potency of Gandhian thought and action: Surely, Gandhiji could have done what he felt best in spite of the Indian National Congress and its government. We know that he led a mammoth struggle against the British; would it have been difficult to lead one against the 'Brown Sahibs'? He could silence a rioting mob. Could he not have put the Congress working committee in order? Indeed, it seems like we did lose the man at a time when he could have made the biggest of differences to the country and its 'depressed' people.

How remarkable it would have been had Nehru, apart from his prime-ministerial responsibilities, adopted a village and worked in it part-time, joining its citizens as they built it up with locally available resources. That would have set a precedent which could have transformed the nation. He could have mattered to the common Indian much more through that example than through all his leadership. Since he was the heir apparent, the nation would have followed him. When the nation was looking for a leader, he chose to be purely a functionary (hard-working, through) in an establishment—the government—which did not project a clear, selfless role to most Indians.

An ageless martyr: Everything is not lost with regard to the Gandhi factor though. The influence of Gandhiji is phenomenal, and whether his sayings are debated with sufficient comprehension in intellectual circles or not, his influence continues to play a deep, almost unfathomable, role in the Indian national life. His is the subtle influence of a martyr's, of an ageless immortal. His memory adds sympathy in public dealings toward the deprived. When the commoner and the politician address the human soul in their struggles, they fall back on him. His set moral standard strongly guided public life then and still works subtly. The feeling of togetherness in the nation, which lies dominant in the Indian psyche, finds yet another anchor in him. A study of the satyagraha offered under his leadership fills Indians with a sense of self-worth. And as far as the Indian nation goes, the position of honor it accords to Gandhiji helps orient its own disposition toward great heights in moral strength, thus obtaining respect for itself.

When one sits back and reflects, a thought invariably creeps into the mind. What if Gandhiji was right all along in matters of progress? What if his vision of rural India is inevitable? What if it is a necessary condition for our progress as a nation?

Or rather, since he had a position of pre-eminence in the Indian psyche that has no parallel in this century, what harm would it do to the nation if it were to draw a leaf out of his book of wisdom? Indeed, why should the 21st-century Indian not give his thoughts the weight they probably deserve? Do Indians have to wait for the West to discover the greater frontiers the Mahatma spoke about so as to follow suit? Mandela, Martin Luther King and now even Obama have spoken in glowing terms of the wisdom of the man. What is the Indian waiting for?

Probably, the Indian of today is missing the depth that is required to see the wisdom of the man. But then, that should not be the case in the land of the Bharatas, for it is supposed to have, in its ethos, the ability to spot wisdom wherever it comes from. Then why does the nation fail to move or even look in the direction pointed out by the Mahatma?

India possesses a great indigenous civilization dating back to 7000 BC, such as recent archaeological discoveries at Mehrgarh clearly reveal. It had the most extensive urban culture in the world in the third millennium BCE with the many cities of the Indus and Sarasvati rivers.

When the Sarasvati river of Vedic fame dried up in the second millennium BCE, the culture shifted east to the more certain rivers of the Gangetic plain, which became the dominant region of the subcontinent.

Gone is the old idea of the Aryan invasion and an outside basis for Indian culture. In its place is the continuity of a civilization and its literature going back to the earliest period of history.

Unfortunately, over the first fifty years since Independence, India has not discovered its real roots. Its intellectuals have mimicked Western trends in thought. They have forgotten their own profound modern sages like Swami Vivekananda and Sri Aurobindo who projected modern and futuristic views of the Indian tradition.

While Westerners come to India seeking spiritual knowledge, Indian intellectuals look to the West with an adulation that is often blind, if not obsequious.

Dr. David Frawley
American Teacher, Doctor, Author, Speaker, Historian

2.4 A CONSTITUTION THAT SYMPATHIZES BUT DOES NOT EMPATHIZE WITH INDIANNESS

The years from 1947 to 1953 were critical to the Indian nation. In this phase, many important decisions were taken concerning the direction that the nation had to take in the form of creating the constitution, wherein it was decided how the Indian team/nation is going to be and how it is going to move ahead. This needs to be revisited; there are certain indicators here which explain why we may have not done true justice to the best of our ancient thought. Let us therefore look back at the context in which the constitution was hammered out and explore what can be done to address any concerns that may need to be taken care of.

The constitution is a key document: When individuals live together in groups, a system of coordination naturally evolves among them. Any such coordination is to be perfected at three important levels: first at the emotional/spiritual/motivational level, next at the level of ideas and third at the physical level.

At the spiritual level, there is an experience of bonding, a feeling of oneness. Citizens share an enthusiasm and a team spirit which thrives on feelings surrounding pride, self-respect and a sense of duty and sacrifice. Interestingly, when that team feeling in a nation has a positive vibe to it and revels in righteousness, that shared sense of righteousness itself acts as a cause for the very existence of a nation. The citizens are enthused to better shoulder their inherent responsibilities. In other words, a citizen/soldier would definitely do more for a nation that stands for righteousness than for one that does not.

At the level of ideas, a nation chooses a line of thought or a method which concerns the manner in which the nation wishes to get itself organized in its pursuit of progress and prosperity. For example, there are arrangements like democracy, communism, socialism, capitalism and monarchy out of which a certain combination is arrived at. This accounts for a line of thinking that is accepted in order to design social, political or economy-related structures.

And finally, we have the most visible 'temporal plane' where the nuts and bolts of the system are pieced together in the form of various institutions and are set into operation in a realistic timeframe.

So, by making arrangements and taking decisions in reference to the three levels, each group or nation sets standards for itself. An outline of how all this is proposed to be done in a nation is generally recorded in the constitution. A team that has its bearings right will focus on excellence; it will be concerned with enhancing efficiency in the output of togetherness by coordinating an excellent team effort.

India too has its own constitution, which is central to the life of its citizens, and for whatever it is worth (hugely so), it has been in force for nearly seven decades now.

This document holds great significance. Every word is important—as has been amply shown in court verdicts. A word here or there or a phrase here or there interpreted this way or that can lead to a world of difference in the practical life in the nation. Among documents in the nation that express the collective aspirations of the living citizens, it is the most important. It reflects the thinking process of the leaders who took care of the nation that had just been born in 1947—which the present people accept as the way forward. Therefore, it decides the nation's fate in a very significant way.

The leaders of the independence struggle decided the way forward. Could that be reviewed today? Where did they really want to take the Indian nation?

Seven decades down the line, the nation can surely make an assessment as to whether there are opportunities to think differently. And it can be done without attempting to find fault, objectively, knowing well that the nation was constrained by various factors that characterized those times. In these times, conditions are different, and opportunities are many. Can Indians do things differently, especially in matters concerning indigenous culture, tradition and learning? Is there some scope to think differently?

Coming of the Indian constitution: During the mid-1940s in India, after World War II, when the possibility of independence was converting into a near certainty, the process of drafting a constitution was initiated. A constituent assembly consisting of peoples' representatives was formed. Some were elected to the body, others were nominated and the thus-created assembly was given the task of framing the constitution. A draft committee made the rough draft. The points were debated upon, and finally, over a course of two to three years, the constitution was hammered into shape.

The document captured in it the philosophy by which the nation was to be governed. The spirit for it was sought from sources like the freedom struggle, indigenous culture, the strength of the character of individuals and other sources available to other democracies in the world. And it set up a political structure suitable for the conditions in the nation.

The men behind it: The men who delivered the constitution were among the best one could pick from the nation, and they came from varied backgrounds too. They represented the broad diversity of the nation. A peep into the mid-thirties gives us a good idea as to who the persons involved in the core of the effort were.

Around 1935, the foreign rulers offered an arrangement that promised a national federation with a central legislative council. The catch was that they wantonly proposed separate electorates for various communities. Though the nationalists did not find this acceptable, they participated in the elections and were elected in a major sweep into the legislatures of the provinces. Now, going by parliamentary standards, this group was supposed to wield 'power', which, incidentally, was a highly watered-down version of the powers which the leaders of an independent nation would have. And the procedure for execution of such power was to be 'majority-in-assembly.' In 1946, when the constituent assembly was framed,

persons who were members of such legislatures elected the representatives to the national house.

An important feature of the election to the assemblies was that it was based on the concept of separate electorates for minorities; hence, these elected individuals also represented lobbies. There was yet another lobby which consisted of persons appointed by the princely states. All these constituted the constituent assembly.

The final picture was that these members of the assembly were to deliver a constitution for the nation on behalf of it. They could well be called the 'cream' of society. They definitely belonged to the 'educated' class and were, predominantly, persons very much associated with the political mainstream.

There were others indirectly involved too. Opinions of learned men in diverse professions were taken. The debates in the assembly were followed closely in the newspapers. And through the newspapers and other public forums, many others had an opportunity to voice their opinions too.

Where the ideas came from: As for ideas to base the structure of the government on, there was no dearth of them. By the middle of the twentieth century, many parliamentary systems had been tried out in other countries. Some had worked for centuries. Democracy was the direction that the world was going, and finding it the best for the Indian system, the Indians thought of a solution along the same lines too.

Long before independence, discussions on what form of government the people would like to have had occurred repeatedly at various forums concerned with national issues. And the trend did take solid shape once the leaders started dreaming of a free India. So, by 1947, a set of ideas shared in common by many erstwhile and then-current stalwarts of the freedom struggle had gradually crystallized.

An early document giving a hint at the possible basic structure of a free India came as a reply to the Simon commission. It was the Nehru Report. Its fundamentals are very similar to what is accepted today—linguistic states, adult franchise, a federal form of government and joint electorates. These basics did not change very much, and they got their due importance in the assembly deliberations.

Next, it was a question of distributing power among the various branches of the government, and that was sorted out through the principle of checks and balances which, again, was used elsewhere in the world too.

Taking help from the 1935 document as proposed by the British, making a note of the condition of the infrastructure present in India and with the help of legal experts in the assembly, a final document was worked out.

Quite a masterpiece: It became the most voluminous constitution in the world. It proposed to make India the world's largest democracy—a multi-party democracy. The nation was to have a federal setup with a very strong central government. Universal adult franchise was to be followed. The prime minister, the leader of the majority in the lower house, was to be the most powerful executive of the country. The executive was to be accountable to the legislative assemblies. A relatively independent judiciary was to be the guardian of the constitution, the interpreter of laws that were framed in the land (the final word in the matter) and the forum for enforcing justice. India was to be a sovereign democratic republic.

Once this was agreed upon, it was passed unanimously. It subsequently came into force. Ever since, with many subsequent amendments, it has been at the center of the Indian public life.

Performance: It has produced mixed results. It has been a remarkable success on the count that the nation indeed has a working democracy with a freedom rarely available in other parts of the world. But there have been tremendous failures as well, and the biggest is that, even today, there is a great amount of despair, poverty and wretchedness. The average Indian has not been able to express himself to the fullest of his being.

Does it really foster an indigenized system? By the middle of the twentieth century, the entire nation had been under British rule for well over a century. The administrative system that had evolved had the definite stamp of colonial rule. The process of change was initiated when Indians had some say in the local legislatures after 1935. Change further happened in a big way when independence finally came and power was finally

transferred to Indian hands and expressed through the constitution. However, were the changes adequate? Did they account for a transfer to genuine freedom for the people? Taking especially the lower level of administration into consideration, could it be said that what came up as a result is indeed an expression of self-rule?

What has not changed is a feeling of subjugation of the masses. If, in the times gone by, it was the government under the British from which the Indian felt all the pressure, now it is the government of the elected representative which stands as an intimidating structure before him. There is no doubt that there have been countless office bearers in this setup who have acted, and continue to act, as benevolent benefactors, but the very fact that there is a need for benevolent benefactors tells so much about the power structure. Even though there are few excesses, it is still an intimidating power structure before the intimidated citizen. And one can get a feel of this if, by chance, he is penniless, without education and/ or is on the wrong side with respect to the men of the system. And it could be disastrous for him if such a person is on the wrong side of the law too.

A peoples' constitution? A very important factor quoted about the Indian constitution is that the common man had a say in the making of the constitution. There are two reasons cited for this. As we have seen, one is that the debates and the day-to-day developments in the constituent assembly were followed up in newspapers. The general public reacted with their opinions, and these were in turn considered by the makers of the law. The second factor was that those who were members of the constituent assembly were generally those persons who were the known 'leaders' of the people. So, they represented in them the aspirations of the freedom fighters and the masses. Owing to this authorship of the common man, the constitution that we have is supposed to be one that is representative of the whole of the Indian population.

Indeed, the logic is strong, but there are still some grounds to question it. First, we know very well that the problem of the safety valve existed and does exist even today. We have seen how the colonial masters used this to gain better control over the indigenous people. Now, this meant that those people who participated in the public debates were the 'educated' Indians. The masses—people who were not educated—definitely did not have a say in matters. After all, they were 'illiterate villagers' who, by accepted standards, knew nothing. Those that knew had to do the work for them. In fact, the point of contention, far from giving the masses the right to design the aspects of statehood, was whether to even give them voting rights. Thankfully, in its magnanimity, the assembly decided in favor of universal adult franchise.

The question is this: were people such as the illiterates truly represented?

There is no doubt that the representatives at the assembly were none other than the who-is-who of the freedom struggle. Questioning their integrity would only be a foolish thing to do. But there is no doubt that there was a difference of opinion between them and the hard-core Gandhians. Both groups wished for the welfare of the masses, but they differed in the approach to the solution. This will make more sense if we look at it from a different angle.

Would the constitution have remained the same had Gandhiji lived after its completion?

We have taken this up in the previous chapter; the ideas propounded by Gandhiji were given little more than lip service in the constitution. True Gandhians who came after Gandhiji received a similar treatment of neglect, for what they said and did was in many ways out of tune with the mainstream trends of the times. And then, there are strong reasons to believe that each leader would not have given his Gandhian preferences the required importance out of lack of conviction or due to the fear of sounding out of tune.

This attitude is nothing unnatural though, and neither does it contain any malice or wanton disrespect to Mahatma Gandhi. Rather, we know very well that most leaders differed from Gandhiji in a very basic sense. Sometimes, they understood what he said, and so, they agreed. But they agreed many times even when they did not understand only because the masses had accepted him as their leader or because what he did was very effective or for the sake of presenting a united front—agreeing to disagree and subsequently sticking by the decision taken by Gandhiji in the interest of collective action. Even Pandit Nehru had his disagreements with Gandhiji.

So, it was very often a matter of 'faith' in him rather than 'reason' that made them go along with Gandhiji. In fact, his opinions and actions were many times even referred to as 'whims and fancies'.

So then, when the onus is on someone who is elected to office (constituent assembly) to act according to his own discretion, why would he toy with an idea which, to him, does not follow the common sense of the intellectual world or, rather, common world opinion?. So, he chose common sense not Gandhi-sense.

Naturally, this lacuna was reflected in the constitution. Hence, the Gandhian ideals present in the constitution are effectively missing their sting. So, if Gandhiji himself was not effectively represented, was the common illiterate villager really represented?

Missing grassroots-level administration: Another fact about the original Indian constitution is that it was incomplete. Indeed, this being so even though it is the largest in the world.

Let us take it for granted that the basic ideas related to the methods of governance were agreed upon, the fundamental rights stated, the directive principles given and the power equations required at the center and states defined. Surely, it was a gem of a document as far as these factors are concerned. But the constitution was almost silent about the institutions that are required at levels below the constitutional heads, right down to the grassroots level.

Obviously, for this, the framers relied on two things: the precedent rule and legislation. In the precedent rule, that which already existed prior to independence would be carried forward. This rule would apply everywhere except when stated otherwise in the constitution. The second thing was legislation. The rough edges in the existing institutions, and in the enacted constitution itself, would be rounded off by the coming parliaments and assemblies in the due course of the performance of their duties.

Local bodies are vital for a nation because of their potential to handle things that cannot be monitored at the state or national level. Local bodies are best suited for pinning responsibilities both upwards on the government and downwards on the citizen, for better implementation of the fundamental rights, for improved and quality participation by people in government and for forcing changes on the system for the better. However, the silence on this issue of local bodies on the part of the constitution and the preference to refer to it in the form of mere directives in a section of the constitution, without giving it any teeth, left some sort of a vacuum.

Of course, the Panchayati Raj Constitutional Amendment (73rd and 74th) is a brave effort at tackling this lacuna, but it still has a long way to go. What happens in the local bodies currently cannot be defined as genuine self-rule.

No solution for casteism: Yet another area where the constitution has been found wanting is in the area of casteism. Has it truly provided a scope for the removal of the ills of casteism? It speaks in terms of wiping out casteism from society. Is it a practical line of approach? Using the provisions of the constitution, policies of reservation have been pursued in a small way initially and then vigorously ever since the nineties. Aspects of it have been inducted in a big way into the constitution and in the interpretation of the provisions made in it. The question remains though. Has it yielded the results which the nation seeks?

Some states want close to 70% of the available opportunities in government institutions to be brought under reservations on various grounds. Political rhetoric apart, does this strategy really bring relief to the downtrodden? The Supreme Court has stepped in and, as guardian of the constitution, has put a cap on this—at some lower figure. But all these efforts seem to have achieved little on the ground.

Some claim that the shackles of caste have been broken now that the lower castes are making a space for themselves in society and have a politics that they call their own. But of what significance is all this?

An assessment of the ground realities show that the nation has not intellectually broken free from the clutches of caste-based thinking; the lower castes have not found in it a true way to salvation, and there continues to be great wretchedness in the lower castes.

What does one do about a 'liberated' lower-caste person who looks down upon his father who in turn has stuck to his old ways? Are such claims to liberation genuine? What is liberation from casteism after all?

Has someone made a correlation study between the various methods of liberation and the effectiveness of those? Is there honesty in such a study or is it all swamped by political rhetoric?

An interesting irony comes to light in what a panchayat president from Vidarbha pointed out during the course of a study conducted there; he said that in today's world, there is a beeline to claim the status of the 'wretched'. He said that in their village, they looked down upon those people who went about answering nature's call by the side of the streets, but the very same persons proclaimed their wretched status and gained patronage from the government. 'What is this government rewarding?' he asked. Looking through this perspective, on the ground, it appears as if it encourages the wretched to remain wretched.

Without a doubt, incidents of untouchability have almost dropped to insignificance. Or have they? The realities are not easy to digest. Instances of deprivation, cruelty and discrimination surface from time to time, and sociologists say that these are but the tip of the iceberg.

The question arises as to whether the strategy adopted in contravention of the Gandhian vision of Eden-like villages is really capable of bringing relief to the section of society that is really hard-pressed? Is this the real way of elevating castes?

Provisions for enhancing virtue: The most serious lacuna, however, is with respect to fostering value systems.

Coming to the ideals of the preamble, we see that they are indeed lofty. The preamble expresses a desire to give the citizens of this land a bountiful nation. The important question to ask here is whether this is realizable for governments within the framework of the vision of the constitution and the institutions it gives birth to—even if the incumbents to office in all public offices in the country are a dedicated lot.

Is such excellence, as is required for the constitution's exalted goals, possible in any country where citizens do not live up to high ideals? And where there aren't enough men with the required merit for the offices? It sets up the Supreme Court, for example, but does it also create a space for a generation of virtuous people who will become talented Supreme Court judges and honest and system-serving lawyers?

The very fact that the constitution accepts the ideals of the preamble implies that it assumes a lot many things about Indians. And in view of the possibility of the absence of a matching idealism in citizens, it also implies that there is a requirement of an environment which stimulates such idealism.

Now then, as expected, the constitution does extol the encouragement of many virtues in individuals and in society, and governments and all kinds of leaders have done their best to carry out this responsibility. In fact, a list of duties has also been incorporated into the constitution through an amendment.

But then, when there is so much corruption in society, when the prime minister goes on record to say that only 17% of the money meant for beneficiaries actually reaches them, when there is a high incidence of crime and when there is this huge mass of Indians who come into the zone characterized by malnutrition, the question arises as to whether such a culture of excellence in its citizens is actually being promoted by and through the constitution.

In fact, the real question is whether it is possible to inculcate such virtue in individuals by overlooking the true merits of the indigenous culture.

Producing the required men of character is possible only when the indigenous culture blossoms to its complete ability—when the various religions, philosophies, great families and outstanding communities it contains deliver men of substance to the nation.

In other words, for the continued effective functioning of the constitution, a support culture meant to nurture virtue is required. How that culture is to be established in a nation must be worked upon if the goal of the nation is to chart a path to genuine progress and prosperity.

The nation's potential: As a document detailing who-should-do-what, there does not seem to be anything too problematic in the constitution, but what is definitely missing is the 'spirit' to keep the wheels well oiled. Somehow, the idealism of the freedom struggle has not passed over to the new setup, and that spirit is seen only in small patches. Though it has produced men of character and substance who have delivered great things for the nation, it has not managed to galvanize every other Indian into the mainstream of life. Corruption, communalism and opportunism have a big say in matters. And in an indirect way, the constitution has been used to propagate the feeling of casteism instead of providing the inspiration to remove it.

Maybe that is expecting too much from a mere constitution, but still, since it forms the foundation of the present nation, one reckons that the missing elements could be a hindrance in the nation achieving success in proportion to its true potential.

It is evident, therefore, that there is only lip service done to what the wise men of yore have said. On the fronts of caste and in matters of nurturing values, there is silence due to the belief that the constitution must remain secular. But then, in striking a balance between trying to remain secular and in building on the traditional strengths and values of the indigenous culture, Indians seem to have bungled somewhere.

Yet to complete the journey from a colonial mind-set to an inspired freedom: The coming of the constitution was truly an opportunity for choosing a direction to move forward. And we have seen how that choice of direction was constrained by several influences that existed in the first half of the 20th century. Wherever the leaders felt apprehensive about tinkering with what existed, they simply carried it forward.

Therefore, as we have reckoned, after the coming of the Indian constitution, the upper strata of the structure suffered remarkable changes. However, deep down, the administrative system largely remained the same as in the colonial period, completely sidestepping the positive elements of the indigenous culture. In fact, it won't be too much of an overstatement to say that the change in 1947 was a mere replacement of foreigners by Indians. Most of the lower level institutions that were carried forward continued to perpetuate the mentality of the earlier rule. New branches and thrusts in administration came up. For example, it is indeed a fact that the district administration now had to take care of development, planning and election-related functions in addition to its earlier duties. But despite all this, in the final analysis, it has remained as the old raj. The vested interests of colonialism were eventually replaced by the vested interests of opportunists who wriggled into positions of power.

A grave charge, one may say, but the institutions in the nation are indeed showing these colors today. The parliamentary setup is finding it difficult to even come up with an effective way to tackle corruption in the government ranks. The intelligentsia seems to be lost as to whether politics should be considered synonymous with evil. Citizens seem to be so content and busy with taking care of the fires in their homes that public life is proving to be a choice not for the best of talents but increasingly for those greedy to wield power and make a quick buck. Somewhere, the nation has got it all wrong, and there does not seem to be any hope unless it learns to go back to the values highlighted by the ancient sages.

And when the nation wishes to go back to the values of this ancient land, who must it take as the guiding lights?

The fact that Hinduism stands for *vasudhaiva kutumbakam* and that universal dharma is what is to be upheld is clearly uncontested; this should give the nation its answer. However, this very answer, though so simple and straightforward, is lost upon the citizen's psyche today. If Lord Krishna and Lord Rama were here today, what would they do? This sleeping giant of a nation can be considered to be awake when it learns to isolate these divisive forces—whether they are based on communism, communalism or community-ism—and talk of dharma in terms of the constitution of India, the wisdom of the ancient sages and the guidance of the tallest of the modern leaders, Mahatma Gandhi.

Section III

Applied Spirituality: Reconverting Casteism Back Into a Boon

This section deals with how the deep understanding of human nature and spirituality eventually was applied to Indian society, what became of it in course of time and what opportunity presents itself to those who diligently work upon the goods it has to deliver.

Degradation is a natural possibility in any system. But that does not mean that the basic principles contained in it must necessarily be wrong. Each generation has its opportunity to use the principles to either manipulate the system to suit selfish needs or live inspired lives. In fact, that is a choice offered to every individual. This is our generation. This is our time. What will we make of this opportunity?

3.1 INTRODUCTION: AN OPPORTUNITY HIDDEN IN CASTEISM

One of the reasons due to which people tend to write off Hinduism is casteism. It is almost as if everything about casteism is nonsensical, atrocities, victimization, unjustified divine rights, dominance… Serious doubts are raised about the original teachers of this faith, about the intentions of the patrons—present and past—and about the validity of the scriptures. But how valid are these commonly held notions about the intentions of the founders/patrons and about diabolical scriptural support to casteism?

Before jumping to conclusions, it is logical/scientific/ sensible that a proper study be first made. And a systematic and rigorous inquiry reveals that there are ways of looking at it by which a deeper and liberating truth emerges.

This alternate perspective suggests that—if spiritualism is anything to go by, if the authority of so-called wise men is anything to go by, if we acknowledge brilliance in the likes of those that are supposedly 'self-realized'—there is definitely an objectiveness about it (independent of personalities, class, sect and individual opinions) which liberates.

Intentions of ancients: But then, it is not easy calling some of the ancients wise, since they seem to be obviously wrong in their decisions. Take the example of *Manu Smriti*: Manu categorized people in seemingly unequal ways. He recommended harsh punishments of pouring molten metal into ears for offenses as simple as trying to learn something that was unauthorized. How could he be called a wise man?

A simple line of reasoning reveals upfront that it could be unscientific and illogical to draw such adverse conclusions about Manu off the cuff. This is because when any classic is studied out of context in another later age, with reference to the values and technology of the new age, it might not appear as sensible as one might want it to be. Sitting where Manu sat, 'turn right' could possibly have been the right thing to do. But today, we may be sitting in some place where 'turn left' could be the right thing to do instead. When this is the case, why blame the classic if a student were to just condemn it as being equal to nothing by saying that 'turning right will take us to hell'? This is precisely what we call as 'throwing the baby out with the bath water'. Is one really sure that in rejecting Manu, he is not throwing out something that could really be the solution to the problem at hand? Can the caste problem be solved if we truly understand Manu?

We can repeat an argument we made earlier. Is it a fair assumption that we, the benevolent wise of the 21st century, are the only wise people that ever lived in all of history? Are we the only ones in all of history who have this all-encompassing compassion that none others had? Are we such geniuses that we know all that the likes of Veda Vyasa, Vashist and Valmiki wanted to teach? After all, these long-remembered scholars/wise men did pay respects to the varna system.

In fact, people very often argue that we shouldn't even consider such things that are so obviously diabolic, ancient and seemingly the source of 'all' the troubles we face today. Indeed, it is easy to conclude as such, but there are reasons to believe that this thinking is not the most logical, scientific or honest way forward.

Playing it fair: It is important to remember that these persons whose books have been revered for more than two millennia designed socio-political constitutions to suit their times—not ours. So then, if we really need to understand what they have been saying, it becomes necessary to extract the core wisdom, i.e. draw out a supposed substratum of timeless wisdom from the political constitutions which they drafted for their respective eras. Only then can we arrive at a conclusion on whether they are really wise.

The wise always speak of highs and lows and rights and wrongs with respect to spiritual matters. But if that is (mis)interpreted by others by ripping it out of its spiritual context and interpolating it into the mundane, whose mistake is it? And if we were to jump to conclusions about the intentions of the original authors by hearing what these ignorant detractors have to say, whose mistake is it? And further, having jumped to such inappropriate conclusions, is it sensible to accuse the ancient authors of being plotters of centuries of atrocities? Were they truly a breed of 'usurpers', woman enslavers and diabolic preservers of material class interests?

This is for the reader to answer for himself. After all, if there is a liberating truth in the claims of the wise, then anyone who takes an unreasonable stance on the same is condemning himself to ignorance. He is blocking the path of his own progress and the progress of those that trust him for guidance. We shall eventually see in the following chapters as to why this is so.

What is a high or a low caste? A caste is a group that follows a certain set of traditions and maybe enjoys a certain status. Socio-politico-economic-religious recognition is given to them.

So then, are there only five groups in all that we need to work upon—the four castes and the *avarnas*? Not at all. There are probably as many as 4500 *jatis*—and that is a conservative estimate. Amazing, one may say. But that is the truth.

The tricky part follows: How does one say which jati among these thousands is forward and which is backward?

Truly speaking, it is decided on the whims and fancies of those that rule the roost. In fact, in the present scenario, 'not' defining the scale of measurement precisely is the trick, since one can continue playing political games.

A century and a half back, this favor was done by the rulers of those times—the colonial masters. And it was easy. Identify the group that produced meritorious individuals who were threats to the colonial rule; call them 'forward classes', and pit them against the others called as the 'backward classes'. And as luck would have it, there was a rough demarcation on the basis of economic and social factors which coincided with this demarcation, and there was also enough going around which could be termed 'atrocities' and was sufficiently potent to whip up mutual hatred among the groups. So, the rulers went ahead and fermented anger and jealousy. This was an extension to the divide-and-rule policy that they cleverly adopted. Today, the situation is different; lines are being drawn to ensure divide-and-rule with the intention of capturing power in a democracy.

Knowing that getting one's caste name into the list recognized in the constitution (in one of the schedules) is the ultimate gateway to the riches that the state doles out, there is a beeline for getting into that list... One can imagine how important it is for people to have themselves called as 'backward' jatis.

Take the example of this group consisting of about a hundred thousand people in Rajasthan. The group has the ability to successfully bring the mechanism of an entire state to a standstill, and it claims that it is a 'backward' class. Now, another class owing its lineage to the iconic warrior leader Shivaji is claiming downtrodden status. Is it not absurd? But it definitely makes a lot of political and economic sense.

The final result is that people are confused. They find it hard to come to a conclusion over whether to mention caste in a national census and whether to parade a low-caste status or a high-caste one.

Merit provides a natural benchmark: But when it is not a question of 'recognizing' certain groups as forward and backward, we do know that certain groups dominate in areas where merit is the criterion. The question is this: how does a group really dominate? And the answer should become obvious by the time the reader finishes the next few chapters.

There are certain objective truths about humans. Great performers are known to have certain tendencies, certain attributes, certain beliefs, certain ways. And this has been a subject of study for thousands of years.

The lessons can be transferred to subsequent generations through direct knowledge or through traditions.

Those cultures that ensure that these lessons are effectively transferred to the coming generations have the natural 'tendency' to groom offspring who show greater abilities as performers.

In the competition of life—in which one has to seize the moment, in which the best is promoted, in which the winner of the running race is rewarded—there is naturally greater success from well-groomed communities. And it is just a matter of course that such communities begin to dominate. The secret therefore is to adhere to higher principles, whatever one's status may be. If this is done, the journey upwards has already commenced...

Hidden in the very heart of the caste debate is the highest of such principles. It is a gem of a solution for the nation, and it can provide true liberation for the lower castes and relief to the higher castes. We shall see what it is.

A problem cannot be solved by the same level of consciousness that created it.

– Albert Einstein

Casteism is an undeniable reality of the Indian system. It is mostly looked upon as an evil which a lot of people would like to see gone. And if it is not condemned outright by someone, that someone is seen as being a part of a diabolic plan of self-interest propagation.

But even among those who do not condemn it outright, there are those who seem to be quite convinced that their bearing is sane, logical and even selfless. Even Gandhiji was seen as going soft on caste. In a one-on-one interaction with Savarkar and Gandhiji, it was clear that their views on the caste system were different. Savarkar wanted the idea of caste to go away, Gandhiji was pointing out the good in it. People claimed that it was not Gandhiji, but others who truly represented the lower castes. And in the same breath, we should remember that he was the foremost among the modern leaders who successfully elevated people from their wretchedness.

Apparently, there are hidden facts that need to be brought to light in this debate. But that requires sincere exploration and earnest and rational exchange of ideas.

This is where the problem seems to lie. If one were to observe the public space in India today, it is apparent that caste considerations are one of those issues which, when taken up, result in a rabid exchange of barking. A lot of people shout themselves hoarse as if their only aim were that no one should talk sense. Ultimately, there is difficulty in raising the consciousness of the debate. And just as one may expect, no one seems to be finding a valid solution to issues related to castes.

Caste vs. jati: For instance, let us consider the fact that the word 'caste' is of colonial India coinage. The indigenous word of approximate usage was 'jati'. These two words are not seen to be synonymous. Those who vouch for the good in the caste system will argue that the word 'jati' had a positive connotation and that the

use of the word 'caste' actually ended up degrading the arrangement. But there are those who oppose this. They say that there were unheard-of atrocities committed under the jati arrangement and that the use of the word 'caste' under 'western rationality' has served to generate liberation praxis for the marginalized. And both sides, quoting real life examples, will stick rigidly to their stands.

And there always seems to be only two sides to this discussion: the 'they' side and the 'we' side. Anyone looking for a genuine solution will be at his wits end to come to grips with it and bring about an understanding between the groups.

Ultimately, the marginalized person, who is at the receiving end of the so-called caste discrimination, lands up in a dilemma: who is the one truly batting for him? Confusing as it is, friends appear like enemies and enemies like friends. Moreover, this seems like one knot which some people seem eager to complicate further rather than genuinely attempt to untangle.

Truth vs. vested interests: First and foremost, one must make an attempt to separate all vested interests from the core of the debate: the point is that vested interests will indulge in anything and everything to win a debate. Let's put it this way. For lawyers who are representing two sides of a contest in court, if they have thrown scruples to the winds, victory is of greater importance than truth (some even believe it is their duty to pursue victory regardless). Truth merely becomes an instrument or a variable in order to obtain victory. Where the truth will give victory, the truth will be paraded… Where it is likely to give loss, the truth will be hidden or only half of it (half-truth) or total lies will be presented. Similar to this is the debate on casteism.

The need to classify and compare castes in political India makes the caste issue a toy, or a weapon, to be used in socio-political-economic games. The notion of repression of lower castes was exaggerated effectively by the political powers that be in British India; and today, it is being highlighted by the 'democratic representatives'.

Not that grave ills did not come out of the caste arrangement, but the shouting that is happening today has also to do with vested interests in the caste debate. In today's situation, we know that electoral victories are designed and carved out through manipulating caste equations—and an election victory is the key to great power and authority. And therefore, everyone is hell bent on propagating their own agenda on the issue. They are more or less shouting themselves hoarse and will counter every sane argument which they feel will kill their position in the power struggle. And indeed, they will do everything they can to position themselves as the genuine champion of the lower castes.

So, it is a game of one-up-man-ship in politics. Prior to independence, it comprised of the divide-and-rule policy, and the colonial masters ranted eloquently on the injustice done to the lower castes. Today, the political compulsion is the 'need to represent more numbers' as required in a democracy. Therefore, the political actors, in making a beeline for political power, play the caste card to the hilt. The caste disparity, therefore, gets accentuated by design. The ills and atrocities that can be credited to casteism are highlighted and amplified and scapegoats are created from among the minority higher classes or from among those who profess faith in spiritualism and religion. The scapegoats are targeted for being the enemies of humanity and the enemies of 'equality'. So much so that there is a rabid barking even at the mere mention of he who authored *Manu Smriti*…

There is this seemingly universal claim that there is a diabolic plot in the Indian scriptures, that there is a strong sense of partiality hidden in none other than the Vedas itself! The Vedas are accused of being a master-schemer hiding behind the notion of high and low castes. Consequently, the lower castes are seen (or rather 'shown') as being victims of a timeless conspiracy hidden in ancient Indian scriptures, specifically the Vedas.

What if we had it wrong? Consider that strong political canvassing is an existing reality today. One must recognize that what appears to us as a reality of the system *has a strong likelihood of being a lie* that has been repeated over and over

again to such an extent that we see no other truth. Let it not be said that it *is* a lie, only that there is a *likelihood* that there is a lie which has been repeated over and over again.

Therefore, knowing that there is this negative campaign against casteism, our present approach to tackling casteism in the public sphere can be considered inappropriate on two counts: first, it is inappropriate to jump to the conclusion that there is nothing but meanness in the caste system and second, even worse, it is inappropriate to resort to scuttling any form of rational exchange of ideas as there will be no chance of arriving at the truth in that case. Preventing a level-headed exchange is not a gainful path to take. Indians definitely need to look with earnestness and open-mindedness if a solution is to be dug out.

Want of clarity: Needless to say, progress on a problem is made when it is understood clearly. Unfortunately, there is little help when a situation like this begs for want of clarity. Political power struggles clearly don't allow for clarity, and it is not just political. Deep down, there are power struggles over factors of production, resources and access rights, and all these lend further reason for the failure of attempts to take forward the debate constructively.

The question which the nation must ask itself first is whether it would really like to take this 'debate' forward by placing it amidst those who have a personal stake of power in it or take it into an arena where it can genuinely reason out the various dimensions of the caste problem and then take a call on what is a sensible way forward and what is not.

Critical for many Indians: At stake is the progress of a huge section of India who we call as the depressed classes. They seem to be sitting around this battlefield waiting to see what the result will be. They seem to be waiting for providence to stretch out a helping hand in the form of doles from the government so that they may elevate their lot. They continue to sit outside, totally uncertain as to whom to really listen to in order to pursue better things in life or to live a better life, to be precise.

In the meanwhile, the political battles continue, and like endless rounds of musical chairs, the nation seems to be hopping from one set of elections to another. Everyone important seems to be deeply entrenched in rhetoric, but there is no result. Most of the depressed classes, over the last sixty years, have remained where they were.

It makes sense for the author and reader to resolve that the debate will be conducted at a level of consciousness that will encourage reason and careful consideration. It is the best way to explore/find a meaningful path for the emancipation of the lower classes.

Diving into the topic, it is evident that the question of inheritance needs to be looked into closely. History has it that the erstwhile caste system was merit-based, and it eventually consolidated into an inheritance-based system. It makes sense to clarify what exactly we can inherit from our parents. What is it that comes to each of us humans with our genes and what does not?

Are humans unequal at birth? To answer this, the start can be made at certain scientifically established facts.

Inheritance through genes: We know that genes provide us with a lot of our inheritance; but there still remains some debate on what the total content of the package is. Since the subject itself is rather intricate, common gentry often attribute musical prowess, the ability to study, the ability to excel in sports, etc. to genes, but subjecting the topic to a systematic analysis helps resolve certain facts.

Physiological factors: One thing for sure is that physiological features do get transferred to children through genes—factors like height, color, hair color, color of the eye, muscle type and blood type get determined by the genetic makeup of parents. But then, there is little reason to suggest that genetic codes define those particular characteristics of individuals which conclusively decide the caste of a person. Caste is basically in the general domain of the emotions, thoughts, mind and action; definitely, the people of a certain caste do not form a separate species or even some kind of special breed within humankind. In fact, if we take the example of blood groups and muscle types, it cuts across all kinds of socio-cultural-racial-ethnic barriers—including caste barriers.

Once an individual is born, his body has a certain degree of flexibility to develop according to the environment in which he grows. Of the characteristics that are determined by genes like height or tooth structure, each characteristic has a certain development-variation range in his life time. The extent to which a characteristic is developed in the course of a lifespan is governed by the amount of nourishment, care, illness, exercise, rest and other factors through which an individual goes, but even this happens within limits that are characteristic of the particular features. For example, there is not much impact possible on the genetically determined color of the iris during the course of a person's lifetime. If he is born with an iris of a certain color, it remains the same all his life. But where height is concerned, the difference of adequate food and inadequate food can indeed make a difference of up to several inches in a person's height. But this deviation from the generic norm too does not get transferred to the offspring; this is supported scientifically by the fact that the theory of 'use and disuse' in the field of genetics has lost out in light of the theory of 'survival of the fittest'.

Thoughts: But what about the way parents think? Do thinking processes get transferred to children through genes?

The study of DNA structures and the methodology of its coding and data transfer do not lend support to the idea. When parents think, the manner in which neurons get rearranged in their brains, on account of the ideas flashing through their minds, will have no impact on the DNA structure in their sperms and ovaries. This means that there will be no impact on the chemical makeup of the genes of the offspring arising from the thinking processes that happen in the minds of parents. There is no reason to believe that something like a learning gene exists, which carries parent's thoughts and memories to children directly.

The mind: The next is the mind. At the outset, it should be mentioned that there are insightful works in Indian spiritual thought which suggest that the mind is in the realm of thoughts and that both thought and mind are two sides of the same coin. But then, even if we go by the common notions of what the mind is, we can reckon a few things. It has been discovered by researchers that there is a link between chemical imbalances in the body and the state of mind of an individual. The studies have not been able to establish the correct cause-effect sequence though—whether it is the chemical imbalance that leads to mind-related problems or the other way around. However, mind science conclusively says that there is much that can be achieved through a change in the thought process of an individual. If he is tutored well, a lot of good can come out of effectively using the qualities of the mind to control the juices flowing in his body. However, there is no evidence to suggest that the qualities of the mind picked up in the lifetime of an individual (or the tendencies of the mind) get coded into genes and get transmitted.

Emotions: A similar argument also arises with respect to the emotional content of a person; there are theories that talk of a chemical basis for emotional problems and vice versa. It is also suggested that the initial grooming and emotional journeys during the formative years have a great impact on personality. And in the same vein, there are theories that suggest that much control can be had over emotions through mind science. But there are no studies that give evidence to the fact that emotions produce systematic, transferrable chemical changes in genes. As of this day, there is no proof in genetics that emotions alter the DNA chain structure in the reproductive cells of parents; so, children do not genetically inherit emotional behavior from parents.

In fact, it is suggested that the mind, thought and emotions are interlinked; if the thought processes are positive, the mind and emotions can be kept positive. And if there is a feeling of positivity in these three, it results in excellent health and high levels of resistance to diseases. But despite this, there is little evidence to suggest that the trio of thoughts, mental makeup and emotions produce genetically transferable changes in an individual.

In turn, this implies that offspring can achieve much more through their own thought process in the sphere of mind and emotions than they can ever be affected by genetic factors.

In the womb: And then, there is the fact that children seem to have the ability to learn at both the emotional and intellectual levels while they are in the wombs of their mothers. This truth was known to ancient Indian sages, and the same has been established in some form in the present scientific era as well. But this, again, is not a biological inheritance; one could rather say it is a cultural inheritance that comes from the culture of the mother and of the environment in which she lives when she is carrying.

So, are we equal at birth? No and yes!

No because

a) the genetic inheritance, which leads to the physiological characteristics of a person, is different for each individual and

b) even at birth, the child has already been through a learning process in the womb.

But then, if we are not concerned about the biological factors which we may overlook in this debate anyway, if we reckon the point of birth to actually mean the point of conception (that is, notionally neglecting the period when they are in their mothers' wombs) and even if we were to believe in something called the karma-of-previous-births theory but relate it to merely inherited physiological characteristics, then the fact is that we are all equal at birth.

Exactly what Manu (of *Manu Smriti* fame) said: 'All men are born equal.'

Cultural inheritance (the mind-related software is acquired): Now, moving away from these established scientific facts, let us dwell on some empirical observations, not too difficult to arrive at, and based on studies of psychologists and suggestions of scholars.

It has been found that the values held and cherished by parents have an impact on the character of children. For instance, deep and unshakable faith and sound value systems held by parents result in children who are exceptionally talented. Not certainly, but there is definitely a high incidence of this. In fact, the converse observation is more certain. Talented persons, in their childhood environment, have had very deep influences of disciplined and faith-bearing (not necessarily religious!) individuals who have had a large say in setting the environment in which they grew. This, of course, is not yet established through formal studies. However, it makes a lot of sense in terms of cause and effect in the spiritual field.

In psychology though, we are on more solid scientific ground. There are studies that indicate that the most significant aspects of peoples' character and personality get fixed well within the initial three or four years of their childhood. For example, they point out that the amount of care and attention a child receives as an infant, say when he has soiled himself, decides the attributes of the child's personality. The 'attitude' aspect of a personality is largely determined by the time he is four or five years old.

Then, there are the skills and knowledge which also get transferred to him as he grows up. To the extent that the environment in which these three attributes are present—knowledge, skills and attitude—is determined by the parents and other family members who come in contact with the child, it is inheritance.

But clearly, this inheritance comes not through the genes. It comes through experience and learning, which happens after conception and during growth. Generally speaking, all the non-biological aspects that characterize an individual as a unique, one-of-a-kind personality are imbibed by him when he grows up in whatever environment he finds himself in; the totality of his experience and learning determines this.

Grooming: Another important point to note is that this imparting of attributes can be taken up by parents with deliberate intent. It is not uncommon for parents to teach their children how to overcome difficulties they are likely to encounter later in life. They share their own experiences or what they have learned from others. And these lessons can be diverse, varying from family to family or even from individual to individual within a family. Some people train their children to take an eye for an eye. Still others say to take two in the place of one. Others say to show the other cheek if someone slaps one cheek. Three different approaches… All are given to children with the impression that if they learn the truth in it, it will be good for them. It is another matter though whether the children bear the fruit of the lessons they absorb. How they act emerges from what they come to believe in after absorbing these lessons, and they bear the fruits of their actions.

The example mentioned above is of course a direct lesson (in this case, it comes from religion), but all lessons do not come directly. There are indirect ones too. A Japanese proverb puts it succinctly: 'Children learn from the backs of their parents.' For example, a parent might want to teach his child to be truthful and may give lectures about it. But the child is more likely to learn from the fact that when the child is headed for a ringing phone, the father says, 'If it is Uncle, tell him "Daddy is not at home.".' Or the child may learn from even subtler suggestions like when an elderly person in the family publicly remarks, 'Oh! Poor honest chap!' as if honesty were a weakness and it were more sensible to be dishonest. And indeed, there are instances where parents think it is desirable for the child to learn to be dishonest and teach it to their children with all earnestness.

Putting all this together, one can conclude that the outcome of influences from parents is quite significant. The child picks up innumerable small lessons along the way and develops ideas, thoughts, attitudes, approaches, emotions, patterns and tendencies which govern much of his behavior in his later years. This means that the family—the first home of the child—and the values cherished in there decide, very decisively, how well he will capitalize on the opportunities that come his way, how well he will play the game of life and how artistic he will be in that game. Indeed, as the wise say, it is a question of how apprised he is of the 'art of living'. Or in other words, this 'software' baggage comprising of knowledge, skills and attitude has a tremendous impact on his productivity, work, effectiveness and inclination to participate in society. Taking it further, if it is a merit-based system that a person is operating in, then we can say that the level of prosperity which an individual will eventually attain depends on the quality of this 'software' that has evolved in him, which in turn depends on the environment in which he was born and brought up.

The significance of the childhood environment: In other words, we can conclude that all men are born equal, but the environment in which they take their toddler steps plays a remarkable role in deciding who they turn out to be and what they end up doing later in life.

Therefore, the childhood environment in which a child grows becomes a point of high concern for a well-wisher. Any well-wisher will capitalize on this environment aspect to deliver the best to the child.

Family traditions: Having seen that the environment set up by parents and guardians in which a child grows decides important aspects of the child's personality, it brings us to the crucial question about families and family traditions. Do family values passed down many generations play a role in ultimately deciding what the nature of the environment in which a child grows will be?

Family traditions include things like the way the members of a group cook their food, way they dress, way they address each other, way they eat their food, way they pray, scriptures they consider authority, values that are nurtured, priorities and choices. They define how a certain group of families perceive themselves and approach life.

When a certain group of families maintained a similar set of traditions, they were all classified together as a 'type' or 'jati' to be precise. The question is whether, in some way, the family environments in such families get patterned in such a manner that children born in such families receive a similar kind of grooming? Is that traditional environment so powerful that there is consistency of characteristics across all progeny of that group? Are such arrangements always successful in producing a certain quality or type or category of individuals? Or maybe a jati arrangement merely increases the probability of producing people with a set of capabilities.

These questions need to be systematically answered, and they constitute a potential area for a lot of research, but even without that rigor of proper scientific research, we can arrive at general conclusions that there indeed are patterns or family types. Certain isolated groups that are not yet touched by modern communication are excellent cases for studying the effect of family patterns. These family patterns are flexible to an extent in the sense that personalities and events have a huge role in deciding outcomes in families. But there are many other factors of tradition and convention, which are transferred almost innocuously or unconsciously by successive generations within a 'type' of family. These traditions may have to do with matters of faith, emotions, ideas, speech or actions. Such a set of families, who constitute a 'type', may be considered a 'jati' when they go about life in a particular way, taking on a certain combination of factors as distinguishable from other groups.

Some interesting questions we may ask about family traditions are as follows:

Q) Are family traditions dynamic?
A) Yes.

Q) Are the family traditions of a jati influenced by other jatis?
A) Yes.

Q) Are the traditions of a jati affected by the culture of a dominating civilization?
A) Yes.

Q) Are the traditions of a jati affected by dominant individuals of that jati?
A) Yes, and to varying extents.

Q) Does marriage within a jati facilitate easier understanding between newlyweds?
A) Yes.

Q) Is human-to-human communication easier within jatis?
A) Yes.

Q) When inter-jati marriages happen, is there a higher chance of misunderstanding and conflict in the early stages of marriage?
A) Yes.

Q) Among newlyweds, which of the spouses is expected to show flexibility to adjust?
A) In the patriarchal system, since the lady moves to the man's house, it is the lady who is expected to adjust. That also means that the groom and his family should show sensitivity. This works out to be logical if the patriarchal system is the accepted mode, and it is true that women are trained like that from the beginning in patriarchal systems. In a matriarchal system, it is the other way around.

Q) Will jatis disappear from the face of the earth?
A) Never. In the most extreme case, at least one jati will survive, i.e. everyone on the globe may end up becoming a part of one jati—a notion that is very unlikely to be accepted/happen. But yes, in a cosmopolitan, digital and global environment, the surrounding walls that tend to isolate jatis are weaker.

Every family will have a way of doing things. There will be differences from family to family. A certain group of families will definitely get an identity of its own if that group has special features (as distinct from other groups) that are common to its members, identifiable over and above the incidental variations that can take place within families of the group.

It all depends on the reference point from which one takes a look, and whatever the reference point chosen, an entire set of families can be divided into groups based on that particular reference point. Certain groups will seem to be remarkably different from that point of reference, and certain other groups will differ in a very minor way. For example, food habits can be used as a reference point for classification. With several such points of reference, groupings will emerge which constitute a 'type'.

Such points of reference are a boon to political dividers. It offers a great opportunity for opportunists to arbitrarily lay down benchmarks (points of reference) in order to say how to distinguish one 'caste' or 'jati' from the other. It is the old game of producing 'they' and 'we' camps according to political needs.

Q) Can we generalize on the characteristics of individuals based on the identity of the group to which they belong?
A) No, because individuals have characteristics that have statistical variation. If we go by individuals and pick up any one characteristic to compare, then we are sure to get an entire spectral distribution among members of a single group. For example, if a certain group is known for producing excellent sportsmen, even that group will have a spectrum of individuals ranging from those very bad in sports to those excellent in sports.

That is, the character of this grouping is not a precise genetic determinant. Rather, there is a distribution described by a bell-shaped curve that is obtained when we plot the number of people on one axis against the amplitude of a particular attribute on the other. Therefore, for any group or jati, if we were to plot the number of persons on the y-axis against excellence in sports on the x-axis, we will get a bell-shaped curve. For a jati that is recognized as being good in sports, the peak will be at the relatively higher end of the sportsmanship axis.

Therefore, generalizing an individual's characteristics on the basis of purely their group identity is prone to end in errors of judgment. 'He comes from that community, and so, he is a good sportsman' is a wrong way of looking at it. 'He comes from that community, so he is likely to be a good sportsman or he is likely to groom good sportsmen' is the correct way of looking at it.

Q) Can these jatis be graded as one being better than another?
A) Yes, but then, the ranking will depend on what criterion is used to rank them. Or in other words, it depends on what the scale along which we are grading the jatis is. It depends on whether we are grading them on the basis of money/possessions, physical prowess, intellectual prowess, musical abilities, output to society or whatever other criterion that we reckon is significant.

Two important points we need to take note of in this context are stated here:

First, the various jatis will get ranked at different positions depending on what scale one chooses to make that distinction. Second, it will only be a comparison of statistical averages. We will be left with several bell-shaped curves in a multi-dimensional matrix, with each dimension representing yet another factor by which castes or groups can be evaluated. The bell-shaped curves will peak at different points for different groups for each of the reckoned dimensions/attributes. So, one jati could be good in one thing, average in another and bad in yet another dimension.

Q) Do individuals use the jati arrangements diabolically for their own ends?
A) Indeed, it is human nature that there will always be some who take advantage of the loopholes that are available. This is an eternal enemy and needs to be checked.

From the above considerations, we can say for sure that traditions vary from family to family. It depends on the lessons which parents and guardians advertently or inadvertently transfer to the subsequent generations. And at all times, one needs to be aware that the quality of what is passed down has a significant impact on what will happen to individuals in subsequent generations of a family or a group in general.

Knowing that the impact of a family on a child is so great and knowing that concerned elders pass on lessons to the next generations through the families, there must have been many wise men of yore who would have worked toward fostering nurturing environments in families. How would they have done it?

The answer is that they would have constructed rituals, habits, rules and such other provisions that constitute components of the political, economic, social, religious and cultural systems of the groups they worked with. They would have done this with the aim that if the patterns they proposed were followed, better environments would automatically be generated in families. In turn, there would be more happiness and better prosperity. Better care would be taken of children. Society would prosper.

Now, is this true? Has this happened?

As far as the works of the wise men go, there are two issues. The first is whether the wise men are truly concerned about their wards. The second is whether the actual solutions they have thought up for their wards are worth anything.

Now, these are again difficult questions to answer, and one may need to consider the wise men on a case-by-case basis. However, it would not be out of place to reckon a perspective about wise men and about the wisdom that arises out of the consideration of the scriptures. Please refer to Appendix G at the end of Part 1 of this book for a discussion on who is wise.

But, in brief, we shall move ahead with the definition that the wise

a) wish good for everybody and

b) know what is good for everybody.

The controversy here would be that there can be no absolute thing called as 'good for everybody'. 'Morality is all relative,' some may say. The eastern systems of wisdom beg to differ. They say that there is something absolute. The discussion in Appendix G throws light on this. But for the moment, the discussion can proceed on the basis that there is a way to decide who is wise and that the wise will have genuine and equal concern for one and all. (Those who cannot yet accept the idea of there being wise persons—well, I would not say it will be pointless reading the book, but maybe, the reader would like to study the arguments so that valid counter arguments could be given (does that inspire?). One can definitely at least make do with the idea that wise people are those 'who seem to genuinely know quite a lot and from whom we can learn'.)

Designing social systems: Having considered that wise men surely have concern for all humans and presuming that they know for certain what really makes a man happy and prosperous and peaceful, it makes sense for us to figure out what inputs they have added into the lives of those that care to listen to them.

For that matter, they have endeavored to put lessons into their children's heads and in their children's surroundings as well. They have advised their young people on how to build families and on how to nurture the next generation. And indeed, they have designated a host of activities, advocated principles and set up value systems which they ask their followers to patronize and follow.

So, in the process of intervening thus, did these wise men truly arrive at something that created an impact? Did they induce ideas that ultimately led to a situation where children were nourished in brilliant ways, which ultimately led to their developing outstanding or excellent characteristics?

The answer is that it indeed did result in a variety of social environments, each producing certain characteristic features in the children of that group. For example, the indigenous Indian varna system (setting aside, for the moment, the discussion on whether it was done by one that was wise or not), which formed the mainstay of society in ancient India, did evolve around a perspective that was deliberately designed. The training in the various families and in the schools of that time was also designed so that the students were groomed to perform their pre-designated duties—of the varna system—efficiently. And the group that followed this system did make it big in Indian society.

Taking an example from Arabia, we can say that Islam was a result of the direct intervention of Muhammad the Prophet. The systems set up there were on the basis of the wisdom that enlightened the Holy Prophet. And it is known to have brought about great discipline in an otherwise chaotic society. In the Indian subcontinent too, there were and continue to exist many such individuals who influence the lives of their followers in significant ways. Therefore, the wise do intervene in society and alter the cultural ecosystems for the children being groomed in it, and it pays dividends to the community or group that imbibes these interventions.

The jatis of India: Multiplicity of groups was a feature of Indian civilization from the very start. Even during the time when the varna system flourished, there were many other groups that existed in parallel that did not belong to the mainstream varna system. Presumably, there were other modes of training and alternative social structures which catered to children of those other groups. For instance, even in the scriptures that catered to the varna system, mention has been made of tribes and forest dwellers that lived and practiced their way of life independent of the varna system. There were examples of other traditions which evolved around the worship of Rudra and of the Mother Goddess. Therefore, there were groups galore, and the totality of this can best be represented in what is known as the jati system, and it evolved in various ways as the centuries passed by.

In conclusion, note that the jati system is not limited merely to what is done to take care of infants or children. Each jati has a way of dealing with everything that happens in a person's life, beginning from the point of conception and up to death and after-life.

And it merely takes common sense to see that a jati (a 'type'), does have a certain consistency in the kind of environment it gives to its children, and therefore, it is not unnatural to find some consistency in the characteristics of individuals who are groomed in a group compared to individuals from another group in the Indian context.

Measuring the depth of culture: In the Indian context, the content of what characterizes groups and individuals is fundamentally estimated in terms of two concepts: *sabhayata* and *sanskriti*. These two translate loosely to 'bearing' and 'learning' respectively. When an individual absorbs higher values, his 'bearing' or sabhayata becomes more noble and gentlemanly. On the other hand, sanskriti stands for his awareness of what the value systems mean and imply and his understanding of its importance. Therefore, sanskriti stands for his learning and scholarship. It is considered desirable for a person to have good sabhayata and good sanskriti. These two concepts give us some indicators by which we can study the validity of the wisdom imparted to groups and the extent to which those values have been absorbed. Therefore, there are ways by which some kind of hierarchy can be established.

Then again, this method of creating a hierarchy need not be considered as an artificial plug-in or an insertion or a designed input. Nature has its own way of selecting what is good and what is not. Certain values—and therefore, groups—are preferred over others in a natural process of selection.

Consider the following hypothesis:

Theory of the 'survival of the fittest culture': Those groups that were able to produce children with outstanding values, character and substance thrived, and the others, which could not, fared badly or even died out.

Down the generations, life has been throbbing with its fullness in this subcontinent, and without a doubt, there have been endless opportunities where excellence has been put to the test. Take the case of a ruler of a small township who needed a minister. He chose from among his citizens and well-wishers. He chose the best, and as it turned out, he chose to prefer a person from among those that had made it their business to sustain a strong tradition of learning. So, other groups lost out. Take the case of attacks by tribes on one another. Those that had put their children through the rigors of training in defense besides the awareness of being duty-bound and fierce in their commitment to their tribe had a better chance of survival. A tribe that did not inculcate these warrior habits in its children got eliminated. And so on…

In the same manner, groups that knew how to cooperate within families, groups that knew how to give stable environments to their children and groups that encouraged virtue in their people fared better than other groups. And this competition and process of natural selection continues to this day. (Do realize that in ancient tribe-based society, people and tribes continuously fought. These efficiencies which individuals and tribes built have therefore been tested to the full, repeatedly.)

Let us take the example of the many churches that mushroom all over the globe. Even as some are taking birth today, others are dying out. The point is that those denominations that are able to truly impart the values which Jesus Christ stood for will survive, i.e. when the children from a certain tradition produce outstanding results in society as a consequence of that church, that method or line gets reinforced and that denomination of church begins to propagate, expand and prosper. In a matter of a few generations, an expanding group will make a mark. If, on the other hand, a freshly-initiated 'church system' has inherent faults or is not able to deliver Christ to its patrons, then it is likely to survive for some time and die out. And yes, besides a church's internal strength, it is also true that external factors decide whether a group will survive. The church can face support or persecution, but ultimately, only those churches or denominations which have developed good internal strength will persist.

And if this is the case of certain groups in the modern world of instant communication and quick travel, it would have been much more significant in the ages gone by. What is happening with the churches is a matter of a few generations, and there have been so many generations in the known history of mankind. The jatis in India are a case in point. The subcontinent has a high density of human population and tribes. Needless to say, each tribe has been severely tested in the test of the 'survival of the fittest culture', and those that continue to exist today are those tribes and groups that have triumphed in that struggle that has gone on for thousands of years.

Therefore, it emerges that if the Brahmins have distinguished themselves and have sustained themselves for so long, it can only be due to the fact that they pass on lessons in their traditions which enable them, as a group, to excel in the struggle for survival. In fact, even the tribes that live in the forests can be credited with evolving practices and traditions that have made them sustain as groups for sufficiently long. The exact opposite is happening to a tribe in the Andamans. This particular tribe has many men and only one living woman. This was probably in the late 1990s when an army doctor was invited by the tribe to administer medicine to this woman. The doctor advised them to admit her in a hospital, which they refused to do. What happened thereafter is not known, but if per chance the woman is no more, that would be the end of that tribe.

An educated Indian would, of course, find the ways of the tribes primitive… But then, it is a matter of relative perception. Any judgment passed on the tribes as such is truly a statement of intolerance toward 'other people' who are not western-educated and who do not share the same views of life as the educated people themselves.

But if one is able to set aside this judgmental perspective, it becomes clear that these tribes continue to exist because they have evolved traditions by which they are able to live together and generate sufficient strength on the basis of the training they impart to upcoming generations.

And on the face of it, there is nothing wrong with wanting to educate or train the upcoming generations, whether by Brahmins or anybody else for that matter. Would we consider it wrong that film star parents teach their children the tricks of the trade and the discipline and work that goes behind success as a star? Or would we consider it wrong that businessmen teach their children the nuances of trade rather early in life?

It is true that film personalities also have easy access to production houses and businessmen have easy access to investments, but it surely is not the only thing that helps them hold their own for generations in these respective fields…

Be it the Brahminical order or the tribal systems of today, one needs to realize that every surviving node of culture that exists in the world today, especially if it has had a long history, has emerged from a trial by fire. The earnest among today's researchers need to explore the strengths that have led to this by fathoming the value of things that are dear to these enduring traditions.

Of course, this also makes for a very strong case for preserving tribal and other cultures in their pristine form. Since these cultures are inspired by the works of the wise of yore, somewhere, somehow, these groups have learned to access their highest potentials.

In the whole world there is no study so beneficial and as elevating as that of the Upanishads. It has been the solace of my life – it will be the solace of my death.

It is the most rewarding and the most elevating book which can be possible in the world.

I believe that the influence of the Sanskrit literature will penetrate not less deeply than did the revival of Greek literature in the fifteenth century.

– Arthur Schopenhauer
German Philosopher (1788–1860)

In Section 1, we saw that the varna system was the mainstay of Indian civilization. This system was built around the inspiration that made the Rishis and saints write the Vedas. And as it has turned out, it is only the Indian civilization that has been in continuous existence for at least 5000 years now; no other civilization across the globe has successfully done that. Clearly, as discussed in the last chapter, the culture developed around the varna system has come out with flying colors when it was tested in real life—it has fared well in the test of the 'survival of the fittest culture'.

But longevity is not possible for a group when people within a group are at loggerheads with each other because the group becomes weak; and this applies to all kinds of groups. Hitler wanted to build a 1000-year *reich*, but it imploded in twenty years. This can be attributed to the fact that his policies divided society and made people commit atrocities against one another.

Maybe a less notorious system would take a little longer to come to naught, but this has been the experience of humanity since time immemorial—any system that nurses evil in its bosom lays the seeds of its own destruction. Mahatma Gandhiji looked at the positive side of the same issue by remarking that 'man is essentially peaceful in nature', meaning that evil is unnatural to him, and hence, institutions built on that basis will not succeed or endure.

But if that is so, why is it that despite the caste system being reputed to be filled with diabolic designs, despite it being thought of as essentially an arrangement for the preservation of selfish class interests and despite it having a record of great atrocities committed on lower castes has it survived this long? How is it possible that certain societies that have been built on the foundation of the varna system have successfully fought degradation? How does this system continue to beat the odds and survive the test of 'survival of the fittest culture'?

The answer is that there must be something solid within this system. There is a core in it which imparts great strength to the system—and most importantly, this core must be consistent with the principle that 'man is essentially peaceful in nature'. What, indeed, is this internal strength of the varna system?

Material strength? For a moment, let us hypothesize that the inherent strength was derived from material factors. Let us suppose that a certain group of people were able to arrange a system which gave material advantages to themselves (higher castes) and that, in turn, gave them advantages of holding power. Maybe it even gave the higher castes the authority to impose unjust rules and regulations so as to create a monopoly over knowledge and exclusivity in education at the cost of the other groups. In other words, let us assume that wealth, power and education were concentrated in certain groups and that that was the source of the strength of the elite classes. Further on, let us propose that just as these upper classes could hypothetically hold their might in society, the varna system has been able to hold its own through the millennia.

The question is whether this explains the facts well enough. Are material advantages sufficient to cause caste equations to sustain, without change, over such long periods, which in turn sustain the varna system in such a way that it ultimately makes the civilization invincible?

A little thought on the lines of how societies perform and sustain in the real world reveals that if material advantage or material knowledge was the core sustaining force, then casteism would have long ceased to be. It does not take too many generations for communities to suffer reverses in military and monetary fortune or for getting opportunities for education and knowledge. Such reverses would have put the so-called lower castes in positions of advantage several times over a span of thousands of years. A very recent case is of the Maratha emperor Shivaji. He did not belong to the warrior clan, but he did eventually wield power. There must have been numerous examples of this kind in ancient India. Chieftains who overthrew small kingdoms, forest dwelling tribes that ran over kingdoms, fishermen groups that took over local rule… Indeed, history does give instances of many such events happening, but despite all that, the caste hierarchy has sustained for centuries in the original format.

That is to say, despite the reverses that happened in the material plane, there is something in the arrangement which kept propping up the varna system and helped sustain the caste equations over long periods. So then, if it is not power, knowledge or material riches that is the deciding force, all of which constitute factors in the material plane, what is that which allowed the system of casteism to sustain for millennia?

Some people claim that it is some kind of perpetual scheme which results in this sustenance and dominance. But that is a judgmental perspective of branding a group of people as perpetually diabolic and crediting scheming dispositions with merits of invincibility. This reflects personal prejudices more than objective analysis. In fact, it is an easy thing to say without having clarity in one's mind. Surely, there is something far more complex.

Getting beyond: Indeed, such tenacity can only be explained by reckoning that there is something in the varna system that has to do with what is beyond power, knowledge or material riches —the obvious bet being that there is an element in the varna system that is spiritual in origin.

From here on, in the arguments presented in this chapter, it is a matter for each person's individual observation and exploration; it is the sincerity and success of an individual's pursuit that determines how much consistency he finds in the claims of the wise. The author is convinced and adds his vote in favor of there being objective truth in the claims of the wise.

It is necessary for the researcher or the seeker to go through the relevant 'knowlerience' (knowledge + experience; courtesy Sirshree of Tej Gyan foundation). Jesus Christ mentions that the one who has 'seen' (or felt or, better still, been through the knowlerience of) the wonder of the 'beyond' behaves like a person who has seen a rare jewel. In pursuit of the rare jewel, he goes about selling everything else that he has so that he may buy that jewel. The object of such pursuit is the foundation of the varna system.

Much has been said about this knowlerience. It is supposed to be a common experience to all of humanity (Refer to Peak experiences, Abraham Maslow, 1970). As a child, each one lives in that bliss, only to lose it out of ignorance as one grows older. The best performers are supposed to be living exponents of that experience when they are in their respective 'zones' while performing. Meditation techniques and yogas (the ones related to transcendence) help people transcend into that state of existence. And teachers/Gurus seek to transfer knowledge and skills related to this ethereal experience to the next generation. It is important to realize that this knowlerience gets passed on to the next generation only if there is awareness of its true value. There must be awareness of its importance in life, and older generations must deliberately nurture their offspring with that awareness. When this successfully happens in a group, generation after generation, that group flourishes with that learning.

Therefore, the hypothesis is that the varna system sustains because it cherishes an experience of transcendence that happens in the spiritual plane. This experience is the core of the varna system, and it is reinforced by the knowledge that is transferred through the generations.

This combination of experience and knowledge is like a jewel stone forming a kernel which is embedded in a casing of precious metal—the jewel stone standing for the experience and the metal casing for the knowledge about it. Without this combination, the varna system could not have sustained.

What proof? On the face of it, we do have proof to indicate that the real substance behind the varna system has to do with spirituality.

There have been tremendous efforts by scholars and political leaders of the present generation and those of the nineteenth century (through reservation, education and all such means) to elevate the lower castes from their wretchedness. But none of these efforts boast of genuine success. Real and effective elevation of castes has happened in India only when the spiritual dimension was worked upon. Real substantial change has happened only through the influence of a wise man. It is only when a group is inspired to adopt principles of better spiritual living and lives dedicated to higher values that the group has risen in stature—and there is evidence for this in Indian history.

One is that of a certain group of Dalits from South India who became Vishnu worshippers in the twelfth century; they are now known to freely intermingle and marry Brahmins in the turn of the new millennium. Another example is that in a matter of one generation, in the ninth century AD, Adi Shankara elevated a group of Dalits to Brahminhood, and they have sustained this stature ever since.

In fact, this is an acknowledged truth in historical circles that groups of people are known to have risen in the jati hierarchy by following spiritual leaders. The spiritual guides of Shivaji were responsible, to a great extent, for elevating his capabilities. And with him, his entire clan grew up in the caste hierarchy. In fact, if someone takes the effort, he will notice that most performers (probably all) that excel in the world reflect higher levels of spirituality and meditation—whether they themselves are aware of it or not.

Therefore, it seems prudent to conclude that with respect to the elevation of castes (and individuals), real and substantial success happens when work gets done in the spiritual plane consciously. In other words, the real game changer, the real driver, the real substance of casteism lies in the spiritual dimension.

Therefore, we can generalize our premise by saying that there is a core spiritual experience and that there is an intellectual awareness about it. When these combine in an individual or in a society, it creates great strength and tenacity. And this is probably the hidden strength of the varna arrangement—that which has led the system to survive great odds and for thousands of years. Therefore, only by understanding the significance of the beyond through knowlerience can one really unravel the true nature and content of the varna system and thereafter, hopefully, successfully work on it.

A difficulty in the proof: This hypothesis may, unfortunately, be just that—a hypothesis—since the proof of the pudding lies in the eating. At the cost of sounding repetitive, it needs to be mentioned here that with regard to spiritual pursuits, the only way one is going to get proof of the objective existence of the beyond is through knowlerience; in other words, if there is no self-experience backed by knowledge of the same, one cannot be given that proof in his hand or in his mind. Each individual has to travel the path himself and experience it himself and only then can he get the proof.

Very convenient, one can say, but given that a reader can still use his intellect and reasoning, extrapolate and arrive at the conclusion that knowlerience is in all probability the key, he needs to extrapolate from the fact that a spiritual experience has been found to be a cross-cultural, global and all-time experience (read *Religious Values and Peak Experiences* by Abraham Maslow). He needs to extrapolate from the fact that a wide spectrum of people have spoken about this in various languages and in various contexts; such contexts are spread over all of human habitation and over the entire known span of human history. (These account for three of the four proofs of wisdom; experience, reason and scriptures. The fourth proof is authority, which is seen in the bearing and confidence of one that is wise.)

Wait for proof? Having considered whatever it is that we are pegging as the central aspect of the varna system as being something that one can only experience and realize for himself, we reach an interesting dilemma:

Is it scientific to carry forward the argument when an intervening step in a theorem has not been proved?

It is not truly scientific. In a sequence of reasoning, one logical step leads to the next, and each are truths in themselves.

What then about those people who do not get the proof for one of the steps in the theorem? Can they proceed? If, as an explorer, I have not knowlerienced the Beyond, can I go further?

But then, it is also not sensible to pause at this point and wait for the explorer to gather proof.

The way out is that since the proof lies in each person observing nature by himself, what can be resorted to here is to describe the further development of the argument and leave it to the readers to obtain the intervening proof. Those that have still to identify the proof of this claim should, for the moment, consider it as a postulate and continue studying the completeness of the theory. The seeker/researcher may keep looking for proof of the same even as he contemplates on the wholeness and consistency of the remainder of the proof of theorem. Keeping to that spirit, we shall move forward by presuming that the postulate about the Beyond is true and that it is the cause of the long-time endurance of the varna system—an objective truth, as the wise men say.

Pursuit of the Beyond produces excellence: The next link in the chain of the argument is that once a person recognizes the importance of transcendence and pursues it, his life becomes sublime. As mentioned earlier (in Christian terminology), living waters flow out from him. His mind becomes capable of excellent focus. He stays in the present, and therefore, his output is the best that is possible from him. In other words, as we have seen in shifting from selfishness to selflessness and from a samsara-bound existence to nirvana, the quality of life improves. The individual not only becomes happier, he also carries a little heaven around him wherever he goes. Not only does he perform better than average, he also inspires those around him to perform better. Invariably, any society that has such a self-realized soul in its midst benefits and performs well. But it does not end here.

Societies that are designed to sustain life for and among the likes of these that aspire for the highest also are ideal societies.

Finally, societies that follow the guidance of such men of wisdom flourish; groups that put this excellence as the goal to pursue improve their quantitative output. Such societies/systems which cater to the needs of the highest aspiration of individuals come in the realm of dharma. The pursuit of the Beyond can therefore mean both the pursuit of the highest ideal for individuals and the pursuit of the highest ideal among societies.

If it is inspired by a wise man, then it is all-inclusive: Let us presume that the wise are interested primarily in the fact that each individual should realize the depth of his potential. They wish for peace, prosperity and freedom from bondage for all humans. When they design systems, these motives would define as to what should be inducted in the arrangements. And do note that any system will be truly complete only if it is designed in such a way so as to maximize contentment, peace, happiness and prosperity for 'all' members of society. After all, the wise are not really wise if they do not transcend human barriers of all kinds.

To accept or to not accept this offering from the wise is in each one's hand. Whoever wishes well for his ward and his community will choose wisely. For consequences will accrue… A person being obstinate about not choosing what the wise recommend is like a bird taking off from a cliff after folding up its wings. It is bound to crash unless it gets freed from its own bondage.

Motives for designing the varna system: The question arises as to whether the varna system was designed by one that was wise. If transcendence is at the core of its longevity, then the hand of a wise man is evident in it. Indeed, the principle of egoless existence is the cardinal principle on which the varna system is based. In this system, the wise have been truly honored to the extent of unquestioned obedience. And their recommendations about how society should be constructed have been accepted and followed.

Hidden in its ways is the pursuit of the highest ideal. The members are taught to dig at their deepest potentials. So also is society constructed so that all members are prodded on to unleash the bliss that is within them no matter their stature as long as they belong to the Vedic culture. By achieving this, the Vedic civilization has produced the resilience and strength that has made it survive against great odds.

A tall claim, one may say. The four-unequal-class-varna format seems to fall at the first hurdle of justice which the modern thinker would put before it: human rights! The truth is that the idea of the caste system turns all notions of equality acceptable in the socialistic world on its head; the Vedic system seems to be essentially thriving on inequality. Clearly, there is a conflict with the way modern intellectuals think.

In fact, the conflict with modern thought runs quite deep. Consumerist culture puts pleasures, facilities, needs, wants, luxuries and their satisfaction for an individual before everything else while the ancient system goes so far as to say that the highest persons in society need to beg for their food and that they should eat only after everyone in the village has had their food. It then goes ahead and says that the persons who are to take care of businesses should deal with large amounts of money, but they should have a consumption pattern which should not be different from the average person on the street. Of its fighters, it says that they should just do their job and expect nothing in return.

These are just three indices, but they are sufficient in themselves to say that the thinking that went into the construction of the varna system is way beyond what is on the minds of modern-day thinkers who specialize in understanding society. The Vedic society, in its design, truly reflected a different understanding of human beings in the minds of its designers. In fact, the above three examples (regarding the highest in society, ideal businessmen and soldiers) show that society was expected to stress on austerity rather than consumerism, and they propose that the path to happiness is a detached approach to pleasures rather than an attached pursuit of it.

All this is hard to digest in two ways. One is that it talks about austerity when the modern man is taught to pursue pleasure for happiness. The other is that, despite all this graciousness, the lower castes, the Shudras in particular, have been an oppressed group in society. Is there, therefore, any truth in the claim that the system was just to everyone?

"India, what it can teach us?"

"If I were to look over the whole world to find out the country most richly endowed with all the wealth, power and beauty that nature can bestow, in some parts a very paradise on earth,

I should point to India.

If I were asked under what sky the human mind has most developed some of it choicest gifts, has most deeply pondered on the greatest problems of life and has found solutions of some of them which will deserve the attention even of those who have studied Plato and Kant,

I should point to India.

And if I were to ask myself from what literature we, here in Europe, who have been nurtured most exclusively on the thoughts of the Greeks and Romans and of the Semitic race and the Jewish may draw that corrective which is most wanted in order to make our inner life more comprehensive, more universal, in fact a more truly human life, again,

I should point to India."

Professor Max Muller (1823–1900)

It is known for sure that the feeling of people being high or low is an essential feature of today's casteism. It is given a lot of importance in practical life. And a major chunk of social dynamics is determined by this. Seeing its importance, it is apt that we study it with care and nail the debate as best as we can. So, what is it that decides that someone is high or low?

If money was the criterion to decide who was high and low, then would a prosperous prostitute be of a high class? And would the situation be altered in anyway if we called her a 'sex worker'?

Or then, would Bill Gates be great? First of all, he has a lot of money—honestly/legally made—and for the most part, in the capitalist world, made through means 'respectable' in society and civilization. Next, he was able to spearhead a great revolution in the industry, and then, as of now, he has dedicated a lot of the money he earned to charity.

Anyway, he has only dedicated his money to charity. There are those who have dedicated their very lives for others. Are they greater then?

And what about suicide bombers? They dedicate their lives too, seemingly having made up their minds to sacrifice their very right to be alive. Are they greater then?

And that takes us back to where we started: let us consider the sex workers who lay down their bodies in service to society, to supposedly depressurize society from some animal passions—for some insignificant trifles they need in order to survive. How do we fix who is great in this?

Is it profession? Let's presume that greatness comes from one's profession; performers of dramas, stage plays and street plays were considered, in most of ancient and medieval Indian history, as among the lowest classes in society, but today, actors are counted among the cream. And teachers were a highly respected breed in that ancient society, and now, that feeling is on the wane; most consider teachers way down the ladder in society as persons who have failed to make it big in other money-making schemes in society.

Within a family, in a patriarchal society, is the man really high? Or as 'liberal modern thinkers' have it, should he really be high? This applies to the women in matriarchal societies too. Or are they all equal as in 'human rights' terminology?

Is the captain of a sports team equal to his teammates or higher than them? To what extent do we apply human rights in this—if there is some presumed inequality in the team? Aren't they all supposed to be equal?

Does one become great by being religious or by being someone big in the religious hierarchy or by being a scholar in religious studies?

So, what should be the criterion: money, political power, muscle power, knowledge, position in various organizations, achievements in society, traditional preconditions, impact of work done, visibility, extent of democratic support? What is it that decides someone is big or small?

If there is one such criterion that we can narrow down to, where does that criterion figure when we compare castes?

Who is the authority to decide? Even for the moment, presuming that people can be so compared, there is another controversial dimension to it. Is it a subjective analysis or is it an objective analysis? Can classification of castes be a personal opinion?

Anyone can turn around and challenge the Mr. X who wrote about highness and lowness of castes and say, 'Who does Mr. X think he is to finally say that this person is great or that caste is great? Or that this person is low and that caste is low? After all, the author is also another person like you and me.'

So, each person, standing in his own place, can come up with his own notions of what is high or low. Anyone can stake a claim over the right to segregate or classify society by drawing his authority from any of a spectrum of principles of authority like comfort in numbers (more people back me, so I have the right to say: democracy), position in a hierarchy (I am senior), government (I am in power), loud mouth (I am an expert in a TV talk show), age (I have more experience), sex (I am a man), caste (I belong to the caste in power), success in society (I have money, fame, prosperity, influence), weight of academic degrees… Standing on the strength of any such authority, he may pass judgments that this is great or that is great. And once we get into this 'I-am-better-than-you' contest, it is like entering quicksand—what really matters then is one-up-man-ship. It is a struggle over whether 'you are great or I am great', and it is, most of the times, a struggle of dogs over a piece of bone or of pigs over a pleasurable place in a sty.

The real substance behind hierarchy in casteism: In the previous chapter, we have seen that the real game changer in the caste system is the spiritual element. Therefore, presuming that it is spiritual experience coupled with knowledge about it that makes the difference, we make the following point: Since the spiritual element is the core of the caste-consciousness, the truly relevant or significant notions of high and low in casteism stem from the spiritual dimension alone; the other non-spiritual criteria are likely to be mere consequences.

Looking at it in another way, we can say that ideas of high and low are designed in the spiritual plane and that they need to be analyzed and understood in the context of the spirit alone. Or in other words, notions related to high and low in the material world are immaterial to our primary concerns.

Only after having seen it from the spiritual perspective can we really be in a position to conclude about the connotations of 'high' and 'low' in a manner that can be successfully or fruitfully applied to society. Therefore, we shall explore the spiritual dimension to try and understand what the content of the hierarchy is. But before we actually go into that, we need to resolve the contents of certain terms or parameters.

The nuances of the debate: When we take up the matter for consideration, we can readily spot two important parameters: the first of these parameters is a feeling of 'greatness', and the second is the notion of 'high and low'.

For example, let us consider the height of a person. Assume that a particular society carries a notion that small is beautiful; therefore, the tall person would be of a low grade, and the short person would be of a high grade. But this is independent of the fact that the short person may carry a notion in his mind that he is 'great', and correspondingly, the tall one may feel an 'inferiority complex' that he is tall. So, the notion of 'greatness' can be considered as independent of the concept of high and low, and the former is a matter of perception or choice. That is, a person can feel great or small over some real gradation in the material world or some perceived notion of being better or less than another, and this feeling is a 'choice' of an individual; it does not matter whether he perceives it about himself or about another individual who he witnesses. So, to sum it up, a person can be huge in size or little (in terms of kilos and inches) in the material plane. Tall may be considered undesirable and short, desirable. This is a notion in society. One may feel great or small about it. This is a personal perception or attitude. Let's take these notions independently as perceived in spirituality.

The notion of greatness: It is hard to beat the genius of Jesus Christ in understanding this. Two of his relevant statements are:

1) 'No one but God is great.'
2) 'It is more difficult for a rich man to enter the Kingdom of Heaven than it is for a camel to go through the eye of a needle.'

In the second statement, the term 'rich man' can be extended to notions of wealth in terms of money, fame, fortune, success, awards, degrees, beauty, etc. So then, it means that any one 'feeling rich' out of having any of this wealth actually shuts against himself the gates of heaven. Therefore, it is Jesus Christ's recommendation that the correct perspective is never to associate greatness to individuals, which incidentally is what the first statement says. Interestingly, he even checked his disciples when they called Jesus himself 'great'.

This theme resonates with Hindu scriptures. According to the Hindu scriptures, for attaining self-realization, it is important to give up everything that one associates with the individual identity (*samarpan*). In fact, there is an inverted tree parallelism in Hinduism which suggests that in the final stage before self-realization, it is important to even give up one's attachment to one's religion (spiritual path). Only then can one attain nirvana. This would mean that all notions of wealth, even if it were an arrogance arriving out of the knowledge of scriptures or out of a reputation of following ritualism in religion, come in the way of 'self-realization'; and incidentally, self-realization or nirvana carries an identical notional description to the Christian concept of 'gaining everlasting life'.

Similar is the case in Islam where individual pride over possession of riches and even pride coming out of being more ritualistic than one's brother is decried.

And if one were averse to these mentions from religion and spiritualism, then there are enough indicators even in common literature to indicate that 'greatness' is a dead end. Let us look at some examples. It is often said that it is foolhardy for a person to 'sit on his laurels'. Another instance is the advice of Sachin Tendulkar's cricket coach to his ward: 'Don't let your head roll off your shoulder.' In other words, don't let pride destabilize you. Still another one goes this way: 'Great men have feet of clay.' All these highlight the same point that the notion of greatness is a hindrance in the path of efficient performance in the world. And the truth is that it doubles up as an obstacle in the path of the ultimate aim of all religions: ultimate freedom, knowlerience.

This would imply that if 'someone' were to accuse the scriptures of facilitating the notion of greatness of certain individuals, then such an individual has no idea about the contents of the scriptures. Similarly, if someone said that he or someone else is 'great' for being accomplished in something religious or spiritual, he too is ignorant.

It can be considered a rule that nothing in the scriptures should make us conclude that the scriptures sanction that one man is considered greater than another.

In fact, it is a tragedy when an educated man thinks he is great. Indeed, he would be a great fool. Pride or the sense of greatness in a person (even because he feels he is more religious than others) is a sure sign of foolishness and ignorance. Not without reason is it said that the truly wise are humble.

Jesus Christ has another thing to say here; he points out that 'the greatest among you is the servant of the rest' (regarding washing of the feet at the Last Supper). This lesson from him also comes with respect to two people praying in a temple: one parading his greatness in his practice of religion and the other standing in a corner and praying out of his humility. The same is also the essence of his famous sermon on the mount. This is a principle which all truly accomplished leaders have believed in. For example, Gandhiji also professed this principle with full faith in it. Interestingly, even corporate Gurus have started talking about the concept of a 'servant leader'.

The irony is that people now have this fancy of saying 'I am a very humble man' while at the same time 'feeling great' that they have achieved humility. Is it not a paradox? 'Great' humble man?

Therefore, let us be firm on this conclusion that the Vedas, if they truly represent the highest spiritualism, by no means say that the Brahmin is 'greater' than the other classes. If a Brahmin carries this notion, he still needs education, and if someone accuses the authors of the system of trying to instill a sense of greatness in certain individuals, that statement betrays the person's ignorance.

So, let us put aside this feeling of greatness or smallness and move on to the more objective consideration of what is high and low.

The notion of high and low in spiritualism: Indeed, there are genuine notions of high and low in spiritualism. In other words, there is some kind of hierarchy, and we shall try to unravel what it actually means. In fact, there are many hierarchies pertaining to spiritualism described in the Hindu scriptures; many of them have to do with levels of consciousness, preference in Gurus or the hierarchy of Gods. But we shall focus on certain notions here that have a bearing to the topic we are considering. They will give us important insights into the support accorded by the scriptures to a positive caste-consciousness.

Gunas: The first of these is a notion of hierarchy that is related to the science of the gunas. It is an established theory used by the ancients for analyzing human personalities. The main postulates of this theory are as follows:

1) All men are governed by three gunas (or characterizations, bearings, modes of existence): *satwa, rajas* and *tamas.*

2) All three modes exist in all individuals at all times; and at any given time, any and only one of the three dominates.

3) The theory thereafter goes on to describe the characteristics of a person who is dominated by each of the three gunas. The general tendency of the person dominated by the tamas state is toward sloth and laziness. The tendency of he that is in the rajas state is intense activity, excessive passion, a liking for an overdose of pungency, etc. The tendency of one dominated by satwa is toward piety, a focus on the finer aspects of life, looking forward to excellence and having affinity for spiritual highs.

4) It is further proposed in the theory that rajas is higher than tamas and that satwa is above rajas. But it does not end here.

5) These three states are further grouped together as states of ignorance. The theory states that the three states are bound states or states in which individuals exhibit ignorance about the true nature of their own selves.

6) Above even satwa is the state of nirvana. This is an unbound state of existence where one realizes one's true nature and is free from the limitations of the mind-body mechanism.

Why the hierarchy in the gunas? As for the hierarchy, that one state is better than another, it actually comes in the form of advice from a teacher to his wards. It is recommended by those wishing good for their wards that the wards should take this hierarchy as the correct journey for life and move upwards along this scale, irrespective of what their job profiles are or what group they belong to.

One may ask why. And the answer is that there is an objective truth about efficiency attached to this.

It is found that those that have tendencies and personal qualities that put them closer to the top of this scale are, by rule, better performers. Given that other parameters are the same, they display greater efficiency, effectiveness and success. Therefore, during the education of wards by the guardians, these desirable tendencies are pointed out as being better.

The question is whether this is the criterion on which castes are defined. And the answer is no. Many scholars like to assign the classification of castes on the lines of this theory, but in truth, the science of the gunas has more to do with personalities across the caste spectrum. For example, when Chanakya looked for someone who had attributes closer to a 'self-realized' or 'twice-born' person, he found him among the lower classes and made him king—Chandra Gupta Maurya. Indeed, one could have a person from a high caste plagued with sloth and a person from a low caste with great love and affinity for divine things. (The highly successful Hindi film *Chandralekha* from the sixties highlights this.)

However, it needs to be pointed out here that family traditions make a huge difference here. In one family tradition, it may be considered a crucial point to communicate to youngsters that one should work one's way upwards in the set hierarchy, and in another culture, that lesson may not be imparted directly. This would mean that those traditions that impel their wards to move upwards on this scale have a greater probability of producing more effective individuals, better families and finer societies.

In the same breath, it is useful to again make mention of the fact that 'nirvana', which is put at the top of the scale, is also considered the highest ideal in Hinduism. One that pursues it is supposed to be aligning himself with the absolute potential in himself. Transcendence to this state of existence is supposed to unleash the highest potential in a person. It is supposed to be pure bliss, and in Jesus Christ's words, 'Living water flows out of that person.' As for the others, they are said to live limited existences (in Hinduism, it is referred to as 'ignorance'; as for Jesus Christ, he says they are 'like trees walking around').

Therefore, this idea of high and low, pertaining to the *gunas*, used in this spiritual sense is basically an objective analysis with implications on the efficiency and effectiveness of a person. Naturally, it is also an indicator of how to attain happiness within oneself and success in society.

Hierarchy of the yogas: Another notion of high and low pertains to the path which a person takes in order to experience the highest that is in him.

When the *Bhagavad Gita* speaks of the state of nirvana, it says that irrespective of the path the seeker has used to arrive at the point, the final destination is the same. Further, he who has arrived at the destination—who has attained nirvana—is the source of all the scriptures. In this sense, all paths leading to the Beyond, or the 'Final Truth', are considered equal in as much as we know that they get the person to the same destination. However, mention is also made of the fact that the soul that reaches this particular state of existence through the path of knowledge and reasoning has traveled a harder and superior path.

In other words, *gyan yoga* (yoga of knowledge) is considered superior to the other yogas like *karma yoga* (yoga of action) or *bhakti yoga* (yoga of faith). Again, yogas can be considered, for the moment, as paths to shift from the mundane to the state of nirvana—from being 'trees walking around' to becoming 'springs of living water'. They may be reckoned in layman terms as some 'exercises' undertaken by the practitioner that fructify him into transcendence.

The question arises as to why this is so. And the answer is that a person who both understands the path that leads to the destination and who also reaches the destination has the twin advantage that he is able to guide others along that path. So, besides the fact that he has already found mergence with the destination and bliss and excellence, he can also be an effective guide. One that merges with the destination through the path of knowledge can also help society design socio-political systems that are best suited to the interests of getting people to target the higher things in the spiritual hierarchy; such societies are enlightened societies or, technically speaking, *dharmic*.

Again, there is a tendency to classify caste groups according to this criterion of high and low; and there is an element of truth in it. Indeed, the fact is that the Brahmins are associated with the path of knowledge

(they can guide). The warriors are on the path of action (the pursuit of the highest is based on action; it produces tangible results). The rest are in pursuit of the highest, primarily along the path of faith. But it is important to see that this is a concept that is easily misinterpreted or taken out of context to demand social status. Any such demand of self-appeasement is not in sync with the final destination, which takes precedence and is the same for everyone.

Ascendency in what one stakes: There is another spiritual hierarchy of importance, and it is based on what one is expected to put at stake for the sake of society. In the path to self-realization, giving up oneself and doing for others are two important markers of progress.

What can be given up can lead to four classifications of significance. At the first level, when you stake your time and services for the welfare of society, you get yourself tagged as a Sudra. In return, you get wages. At the next level, when you stake your properties into a business and set up enterprises for the welfare of the nation, you get profits in return. The tag is Vaisya. Then at the next level, you stake your life in the service of others. You are a warrior and get to wield power in return. That makes you a Kshatriya. At the highest level, you have given up everything, even your ego, and have dedicated yourself to learning and living on the mercies of the society and the divine. No wealth and bare necessity level of possessions… You get to guide society and are respected by society at the highest level. (But does it matter to one?) That gives you the tag of a Brahmin.

So, the Sudras and Vaisyas target the highest through faith. The Kshatriyas are expected to traverse the yoga of action. And the Brahmins traverse the path of knowledge. Equity lies in the fact that the goal arrived at is one and the same: the highest goal of the Bharatas. Note that the classes are in service to one another, and it is a privilege to belong to the four-class-team.

How this notion got applied: A notion like this gets applied according to the social context and according to the technology of the times in which the system was instituted. During the times of the revelation of the Vedas, just a few in society could travel the path of knowledge as others needed to occupy themselves with the tasks of fighting or working for society. This did create an exclusive club, but of tremendous benevolence. It was upon the small exclusive club to guide society in maximizing spiritual gains; and this small group suggested, for different categories of people, alternate paths to the destination. The path of action was therefore predominantly recommended to a select group of warriors and performers, and the path of faith was naturally recommended for the rest.

So, what is the implied hierarchy that gets instituted here? It is that it is good to listen to those that have benefited from knowlerience. It is important to see that the notion of what is better is an objective fact determined by effectiveness, joy and efficiency; and it has to do with knowing what is technically sound in designing a society tuned for the highest ideal.

Therefore, insisting that one caste is higher on this basis needs to be done merely from the point of view that, in the process of a group/society wanting to raise the bar for itself (which every sensible group wants to do), one sub-group that is pursuing the highest ideal through the difficult path of knowledge will eventually turn out to be the better bet for guiding society.

In other words, this classification of high and low is again a recommendation regarding spiritual prioritization by sensible guardians to their wards. And the same has been traditionally communicated through all kinds of training frameworks, whether in religion, secular education or in the families that practice Hinduism. Loosely, it can be said that Christians are taught to pay respect to the priests because these people are made to study about Christ and his works in depth. And the Americans are taught to respect their marines and veterans because they put 'their lives on the line' (the second highest level).

And interestingly, referring back to those times in which the Vedic system flourished, there were other societies that existed alongside. Those societies were not inspired by this Vedic ideal/understanding. They were referred to as 'those that do not belong' or avarna or non-varna. Typically, they may have had their own way of pursuing the highest ideal, but that would be in a way that is different from the way of the group that upheld the Vedic inspiration. In that sense, as of today, all non-Indians are avarnas. Now, we can hardly conclude from that that there is no excellence elsewhere in the world.

We therefore come back to the argument that Vedic systems talk essentially about inherent equality among all human beings and of using an appropriate path toward 'self-realization' that is suitable for the kind of work one is expected to be associated with while operating in the material world. It is interested in establishing a socio-political constitution which does little more than say that when one is in this Aryan organization of individuals, the 'superior' person automatically gets the right to call the final shots—superior, essentially in spiritual merit. That authority gets endowed by nature itself through wisdom.

Before going any further, one needs to specifically take note of the fact that that which is considered to be the ultimate goal of all humans, the highest that the Vedas has to offer—nirvana—is made equally available to all classes or jatis irrespective of what earthly activity they are associated with. This pursuit of the ultimate beauty of human existence puts the notion of material riches at a far lower priority. Therefore, in as far as the most important thing with respect to the Vedic civilization is concerned, there is essential equality among all individuals of the group. It is a matter of chaff that people are provided for unequally in order to take care of their respective responsibilities as 'trustees' (Gandhiji's principle of trusteeship is based on this) on behalf of society.

(A parallel principle in the modern thought process is the term 'dignity of labor'. One can therefore understand why the thing that really matters is 'how one serves' and not 'where one serves'. 'My father made such shoes that his patrons never had a complaint for the normal duration of the life of a shoe.' – Abraham Lincoln taking pride in his father's work.)

Of Gods, Devas and Asuras: There is still another idea which is used to discriminate among people, but again, it is essentially an idea with spiritual content. This is about the reference to the triad of Gods, Devas and Asuras. These three categories are very often confused as representing the Supreme Truth, Aryans and indigenous Indians respectively. The interpretation is erroneous when looked at from a spiritual perspective. The categorization has an interesting Hindu concept to it.

At the highest level is the trilogy of Hindu Gods: Brahma, Vishnu and Maheshwara. They are supposed to be in the realm of 'self-realized' souls or transcended souls. These Gods are anchored in this highest state and know no return to the human individual ignorance unless they wish to manifest.

The next category consists of the Gods who belong to the world of God Indra. They are characterized by the fact that they have the human element in them. They pursue the highest through their penance and efforts, and having realized the final aim, they relish the same. This relishing is a human trait. Hence, they slip back to the lower worlds and become human. They see misery yet again, and therefore, they toil with penances once more in order to work into the higher worlds. Therefore, this group is one that is tuned to the highest but is not quite there. They keep traveling up and down.

The last is the group of the Asuras. This group is characterized by the fact that they are egoistic, are driven by their minds and have a strong inclination to their individuality. They believe that they are doers and see no truth in the Beyond. Even their worship has an element of 'I did penance and got this boon from God'. The 'I' is important. The legend/story of 'Narasimha' brings out the dynamics between the three categorizations nicely.

The interesting thing about this hierarchy is that in delegating responsibilities and authority, it is suggested that one ought to give power and authority to the Devas and not to the Asuras. Or in other words, those that are given authority in organizations should not be those that are driven by their individual minds and egos but preferably those people who have a natural urge to work toward the higher levels of consciousness. The reason being that the chances of prosperity, happiness and success are bettered in an organization when this principle is adopted.

Again, this is a characteristic that applies across the castes. And yes, it does lay down a hierarchy which teaches the student that he needs to give up his ego, strive for what is higher and pursue the attainment of nirvana, the best he can do with his life.

Of gunas, yogas, stakes and ego types: We have listed four notions of big and small that are relevant in Indian spirituality which seem to have an impact on the caste system. These are the three guna states, the preference of a path that leads to final liberation, what one stakes in service of others and rising above egoism and individuality. All four are essentially spiritual concepts and are more concerned with trying to give liberation to man and trying to take him toward nirvana rather than to say that one group (or person) is greater than another group (or person) in the material world. These ideas of high and low are all objectively grounded in spiritual realities, which relate to contentment, peace and happiness in individuals and societies.

These cannot be considered synonymous with inequalities in the realm of religious rituals, socio-political responsibilities, religious hierarchy and the like. These material inequalities are in the realm of chaff and have to be seen merely as differences in 'responsibilities' (trusteeship responsibilities, if one may) in society. This notion of big and small contained in the spiritual factors condemns no group on the basis of location, race, gender or caste. All matters of high and low that are recommended by the wise are instituted in order to determine whether people are working toward the higher planes in spirituality or not. The rest are truly not significant.

When a spiritualist says high or low: One last point before we close this argument. Consider the poem in which it is said, 'The cow jumped over the moon.' Can we really look at the poet and say, 'What you say is total nonsense since you have no idea of what a moon is and what cows are.' Technically (or scientifically speaking), the poem is wrong, but it is important to note that these are not the questions you challenge a poem with.

Reckoning along the same lines, when someone from among the originators of the Vedas talks about high and low, it is not apt for us to literally interpret these spiritual notions of high and low as identical with the notions of high and low that people have entertained in the material world—especially in the practice of caste-based atrocities.

The spiritual experience is hypothesized to be beyond the senses and the objects of the senses. Therefore, one can do poetry and not science or social science or political science in this domain. Just like the little poem quoted above makes poetic sense, the sayings of wise men make spiritual sense. When high and low is being discussed with respect to castes, it is about the devout striving to experience something that is higher in spirituality. It must not be interpreted as a device to primarily determine rank in matters of possession, status or politics.

Elevated in spirit: Therefore, going by the discussions that have happened in the last few chapters, certain points may be concluded:

a) There is no inherent biological or genetic component that makes one group better than another.

b) High and low is all about recommendations of trainers to their students, and more importantly, the training is for spiritual uplift.

c) The only spiritually authorized discrimination in terms of high and low deals with the distance of the practitioner from the final spiritual goal.

d) If someone uses the spiritual constructs to score brownie points over others in the material world, then that person is merely misusing the benevolent constructs of the ancient sages.

e) If a certain person says he deserves a better deal on account of being a person of high caste, then that claim must be accompanied by his standing up to incredibly high principles. And these principles are no laughing matter: altruism, sacrifice, begging from five houses for meals, doing one's duty without expecting anything in return, etc. And if he has not lost his ego even after successfully doing all this, it boils down to nothing.

Ultimately, the only ranking that is of substance, in as far as the overall Indian system goes, is that which determines how close a person is to the highest spiritual experience. It sets up everything. Those jatis that facilitate this in their members rise in the caste hierarchy.

What is the specific logic on the basis of which castes are defined as backward and forward in the public domain in India? No one knows. And in just the same manner, there is no clear logic/thinking on what constitutes a good attempt to elevate the so-called lower castes from their wretchedness. That is, no one seems to know what the starting and ending points, with respect to the elevation of castes, are.

Even though a lot of sincere attempts do go into getting rid of the caste-consciousness, most are misdirected and are destined to fail in the long run. Though, of course, many of these attempts must still be lauded.

But in the final tally, owing to the kind of situation that is created in the public space in India, the lower castes remain where they are, unable to find any way out of their wretchedness. They need clarity of thought and direction in order to move ahead, and that is not readily available to them. In fact, the detractors appear to be certain myths in the liberation praxis of the lower castes, and this needs to be busted. Hopefully, that should make the lower castes stop looking for fish hand-outs and start going to fishing schools instead.

Myth 1: Wipe out the entre caste system, and attempt to replace it with a uniform alternative. It will solve the problem.

The Vedic system may essentially be good at the core, but in some distorted form, this scriptural core has been interpreted to support the negative traits of the caste system. This, in turn, has led to a lot of heartburn in Indian society. So, what is it that can be done about it? The answer entertained by a significant percentage of reformers is that we need to wipe out the entire system and replace it with some uniform alternative.

But when called to reason, one wonders if it is the sensible path to take. And the ponderable points can be summarized as follows:

1) The erstwhile system emerges from what has been taught by elders to their wards and offspring as the better way of living, and as such, it is a result of accumulation of knowledge. This knowledge is about how one can make his life sublime and be more effective and happy. There is a promise of success and prosperity and of better chances of victory; there is a promise of building up better teams and communities. The question is whether it is sensible to learn from it or, alternatively, jettison centuries of learning and go about re-inventing the wheel.

2) The preliminary question is whether we are assessing the value of the existing system correctly. Every system needs to be applied and tested in its fullness. If it is half-applied, out of context, and then tested for its potency, it is both unfair on the system and improper on the part of the one that tests in that manner. Is the caste system applied correctly and only then tested? Are the ones who are to play important roles in the setup aware of their responsibilities? Are they executing their duties correctly? Do they understand the system in the first place?

When there is half-hearted application or when an old system is evaluated in a new age without trying to understand what it stands for, how can we conclude on the usefulness or uselessness of the system? And how correct is it to pass judgments on it?

3) Something that was relevant to the technology and context of society 3000 to 4000 years back would definitely need re-adaptation to suit the needs of the present time. Has this adjustment been done before its application and subsequent assessment?

4) Next, let's say that we manage to throw out the erstwhile system completely (which seems impossible), would society, relieved of the centuries-old system, be able to develop the requisite alternative strengths to hold its ground in the world order? Can this new arrangement ensure that families stick together, children are taken care of, old people are taken care of, there is harmony in society, each and every individual is covered by the benevolence of the system and there is good understanding between people and nations? And can one guarantee that there

won't even be freak cases of groups taking undue advantage of other groups in that new set up?

5) Can there exist a vacuum in place of the caste system, or will it be taken up by another order? What would this new system be like? Would it really develop into something good or will it develop into something worse than what existed?

5A) Can a new system be evolved for the Indian subcontinent without understanding the eloquence of the ancients? Can a new system be evolved by displacing the systems and arrangements made by the ancient thinkers?

6) And if a new arrangement were possible, it should be on the basis of what the thinkers and researchers of today come up with. It should be based on the language of human rights and how the various nations, including India, adopt and protect the same. It should be based on value systems inculcated in schools and colleges, through the advice given by teachers and parents. It should be based on personality development initiatives, through getting people inspired by sports stars and film stars and through making people listen to corporate Gurus and other 'better living' authors. And it should be based in some way on spiritual learning through privately conveyed religion as well (which thinkers of modern time suggest should have no role in public life).

And from the way modern thought is evolving, it becomes evident that we are almost closing in to complete a circle. We are again dabbling with the same kind of components which the benevolent human mind has been engaged with for millennia. There is increasing evidence to show that psychology is giving way to mind science and mind science to spirituality. The next logical step in the argument is definitely the quieting of the mind and meditation (this is almost becoming a fad today), and then, we will finally have the discovery of the Supreme Self which is supposed to lie just beyond the highest form of meditation. Are we not back at square one then? That is where the ancient masters started.

7) If we are able to see through the scheming of the detractors, it becomes evident that in essence, the caste arrangement has tremendous benevolence within. Any arrangement can be misused by opportunists; and if a system can be misused by opportunists, it is indeed

a weakness of the system. The caste system is prey to this, but it is better to look at the system as a glass half-full than as a glass half-empty. The reason being that without its positives, one can call to doubt whether the success of many of the ancient Indian empires, in terms of the prosperity they brought to their people (like the Vijayanagar empire for example), was possible.

Can we explain why Islam in India is more at peace with itself in comparison to other nations of the world without giving credit to what is being transferred down the generations of Indians within families? Spirituality is very much a part of the family traditions of the people who live in the land where the Sindhu and Ganga rivers flow. Without the stress on learning that is prevalent in indigenous culture, would Indians be such success stories in the global intellectual circles as it is today in IT, for instance? Without the traditions that are passed down the generations of Indians through families and castes, could India have some of its greatest strengths? The level of character building that exists within families, the relatively high level of stability in families, the general environment of peace and happiness despite the adverse economic, social and political arrangements in many poverty-stricken circles—all indicate great resilience in the indigenous culture.

What results from this consideration is that, in the public sphere, the planners would be headed in the wrong direction if they simply ignored indigenous content. Indians need to think of ways by which they can benefit from the strengths of this ancient arrangement, expand the culture's merits and suppress its demerits. The alternative of trying to wish the system away must be discouraged at all costs.

Myth 2: Education will lead to a casteless society.

Myth 3: Professional education and economic development will lead to a classless society.

First and foremost, it has come to light that it is the educated who are more rigorous on caste. Open one of the matrimonial pages of any of the popular English dailies in India, and this myth will pop up into one's face; definitely, it is the educated who both advertise in and read these papers.

Even if education were to lead us to a casteless society, what would that society be like? Would it consist of families like what the former President of the USA, Obama has—parentage from two different races? Standardization is a great idea, alright, but can all families be standardized as nuclear families across all citizens? Maybe some people will say that they prefer electronic families and single parenthood. Or do we fancy that all of us are destined to have a jati like the one to which the Queen of England belongs? Unfortunately, for a jati like the queen's to sustain, there is a need for maids and servants and a lot of gentry. So, if somebody is to be a maid, how can she also be a queen? Hence, everyone cannot be of the same jati as the queen. Then, of course, we could come up with a classless society which the communists speak of. Attempts were made, but as George Orwell predicted in his book *Animal Farm*, it turned out that some of them were 'more equal' than others and that 'the pigs became so special and important that they freely interacted and partied with men and there seemed to be no difference'.

Even in the communist experience, the possibility of creating one caste or jati did not succeed. In fact, as discussed earlier, the concept of just one jati is a myth. There will always be differences in the way families do what they do. There will be numerous yardsticks by which it can be said that a certain group of families constitute a distinct jati in comparison to others. No amount of education, professional or otherwise, will get rid of this. Professional education may move someone up the economic ladder, but it is difficult to conclude that despite being in the same profession, two people from distinct jatis will be identical. Rather, because of the grooming that happens early in life, they maintain their uniqueness of mannerisms.

The jati arrangement in India has entered a dynamic phase today; because of education, democracy and capitalism, there is a shift from traditional jatis. New ones are being created simultaneously. New parameters are being added to the list of differentiating factors. Education is one of them. Rank and designation is another. Government or private service, rural or urban, traditional or modern, vernacular or non-vernacular—all

of them add to the complexities. But that makes it still more fractured.

Differences are a law of nature. There will be different types of mannerisms, and this fact will forever be true. And indeed, a group of successful families will continue to dominate if they continue to preserve a nucleus of wisdom—about inspired higher living—and transfer the same down the generations.

Myth 4: There is poetic justice in lower castes being given power and authority today.

How logical is it to hold A responsible for the crimes committed by B? And would it be okay if A were the great-grandson of the B who committed the crime?

And if the great-grandfather B did commit crimes against C, then does it mean that C's great-grandson D will get poetic justice if he is given a head start in the 100m dash? Absurd logic...

Let's say that Genghis Khan murdered and looted in Delhi in the twelfth century. How much sense does it make for Delhiites today to 'return' to Mongolia in order to pay back in the 21st century? If ages back, two forefathers fought over something, what is the need for the present generation to fight as well?

In the event the two nations do fight, then it could be on one of two grounds:

A) Over the fact that their great-great...grandfathers fought; that the Mongolians invaded the Indians, so Indians are going to pay back in equal measure

B) Over the fact that a certain issue that they fought over is still alive today; say some imaginary boundary dispute was alive then and is alive now (of course, there was no question of it then, and there is no question of that now with Mongolia; let's just say there is)

If the fight is over issue 'A' alone, then the argument is absurd. To say that I would like to be compensated for the atrocities someone's grandfather committed against my grandfather makes no sense in law, definitely not in terms of human rights and not in spirituality either. This payback for past crimes done by ancestors is generally a bogie raised by political gamesmanship.

The law does make some provisions where legal inheritors are made responsible for bad debts. But to take it to the extent of settling crime scores and getting the grandchildren to spend time in prison for crimes of the grandfather is taking things too far...

It feels like poetic justice, but it is not. Far from it, this is plain bullying by people of this era of another set of people of this very era—using a 'revenge' pretext.

And getting back to Genghis Khan, if the fight is over some issue like the case 'B', i.e. if it were a running feud over possession of some land or property, then, as a mature generation, it would make sense for the two nations to sit together and see if the problem can be sorted out through diplomatic means—through mutual understanding or some means other than going out for an open invasion. The dispute need not be handled the way the forefathers went about handling it.

So, the same principle applies to the issue of caste suppression too.

Nothing in our logic should support someone even hinting that the present high castes should 'pay back' for things done by their ancestors. If Indians believe in the Indian constitution, then it must be remembered that Indians have decided to start with a clean slate. And each individual citizen begins his innings at the point of conception/birth. In fact, an individual is even not called to answer in full measure for the crimes he commits as a minor, let alone crimes that were committed when he was not born.

As for the other idea that problems are in existence as of today—that there is suppression happening even today—the answer is to look for ways to put an end to the atrocities. It must be tackled by confronting those people who are doing it and flashing before them the provisions of the constitution that tell them to stop. If these people are doing it for economic gains, then that must be addressed. Is education being deprived today? Address that issue then. If spiritual pursuits and education will help the groups develop, then make arrangements for that. All of this has to be done in today's context by assessing how each group is making use of the opportunities which the constitution of India places before it. The idea is to make those responsible for current atrocities pay for their mistakes, and it should be done within the four corners of the constitution of India.

It is absurd to say that the constitution of India intends to treat people on unequal terms based on inherited traditions of excellence. An individual's traditions teach him to struggle and excel; does that mean that he should get less preference? Or if there are certain groups that do not inherit family traditions of learning (that can, in turn, ignite excellence in the children) and are not inspired to make efforts toward excellence as a consequence, should they be given crutches and jacks? Should standards be lowered only for them? It is an illogical approach to fairness and justice at a time when the constitution of India has allowed free access to knowledge. Consider the following points:

i) If it is true that all Indians are born equal, and despite this, if some group or the other dominates, then we must realize that that particular jati dominates merely on account of its discipline and the training it imparts to its wards.

ii) The other option is to agree that the constitution of India presumes that Indians are 'not' born equal at birth and that Indians carry with them genetic factors that pre-determine the quality of each caste at birth [sic]—not true of course.

iii) Saying that the more meritorious must be discriminated against on account of historical reasons is an error of judgment because such persons are not answerable for the crimes of their forefathers.

iv) Insisting that members of a meritorious group should step back from contesting for a percentage of offices in society indicates ignorance; it is proof of the fact that one does not understand what effort it takes to train an individual to be an asset to society. It is like saying, 'I don't know what these members of the cricket team did that they play so well, but at least two or three seats in the team should be reserved for those of weaker communities.'

v) Gandhiji, in his wisdom, advised against this in a famous remark. He pointed out, 'If there are ten positions of importance in society and when fairly contested if all ten positions were to be ultimately won by Muslims then be it so...' Apparently, that applies to any other group or jati, including the Marathas of Maharashtra, Lingayats of Karnataka or even Brahmins or Indians.

vi) 'Fair contest' is an important criterion in nation-building, and it is one's dharma to ensure that all contests are fair. Anyone can get selected, provided there is no bias and the competition is appropriate and fair. One doubts whether the constitution of India has anything else to say.

And as far as atrocities against the lower castes go, a truth emerged out of a study in South India. It showed that atrocities on lower castes were meted out by the chaste Hindus (the land-owning and business classes) and not the Brahmins, meaning that atrocities come from material considerations rather than spiritual ones. This means that those crimes cannot be attributed to groups on the basis of spiritual segregation. Rather, it happened in very human struggles where people ganged up and fought over material resources. So, the notion of a historical wrong itself hangs in question. Did the system do the damage, or did the degradation of the system by greedy individuals do it?

One should realize that there is no poetic justice in cowing down those that dedicate themselves to higher principles and higher standards. Using any such logic to counter merit is just the perpetuation of injustice and wickedness by another group and in another form—and it should not be encouraged in our age and time.

In a dynamic situation, merit alone is rewarded; don't attribute this to ancient crimes committed. When people live together, a political arrangement is necessary; it involves handling power, and there cannot be a situation where there is no power or that it goes un-shouldered. The real question is who occupies that power? And the answer is that the one who is most eligible and suitable, as dictated by essential human nature, gets it most of the time. This is a natural process.

It is a way of nature that it pulls down merit-less systems and undeserving persons. When this is the case, the reason for the high incidence of any group being on top is that the group brings merit to the institution in question.

People blame their downtrodden status on subjugation that was plotted and planned; the true picture could be something else. There was open competition, and groups with a tradition of learning (Vedic) produced a greater number of winners than other groups. To a certain limit, individuals suppress each other. Some battles may go in the favor of scoundrels. You will definitely come across powermongers in any setup. But the war is eventually won by the meritorious.

The enduring systems that sustain are usually those which have the gift of meritorious persons who are not powermongers. Any caste that teaches its children to be fair-minded, honest, just, strong and firm will definitely have many of its wards in the highest positions of successful organizations, kingdoms, nations and companies. Groups thrive because of them. It does not matter which caste that meritorious person belongs to.

The only reason that the downtrodden remain downtrodden in the long run is that such groups fail to learn from the behavior of the meritorious among them and inculcate those merits in the forthcoming generations. They fail to preserve traditions and value systems that elevate people spiritually. It is because they have not moved along the paths that lead to the final freedom with great conviction. It is because they fail to learn from or pay heed to the 'wise'.

Now for the most interesting twist… Even if there is to be poetic justice for crimes of great-grandfathers, there should be a crime in the first place. There are no crimes save those done by greedy individuals. Communities don't commit crimes. There is no question of poetic justice against a community at all. Communities that commit crimes cannot dominate; they can dominate only on the basis of their merit, the service they render to society and their usefulness to others. Poetic justice must only lie in saying that the meritorious must win; the meritorious must lead us. It does not matter which community they come from. It is the same poetic justice of Mahatma Gandhi's ten Muslims.

There is no poetic justice in making someone non-meritorious take up positions of merit. Whether it was Valmiki or Chandra Gupta Maurya, they rose up and attained their places out of their own merit; it cannot be seen as poetic justice. There is no poetic justice in doing injustice to groups that make their wards persevere toward higher efficiencies. There is no poetic justice in rewarding those groups that fail to raise the bar for themselves.

There is no poetic justice in compromising the excellence of a nation. There is no poetic justice in punishing me for the sins of my forefathers. Read the requirements of the times and adapt to the requirements.

There is definitely poetic injustice in misleading a group of people by telling them that others are responsible for their wretchedness. If one recommends that the lower castes should take revenge, please say so. There would be at least no hypocrisy, and one can readily take a decision as to whether it makes sense to do that or not. But hiding this behind a term called as poetic justice only drags everyone into the mud. It confuses the lower castes and stops them from learning to be the masters of their own destinies.

Myth 5: Reservation will lead to elevating castes.

The Indian state has arrived at some kind of reasoning for the upliftment of the so-called lower castes. Much of this is centered on the idea of giving reservations in every imaginable place for all groups. Can this line of thinking truly work? Is it really producing elevation, or is it creating more problems for the downtrodden? There are many issues to this:

It makes a change for just a few: Through the reservation policy, those who benefit constitute a miniscule proportion of the deprived classes; even if the efficiency of getting vacancies filled were to be 100% and if creamy layers were to be eliminated, would it really lead to the elevation of entire communities?

Credible leaders did not favor it: The truly tall leaders of the Indian freedom movement have asked for the policy to not be carried forward. Is it appropriate to ignore Gandhian views on this? Are we showing too much arrogance in claiming that we know better than what Mahatma Gandhi knew? Even Dr. Ambedkar suggested no more than ten years of such a policy. In fact, even Mr. Kanshi Ram had reasons to say that the policy of reservation was not suitable. He said it was like 'running with crutches'.

Track record of the policy: Has it really helped when the nation followed the path of reservation for the last so many years? It takes much more hard work to make the downtrodden improve their lot. It is like offering tidbits to a few with the hope that they will grow and then get their brethren to grow. Does it really happen that way? What do statistical studies show?

A lower-caste individual who is given great responsibility by lowering the admission standards for his case and a lower-caste individual who earns a position through fair competition in the general category—which of the two individuals really contributes to the elevation of his caste? The praxis of liberation and development currently suggests that the lower castes need to be given reservation to be able to stand shoulder to shoulder with the others with whom they compete. In fact, the truth is otherwise. A lower-caste person who occupies a position on his merit stands shoulder to shoulder with his peers and stands up tall to the completeness of his being; however, one that is put artificially into some position through the lowering of standards for him on account of caste considerations experiences low self-esteem among his peers and carries it for the rest of his life.

Is there elevation without elevation of self-esteem? The doles given out by the government are to needy people. It does not stimulate self-reliance in communities; rather, it makes them dependent. When a feeling of dependence seeps in, where is the chance for self-esteem?

Rewarding what? As mentioned earlier in the book, the sarpanch in Vidarbha had a point when he said, 'What kind of government policy is this where people are falling head over heels to say, "I am more backward than the other person," and the government is rewarding those who win that contest with something here and something there? We look down upon these people who use the streets to answer their nature's calls.'

Indeed, if the idea is to uplift someone, how does one do that by rewarding wretchedness? Somewhere, the message that is going out is wrong.

Myth 6: The so-called lower castes have suffered for centuries, and that is why they are where they are now.

The arguments we have looked into so far are sufficient to suggest otherwise. Dominance of groups by atrocities is impossible. Dominance of groups happens only through spiritual elevation. Opportunities for power-wielding by all kinds of jatis have happened countless times in history. Those groups that did not organize themselves well bore the brunt of the constant tribal warring and inter-kingdom skirmishes. They have landed up in the bottom because of this. To give an 'individual human character' to entire communities and talk about one community (as if it is an individual) suppressing another community (as if it is another individual) is a very simplistic way of looking at things.

As long as we keep to this myth, we refuse to acknowledge the real reason for the downtrodden nature of the downtrodden. That, in turn, means that we will not show them the true path for their progress. If they have no inheritance that will help them excel, then there are enough live Gurus who can guide them to the highest ideal, help them tap into their highest potentials and help them excel at merit-based competitions. They need to pursue yogas that can take them to the highest ideal. Those elements in their indigenous culture that help them rise in yoginess should be nurtured and fostered.

Myth 7: Emancipation of the lower castes is possible only if lower castes represent lower castes.

Sounds like music in a 'representative' polity like democracy, but there is an inner contradiction that is very serious and needs to be properly understood. A person who professes this idea with full belief is unfit for representing his caste and that too in exact proportion to the intensity of his faith in the idea of representation.

The reason being that he is too short-sighted to see that there is a selfless perspective of universal brotherhood; it is this selfless perspective that forms the core of the spiritual content that can truly elevate the caste. When members of a caste pin their faith onto leaders who claim leadership just because these people are from their caste, they play ball to a divisive game. They may fall in line with the leader to protest and may sustain the protest till energies last, but ultimately, they will see no real progress in their position in society.

Individuals and groups excel and prosper only when they discover the secrets of universal brotherhood. What is truly needed for them are leaders who will lead them toward self-dignity in universal brotherhood rather than those who imprison them into labels and make them fight as reactionaries to imagined scoundrels and diabolic

usurpers of the Vedic legacy. A valiant caste leader definitely makes sacrifices for his caste, but sadly, he leads them to a point where genuine progress may not happen.

These are the 'narrow' representatives. A caste can progress only if it finds 'open representatives'.

A good caste leader will be one who leads the caste to the wise; the wise, in turn, will lead the group to discover its true internal potential. The punch line is 'wise'; emancipation of the lower castes can happen only under the guidance of the wise; and the wise have no caste.

Myth 8: Intolerant shouting will lead to emancipation.

Is it good to herd a jati together to shout at other groups and 'protest' in order that one may find emancipation?

If there is nothing else the group is doing, then this does count; it is better to shout than to just sit silent and bear it. After all, someone may see the baby cry and do something. But there is so much stacked against this strategy that it is more or less bound to fail.

This is because the raising of an individual's spiritual caliber comes from the quietness of the mind, from a meditative state. The idea of intolerant shouting takes one away from quietness. Therefore, in an attempt to elevate itself, the group will be resorting to a method which actually blocks the chances of members of that group attaining greater spiritual heights. Thus, it makes it more difficult for the members of the group to find higher levels of efficiency, performance and abilities.

The next important point is that when a group shouts at someone or something for its own emancipation, it is knocking on the wrong door. In truth, the emancipation of a caste happens when it adopts high principles, it tunes itself with the highest, it enjoys the thrill of heaven in its dances and songs and the members of that caste rise up to sacrifice and mutually help one another. It should realize that the answers are in the potential which its own members have. It is not to be sought from outside; it needs to be dug out of the caste's own limitless capabilities.

In shouting at someone else, the belief expressed is that 'there is nothing in our hands', that 'the other has to give it to us' and that 'they are not doing so'. The onus is put on the other. Now, the other can, at the most, cow down a group with its control over political power and economic resources. But it is an established truth among humans, beautifully brought out by Mariam Anderson when she says, 'As long as you keep a person down some part of you has to be down there to hold him down, so it means you cannot soar as you otherwise might.' So, the net effect is that both are in the pits. And this cannot go on for long.

When a group gains in merit out of its own resources and is ready to soar, no one can hold it down for any significant length of time. Nature takes its course, and the group automatically grows up and shines. The take-home lesson of this discussion is that there is no point shouting at the other; true emancipation happens when a group looks inward. When it turns outward and puts the onus on (or accuses) another person or group, it releases into the universe a belief that it can only beg or struggle in dependence; it humiliates itself and is blinded.

'When the blind leads the blind, both of them fall into the ditch.' This is a saying from Jesus Christ. He points out that if someone takes a judgmental attitude, then it is like a person who has a log in his eye trying to take out a speck from someone else's eye. A person who is shouting at another person or group—or the government even—is being judgmental. The point is that when a person is blinded by judgment and unforgivingness, he fails to see wisdom. In other words, he puts hurdles on the way to realizing his and his group's highest potential. He closes the way to personal liberty for his group's members. He fails to see what can truly liberate the group, and it will lead to perpetuating that particular jati's wretchedness.

Note that all the points mentioned above hold true only if it is indeed true that it is spiritualism that is the game changer in castes. These can be understood only if one realizes important truths about human beings. It is suggested that the points should not be taken for their face value, nor should they be rejected out of intolerance. For if what is said about this myth is indeed true, then the real route to emancipation lies in picking the correct attitude.

Myth 9: The constitution essentially calls for showering additional benefits on scheduled classes and tribes in order to treat them as equals in the spirit of the fundamental rights enshrined in the constitution.

Let us summarize all the important arguments made so far while tackling this myth.

What is the definition by which a certain group or jati out of the 4500 may be considered as backward so that it may be included into a schedule? And what is the basis on which a certain group may be declined inclusion into a schedule? Is it just because some sometime long back, someone decided so?

Are the backward jatis truly backward because of a genetic defect, or is it that they are inadequately trained as they grow up?

If all children born are equal at birth, then why should a child of a certain group be considered backward merely on the basis of a label that is attached to it at birth? And should another child be discriminated against because it is labeled as 'non-scheduled' at birth?

What mistake is it of this other child that its great-great-grandfather supposedly committed atrocities against the great-great-grandfather of the first child (and we have seen that this is truly a dud story—since even in that generation a long time back, those that stood up to the competition took the plum posts in society; it was not crime but rather merit that lead to dominance).

If it is indeed true that the game changer is the spiritual dimension, and if it is the absence of spiritual fineness in the parents which leads to the child being handicapped, then can or should the constitution really intervene effectively to change the status of the downtrodden since it claims that it is irreligious?

Is the constitution inventing a policy such that the training that happens between the conception and the schooling of a child will decide whether the child will receive special benefits from the government? Is the constitution saying that if the traditions are outstanding, then there should be negative discrimination against those children? And if the value systems are not good, then there should be positive discrimination in such cases?

If that is so, how will it decide what is good tradition and what is not? Is the constitution inventing a policy of 'historic wrong' needing to be compensated by a 'present wrong'? In which case does it truly represent a constitution that treats all as equals?

In conclusion: Clearly, these are rather uncomfortable questions which people do not want to answer, do not want to probe into and maybe do not even want to hear about. But this is the truth, and it needs to be addressed if we need to understand how to bring the downtrodden up. If we take pride in our constitution that it creates a nation of equals and that it is supposed to be secular, then this idea of positive discrimination without a doubt is not the proper direction to take. Especially the way the state is going about it by applying some fuzzy logic, not willing to put things in black and white or take a statistical and scientific look at the results of the policies it has adopted…

One wonders whether people who support such myths are really serious about bringing up the lower castes. In fact, it is people such as these who amplify hostilities within local village communities and communities whose members would otherwise like to develop by helping each other and benefit mutually.

The nation's approach to the emancipation of lower castes needs a serious rethink.

Admittedly, there are a lot of places in the hinterland in India where there is a grave need for a struggle to elevate castes; but does this process have to be a path of confrontation? Indeed, if one finds that there is no option other than to sit down helpless and sulk, it is better he takes up a path of confrontation—that takes courage too. But is that option necessarily, really? The scope in the political arrangement of today is remarkably large, especially in comparison to colonial or even pre-colonial times. In the present arrangement, there are great opportunities to look forward to.

The case for perpetuation has weakened: We have seen that the decisive component in the caste structure in India is the spiritual factor, but this factor is powerfully positive. The negative elements, however, arise from material factors, and these factors need to be tackled to dilute caste problems. To understand this, let us first reckon what these material factors were and what role they played in holding up a rigid, compartmentalized society.

The four material pivots that gave strength to the erstwhile system:

The first and the most important one was exclusive scholarship. Through the tradition of learning that existed within a family and through other specialized institutions meant for training, a great deal of knowledge was transferred down the generations. This knowledge, gathered over centuries of experience of the forefathers, was exclusive, and it gave the learned castes a definite advantage over other castes that did not benefit directly from that learning. And the difference can be remarkable. Because, apart from other things, that learning makes the wise induce traditions into society thus altering the environment in which a caste dwells. So, those that are nourished as children in that environment are benefited in unknown, subtle ways. It is known that men are born equal; it is education, both spiritual and temporal, that makes the difference. Putting it in HRD terminology, exclusive education was instrumental in providing information and

in the development of IQ, EQ and SQ among the wards of only certain groups.

The second factor was political monopoly. The militant class and the class dealing with knowledge shared a relationship of mutual help in the political setup. According to the constitution of monarchy in India, they were to aid each other in their work. Kings had to patronize the men of knowledge, and the men of knowledge guided the kings and helped them in matters concerning the spiritual health of the kingdom and advised them on matters related to management. There was rivalry too. Many times, the class of scholars took over the reins of government, and there were instances when the rulers acted independent of the scholars. But generally speaking, through the centuries, these two worked in a partnership of some form or the other. It helped in the sustenance of the interests of both classes. Both selfish individuals, who worked for their own betterment, and selfless ones, who in their heart of hearts had the subjects' interests above everything else, found elements of the system useful to their aims.

The third factor was economic, including control over resources. Through taxation, the militant class was powerful. Scholars received the patronage of both the ruling and the moneyed classes as the social order required. Then, there were those who had money since they were controlling various professions. And finally, there were the rest who were outside these three economic slots. This implied a compartmentalization in terms of possessions, whose rigidity was offset only by the wisdom that was contained in traditions and practices. And when there was rigidity in the caste hierarchy and ill-will in caste relations, money became a 'hard factor'. When money became too important, the lower castes were especially more vulnerable.

Finally, there was the factor of heredity in profession. It is not uncommon today, in the age of universal education, for children to take up their parents' profession. It should have been the obvious route to take in the centuries gone by. Should it then be surprising that the positions of authority became hereditary? Then again, in the light of the terrible evils of wars of accession, it was the best option for transfer of power among kings. This meant that even the learned benevolent found it sensible to support accession by heredity in a monarchical system. So, eventually, heredity came to stay, and it fortified the compartmentalization of society.

To dilute the impact of the rigidity of caste-consciousness: Now, if the above four are the sources for the material strength of the 'problem' dimension in caste-consciousness, then, in the event of wishing to remove it, these four need to be tackled.

As for the first factor of exclusive scholarship, if learning does carry in it the wisdom that can elevate castes, then there is now an opportunity to share that knowledge with everyone. Modern technology provides the scope for the required universal education. Knowledge need not be restricted to certain classes like in the ancient days; it can be made universal. Numerous modern-day Gurus give this education directly to the faithful.

As for the second factor of political monopoly, the constitution has nullified the scholar-militant nexus that existed earlier by eliminating monarchy. The outcome is that the political power which aided the sustenance of a rigid caste system is no more there.

As for the last factor, namely heredity, the perpetuation of the exalted status of an incompetent heir is becoming harder and harder. Merit is now a part of this system which the constitution envisages. This will remain so long as universal education, capitalism and the free market dynamics remain with modern India. In keeping pace with the developments in the global order, even as the globe continues to shrink, one needs to continue to work in order to preserve one's advantages. Incompetence can result in the wiping away of large inherited fortunes. Similarly, diligent working does take people to great fortunes and into higher echelons in society. This is happening even now.

But caste problems on account of economic factors continue even today. And for correcting this, work is required. A strong thrust in the form of self-rule initiatives

by people at the grassroots level in sync with efforts from lower levels of administration may help solve problems. Even increased number of grassroots-level entrepreneurial ventures can help offset these problems.

But over and above all these, if pursuit of 'wisdom' is the solution—tried and tested—then it is an alternative which is a far more fruitful path for the downtrodden to take. It will do wonders for them, their families and their communities, and it can raise the soul of the nation to greater heights too!

Know what it takes to rise: The question is how many average citizens, mere mortals, know what discipline it takes for a superstar to be where he is today. What is the work his parents may have put into him? How many of us know what discipline with respect to handling money it takes in order to be able to hold one's own in a business environment? Had we known, would we not have trained our wards accordingly?

The same applies to all kinds of groups which people envy. Why do we not go to a person from a lower-caste family and ask him, 'Do you know what kind of discipline a high-class family puts their children through?' Instead, it is easy to sit complacent and say, 'The higher classes rule the roost because they have access to political power, because they usurped education rights, etc.'

A fair thing to say, nonetheless, because one from the lower castes (and even from the upper), in his limited awareness, may simply not know what kind of work goes into grooming such children in higher-caste families. But learning that should be a lesser problem in this modern era of universal learning, and one must endeavor to understand how all this is connected.

Freedom must happen in the mind first: A certain self-defeating attitude that exists among the weaker sections needs to be stopped in right earnest. One should not shift the blame for one's plight onto the actions of others blatantly.

One who is free does not complain that others are responsible for his plight. For true elevation or liberation, there is a need for one to take complete responsibility of himself. One that takes up responsibility is found working by using his resources, using assistance he gets from others, taking the opportunities that come along his way, being fair to others around him and moving up. The very fact that he is doing this indicates his elevation to higher standards.

Instead of this, to start with the premise that one is helpless, that this helplessness is because of the actions of the higher castes and that too because the higher castes have troubled the lower castes generation after generation for centuries is not the way forward. It is equivalent to shifting the blame onto others and refusing to work one's way up. And this is tragic—passing the buck on matters of one's own development. This should never be encouraged.

Anything that induces such a persecution complex in the downtrodden actually emasculates him and lowers his self-esteem. This approach never leads to the kind of liberation that we seek for the downtrodden. Therefore, all those who profess to help the downtrodden but shift the blame for the plight of the downtrodden onto the higher castes or to the government are really doing them a disservice and holding them down—a perfect case of a professed liberator who is actually a jailor.

One needs to remember that one cannot blame someone else and experience liberation at the same time. Liberation comes from taking responsibility, and this responsibility and liberation elevates a caste.

Teachers of mind science say that if you eventually want to be a CEO of a company, start acting as one. Inculcate in yourself, early in life, those disciplines that are required to hold a position of that stature, and eventually, you become eligible for it and duly find yourself there. The solution for the caste problem, therefore, is to first experience liberation; it is about getting to be responsible for oneself. The day an individual says that he is in charge, the day he says, 'I am responsible,' he has turned around and has taken his first step toward his emancipation.

Therefore, to summarize, the constitution has already provided the environment to weaken the power nexuses that used to back the caste arrangement. The present technology is such that education is universal. The implementation system is also technologically advanced; therefore, it is easy to monitor the efficient functioning of grassroots-level systems. All these factors point out that there is little to fear from the caste system.

All that one needs to do is change the way one thinks and earnestly pursue the higher things in life by taking up responsibility.

Preserve self-dignity and build on indigenous strength: Some years back, Mrs. Sudha Murthy of Infosys fame was distributing some school-related stationery and clothes to children from a tribal area as part of an outreach program of the Infosys foundation. In due course of the ceremonies, after the gifts were distributed, the headman of the tribe came forward and offered to Mrs. Murthy a bottle of some herb extract that was obtained from the forest. A hesitant Mrs. Murthy said it was alright and gently declined the gift, but she was surprised by the answer. The tribal leader responded by saying that if she did not take his gift, then they, as a tribe, could not accept the gifts she was offering them.

Mrs. Murthy, in all her magnanimity, refers to this as a very humbling experience. It teaches us something important. In this setting, the tribal leader felt not an inch smaller or bigger than Mrs. Murthy. He represented a tribe that stood tall. But what would his fate in a city be? If the very same leader came to the city in search of his livelihood, he would be considered to be at the very bottom of the heap; even a second- or third-standard pass would look down upon him.

It is the handicap of the educated mind to feel that they (the Adivasis, for instance) live lesser lives. They should not be encouraged to think along the lines of individuals needing to be deconstructed and rearranged into a westernized thought process. They must not be stimulated to have contempt for what their ancestry contains. In fact, if they can be allowed to live dignified lives without hegemonic interference in their own cultural settings, it would be the best that can happen. In such an instance, there would be no question of them being judged for being big or small. Any development should be affected without disturbing that feeling of self-worth in them. As we have seen, if their cultures have survived for centuries, there is bound to be in them elements that pertain to the pursuit of the highest ideal through yogas that they are familiar with. These need to be highlighted and encouraged, and with minimal corrections, excellence can be attained.

Since the spiritual dimension forms the benchmark for development, it is through their own realization—that it is expected of them to work harder to higher values, to higher principles, to better discipline and to accomplished education and skill—that they can be emancipated. This would make them better performers on an average. This will open the gates to their own salvation.

Such an arrangement, if it can be achieved, which prods every individual to excel in pursuit of open merit, will take the nation even closer to the Vedic ideal.

Am I compelled to be in the varna system? To be or not to be a part of the varna system is the choice of the individual. The Vedic culture is the culture of a group that nurtures the high values of the Vedas. If one does not like it, please feel free to walk away. There is no need to follow the idealism of Brahminical society. In fact, if one is under the impression that the Brahmin (a human being) is the gatekeeper to heaven and that his refusal to open heaven's doors will doom one to hell, then the advice to him is that he has no idea of what the Vedic civilization seeks to transfer to him. He should rather give up trying to be a part of it. There are other doors to heaven. In fact, all genuine Gurus are doors to heaven. Several even live today (in fact, in Sikhism, gurudwara actually means 'Guru—the door to the Ultimate'). The Brahmin can be dispensed with in such a case.

In an adulterated Vedic society, a Brahmin may use his position of eminence to score brownie points in the material world. This is a tragedy in that particular Brahmin's life, and it is bad luck for the faithful who depend on him. But, in essence, for all the varnas, the pathway to heaven is always open through bhakti yoga and karma yoga, which cannot be blocked by anyone but oneself.

Ultimately, in Brahminism, the Brahmin is only a facilitator. Grace comes from heaven. Besides, the realization of the Highest results from one's own efforts in the yogas. A Brahmin fails in his duty if he fails to recognize and respect yogis who attain the Supreme through karma yoga or bhakti yoga. Therefore, there is essentially no inequality in the Vedic society.

The aim of the Vedas is to cajole all members of its society toward the highest ideal, irrespective of what varna they belong to. All those that are properly guided on this and, therefore, believe this, bear the fruits of this learning. They learn to uncover their individual divine plans in the grand design of a benevolent system, in dharma. In their pursuit of dharma, they realize the highest that the Vedas promise. Therefore, irrespective of what one's designation in the varna system may be, it is essentially a privilege to belong to a group that facilitates its members to get the best that man can get.

For the faithful of today: The secret of egoless existence is the cardinal principle on which Brahminism is based. Recognition and reverence of this eternal principle does indeed elevate the state of existence of people and does raise the output of a group that nurtures the principle on average.

This means that a person who considers himself part of the Vedic civilization should not entertain in himself notions of being constrained by human beings. By being part of the culture, he declares his belief in the highest that the Vedas point to. He believes that through the pursuit of the yogas, he can attain the highest that is available to humankind—and he pursues it. He knows that true fulfillment in life lies there and there alone. He takes the help of those that he knows are knowledgeable and works toward the highest even as he continues to carry out his responsibilities in the world. With the knowledge that he too can have all that is there to be had, he sees equal potential for the ultimate gain even in his small responsibilities and works toward realizing that potential—all because he has full confidence that the wise have advised him well.

In fact, this is the beauty of being a Hindu. Irrespective of what role he plays in society, his mind is fixed on the highest; he honors it completely. He celebrates it in his festivals, and he looks for fulfillment in life in its pursuit.

This brings us to the important question: How should the varna system be represented and seen in the present context? The answer is that with changes in economic, social and political structures, technology, transport and communication, the setting/era has completely changed. But what has not changed is the fact that humans still continue to be humans. We still continue to have the Divine Spark within us. Fulfillment for us moderns too is dependent on the spiritual dimension. Even while we work and vegetate, the impulse to find our spiritual depths is not gone. Dharma and moksha continue to be motivators of our existence. What impelled humans in the monarchy-based varna system continues to impel us today in the democratic order.

Today's democratic order, interestingly, has the potential for reversion to the earliest Vedic ideal of vertical mobility. As Indians work within this order, irrespective of the roles played, they must ceaselessly pursue the best that the Vedic system promised. Inspired by the Vedic ideal of moving up in the spiritual plane, Indians must rise up to be lovers of dignity of labor, persons having no duty working dedicatedly for the rule of law, connoisseurs of art, music, dance and sports, admirers of true sportsmanship and upholders of justice.

As humans liberate themselves and enter detached spheres, they build little heavens around themselves, and when Indians see this as the promise of the Vedic civilization, Hinduism will again blossom into being the nursery of world culture that it has essentially always been.

It is already becoming clear that a chapter which had a Western beginning will have to have an Indian ending, if it is not to end in the self-destruction of the human race.

At this supremely dangerous moment in human history, the only way of salvation for mankind is the Indian way.

Dr. Arnold Joseph Toynbee
British Historian (1889–1975)

Appendix

A: DETRACTORS WILL USE PASSIONATE SHOUTING

Finally, life is a game that unfolds before us, and certain people can play wicked games in it; being aware of these helps in enjoying the game better while not getting trapped into their attitude.

Listeners are of many types. Apart from a whole spectrum of those who will listen at various levels of keenness, there will be some that approach negatively. Some of them will not understand; some will not try to understand; some will not listen and others will try to not let the speaker speak. All these are possible. Clearly, when Jesus Christ was narrating the parable of the sower, he was making the point that however good be the intentions of the one that tells a truth, or tries to explain something important, not all will benefit from it in equal measure. As he says, some of the seeds tossed by the farmer into the field will fall on the rocks, some among the thorny bushes and others on the pathway. These seeds will eventually be lost. But a lot of it will also fall in good soil and will produce grain. Some, tenfold; some, hundredfold and some, even more… One must not expect that everyone is going to understand the beauty of an idea, however brilliant it might be.

At the outset, two categories of people can be discounted from the list.

Again, this is a passage from Jesus Christ:

Do not give what is holy to dogs—they will turn around and attack you. Do not throw your pearls in front of pigs—they will only trample them underfoot.

The Bible, Matthew 6:6

Apparently, the pigs are the kind of people who are predominantly lost in the pursuit of kama. They are motivated by it alone and dedicate their lives to pleasures and laziness. They represent more or less those who are inclined to sloth and have a strong tendency toward being tamasic in nature.

Indeed, when beautiful things are said to them, they will see no worth in it. They will stamp it and continue with what they were up to.

The other category of dogs includes those who have a combination of the following three: 1) a strong tendency toward being rajasic in nature, 2) predominantly pursuing artha and 3) a tendency to be reckless and wicked while doing so. These people will be intolerant toward what is being said and what is going to be said. These are persons who will resort to pre-judgment and may resort to shouting to scuttle anything related to a reasonable idea that is brought out. Shouting does not necessarily mean creating a din; it could also be equivalent to creating a mental block within oneself and an unwillingness to listen. Whether they express themselves in words and deeds or not, the attitude they carry can be described as 'will turn around and attack you'.

In relation to this, there is an interesting category of people who say things like, 'If you cannot convince me, how will you convince the world?' while they have not even cared to listen to what is being said. It is important to realize from these facts that the reception of an idea does not necessarily depend on the quality of the idea alone.

Be it pigs or wild dogs, these people need to be condemned outright, if the agenda is the pursuit of the truth. People like them make an appearance when political victories become the driving purpose of one's vision and mission at the cost of truth and wisdom. They may wish to represent on the basis of all kinds of chauvinism varying from race, sex, religion, ideology, caste, tribe, class, nationalism, language and age to region. But then, it will be the blind leading the blind. Short of wisdom, nothing will produce enduring prosperity and peace. Those that shout in intolerance, unable to bring forth reasoned thought into discussions, must always be taken with a pinch of salt.

If one has such tendencies, it is time to realize that one can indeed work on them. Being open-minded to the truth opens many gates.

And yes, victory will eventually happen on the side of truth.

B: PANDIT DEENDHAYAL UPADHYAYA'S VIEWS ON DHARMA

The following is an extract from a series of lectures given by Pandit Deendhayal Upadhyaya in April 1965. One can see that he has not interpreted dharma in the limited sense of something that has to be within the confines of religion, monarchy or Hinduism. He also argues that the constitution is a subset of dharma. One can also notice that his approach is empirical. He speaks from a gut feeling as against reasoning on the basis of core ideals or basic principles. And he is quite on the mark. Clearly, he is giving divine authorship to dharma, and he argues that it needs to be alive and kicking and in the 'now'. It is being added here to support the arguments in the book and to show the general direction that dharma truly points out to.

…On the one hand, we used the word religion as synonymous with Dharma, and on the other hand, increasing ignorance, neglect of our society and Dharma, and greater acceptance of European life, became the outstanding features of our education. As a result, all the characteristics of a narrow religion, especially as practiced in the West, were attributed automatically to the concept of Dharma also. Since in the West, injustice and atrocities were perpetrated, and bitter conflicts and battles were fought in the name of religion, all these were listed en bloc on the debit side of Dharma. We felt that in the name of Dharma also, battles were fought. However, battles of religion and battles for Dharma are two different things. Religion means a creed or sect; it does not mean Dharma. Dharma is a very wide concept. It is concerned with all aspects of life. It sustains Society. Ever further, it sustains the whole world. That, which sustains, is Dharma.

The fundamental principles of Dharma are eternals and universal. Yet, their implementation may differ according to time, place and circumstances. It is a fact that a human being requires food for maintaining his body. However, what a particular person should eat, in how much quantity at what intervals, all these are decided according to circumstances. It is possible at times that even fasting is advisable. If a typhoid patent is given normal food, the consequences may be disastrous. For such a person, keeping away from food is necessary. Similarly, the principles of Dharma have to be adapted to changing times and place.

Some rules are temporary and others are valid for longer periods. There are some rules regulating our conduct at this meeting. One of the rules is that I speak and you listen with attention. If in contravention of this rule, you start conversing with one another or addressing the gathering at the same time, than there will be disorder; our work will not progress: the meeting will not be sustained. It can be said that you have not observed your Dharma. Thus it is our Dharma that we observed the rules by which the meeting proceeds smoothly. But this rule is applicable only as long as this meeting lasts. If after the meeting is over, even when you reach home, you continue to observe this rule and do not speak, a different problem will arise. Your family might have to call in a doctor. At home, the rules suitable there will have to be observed. The complete treatise on the rules in general and their philosophical basis is the meaning of Dharma. These rules cannot be arbitrary. They should be such as to sustain and further existence and progress of the entity which they serve. At the same time they should be in agreement with and supplementary to the larger framework of Dharma of which they form a part. For instance, when we form a registered society, we have the right to frame the rules and regulations, but these cannot be contradictory to the constitution of the society. The constitution itself cannot violate the Societies Registration Act. The act has to be within the provision of the Constitution of the country. In other words, the Constitution of the country is a fundamental document which governs the formulation of all acts in the country. In Germany the constitution is known as the "Basic Law".

Is the Constitution too, not subject to some principles of more fundamental nature? Or is it a product of any arbitrary decisions of the constituent assembly? On serious consideration, it will be clear that even the Constitution has to follow certain basic principles of Nature. Constitution is for sustaining the nation. If instead it is instrumental in its deterioration, then it must be pronounced improper. It must be amended. The amendment is also not solely dependent on majority opinion. Now-a-days the majority is much talked of. Is the majority capable of doing anything and everything? Is the action of the majority always just and proper? No. In the West, the king used to be the sovereign. Thereafter when royalty was deprived of its so-called divine rights, sovereignty was proclaimed to be with the people. Here in Our country neither the kings, nor the people, nor the parliament have had absolute sovereignty. Parliament cannot legislate arbitrarily.

It is said about the British parliament that it is sovereign and can do anything. They say that "British Parliament can do everything except making a woman a man and vice versa." But is it possible for the parliament to legislate that every Englishman must walk on his head? It is not possible. Can they pass an act that everyone in England must present himself before the local authority once every day? They cannot. England has no written Constitution. They regard tradition highly. But their traditions too have undergone change. What is the basis for making changes in their traditions? Whichever tradition proved an obstacle in the progress of England, was discarded. Those which were helpful in the progress were consolidated.

The traditions are respected everywhere, just as in England. We have a written constitution, but even this written constitution cannot go contrary to the traditions of this country. In as much as it does go contrary to our traditions, it is not fulfilling Dharma. That Constitution which sustains the nation is in tune with Dharma. Dharma sustains the nation. Hence we have always given primary importance

to Dharma, which is considered sovereign. All other entities, institutions or authorities derive their power from Dharma and are subordinate to it...

Clearly, from the above passage, what seems to be missing is to say that dharma is the will of the Universal Soul. The Universal Soul is timeless; it sustains nations; it sustains humanity. Constitutions of nations are to be made in harmony with the same. The Universal Soul is, after all, the same that is in all of us. Clearly, he is avoiding the mention of the core principle and is taking the argument forward on the basis of facts that are commonly argued upon in intellectual circles. He is indeed moving inward from the periphery. That is, he is able to churn out the essence of the notion of dharma by merely focusing on the world that is perceptible to the senses through his lifelong efforts—yogic practices—or learning. In which case, again, he is quite on the mark.

Following is a passage again from the same work, *Integral Humanism*, in which he reveals how Manu was eventually handed the task of laying down the dharma of his times. In other words, he was asked to lay down the constitution for that time.

...Later on interruption and disorganization came into existence. Greed and anger dominated. Dharma was on the decline and the rule "might is right" prevailed. The Rishis were perturbed over the developments. They all went to Brahma to seek counsel, Brahma gave them a treatise on "Law and the Functions of the State", which he had himself written. At the same time, he asked Manu to become the first King. Manu declined saying that a king will have to punish other persons, put them in jail and so on; he was not prepared to commit all these sins. There upon Brahma said, 'Your actions in the capacity of king will not constitute sin, as long as they are aimed at securing conditions under which the society can live peacefully and according to Dharma. This will be your duty, your Dharma. Not only that but you will also have a share of the Karma of your subjects, whereby you will gain Dharma considerably if your subjects maintain conduct according to Dharma.'...

Those who are wary of the use of the icons of Hinduism (like Brahma, for instance) can simply take this to mean that a deep process of prayer, meditation and discussion unraveled an 'inner voice' which said Manu had to persist with laying down the rules, regardless.

C: NEED TO UPHOLD DHARMA (K. Subrahmanyam; as it appeared in The Speaking Tree; Times of India; February 3, 2011)

Hindu tradition is based not on acceptance of particular Gods, dogmas, revelations and religious structures but on reverence for Dharma which is the rule of law and the ethics of the age. In the Hindu way of life there are no God- or Prophet-given laws. Dharma is not immutable but is liable to change to be in consonance with changing times – hence, the concept of yuga dharma. Today's ethics, formulated by the constitution, is secularism – that is the yuga dharma. Violators of it cannot be considered Hindus; they can only be looked upon as enemies of the Hindu way of life.

The true Hindu way of life is in danger today but not from those who follow other religions. It is threatened by those who want to imitate others and abandon its essence, because they have misinterpreted it through the prism of dogmatic faiths. For those who assert 'Brahmasmi" and 'Tattvamasi,' it does not matter if the temple at the birthplace of Rama comes up a few years or a few decades later, if it comes up at all.

Why is Rama the most popular of all the nine avatars? Because he was a Maryada Purusha, who gave Ram Rajya (good governance) and defended Dharma (rule of law). Rama cannot be venerated by those who transgress Dharma by killing innocents. A way of life which highlights the birth and death cycle, allows one the freedom to worship God in any form or not to worship at all, proclaims the cosmic universality with its Advaita cannot be reconciled with the killing of innocents.

The Hindu way of life will survive because it is the natural, free, inquiring way. The reverence for life, which is the essence of birth and death cycle, the worship of Ishta devatas and the ability to see God in all things living and non-living, has to be restored. The temptation to imitate others by trying to straitjacket the free Hindu way of life into structural frameworks must be resisted. Dharma – the rule of law – must be restored. Ram Rajya – good governance – should be established and nourished. The Hindu way of life is not the same as accepting an organised religion. Therefore, this way of life can be propagated, cherished and practised without having to come into conflict with other religions. Comparing the Hindu way of life with other religions is like comparing apples and oranges. The Hindu way of life is the essence of secularism. Its thought processes and philosophical reflections are meant to be observed privately; in public, Dharma, the rule of law, has to be respected.

Recently, the prime minister referred to two kinds of Hinduism – one of Vivekananda and the other of the self-styled "Hindu" extremists. The latter is in the same class as the extremist clergy of religions. There is no difference between those Hindu extremists and the fundamentalist clergy of Semitic religions. Part of the problem is that the Hindu way of life has not been explained to our children as a secular way of life and that it is not the practising of a religion as understood elsewhere in the world.

The writer (January 19, 1929-February 2, 2011) was a strategic affairs analyst and a consultant editor with the TOI. This article is abridged from the article 'Dharma Was Killed in Gujarat Violence', published on April 4, 2002.

www.speakingtree.in

D: SWAMI VIVEKANANDA'S ADDRESS TO THE WORLD PARLIAMENT OF RELIGIONS: SEPTEMBER 1893

Sisters and Brothers of America,

It fills my heart with joy unspeakable to rise in response to the warm and cordial welcome which you have given us. I thank you in the name of the most ancient order of monks in the world; I thank you in the name of the mother of religions, and I thank you in the name of millions and millions of Hindu people of all classes and sects.

My thanks, also, to some of the speakers on this platform who, referring to the delegates from the Orient, have told you that these men from far-off nations may well claim the honour of bearing to different lands the idea of toleration. I am proud to belong to a religion which has taught the world both tolerance and universal acceptance. We believe not only in universal toleration, but we accept all religions as true. I am proud to belong to a nation which has sheltered the persecuted and the refugees of all religions and all nations of the earth. I am proud to tell you that we have gathered in our bosom the purest remnant of the Israelites, who came to Southern India and took refuge with us in the very year in which their holy temple was shattered to pieces by Roman tyranny. I am proud to belong to the religion which has sheltered and is still fostering the remnant of the grand Zoroastrian nation. I will quote to you, brethren, a few lines from a hymn which I remember to have repeated from my earliest boyhood, which is every day repeated by millions of human beings: 'As the different streams having their sources in different paths which men take through different tendencies, various though they appear, crooked or straight, all lead to Thee.'

The present convention, which is one of the most august assemblies ever held, is in itself a vindication, a declaration to the world of the wonderful doctrine preached in the Gita: 'Whosoever comes to me, through whatsoever form, I reach him; all men are struggling through paths which in the end lead to me.' Sectarianism, bigotry, and its horrible descendant, fanaticism, have long possessed this beautiful earth. They have filled the earth with violence, drenched it often and often with human blood, destroyed civilization and sent whole nations to despair. Had it not been for these horrible demons, human society would be far more advanced than it is now? But their time is come; and I fervently hope that the bell that tolled this morning in honour of this convention may be the death-knell of all fanaticism, of all persecutions with the sword or with the pen, and of all uncharitable feelings between persons wending their way to the same goal.

E: EVALUATING THE SPIRITUAL ATTRIBUTES OF A LEADER

When people make a statement that they are secular or when a political party makes a claim that it is secular, there are many connotations to it. One needs to assess what is being said at many levels, and only then does a clear picture emerge. Only when one goes about resolving the various factors related to spiritualism does one realize that there is so much complexity arising from various factors.

Let us tackle the following topic: Analyse the public and private bearing and views of an individual from the standpoint of all issues related to spiritual matters.

The answer is that it can be obtained by locating the position of the person along the following parameters:

Parameters	Variables						
Guna	Tamasic	Rajasic	Satwic	Self-Realized			
Spiritual depth	Asura	Deva	Self-Realized				
Religious inclination	Antipathy	Apathy	Neutral	Affinity	Fundamentalist		
Religious affiliation	Revulsion	Namesake	Practicing	Dogmatic	Evangelic		
Religiosity	Criticizing	Ignoring	Avoiding	Non-Practicing	Practicing		
Militancy	Admissible, willing	Admissible, not willing	Not admissible, willing	Not admissible	Undecided		
State religion	Admissible	Not admissible	Makes no difference				
Religious interference in state	Not tolerated	Only advise	Tolerated	State by religious tenets	State run by religious		
For other religions	Affinity	Have rights	Neutral	Apathy	Tolerant	Intolerant	Persecution
Political rhetoric	Narrow Representative	Open Representative					
Values in public life	Through private religion	Through state religion	Through human rights	Through education	Through enforced laws	By selection by merit	Through indigenous culture

Note that it also depends on changing moods, and as far as other religions go, an individual usually has different approaches to different religions. Then, there is the element of hypocrisy where the public face is different from the private one. Confusing as this is, there is even more. So, how does one evaluate a leader then?

The author recommends just two measures: open representative and dharmic. That is the most valuable combination.

1) Is the leader a 'narrow representative' or an 'open representative'?

2) Is the leader 'dharmic' (primarily system-centric and belief in rule of law)?

F: INTER-CASTE MARRIAGES

Officially, the only advice given about inter-caste marriages is that a lower-caste girl may marry into a higher-caste family and that a higher-caste girl must not marry into a lower-caste home. One needs to understand why this advice is given:

For better or for worse, it was the patriarchal system that existed in the country—in most of it, at least. The ancients have therefore constituted society along these lines. What was the arrangement made by the wise of that age for patriarchal families?

The basic consideration is that in all teams consisting of individuals, there is some kind of arrangement or discipline required to run the system efficiently. Practical observations clearly show that organizations with all persons equal and having equal powers end up as disasters. The worst part happens when there is a difference of opinion and no one wishes to budge from a taken position. The sensible way out is to have an organization among equals but with unequal powers. A leader is appointed, who has special powers. And this leader or captain is expected to mouth decisions on behalf of his team. He may be expected to carry a veto, or he may be expected to voice the view of the majority. Whatever may be the arrangement the group finally arrives at, it also tries to ensure that the leader does not run rough-shod over the wishes of his teammates while at the same time protecting the interests of the group. Once such a special position is designated in a group's constitution, attempts are made

to ensure that the leader is meritorious, is acceptable to the group, is naturally wiser, has the tendency to consider maximum views, acts selflessly and so on.

In the specific case of families, when the wise wish for their success, they must find solutions and recommendations in the context of the prevailing society, times, technology, etc. Now, if patriarchy is the accepted mode, then solutions should be found suitable to that and protective measures need to be taken in the said context to ensure that there is no injustice to any person of that community arising from that arrangement besides the aim that the community must flourish.

Therefore, what is the arrangement that was eventually recommended? The answer is as follows:

Let the captain of the family be a male member.

Let him be older in age and higher on the spiritual plane so that he has greater efficiencies and he can be naturally accepted as a leader in the family.

Let the captain of the family have the veto so that in case of conflicting views, the leader's word will stand.

Let the leader be as democratic as possible. Let him think of others in the family first and then himself. Let him be truly meritorious. Let him be trained to be a worthy leader of a family.

Let the others give the leader his special place and authority and work within the laid parameters.

The other members also have powers, which have been traditionally agreed upon, which they can use in case things go out of hand.

These family arrangements and the relative powers and privileges of the sexes, of the parents and of the children have subtle variations in the various castes. And as one grows up in one's caste, one gets familiar with the responsibilities of the sexes as is ordained in one's tradition. Through this grooming, he believes that he needs to behave in so-and-so manner when responsibilities are to be shouldered.

Castes have arrangements for conflict resolution, beginning with mutually trying to sort out the issue, taking matters to the elders within the family, to the elders of the caste, to the spiritual leaders of the caste and finally to the courts of law.

Since arrangements in different castes differ, and since one is adept with the ways of one's own caste, he is advised to marry within his caste—strongly recommended. In the event of marrying outside the caste, extra efforts must be made by both sides to understand each other's culture and come to a common understanding on what each one's responsibilities are and then alone step into marriage.

In any case, in the patriarchal system, it has been decided that the bride goes over to live at the groom's place. In which case, the bride is expected to show flexibility for adjustment while joining a new culture. The girls are therefore trained for this in their upbringing. They are therefore ready and flexible for possible drastic changes at the point of marriage. But that does not take the onus out of the hands of the bridegroom's family; there is a need for them to show immense sensitivity when a new member joins the family.

The recommendation for women to marry only into a higher caste becomes relevant here for two reasons. The first is that knowledge and sensibilities are higher in the higher caste, and therefore, her reception at the new family is cushioned and there is a movement into a better environment (spiritually). The second is that since she is moving into another family in which she needs to play vice-captain to the man of the family, the man needs to be better accomplished than her so that he can be a natural leader in the family and the wife can be willing to assist and obey if needed.

Clearly, all such advice is in the better interests of the woman, in the better interests of excellent families, in the better interests of children and in the better interests of good societies. That people have reduced this into family ego problems, possession politics, honor issues and humiliation issues. Revenge is an unnecessary aberration.

Needless to say, the idea of high caste and low caste in this context refers only to the Vedic civilization in which spiritual accomplishment is considered higher in the higher castes. But then, for the sake of better partnerships in marriage, it is recommended that the man be more accomplished in other ways as well so that obedience, in case of conflict, comes naturally to the vice-captain without loss of dignity.

It is strongly recommended by the author that, in these matters, the woman needs to be guided by the wise and the wise alone. To date, there are a whole lot of feminists out in the world to bring justice to women, who want equal rights, who want human rights, who want to be no lesser than men and so on. Even in schools today, a lot of stress is being laid on giving up the traditional pattern of women-anchored families. Ideas that rebel against patriarchal arrangements are being fed en masse. The result is a confused perception of life where one cannot decide whether going modern is going forward or backward, whether one has to insist on the man contributing to housework, whether the man should leave it to the woman alone, whether housework is the maid's work, whether there should be one career in a home or two and whether home is a career or a task.

Only time will tell what solution will eventually evolve. In the meanwhile, each one needs to work on his own solutions. What is very important though is that one needs to be sure that when in doubt, he is listening carefully to and taking advice from someone that is truly wise.

As of now... Ladies, if you are living in a patriarchal system, please marry a person who you feel you can obey without question if it suddenly comes to that. Else, do make an agreement before marriage as to how stalemates will be resolved. Men must learn to rise in stature, and they can do that by increasing their spiritual quotient alone.

G: WHO IS WISE?

This has been a timeless question. Is Karl Marx wise? Is Veda Vyasa wiser than Marx? Is there a scale by which we can decide what is truly wisdom and who is higher on the scale and who is not? And most of all, is there a need to listen to the wise at all? Why should I rely on the wise to make my decisions? Why not do my own thing? Consider the following:

1) Let's say that there is a difference between what my parents say is good for me and what a wise man says is good for me. The question arises as to who I should listen to. My parents know me personally and know what I require. But the scriptures suggest that one should rather listen to a wise man.

If the wise man is truly wise—in that he is not just a scholar but also a self-realized soul—then listening to him is supposed to be the more sensible option. The logic is that the parents do want the best for their child, but then, do they know what is best for the child? On the other hand, the wise man too wishes the best for the child, but over and above that, he also 'knows' what is good for the child. That sounds like a tall claim, but it is probably true.

2) A very interesting anonymous verse goes as follows:

A man who knows not, and knows not that he knows not
He is a fool; shun him

A man who knows not, and knows that he knows not
He is a simpleton; teach him

A man who knows, and knows not that he knows
He is asleep; wake him

A man who knows, and knows that he knows
He is wise; follow him

Here, the reference is being made to knowledge of the Supreme Self and God. That is what is supposed to make one wise. What then of the others? How can it be fixed that they do not know enough? More importantly, how does one convince them that they do not know enough?

Let alone the knowledge of the self. Any knowledge for that matter is not known to a person until he comes to know of it! A strange thing to say, but it is profound and true. When a person insists that he knows everything and wants to learn no further, he is playing tricks on himself. He knows everything until he discovers something new, and then, again, he knows everything. The truth is that 'he knows everything that he knows'. And that applies to everyone at all times.

The interesting outcome is that the person who 'knows not' will not be in a position to know 'what' he knows not, and when he acts from that perspective, one really cannot say he is wrong. Is it wisdom then in forgiving a fool for his ignorance? And what if there are a lot of people who say that there is no such thing as a truth that makes the wise men wise?

For all the good which democracy gives, this unfortunate ill should also be accepted in that package. Knowledge is recommended to be kept outside the confines of majority-ism. It is best to pay heed to the minority of wise men on such matters; in fact, if this is achieved in a democracy, it seems that it would strengthen democracy further.

3) Fortunately, science has a way out of it. Scientists do not win their cases through shouting matches, power dynamics or by strength of numbers (though of course, some do play these games). They propose experiments and come out with predictions which are tested for their accuracy. Successful prediction of results and the developing of applications that are based on their theories help in establishing the authority of their theories.

The subject of spirituality and wisdom, however, does not have an effective and established scientific method, and the resolving of intellectual issues related to spiritualism has been found to be difficult. In any case, there is some parallelism, and this similarity can be used in some way as a means for resolving intellectual issues related to spiritualism as well. Consider the following:

a) Some of the ancient Indian sages have proposed models that have a greater ability to predict human behavior than the models and theories proposed by modern-day experts on the subject of human nature.

b) When lessons from the ancient texts are applied—in the way they must be—there is evidence that they do give relief to the practitioner.

c) Individuals who have used the lessons—truthfully and effectively—have shown demonstrable improvement in their abilities, bettered their relationships, shown greater ingenuity in their approach to problems and issues and done well in life generally.

These facts indicate that, at the level of 'application' and 'predictability', the ancient texts seem to be performing admirably better than modern scholars. And even though this proof cannot be considered with the same sense of finality which is characteristic of proofs in the scientific world, they do constitute enough reason for adventurers and explorers to inquire further and attempt to arrive at the truth.

4) And there is one other dimension to this which is interesting and relevant to the context of wisdom which we are considering. As explained through a parable (the talents) by Jesus Christ and directly by many of the Gurus, it is said that it is only when one climbs higher in the ladder of wisdom that one gets better insight into the beauty and truth revealed by the scriptures. Therefore, such a person

with a higher level of consciousness seeks to remain where he is or wishes to climb even further up with much greater vigor than he did when he was way down in the ladder. In fact, the higher up he is on the ladder, the greater the energy available to him to work upwards.

It is another way of saying that those who have more will be given more.

This conversely means that those who are far from seeing what is supposed to be seen also have a lesser ability for seeing what is supposed to be seen. It is like when a person is close to a huge billboard. His eyesight starts becoming clear. The closer he gets, the better he becomes at reading, and he can read even very small scribbles. The more he reads, the more the treasures of the billboard are revealed to him. But when he is far away, his eyesight drops, and it is difficult for him to understand how his eyesight will improve when he reads some billboard that is far away.

5) Another relevant point that can be considered here is a litmus test which Jesus Christ lays down—a test for wisdom one may say. Anyone can use it to make an assessment, and it goes as follows:

'You will know who comes from The Father from the work they do…'

According to this, the best judge of wisdom is to see how people behave—look at their work, and it will become apparent. This means that one who chirps continuously about God, sticks to religious dogma or practices his religion to the hilt need not be truly wise. The test is to watch him in a situation in life and see what he does (the same concept of Karma Bhoomi).

6) Talking of ancients trying to arrive at an answer about wisdom, we have Socrates and Plato in the classical treatise titled *The Republic*. It contains an excellent exploration into the attributes of wisdom. But far more powerful and holistic seems to be the exhaustive description contained in a poem that was composed even earlier—earlier than 700 BC—in India.

The Bhagavad Gita, Chapter 2: 54–65:

Arjuna said:

54. What, O Krishna, is the description of him who has steady wisdom and is merged in the Super-conscious State?

How does one of steady wisdom speak? How does he sit? How does he walk?

The Blessed Lord said:

55. When a man completely casts off, O Arjuna, all the desires of the mind and is satisfied in the Self by the Self, then is he said to be one of steady wisdom!

56. He whose mind is not shaken by adversity, who does not hanker after pleasures, and who is free from attachment, fear and anger, is called a sage of steady wisdom.

57. He who is everywhere without attachment, on meeting with anything good or bad, who neither rejoices nor hates, his wisdom is fixed.

58. When, like the tortoise which withdraws its limbs on all sides, he withdraws his senses from the sense-objects, then his wisdom becomes steady.

59. The objects of the senses turn away from the abstinent man, leaving the longing (behind); but his longing also turns away on seeing the Supreme.

60. The turbulent senses, O Arjuna, do violently carry away the mind of a wise man though he be striving (to control them)!

61. Having restrained them all he should sit steadfast, intent on Me; his wisdom is steady whose senses are under control.

62. When a man thinks of the objects, attachment to them arises; from attachment desire is born; from desire anger arises.

63. From anger comes delusion; from delusion the loss of memory; from loss of memory the destruction of discrimination; from the destruction of discrimination he perishes.

64. But the self-controlled man, moving amongst objects with the senses under restraint, and free from attraction and repulsion, attains to peace.

65. In that peace all pains are destroyed, for the intellect of the tranquil-minded soon becomes steady.

These aspects do point to who is wise. The script from the *Bhagavad Gita* is a scholarly elaboration of the idea. And when one considers it in depth, it becomes evident that it is not talking of individuals, but rather about principles. These are timeless. Invariably, the wise of various nations easily fit into this description. This is again a good revelation of the approach of Hinduism. It stresses on wisdom and principles in general. It talks about all religions.

Panchayati Swaraj: Freedom at the Doorstep

The part deals with a possible practical manifestation of de-centralization so as to offer effective freedom to the villages of India. It combines the vision of Mahatma Gandhi with a tried, tested and successful implementation of community living that existed in the successful reign of the Cholas.

Dedicated To
Fr. Agnelo Pinto SJ,
Fr. Patrick D'lima SJ
and
My Teachers at St Paul's High School

Tell me and I forget; Teach me and I remember… Involve me and I learn.
Benjamin Franklin

Involve the villages of India and its citizens in their own development.
Let it be their responsibility.

Foreword

Wisdom comes from experience. Experience involves attitude, aptitude, analysis, ability and awareness. If man can emerge successfully from his experiences, then he will be able to understand what freedom really means. This involves reconstruction of ideas related to existence and experience. It requires trust—trust in the capacity of common men to build an economically and socially strong India, trust to carry on development from grassroots level.

This is the undercurrent of 'Panchayati Swaraj'; a short but meaningful and relevant treatise by Mr. Nixon Fernando. The book is a reflection of the faith, dedication and conviction of the author on the power of common man. Analysing the concept of freedom and self-government in their various dimensions, Mr. Nixon Fernando has brought out an authentic and practical approach to solve politico-social issues. Explaining the corruption and manipulation involved in power struggles at all levels, the author is hopeful that given the right freedom and right conditions, humanity will enjoy real freedom. He rightfully believes that a decentralized, self-awakening and systematic contribution by local governing bodies—panchayats—will be able to destroy the narrow loyalties and temptations to outshine.

Indian culture and way of life is an indivisible part of the system of local government. Any purposeful and meaningful system will have the needs and aspirations of the common man as its focus, the beginning and the end. Inequalities between the rich and the poor, the powerful and the powerless, the knowledgeable and the ignorant, are the source of discontent among human societies. Mr. Nixon Fernando has analysed these inequalities very logically and has suggested a building-up from the lowest rung of development.

I congratulate Mr. Fernando for his refreshingly unique approach to the governance of panchayats. The title 'Panchayati Swaraj' is unique because it reveals that only within the local self-governing bodies the future of India rests. This book is a very valuable contribution, by Mr. Nixon Fernando to remove the apathy and indifference with which those in power look at development issues.

Dr. Lalitha Ramamurthi
Chairperson, Gandhi Peace Foundation, Chennai
President, Institution for Development Education, Chennai
Former Senior Research Fellow, Madras University
Chennai, November 2010

Preface

I was walking down a street in Chennai a few paces away from a small roadside shrine when I saw someone smashing a coconut as an offering at that shrine. Almost immediately, a young emasculated man in tattered clothes scurried about picking up the broken pieces of the coconut; apparently, it would provide him a morsel to ease his hunger. Similarly, I came across a poor woman carrying a two- or three-year-old child in her arms near a busy bus stand in Pune. She had chanced upon a half-eaten pod of corn, and she was feeding the little child with it. The tenderness with which she was nurturing her child was readily visible. It was also evident that she herself was hungry and that she was compassionate in her offering to her child—a few mouthfuls of corn so that the child would have something in the stomach. This is not an unusual sight given the levels of poverty in India, but on both occasions, when our eyes briefly met, the hurt pride was clearly visible. They did not particularly cherish being in that predicament. Their life situations had them cornered, and these bits of food were straws they were clutching on to.

I have heard a saying about the plight of villagers along the following lines: 'He was a sarpanch in his village, and now, he is a security guard in the city.' The deal is not at all good for the villagers of our nation and for the poor in general. This has often made me wonder what could have gone so grievously wrong.

Could these people have done something about it? Lost in the city streets, they were merely surviving. Life was dishing out to them like a rough sea would to a piece of floating wood. What could they have possibly done?

And yet, I am sure that there is a solution to this. Much of this wretchedness can be removed by energizing our villages. Individually, there is an incredible energy in them that can be tapped into, and even better than that, they can do amazing things for themselves and for others as a part of teams…

There is an interesting indicator for this. We know that the present format of annual Ganesha celebrations became popular only in the beginning of the twentieth century. The person to whom this is credited is the freedom fighter Bal Gangadar Tilak. The British did not want to interfere in the religious life of the locals, so they did not do anything much to stop these celebrations. After all, what threat could a bunch of harmless worshippers pose to the British government? They allowed it. But we must credit it to B. G. Tilak's ingenuity that it was a great demonstration of what Indian people can achieve together if they get an opportunity to organize themselves around a positive idea. Look at the competitiveness and scale of what these small teams achieve. The best of the huge Ganapati and Durga pooja pandals are designed to last for a maximum of just fifteen days. And one can see the kind of organizing and mobilization such feats take. Much more can be achieved if, instead of this task, the villagers are tasked with the more permanent goal of their development and prosperity.

It only takes a look into the kind of competitiveness neighboring villages enjoy. They fight it out like crazy over inter-village sports and other inter-village rivalries. The lengths they go to protect their village 'pride' on matters close to their hearts has to be seen to be believed. And a well-wisher statesman would surely come up with ingenious ways to redirect that competitiveness toward the emancipation and development of those very same villages.

A special note: When the alumni of the '85 batch of St. Paul's high school, Belgaum, had their silver jubilee reunion in 2010, the late Fr. Agnelo Pinto, who was the principal when we were in school, addressed us. He was bothered about the plight of the villages which were situated less than forty kilometers from our school and wanted us to do something about it. I sincerely hope this book will move things in a direction that will offer solutions for these villages and others like these in India and abroad.

Introduction

AN IDEA WHOSE TIME HAS COME

Rural India is rich with God-given gifts; there is a lot of energy, potential, ability, great enthusiasm and passion. All we need is a method to channelize this huge force into the 'recognized' development process of the nation. The tone or attitude with which the government addresses the villages must change. Instead of the governments suggesting to the villages things like 'fingers on your lips and sit down; we will do for you', they must say 'go out and play and do your thing; we will help you'. The nation must shift its strategy and approach. It was trying to 'give' panchayati raj; instead, it should help people develop a panchayati swaraj on their own. This involves unlocking and freeing the minds of the citizens from an enslaved thinking; it must be changed into a responsible kind of thinking.

The Indian nation cannot truly prosper if only a few of its citizens are prosperous; everyone must have a share in it. India cannot progress until it finds some way to ensure that the sixty percentage of its population which is situated in the rural areas has an adequate platform to launch itself to prosperity. Most experts also agree on this. They are also sure that the freedom of the villages to express themselves—to follow their dreams—is the best possible platform for them to achieve prosperity.

No nation has ever become great when its citizens were treated like powerless beings that had to depend on handouts given by the government. The people of the nation make the nation; and if that nation of people has to reach greatness, then it must do so on its own feet. In fact, every village can achieve prosperity only on its own feet. Let the villages have the vision, spirit and scope to 'achieve'; and all can witness the wonders that will happen in India.

No doubt, there have been sincere attempts from various governments to achieve freedom in India from the grassroots level, but these efforts have not truly reflected the spirit of Gandhiji's self-reliant and freedom-inspiring wishes. The governments have sent many reformers, helpers, government officials and government servants to the villages to do good for the people. But have they ever believed that the villages can do good for themselves?

Attempts have been made to give freedom to Indian villages ever since India achieved independence, and this is not a first-time thing in the world either. Systems that give freedom at the grassroots level have been tried and tested even before thousands of years. There are examples of these from across the world that we can refer to and learn from. And having learned these ideas, if we were to adjust these ideas to suit (1) the present situation and (2) the wishes of the father of the nation, India can indeed be transformed.

The power of an idea: At the core of this part of the book is an idea—an idea to do things differently. It goes like this. As a nation, we are already walking. We are broadly headed in one direction. Why not just change the direction a bit? A little change by a few degrees, and the end result may be surprising. The idea which gives a 'different direction' is what is being highlighted here.

A simple idea, if it is really good, can achieve wonders: To understand how powerful an idea can be, let us consider an important turning point in history created by one such simple idea. This idea was brought to light by Adam Smith who is referred to as the Father of Modern Economics.

In the early eighteenth century, a factory in England made needles. Making a needle involved several processes like melting the iron, pouring it in a mold, polishing, etc. A skilled worker at that time could manufacture up to twenty needles a day. Then, there was an idea: division of labor.

'Instead of one person doing all the jobs, let one step of the job be done by one person, the next step by another and so on.'

The effect was that production went up by 1900%. One person could make twenty needles in one day earlier. When he joined hands with others, he made nearly five hundred needles! Not a total of five hundred, five hundred needles per person per day. Thus, the company definitely made a lot of profits just by using this simple idea of division of labor. Many factories followed this principle; it led to the industrial revolution. A lot of things were produced and manufactured. Many other things became inexpensive for the public. Earlier, only kings and nobles could afford to buy some particular things, but with the industrial revolution, even poor people could buy those things.

Just give it some thought. Imagine you come up with an idea by which a woman who could make twenty chapattis in an hour can now make five hundred in the same time. What implications could that have?

Sensibly teaming up with others can produce results that are good, but it can also produce a dramatic change beyond all expectations. That is the power of a good idea and the power of a team.

So, does the idea of effective decentralization belong to this category? If we Indians get it right, can this idea lead us to unimaginable results in India? Is there enough strength in such an idea?

Indeed, there is!

The purpose of the present book is to point out such a set of ideas. A set of brilliant, tried and tested ideas from the past that is capable of creating a revolution in India. The nation can

1) Address the removal of poverty in a huge way and
2) Take a great step forward in bringing about good governance.

India needs a lot of work today. A large section of the Indian population needs support for development. And most leaders and common citizens have an unfortunate belief that the development of all such poor people is practically impossible and can never be achieved in the present Indian context. Everyone is also aware that whatever little that is happening is not widespread and fast enough. They are resigned to the fact that people will suffer in the meanwhile.

But if we see closely, there is a lot of creativity and capacity for effort that is available in the villages and not being put to use. If the creativity and human resource of six hundred million people from the villages is used properly, it can produce dramatic results. A lot of problems can surely be removed from our nation by using this resource and channelizing it properly.

In the average Indian, there is no such thing as a lack of talent or sincerity toward the cause of a better world. There are those who really work their hearts out, even willing to die for the nation. Despite this, very few people see a bright future for the millions of Indians at the bottom of the pyramid. Is it not tragic?

Are we making a mistake by not organizing all this talent properly?

People may not agree that the idea of 'decentralization' will work. They will say, 'Anyone who says that decentralization will solve the problem is flogging a dead horse.' And yes, obviously, there is a possibility that the author is wrong and that no such brilliant idea exists.

But then, what if it does? What if the present tried and marginally successful decentralization is different from the decentralization that was known to wise men long ago? What if there really exists a different set of ideas that can unleash the power of ALL Indians?

What if India could be taken forward in a different way? Just make seven lakh powerful teams in the seven lakh villages of India. Can this be achieved by just changing the approach and focus, by just changing the idea of how we should move forward?

Is it possible that we Indians can take the two crore plus pending cases in the courts that cannot be solved within the next three hundred years by the present system and dispose them in no time—say one or two years. Just imagine how much relief it can bring to society.

At the core of what is being suggested in this book is a vision propounded by Mahatma Gandhi. In fact, we will start with that vision. His methods have the potential of unimaginable results as expressed above. History bears testimony to the fact that Gandhiji transformed a small resistance by leaders into a mass movement for freedom. Great things are possible when citizens join in!

Conceiving a journey back to freedom: Colonial India centralized an otherwise decentralized system through systematic neglect and withdrawal of patronage (we shall see the details in Section III of this part of the book). And the changes that were introduced after India achieved independence did not undo the negative effect of the colonial rule. In other words, the freedom of the average citizen was not restored during independence.

In the pursuit of freedom, there is an unfinished agenda which the nation must take care of now. Indicators of better alternatives are available to us from history, and these ancient examples give us excellent ideas to pursue. These need to be implemented less in the letter and more in the spirit. That is, discretion is required; the ideas need to be adapted for today's times, for today's technology, without the glaring negatives and without violating the constitution of India.

Let us begin by conceiving what this freedom will possibly look like.

Then, we shall go into understanding the six pillars of freedom that need to be nurtured in the local communities of India and how they will implement it.

Finally, we shall look into the thought process that leads us to this question: Are our villages truly not free? Are there examples where they had it better? Can we pick up ideas from the West? Where is the actual battle to be won? What are the two cardinal principles we must adopt for villages shifting from dependency to freedom? What must external agencies do to support this transition from dependency to freedom?

Let us begin our journey by carefully understanding what Mahatma Gandhi said about the villages of India. Then, we will try to understand what it means in today's context through the story of a village that strives to reach its Gandhian destiny.

Let inspirational thoughts come to us from every side.

– Rig Veda

Let wisdom guide our every step.

Section I

The Vision

1.1   THE VILLAGES OF INDIA IN THE EYES OF MAHATMA GANDHI

The villagers should develop such a high degree of skill that articles prepared by them should command a ready market outside.

When our villages are fully developed, there will be no dearth in them of men with a high degree of skill and artistic talent. There will be village poets, village artists, village architects, linguists and research workers. In short, there will be nothing in life worth having which will not be had in the villages.

Today the villages are dung heaps. Tomorrow they will be like tiny gardens of Eden where highly intelligent folks dwell, whom no one can deceive or exploit.

The reconstruction of the villages along those lines should begin right now… The reconstruction of the villages should not be organized on a temporary but on a permanent basis…

Displayed on a panel at the Birla House where Mahatma Gandhi was martyred.

'My idea of village Swaraj is that it is a complete republic, independent of its neighbours for its own vital wants and yet interdependent for many others in which dependence is necessary. Thus, the first concern of every village will be to grow its own food crops, and cotton for its cloth. It should have a reserve for its cattle, recreation and playground for adults and children. Then, if there is more land available, it will grow useful money crops, thus excluding ganja, tobacco, opium and the like. The village will maintain a village theatre, school and public hall. It will have its own waterworks ensuring clean water supply. This can be done through controlled wells or tanks. Education will be compulsory up to the final basic course. As far as possible, every activity will be conducted on the cooperative basis. There will be no castes such as we have today with their graded untouchability. Nonviolence with its technique of Satyagraha and non-co-operation will be the sanction of the village community. There will be a compulsory service of village guards who will be selected by rotation from the register maintained by the village.'

– Harijan
July 26, 1942

For the elderly gentleman, the ride from the city to his old village was much smoother than he had expected: first in the comfortable bus to the PURA (Providing Urban-amenities in Rural Areas) headquarters and now in the little electric van heading for the village.

In this second leg of the journey, he was sitting at a vantage point by the side of the driver. And there was a curiosity and deep interest visible in his face as he kept looking at the passing sights.

The driver sounded very apologetic, 'Very sorry that we had to wait for some time for more passengers; usually, it is not a problem…' he trailed off as the elderly gentleman dismissed the thought and continued to look at the greenery and the wonderful sights.

As the van reached a high ground, he caught the first glimpse of the village. It was a remote village visible at the edge of the reserved forest, and the green hills in the background gave a golden glow, flooded as they were by the warm rays of the rising sun.

'Your vehicle is in very good condition for something that has run 70,000 kilometers…' the elderly man said.

'Oh, that's our village mechanic's work,' the driver replied. 'He can repair virtually anything, and he knows how to keep this beauty fit and fine. He has a certificate in repairing automobiles… And you may be interested to know that he has even come up with his own version of a solar car which can be driven while you sit at his computer at home.'

The elderly man lifted his eyebrows. 'That sounds pretty good,' he said appreciatively.

As the elderly gentleman was saying this, they passed by an old temple just outside the village, and a pleasant nostalgic smile crept across his face.

'It still is home, after all…' the visitor thought. It was twenty years now that he had left the village to go out and earn money, fame and success. He had initially kept up with the changes through the electronic connectivity system that had been established, but then, he had

eventually lost track. This time around, he was seeing it all with his own eyes.

Looking at the driver, he said, 'I actually came to pick up some door fittings and iron grills which my son had ordered a week ago…'

'Ah yes, you cannot get more personalized and beautiful pieces than these anywhere… You know, Naseer's workshop gets orders from abroad as well!'

'You mean there is a market for this iron stuff there too?'

'Oh yes! When there is beauty, there are always buyers…'

As the old man got off the vehicle, he gave a stunned look. He could not believe his eyes.

The reaction amused the driver. He said, 'Naseer's office is over there close to the temple of the village deity; you won't miss it.'

'Are you sure this is my village?' the elderly man asked looking around without expecting an answer.

The driver smiled, 'See you then. Hope I meet you on your way back.' So saying, he revved up the motor, waved and buzzed away toward the next village.

The old man kept looking around without losing his sense of surprise. He could hardly believe his eyes.

'This can't be the village I left behind when I left for work,' he kept saying to himself.

The houses were beautiful. They looked prosperous; even the smallest houses now had either a tiled or cement roof. The design of the houses and the vivid colors expressed that the owners were connoisseurs. And there was an artistic, constructive mind that was doing the design part… The houses were built intelligently.

He did not have to walk much to get to the temple, and once he reached there, the office was indeed easy to spot.

'This office could make a brigadier proud,' he mused out loud as he entered the open office door. The display was exquisite, and it even had an exclusive display cabinet for all the awards and trophies which Naseer had obviously won. Each piece on the display had a touch of class in it— faces, animals, symbols, names… You name it, and it was there. The beautiful part of it was that each piece seemed to have been made with a lot of love and care.

'We make a piece or two extra in some cases so that we can display them here,' a young voice suddenly said.

The old man turned around, as if broken from a trance, to see a smart young lad in his mid-teens. 'Oh! Sorry, Sir. I didn't mean to startle you. Can I help you?'

'Yes, I was supposed to pick up my stuff today. Is it ready?'

'Ah yes! My father said you would come. You can come and take a look at what we have done for you.'

They went to the workshop, and he showed him the work. It was exquisite. Quite nearly the way he had asked for it—lion heads for the handles and grill bits that were designed like a creeper with leaves and flowers. The edges were perfectly rounded off. The shine was perfect.

'These are made of brass. Those grills are iron,' the boy said.

'Yes, indeed,' the elderly gentleman said, still feeling the pieces with his hands.

The young lad, hitting something like a sales pitch, said, 'Once you put them in place, you will have nothing to complain about. The measurements for the knobs and door handles will be accurate to within a millimeter. We guarantee that.'

'It's beautiful. How do you manage to design such stuff?' the elderly gentleman asked.

'Oh! We have a village full of artists. You will get one or two in every household here. Some of them work for us. They are asked to work on chalk, wax or clay. Some artists also help in visualizing the description given by the patrons in picture form, and then, these two-dimensional pictures are converted to 3D molds. Converting those molds into metal is the work of the workshop. We even have a spectrum of metals to choose from,' he said.

The money had already been paid through the internet, and there was home delivery for his town as well. All that was left was for Naseer to pack it up and have it dispatched.

'This stuff is good,' the visitor thought aloud. 'It carries a feeling of grace and peace in it. There are so many places where one can put these things. I should order more.'

'Oh! Thanks for the compliment,' the young lad smiled.

'You are welcome,' the elderly gentleman said, and his attention turned to the important thing he had come for. 'Could you direct me to Krishna's house?' he asked the young lad.

'You mean the one who runs the music center?'

'Yes, he's the one,' the elderly man nodded in reply.

The young lad said, 'Sure, it's pretty close. Let me show you…' and led the way.

As they walked along the street, the young lad said, 'I was telling you about our artists, right? You will also get very good paintings for display in our village, if you want them. In fact, I suggest you have your own portrait made; it will not take you long, and the price is reasonable. The landscapes are very beautiful too. If it is oil, it will cost you some money, but watercolors will not cost much. I suggest you grab it. Your descendants will make a lot of money from it,' he said with a degree of seriousness.

'You paint too?'

'No, not at all,' he replied. 'It is not my cup of tea. I am more of a sports-lover. I prefer my games, and we have a score to settle in the coming tournament.' His voice revealed resolve and determination as that thought crossed his mind. Soon enough, the young lad led the way through the front door of a house and into the courtyard, calling loudly, 'Kaki! Hello! Anyone home?'

A sweet voice responded, pretending to admonish, 'Why do you have to yell, Saleem? You'll bring down the roof.'

It was a pleasant young lady in her early twenties who came to one of the doors comfortably dressed in a blue-green salwar kameez with a pen and a book in her hand. Her mock anger was a giveaway; and she stopped short on seeing the elderly man. She greeted him with folded hands, and a questioning look went toward the young lad.

'Ah, Sital… Here, Uncle wants to see your dad…' he said quickly.

Immediately, a knowing coy smile flashed across her face.

Saleem looked at her quizzically but seemed in some hurry, 'Bye… Got to go! Sital, take my advice. Give up your idea of writing those silly poems. Can't you think of something useful to do?'

She responded with some pretend anger, 'Better than running around like mad men behind a ball for an hour or even two hours.'

Saleem was not interested in hearing what she had to say; he turned to the elderly man and asked, 'May I take your leave, Uncle?'

'Yes, Saleem. Thank you very much.'

'Oh, you are welcome any time. Bye, Uncle! This girl will not improve,' and he doubled away, making one last face at Sital. She smiled in return.

Sital paid her respects to the elderly gentleman by touching his feet, and the man blessed her by saying, 'May happiness and prosperity always be with you.'

'He is a light in our lives,' she told the elderly gentleman. 'Did he trouble you too much?'

The elderly man smiled back as he shook his head for a no. 'On the contrary, he was very helpful,' he said.

'Do take a seat. I'll get some water,' Sital offered. 'Would you like to have some tea or some breakfast?'

'Oh yes, sure,' he replied.

'Daddy is at the farm with *bhayya*. Ma will soon be back from the temple. It's about time.' She then asked, 'How was the journey? How is Vijay's grandma? And everyone else?'

'Ha, just fine. The journey was great, and everyone is fine. I wanted so much to see you all. And coming back here is so nostalgic. But I can hardly recognize this place. The change is fantastic.' Sital could only shrug her shoulders, not knowing what to say.

'What was all that about running behind the ball?' the visitor asked.

'Oh, that! Just pulling his leg,' she smiled. 'The truth is that we make it a policy in our village to encourage games. We believe it produces men of quality and substance. And it improves the standards of health in the village too.'

'It is pretty much the same in the Americas,' the elderly man added. 'They have a culture of encouraging sports. I guess we are catching on now.'

She smiled and asked, 'Will you be waiting for the poetry session today?'

'And what is that?' the old man asked in return.

'Well, I think it had just started when you went abroad. You must remember the teacher who used to teach children Hindi and English…'

The old man's face lit up with the memory as he nodded in agreement, a glass of water in his hand. Sital continued, 'Well, he thought the best way to get people to learn was to make them sit together and recite poetry and discuss it. He started it as a weekly meet with school children and some youth. The priest and the postman also used to participate. You might know them, I think…'

The elderly man nodded in agreement.

'Well,' she said. 'It started with discussing the poetry of famous people. We went on to read and discuss the great epics, some spiritual texts, personality development book extracts and many more. It grew from strength to strength. It has turned out very well now. Some outstanding poems have been written by our own people. One of us managed to publish a bestselling collection. Another one of us is popular in the stand-up comedy circuit and has the nickname 'Joker Poet'; it all started here,' she said in a matter-of-fact way.

'So, what do you get from it?' the elderly gentleman asked.

'I love it because it makes me look at life in so many different ways. And it helps me participate in what we call the timeless song of the poets,' she said, her face glowing with the thought.

'Okay. Tell me about the houses. They all look so pretty. This one feels so comfortable,' the old man said and moved to the door to take a closer look.

'Ah, well, it is probably because a lot of thought goes into it actually. We have one architect from our village and three people in the next village who have developed a reputation for designing excellent structures. Three of them are diploma holders in civil engineering, and one of them has just completed architectural engineering at the age of 42. They are in some kind of network on the internet where they exchange ideas on buildings, materials, design, air circulation, water cooling, well maintenance, gas plants and so on. Their contacts are from across the world. You name a thing, and they can build it. Generally, they work in a team, and that brings good results, I think,' she said, with her eye on the intricate carvings on the window frame.

'It is beautiful too,' the old man said, running his fingers through the designs, and he suddenly changed the topic.

'You speak such good English. How is that?'

'Oh, thank you,' she said and added, 'Practice makes one perfect. If you go around in the village, you will see that most of the youngsters are good in three languages. Among the seniors, most know two languages proficiently. The rest will be fluent in Marathi but will be able to understand Hindi. Unfortunately, they have to use sign language if they have to talk to someone like Unni Uncle.'

She paused for a moment and then said, 'I also tried to learn French, but I could not make progress because the teacher could not continue the course. But I am working on it. Ravi Uncle knows seven languages. Not French though, unfortunately.'

'Ravi?' the elderly gentleman asked.

'He is the supervisor at the food processing unit of the village,' she replied. 'He is supposed to be very good at five of the languages, but he writes poetry only in Marathi. He also directs plays in his spare time…' As she was saying it, her mother walked in through the front door.

Apparently delighted to see the elderly man, she exclaimed, 'Oh! America Uncle!' With a broad grin, she said, 'I hope you had nice travel' as she paid her respects by touching his feet.

'Had a nice journey,' her daughter corrected.

'A nice journey?' she asked the gentleman, smiling, and he nodded.

'Yes, it was very comfortable.'

'So, you are working on your English?' the visitor asked, and she nodded in agreement.

'Just a wish,' she said.

Soon, the two of them shifted into comfortable Marathi and began exchanging notes of the years that had passed by. Meanwhile, Sital went into the kitchen to take care of breakfast. All she had to do was warm it up in the microwave oven, and soon, the three of them were done with their breakfast.

'Sital, tell me… Is the elderly school teacher still here in the village?'

'Yes, indeed. Would you like to go and see him?'

'Oh, that would be great. Can you take me there?'

Sital looked at her mother.

'Okay, go along. Take him there, but bring him back in time for lunch. I'll just phone to tell the teacher that you are coming,' her mother said. 'And remember to take grandpa through Unni Uncle's laboratory,' she added.

They set out and reached the laboratory soon enough. But it was latched shut.

'I guess he has gone out to the hills,' Sital said as she opened the gate to let herself in.

She explained, 'Unni Uncle retired from ISRO as a scientist and decided to set up a small research lab in the village. It was his dream project. He wanted to work on biotechnology and its contribution to forest upkeep. It began as a shed he set up here, and he used to travel up and down from the PURA headquarters where he used to stay. Then, the children and some women in the village got involved in his research activities. Then, the village school and even the science college at our PURA headquarters started coming here to do projects. Now, it is a wonderful resource.'

'But how did this lab get built up like this?'

'Well, that is a long story, actually. Initially, no one cared much, and Unni Uncle himself was only interested in having a piece of land and access to the forests. He used to hire one or two people in the village, and so, the people of the village let him be. But a change came when the children got involved with him… Or maybe the other way around… He would make us ask all sorts of questions about science, and he would actually show us how things worked. We all used to have a great time.'

'I still remember the day he showed us a fountain with a soft drink and mint chocolate. But it was a waste of a good soft drink. Then, he showed us how to make a rocket. Amit nearly burned down his own house, and Unni Uncle had to hear a lot from Amit's daddy. Luckily, Unni Uncle knows little Marathi. So, it all ended up very funny,' she said, giving an amused smile.

'What does your uncle do here?' the elderly man asked.

'The biggest thing he did for us was the fruit extract from the berries that were picked up in the forest. He showed us how to extract the juice and convert it into syrup and package it. It became a raging success. After that, money flowed into the village. It is cited as one of the reasons the village developed so much. Then, as we children grew, he got many of us involved in serious experiments. We even helped Uncle set up this modern lab, and now, he has a name at an international level.'

'So, you all are paid for your work?'

'Most of us volunteer when he asks for help because we understand the value of what he has done and still continues to do. This farm that you see has the rarest of herbs, and most of them have medicinal value. We help him grow it. It is taken up to the hills, and the hill people plant it everywhere. So, if you go up the hills, it is full of it in small patches and in natural settings. It is systematically harvested, and that forms the main base of income for the hill people. The hill people give us the forest produce for processing and marketing. So, it comes as a complete cycle. This arrangement is great, and his efforts are at the heart of it.'

'That is not all,' she went on. 'He has helped two of the children who used to work with him pick up their Ph.Ds. As for the farmers in our village, he works in partnership with them in their farms. Together, they try out new things, manures, pesticides, seeds… If you noticed as we entered the village, multi-level cropping is taking place in those farms by the side of the old temple. Scientists from a research center in Brazil came to see it last January. And you might know, many of the farmers have at least a diploma in farming. And all of them have done up to the C-level certificate course…'

'Certificate course?'

'Yes, in farming technology. Ah, there we are! Do you recognize that person standing next to that jeep?' Sital asked.

'Oh, yes! You cannot miss him, can you?' the elderly man smiled.

As they approached him, a broad grin of recognition came across the teacher's face. It was quite weathered with age, but the gracefulness of his happy years was visible on him. He had lost none of his old charm. The elderly gentleman greeted the teacher with folded hands, a broad smile and a mischievous twinkle in his eyes. The teacher greeted him happily, clasping the folded palms of the visitor in his own.

'My dear friend, what a delightful surprise!' the teacher said

Sital could literally feel the vibes of their delightful meeting. The excitement in the air was to remain for a long time after that. The young lady paid her respects to the teacher. And the teacher said to them, 'Come, let's go inside.'

Addressing the elderly visitor, he added, 'Like to have something? The mango season has left us with the choicest of juices and sweets this time. It's been a plentiful harvest.'

'Grandpa just had breakfast; I don't think he will have anything. Will you?' she asked the elderly gentleman.

He shook his head for a no, and she offered, 'I'll get some water for you two.'

'Okay, Sital. Bring some of those sweets also—just in case—and pull a chair for yourself. Ah, and the book on French that I promised you is on the reading table. Don't ask how I managed to get it! It's borrowed for your use.'

Sital disappeared into the house with a squeal of delight while the two of them made their way to the two garden chairs kept in the shade of the huge mango tree.

'You all have achieved a miracle here,' was the first thing the elderly gentleman could say.

The teacher replied, 'Come on! You know that even you are responsible for this. The money you had sent initially, when I asked for it, made a huge difference.'

'No, no! That was hardly anything,' the visitor protested.

'No, young man. It mattered a lot when we started. We literally had no financial strength at that time. It was not that we were not happy; happiness is something that is within each of us. But the way we were living was not the best we could be.'

'Yes, indeed. I vividly remember this place from that time,' the elderly visitor said looking at some kittens playing at a distance. 'In the summer, we had to walk three kilometers to get drinking water and another three back. Then, there was that twice-a-day bus which used to come to the next village—once in the morning and once in the evening. But there were none to our village. The lands were barren except for a few trees here and there. And then, there were the dry rain-fed farms. We had the Dalit shanties on that side…' he said, pointing out at what could now easily be a part of a suburb.

'There was that liquor den beyond that other hillock as well,' he said, turning toward the little hills.

'The slopes of the hills were barren except for one odd bush here and there and some grass. We would have to get fuel wood from the forest—or whatever you could call that barren place—and there would be such trouble over it. There was the problem of single-meal families, literally living on the edge of survival. To study beyond tenth standard, one had to travel twelve kilometers. There were only two TVs in the entire village. As for electricity, the poles were there and the wires were there, but there was hardly any power supply. Then, there were those endless quarrels with the fair price shop over the availability of grain and kerosene. And do you remember how we lost my niece and her child because we could not take her to the nursing home in time? Three hours by cart… She could not have made it. And now, look at this! How did you turn it all around?'

The teacher was apparently transported into the past, and he looked to be in a reverie when he thoughtfully said, 'One lesson I learned in this entire process is that you should never underestimate the power of a team.'

As he was saying this, Sital walked toward them balancing a tray on one hand with some water and sweets on it and a chair on which she had placed a little book in the other. They helped her place the tray on a small garden stool and moved their chairs to make place for her in the shade, and she adjusted her chair into place.

'Thank you, young lady. Grandpa has been telling us how this place was when he left,' the teacher said as he offered some sweets to the visitor.

'I heard that things were very difficult then,' Sital said

He smiled and continued, 'So, as I was saying, it all began to happen when everything fell into place. We had this village which had the human resources of nearly 2000 people in all, but we had nothing to put them together and work at something. Then, by sheer coincidence, some persons reached here. Naseer was invited here by his friend Krishna when there was trouble in his home state.'

'You mean Sital's father?' the elderly gentleman asked.

'Yes, our Krishna,' he said and then explained. 'Naseer had a manufacturing unit which was destroyed in a riot. He came here for some time to be in a quiet environment, but he eventually settled down here. It was he who taught all of us what we know about manufacturing, business and marketing; his foresight and vision were a great asset. Then, there was Unni, an encyclopedia of knowledge. Then, of course, we have the village priest; he knows when to say something, what to say and how to say it. He was able to make people listen and do what they were expected to do.

Also important at that time was the announcement by the government that they were going to set up PURAs. And finally, there were numerous government schemes about which I knew quite a lot, and I had some students in the government who kept me informed about what I could bring for the village. We had the money you sent. We got some more from donors and NGOs, and we pooled in some money from our savings. When all this came together, things just began to happen.

I got my hand on some literature on PURA. I spoke to several other teachers and then to some sarpanches. When we spoke to the Block Development Officer, he just gave us a vague idea that if there were to be a PURA, then eighteen neighboring villages would form our unit. He gave us the list of those eighteen villages. We had a meeting of all these sarpanches, and then, we started making plans. There was a need for facilities which one or two villages could not afford by themselves, so we started sharing. While the funds for schools were diverted to three different schools in these eighteen villages, we set up hospitals in four others and a special hospital in the PURA headquarters. Then, as if by magic, a lot of facilities started being set up by private commercial players all over. The government gave us roads and electronic connectivity. Our village eventually got a school. For the nursing home, we need to go to the next village, but we have a health worker with us.'

'Remarkable, indeed,' the elderly gentleman said. 'But you still have not told me how everyone cooperated in the effort.'

The teacher said, 'Oh that… It all started when the water problem reached its peak, and we had to ration the drinking water that season. There was a fight that night… But ultimately, the outcome was good. One of Unni's friends, an expert in water resources, was visiting him that day. To date, Unni says it was just a coincidence that he was in the village, but we don't think so. He was from

Sangli. He knew Marathi well, and apparently, he knew this whole business about water. When he spoke to the villagers, it was like magic. They sat and listened to him spell-bound. The very next day, we started digging. It was nice to watch. Even Sital here went up that day. She was probably in her second or third standard, I think, and she dug her own little water bund.'

'Yes, Grandpa. I remember; it was so much fun,' Sital said.

'Well, I hope it was fun for the others too,' the teacher replied.

'It was like a picnic,' she said, smiling.

The teacher continued, 'That event made a great difference; after that, we went up once a week for six weeks and did voluntary work, and the energy did not sag for quite some time. Two thousand people up on the hills. Mind you. If they put their minds to it, they could have moved the hill; these bunds were small things. The very next summer, our wells did not dry up. That was a stroke of luck because it is difficult to get results so fast. Anyway, we hit a high note when two or three years after that, people started coming to our village to collect drinking water; there was no looking back after that. Three years after when Unni's friend had given the talk, the villagers started pestering Unni to call him once again. Unni's friend knew more than just about water conservation. We got all kinds of knowledge and inspiration from him, and then, it slowly took off. We gradually phased out firewood and used alternate sources of energy; the direct result was that trees started appearing on the hills. We forced all the children to school; we arranged for work and livelihood for everyone. We kept sending one person or the other from the village for some training or the other. Soon, we had trained mechanics, builders, artists, sportsmen, farmers, dairy specialists, poultry specialists... You ask for it, we have them. Then, Unni and the hill people happened...'

'Sital told me about that...' the visitor said.

And the teacher continued, 'And after that, we have never looked back. Anyway, I should tell you that a lot of deliberate planning went into it. There were committees responsible for even planning how to balance the imports and exports of the village. We wanted a balance so that profits were generated for the village and its members too

because things would not work out otherwise. We have come a long way,' he smiled.

'I think such places are called Edens,' the visitor offered.

The discussion veered toward his work, his journeys in America and finally his settling down in India with his son in the town.

'So, one of the reasons I came here was to look for a match for my grandson Vijay,' he said looking at Sital, smiling mischievously.

Sital was a picture of pretend disinterestedness, 'Why would he want to marry a village girl like me?' she said leafing through the French book in her hand without any purpose.

'Are you serious?' the elderly man asked. 'I am worried about the other way around.'

Sital raised her eyebrows in surprise.

The elderly man said, 'You have all the best amenities that a city can offer within twenty kilometers from your house. You have this space for playgrounds. You have generous space to build your homes. Your education in the three R's and in the spiritual and social dimensions of life are not in any way wanting. You even have a French book in your hand. What else do you want? If you are on the lookout for universities or professional colleges for your children, there is of course a need to stay away from home. But even people in the city have to do that.

And in the city, you could even end up traveling for an hour just to reach your work place or to get to the college. To give to children all that the city affords, most of the time, both the mother and father have to work at their respective jobs in a continuous cycle from dawn to dusk. And in such cases, the pressure on the woman is really very high. I agree there is work here in the villages too, but it is more balanced, and the responsibilities are better shared. And it is done in an environment that agrees with our traditions. Moreover, this village is your extended family. You can walk into anyone's house; everyone participates in all occasions in peoples' lives. You can sit and write poetry in the quiet forest or in the farms, and here, you can even drink water from that fresh stream...

Now, if you were to go to the city, 99% of the people who pass by you will be strangers. You will gain some kind of freedom and anonymity, but you will lose the warmth of these people and the nourishing touch of a closed society. I am not saying that you won't get true and good friends there, but it is a different life. And in any case, if you really want to get to the city, I took less than an hour to reach this place. So, even the city is not beyond your reach from here.'

Sital shrugged her shoulders and smiled.

The teacher was reassuring, 'Don't worry about her. She will adjust; this lady is tough. Or there is another great idea; why don't you all shift somewhere here in the meantime?' he said

And as Sital blushed, the elderly gentleman replied, 'That is a possibility I have started to think about rather seriously now. This place is a real nursery of life.'

Soon enough, all three of them got up to head back to Sital's home for lunch. As they were getting ready to go, the elderly man gave voice to something that had been at the back of his mind, 'I don't see many people around.'

'Oh that,' the teacher said. 'It is a holiday, and there is a fair going on in the next village. The final match of the cricket tournament is happening today, and our boys are playing. Everyone is out to cheer them on.'

'What about you?' the elderly man asked.

'Well, we will move after lunch. Krishna will be taking us in his vehicle. You are coming along,' the teacher said firmly without offering him a choice.

'Will you be coming too, Sital?' the elderly gentleman asked.

She apologetically replied, 'No, Grandpa. I will skip. I have some work to do for today's poetry session. But I plan to watch what I can of the match on cable TV.'

The teacher bolted his door shut and informed his neighbor of his departure. The three of them then set course for Sital's home, walking in the shade of the huge trees.

'You must have had good support from the politicians too,' the visitor said.

'Well, yes and no,' the teacher replied and went on to explain. 'Initially, they were the biggest hurdles for us. They would come and feed on their vote banks. They would say and do things such that various groups in the village sincerely believed that the others were enemies.

But you know that saying about fooling people… Sital, what is that?'

'Wolf, wolf…?' she asked.

'Ah, that too. But I was mentioning another… You can fool all people for some time, you can fool some people all the time…' And Sital joined in a chorus, 'But you can't fool all people all the time.' And they smiled at each other.

The teacher continued, 'Eventually, wisdom brought light on the people that these politicians came only when elections came. They said they would do all sorts of things but did nothing really substantial. Well, how much could you expect them to do for just a few votes? They would get all of us excited before the polling, and after it, they would disappear until the next elections were around the corner. But things began to change when we learned to stick together.

When the change came, everyone accepted the situation that they were in and did not blame anyone else for it. Then, we all started looking ahead together. Ten years from then, those shanties disappeared, and you can see what remains of it now.'

The elderly gentleman kept his eyes fixed on the houses as he listened to the teacher and said, 'Indeed, it is a most amazing transformation. I just could not believe it when I saw it for the first time.'

'And Grandpa, I told you about two of them who have done their Ph.Ds, right? That two-storied house painted in blue and white belongs to one of them.'

'Ah, Rahul.' The teacher added, 'You won't believe it… He took a vow that he would take admissions only in the general merit category. He got many scholarships but never took even a single reservation seat. Now, he holds an Associate Professor's post at the university on the strength of his own merit. We are all delighted for him, and he is highly respected for his achievements. No one can even say that he is from the same group who about twenty odd years back were scavenging, had one meal a day and did not know what it was to take a proper bath. That is why I say that that day was like magic when Unni's friend spoke to us. Once we became a team, once we realized that we were all trying to do some good to each other by helping each other, once we saw that we were really trying to get livelihoods for all of us in the village, things slowly changed. The priest was a great help in this.'

'And the politicians?' the elderly man asked.

'Once we got together, we started to fool all the politicians. Then, the politicians became wise. They realized that if they helped the village as a whole, they would get votes. They then did exactly that. After that, it has been a good partnership with the politicians, and they have good connections. A lot of good has been done through them, and we are thankful to them. But they cannot fool us now, not by dividing us.

We have our differences, but we have evolved ways of facing such situations by trying to focus on the solution rather than the problem. We sort things out among ourselves. We may even fight among ourselves, but when we deal with outsiders, we remain united. That is our strength.'

Soon, they reached Sital's home and had a delightful lunch with the entire family. And then, things happened according to plan…

The day was hectic indeed. Lunch was followed by the excitement of the cricket match. The elderly gentleman had not played much of the game, but the electric atmosphere got the better even of him. Then, there were celebrations. Dinner was over only by 9:00 PM, but they decided to hold the poetry session anyway. It was a great experience. Folk songs, some jokes, poetry and special of all was the little surprise Sital had in store. She had a poem titled 'Starry eyes', and it was a little embarrassing for him since he was the hero of the poem. The poem got the wildest applause, and one could not make out whether it was for the hero or for the writer. But he noticed that the villagers saw him in a different light after the poem.

He called up home a little later, and as he spoke to Vijay, he said, 'You know, Vijay. I know for sure that I am at home. Not one of my blood is around me, and I am still at home!'

An hour or so later, as he lay in bed at the teacher's house, looking at the stars through the first-floor window, a feeling of great delight and gratitude engulfed him.

'This is splendid,' he thought. 'This is a full life; this village has finally arrived at Mahatma Gandhi's dream. Vijay would have to do a lot to give this girl a home and community as beautiful as this in his city.'

What was the purpose of the story?

Students of a school, who were in their final year and about to pass out, were asked to fill up a questionnaire which, among other things, asked them questions about who they were, where they came from, how they were doing as they were finishing school and what they aimed to achieve or be in life.

Thirty years later, these responses were assessed again to find out how the same students had done over those last thirty years. The statistics threw up an interesting fact.

The researchers wanted to find out which of the students did well in the thirty years. They wanted to compare the performance of the students in their school days and see if the same 'best' students also did well in their lives.

One would have expected the smart ones, the achievers in school, the heroes, the top players, the favorites of the opposite sex, the favorites of the teachers and the rank holders to have achieved much in life. They were surprised that such 'success' at the school level did not naturally imply that they would be successful later in life.

There was one factor, however, that was common to all the students who had achieved success in life later on. The common trait was that they all had an 'aim' when they were passing out from school.

Those who had distinct aims at the end of their schooling were, thirty years later, more or less where they aimed to be in life. If they were not there exactly, then they were there approximately. As opposed to this group, those who did not have an aim generally drifted about and did not make it anywhere big in life, even if they were really smart at school.

So, is an 'aim' important in life? Apparently, yes, if this research finding is correct.

This was an empirical finding or, shall we say, an experimental finding using statistical methods that tells us about the importance of having an 'aim'.

Mind science too comes to the same conclusion. Mind science compares the effect produced by having an aim to the effect produced by a convex lens. When the rays of the sun are made to pass through a convex lens, the rays are focused to a point. At this point, the heat is so intense that things can be burned by that tiny dot. An aim in the mind of a person produces a similar effect. Just like how the rays of the sun are converged to a point, the efforts and energies of the person who has an aim are converged toward that aim. The person with the aim allots his resources of time, money, things, relationships and enthusiasm toward the aim, unconscious to him, and the result is remarkable.

Such a focus of work, energy and resources can burn a path to achieve even difficult aims. It can burn a person's path to success. It helps in putting together the resources in our command to achieve what may even seem to be an impossible thing to achieve. We can therefore understand why those students who had an 'aim' ultimately, thirty years down the line, managed to achieve success.

From individual aims to team aims: Now, that was for individuals. The same thing can also be extended to groups and teams. When members of a team push in the same direction, a thing moves easily, and if each of them has the same aim and all their energies are being channelized in the same direction, then the results can be remarkable.

Such a common aim would assist in harmonizing a team effort. The members would become focused. They would take up individual tasks that can be added up together to create a team task. This would ultimately lead to a powerful and deliberate movement of the team and its individuals toward a pre-determined direction.

From this, we can conclude that if the well-wisher of the village wants to implement panchayati swaraj and if it has to be achieved by a group of people who are a team, then the place to start is where the group is ready to set an aim. Whether this aim is suggested to the members of the village or whether it is generated by themselves (this book suggests a combination of both), as long as the team has a good aim or a goal that they can look up to, then wonders can be achieved. It does not matter from where the team gets an aim; what is more important is that once the members of a team have decided upon an aim, it becomes their aim. And once it is their own aim, that alone will make things work. It is therefore important that it must be their own aim.

So, with respect to self-rule, what should that goal or aim or image be that should be placed before the Indian village citizens so that the members in the village become teams and start developing their common goals? What must the well-wisher suggest to them so that they channelize their energies and move powerfully toward success and self-rule?

There cannot be a better foundation for this than the one that Gandhiji propounded, which was highlighted through the story. It is indeed worthwhile probing into the various nuances of what was on Mahatma Gandhi's mind.

There cannot be a better person than Mahatma Gandhi for giving directions to the nation on this. First of all, he had a mind that understood India far better than any of his political contemporaries. He had a spiritual bend which few other political leaders had, and he had a grasp of political and administrative realities which few other spiritual people had. He was a man of action, and his action plans have invigorated millions into coordinated action. His thoughts have inspired some of the greatest minds and personalities of the present age. The sensible path to take, therefore, is to understand what this vision is all about, perceive this in the present-day context and then present that aim as a benchmark or standard upon which the village teams can build further.

If the citizens of the villages realize that the aim comes from Mahatma Gandhi himself and if they get convinced that it applies to the conditions in which they live, then it is likely that they will accept this benchmark and adapt it for their requirements.

Using a mind-science tool to present the vision in an acceptable form: The passage from Gandhiji, which we considered, is indeed amazing in its depth. But unfortunately, the words used there have been used by a lot of other individuals in various contexts in ways that confused its meaning, and therefore, there is a definite chance that one can miss the importance of this particular passage. It may even sound like a fantasy to some, and it may sound like it is an impossible thing to achieve. That is what a process of practical vision-building must overcome. We need to extract the maximum potential of this Gandhian vision by presenting it in a way that everyone can understand. It should be digestible, and it should reveal how it is possible. It should give a common aim to the villages so that they can work on it and create their own set of aims, goals or vision.

So then, you know why we had the story... Something visualized like that has a potential beyond mere words (mind science suggests visualization over the use of words).

At this point, let us reckon an important law that is known to the experts of mind science. It goes like this: 'Everything created by man is created twice, first in the mind and then in the physical world.'

When a dreamer thinks of something and sees it in his mind's eye at that time, it gets created for the first time. Then, he works on it, and only later does it get created in real life. This is the second creation.

Experts in the field of personality training and mind science tell us that words, images and emotions can be very powerful tools in Neuro-Linguistic Programming (NLP). When a goal gets created in the form of words, images or emotions, they can be transferred into real life in a very powerful way. The achievement levels can be high. So, the idea is to create a vision in words, images or emotions in the minds of the village citizens first—the first creation. Then, what is finally created in the minds of the villagers will be created in the real world in the villages— the second creation. Further, experts also add that more powerful than words are images, and more powerful than images are emotions. So, the idea is to create in the minds of the village dwellers a vision about how villages have to really exist in terms of the more powerful tools of images and emotions.

Leaders have used this device/tool knowingly or unknowingly in their communications with their followers through the ages. Even Gandhiji's words that we have seen above can serve to trigger such thoughts in the minds of village citizens. Therefore, Gandhiji's words are the creation of a vision in terms of words and images.

The purpose of the story was to translate the vision into images and emotions.

How that story can be used: If the reader reads this story when his mind is quiet and calm, it will help him dream up something of a similar kind for his own village.

A few things about the story are mentioned here:

a) There is tremendous flexibility that can be adopted in this visualization. It depends on the individual who is reading it, on the experiences he has had in his life, on the physical settings of the village and on the team that the village is composed of.

b) This dreaming-up is an exercise which the architects of successful modern Indian villages need to do for themselves first before they share it with the members of the village. They need to figure out how their own villages would look in ten- or twenty-years' time and share it with all others in their communities.

c) When the members of a village have such an effigy of their village in their minds, it will act as a goal/aim/focus; and it will only be a matter of time before the dreams are realized in the real world.

A simple way of using this story is to merely narrate it in a village forum when the entire village sits together. This can be followed by a discussion to figure out what Gandhiji might have wanted for the village.

A leader is innovative, and he will know how to adapt the story and the vision contained in it to suit the setting of his village. Let us hope and pray that many leaders will rise from the villages so that the villages can see their potential, develop aims and ideas in their minds and rise to meet their potential.

Section II

An Expose of the Vision

Let us interpret this vision in some more detail, closer to achievable goals.

Taking inspiration from the vision statement of Gandhiji, we must attempt to expand the vision on the basis of ground level goals to be achieved in the villages of the nation. We shall make an attempt to do this in this section.

Let us for a moment assume that the members of a village have understood the significance of freedom and are therefore sensitized to the need of pursuing it. They understand that the responsibility rests on their shoulders and wish to shoulder that responsibility well. How are they to go about it?

After a study of various village success stories—with ideas coming from our ancient past, taking into consideration Gandhian thought, fixing our reference point in the indigenous value systems, with awareness of the need to march in unison with modern technology, with awareness of the need to dovetail our grassroots-level political system into the nationwide structure set up by our constitution, taking advantage of modern ideas of management and mind science and in consideration of the high potential of the people in Indian villages—six areas have been found critical to nurture village freedom as indicated in the mind map.

If a village team makes suitable advances and achievements in these six areas, they can get really close to the object of Gandhiji's vision. The first of the areas has to do with transparency; this is a very basic need that has to be met if genuine freedom is the goal. The next three, economy, culture and health, are more or less self-explanatory, but they still need elaboration. The next one, government, is about innovating even more than the 74th amendment of the constitution has done. Finally, the sixth is about a forward-looking village that aspires for excellence. A village team needs to ensure that substantial progress is made in each of these areas. If this happens, then a solid foundation can be laid for a movement toward freedom. In this section, we shall go into each of these freedoms systematically.

NOTE: Please refer to Appendix A of this part (Part 2) of the book for the relevance and detailed rationale of each freedom referred to in the following six chapters.

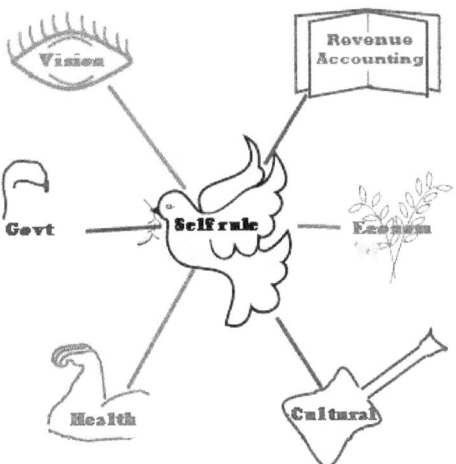

This is based on transparency. All village success stories in India use transparency as a vital keystone. In such successful villages, if computers are not in vogue, they use the walls of the panchayat buildings and other public walls in the villages to put up information for display. What the village policies are, who has been receiving benefits and what funds have come into the village are examples of such information.

Let alone villages, all nations and leaders who follow the principles of transparency have prospered. A righteous leader is usually transparent in his dealings. Therefore, transparency facilitates the emergence of good leadership in a village, and it also helps in the creation of an environment that minimizes corruption.

The other dimension contained in this freedom is the principle of systematic accounting. When proper accounts are maintained, it reduces friction and unnecessary litigation to a great extent. We shall see more of this as we touch upon the various components of this freedom.

The central resource in this is a universally accessible computer (or computer network) alongside suitable documentation, which holds all vital information concerning the village within the village itself. This data should be updated under the direct administrative control of the village body and should always be available for reference by any member of the village community.

The factors that are listed under this freedom do not readily appear to be freedoms. For example, writing accounts or documenting clearly who has received what benefit cannot be categorized as freedoms in themselves. And yet, they are important ingredients for the setting up of freedom in a village. When a village successfully ensures that the components of Revenue Accounting freedom are implemented, it lays strong foundations for building up freedom. Therefore, these may be treated as freedoms themselves.

Accounting Freedom 1: Land Records
A village should have a complete record of the land holdings in the village updated to within a week of the last changes made in the tahsildar's office, preferably computerized. It should be available for inspection at any time and accessible to all members of the village community.

Success stories and action: There are no rules against maintaining such records at present, but it would be worthwhile if such a requirement is codified in the statutes so that there is harmonious transfer of data between the tahsildar and the village. There is a case of successful computerization of land records in a district in Karnataka, and there is an example of a village called Dhamoli in Vidarbha, Maharashtra where the villagers maintain land records. A marriage of these two ideas can help in transformation.

Accounting Freedom 2: Taxes (a record of taxation and expenses)
Every village should have a complete record of taxes and revenues recovered from the village. Whether it is the revenue for land, dwellings or other constructions or for the consumption of electricity and water... Even arbitrary collections for festivals... Proper audited records should be maintained for suitable inspection by revenue officials who visit for government audits and be made accessible to all members of the village.

Success stories and action: Most successful organizations, especially companies, have had excellent accounting systems. Also, as evident in the Uttaramerur inscriptions (we see this in detail later in the book), successful nations do initiate systematic processes where there is transparent accounting. Modern prosperous nations too ensure that organizations within their nation keep proper accounts. (Maybe if such a requirement is insisted of the political parties of India, a major hurdle will be removed from the nation's path to progress.)

A standard procedure of accounting needs to be used, preferably also computerized. The requisite skill must be quickly gained by accountants in the village. Proper opening and closing of accounts books must happen. Standards will surely be developed; standards used in the industry could also be adapted.

Accounting Freedom 3: Scheme List

The village should possess a complete list and details of the schemes of the central and state governments which are available for the development of villages and their citizens. Also, once government help is received, the village administration should maintain records of the status of such help being given to the members of the village.

Success stories and action: Most successful villages have used this as a basis for their development. They not only receive funds from the government but also from NGOs. When such data is put up on the village walls, everyone knows who has received what benefit; and it makes it more difficult for politicians to misguide and for opportunists to swindle.

The village success stories of Ralegaon Siddhi and Hiware Bazar in Maharashtra are based on the receipt of government and NGO funds and their proper utilization in the respective villages. These villages have their panchayat walls filled with the names of beneficiaries of certain schemes. This is an important foundation stone for freedom and progress in a village.

Accounting Freedom 4: Census

The village must maintain a complete data bank of the members of the village, stored in a computer and based on a pattern given by the state.

Success stories and action: Most successful nations have proper records of every individual citizen of their nation. Their social security number gives access to relevant certificates and data in advanced countries. It is possible to maintain confidentiality as followed in these cases. In any case, such processes are already happening in India. The election ID, ration card and aadhar card are relevant examples. But clarity is required within a village. A village must have authorized updated data at its fingertips.

Both ultimate freedom and penultimate freedom are more dependent on matters of the spirit; therefore, matters of the spirit are of primary importance. Even so, the material aspect and money are important in the pursuit of freedoms and must be accorded their due. The economic status of every village needs to be sound. It is an important component for the freedom of a village. It includes things like using the resources economically, producing those things which give them a competitive advantage, making arrangements for all the inputs that are required to sustain a stable economic process and ensuring that the village fits competitively into the larger scheme of economics of the nation and the world. This set of freedoms pertains to the ability of the village to survive and thrive in the economic scenario of the 21st century. There are five areas of focus in order to achieve this freedom.

Economic Freedom 1: Adaptation and Integration

The village should display an ability to understand the economic need of the time and should quickly fine-tune its processes in order to thrive in the commercial setup of the economy.

Success stories and action: This freedom is driven by education, information transfer, responsibility-shouldering by the village, teamwork and general awareness. If a village works on improving its communication and information-updating channels, it is bound to keep pace with this aspect of freedom. The opportunities are large. Besides the primary industries, manufacturing, tourism and IT-based services must be explored. Three connectivities of the PURA model—physical, electronic and knowledge—must be ensured so that proper economic integration is achieved. Digital connectivity is rapidly ensuring electronic connectivity and facilitating knowledge connectivity, so much of this work is already happening. Incidentally, economic connectivity is considered as the fourth of the connectivities proposed by the PURA model. To be economically connected is the channel. 'To plan for economic integration into the national and international economy while maintaining its own core competence and identity' is the freedom; else, the same connectivities can facilitate the degradation of the villages.

Economic Freedom 2: Employment

The village should strive to attain hundred percentage employment for all eligible members of its workforce, and in the process, it must succeed in attaining a high national average for gainful employment. The employment must suffice for all families in the village to rise above the need for food, clothing and shelter and have enough for security, health, hygiene, education and cultural involvement.

Success stories and action: Action would include taking initiative in developing some industries within the village, providing capital for the same, bringing in government schemes which facilitate economic activity, arranging for trade and commerce, facilitating commercial partnerships, providing contractual employment, assisting in developing a client base outside the village, increasing the number and extent of services provided to its members in the village and all such things that help the village maximize employment. The barest minimum is that at least one person in each family should definitely have a steady income all-round the year.

Ample success stories exist in villages that have successfully fought unemployment. There are also stories of unique businesses that were created from scratch. There are also novel examples of creative products that can be manufactured and used in a village setting. Certain government agencies and NGOs also specialize in the facilitation and development of rural industries. The internet is a great source of access to such information. All it perhaps needs is a focused approach and a will to solve the problem. Technologies, financial support, resources, training, etc. are available to various extents and can be tapped into. External agencies can offer support, but the will to improve must come from the village teams. The possibility of P-V and G-V partnerships (Private-Village and Government-Village) must be explored fully.

Economic Freedom 3: Financial

The village should ensure the proper health of its financial sector; both lending and repayment must be efficient and effective. It should ensure that finance is available at reasonable rates of interests for the village dwellers. It should ensure that the processes involved are also reasonable and fair.

Success stories and action: Rural banking is taking off in a big way, and it is important that the villages ensure a culture of timely repayment. This will encourage low-cost lenders to operate effectively in the village environment. The Grameen Bank model is a great boon. But it needs to be implemented properly along with the right culture. The idea that each individual must have an account is a great foresight and must be pursued vigorously though it has hit some hurdles. It brings in transparency and auditability. It will also help in sound planning. The village team must ensure that at least one bank sets up shop in the village or at least actively services the village and that the probability of bad loans goes down to nil.

The possibility of enforcing the ancient tradition of *Daamdupat* on local lending agents in terms of gold value—which would take care of inflation—should be explored with more seriousness. Such traditional solutions could ease a lot of misery in the villages, which makes lending quite ethical.

Economic Freedom 4: Technological

In the pursuit of manufacturing clean, quality and useful products, the village must have knowledge about and access to the best of technologies that are applicable in their situation. All commercial and other activities in a village that may contain applications of science and technology must happen on par with the latest available across the globe. All village institutions must reflect this pursuit. Encouraging a culture of innovation and rewarding such innovations generally ensures this indirectly.

Success stories and action: Pursuit of this technology would include the gaining of knowledge about agriculture, animal husbandry, fisheries, forestry, etc.; the latest in each field must be made available to the people of the village. Such new technologies may also need new skills,

so arrangements must be made to ensure that such skills are learned quickly.

It should be the responsibility of the village to remain alert for all such possibilities and to be willing to experiment on such new initiatives regardless of whether the offers come from the industry CSR, NGOs or the government.

Each village should have a culture of encouraging and absorbing innovation and must develop well-established procedures for strategic adoption of new technology. When some people take the risk to try out something new, this should be supported by the village community as a matter of policy. This can be in terms of financial help or by giving volunteers.

However, despite all the good which technology promises, the spirit of freedom must always ensure that people are always first. Technology is next. One must not only show keenness to be updated but also show sufficient prudence to keep people and the environment at a higher pedestal than economics and technology. The initial phase of development may require low technology and human intensive industry, but the villages must rise quickly to high technology after universal employment goals are successfully achieved.

Economic Freedom 5: Resource Economization

Every village has immense resources, whether it is of man, material, produce, raw materials or simple gifts of nature. And these must be allocated in such a way so as to maximize the use, minimize the wastage/degradation and, wherever applicable, ensure rejuvenation for future generations' use.

Success stories and action: This will include things like adoption of efficient technologies, minimized use of fuel wood and using other fuels instead, efficient use of water, conservation of soil and rejuvenation of natural resources.

Another aspect in this would be to share resources through common ownership (mostly capital goods/technological applications) so that capital goods do not remain idle for long periods of time. This would help those who have limited finances. Such common possession would also be assisted through processes of centralized maintenance.

Certain villages in Maharashtra practice 'Block Water' (stoppage of running rain water so as to allow water to seep into the ground). Some communities in Rajasthan do not touch the innermost core of a forest even under the worst drought conditions and migrate instead so as to not use those resources. There are also outstanding examples of water conservation which villages have achieved through partnership with the government or otherwise both in the present world and in the centuries gone by. Outstanding models of waste management (economically) are already functional in South India and can be copied.

In many ways, this is just about having a mentality or a culture of conservation. If that attitude is developed and patronized in a village, it is assured that innovative solutions will emerge, and the world will move forcefully away from the present forecast of environmental doom.

This freedom indicates the thirst and yearning for the aesthetic sense in man—his passion for excellence. This is a measure of how intellectually and spiritually sound a village is; it is a measure of the *quality of its freedom*. It deals with the merits it possesses with which it protects the rights of its citizens. It deals with how well it nurtures its human resources. It is a measure of the ease with which it overcomes any divisive influences. It is a measure of its maturity in dealing with problematic situations and conflicts. It is also a measure of its patronage for arts, crafts, sports and games.

The totality of this can, even now, be experienced in the environs of a village. To those compulsively lost in the arithmetic of material possessions and development, much of this will sound meaningless. However, completeness and fulfillment in life lies almost exclusively in these aspects of culture. If any particular sub-group in a village experiences fear because of its label, if criminals act fearlessly and with impunity, if there is adharma or a lack of rule of law and if there is unashamed corruption and a lack of the sense of nobility, then all these indicate that a village has not evolved intellectually, spiritually or culturally.

The vision of Rabindranath Tagore aptly describes how that environment has to really be.

Where the mind is without fear and the head is held high
Where knowledge is free
Where the world has not been broken up into fragments
By narrow domestic walls
Where words come out from the depth of truth
Where tireless striving stretches its arms towards perfection
Where the clear stream of reason has not lost its way
Into the dreary desert sand of dead habit
Where the mind is led forward by thee
Into ever-widening thought and action
Into that heaven of freedom, my Father, let my
country awake.

Cultural freedom can be pursued under five headings.

Cultural Freedom 1: Education
For a start, every village has to ensure that all the children in the village are put through the formal process of basic schooling. It should coordinate with the neighboring villages to establish institutions that a single village cannot afford. It must support efforts of the government and private agencies at setting centers of learning in the taluka or district neighborhood of the village. It must participate actively, through the parents of the students and through the village elders, in shaping that part of the syllabi in schools which has to do with indigenous culture and values (all secular). In a holistic sense, education is the totality of culturing that happens from birth to death. It is not just about what is taught in schools. A village should therefore develop its own vision of total education and implement it in a way such that its human resources are upgraded constantly.

Success stories and action: Though hundred percentage basic education may not be feasible at the moment, a lot is expected to change. A shift from a supply-and-push approach to education must change into a demand-and-pull model. With pull from the villages and push from the government, remarkable things in the environment can be achieved. As the village takes responsibility upon itself and as prosperity sets in, a greater amount of time and effort can go into the education of the citizens. As Gandhiji said, what we see now is dung heaps. Imagine what swaraj villages will be like…

It is important that the basic requirement of studying up to tenth or preferably twelfth class must be met in all citizens at any cost on top priority. This is the best place to start. Eventually, as Gandhiji famously says, 'When our villages are fully developed, there will be no dearth in them of men with a high degree of skill and artistic talent. There will be village poets, village artists, village architects, linguists and research workers…'

Cultural Freedom 2: Skill Sets

The village must ensure that there are enough skills in the village to ensure two things. First, each individual must be skilled enough in one way or the other so that if and when he is confronted with the need for earning his livelihood, he must not have any difficulty. And second, the totality of skills available in the village (in its various citizens) must be adequate to provide all the basic services needed for the village to thrive. The village must strive to ensure that there is no monopoly in any of the required skills.

Success stories and action: There is a requirement of conscious effort when planning for the skills of a village, and it has to be done by the village management itself. Skills that are not available in a village should be made available either through borrowing people from outside or by sending out village members to learn relevant skills from trainers and training institutes outside. Having obtained the relevant skills, there are different ways by which such skills can be transferred down the generations, and the leaders of a village must develop a plan to ensure that the entire spectrum of skills is available in the subsequent generations as well.

Even for upgrading skills, the initiative must come from the villagers themselves. For example, if a teacher has been working in the village for some time, it would be nice if the teacher gets some additional coaching on counseling. In such cases, the village itself must sponsor and send the teacher for training. Farming, equipment maintenance, animal husbandry, business skills training, medicine, law, traditional medicine and water management are all areas in which people must be sent for higher training in a timely manner so that there is continuous improvement. The community must understand the importance of this and bear the costs.

As for the youngsters, who are in the process of being educated, the village must ensure that they have the opportunity to pick up the requisite skills needed for success in the future. This can either be integrated into the school syllabus or there can be separate training centers for it.

Cultural Freedom 3: Traditions

The village must ensure that it upholds and provides continuity for its traditions and at the same time have the flexibility to gel with the present age and times. It must take up those activities that have been transferred through the generations and ensure patronage for them. This includes traditional sports schools, temple festivals, art forms, festival rituals, conflict resolution methods, temple dances, storytelling, dramas and other activities based on the scriptures. Upholding the traditions also relates to the values a village cherishes with respect to a host of things like marriage customs, the elderly, women, children, spouses, teachers, guests, monks, government agents, etc. But even while traditions are upheld, human rights must also be protected.

Success stories and action: The Indian nation, having enacted unto itself a constitution, has set course along a particular path. This requires the concerned stakeholders to review the traditions that are used in a village in the light of what the nation seeks to achieve through its constitution. Without damaging what is inherent to the soil, there is a need to move away from that which violates the constitution.

But this needs to be done while considering certain important truths:

➤ The literate—from KG to Ph.D—are not necessarily wise.

➤ All scholars of ancient texts are not necessarily wise.

➤ All those who wear saffron and other holy colors are not necessarily wise.

➤ All those who have worked themselves into positions of political authority are not necessarily wise.

➤ Actors and sports stars are not necessarily wise.

➤ All those who have economic power are not necessarily wise.

The truly wise come few and far between and take the nation by storm. While a virtuous and scholarly head of an organization (or nation) struggles along with the members of his team, a wise man wins the hearts and minds of the masses who are marching with him. Traditions are set by the likes of these wise men. To search and find such people, and to follow them, has always been the highest aspiration in the Indian subcontinent. The value of this should not be lost on the administration of a village.

Cultural Freedom 4: Freedom in the Arts

Art must be considered as an integral part of the existence of the village community. It must sponsor art-related events to the highest extent possible. It must ensure that all children are groomed in at least one of the arts from an early age. As such, it will ensure that teachers of the arts are patronized in the village and that every attempt is made to help the teacher take that particular art to its spiritual heights. When creativity and art merge with daily work, it also lays the foundation for economic success.

Success stories and action: 'We do everything creatively and at excellence.' This attitude should be patronized in all activities in a village. Arts like culinary arts, performing arts, handicraft, poetry, literature, painting, *rangoli* and fashion need to be encouraged as an integral part of life.

When arts are combined with spiritual themes, the effect is heady. Folk arts, classical arts, dramatics, prose, poetry and storytelling form effective vehicles for transfer of wisdom. Hence, activities of this kind should be sponsored, and live performances of these by either professionals or amateurs must be encouraged.

With the understanding of art as a priceless possession or with the awareness that human fulfillment happens only through the satisfaction of the metaphysical nature of man, the village team must give top priority to encourage art of all kinds.

Cultural Freedom 5: Spiritual

The village must resonate with the spirit of vasudaiva kutumbakam (the world is one family). It must place the commonality in man to be bigger and far more important than all differences; if the spirit is substantial and is one in everybody, then the differences of race, sex, caste, religion, tribe, thinking and physical attributes are far less important than the oneness of spirit. In brief, the village must facilitate its citizens to realize that the spirit is more important than the material. It must practice the principle of 'specific religion in private and secular spiritualism in public'. It must also ensure the timeless principle of separation of religion and polity; authorities in religion and polity must be different individuals, and the teams that manage each of these should be separate and independent. And yet, the actions of all political leaders must be guided by secular spiritualism.

Success stories and action: Religions and religious institutions are designed to deliver the spiritual quotient. But they are not exclusive means to ensure spiritual growth; spiritual growth can also be nourished by and through the arts and all kinds of sports. Formal education is also possible in spiritualism. And there are a host of secular spiritual practices and traditions possible in society which can provide benefits to all individuals and societies.

Toward the task of winning spiritual freedom, a good leadership in a village should arrange to nourish its citizens with the best lessons from every good source. It should have its mind focused on enhancing the spiritual value of the village. It must give due importance to the spiritual component of life in its plans and ensure that spiritual activities get enough patronage with due sensitivity to all communities involved.

Therefore, in order for the members of a village to live a life of higher quality, it is important for the village community to take up initiatives that will enhance spiritual goodness in the citizens of the village. These initiatives can cover a range of socio-religious-cultural traditions and practices like patronization of the arts and sports, support for temple festivals, encouraging folk and classical arts that use the scriptures as a foundation of various activities and community prayers.

The village must ensure that its citizens have fitness levels that compare reasonably with those of the best of amateur sportsmen competing at the state or national level. These national or state amateurs may overcome common village citizens in skills, but as far as fitness is concerned, there must be little to separate the two groups. There are three kinds of challenges with respect to health, which are enhancement, maintenance and repair. All these functions are important and can be covered by taking up the various dimensions that come under this heading.

Health Freedom 1: Sports

The village must take up sports initiatives by becoming sponsors and supporters (for sports, sportsmen and sports Gurus) and also by organizing sporting events. Important village occasions like local temple festivals, anniversaries or common festivals must have sports competitions/displays as part of the proceedings/celebrations. Local facilities must be made available for training and coaching. Time and resources must be specifically diverted so that there will be reasons for the children and youth to practice and excel in some sport or the other all-round the year. Awards and trophies must truly bring honor to those who excel. Those found outstanding must be pushed to represent the village at higher levels of sports and games.

Success stories and action: There are many outstanding villages in India who have had success in sports like boxing, wrestling, *kho kho* and *kabaddi*. The list is long. These are very good examples to emulate.

The village sports committee must understand the spiritual dimension of sports besides the health and social dimensions as well. This will ensure that patronage will be taken up with unflinching commitment. The outer expression is that sports is a showpiece of the village; the inner dimension is that the village has achieved surplus and freedom, and as a result of this, it has allocated time and effort for higher pursuits.

Health Freedom 2: Health Care and Wellness

The village must develop within itself a culture of healthy living. It must undertake activities that will help its citizens attain and maintain themselves in the pinkest of physical and mental health. In a sense, this aspect of freedom will reflect a pro-active approach with respect to illnesses. As it is said, a stitch in time saves nine. If efforts are routinely applied in the direction of monitoring good health and taking pre-emptive measures, it will have two important benefits. It will improve the quality of living, and it will reduce expenses on medicine.

Success stories and action: Two important areas to focus on would be education and support related to the entire human biological cycle and innovative assistance in discouraging health-damaging practices and habits. The village should also actively encourage and facilitate various wellness regimens based on *yogasanas*, breath control, meditation, aerobics, laughter clubs, mind science, personality development, etc., thus leading to better all-round health.

Health Freedom 3: Hygiene

First, the village needs to ensure hygiene with respect to public places, public utilities, production spaces and other common requirements of society. Second, it should promote better hygiene within families and in individuals. Hygiene standards in spiritual/religious contexts are significantly higher in the Indian context; these must be extended effectively into home spaces, manufacturing spaces and public spaces.

Success stories and action: As part of its responsibilities, a village must meet the set standards of public hygiene as indicated by external agencies from time to time. All steps related to the management of communicable diseases must be taken up with both effectiveness and speed. The best practices of sanitation must be adopted and implemented efficiently coupled with the best of conservation efforts. The village must define and implement clear rules on what is allowed and what is not acceptable using the powers it is authorized. This will have to do with everything related to open defecating, spitting, waste disposal, garbage, gutters, drains, food making, washing, village water bodies, etc.

As for individual hygiene, it must facilitate education and training. It should also facilitate the process of obtaining tools and facilities (for example, toilets and cleaning materials) that individuals can use to nurture better hygiene standards. It must ensure that the commercial brands operating from the village adhere to higher hygiene standards, thus promoting the brand value of that particular village.

Health Freedom 4: Nutrition

The village must address both the issues of quantity and quality of nutrition. Initially through promoting the government and NGO schemes and eventually through proper arrangement of employment for every family, a village must ensure that there is no starvation unless by an individual's own choice. As for quality, all traditional recipes of the village must be preserved. Medical practitioners and sports Gurus besides householders and traditional cooks are good reservoirs of knowledge related to food; they must be patronized. The village must attain the required nutrition status with the help of external support agencies.

Success stories and action: A village must ensure richness in the knowledge of nutrition through preservation and propagation of traditions related to sports and the culinary arts. It must coordinate with nutrition specialists and nutrition agencies to have the staple food in the area scientifically analyzed and recommend changes in food and also the method of cooking to the members of the village. It must assess the availability and non-availability of nutrients needed for a balanced diet and ensure that the village produce/ market has enough diversity to meet the basic needs. The village body must also facilitate the availability and use of traditional herbs and medicines in the village, preferably along with experts in traditional medicine. The use of traditional herbs can eventually develop into an industry if the ancient traditions of healthy living and healthy sporting are systematically supported.

Indian traditional institutions like Ayurveda, *acharyas* and coaches have what it takes to meet the requirements. There have been cases of success in the Indian context with villages achieving great milestones in the fields of boxing and wrestling. They have found international recognition and acclaim. There are martial arts traditions too besides the other sports and art forms that are rich in this wealth. These are great sources to study and improve the performance of each village.

A village must record the number of children with malnutrition present in its domain as a great affront to itself and shoulder full responsibility to ensure that hunger is not heard of within its boundaries. Rather, we should note that great sportsmanship does not come from an empty stomach; if a village has an outstanding sports culture, then it has already addressed its hunger issues.

Health Freedom 5: Medical Care

A village should be self-sufficient in meeting its basic healthcare. It must also build a strong connect with specialized facilities that are available at the higher levels of administration. It must ensure that the poor are adequately covered through the various systems of medicine available. The burden of medical expenses must be lightened on the individuals by getting them access to the various facilities and schemes available through the government and the various types of insurance.

Success stories and action: From the assortment of traditional medicines like Ayurveda, Allopathy, *Unani* and Homeopathy, a village should have a minimum of at least two available within its boundaries for basic medicine. Citizens must have a choice of affording at least one low-cost option which is reasonably effective for treating basic illnesses. Basic medicines should be readily available at hand. Each village should preferably have its own dedicated nursery of required medicinal herbs and should be able to obtain the rest through purchase or barter from neighboring villages. A facility for physiotherapy should be an integral part of the sports traditions in a village. The local units must have very strong links with specialized institutions at the next level, and this should be supported either through a corporate movement, the government itself or through insurance so that medical care for everyone is assured.

It is important to watch over healthy individuals through regular visits by a family doctor and have the citizens closely monitored for maintaining their good health. These family doctors must serve more like 'maintenance doctors' than 'repair doctors' though they are certified for the latter. A doctor should be paid for just being there to look after healthy people, not only when people are sick. A fixed monthly charge per family going toward the salary of the doctor should be an option that a village must implement.

Dr. Devi Shetty's ideas as implemented in the chain of 21 centers set up under Narayana Health appear to be a very good solution in the present context. Anand Eye Care is another model that is doing great service to rural areas and the poor. But in some way, if these can also incorporate the riches of traditional medicine and/ or if similar systems can be set up for other systems of medicine, then even these other systems can be preserved and kept relevant to civilization. A healthy mix must be patronized by the government at all levels so that no monopolies operate in this sector.

Typically, a free nation controls its own legislature, executive and judiciary. But that does not mean that if that nation were a part of a larger nation, it would have lost its freedom. Taking the example of the Eurozone, we can see that certain powers which a smaller nation enjoys can be conceded to larger authorities without diluting the freedom which a citizen enjoys—it would rather effectively enhance a citizen's freedom. There are very good reasons for small and righteous political domains expanding into bigger units, and even spiritual lights have promoted this. A wider political domain brings greater stability and lightens the burden on citizens. The existence of a higher authority therefore need not be seen as an imposition. It is more about a balance of government power in which the various levels of government have both the rights and responsibilities that help enhance the freedom of the individual citizen. In an outstanding system, even the lowest of such formations, which is defined by a local community, will have a sense of nationality. They will have rights and responsibilities and will facilitate the freedom of individual citizens.

In the Indian system, the panchayat has traditionally been the lowest formation. To maintain the balance of governance, the panchayat too must enjoy legislative, executive and judicial power in a way such that the freedom and self-expression of its citizens is ensured.

Of the six freedoms, this is unique because this needs the sanction and authority of the government at the higher level—within the confines of the constitution. The other freedoms can be obtained by the citizens of a village by teaming up and working for themselves. But 'government freedom' is to be 'earned' by them, and it needs to be 'given' by the Indian nation state when that village becomes worthy of it.

The local government is important because it is capable of the highest impact on an individual citizen. This is the zone where an individual can best express himself in bettering his surroundings. It is the sphere where he can be taught to be responsible for others and for his nation. Here, he can also be taught to select the right candidates for the state and national leadership. A government OF the people, BY the people and FOR the people can happen at the higher levels. But a government WITH the people can best happen in the local community.

Government freedom means the effective transfer of legislative (rule-making), executive (administration) and judicial powers, which concern a village's governance, into the hands of the village itself. It requires the setting up and effective running of grassroots-level governance institutions and adequate training for the local people so that they can man these institutions. The institutions must cater to a modern village republic—meaning that people must be completely responsible for their welfare, development and governance. It also requires the setting up of a proper audit mechanism by the state government so that it can keep an eye on the local institutions and ensure that they comply with the national laws and aims.

This shift into institutionalization can be considered as a shift into exponentially increasing the number of minds that are contributing to the welfare of the village members. It will be an added bonus when these minds are not borrowed from outside but are rather born in the village itself. Action will naturally follow on the basis of the ideas that are generated by such minds. And with an effective design and audit of such institutions by higher authorities, we could end up seeing villagers having the freedom to take decisions and work for their own betterment.

Governance Freedom 1: Legislative

A village must make village policies and village rules that are applicable to itself through its Gram Sabha, provided of course that these policies and rules do not violate the constitution of India. These rules must preferably be briefly recorded in writing, and a copy of the same must be maintained at the taluka head office and taluka court.

(These provisions are still to be made in the administrative setup at the taluka level.) The Gram Sabha should also oversee the functioning of the village executive, and as such, it should lay down the norms on which basis the executive will take forward the goals of the village. Some important operational decisions can also be taken through the Gram Sabha.

Success stories and action: For such a thing to happen, the Indian government and state governments must set the limits to which the village can legislate. It must also make arrangements to ensure that these drafted rules are effectively audited so that there is compliance with the constitution of India. At the heart of the effort should be the Gram Sabha. It will be seen as a meeting of all eligible voters of the village. Like general bodies in the case of companies, these Gram Sabhas will control the executive bodies of the village. Surely the 73rd and 74th amendments will form the platform on which this devolution of power will be affected.

A village will be given legislative freedom only after the state government is assured, through its auditors, that the members of that village deal with each other in a manner that does not violate the constitution of India. The villagers will, therefore, have to earn the right to be in charge of this and other village-level institutions.

Governance Freedom 2: Executive

The executive will be elected on the basis of the laws of the land, preferably drafted at the village level on the guidance of the templates/patterns recommended at the state level. However, these executive bodies can be considered operational only after the requisite clearance and recognition is done by the state government. All those who serve in a village—in the public institutions there—should come under the administrative control of the village executive; this would include doctors, health workers, teachers, other village panchayat staff, knowledge workers, etc.

Success stories and action: Even a company has some freedom to choose what administrative structure it wishes to have. Likewise, the villages must have a degree of freedom in deciding what kind of local government setup they want. It should not be centrally imposed in all its details. Villages should be free to use their creativity to come up with an arrangement that is suited to them. Broad outlines can also be laid, and there are such established models of administration which can be highlighted for adoption. One such model is the system that was used in the Chola period (Uttaramerur); and there are many other examples from across the world operating even to date (Kibbutz from Israel, for instance). The communities should therefore be given flexibility for this. This means that local communities need to be empowered so that they can adopt their own systems depending on their traditions and culture.

A free village should also have the freedom to choose its own executives without any specific or categorist imposition from the outside—I can choose the best from my village, whoever that may be. An outside agent must not decide that so-and-so is not eligible unless, of course, by the law established on account of a criminal conviction.

We also know that an integrated village is the one that can bestow most benevolence on its members. Further, when united, they can rise to tap into the village's highest potentials. It is relevant, in this context, to note that the founders of the nation had a vision that elections to the municipalities should not be held along party lines, which would imply that even panchayat elections should not happen along party lines. In other words, their idea was that the village administration should not be divided within itself along party lines.

One way the villages can ensure this is to use the system of 'drawing lots' as was the case in the election system suggested by the Chola rulers at Uttaramerur. That arrangement will definitely fit the profile of an integrated village of equals and stop the divisive interference of external agencies in intra-village matters. Let's watch. The Indian mind is extremely creative, and wonderful ways will definitely be found to ensure that villages stay integrated despite all attempts to sow discord and division.

Governance Freedom 3: Judicial

Each village must have a nyay panchayat consisting of five members. Every member should have passed a certificate course conducted by a judicial commission developed for this purpose. The course should be such that even an illiterate person can get certified. The village Gram Sabha will elect them for a fixed period of ten years, and one person will retire and be replaced/renewed every two years in rotation. This initiative will be mostly honorary on a cost-covering basis, which the village should mostly bear.

Success stories and action: The immediate course of action should be the village shortlisting five of its elders, who are not in the executive body of the village, as village magistrates (for the first term). Thereafter, a systematic and transparent procedure for efficient functioning can be developed. Also, a permanent caveat can be put in the courts immediately for all cases going to the formal judicial system which the nyay panchayats have already heard. Besides this, the formal courts at the lowest level can respond positively, considerate of the decisions of the nyay panchayats. Over and above that, the village community may put pressure on its citizens to resolve issues in the local nyay panchayat itself—though, of course, access to the main courts will not be denied.

However, there is no doubt that for affecting this arrangement, there is a need to restructure the infrastructure at the taluka level to cater for such lower judiciary. This can be achieved only when the three branches of the government at the national level (especially the legislative and judiciary) come together to implement such an arrangement.

Governance Freedom 4: Integration

A village community must integrate into the national processes that spring from the constitution of India. There will always be institutions such as political parties, non-governmental organizations, the government, media agencies, commercial institutions, neighboring villages and higher panchayat-based organizations which will play an important role in the dynamics of the village environment. It will be in the interest of the nation if the village can retain a distinguished identity while at the same time dovetail comfortably into this existing political-economic environment.

Success stories and action: The level above the panchayat which is equivalent to the *mandala*, the PURA headquarters or the taluka, is very important in the sustaining of freedoms at the lowest levels. A great deal of political, executive and judicial work besides social, commercial and development work should be handled by active non-government and government workers. The villages must facilitate all such processes and come more than halfway to encourage productive work in all fields within their domains.

Whether it is about taking advantage of government facilities, NGO efforts, commercial opportunities or political parties' actions, most successful village movements have achieved their success by taking advantage of both their internal energies and the opportunities offered to them by their environment.

A thriving village community must have a team 'will' that is emancipated. This will give it an ability to look forward into the horizon with a sense of positive anticipation and purpose.

For this, the village, as a team, must collectively develop a vision toward realizing something it is destined for, something that the village team will delight in, something that will make it special in its own way, something that is an expression of its nationality, if one may.

The village must first aspire for freedom and self-rule. Besides this, even to give wings to that aspiration of freedom and self-rule, it must pay special attention to three categories of goals that hold special significance.

These three visions collectively developed by a village, through consensus, should be held commonly by the village community as benchmarks for finding fulfillment. Help from external experts may be taken in the process of thrashing out ideas. The resultant vision will act as a guiding light for the decision-makers of the village and an inspiration for all citizens.

Such vision should in no way impede the pursuit of excellence by individuals while at the same time being focused on facilitating excellence at the team level.

Vision Freedom 1: Environmental

A village community must develop and have a futuristic vision about its environment. It must participate positively in the global effort to fight environmental degradation and global warming. The vision must guide its entire decision-making and provide clarity in the minds of the average citizen in the village about this priority. Commitment toward environmental protection must be demonstrated in the great lengths to which the village will go to take care of the environment.

Success stories and action: The village must have clear team goals regarding the aims of checking soil erosion, growing trees, finding alternatives to fuel wood, checking runoff water, raising the water table, improving the fertility of land, developing self-sufficiency in alternate energy, waste disposal, organic fertilizer, organic pesticide, etc. Guidance from experts must be taken in formulating the environmental goals.

The benchmark for this vision should be 'better land, water, resources and environment for the future generations'. The vision must be something voluntary and expressive of freedom. It cannot be forced onto a village. At best, external agencies will facilitate the generation of the vision by offering templates, which the village administration can adapt to its own needs.

Vision Freedom 2: Developmental

The village should have extensively discussed and arrived at the rough contours of a plan for the development of the village, thus giving form to the common aspirations of a team. It should include making a list of projects relevant to the better future of the village. The projects should be listed in order of their importance, and all plans and estimates for each project should be in place, waiting only for the exact moment or for suitable resources to make these projects roll. It should pass the same in the Gram Sabha and adapt it as its vision for the future.

Success stories and action: There are many examples of villages that have successfully pursued development. These models can therefore be applied, and some of these are easily replicable. These need to be studied by each village, and suitable models can be developed with reference to themselves.

NGOs, visionary leaders, political parties, government agencies, non-resident villagers and international agencies will all help and facilitate. However, the final draft must come from the village leadership itself. It must be convinced of the direction it wishes to go. The team that is going to execute the plan is the village itself. Therefore, it must listen with large ears, but eventually after due diligence, it can take its own call on what is good for itself.

Vision Freedom 3: Contributory

It is important that the village cherish dreams of contributing to the nation and the world. Alternatively, it should patronize individuals and institutions within its boundaries who seek to make such contributions that the village can be proud of. It should look forward to send Olympians, soldiers, administrators, leaders, scientists, etc., in the service of the nation and the world.

Success stories and action: A village must target excellence, to be the best in what it does and to instill the thirst for 'being the best' in its citizens. Its citizens can contribute to the nation and the world only if they are world-beaters. A village must attempt to raise itself high in skilling, education and team-building to heights such that its citizens gain recognition at national and international levels. All this can be achieved only if it is in pursuit of a vision in which it sees its citizens achieve great things in the world outside.

The village may specialize in a certain area if it has strengths in something specific. But it must be worth the effort, and it must be something that gives the village energy and pride.

In the Indian villages of the 21st century, the potential to be better is truly large. Recognizing their current status as dung heaps contains in it the promise of what they are otherwise supposed to be: where is 'dung heap' and where is Gandhiji's 'Garden of Eden'? It coaxes them to be ready to change their thinking radically in order to bring to fruition something that is supposed to be dramatically different from what exists today.

Mere recognition of this disparity brought out by Mahatma Gandhi opens up a new world for the villages. It tells the villagers to sit together and work for what is still to be achieved.

'So, has my village achieved the six freedoms?' We have considered six freedoms in this section. Why six and why not seven or any other number? The answer is that it is ergonomic to categorize it as such. And almost everything that matters can be inserted into one or the other headings of the freedoms required. It is not the number that is important; it is about what this package can deliver.

What is this package of freedoms supposed to deliver in the villages? What is the idea of needing to put it into such a form and call it 'freedoms'?

A vision is the start: A vision is the starting point. It helps in realizing the defects of an existing system, and it points toward what it otherwise can be. It helps in deciding to do something concrete about the existing situation and about 'being the change one would like to see'. (We shall analyse this further later in this book.) As we have seen, that vision has already been created by Gandhiji when he laid out that the villages must transform into little gardens of Eden where highly intellectual folk live. And the same applies to Rabindranath Tagore's vision when he spoke of the spirit of freedom. Taking that vision forward till it materializes into practical-completed-working projects on the ground is the task at hand.

What is a project? A project is a kind of cluster of tasks that a person or a team takes up so that some desired outcome is achieved in the real world. A project is properly defined only if it is limited by two markers—one at the starting point and the other at the end—and if it is set within a timeframe. For example, let's say someone is building a car (this is a specific target, a project). Then, he says that he will build it in eight weeks (this is a time-bound project, which will, in turn, involve many sub-goals). The advance is paid, and he starts the work (commencement of the project). Then, someday, the car will be built, tested and the key handed over to the one who ordered the car (this will mark the end of the project). Similarly, each project should be specific, time-bound and have a defined start and end point.

A plan is a general term that can be used to define a collection of projects, all of which are seeking to attain some overall aim. A vision is what inspires the creation of a plan and the setting up of projects.

In order to effectively get into action in the real world, all aspirations need to be represented as visions, plans and projects. Detailed plans have to be worked out by those who wish to 'shape their own destinies', which should include a series of projects to take them from where they are to where they wish to be.

In other words, this conceptualization of six freedoms must (1) break up a vision into smaller achievable goals and (2) generate inspired enthusiasm in the village citizens to move toward their highest potentials. These six freedoms take this process one step forward.

The challenges of moving from vision to project implementation: The vision must spur people to action. It must aid the creation of teams who will take on projects and execute them. The challenges in this can be listed randomly as stated below:

➢ Each village must have a plan.
➢ The plans must qualify as true and practical visualizations, giving form and structure to Gandhian/Tagorean visions.

- The plans have to gel with the times; they need to take into account current global realities.
- They should cater to institutionalization at the village level, which will complement and supplement the institutions set up by the constitution of India and the parliament.
- The plans should ensure that all related activities proposed are established on the substratum of traditions and culture of the people.
- Harmonization should be achieved through a win-win for the state and the citizens.
- The plans need to capitalize on all kinds of conventional and unconventional resources of men and materials and deploy them judiciously in order to obtain the greatest mileage.
- The NGOs and the government should be able to catalyze into use the huge amount of resources available in the workforce in the villages.
- The present political setup must learn to see victory in taking that vision forward; the leaders and parties need to compete in an environment of constructive one-up-man-ship toward this end.
- For the villages, the plans need to be invigorating and absorbing; they must be in competition with other villages to attain better indices of freedom.
- The plans should be presented in a way such that it is be easy for village teams to focus their efforts. There should be a memory tool so that it will be easy for people on the ground to remember.
- It should help in the defining and classification of administrative responsibilities in a village.
- A comparison with a vision document should help a leader/administrator readily spot areas where focus is required.
- A plan document must serve as a basic standard for easy communication of ideas across the nation.

This array of challenges or parameters will have to be considered when one is drafting a plan to change the destiny of a village. The six freedoms create the groundwork for this to happen. These are comprehensively listed in the following mind map.

Village freedom mind map:

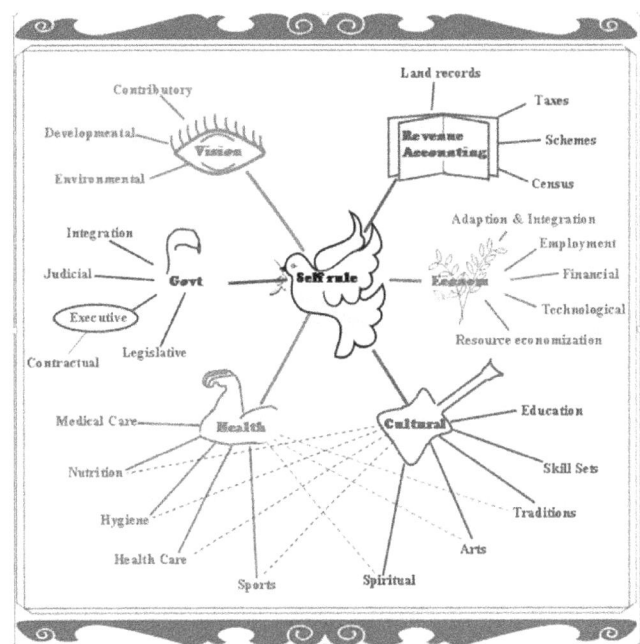

What is the thought behind generating this village freedom mind map? Mind maps have the following important advantages:

a) They can be used to represent the relationship between many individual items that share some commonality.

b) They are one of the best ways to remember many things that can be categorized in some particular way.

c) They are excellent tools for analysis.

d) They are excellent facilitators for communication.

A mind map is usually constructed such that the sequence of ideas commences from the 1 o'clock position and moves clockwise to the 12 o' clock position. So, the first item in the map that is presented here is 'Revenue and Records' and the last is 'Vision'.

This mind map is useful in the following ways:

1) The freedoms that we defined in the previous chapters have all been depicted at once in the map. It gives an assurance that it is comprehensive, and so, it can be used to make people think holistically.

2) The mind map helps in getting an idea about how the freedoms are connected.

3) It facilitates in crystallizing the thought process quickly. It helps a reader narrow down to relevant

areas of priority in the setting of his village so that those can be highlighted.

4) It assists those attempting to spread the discussed ideas by offering greater effectiveness in communication.

5) It provides an outline along which the village team may distribute their responsibilities, and concerned teams of people can have focused discussions on the chosen aspects and take better decisions.

6) It also provides a basic idea about how it may build up its executive team. A village can make teams responsible for various major aspects listed in the mind map and use it as a basis to form village committees.

How to use this mind map and point in the direction of freedom: Facilitators of freedom must understand this mind map and, if necessary, cut and paste a little bit here and there in order to customize it for a village.

They must remind the members of the village that the nation's hard-won freedom is not complete and that a village must stand on its own feet in order to be counted as a Gram Swaraj. Then, they must share the map within the village team and use it as a tool to discuss matters. They should say what has to be achieved in order to keep in line with the wishes of the Mahatma—specifically, what must be achieved under each heading.

They must be able to redirect the competitive energies of the villages (wherein each village tries to outdo neighboring villages) and channelize energies into development activity which will take them to freedom. They must say, 'We should outdo the other villages in all the indices of freedom.'

A facilitator must therefore use the mind map to develop cohesiveness in the village team along the parameters of both vision and action. Having constituted the teams and having decided on the areas to focus, the team must come up with and execute a series of projects that will take the village in the direction in which it wishes to move.

What the village must do:

Step 1: Swaraj Seedling(s)

This is the stage in which awareness of the idea comes to the village. A small group of about five people pour upon the idea of village freedom and study different village revolutions from all over the country and abroad.

Step 2: Freedom Nursery

In this stage, the seedling expands and joins with all the other seedlings in the village. Together, they split themselves up into small groups, each focused on one or the other of the six freedoms. Each freedom team looks into its area of specialization. They look outward for solutions available from across the world. They look inside their villages and see where their weaknesses are and how these solutions are relevant to themselves. They start making a list of projects that need to be taken up in the village. They all come together, discuss the six freedoms and try to create harmony with ideas from the other groups.

Step 2a: Freedom Nursery Presentation

The Freedom Nursery presents its findings and understanding to the village executive first and then to the Gram Sabha.

Step 3: Village Freedom Council

The Gram Sabha listens to the presentation, understands it and sanctions the creation of a Village Freedom Council which is a formalized structure of the Freedom Nursery. It consists of the core members of the Freedom Nursery including other members as the Gram Sabha deems fit. The Gram Sabha grants permission to the Village Freedom Council to invite help from NRVs (Non-Resident Villagers), NGOs and government agencies.

Step 4: The NRV Meet

The Village Freedom Council, with the blessings and support of the Gram Sabha, invites all NRVs, NGO representatives and local government officials and has a two-day discussion/seminar on the pursuit of freedom of the village.

Step 5: The Village Swaraj Master Plan

Based on the proceedings of the NRV Meet, the studies and analyses that have happened before that and due consultation with all stakeholders from within and outside the village, the Village Freedom Council comes out with a Village Swaraj Master Plan. This master plan sets clear priority on what projects must be taken up immediately, in the near future and in the long run. It also has a list of projects ready on paper so that when the opportunity comes, in terms of time or money, it can be implemented quickly.

A very critical reform required for the pursuit of swaraj: The importance of this cannot be overstressed. All commercial establishments know very well that a person who wants to buy but does not have money is useless and powerless. The same thing happens to a village. If a village must have swaraj, then it is possible only if it has the ability to spend money according to what it thinks is important. The village government must have adequate command over resources so that it can direct its activities toward what is good for itself. Giving it no financial authority is as good as making a toothless and clawless tiger. It can do little other than throw around its weight. If the government at the center or the state does not put money into the hands of the village directly, then it must at least allow a small tax of 10% to be levied in the village.

The important tax reform: The taxes collected from the farmers of villages of erstwhile kingdoms that existed in the past centuries in India varied from half the produce to $1/6^{th}$ of the produce of the land. This was not a fixed value though—not even within a single kingdom—and it could vary by the year. Much of it depended on how the weather fared in a particular year; in periods of drought, the taxes would be reduced to as much as $1/10^{th}$ or even be waived.

As of now, agriculture taxation is not done in India for political reasons. But this fact can be used as an opportunity to put money in the hands of the village community. A standard 1/10th of the income of each earning member of the village community and 1/10th of the produce of each farm should be collected and set aside for usage by the village leadership. Every earning member should be taxed since that induces a sense of belonging and equality. This money should not go out of the village.

The figure should not be significantly more than 1/10th since no contribution goes to the state. The entire process needs to be carried out by the village itself, and proper records should be maintained. Such records will be kept open for annual or biannual state audits, when auditors either from the tax department or the Comptroller Auditor General visit the villages. The village may decide how it wishes to spend the revenues. However, it should be on the basis of broad outlines, and these outlines should be previously scrutinized and approved by the state administration.

There should be no doubt that an organization becomes powerless if it does not have financial power in a world (capitalist) where money plays a vital role. It is only when the village attains financial freedom that it can independently think of its own progress and shoulder the responsibility of the freedom of its members. If the center and state government do not allow this taxation, then they must put all funds directed to village development squarely to the decision-making authority of the Gram Sabha.

A caution for tax reform: When the plan is to tax farmers, we may encounter many persons who stretch the notions of equality to suggest that this taxation should be increased to higher levels in order to enhance uplift. If such radical changes are not rooted in the traditions of the people of that locality, then it is equal to that of a violence committed against them. Wisdom lies in avoiding such drastic measures. The aim should be to work within the perimeters of the Indian constitution and the traditions of the local culture. The spirit of 'trusteeship' and the wisdom contained in the concept of dharma should prevail. When this happens, there will be no need of violence, force or compulsion, be it overt or covert.

Our possessions belong to the brave who put their lives in the line of duty: In freedom, one must never forget that all possessions held within the country are permissible or rather possible only because there are martyrs and brave people who have pledged their lives for the defense of the nation against internal and external evils. In a world of timeless heroes, attached possession of such wealth with the purpose of self-aggrandizement is considered a sickness.

If the spirit of nobility prevails, instead of self-aggrandizement, therein lies majesty which cannot be measured in terms of material wealth. If a village is truly free, then that sense of nobility will be sensed in the very environment. The wealthy will use part of their earnings to patronize noble causes within the village and outside. There will be no 'needy' in that village then. Therefore, the satisfaction of 'needs' in a village should not be achieved through bitter wrangling over material wealth. Rather, it should come from a sense of self-help, nobility and fullness that represents true freedom.

Section III

The Nuances of the Pursuit of Freedom

In this section, we will focus on a set of ideas that explore the factual position of the villages of India. Are we really free? What does the evidence show? Do the majority of Indians have an attitude of freedom? If there is a slavish mentality from where does it originate? Is it reversible? Are there alternative ways to look at it? As we explore the significance of each, various dimensions of the pursuit for the second freedom become evident. These ideas not only firm up our faith in the possibility of a process, they also give very good markers and pointers for productive action. Let us explore these ideas and see what possibilities they offer us in our pursuit of panchayati swaraj. How did the present situation in rural India evolve, and where do we go from here? Does the situation indeed point to the pursuit of the six freedoms?

The people who are generally elected to power in India have almost given up the idea of decentralization. Most, including a lot of intellectuals, think decentralization is a great idea but that it cannot be implemented. They are correct from the usual points of view that rule the roost today, but at the same time, it is also a fact that we are not using much of the wisdom that comes to us from our ancient sages and influential past leaders. In fact, we are not even really using Gandhiji's ideas. The lessons coming to us from all these sources seem to indicate that if we use all that knowledge, remarkable things are possible. All we need to do is explore these ideas, and by doing just that, the answers that we have discussed for today's problems become visible slowly and surely. The pursuit of effective decentralization emerges as the best strategy for the release of the potentials and energies of rural India.

3.1 IDEA 1: THE CONNECTION BETWEEN DECENTRALIZATION AND SUCCESSFUL KINGDOMS

What is the difference between magisterial duties and judicial duties? This question hides a great secret about the possibility of self-rule in India.

To understand this, let us go to the origin of the word. In India, the word was used in connection with collectors; collectors initially had to do some 'magisterial' duties. Then in the 1790s, the district judge was appointed, and all judicial and magisterial duties were shifted to them. In due course, possibly around the 1820s, magisterial duties were removed from the district judge and transferred back to the collector. Much later, post-independence, the magisterial duties of the executives (which included collectors, tahsildars, etc.) were decreased.

'So, what does it mean to be a magistrate?' and 'What is that which is classified under the term "magisterial duties"?' are questions to be explored further. It is only natural that we look back into the English tradition to find out what the original idea of 'magistrates' was all about. And indeed, something interesting turns up.

i) 95% of all judicial officers in England are magistrates, and only 5% are judges.

ii) Magistrates are not qualified in law, while judges are qualified in law. Judges first become barristers through seven years of learning. Magistrates, on the other hand, are common people who are not law-educated. They may be educated in other subjects. These common citizen aspirants fill out a form and possibly go through a small test to qualify as magistrates. Both categories (judges and magistrates) undergo training when they are on their job while judging cases.

iii) *Magistrates are not paid!* (Surprise, surprise!) Their service is voluntary. They can claim travel and other incidental expenses, but they do not receive a salary.

iv) Magistrates always sit in benches of three to hear cases. A bench, as far as possible, represents great diversity in terms of race, creed, age, abilities, ethnicity, etc. For the junior magistrates, it is training. Despite that, each magistrate carries one vote for judgments, and the result is based on majority.

v) There is an established nationwide system to organize and manage the magistrates and their cases. And there is *legitimacy*; the judgments passed by them are legally valid.

vi) But magistrates do not handle all cases. There is a defined set of cases which magistrates can hear—cases that relate to minor crimes and civil cases. The important part is that there is a demarcation or a line that defines what magistrates can hear and what they cannot. There are rules; there is a system.

Of these points mentioned above, we must pay particular note to the fact that magistrates are not paid. This means that this system of delivering justice is based on voluntary effort. If one pauses here and thinks about it, it will become clear that the poorest of the poor will benefit by this. You would not have to travel too far to be heard for small issues. The next important advantage is that the regular judges are freed up to hear only the demanding cases; the simpler cases are heard and settled before they are brought to these higher courts. And solving small cases at the community level itself makes a lot of sense because it can be quick and accurate—provided that the system is running properly.

Do note that this system is very similar to the erstwhile panchayat system of India. Like the magistrates, the panches are not lawyers. Instead of three, we have five. But the difference today is that there is no system in place to control them or tell them what their limits or duties are.

Chanakya's idea of decentralizing judicial power: Let us now shift our focus to a lesson from ancient India. It comes to us from Chanakya. Now, the solutions Chanakya has given are tuned to the technology and (was based on the) situation of his times (fourth century BC). However, there are basic principles that apply at all times. We shall consider one such principle related to the judicial system and explore how that principle makes us look in a different direction today.

Let us presume that the issue at hand is a land dispute. Two people are fighting for ownership of a piece of land, and the system (monarchy during Chanakya's time) must settle this issue. For a moment, if we were to use the normal thinking of today, we will expect Chanakya to have given rules for a super benevolent king to follow so that he can be ready to stay up day and night to provide justice. In other words, he must have had a huge collection of judges to sort out the problems.

One cannot be farther from the truth. To make a long story short, he more or less tells the two parties to first sit together to try to solve the problem. Next, in the event that they cannot solve the problem between themselves, he asks them to go and look for someone wise, who is acceptable to both, to mediate. And if it is still not resolved, then the two parties may take it to the local formal court. If no settlement comes out of it, then the land gets transferred to the king for him to dispose as he pleases.

One may say that it is a diabolic strategy for the king to become rich. But after dwelling on it for some time, it becomes clear that there is a sound strategy hidden in it. It makes sense from several points of view, and it was possibly the best solution for those times. There are many principles of sound administration hidden in this strategy.

First of all, there is good encouragement—or rather pressure—on both contestants to have the problem resolved at the lower levels itself. Else, both stand to lose. Thus, by putting pressure on the contestants, two distinct advantages can be seen. One is that justice becomes affordable because a case like this is likely to be settled more quickly, and that brings us to the second principle that it frees the officials at the higher levels to take care of other important work.

Another positive is that when someone can officially arbitrate between the two, the settlement gets officially recognized. This is likely to resolve many problems that occur due to ego clashes. A fourth advantage is that it enhances people's participation in each other's lives, and therefore, it enables greater community strength.

Also, if a contestant knows that there is a real danger of losing his land at the next higher level, he may be willing to accept a difficult compromise as there might be no other easy way out (it may appear unjust, but it could be the best way out).

When we look at this from the authorities' perspective, it means that the rulers are placing a lot of faith in the abilities of the people at the lower levels. They believe that people can solve most of their own problems. This strategy of placing faith on the people is extremely good because faith is eventually rewarded. It is human nature that people definitely rise to meet the challenge in front of them. People will study up about law, learn the tricks of the trade and also use their ingenuity to find solutions— only if they are given that task.

Even if they are not capable of it at that moment in time, the faith will ensure that they eventually grow up to fill that bigger shoe—again, provided the authorities place that trust in the common man.

And then, what will the king do with the land that so comes to him? He should put his higher officials on the task to see if there is justice in either claim and dispose it accordingly. If the problem remains unresolved even after that, the law of the land will apply, and the king will have the right to keep the land or dispose it according to his own political needs.

What we can gain from this example is that we need to place our trust in common citizens. We must encourage common citizens to believe in themselves so that they can solve the problems that happen in their surroundings.

This belief in the lower levels need not be restricted to the judiciary. The two examples considered here, one from traditional Britain and the other from ancient India, pertain to the judiciary. But the same principle can be applied in other aspects of life like governance, polity, education, taxation, etc. Generalizing, it can be said that there are such lessons available in other aspects of the life of a community as well. And the best of them suggest that it is all about transferring responsibility and power to the communities so that they can nurture an environment of self-reliance and freedom among themselves.

Looking back at the Indian system, let us do a reality check. Is the Indian system of government currently using methods that encourage self-reliance in local communities and in common citizens? No, it is not! And this was how it was when the British government ruled India as well; before the British, the situation was different under the better rulers of India.

The colonial rulers appointed 'magistrates' in India, but the arrangement they made in India was not the same as in Britain. The magistrate in Britain took care of his village; the magistrate in India, however, was to take care of thousands of villages. Instead of making magistrates at the level of panchayats, the colonial rulers made magistrates at the level of the district collector.

By setting up such a system, they could 'claim' that they had set up a judicial system consisting of magistrates in the country. And by ensuring that the magistrate was at a very high level, they could also say that the 'natives' were not fit to rule themselves. In their opinion, Indians did not possess even enough merit for being appointed as magistrates.

And it was easy to say that because not many Indians were 'educated' at that time. More specifically, there were few Indians who went to schools which the rulers recognized as 'educational institutions'. It is easy to say that one needs at least a little knowledge of law (British law) to be a magistrate. Not many, if any, Indians had that knowledge.

Hence, the magistrates of England and the magistrates of India are similar in the fact that both are not officially educated in law. But besides that, there is no similarity. In Britain, the magistrate is a common man; in India, he is a ruler. In Britain, the magistrate is part of a grassroots-level process; in India, he is part of the ruling elite. In fact, the newly imposed system of magistrates and judges even destroyed the erstwhile grassroots-level judicial process in India.

The indigenous grassroots-level judicial system: There was an indigenous judicial system that existed in Mughal India. That system continued to operate even after the Mughals, but with the coming of the colonial rule, it was pushed into the background. There was no support for it from the rulers. It became 'unofficial'. It

became illegal. It was not considered to be part of the mainstream process, but the rulers tactically allowed it to exist. Such traditional courts had to rely on the whims of the individuals who represented the administration for patronage. It was not established by rules and laws; instead, it was allowed to exist at the mercy of the rulers.

Gradually, the traditional system became weak. It was eventually lost when the constitution of India came into force because the constitution did not give it an official recognition. There is no process today by which the nyay panchayats are considered as part of the main system of judiciary in India. Mostly, these systems are called katta panchayats and are condemned. There is some effort going into recognizing these systems in some states, but they do not have official sanction of any substance. At the most, they are taken as arbitration processes.

The courts of India have been unnecessarily loaded with huge amounts of work. We have merely been expanding the courts system in the country by adding more sessions courts and special courts and so on, but have we thought seriously about the option of grassroots-level courts—about giving power to the people?

And who is to blame for it? The courts? No, not them. The task is for the rule makers—the legislators—to redesign the judicial system at the grassroots level, develop ways by which small cases can be handled in communities and make the present courts free to deal with larger issues.

When comparing our present system with the two examples we considered in the beginning of this chapter, we see that the judiciary in India is unnecessarily loaded at the top. It is a great ideal to say that even the highest court in India, the Supreme Court, is open for justice to all citizens of India. It is also great to have an ideal which says that 'learned' judges will hear and dispose cases even at the lowest level, but we also need to be practical. If we end up with an arrangement where time is stretched like rubber and huge holes are cut into our pockets in pursuit of such high ideals, then of what use is it? The nation must work out an optimum solution. We need to have a system that will be respectable and deliver time-bound justice at a low cost.

So then, why not take a leaf out of the wisdom of others? Why should we not be inspired by them and see if we can improve the arrangement for ourselves? Take the British courts as an example. Just imagine. If we could produce so many more courts that the present number will reduce to only 5% of the total for a little additional cost, that would be a revolution of sorts! That is, for every court that exists today, if we can make nineteen more courts with just a little additional cost, then why not? And there is enough historical evidence to show that this alternative can be made to work.

The suggestion is definitely to give 'formal' status to the nyay panchayats in a practicable way. Can these grassroots-level courts be redesigned to be made suitable for our times? Can an illiterate person possess enough wisdom, training and experience to be considered fit to hold court for matters pertaining to his village? Can the formalities be designed such that illiteracy too does not matter?

With creative inputs from experts in law, philosophers, social scientists, historians, anthropologists, experienced activists, experienced bureaucrats and leaders who are close to the soil, it must be possible to design something that is effective, low cost and worthy of respect.

For example, even as the system stands now, let us consider one small change. Let there be a permanent caveat that when a case comes from the villages to the lowest formal courts of India, the nyay panchayat representative of that village will also be given a compulsory hearing. Even this small step can put enough pressure on people to take the nyay panchayats seriously and accept the legality of the solutions offered by them.

Better yet, if we put in a formal structure, give powers to the panchayats, define the limits to which they can operate, create a proper audit system to ensure that the panchayats stay within their limits and keep their decisions open for review by higher courts, we could have an effective system at the grassroots level. This will take the informality out of the illegal katta panchayats, bring the process to the open and have them subjected to the law of the land. The most important outcome will be that justice will come at virtually no cost. Community ties can be enhanced. Strong indirect pressure can be applied on the villages to get themselves educated, and finally, the higher courts can be relieved

to work on more serious cases so that they can offer time-bound justice.

The arrangement is automatically a HR person's dream-come-true. Where people have no work, jobs are created. Where there is no service, one comes into existence. And if the whole affair is carefully drafted, it can become a great trigger for the education and self-reliance of the general population.

That this discussion is centered on the judiciary is only incidental. The same principle can be extended to other spheres of life. The idea can be generalized to the other two legs of the government too—the legislature and the executive. There is scope in present India to institute grassroots-level systems in the legislature, executive and judiciary that can give greater opportunities for self-expression.

We need to look at a set of assumptions in vogue today in relation to administration, which is not conducive to freedom:

1) There is an assumption that all government services available in villages should be standardized in full detail across the entire state or nation.

2) There is an assumption that services available at all levels—including the grassroots level—should have a monetary framework.

3) There is also an assumption that the minimum eligibility criteria for individuals to join in a process of institutionalization should be fixed at literacy.

All this is needless self-limitation. These are boxes which we put around our creative thinking. There is a need to think out of the box, so to say. There is a need to develop a playfield within the villages where legitimate authority is granted to its members to take on tasks of governance, economic emancipation and such others by themselves. A free nation rules itself. A free village must also be able to manage itself.

Therefore, we need to work while keeping in mind that there is a lot of scope to move forward by just re-organizing and legitimizing processes in villages. We have to first define the limits of the scope and where the local communities have to operate freely; then, a formal, self-sustaining grassroots-level system can eventually be established across all villages in India.

The two practical examples of judiciary we have discussed in the beginning are taken from political success stories. One of them is Britain, a nation which went on to spread its influence far and wide in the world. The other is the Mauryan empire that stretched across the length and breadth of India even at a time when technology was far behind what we have today. These two nations have immense achievements to their credit. Can we conclude from this that this ability of the system to make the grassroots take on administrative responsibilities is one of the attributes of a golden age?

Not just yet... Let us keep this at the back of our minds while we look for more examples, if there are any.

One example is the remarkable Mughal rule. At its peak, it had dominion over a kingdom that spanned from what is Afghanistan today all the way to Bengal, from the Himalayas in the north to the Deccan Plateau in the south. At the heights of its glory, it created the Taj Mahal, truly a wonder of its age. The remarkable expansion of the Mughal rule happened under Emperor Akbar. An important component of this success was his excellent handling of governance and taxation. It is said that Raja Todarmal, who worked for Akbar, was to a great extent responsible for implementing many reforms during his time. Incidentally, even before Raja Todarmal was Sher Shah Suri who preceded Akbar's father as the ruler of Delhi. It is said that Sher Shah was the original genius in administration. What Sher Shah started was merely carried forward by Akbar.

As we close this chapter, we may summarize the first idea thus. When there has been effective decentralization leading to liberty for the people in some past kingdoms, those kingdoms have had demonstrable success in the political arena. Therefore, if we indeed affect decentralization the way it was done in the case of the judiciary in the examples we considered, we can reach deeper into the great potential we have as a nation.

Even greater than the Mughal system is a remarkable system used by the Chola kings of South India. Historians refer to the villages of this empire by the term 'village republics' as they had the flavor of 'freedom at the doorstep'. It is a place from which great inspiration and critical lessons can be drawn for our systems today.

But before we get to that, let us look at an interesting question related to the ignorance of rulers. Is it possible for a king to have great benevolence and yet do great damage to his people? We shall see that in the next chapter.

3.2 IDEA 2: BENEVOLENCE IN CENTRALIZATION IS IGNORANCE PERSONIFIED

Once upon a time, there was a kingdom which had self-sufficient villages. The king had passed away, and the prince had just taken over the reins of office. He knew himself to be greatly magnanimous; he wanted to rule his kingdom even better than his father and hoped to divert all his energy and resources toward the happiness of his people.

In due course, he got some complaints of irregularities. The complaints were numerous, but it was natural for a kingdom as large as his. There were thousands of villages, and even if there were complaints from only a small fraction of them, it was represented as a significant number at his level. He wanted even these complaints to be checked, so he decided to keep one arbitrator permanently in each village. He hired many new arbitrators, had them trained and placed them in the villages. Naturally, these arbitrators, who were on the payroll of the king, began enjoying an elevated status in the village.

Finding that some villages did not have the human resources to handle simple tasks in the villages, he appointed accountants, doctors and teachers. Pretty soon, he found that he was running huge bills toward their salaries. Since it was, after all, a benevolent dictatorship, and since the expenses were mostly for welfare, he decided to hike the taxes. Else, he would not have money to run his benevolent state. But he met with resistance from the people. There was unrest, and wherever there was unrest, he had to station his soldiers to keep the people in check. And soon, he was ruling the nation pretty much with an iron hand.

Soon, he passed away, and the next in line became the king. But now, the people were complaining that the services which the king was making available for them in the villages were irregular and of sub-standard quality. The villagers saw themselves as different from the paid employees of the king and felt a general resentment toward them. It was not long before the nation became weak, and the ruler was declared a failure.

The surprising thing is that it all started with a benevolent king, and it ended up in disaster. The point one should not fail to notice here is that the benevolent king was well-meaning but stupid.

There are several blunders he actually committed. The first was that he did not have faith in his people. Accepting aberrations, he should have merely fine-tuned only the troubled villages so that those specific problems could be taken care of. Given a chance, they would definitely have bounced back. But rather, he had this notion that these 'good-for-nothing' villages had to be taken care of.

The second blunder was that he was under the naïve impression that, being the king, he had to do things for his people, almost as if he was the only doer around. He had this impression that everything was happening because of him. The truth was that the king was merely playing his part. Of course, he was playing an important part, more important than all the others probably. But to think that he was making it all happen was his folly.

Next, he was committing three human resource blunders.

First, he was trying to run thousands of villages through remote control. He was trying to control thousands of personnel through his personal individual intervention. This would put tremendous strain on him (which he was willing to take on, out of his benevolence), and it resulted in the creation of a monstrous bureaucracy, which had to be held together with an iron hand.

Second, he was inadvertently replacing the human resources contained in entire inspired villages with the human resources of a handful of paid workers. Scores of villagers would have been working earlier, taking very little pay—and most importantly—inspired. The paid workers would be hardly a handful in number. They were doing their job, working for their pay or working out of fear. At best, they would be working inspired. Where is the comparison? A handful of (rarely) inspired agents against hundreds of inspired home-hands…

The third disaster was that he was creating a new class of people in the village. This class would be seen as alien by the villagers as if they were implants of the king. This feeling would arise even if the people were taken from the stock of the village itself. Ultimately, this would be a source of discontentment against the king.

Therefore, it is not surprising that the king who started out by trying to be benevolent actually turned out to be a disaster, a human resources disaster.

Without a doubt, the above criticism is directed at the system we presently follow. How absurd it is for us to think that all judicial problems will be solved through the formal courts right from the Supreme Court down through to the Class 2 judges. In fact, the government, (luckily) cannot even dream of providing judges in each village. Then again, it wants to set up schools in each village with teachers paid from its coffers. It wants Gram Sewaks to go around the villages. As well as sanitary workers and doctors who are not answerable to the village community but to the government that controls them from far away.

This arrangement is wrong. It is a human resources disaster. It is a result of colonial thinking.

It is time to throw out this colonial thinking and place more trust in the people and their capacity for inspired action. There is a need to operate on a more positive principle of 'faith in the abilities of the commonest Indian'.

Let each village team run its own show!

There have been examples, in this very land of ours, to show that there is a lot the common citizen can do. Some people say that times have changed, that people have changed and that the present generation will not live up to such values or that they cannot have such merit that they can run their own show. This is a fallacy. If at all someone is authorized to comment on this aspect of human behavior, it should be anthropologists or genetic engineers. Either of them will certify that there is no reason for us to believe that humans have evolved so drastically over the last century or two. Changes in a species happen only rarely after several hundred or more generations, and substantial changes happen only after thousands of generations. All this would mean that the essential nature of man has not changed in the last few thousand years. Many of the tried and tested solutions of these past centuries can be applied today with suitable adaptations. What motivated our ancestors can motivate us even today. We need to see how villages were self-motivated in those times and recreate that opportunity today.

To conclude, the second idea is that there is no need to rule from above or for kings and politicians to be benevolent from a distance. People can do their own thing. Let people have the freedom to take care of themselves, and they will, in no time, rise up to the task.

Let us take a look at one of the excellent precedents from our nation in the next chapter. It definitely offers pointers as to what can be achieved in small communities anywhere in the world.

The Chola kings ruled in South India between the ninth and twelfth centuries AD, and they were successful as rulers. We can say this with conviction by comparing them with a number of other rulers who existed in the same area before and after them and with those who ruled other areas in the same period. The Cholas are the only South Indian kings who went as far as the Gangetic plane on conquests and the only Indian kings to have established a rule outside the subcontinent; for instance, they crossed the Bay of Bengal and set up a rule at Bali in Indonesia.

By all means, the aim is not to exaggerate the military might of the kingdom or to propose aggression; rather, the aim is to point at the inner strength of the kingdom. In the technological setting of those times, for a kingdom to be capable of such conquests, together with having a long period of stability extending over centuries (unlike tyrannies), this would have been possible only after ensuring, through its good administration, that its citizens enjoyed peace and prosperity.

Now, to what can we credit this unusual excellence?

Many reasons are possible, but there is evidence to believe that there are two primary reasons for this success, out of which one of them fits into our context of local administration directly.

In passing, we can just make a note here that the other reason for the success of the kingdom was the great awakening which Adi Shankara epitomized. With respect to this, it is sufficient to say that such an awakening is capable of producing men of great integrity and ability. And it can continue giving that strength till such a time that the awakening does not get entangled in dogma and ritualism. (This hypothesis is yet to be proven, but there is plenty of empirical evidence.)

But that apart, the other important cause which led to the stability of the Chola nation was the system of administration of that time at the grassroots level—which gave the citizens control over their own destinies.

Inscriptions: Two inscriptions have been discovered at a place called Uttaramerur in present-Tamil Nadu, close to Chennai. The authorship has been attributed to the Cholas, and the date has been fixed around about the eighth century AD. Engraved on them is a reflection of how grassroots-level administration was carried on at that time.

There is no need here to dwell in depth on a subject on which experts have done exemplary work. It is better if a reader is referred directly over to them so that those who are keen may see the relevant details for themselves. While a search engine will easily give enough information on the internet, following are a list of three sites that can be referred to for the specific reasons listed:

To understand a little about the Chola Empire, one can refer to the following site:

http://en.wikipedia.org/wiki/Chola_government

For an exact translation of the inscription, the following site is fine enough:

http://www.geocities.com/ifihhome/articles/uttaramerur.html

And the following site gives an expert opinion on the inscription and related issues:

http://tamilartsacademy.com/articles/article01.xml

But for our limited purpose, we shall very briefly consider the following. The inscriptions go on to elaborately describe the process of election in a village. In fact, it is an agreement which the people of Uttaramerur promise to live by. It seems to have been done as part of an administrative process that was being initiated under the Chola king of that time. We shall pick up some implications of the 'agreement' and see what lessons there are for the freedom of modern-day villages.

1) There are two elements in the document which are related to authority external to the village. The first is a letter from the king on which basis the agreement is being drafted. The second element is the arbitrator (apparently deputed by the king)

who supervises what happens during the elections. Broad outlines and boundaries of authority are drawn up within which a process of building grassroots-level institutions takes place in the village.

2) From the scheme, it appears as if all villages in the kingdom were to have three important committees: the annual committee, the garden committee and the tank committee. These committees needed to handle money, and proper accounts had to be maintained. The exact formation of the committees for each village seems to have been achieved through slight modifications of a given standard. The inscriptions at Uttaramerur seem to represent the agreement modified to suit Uttaramerur.

3) The authority of the king is evident, since he monitors the elections through the arbitrator. The result is that the elected body has the sanction of his authority. The elected committees are definitely answerable to the people of the village, but they are also answerable to an audit by the king.

4) There was an established system of accounting. A professional accountant was to be hired and placed under the command of the executives of the village. There was a procedure called 'closure of account'. It implies that the established accounting system had some set standards which had to be followed and which could be audited. The inscription declares that the next accountant could be hired only after the previous accountant closed the account. This indicates that care was taken to ensure that there would be minimal corruption and that responsibility for misdeeds could be properly fixed.

5) The inscription also throws light on people who were eligible for contesting for positions of authority in a village. The criteria disallowed persons who were involved in anti-social activities and office irregularities from contesting in elections. Even close family members of guilty persons were not eligible to contest. These relations also included the first cousins and uncles; this indicates that, unlike today, there was a legal premium placed on family and extended family values.

6) There was also a premium on education, in the sense that only those persons who were educated to a certain extent could offer themselves for selection. Also, only those owning a minimum amount of land (farmable) had the right. And again, they had to be residents of that place, in the sense that they had to have a dwelling on that land.

Well then, did it exclude anyone from participating in the process? Based on their caste, for instance... The answer to this is not clear. However, it can be said that once someone was eligible for being selected, it was just a matter of luck. A draw of lots would decide who would be elevated to power in the village. And there was one candidate for each ward.

Also, the process was rotational; those who had held a post in the recent past were not eligible. So, everyone got a chance, and all were considered fit. This would also have ensured that the people of the village were all generally educated about the processes involved in administration. Merit was a criterion only after the entire executive team was elected. Once the members of the team were finalized, the team members would choose from among themselves as to who would lead and who would form part of which committee. Indeed, as the historians say, it was a village for enlightened equals.

7) The age limit for contesting was between 35 and 70. Therefore, only seniors were eligible. Chances are that this was because younger persons were required for service in the government machinery. Or maybe, they were considered too young to shoulder responsibilities.

8) It also looks like there was a clear process for collecting taxes, sharing resources and paying the king's share to the king. All these were to be made transparent through the process of systematic accounting. Therefore, just as the arbitrator came in to the village to supervise the election process, there would also definitely have been regular audits of accounts.

9) It is also evident that there was some procedure for keeping records of misdeeds which advised that some people were ineligible for office. This also means that there was an accepted definition of law and that there

were processes connected to judging and punishing. The system was so well-defined that individuals' misdeeds were recorded and kept for reference for a later date. Indeed, it is remarkable.

These were actually self-sufficient villages. It is said about them that the only thing they looked to the king for was protection. Evidently, that is not the entire truth. Since, through the king's directives and his representatives, he was responsible for starting and protecting grassroots-level processes. Through time-to-time monitoring, he was ensuring that things were flowing smoothly. But it is important to note that the entire show was of the villagers. The initiative was theirs; they took care of themselves, and therefore, they could be called republics. The setting up of such a system seems to indicate that it was based on deep thought and wisdom. It was a practical arrangement, and the spirit of it is good.

When the villages were organized in this manner, even the king benefited from it. If the villages looked after itself and paid its dues to the king without corruption taking its toll and if societies were living in the spirit of the laws, then the king had no need to interfere. He was free to concentrate on his own sphere of activities. Therefore, when the people were thus free to express themselves in their community-based institutions, stability naturally prevailed in that nation.

The prosperity of any nation shares a direct relationship with the status of the common citizen; both rise and fall together. Or to be more precise, when the status of the citizen improves, the nation soon prospers. Similarly, as the status of the common citizen goes down, the fortunes of the nation soon dips too.

The growth phase of the Mughal period clearly shows that the people were liberated from the clutches of the lower administration. And a rule of law—a liberal but firm law—was established. The reforms of Sher Shah Suri were instrumental in the liberation of the people, and that liberation formed the basis of Akbar's success. Obviously, the perpetuation of the Mughal rule over such an extensive area, and for such a long time, owes itself very much to this. And interestingly, the Mughal rule is also an example for the opposite effect. Under the later kings of the Mughal dynasty (especially Aurangzeb), many of the reforms of Akbar's times were rolled back. And it led to the degradation of the status of the people, and this, in turn, formed an important cause for the downfall of the empire.

In fact, this seems to be the truth in most successful empires, maybe all—the liberation of the common man leading to stability and prosperity.

Summarizing the third idea, we can say that a visit to Uttaramerur shows that there is the possibility of a little republic in each village of India. When the onus is on the villagers themselves, they can rise up to meet relevant challenges. They can not only take care of themselves but also go on to provide resources of men and materials for the nation. All that is needed is a government that understands that this possibility exists, believes in it and takes upon itself the role of the external agency that will initiate and nourish such village republics.

There are other examples of self-rule villages like the one we have just considered. And there are important lessons that can be drawn from these. We should not do a copy-paste; rather, the past needs to be analyzed for underlying principles that can be applied universally, irrespective of the era. If some principles were valid at some time in the past, they should be relevant now too. Let us give some thought to such important principles that will guide us in finding solutions for the present-day situation.

These principles have to do with the characteristic relationship that needs to exist between the nation, state and village. These may be termed as the two cardinal principles for facilitating self-rule that need to be adopted when we take up the process of building freedom-giving institutions at the grassroots level.

The first cardinal principle: Following is a passage that dates back to the freedom struggle of India, sometime in the 1930s:

> *The old Panchayat rule in India may be said to be a somewhat imperfect but honest attempt in this (non-violent, rule-by-all) direction. But in the absence of any coordinating arrangement between the various panchayats that attempt must be regarded as unscientific, and inadequate for our present-day needs.*

> *Vinobha Bhave in Swaraj Shastra*
> *(which he dictated while in prison)*

The chapter in which this passage appears in his book deals with the classification of different kinds of administrations/rules as he sees them. However, this observation made by him helps us draw some important inferences in our context. First of all, he does admit to the existence of a panchayat system that was tuned to higher values of human living. But besides that, he mentions that there was an absence of a coordinating arrangement between the various panchayats. This, he says, made the process unscientific. His mentioning of this implies that

he felt the need for a coordinating agency to make the panchayat system scientific. A little thought shows how this is true.

A single panchayat, all by itself, is merely an outcome of an agreement for cooperation among a group of families living together—that they will run their togetherness in some pre-determined manner which they have agreed upon. If such a community is left isolated and is not influenced by people from outside, then this 'arrangement' will continuously evolve and change according to the personalities involved. There will not be permanence. The team can improve or degrade, and it will be difficult for those who are in the community to decide as to what needs to be done. In other words, if there is no benchmark with which it can be compared, it is free to take any shape and change wildly in both content and quality.

In fact, the concept of a panchayat really makes sense only when we set up a standard or a benchmark which can be followed by many local communities of a state or a nation. It must be designed in such a way that it will help both, the people of the village and the nation at large. It must be defined in terms of what must happen inside a community and what must happen between communities. In Mr. Vinobha Bhave's perception, such a process of scientific standardization did not exist in India as far as he knew, both from history and as far as he perceived in his surroundings.

Be that as it may, we are now aware that in various phases of Indian history, such standardization and some kind of coordination system between panchayats did exist. The rulers of many ancient kingdoms were responsible for ensuring that such coordination existed. The Uttaramerur inscription is proof of such kinds of standardization.

So then, a question arises as to why it was not in existence when Mr. Vinobha Bhave wrote in the 1930? In the 1930s, the colonial powers were in charge. They had been influencing the nation as rulers for more than a century and a half by then. Chances are that it must be something they had done

A fact known to politicians today is this: if one wants to kill a program initiated by a previous government, all one needs to do is stop all the funds flowing to that program. It dies its own death. Or take the example of the various sports in our country. Those that get sponsorship are able to survive; those that don't get any money don't survive. Take yet another example. Let's say there are two cricket federations fighting it out in India. Which would be the 'real' federation? Obviously, it will be the one that is 'recognized' by the International Cricket Council. One could check it out if desired. Let us say the ICC suddenly recognizes the rebel league as the real thing. In a matter of a few months, once people get the idea that the change is for keeps, all the 'star' players would shift to the new rebel league. The original federation would eventually disappear.

There are thousands of examples to show how any institution in public life gains endurance when it is 'recognized' and 'patronized'. Conversely, an institution gets automatically stifled, emasculated or even killed when patronage is withdrawn. The same applies to the panchayats too.

When the modern systems were established and consolidated in the administration of British India, patronage to traditional and indigenous systems was withdrawn. Therefore, by the time Mr. Vinobha Bhave was looking at the system, he was merely looking at the remains of a long-lost system that lay scattered around him after more than a century and a half of colonial rule. We shall see how the colonial system did this in great detail in the coming chapters, for it gives us an idea of how we can reset the clock and move forward. But for the moment, we shall take it at face value and say that patronage to the earlier panchayat system was withdrawn.

Therefore, if a panchayat system needs to succeed, there is a need for it to gain recognition and legitimacy. Politically, it needs to be respected for its decisions. Its judicial powers need to be recognized. It needs financial support. It needs economic freedom. Having ensured this, and only after having ensured this, can we even start evaluating the value of the panchayat system. Therefore,

we can briefly state the first of the cardinal principles as follows:

The panchayat system, which should be instituted first, should also be accorded recognition and patronage.

Fortunately, this process has been initiated post-independence through a long-drawn process ending in the 73rd and 74th amendments of the constitution, but it still needs to be taken to its logical conclusion.

The second cardinal principle: Let us take the example of McDonalds. Let's say that the first McDonalds fast food center, which came up in some town or city of the US, made a lot of money. The owner decided to expand into other cities and into the world, and so, he set up franchisees all over. He made a deal with each franchisee owner by which he got some regular amount of money and let them do business on his behalf. So, all he did was sit at home. And the money kept coming!

Well! Well! Are we not missing something? If that is all he did, then he would have become a pauper in no time! His clients, having visited McDonalds outlets in other parts of the town or in other cities, might not have liked what they ate there. And so, disgusted with the food, they would have possibly kept their distance from even the original outlet. Indeed, if the McDonalds franchisees in India decided to sell only dosas and nothing else, there would be nothing similar to the original outlet except for the name.

It does not make sense having a franchisee arrangement if there is no standard set up from a nerve center and if there is no regular monitoring from that nerve center. Only this standard setting coupled with monitoring will complete the system/organization. If McDonalds does this successfully, wherever any of its American patrons go, they will get to eat almost the same food. If the original food was perceived as good, then the franchisees would also be seen to be serving the same good food. The organization/company would grow and prosper. This is the story of all franchise-based companies all over the world.

This is a simple principle which modern companies use. It is not a new one though. The idea has been used for centuries in relation to the Indian system of panchayats. A wise ruler would let the panchayats operate freely within a set of clearly defined rules, and then, most importantly, he would come back to regularly check whether the panchayats were operating in tune with the scheme. In other words, he would audit the records and performance of the panchayats to check whether they were maintaining the standards he had set for them. He would naturally get feedback, and he would explore corrective measures to improve the system further. If everything was going as per his plan, then he would rate his governance a success.

This reasoning leads us to the second cardinal principle:

A panchayat system is complete only if it is subjected to regular and effective audits.

We desire various goals for the villages of India. Some of them can be listed as follows:

➤ All persons in the village must be treated equally in accordance to the merit of their own actions.

➤ No one must be deprived of what is lawfully his.

➤ Each one must get equal opportunity for studies.

➤ Rule of law must be upheld in the villages.

➤ No section of society defined by caste, sex, religion, race or age must be discriminated against.

➤ The village must have a development plan and work on it.

➤ Villages must meet their environment-related goals.

If these goals need to be achieved, then all of this has to be coded into the laws governing the village and enforced through time-bound audits. These audits need to be semester audits or, at the worst, annual audits.

All government systems at the taluka level need to have this audit mechanism as one of their prime responsibilities. At the taluka level, the government should have a proper reward and punishment mechanism to ensure that the village communities, through their panchayats, stick to the scheme of progress as broadly designed for the villages of the country.

In conclusion, we can say that when our goal is a grassroots-level system that is holistic and that targets excellence and when we seek something that is desirable for creating and sustaining freedom, it cannot be arrived at by merely initiating a panchayat system. The panchayat system is complete only when it is followed up with the two cardinal principles.

i) Grassroots-level institutions have to be given the requisite authority or sanction of law so that they can do their own thing. The higher authorities need to hold the hands of those working toward accomplishing their responsibilities at the lower levels. Local governments must be respected and patronized.

ii) In order to ensure compliance to rules and the constitution, arrangements need to be made so that their activities may be audited systematically and regularly.

These two principles need to be ensured if a dynamic grassroots-level process is to be sustained in India.

3.5 IDEA 5: A QUESTION TO VILLAGE CITIZENS: WHEN DOES ONE QUALIFY TO BE CALLED FREE?

Freedom has many connotations. It means something to a prisoner, something else to a spiritual person, something else to one who is struggling to get rid of a loan, still another thing for someone who is enslaved and something else for someone who has a bad boss. In the context of a nation, the term 'freedom' can also be seen through different perspectives. Let us check out some of the underlying principles.

Index 1 – The irresponsibility dimension of slavery: The story in a movie went something like this.

There was a certain retired teacher who was trying to get his pension released, and he was a deeply troubled man. It was a question of whether he should pay a little bribe to the man in the middle so that his papers could get through. Whether he was not willing to pay up or whether he did not have the means, he could not satisfy the official. The poor old man's papers were stuck, and he had already run many rounds of the concerned office.

Now, what is the solution to this problem? As the story unfolds, it is revealed that a student of this teacher happened to have become a minister. When the honorable minister got to know of it, he came down, like all Holly, Bolly, Molly and Kollywood heroes do, took the concerned official to task (filmi-style) and then, of course, the pension is released. And after some more melodrama, the audience goes clap, clap, clap…

What kind of solution is the storywriter offering in the context of this movie? Let us check it out. If it takes a minister to solve the pension problem of a retired teacher, it means that there should be ministers available for all retired teachers, just in case they encounter a similar problem. Or conversely, if we say that this particular minister should take care of everyone who is stuck for his pension, then it becomes a process of centralization of responsibility. Stretch that a little further, and we will have to assume that one prime minister should ultimately be responsible for everything—building schools, sweeping streets, setting right the drainages of cities and even getting pensions released. All this for a population of a billion plus people…

So, why, one may ask, is the prime minister not finally responsible for everything?

No! If freedom lies in the fact that we have our destinies in our own hands, is this loading of responsibility on the government the way out of our problems? 'The minister will solve our problems…' Is that not the wrong approach? The prime minister is surely responsible for his role in the government. But as far as the entire nation goes, he is as responsible for it as each one of us is.

If we, each one of us, have not taken charge of the problems which the people around us face, are we really free? When do we really say that a boy has grown into a man? When his body has grown big? When his brain has grown enough? When he is able to earn a livelihood for himself? Or when he takes up responsibility for the things around him?

It is in taking responsibility that one gets to be in charge of life.

Indeed, in the pension case, it is evident that only the minister was a free man. Ideally, those in the teacher's close vicinity, who have related duties in the capacity of administrators or citizens should have taken up responsibility. The local leaders, the head of the concerned department, the local citizen, the local representative of the ACB, the local policeman, the colleague of the concerned official—all of them could have done what it took to resolve the issue. Where is the need for a minister to come and interfere with things happening in a low-level pension office? A minister needs to be busy taking care of things at his level.

Moreover, he is also not letting the locals take up their responsibilities! If a minister is going to come down and do that work, it gets stamped as the minister's work/duty. When this is so, it is natural for the locals to feel that they are not responsible and that they are powerless. Each official feels that he is too little to handle it. He, therefore, may not even interfere, saying that it is not his business.

This is the habit the common citizen has been beaten into. He expects some high, powerful hand to come down from somewhere far and get things moving in his surroundings. When people do not take up responsibility for the things happening in their surroundings, are they really free? As a nation, then are we free?

Some spiritual masters point out that one must cultivate an expanding sense of responsibility. One must take responsibility for his actions, his relationships and for the things happening around him. This is a call to freedom from one's highest inner nature—to take up universal responsibility. This perspective carries a deep sense of freedom, and anyone who avoids it is slavish.

This, which we have dealt with, is the irresponsibility dimension of slavery. The truth is that most villages of India do not take up responsibility. They have been beaten down into thinking that it is all somebody else's responsibility. They have been taught to accuse someone else for the wrong that is happening in their village, for the things that they are missing out on. Based on this, is the average Indian citizen not slavish?

Index 2 – A feeling of being subjugated: The next index of slavery is the existence of a feeling of being subjugated—in slavery.

Take the example of holding strikes. It seems so easy. Whenever there is a problem, go on a strike. If this is a free country, is there a need to strike? A strike is actually the use of force or resistance so as not to allow the normal functioning of a society. It is about stalling or derailing a constructive process. It is a force used against another force. What is the other force? Is it not what the people perceive as the authority of government officials?

Now, is there a different way of looking at it? In Japan, there is a novel way of protesting. If employees find that the management is not doing something right and they wish to voice their protest, they will not stop working. They will work while wearing black badges. And they will refuse to take pay for the days on which they protested. This indicates great maturity and a sense of freedom on the part of the workers.

If, on the other hand, people think it is a dog-eat-dog world and that people need to twist each other's arms to make the other do their bidding, then it means that such minds see the world as consisting of masters and slaves. Such minds harbor a vision in which two groups of people, namely the management and the employees or the government and the citizens, are actually opponents or competitors for a single pie.

This means that the citizens actually think of themselves as slaves even when things are going normally in society. That is, they harbor the thought that they remain within the law because they have been beaten down into it. They might think that if they were actually free, they would want to do something else. This means that it is not the citizens' law. It is something which some external interest has imposed on the citizens. This is a sure sign of slavery.

Take the naxalites, for example. After all, they are also citizens of this nation. But look carefully at the way they are dealt with by the state. Naxalites have set themselves up as a force-of-reaction to what they see is the ruthlessness of the system, and both sides are fighting it out in kind. Their very existence as a reactionary force proves that they see no alternative except to fight force with force. That is, they see injustice and terror being forced on them; they see slavery being imposed on them. For them, the use of arms is an expression of their thirst for freedom.

Now, what is the freedom they really want?

Would they have felt a need for force if there was awareness in them that the state is not a ruthless enemy but rather an extension of themselves? Maybe their own government is not delivering and is making a lot of mistakes. Even that would have been acceptable to them… Instead, they see this system as their enemy that is out to enslave them. So then, is their perception that this is a slave country and that the government is an enslaving mechanism wrong?

What about Kashmir? Is it a free country? It is supposed to be freer than the rest of the nation because, after all, it is the only province in the union which is supposed to enjoy a 'special' status in the constitution. Just imagine—one notch above democracy! Now, there is a huge force being put in place to keep the peace there. Would a still worse status not befall other areas in the nation if something adverse were to happen there too? Take the Punjab experience for instance. Take the naxal areas, Nagaland, parts of Assam… The question is why the state is being seen as a foreign object trying to impose itself? This is not freedom. Conflict of this kind is an index of slavery, of something still wanting…

What about the poor tribals? There are pockets that experience starvation in the country. Such pockets experience the worst kind of exploitation at the hands of all kinds of people. They live not with love for the police but in terror of them. When naxalites become active in their areas, they hang in between the frying pan and the fire. A typical recent example was Buldana. Forest dwellers were simply driven out of the forest lands in which they were dwelling. Well, that is what the law permits. But then, where is the sensibility? Is our law that ruthless?

Take villagers, for instance. They form more than 60% of our population. Where do they stand in the scheme of society in the nation? God forbid! What happens if the poor villager lands up in the hands of the money-spinning variety of doctors and any of the unscrupulous ones among the lawyers? What happens if, for some unfortunate reasons, he cannot earn profits in his traditional occupation?

Without a doubt, all these examples show that there is a widespread experience of being subjugated under a law, a law that may not necessarily be seen as benevolent or as the citizens' law. A huge percentage of the population still feels this subjugation, and this is another dimension of slavery.

Index 3 – The question of rights: Let us start with the premise that a man is living in a free country if his rights are protected. That is how it is perceived in the scheme of human rights. The constitution of India lists certain fundamental rights which it assures to its citizens and others. We know that the legislature makes laws. The executive runs the nation or state according to those laws. And if something goes wrong, then the courts can be called to resolve matters. Therefore, if the citizen has rights, it means that the legislatures are supposed to be sensitive to the needs of the citizens. The executive is to be indirectly in the control of the citizens. The leaders, his representatives, are supposed to run the government. And the judiciary is supposed to ensure that the citizen gets his right when he goes to the courts asking for relief.

Now, is all this really available to the average citizen? The average Indian citizen effectively does not make his own laws. He hardly understands the thousands of laws that are made in his name. Second, he has hardly any control over even the government staff who is appointed to operate within his panchayat limits. He can do little about a bad doctor, an irregular teacher or a tyrannical policeman. He has virtually no control over the expenditure of his panchayat. Or to be more precise, his panchayat has virtually no money to spend as it likes. And for a dispute that he wants to settle, he needs to go all the way to the formal courts. In these courts, the processes are laborious, time-consuming (it takes the span of a generation, on an average, to settle an issue) and costly. God forbid if he lands in jail! He could stagnate there without trial for years. So, when we sum it up, he has a legislature that makes laws that are not according to his wishes… He has an executive that is actually not answerable to him… And he has a judiciary that is too costly and time-consuming for him…

The panchayat is ideally the best forum for citizens' self-expression. But experts agree that the panchayat is the most powerless institution created by the constitution of India. Therefore, what rights does the citizen really enjoy? In fact, even the panchayat is being used as a means to run things from above, to perpetuate the 'raj' from above. In such a scenario, what is the position of the villager's rights?

If he effectively does not have the legislature, executive and judiciary of his community on his side, is this freedom then?

Index 4 – The highest freedom:
Where the mind is without fear and the head is held high;
Where knowledge is free;
Where the world has not been broken up into fragments by narrow domestic walls…

Rabindranath Tagore

Is this a description of the freedom which the majority of Indians experience?

That passage from Rabindranath Tagore continues as follows:

… Where words come out from the depth of truth;

Where tireless striving stretches its arms towards perfection;

Where the clear stream of reason has not lost its way into the dreary desert sand of dead habit;

Where the mind is led forward by thee into ever-widening thought and action…

Into that heaven of freedom, my Father, let my country awake.

This part of the poem refers to the final freedom, the domain of wise men. It is that freedom which cannot be bought for money. It is the heaven of the artists. It is the nirvana of the sages. It is the zone of the sportsmen. It is the bliss of childhood. It is the life of the twice-born. It is the joy of dancing. It is the ecstasy of music. It is obtained by working inward into oneself, and in it is a freedom that transcends all castes, religions, labels. To know the secret of this knowledge is freedom from all bonds; it is supposed to be a delight that no thing or individual can take away. It is that which does not fear even death. It is a short circuit to heaven without having to deal with intermediaries. This is the final freedom.

Though this final freedom is not the subject of the present study, it is the inspiration for it. When a nation, a society, a community or a family does not yearn toward that highest freedom, can it be considered free?

To summarize:

1) When the people of a nation do not take up responsibility for the bad things happening in their surroundings, can we call it a free nation?

2) When people have a general feeling that they are being intimidated by the state and its machinery, are we really free?

3) When the citizen does not have control over his destiny even in the panchayats and when his human rights cannot be protected because the three arms of the state are ineffective and unresponsive, is the citizen free?

4) When there is no yearning for the highest freedom and when one is not in an environment that stretches him to touch his highest potential, can we call it freedom?

The answer to this predicament lies in tackling each of these weaknesses in the best manner we can. First of all, the citizens of the nation must take up responsibility. Today, the political arena is loaded with blame games, and everybody and everything can be blamed. Beginning from the Vedas, Buddha, Manu, Alexander, Chanakya, Muhammad of Ghazni, Babur and the British to Savarkar, Gandhi, Nehru and Godse… This is a form of intellectual slavery. Find a scapegoat so that we may shift blame onto someone or something, and in the bargain, do nothing about what has to be done. Such a blame game does not gel with the spirit of a forward-looking freedom. The question is: What needs to be done now?

Has the citizen learned to take up responsibility? Can we have a political ethos that reflects the citizen taking charge of what is happening around him? Next, having taken responsibility, the citizen must ensure that the state is an extension of himself. He must participate in the relevant processes and ensure that the system does not impose itself on any individual or community. He must exert control over the legislature, executive and judiciary in his immediate neighborhood and ensure that it is doing its job of protecting the rights of all the people in his village community. In this environment, the village community and its members must celebrate the heights of human spirit.

When all this happens, we can say that the nation has risen to freedom.

Anyway, the attitude of enslavement that exists is not the inherent character of the Indian civilization as some people claim it is. A brief look into the nation's history over the past two centuries will indicate that some unwanted changes happened. If these can be rectified, then a free nation can emerge and begin expressing itself. This can happen like it has happened several times in the past when distinguished leaders raised their respective kingdoms to freedom. In the next chapter, we shall take a look at the changes that happened during the enslaving colonial rule that led to the nation's degradation.

3.6 IDEA 6: CAN THE INDIAN ADMINISTRATION NURTURED IN SLAVERY NURTURE FREEDOM?

Foreign vs. native: In the beginning of the twentieth century, when Pandit Jawaharlal Nehru was studying at a college in England, he encountered a life-changing moment. He discovered that he was not a British citizen! Nehru found that his collegemates would not accept him as one of their own. Though India was part of the British Empire, he, an Indian, only enjoyed second-class citizenship.

To be fair to the leaders of the Indian independence struggle, they did give the colonial powers a chance. They were not against the rulers from the outset or right in the beginning. In fact, they thought of their rulers as 'our rulers', but it came as a rude shock when they realized that there was a strong sense of alienation.

The Indian National Congress came into existence in 1885. At that time, the people who formed the Congress essentially believed in the righteous potential of the British Empire. They came together with the intention that they would place before the rulers the concerns and needs of the Indian masses so that the rulers could take informed decisions. But soon, disillusionment grew. The moderates lost steam, and the extremists took over. The extremists were defined as extreme because they were very clear that they did not want the colonial rule to continue. Even the moderates' Home Rule Movement asked for autonomy.

This change was also seen in the bearing of Gandhiji. In the initial phase, he insisted that he had no problem if the British ruled over India, provided they ruled like ideal rulers. But in the end, in 1942, his call of 'Do or Die' and 'Quit India' indicated no faith whatsoever in the British right to rule over India. He wanted India to be left to its own means. The British could leave…

These are just examples to show that something inherent in the system compelled the very best Indians to change their views about the nature of the British Empire. Indeed, a close look at the colonial rule only leads to the conclusion that it was an 'alien' system. This part of their empire was a 'colony'. The Indians were the 'natives'—maybe a little better than 'slaves'. It was a matter of race, of education and of not being English and European. For example, when the empire grew in size in India, the number of indigenous British citizens also increased. The intermingling of races naturally took place. Formal marriages happened. Seeing this, there was an order from the crown that the officers were to take their women with them. This can be seen as an attempt of the crown to ensure the morality of the soldiers; on the other hand, it can also be seen as an attempt to keep the races from intermingling. There was this strong underbelly of differentiation that governed affairs in colonial India. The aim was not to come to India and settle down. It was not to make this a home. The rulers were on a trip to a 'foreign land', and they just wished to go back 'home' wealthy.

The aim of this discussion is not to get all Indians worked up and angry. It was how they, of that generation, lived their lives. The present generation has its choices to make, and it must be done with positivity. But it is important to recall these things because the negativity of the past was built into the institutions created at that time. This negativity continues to have an impact today, and we can change it. Aloofness can be replaced by the spirit of oneness.

Institution-building by the colonial masters: The rulers belonged to a small nation that was situated thousands of miles away. Those who came over to rule India were few in number, compared to the huge population of India. The geographical extent of India was also large. Now, if these few people had to hold on to the vast empire, there was a need to devise means to keep the local population under check. There was no question of them trying to empower the ordinary Indian; on the contrary, the rulers did everything to keep the indigenous population weak. And this was constantly in the back of their minds when they took actions in India and when they built up organizations and institutions in India.

Evidence for this can best be seen in the policy of education which was initiated by the rulers. There was an education system that existed in India before the advent of the rulers. That system was ignored. That system needed the protection and patronage of the rulers. However, the new rulers did not support it. It was, therefore, pushed into the background. A new system was introduced instead. This new system had the aim of 'producing a breed, Indian in blood and western in thinking and mannerisms'. The graduates of this system were employed in the British establishment in India.

The good part of this system was that it brought international education of the 'European' kind to India. And it did the same thing to a student that it did to a student in Europe. But it also created a group of Indians who stood between the rulers and the great mass of Indian citizens. The impact of this change continues in India today, long after independence has been achieved. And this impact is huge.

A very interesting lesson to be learned when traveling in nations like France, Switzerland and possibly in most other European nations as well is that the English-speaking have no great advantage in these nations. It is like a Marathi-speaking person traveling to Bengal or Gujarat. While communicating in these other European nations, the substance of the person, his personality, his mannerisms and his bearing matter a lot. The ability to speak English does not automatically mean an elevated status, like it does here in India. Though of course, there are advantages that arise out of knowing English. In other words, in India too, there is no need to conclude that everything non-English needs to be looked down with disdain. The rural Indian should be valued for his inherent qualities and behavior in a country like in Germany or France, even if he knows no English.

The negative way of looking at the vernacular has been put into our heads with the introduction of the modern system of education in India. Even seven decades after having gained independence, we have not broken free from this mind-set. Instead, we are stuck with the notion that an English-speaking person is naturally several notches higher than someone who speaks the vernacular.

There is an air of status in being educated. Even a fourth- or fifth-standard pass that has been churned out of the present system of education system thinks of himself as elevated in comparison to the illiterate native. It is a ploy to deny self-respect to the majority of the population of the country, which was deliberately included into the design when the new system of education was introduced in India.

Just as it has been done in the system of education, other aspects of life in the nation too have thus been affected. The military, judiciary, economy, religion, culture… Everything was subjected to this alienation. Even the manner in which Indians perceive their own history has been affected.

The true colors of the bureaucracy: Now, in the context of what we are considering, let us think about what happened when the bureaucratic system was set up in India. The system of administration that was set up by the rulers (they replaced the older system) also had the same flavor; the alien nature was infused into the administrative system as it was built up.

Would this system ensure stability? Yes, it would. But would it be people-empowering? Surely not… It is true that there were statesmen among those who actually built the system. It is true that they used the knowledge of administration that they carried from their nation. They did also use some aspects of the system that existed in India prior to their coming. Despite this truth, it was a logical outcome that they would tweak everything to meet the aims of a colonial power.

The steel frame (the bureaucratic setup) came into existence to hold up the British rule in a country that was considered 'foreign' to rulers. It was not constructed as a scaffolding to build a prosperous Indian subcontinent. The system that eventually emerged looked down upon the people and kept them emasculated rather than empowered.

Without going into the question of 'how can we say that?' at the moment, let us rest this argument by concluding the following point:

We know that the British thought of this land as a foreign country. The systems established were set up and fine-tuned to cater to an imposition rather than to reflect a nourishing partnership with the local population. The local systems of education and administration were literally displaced or, at best, left to survive on their own—without any official sponsorship.

The next question… Did the system that came into existence and held up a 150-year 'foreign' rule change when India got independence?

After independence, the highest level of government was reorganized. The colonial system went away, and a new system described in the constitution of India came into force. The holders of power were also Indians now. And these leaders were 'elected' into power by the people of India. However, below the constitutional authorities, in the middle and lower executive structures of the government, few changes of real substance were made.

For one thing, some responsibilities were transferred from the bureaucracy to other agencies. For example, some magisterial powers were transferred to judges. Also, three important functions were added to the bureaucracy. First, they became agencies to deliver various schemes pushed downwards from ministries. That is, the number of welfare measures they had to handle became large. Second, they were given the task of assisting in the election process. The bureaucracy is the arm of the government that becomes subject to the election commission in the holding of elections. And finally, they were given the task of assisting in the planning and development processes at the lower levels, chiefly through the panchayati raj institutions.

Therefore, at independence, the functions which the bureaucracy had to shoulder changed. However, in all these changes, the 'steel frame' was not taught to 'think' and 'feel' differently. There were modifications made to the content of responsibilities but not to the attitude/nature of responsibilities. Even today, the system retains its ruthlessness and alienation, though in a toned-down form. The best proof for it is in the way the police force is expected to deal with the citizen.

In Britain, children are encouraged to go to a friendly policeman and probably exchange a flower with him, if they fancy it. Why was that kind of understanding and sympathy not conceived in the relationship between the policemen and children of India?

A policeman should ideally carry the following attitude toward an offender: 'I understand you have done a mistake and therefore have been penalized by the system. I have nothing personal against you; I am merely doing my duty on behalf of the system and I shall do it to the best of my ability. I wish the best for you when you face the law, but the law you must face.'

The designers of the US policing system sought to inculcate this spirit in the police force of the United States. Proof for it lies in what the policeman has to do when he arrests someone. The policeman is expected to clearly state to the person being arrested that the person has the right to be silent and that what he says could be used against him in a court of law. This simple task is aimed at depersonalizing the event of the arrest. It is supposed to reflect that the law is the 'actor' here. A policeman need not have any 'extra' attitude toward a criminal. The offender is still a human being who is being put through the motions of the law.

It is the same spirit that is reflected in our Indian ethos which bears no ill-will to anyone and merely says, 'Let the individual bear the fruits of his own deeds…'

However, this is not the way it is being perceived in the present police force. The police force is not seen as an extension of any local community. Instead, it is perceived as an 'enforcing' agency that must intimidate the citizen and keep the average citizen in check. There is a sense of elitism, of looking down on the average Indian, of 'policing' him into submission and of getting people terrified into keeping with the wishes of the rulers of the land. This is a basic characteristic that has persisted in the police force since the colonial era. And the same sense can be experienced in some form or the other in the entire executive, legislative and judiciary arrangement in India.

In addition to the sense of alienation, there are other serious problems. One significant one is that the administrative structure remains subtly suspicious (which gets pronounced in certain areas like the naxal belts, for instance) and deeply wary of the indigenous people.

Yet another one is that it thinks of the indigenous people (who are not put through the formal education stream) as not worthy of being given responsibility, even over their own grassroots-level institutions!

All these are attributes that expose the remains of the erstwhile system, alive and hidden deep within the administration that exists today.

There is, therefore, a need to see that the entire bureaucratic setup is put through a filter to take away the negative aspects of alienation, disinterestedness, suspicion, weariness and disdain. Everything that has been constructed in the colonial era must be taken with a pinch of salt. There might have been even better things that a more indigenous rule might have done—over and above the good things the British rule did in India.

There once was a king who had five squabbling sons. He sent them to an old man and requested, 'Teach my sons to be united.' So, the sons went to the old man, and the old man handed over to them a bundle of twigs which were neatly tied up with a string. 'Could you break this for me with your bare hands?' he said, and the bundle was passed around. Each of them tried, and even the best of them couldn't break it. Then, he untied the string that held them together and gave a twig each to the sons. They broke it easily.

This story has an interesting symmetry to it. Looking at it from the sons' point of view, when the sons teamed up and split up the work, they achieved it easily. The other part of the symmetry is the view from the twigs' angle. As long as they were held together with the string, they were invincible. Both suggest that there are immense gains for being united. Another interesting angle to look at is that the person who separates the twigs by removing the string is an enemy of the twigs and the one who ties up the twigs together is a friend.

Therefore, those who make efforts to put the villages together as a team are friends of the villages and those who divide them into splintered groups are enemies. A united village has much to gain. The total extent of how much is possible is difficult to estimate. The wise say that when we talk about teams, one and one make eleven. A village that has teamed up can do incredible work, much more than the sum of the individual contributions of its members.

Consider a bus that is under repair and needs to be pushed. Just three persons, pushing at it, can make it move, provided they are pushing together according to a sensible plan and to the best of their abilities. And it is also possible that fifty people pushing at the same bus from all directions with all their energy cannot make it move. Similarly, a sports team, a bunch of ordinary players, working synchronized as a team, can even upset a team that has professional players who are individualistic and not synchronized. Anything that can put a team together

and make it work toward its wellbeing like a coordinating thought process, agency, idea or inspiration is what one must look out for.

On the ground, there are many examples of wonder villages which have teamed up and produced outstanding results. These villages have been usually led by inspirational leaders. And the results are there for us to see. An example is the village Kattanbhavi in Belgaum district. It has an inspirational grassroots-level leader by the name of Shivaji. If one stands on the hillock that lies on the way to the village, one can literally see the remarkable difference the village has made. The forest on the side of Kattanbhavi is green and full of trees while the same forest on the other side, adjoining the next village, is barren. The water table in Kattanbhavi has risen while it is depleting in the surrounding places.

Take Baba Amte's village for instance. It is a green oasis in the heart of a drought-prone land. Indeed, when a team works together, it can come up with wonders. Take another example of the REDS, a welfare organization working in Tumkur district of Karnataka independent of the government. They have set up what they call 'Dalit Panchayats' which team up the marginalized groups. It helps them mutually resolve their issues and support each other in growth. This movement has grown to cover hundreds of villages. It has grown so because the people themselves realize that in working with and through their teams, they are getting empowered.

But these and many like these are exceptions. We can count a mere few from among the seven lakh villages of the nation. Consider the following analogy. There is a huge barren land where seven lakh trees can grow. But most trees are not taller than bushes, and there are only a few tall trees standing up here and there. When we go close to each of these huge trees, we see an inspirational leader watering that particular tree daily.

Why is there no rain in this barren forest? Why is there no system where all the little trees are watered daily through pipelines and they all start growing into huge trees? Why is there no water released into the barren land from nearby dams and tanks?

What we are referring to here is the 'environment' in which the villages of India exist. The system of governance in the nation is not the kind that will pour water so that the stunted trees can grow to their original size. In fact, even where there are inspirational leaders, it looks like they have to struggle uphill. They have to fight against the system in order to water the tree and make it grow. Powerful people are either neutral or opposed to village members joining hands, making teams and addressing their own problems.

The government machinery is huge and has great capacity for action. When Anna Hazare and Ilango are doing such fine jobs in their respective villages, the government can do a lot of things to ensure that such work starts getting replicated everywhere. For, after all, what more does a government want than a village that has started taking care of itself and to which it need not give too much subsidies or spend on any development measures? Then, why do such villages still need to 'struggle'?

Instead, is it possible to make teams out of our villages? Are there ideas that can ensure that the political system, the system of governance, the national administration and the state administration start inspiring the villages to become teams and start delivering results? Indeed, there are such ideas, and we have seen some of the examples in ancient kingdoms in the last few chapters. Something similar should be possible now.

We need to go into this further. What is it about our national environment that does not allow the villages to flourish? The environment that exists is not one that wants to put people together into teams and empower and energize them. In the Chola period, the king 'wanted' the Uttaramerur team to work together. He 'made' them work together. In the present age, the political and government process splinters the village and makes them powerless. Let us look into this further in the next chapter.

We have seen that as time passes, a nation and its various institutions advance in a direction that matches the spirit and motivation of its leadership. A king tuned to niceness will try continuously to add nice things to his kingdom while one that is decided on being nasty will add nasty institutions to his kingdom.

If the purpose of a certain ruler is to be a 'terror' and benefit economically from that authority and if he relies on power and force to achieve this, he will try to keep the people weak. Whatever he does in his role as administrator and whatever institutions he tries to build will be such that they take away the capacity of resistance from the citizens. For that, the first thing he does is ensure that the citizens are not allowed to form teams because teams give incredible strength to common citizens. Any team that is nonetheless formed will be closely scrutinized, and people will be made to work against one another. Those institutions that make citizens strong will be discouraged. Those institutions that give citizens internal strength will be decried. What they cherish will be belittled if not ridiculed. Their team endeavors will not be given patronage.

Is this true about the system that we have today? Let us check.

The true strength of a nation lies in its culture (refer to *Towards the Kingdom of Heaven*, Bharitiya Vidya Bhavan, 2000, by the same author). If the culture is weak, there will be infighting, and in a matter of years or decades, that culture and its people will disappear. So, for a strong nation to exist, there must be a strong culture, and that culture needs to be nourished. This is done by appropriate patronization, at crucial places, so that the civilization can be sustained. One such aspect of a civilization which needs nourishment/patronization is the indigenous education system because the education system transfers culture down the generations. Removal of the indigenous education system serves to weaken indigenous culture and peoples.

If we do a reality check, how many of our institutions of education today are of indigenous origin? How many of them draw their inspiration from the traditions of learning that developed around Islam, the Vedas or the Buddhist, Jain and Sikh schools of learning that evolved at least several centuries ago? Are these alternatives recognized as legitimate institutions of learning?

There surely are such schools scattered across the nation. But are they considered mainstream?

Take the other example of indigenous industries. Indigenous industries have the ability to give strength to the people of a nation; a leader that seeks to weaken the potential for resistance will break the back of a nation by systematically finishing off the indigenous industries or by preventing new industries from being built. In addition, if he finds his own commercial interests threatened by the local industry, he will try to destroy it. This was actually done to Indian industries, rather ruthlessly too (like in the case of muslin where thumbs of the artisans were supposedly cut off).

In the process of trying to facilitate continued dominance, it is natural for an alien power to do certain things like the following:

i) The political institutions existing at the local level would lose recognition. In their place, a host of agents who are under the control of the alien power would obtain total control over the life of the people. This would enable these external powers to control the subject population through the so-created intermediaries.

ii) Indigenous economic institutions would be replaced by new ones that can help in changing the balance of power.

iii) The indigenous dispute resolution mechanisms would lose recognition. For every small quarrel, it would be obligatory to go to the higher levels for resolution of conflict. Such new courts might not be adequate in numbers and possibly be corrupt too. And to cap it all, erstwhile judicial practice would be declared clandestine or illegal.

iv) There would be no official declaration of responsibilities on the functionaries at the grassroots level. The representatives would not be expected to come together to tackle the problems of the people who live in the neighborhood.

All of these are realities of pre-independence India.

Ever since independence, the Indian industry has recovered to an extent. But the situation in rural India has still not changed. The remains of this build-up still continues to play a role in our nation today. For instance, the industrial backbone of rural India is as good as non-existent.

Therefore, to summarize Idea 8, we can say that the pre-existing systems were ignored or adversely molded and weakened in order to meet the requirements of an occupying force.

Now, is there evidence to show that this was done either deliberately or inadvertently to break the indigenous local communities? Can facts show that the degradation took place when new institutions were created?

Indeed, there is proof. At least in the aspect of rule at the panchayat level, there was a revolution of sorts that took place under the colonial rule. It weakened the Indian citizen remarkably. We shall take this up in the next chapter.

A look at Indian history between the years 1757 and 1793 AD is extremely useful. The happenings of this phase had a very significant impact on the future course of administration in India. This phase marked the beginning of the British takeover of the nation. The setting up of the steel frame, the judiciary, the armed forces and the police force began in this period. The subsequent growth of the empire and the coming of other arrangements like telecommunications, railways, education and even the formation of the nation followed this phase. But there was also a revolution of deep impact which took place in these thirty-five odd years. A process was initiated which eventually led to the near wipe-off of the grassroots-level movements.

The grassroots-level movement that existed earlier was very potent. It is said about ancient India that even when there were periods of political turmoil at the highest level, people enjoyed a certain degree of insulation from instability at the lower levels. That is, even when kings fought over each other's domains and even when one ruler was replaced by another from another clan, the people at the grassroots level continued to have an environment that was quite secure and insulated from such adverse happenings in the higher levels. Historians attribute this stability to the robustness of the processes that existed all along at that level. This stability took a direct hit when the colonial rule came into being. The freedom at the grassroots level was virtually lost, and it made the common Indian citizen highly vulnerable by stripping away the shield of the local team that protected him. Let us see how this happened.

In 1757, the East India Company, under Clive, won the Diwani rights of Bengal through its victory in the Battle of Plassey. Subsequently, a set of 'collectors' were appointed. They were possibly named 'collectors' because their primary duty was to collect tax, but they were to look after the complete administration of their respective districts. A comparison can be made of this arrangement with the system that existed earlier under the Mughals. The area of influence of the *subedars* of the Mughal rule coincided more or less with the area of influence of the new collectors.

In that earlier administrative setup, there were *zamindars* who reported to these Mughal subedars, and so it followed that there were zamindars under the collectors in the new colonial administration too. The zamindari system continued to be in vogue even up to the 1950s (it was subsequently dismantled through land reforms in free India). In Pakistan, the system exists even to this day.

Now, does it mean that the zamindari system that existed under the Mughals is the same that exists in Pakistan today? The answer is no. The character of the zamindari system changed color through the decades and centuries. The phase from 1757 to 1793 marked a period of total change. The zamindari system before and after this phase were same only in name; in content, it changed drastically.

Thirteen years after the British administration took over, there was a great famine in Bengal (1770). People died in hundreds of thousands. The accepted explanation for what happened subsequently goes something like this:

The British administration did not have enough manpower, and therefore, it was not able to effectively oversee the entire process of administration. There happened to be a nexus of corruption between the land-owning class and a group of unmonitored corrupt colonial officers. Through this corruption, great personal fortunes were made. A little of this fortune was built up at the cost of the rulers, but much more was made at the cost of the local population. The result was that the indigenous population was rapidly impoverished. The new set of land owners, who were introduced as an outcome of the administrative reforms (or deforms rather), were ruthless. They were only focused on their money and did not care to nourish the lands under them. So, the productivity of the land dropped and, when the weather was bad in one particular year, the impoverished population did not have the resilience to withstand it. This combination of natural disaster and bad administration thus resulted in the human catastrophe.

This disaster made the administration take action. Warren Hastings, the then governor-general, introduced a new system of five-yearly inspections and temporary tax farmers. This proved to be porous in that the tax could not be effectively collected. In addition to this, the situation on the ground did not change much. Therefore, on the advice of Cornwallis who came for a study in 1786, the East India Company court of directors first proposed a permanent settlement for Bengal. After subsequent debates and discussions, in 1790, the court of directors issued a ten-year settlement to the zamindars. And in 1793, the same was made permanent. This permanent settlement system was found more or less satisfactory from the point of view of the administrators, and so, a similar system was adopted even in some nations of Africa besides other parts of India.

A revolution of sorts: So, what was this change that really happened to the local citizens in this period?

In the system that existed earlier under the Mughal rule, the zamindar was not the real owner of land. A system of land ownership did exist, and it was overseen through indigenous laws. The zamindar had a huge house situated on a large estate, but only the estate was his. Beyond the estate, he had an area of influence in which his prime duty was to administer—to take care of the police, military and judicial responsibilities for that area. This administrative area/domain extended much beyond the limits of his estate. Beyond the limits of the estate, there were other citizens who held the rights to the land, and they paid tribute to the emperor through the zamindars. The zamindar therefore held authority on behalf of the rulers. Take for instance, the zamindari *adalats* (courts). As the name suggests, the zamindars were tasked with judicial responsibilities. And such power ensured that the people who lived in a zamindar's area of influence had somewhere to go to in order to seek justice. And the zamindar responded on behalf of the king. In other words, the zamindari system was more or less a grassroots-level arrangement meant for administrative responsibilities of all kinds.

The zamindars ideally catered to what can be called a 'good administration', and their success or failure was measured on the basis of how well they did this job. Whether it was maintaining law and order, resolving disputes or fighting crime, everything was taken care of. But most importantly, the success of this arrangement directly depended on the blessings and support of the crown. It also seems evident that they had a hands-off approach with respect to village communities and allowed villagers to administer themselves according to agreed standards.

It is up to students of history and public administration to study the details of this arrangement. Surely, by studying these, we will gain useful insights into how administration can bettered today. But our purpose is to understand the basic spirit of the changes that happened to this system and to see whether these changes were revolutionary in nature. For this, we shall concentrate on one important change that resulted in the transformation in that period. This change is a combination of three effects:

1) the change in the money-lending system
2) the change in the pattern of land-holding
3) the change in the authority of the zamindars

The change in laws related to borrowing and lending: The system of borrowing and lending that existed at that time had a peculiar feature that was different from what we have today; it consisted of a rule known as 'Daamdupat'. This notionally translates into 'twice the principal'. That is, let us consider that Person B has borrowed a fixed amount of X from Person A. Now, B starts paying back according to what they have agreed upon. In the process, as time passes, let us presume that B has paid back twice as much as X, which he had initially borrowed. If he pays back 2X, then the law of the land states that based on the Daamdupat principle, the loan is considered as repaid in full. This rule was enforced by the village-based system and overseen by the zamindar.

Following the Battle of Plassey, in four decades of British rule, the system was changed. A new system of banking, as it is in use today, was introduced. For the first time, people were confronted with endless loans based on simple and compound interest. Daamdupat did not receive the support of the new system. It lost its legal cover, which meant that there was no limit to repayment now.

When historians analyse this change, they say that the status of the money lender suddenly changed; before the system came, the money-lending class was subservient to the village administration. But with the new rules, the money-lending class started earning a lot of profits and became rich and powerful.

The rulers, as far as possible, adopted a policy of not interfering in the internal matters of the locals. So, they were not concerned that some people had become suddenly rich and that the power equations in the villages were changing.

It is true that the nation shifted to a more modern system of banking and that this was a good step. But it was as not simple and straightforward as that in its impact on the indigenous system. This change, coupled with the other changes, led to a dangerous combination.

The change in the pattern of land-holding – Permanent land settlement: We have seen earlier in the chapter how permanent land settlement came into force. In the pursuit of their interests, the rulers brought in land reforms. Through the various edicts pertaining to land ownership, which culminated in permanent settlement, the lands were finally transferred to the people who could 'buy' the rights. Taxes were collected from these 'owners', and in return, they were recognized as the owners of the lands. The owners of the lands, on their part, had to squeeze the farmers under their domain and bribe the higher officials who supervised them in order to survive. The corruption was eating into the profits of both the owners and the government itself. After permanent settlement was enforced, the rulers and land owners were able to enjoy some freedom from the corruption of the officials. After paying the dues to the government, the owners were left free for a considerable period of time, and the officials could not trouble them. The owners were free to make the most of the land and the farming class that was under their area of ownership.

So, when permanent settlement was imposed, the rich people became owners. Two things happened. First, ownership was 'settled' in certain owners' names. Second, traditional land holders were replaced by a new set of people who were not so familiar with the idea of holding and taking care of land.

The change in the authority of the zamindars: Under the new rule of the colonial masters, a new class 'Zamindars Mark II' came into existence. Unlike the earlier zamindars, the new ones did not have judicial, magisterial, military or police powers. Officially, they were only land holders. If they could exert some local authority on the indigenous people, it was their own lookout. Unlike the earlier rulers, the colonial masters did not give the zamindars the authority or approval to exert the powers which the earlier zamindars exerted. The 'ownership' gave them rights, and they could lawfully tax the people under them.

Combined effect of the three: The money lender who was once under the control of the local self-rule authorities, or panchayats, now broke free. He was not answerable to the local administration any more. He was accountable to the new laws.

Since he was rich, he bought the tax rights that were being offered in the new system. He had invested in order to get his rights, and so, he was interested in his returns. He took from the farmer who was tilling the land. Since he did not know the ways of the traditional land owner, he did not care to nourish the lands the way the erstwhile zamindars and land lords used to do. An element of irresponsibility crept into the administration. Earlier, the zamindar took up administrative responsibilities. Land owners also took up the responsibility of nourishing the land. In the new system, neither of this was present. Ultimately, the tillers of the soil had very little to survive on, and when the season failed, the disaster of 1770 took place.

Thirty-six years of total transformation: As seen above, the changes in the money-lending and land-holding rules led to the decay of the system of grassroots-level administration that existed earlier.

When we take stock of this and all the other things that happened in those thirty-six years—nearly two generations—we see that there was enough and more time to completely destroy the erstwhile system that existed. In the new arrangement, the local disputes were to be settled in courts. Complaints had to be lodged, and cases had to be filed. Any indigenous judicial mechanism that earlier existed or continued to exist at the grassroots level had no legal sanction. These were considered to be just some kind of 'local arrangement of the natives'.

Is that not how we refer to 'katta panchayats' today?

The earlier local arrangement for administration under the zamindari class was therefore replaced by a zamindari class that almost exclusively dealt with money. The modern system of administration thus took birth.

The inherent nature of the colonial rule process: So then, are we indulging in British-bashing? It is not necessarily so. It is not about a tribe of people and their wickedness. Rather, it is about a new system and how it survived and thrived in a 'foreign land'. The British venture in India was a business, and a business is only interested in making profits. It knows little about governance other than enough to manipulate kings and statesmen so that it can maximize its profits. It is the very character of a business that it wants to profit and that it wants that profit to sustain. The institution that took over the Diwani rights of Bengal was the East India Company, and it was a trade organization—a business. It was not the crown of England doing business. It was a business that was doing the work of the crown. So, giving due credit to the British individuals of merit and to the British culture that has its excellent points, we need to see that the machinery set up in the Indian subcontinent was not exactly the best that could be designed for India.

Then again, we have seen at length the attitude that was used when all the other systems were subsequently established in India. It is difficult to say whether the British did not have faith in the indigenous system, whether they were genuinely ignorant of it or whether they felt it was too good and had to be worked against. Whatever be the belief, the net result was that the indigenous system was never patronized. And the existing grassroots-level system got pushed toward a slow death.

In 1857, when the first rising happened, it was already ninety years since the Battle of Plassey. Almost all of India was now under colonial rule. The new systems of administration, education and the judiciary had been established across the subcontinent by this time. And for another ninety years after that, the Indian probably had no idea of what it was to have a legal, indigenous, local self-government.

In this phase, untold misery was wrought on the farmers. For instance, there was the case in the late nineteenth and early twentieth century where, in order to maximize their profits, the zamindars forced the farmers to grow cash crops even though it resulted in the loss of the land's fertility. Indigo plantation in particular created a lot of misery for farmers in the early twentieth century.

Consider a poor farmer who is in dispute over a piece of land with his neighbor. The 'official' or 'recognized' starting point for seeking relief is the second-class judge operating at the taluka level to whom he needs to go through a lawyer. The lawyer would be able to deliver the goods effectively most of the times only if he were talented. This fact makes the farmer's right to obtain justice subject to the condition that he should have the money to buy the services of a talented lawyer. The whole thing is so cumbersome that one would rather let things be.

So, the farmer of that day was taxed to the maximum. He had no system of law and justice that he could fall back on which was within his means. Under such circumstances, where was the chance that the farmer could rise above subsistence? He was just looking for survival, and there was no question of dreaming of systems that would give him freedom and self-rule.

Has the system been corrected ever since? No! It has not been reset.

No real sense of freedom and self-rule exists even today. There is no worthy administration within his reach which the village dweller can call as self-rule. It is the power wielders who rule the roost. A village citizen is just about expected to take care of his family and his work. Those that get into positions of power, on the other hand, 'enjoy' power.

Now, that would imply that there is a possibility of something better which the villager could have even today. Does such a thing exist?

We have considered the ideas of judicial systems from native Britain, Chanakya, Sher Shah Suri and Uttaramerur. In fact, we have seen that some undoing of the indigenous system happened at the start of the British rule in India. All of them serve to show that there are indeed opportunities. It is how we decide to apply them that will make the difference. And the difference can be truly substantial.

Section IV

Tackling the Forces That Can Impede

In Section III of this part of the book, we have considered ideas that indicate that there is a strong case for reorganization at the level of the grassroots. The teams of grassroots-India have been disenfranchised. There is great scope for reform and positive action.

We have seen in Section II that the villages have their work cut out for themselves. We shall also see in Section V how external agencies have a lot of scope for action and how, if well directed, they can truly facilitate transition to the second freedom. But before we get to that, we need to consider certain enemies of freedom that need to be sorted out.

These negative forces are basically attitudes which the concerned people hold in their minds. We can call these as mental blocks. Those who want to facilitate a journey to freedom must be aware of these and also of how to tackle them. The best part is that awareness of the play of these negative forces itself is a big cure. We shall call them 'the four enemies of freedom'.

These enemies of freedom need to be listed out because the fight against them must be systematic and well-considered. If these enemies are enumerated, then those intending reform can team up and act in unison when confronting these adversities.

The administration in India is deeply centralized. A minister at Delhi even decides who should get a petrol bunk and who should not. It is not uncommon for ministers and MPs to decide who will be the person to get a house or a well or a toilet as part of the government's gifts. It may seem to be a normal thing because it happens every day, but if one imagines the scale of things correctly, one will see how ridiculous it is. Let's say there are 130 crore people in India and about 800 MPs. This means that there are around sixteen lakh people for each MP to take care of. If we fill these people into buses of fifty seats each, then we will need a total of around 32,500 buses. If each bus is seven meters long, and if the buses are made to stand one behind the other, then these buses will cover a distance of more than two hundred and twenty kilometers. This is more than the distance from Pune to Mumbai or almost as much as from Delhi to Agra. If an MP is busy with giving toilets to people from ten of those buses every day, then he will need nearly 10 years to visit all the buses. You can see that by thus indulging in individual matters, he is following a system that is not really concerned with the problems of the nation. Rather, he is only taking care of those people who come into close contact with him.

Truly speaking, this process of centralization takes place at other levels as well. Power hoarders do not want to let authority and power exist at lower levels. Authority is not devolved from the center down to the district level and from the state to the taluka level. Even if it is out of a mistaken sense of duty, MPs and MLAs want to take care of everything. It becomes so top-centric that nothing is initiated at the grassroots level. And if, by chance, someone takes some initiative in a village, then it is considered a very surprising thing or a highly noble thing.

For example, a group of villagers built a railway platform for themselves because they wanted the train to stop near their village. It became national news. Why should this be considered as news? The whole picture is wrong. Citizens are supposed to help themselves! They have to solve their own problems. If there is a problem in India, we don't expect America to come and solve it for us. Similarly, if there is a problem in a village, then the members of the village are the ones who should take responsibility for it. At least, the members of the village should consider themselves as the ones responsible for taking the first steps to solve that problem!

As for a minister, he thinks that he is a 'benevolent benefactor'; rather, he believes that every person who comes to occupy a minister's position should be a benevolent benefactor. In his mind, he holds a strong belief that most of those who dwell in the villages in the country are incapable of solving the problems they face. In fact, he thinks that they cannot even understand what problems they face. So, he believes that he has to 'do' things for them.

We need to pause here and take into consideration the complete picture of the nation. When we think of the government as a whole, is it not too heavy a load on too few a people?

The responsibilities a citizen must take up in society can be divided into three parts. The first one is to take care of himself and his family. The next is for him to participate in a profession of his choice so that, in the process, he may contribute to society indirectly even if he thinks he is looking after his own interests. The third set of responsibilities concerns the work that must be done for the team that constitutes his community. For the community to achieve its aims, there should be people contributing in the team effort…

Imagine, for example, that there are a hundred people living together. Is it right to tell ninety-eight people that all they must do is take care of themselves and do some 'job' that is on offer in society and that they have no role in taking care of the 'team' of hundred people? Can we put the responsibility on merely two of them to 'serve' the team on behalf of all the others?

What good is there in the idea of depending on two crore people hired by the governments at all levels (there are around two crore government employees in India) to take care of about 130 crore people? That stands for a worker to beneficiary ratio of about 2:100. It is actually absurd. And the worst part is that most of those who fall in this two percentage are ultimately involved in taking care of themselves and their families too. They merely do their 'government job'. Only a few people like some outstanding soldiers, policemen, statesmen, bureaucrats and genuinely service-minded professionals rise above the mundane.

The question we must ask is whether it should be the responsibility of the government or the villages themselves to take care of the six lakh plus villages of India?

The present kind of setup is highly inefficient in its tapping of human potential. Deep analysis also shows that the politico-bureaucratic arrangement is corruption-prone. It is detrimental to excellence, and it is also spiritually unsound. We also saw in one of the chapters in the previous section that it is a grave mistake to think on the lines of a society that is built up by pushing the responsibility onto the government. Even within the government, the responsibility is pushed up the pyramid and even beyond.

There are two causes for this kind of approach existing in India.

The first is that the leaders have no other way. This is the way it has always been. This is the way it was transferred down to them by the earlier leadership. They have not figured out that something like the Uttaramerur solution is possible and that villages can shoulder much of their own responsibility. So, they continue to play their 'generous' parts as if only they are responsible for doing everything for the people down under. They have no idea that, in their magnanimous approach, they are doing great harm.

This second cause for taking a centralized approach is a systemic problem. The party system and the political arrangements around political candidates, at all levels, require workers. How are these workers to be rewarded for their services? If this direct intervention of ministers does not exist, how will political parties be able to sustain the huge workforce that is required? The system allows power wielders to do small favors to these followers and to those who give political donations. Such arrangements, of taking care of small things, also enable the 'leaders' to collect cuts/commissions. This income is vital to meet the expenditures for the next elections. How can power be sustained in the hands of politicians without the resources that are needed to win elections? Therefore, since this system of 'centralization' is favorable to the people in power, there is a strong wish from these power wielders to keep the system as it is. Though this is the root source of corruption in the society of today, even the well-meaning among the politicians are pressurized to resist any reforms in this matter.

If centralization gives power and if decentralization threatens the roots of their own existence and their continuance in power, why would the leaders want to go for decentralization? This, therefore, is the second aspect of the first enemy.

Summarizing the two, we can say that leaders think they have to play the role of 'magnificent benefactors', and hence, they want to sustain a centralized system to deliver their goods.

Therefore, the first enemy lies in the attitude of leadership, in leadership thinking of it as benevolent and the villagers as incapable. This translates to its need to keep things in the existing status quo because centralization assists in its perpetuation. We can term this enemy as the 'benevolence of (ignorant) kings'.

Fighting the first enemy: The reader is cautioned to objectively consider the secular wisdom contained in what follows. The idea has the potential to give the patient pursuer of truth a rewarding insight. The passage that is being referred to below appears as a question and an answer from an ancient text originally written in Sanskrit.

The question is this: 'Who is the greatest benefactor?'

Let's not get to the answer directly. Instead, let's pause for a moment and ponder over it. Who indeed is the greatest benefactor?

A mother? After all, she brings her baby into the world and does so much for a person. What about the father? He can make a great difference to an individual too. Then, we have the king. Indeed, why not the king? He is the one who can have the widest impact and give the costliest of gifts. We can also think of scholarly men. People who benefit from such as these gain tremendously and develop the skills to live better lives, so scholars can be the greatest benefactors. And again, as of today, we can possibly rate either Mother Theresa, the president of the United States, the secretary general of the United Nations or even the Bill Gates Foundation as the greatest benefactor. Maybe, the Pope… We can easily come out with a poll and find out what the people have to say. But what was the answer suggested in the scriptures?

'Dharma!'

This is taken from the *Prashnottara Ratna Malika* authored by the renowned Adi Shankara.

Dharma? How can it be dharma? And what is dharma in the first place? The interesting part is that this aspect of dharma—that it is the highest benefactor—helps in understanding it better.

It is similar to the 'rule of law'. The difference being that while we speak of the rule of law, it is the constitution of a nation that is paramount. But in the case of dharma, it is the common soul in each of us that is paramount. If one plays his role in society for and on behalf of the constitution of India, then he is supposed to be maintaining the rule of law. If he does his part for humanity, for the common soul, for God, for (the True) Allah—in a system that is designed according to the wishes of that Supreme Power—then he is upholding dharma.

Without getting too preoccupied with the spiritual part, we can easily take the digestible or simplified version of it, which would be this: 'The greatest benefactor is the rule of law.'

Is that true? Well, at least, the western world believes in it. Democracy swears by it.

Come to think of it, when there is rule of law, the ill-effects of its violation are not there. So, if the law is designed appropriately and if the law itself provides for fine-tuning to make it even better so as to allow for adaptation with the changing times, then every citizen would indeed get the best that is practically possible. He would not have to plead before any individual. All he has to do is his 'duty' in the 'rule of law', and the law will take care of him, his family and his interests.

The concept of *farz* that is common in the Hindi heartland has shades of this idea. When everyone does his duty or farz—a duty that has been designated on the basis of the established constitution of the society and the highest principles—then that is the highest which a man can do. The rule of law will automatically come into play, and each individual will get his due.

Therefore, the greatest benefactor for Indians today is the rule of law that is contained and symbolized in the Indian constitution! From the constitution springs all our laws. It represents the highest aspiration of the people of the subcontinent. It represents a pursuit of collecting the best from all the worldly constitutions in order to get the best that Indians could possibly ask for.

Therefore, we say that it is the constitution of India which is the doer—the benefactor—the thing that gives generously to all Indians and others. As for the individual-minded 'leader', when he takes it upon himself instead and when he starts to think and act as if he is the giver, the doer and the benefactor, he has to be treated with the greatest of suspicion.

Such a person is either ignorant or is a thief who has his own agenda. If he does not want your money, your loyalty or your votes, then he wants, at the very least, your appreciation which he would like to buy using the power at his disposal.

On the other hand, a person who works to uphold a system of rule of law is the real hero. When we thus separate the thieves from the heroes, the first of the enemies is automatically defeated.

We can take up here the case of the minister who resolved his teacher's pension issue. When a personal problem is taken to genuine ministers, they will use that problem to generalize the situation. They will look into the system for faults and think of establishing a system so that others in the same predicament will receive justice. So, all retired teachers and further still, all retired personnel will receive justice.

Therefore, what we need now is leaders who will uphold the rule of law, who will uphold dharma, who will keep their farz above everything and who will work toward establishing a system that is responsive to problems. They should not be leaders who project their individual interventions as solutions. Hollywood and Bollywood solutions of heroes single-handedly bashing up villains won't work.

There is only one way to tackle this enemy. The leader must be made to understand the difference and must play his part in the rule of law rather than feel the strong urge to interfere personally and try to be benevolent.

In the same way, people should learn to recognize and appreciate the upholders of the rule of law. They must also understand what 'dignity of labor' is. They should realize that 'how' they serve and not 'where' they serve is important. They must know that they work for the same rule of law and that they are therefore equal to everyone else who does the same.

A true leader is therefore one who sets an example in upholding the rule of law. This is the central theme of our Indian epics. This is the heart of the Indian ethos: upholding dharma. Defeat the first enemy by stressing on the upholding of dharma, of the system, of the rule of law.

This enemy is even bigger than the first, and it complements it. Hammered into the present system, the Indian citizen does not easily think in unique ways other than being 'slavish'.

The colonial legacy has ensured that there are no demands made on the average Indian citizen in the political arena. For more than two centuries, he has had a very limited official role in the village government. He was expected to do little more than work for himself, earn money and take care of his family. He used his spare time, at worst, to get drunk or, at best, to nurture a village sports team, do some work for the temples, chat with his many friends or enjoy life in other usual ways.

There are examples of politically productive individuals too, those who go beyond their homes and do what is needed for their villages, state and nation in the areas of politics and governance. They fall in two categories. One set becomes the instrument of the state, and having taken official positions, they help in the continuation of the raj. The other kind act from an enlightened standpoint, and whether they are office bearers or merely citizens, they genuinely participate in improving the government of the village. However, these people are considered as the exception and not the norm. The official position of the Indian system is that citizens have no effective role to play in the political arrangement in the village—except for casting votes and playing some supportive role in the criminal law (also, only a rare few are aware of this latter part). A list of duties has also been added to the constitution by an amendment, but it has not served to transform the attitude of the average citizen.

The challenges confronting the village in which the citizen lives are not directly placed on the citizen's shoulders. Instead, every government has promised the villagers that 'the government will take care' of their problems. So, they tell them to 'just vote'. This approach has been common in the Indian system ever since the Indians took control of the government in the wake of independence.

The belief that villagers are incapable: When the Indian parliament came into existence, it was made up of a special class of people. It represented the English-educated gentry, foreign returns, lawyers, Ph.D holders and the tallest leaders of the freedom struggle. And in comparison to them, the poor, illiterate villagers were nothing. They were 'native' Indians who were yet to be educated. It was difficult to trust them to do something in politics.

Just before we got independence, the then prime minister of Britain, Winston Churchill, went so far as to say that the barbarians (Indians) would be killing each other if the British left. He did not believe that the Indians had the cultural strength or the knowledge and understanding to handle something as complex as the administration of India. The Indian leadership, which took over from the British, had a better view of the indigenous Indian, but apparently, they too thought on similar lines about the village dweller. They said that if the illiterate masses were given the power to run their communities, some of them could be nasty toward their fellowmen and end up harming each other. So, through the constituent assembly and the parliament, they built a system which could only think in terms of 'doing for the villagers' rather than that the 'villagers could do things for themselves'.

In fact, at that time, there was even a debate as to whether the illiterate commoner should be given the right to vote! When this was the kind of faith the leadership had in the capabilities of the villagers, the villagers too did not expect much out of themselves. When the leaders thought little of the common citizens and when the common citizens did not think much of themselves, there was no chance of setting up self-governing communities at the grassroots level.

People have sometimes risen with the help of the workforce of some NGOs and excellent grassroots-level leaders. They have demonstrated that they can take on responsibility for themselves. But this has always been considered as something abnormal. More often than not, when the leadership that put them on their feet goes away, the people go back to where they started, thinking little of themselves all over again.

Villages left leaderless: The system has another peculiar characteristic of taking away village leadership. A village can rise up to shoulder its responsibilities only if it has leaders from among its citizens. But such leaders disappear in no time. And there is a cause for this that comes from the political system.

No sooner do leaders rise and assert themselves, and make their presence felt, political parties reach out to them and suck them into their fold. Every such grassroots-level leader gets a cake that matches the size of his ability. The younger village leaders become the grassroots-level workers of the political parties, and the bigger leaders get bigger positions in the political hierarchy. While this induction suddenly gives the leaders reach, recognition, visibility, power and possibly money, the village itself loses a leader who can represent the village as one unit. This is because the village leader begins to speak the language of one of the opposing political parties.

The result of this kind of sponging out of the leadership is that it brings to an end the initiatives of village teams. Village teams more or less disappear in no time. Once the village community initiatives are gone, the members fall back to the original routine of dependence on outside forces. The village that cannot be a team cannot take up responsibility. The village again starts waiting for goodies to fall from above. This time, the route through which those goodies come will be the new representatives of the political parties who are from their own village.

New players, old raj: After the 73rd and 74th amendments to the constitution, a new system was indeed brought in. But even in this, the old feeling of incompetence continues to exist in the citizens. The new system is not a self-rule; it is still a 'rule' by the panchayat. These elected people, though they belong to the village, mostly become mere agents for external forces. The old raj remains effective. Power flows from above. People retain the same old attitudes of 'I-am-not-responsible-the-panchayat-is' and 'I-am-incapable-and-dependent'. The newly elected people merely become the channels through which such help is asked for from the powerful people and the institutions existing outside the village.

It takes rare grit and determination for those who are elected to become real expressions of the strength of village autonomy. Again, those who thus successfully break the mold are considered 'special people', 'different leaders' or 'great leaders'. Where such leaders are missing, the village is unable to assert either its autonomy or its team spirit. The slavish mentality of the citizens thus continues to persist even though the new panchayati raj institutions have come into existence.

Perpetuation of a slavish mentality: Ideally, with the nation becoming free, the citizens should have started developing a responsible and self-dependent attitude. However, the 'dependent' mind-set has continued even after independence was won. To understand why this is so, we need to go back to the times when the nation was born.

Gandhiji had just passed away. At that time, the people of the nation were caught in a dilemma between the leaders who were 'non-political Gandhians' and the 'political Gandhians' who, in turn, were the political face of the freedom struggle. These political leaders had now taken up to wielding power at the center.

Pandit Nehru was the heir apparent, and he was walking the path of centralized progress. He was working on centralized planning and on building monuments that were to be the temples of free India. He was placing faith in his parliament to deliver the goods. Needless to say, that dimension of progress was necessary at that time. But there was a lacuna on another side. He never walked a path on which the free common Indian citizen could walk.

With Gandhiji, it was different. If Gandhiji defied the salt law, the common man also defied the salt law. If Gandhiji burned foreign clothes, the common man also burned foreign clothes. If Gandhiji took to spinning *khadi*, the common man also did the same in his own way. Following these lines, the post-Gandhi non-political Gandhian leaders were laying out a path which the common citizens could follow, but they were working almost unnoticed at the grassroots-level. The common man did not follow and do the work of these non-political

Gandhians. Besides this, there was no burning issue or storm or a visible common enemy that could give a feeling of a want of revolution. There was no charged-up atmosphere in which the average Indian citizen could get spurred on to action. The visibility was with the political Gandhians. They could see Pandit Nehru, but they could not follow him. Nehru went on to do the job of a prime minister, and people did not have a role like the prime minister's where they could work like Nehru. So, the masses kept themselves to the task of earning their bread and butter while it was left to the leaders to 'do' things for them.

The Indian leadership at that stage merely 'encouraged' the citizens to work for their villages. That leadership became the boss of the government mechanism. It took on the task of 'commanding' the bureaucracy and of inspiring the government servants to do a good job. It was inspiring them to 'serve' the citizens of the nation. People were hired and put to work in the villages as development officers. But such an arrangement only went on to confirm the belief that the village citizens were not capable of shouldering responsibilities. This was not the village taking care of its own welfare. This was just an arm of the government trying to help the villages.

The vision of Gandhiji was lost somewhere in all of this. And even after the formation of panchayats, the Gandhian spirit could not be incorporated into the thinking of the average citizen. The common man never got into doing things in his village like Gandhiji expected of him.

This ignorance of the villager is the second enemy of the spirit of freedom. The villager does not realize that he has a responsibility toward his community! He is not even aware that he has, in his person, the capacity to take on such responsibilities.

Thus, the second enemy is the slavish attitude of the common citizen. In this, he does not realize that he is answerable for the success of his village. He holds the belief that he is incapable and clings on to the hope that some Bollywood-type hero will come down and solve the problems he sees around him. We can therefore define this enemy as citizens with low political self-esteem and an underdeveloped sense of political responsibility.

Fighting the second enemy: An anonymous passage from the ancient Indian scriptures helps to look at things differently.

A fool is respected in his home. A king is respected in his kingdom. A wise man is respected by all men and for all time.

According to this author, every citizen has a role to play in society. He who merely restricts himself to his home, satisfying his own limited needs, is supposed to be a fool! (In Hinduism, it is referred to as an outcome of ignorance.) It is a duty enjoined on humans by their spiritual nature that they at least be kings in the sense that they think of and work for their village, taluka, state, nation, company or the world at large—anywhere where they can take up some responsibility for others. Even above this is the sense of universality. Citizens are asked to rise above their individualities and above the tribe they belong to and enter the domain of the wise, where they attain oneness with all of humanity—of the past, present and future. This is the highest that they can achieve. The best of men are supposed to act from this perspective.

The important point is to see that this is not about a clever or cunning ruler brainwashing his people into doing work for others. This is instead about the true spiritual nature of man. The belief is that this compulsion to be selfless and away from being self-aggrandizing comes from our deepest natures. This passage is therefore only a pointer showing which way is up and which way brings more contentment in life to human beings.

This, of course, is a debatable question—but it is a debate only for the modern world. In contrast, the best of ancient Indian wisdom has answered this question for itself and has made up its mind on this issue. The basic culture and traditions of the indigenous culture, which are still alive in the villages of India, teach the citizens to reach out beyond their personal interests.

Therefore, the villagers will do well in realizing that both the tradition into which they are born and their inherent natures compel them to start taking up responsibility for more than merely their families. How can they see wretchedness, child deaths, dowry deaths, ill health, persecution, discord, discrimination and so many ills in their immediate neighborhood and keep quiet about them?

In contrast, the system that has been in operation for more than two centuries now has always encouraged the common Indian citizen to ignore the happenings and remain uninvolved. But if freedom is what the nation seeks and if we Indians have to be masters of our own destinies, then we have to break free from this legacy of the colonial past. We need to take up our responsibilities.

The village citizens need to be part of the village team and meet the village's goals. It is usual for a village citizen to put his eight plus hours of work to take care of his living and his individual goals. But, in addition, he must also put in at least a half an hour or so of extra work each day which is focused on the welfare of the society around him. He must not expect anything in return for this contribution. Instead, it is an obligation that comes from being human, from being part of the local community and from being seekers of freedom. (One successful Indian village has made one hour of unpaid community service mandatory per week.)

If all the children in the village are not educated, it is the problem of the village citizen and his village team. If there is no adequate healthcare in the village, it is his problem. If the lower castes are not learning to live better lives, it is the entire village's problem. If the village cannot boast of even a single sports team which can make a mark somewhere outside, it is again the village's problem. If the nation has got excellent soldiers, doctors, engineers, renowned scientists, artists, sportspersons and outstanding leaders from that village, then the entire village has reason to be proud. A citizen can then find that he has played his role well in the process of grooming them.

When the common citizen understands the truth about his highest nature, takes up responsibility, goes that extra mile to facilitate his village team, begins to believe in himself and his team and acts on the challenges confronting the village, without waiting for a savior to arrive, the second enemy is defeated.

Man always coordinates his activities with his fellowmen through institutions. If institutions do not exist, then teams do not maximize their potential and members lose out on a lot of advantages.

The best example, again, could be the story of the needles associated with Adam Smith, which we considered earlier in the book. Break up the job. Create a department for molten iron, another for drawing wire, another for punching holes and curing and still another for polishing (that is probably the way the departments of production are broken up). And then, you have your production skyrocketing. Similarly, in a village, you should have a committee for education, another for accounts, another for judiciary, another for water bodies and so on. Each of these units has a role, a power and a responsibility. When the role, power and responsibility are officially recognized by the overall system, then the activities of each unit become 'legal'. The village citizen can use these units/institutions as tools to coordinate productive action and take on challenges in his neighborhood. Legal recognition is crucial. Since the units/institutions have the protection of the law of the land, they empower the village teams to solve their own problems.

What is the scenario in the villages of India? Do the villages of India have effective institutions?

Insufficient change at independence: Before independence, the bureaucrat was a ruthless and sometimes merciful hand of the British rule. He ruled; he judged; he maintained law and order; he showed mercy; he kept things under control… It was actually a one-man show, and everything moved to his tune. As we have already seen, the Indian leadership, after independence, went about expanding the bureaucracy into new areas of which the most important were welfare, planning and development. The new bureaucrat was tempered with the benevolence of the new political leadership. So, though he still continued to be a one-man show, the difference was that he was now under the command of the president of India rather than the queen of England. He was to act according to the rules laid down by the constitution. The constitution, in turn, bestowed certain fundamental rights on the citizens of India, and therefore, the bureaucrat had to protect those rights in everything he did.

Indeed, this shift in power from colonial rule to constitutional rule brought in great changes. If one takes a look at the Indian national data from 1900 to 2000, a remarkable change is seen happening at 1947. For example, the statistics and graphs pertaining to industries, infant mortality rates, level of education, population growth and gross domestic product (GDP) over the past century show an almost miraculous bend for the better at the point of independence. Therefore, independence marked a quantum leap toward prosperity for Indians.

And even though this remarkably positive transition happened at independence, an important dimension was missed out completely. If that lacuna had been addressed, it would probably have resulted not just in reform but rather in a quiet revolution. This pertains to village communities having the means to control their own destinies.

The omission of Gandhian concerns regarding decentralization in the constitution was criticized even at the time of its creation as being equivalent to a fraud committed on the people of India.

We have seen how the Indian leadership did not believe they could trust the common citizen with the power and authority to rule themselves. Belief in this naturally made them decide not to give form and structure to grassroots-level administrative institutions which could otherwise give power to the people. They opted to leave things simply as they were before independence after incorporating some small benevolent changes in the structure. They surely did address the issue of local self-government for the people, but they also ensured that the government was not compelled to implement this. People who know how the constitution is structured will know that Section IV is called the 'Directive Principles of State Policy'.

This section contains a description of how villages are to be administered, but one must also remember that everything that is contained in Section IV is only a 'Directive Principle' which can give guidance to the government to govern better, but governments cannot be forced to implement these guidelines.

Also, the bureaucratic arrangement which was called the 'steel frame' was left as is. At independence, the rulers of free India felt the need for its continuance so that they could ensure stability especially when the nation was taking baby steps. There was hardly any infrastructure worth its name, and partition was happening or had just happened. Surely, stability was a need of the hour at that time.

Putting the two together, we realize that villages were not given autonomy and that power continued to flow from the bureaucracy. This ensured that nothing really changed on the ground. The villages remained enslaved. Freedom merely meant that the villager had the right to choose his leaders. This chosen leader would, in turn, be put in charge of that 'steel frame'—a steel frame that was, at its core, the same old colonial arrangement. To sum it up, the grave mistake the leaders of free India committed was that they did not institute an effective self-rule process at the grassroots level.

> *... one could safely conclude that the Gandhian ideal of village Swaraj was not given proper attention in the major part of post-independent India. It is more surprising that the Constituent Assembly which primarily comprised freedom fighters and ardent followers of Mahatma Gandhi, failed to give due consideration to his concept (of gram swarajya).*
>
> *Panchayat Raj and Gandhi's Vision of Village Governance*
> *Ram Chandra Pradhan and Siby K. Joseph*
> *2013, Dialogue, Volume 15 No. 2*

Reforms that did not measure up: To correct the lacuna, the parliament and executive came up with many measures. Starting from the time of Pandit Nehru and ending with Mr. Narasimha Rao's time, various steps were taken with the aim of invigorating the villages. This ended in the two amendments to the constitution (73rd and 74th) that were made in the early 90s. Based on the changes introduced, various states of the nation framed relevant laws. But in all of this, even if the intentions were clean and well-meaning, the sentiment underlying the arrangements said, 'I am sorry, dear villager. I don't trust you to handle yourself or your own administration.' There is an exception though. In the communists-ruled state of Kerala (in the late 1960s), power was truly devolved, and the grassroots-level institutions did do remarkable work. But this interpretation of grassroots-level power had some inherent weaknesses, wherein it discouraged enterprise. But other than this, in the rest of the country, the result of the decentralization efforts is not very encouraging.

As of today, the villagers do not even have the freedom to choose for themselves whether they want a man or a woman as the elected leader or whether they want to elect an upper-caste person or a Dalit. It does not matter what their indigenous culture and traditions are. The villages of India are to be tight-fitted into the standards set on the basis of western notions of progress and prosperity. Equality of humans and equality of the sexes are defined in a way that is not in sync with the best of ideas in the Indian civilization. Citizens are encouraged to focus on their rights (and make demands for those rights) while, in contrast, their culture and traditions ask them to bother more about dharma (duty). The villager is made to confine himself to take care of his spouse, parents and children. He is not expected to contribute toward the governance-related matters around him. Very often, 'educated' people come to him and speak down to him saying that his traditions are barbaric and that his faith is little better than superstition.

Further, the government has kept the doctors, teachers and other village-level workers on its own payroll. The feeling is that such professionals cannot serve under the panchayats. It has not given the panchayats financial power in adequate measure. Panchayats have just a measly sum to spend. They cannot hire their own contractors. They can barely plan for their own progress, and they have no authority to adjudicate.

This can be contrasted with the example of the village republic of Uttaramerur. We have seen that the king's government there played the role of an auditor while the initiative was in the hands of the village. The systems which set up the grassroots-level administration in Uttaramerur literally told the villagers, 'Let me see if you are taking care of yourself properly.' The village had a certain 'government space' in which it could operate. It had established systems of accounting, elections, a taxation authority and committees for various tasks; it could use these institutions to tackle the problems it faced. The village was responsible for itself.

So, while the erstwhile system told the village to take care of themselves properly, the present system says, 'Okay! Relax! I am doing my best to help you.'

In the present system, the credit or discredit of having done something, therefore, lies in the hands of the government. The people do not have their own forums to do anything substantial. It can be said that people can only stand by the wayside and applaud or complain or struggle. The showpiece law-making and government-running institutions that have been created in the grassroots level are weak and have minimum influence and power. Grassroots-level judicial institutions are absent. Or in other words, there are no institutions available in order to sustain a grassroots-level movement. The absence of institutions that would otherwise constitute space for self-expression is the third enemy in the present setup.

There is a need to create that space. The village has to be the citizen's playground. The institutions in his village meant for village development need to make demands on his abilities. The institutions must target bringing prosperity to the community. Every member of the community must be obliged to play a constructive part. And even as the citizen gets accustomed to playing roles in the village-level organization, he must seek opportunities to serve in higher level forums operating at the taluka, district, state, national and international levels.

Therefore, this third enemy can be defined as the absence of grassroots-level institutions and, consequently, the absence of the average citizen's contributions to the overall system of governance of the nation.

There cannot be better proof for the existence of this enemy than the fact that all team initiatives at the grassroots level face uphill struggles. In a good nation, the political

setup, the NGOs, commercial interests and the bureaucracy should be delighted when someone from the grassroots level takes initiative. They should go all out to support him and ensure that his enthusiasm spreads to others around. They must also ensure that if a village has had a success story in self-emancipation, then the same model must spread to other villages and to other regions of the nation too. But more often than not, the situation is just the opposite; these forces become the opposition against which indigenous movements have to fight an uphill struggle. These forces, more often than not, prevent the existence of grassroots-level institutions, and if they do exist, they prevent them from being able to deliver their goods. These higher formations are not tasked to uphold such institutions. They are either inspired to discourage them or, at best, ignore them.

Fighting the third enemy: The nation needs grassroots-level institutions. The nation needs its citizens to have a spirit of wanting to have self-reliance. The nation needs a system that will encourage initiative in the villages and empower those that show responsibility.

The only way to achieve this is to change the present system by setting up meaningful units, institutions or forums at the lowest level and empowering them to play a constructive role in the grassroots-level dynamics.

In order to achieve this, the real work must happen at the lowest level of the state which interacts with the village republic—taluka level, block level or PURA level, whichever it may be. This level must be the main focus of efforts and can also be called the 'chief governance catalyzing unit'. The chief governance catalyzing unit must cater to three basic aims:

1) The catalyzing unit should have the ability to formalize instituted/setup processes in the villages that stimulate self-sufficiency, self-reliance and autonomy.

2) It should have the ability to take on an audit process to ensure that these institutions that are formalized in the villages are scrutinized and are functioning strictly in accordance with the word and spirit of the Indian constitution.

3) It should have the ability to apply corrective measures where things are not going according to the constitutional plan and also play a nourishing role where self-reliance is making its presence felt.

The principles on which the catalysis must focus on are as follows:

a) Ensure transparency.

b) Immense amount of knowhow must get pumped into the villages (not necessarily through schools).

c) Place great trust in the abilities of the villages.

d) Give enough scope to villages to have their own local laws in agreement with their social setup and traditions.

e) External agencies must primarily use the methods of suggestion, motivation, advice, encouragement, social reform and spiritual reform to achieve the objectives of village self-reliance.

f) Some degree of benevolent arm-twisting, compulsion or force can be strategically applied from outside, but only what is legally allowed. The constitution of India cannot be violated.

g) The process needs to be taken forward firmly in a step-wise manner but as quickly as possible, and it should (and can) be done only through the highest principles of management which the nation's rich past has to offer.

h) In each village, the members of the village must team up with NRVs.

i) NGOs must offer whatever help they can, but they must join in the harmony and always keep the bigger picture before them.

j) Political parties must alter their strategies so as to align with people's liberty and long-term goals.

k) The political leadership must seek to do its part in the rule of law, delighted to play its part in the process of change, with the highest goal in mind.

l) Intellectuals must dig out practical solutions from the knowledge resources at their command to create and fine-tune lasting institutions.

m) Servants in spirituality must ensure that people rise in service of humanity.

n) The bureaucracy must take full advantage of its vantage point in order to leave a mark of excellence in governing.

Only time will tell what kind of challenges emerge on the ground. But if the ideas that have been analyzed in this book are any indicator, overcoming the challenges should not be an issue. In conclusion, it can be said that if there are no government-'recognized' institutions functioning and empowered in the villages, then grassroots-level freedom is not possible. This is the third enemy. To remove this enemy, historical blunders need to be undone. Institutions that indicate self-reliance need to be built up. The injustice that was done to Gandhian thought must be undone now. Gandhiji wanted the villagers to control their own destinies, and this is not possible if they do not have powerful institutions.

We, the citizens of India, want our nation to experience true freedom even in the vast majority of rural poor. The alternate idea of trying to drive prosperity from above has had its chance. Seven decades is a long enough time for 'doer leaders' to have set up a strong edifice, and it is time to get into the details. What they have done is there for us to see, and it is limited by the fact that a team effort involving common citizens can produce far better results. Let it be the citizens' turn now. Give them the institutions, and they will surely rise.

The fourth enemy is divisive and judgmental thinking, which is capable of clouding the serene calmness in an individual. It does this by provoking a bloated ego in him that is agitated and judgmental and makes him prone to committing errors he eventually regrets.

In order to understand this, let us first reckon two of man's great strengths.

The first great strength:
The most powerful moments in the life of an individual are the quietest ones. This is a great secret which the ancient Indian wise men discovered and recorded in their scriptures to pass it down to their children.

If a person has played any game regularly or observed it carefully, he would know that the best performance on the field comes when the body is dynamic in its activity, the mind is deeply involved in excellence and the player has a feeling of serene calmness. Take artists, for example. The most beautiful of works they produce always come in the quietest hours when the mind, body, pencil, brush and paint flow majestically in some unexplained harmony.

Such moments of calmness come at the end of a prayer. Sportsmen enter the sports field with a prayer for this very reason. Most of the outstanding players do pray. As for the rest, they know how to be in a mood of serene focus without actually praying. Students of Indian classical performing arts are taught to handle their musical instruments with sacred respect; the instruments are seen as tools that help musicians find access to the highest. In fact, musicians and dancers who excel give themselves up, let go of their centers and humble themselves before their art. Only that—and nothing else—brings the best out of them. This prayerful bearing brings out the quietness in them. It puts their minds at peace, and those who are thus surrendered to the highest principle can wholeheartedly work in brilliance.

Take political leaders, for example. Even Hitler was originally an artist with some promise. He knew how to work with a calm mind even when he was giving hate speeches and agitating everyone around him. As Rudyard Kipling says, 'If you can keep your head when all about you are losing theirs and blaming it on you…' (an extract from the poem *If*)

Take Dr. Ambedkar, for example. He achieved great heights in life not because he had a mind which was agitated and easily made angry, but because, when people around him did wicked things, he could ignore them and work with diligence on his studies and at the tasks entrusted to him with a calm mind. The good results which he brought out through such brilliance made him capable of successfully captaining the team that drafted the constitution of India.

In this 'experience' of outstanding performers, there is true joy. The joy of music, the joy of dance and the joy of diligent sportsmanship all come only by a calm disposition and a mind tuned to excellence.

Why else would there be so much stress on meditation in spiritual practice? Why else is it found that those that take up meditation as a practice find their concentration improving and their successes multiplying? Why else would the noblest of families stress on the finer aspects of life, like music and dance, as an important component of their children's grooming?

Indeed, a calm mind is a great asset.

Another great strength: The togetherness a person shares with those around him is a great strength. We have seen in the introduction of this part of the book how teaming up with others can produce not only good but rather dramatic results. When people act according to a plan simultaneously, they can remove unnecessary clashes in functions. They can also benefit from 'specialized division of labor' and develop efficiency. Humans prosper when they complement each other in completing tasks as teams.

There is even more. The sharing that people have with others has even deeper significance. The basic unit of society, the family, is proof of the fact that man as a species has evolved into a social being. For man, life is not just about his material goals. He draws his contentment and satisfaction from friendships, peers, children and even acquaintances. Interestingly, he gains great satisfaction from doing work for all of them—mostly when he does so without expecting anything in return. Therefore, his ability to relate to others and build successful teams with others, in accordance with a gracious heart, is a great blessing. In this, he shares an 'inner connect' with the rest of humanity, and it is this that gives him that contentment and satisfaction in his relationships. This connect that he has with others is the other great strength.

To summarize, an internal calmness that bestows a terrific presence of mind (lotus eyes, so to say) along with excellence and the ability to connect at a deep level with those around are two strengths that go a long way in making a person's life meaningful and successful.

What is the fourth enemy and what does it do? The fourth enemy is therefore anything and everything that is capable of clouding that serene calmness in an individual by provoking a bloated ego that is agitated and judgmental. It works by depriving a person of both these key strengths we just discussed. It robs his calmness from him and makes him agitated and mediocre. And it builds walls between him and those close to him and deprives him of both team benefits and contentment.

This fourth enemy can be triggered in people by riling them up into anger. The modus operandi is to feed on people's fear, worry and security concerns. This is achieved by projecting before these intended victims the notion of an 'enemy'. One way provocateurs do this is by passing on real, half-truth or fictional information about a third party (person or group) and 'expose' the other's (third party's) evil-mindedness. But the provocateur must do this in such a way that it triggers adverse emotions and agitation in the listener.

The only thing the provocateur needs is 'other' people who have any label that is different from 'our' label—any label will do.

This is how it works. A member of Group A has come to speak to an audience, and he agitatedly puts forth so-called facts about the 'other', Group B (a third party).

Apparently, such speakers speak in full vigor only to a crowd in which the majority belong to their own group. Alternatively, such a person will speak to an audience in which the only ones that can create harm to him are from his supposed 'own' group.

Now, for those who are listening to A, if the listener is in the same group as the speaker, he can be roused into the 'hate' that 'all B's are bad'. And if the listener is from Group B, then a feeling of hatred is directed either at the speaker himself or at A's. In all these cases, the provocateur has won. He has successfully put the fourth enemy into the mind of the listener (both B and A). That is, success [sic] in his endeavors lies in the fact that he has generated thoughts of hate in both camps A and B.

Now that he has highlighted that the 'other' people are evil and have so-and-so evil designs, he takes the next step. He construes the angry reaction of his own people as a positive thing happening in 'our' 'brave' (he does not mean it; he is just stroking their egos), 'patriotic' and 'courageous' people. 'His' people are thus forced into taking action to resolve the 'issue'.

One must note the trickery here. These words like bravery, patriotic and courageous are not being said in the context of a courageous heart. This use of the word 'bravery' is about an attempt to forcefully elicit or provoke some headless action. In truth, the follower is being constrained to conform. He is being provoked on the basis of his loyalty to the 'label' to which he belongs. Such followers take action after compromising their peace of mind and stepping all over their relationships.

Therefore, the fourth enemy is a thief. The aim of the provocateur who plants the fourth enemy is to knock a listener off balance and steal from him. It could be the listener's loyalty which the speaker is after or his money, vote, muscle power, praise or merely the permission to add the victim's name to the list of his followers.

Maybe the provocateur has his own axe to grind against the 'enemy'. Maybe he is just confused. Or maybe he has someone's goose to cook and his own nest to feather. Whatever be his motive, he indulges in the act of knocking a follower off balance with the intention of making the follower's agitated mind do things that it would otherwise not do. An agitated mind dwells in the realm of the duality of 'tolerance and intolerance' and is deeply involved in measuring/judging people and being suspicious of them.

If this is so simple and straightforward, why is it that people still fall into this trap? The answer is that in such an instance, the attention of the victim is diverted. Consider this. If Bugs Bunny (second party, provocateur) wants Donald Duck (first party) to be angry with Mickey Mouse (third party), what would he do? He would go to Donald Duck, stroke his ego a bit by saying that he is a tough and no-nonsense fellow full of courage. Then, he would slowly turn Donald's attention to Mickey Mouse. And then, he would 'inform' him about all that Mickey Mouse is doing (or not doing), which are all 'designed' by Mickey Mouse to make Donald Duck a lame duck. When this is happening, Donald Duck's attention is not on Bugs Bunny. It is on Mickey Mouse. Bugs Bunny is pumping loads of misunderstanding in between Donald Duck and Mickey Mouse all along, but Donald Duck is too busy and angry and all riled up and thinking of 'bad' Mickey Mouse. Donald Duck fails to see what Bugs Bunny is doing.

Thus, the fourth enemy operates by piling up 'misunderstandings' in society and ensuring that people are so agitated that they cannot see the truth. And this is done in such a way that the one who plays the mischief appears to be a well-wisher and a friend.

Effect on people: Once an individual has a 'log' firmly covering his eyes, then his heart is hardened. As an individual, he loses his connect with other people. And this weakens him in two ways. First, he is working at cross purposes with the calmness of his mind. Therefore, his personal efficiency drops, and his team-making ability is reduced. Second, out of a hardened heart, he gets little satisfaction from his relationships.

He is not at peace owing to an agitated mind. There is a firm and tacit aversion of the truth, and it is as if blinkers have been attached. The agitated mind scuttles everything. When anger comes and takes hold of a person, it makes him act in a manner that could be injurious to himself and beneficial to the trickster. On most occasions, the negative results appear immediately. Even in other cases where

positive results seem to appear immediately, the results are found adverse in the long run.

The lowest ebb of this happens when people take 'decisions' when they are in the grip of an agitated mind. Invariably, such decisions are of a much lower quality than those taken by a truly calm and balanced mind. In fact, the best way to destroy a person is to get him to lose his calm and balance at a time when he has to make serious decisions or do something important. One place where we can see such a thing practically working is sledging, which some sportspersons use on their opponents.

It is said, in the scriptures, that there is great danger that a person puts himself into when he is destabilized. And when he wakes up from his folly, the damage is very often already done.

The fourth enemy comes in various forms: Anyone who leads an individual away from calmness and into agitation, wickedness, anger, discontent, hate or ill-will is not a true friend of the individual for the only reason that his influence is making the individual lesser then he can be.

Take Hitler, for example. He was doing it all for the people of his fatherland and the Aryan race—that is what he claimed. But in riling these very same people against the Jews and against the Gypsies and the infirm, was he truly being a friend to them? How can a person who takes you away from your best strengths, makes you act as a headless chicken and makes you do things that you eventually regret be acting in your interests? But many of those who did stand by Hitler thought he was taking care of their interests. Or they were too terrified to even think of going against Hitler.

Consider here three instances of the fourth enemy.

The thief in the guise of a friend and well-wisher: Anyone who promises that he will lead people to prosperity and happiness but blocks humaneness from the heart and calmness from the mind is in fact a thief. He wants to weaken the gullible listener, and in that moment of weakness, he wants to take away something precious the listener has. And though he is a thief, he will come in the form of a well-wisher and friend. Indeed, all dividers who have sown enmity among groups of people and who have led nations to their doom have always presented themselves as friends and well-wishers—as salvation for their people. But are they a way to salvation or are they a promise of doom?

The false Gurus: Similarly, such examples are also found among those tasked to act as spiritual guides. Some of them promise the joys of heaven by spitting hate, tolerance and intolerance against fellow humans of other creeds. They could even promise prosperity to their followers by making them do wickedness to 'others' who 'deserve' it. They might attempt to get followers to place their trust (misplaced) in their leadership by highlighting the mutual association with a particular label. (I am of XXXX label. You are also of XXXX label. Don't trust anyone else.) They speak the tongue of dividers. They operate from the egoistical position of being a part of XXXX group, having little to do with the universal truth that is present in all men. A Guru erodes ego. The false Guru builds it up. In fact, a true Guru from the XXXX (spiritual) group would help people get rid of even the XXXX (spiritual) label if it was building up an ego in the disciple.

The self-centered label-representing-leader: The most difficult provocateurs to spot are the 'rights-representatives'. They are the worst because they come justifying that they are righteous, selfless and legitimate entities in a democratic environment that protects 'rights'. They say, 'You belong to YYYY label. When you belong to this YYYY label, you have these yyyy rights. Let me represent you in your attempts to get your rights.' In the process, more often than not, they sow differences in people's minds. They enhance egos, and they infuse persecution complexes and end up spreading mind poison in society.

According to people such as these, women will not get justice unless 33% reservation is made for them in the parliament. The various castes and communities which they represent will not get justice if they themselves—the 'representatives'—are not present in the parliament.

When the reader first reads this, he might say, 'This is all true. This is the natural thing to do in a democracy! This is how we protect human rights. This is how we make parliaments. This is how we elect representatives. This is the norm'

No! It is not the norm of human nature. It has been reduced to that in the present-day scenario. We have been hammered into believing this as true. If we accept this principle, then it means that true justice will be achieved for everyone in India only when each and every one of us is present in the parliament! That is impossible.

Therefore, since each of us cannot sit in the parliament, can there never be universal justice in India? Is there not something wrong in this?

We know that there can be justice for everyone. Our traditions and culture believe this is possible. It is supposed to be possible if we have a leader who is of the mold of the legends of ancient India. Why are we looking at ancient India? Do consider a very modern context. When President Obama was on his first campaign for presidency, two youngsters held up a banner with the message about 'blacks getting justice' in the stage background at one of the conventions. It took Obama by surprise. But such a banner never made its appearance again in his campaign. Clearly, there was a genuine leadership in operation in the Democratic Party campaign at that time which saw an end to the divisive idea. Accentuating that sentiment of division was never the way forward even if there was a question of rights of the blacks. Obama did represent a united and peaceful United States. This does not mean that Obama's leadership was totally enlightened. But definitely, it indicates that it was inspired by an enlightening idea. The lesson for the others is that there is a genuine possibility for success when one pursues the higher ideals. And India has inherited some of the best ideals known to man.

The original idea of 'democratic representation' was meant to carry this 'universal appeal'. In contrast, the sectarianism that is dominating today is something wrong. And this must definitely revert and return to the pursuit of the higher ideal if India is to find its right place in the world.

Thinking 'I can trust no one except myself' is the exact opposite sentiment to the 'trust' that is required when we send a representative to a powerful house like the parliament. This faithless and selfish environment produces bad leadership, bad followers and bad politics.

Such 'representatives' are not eligible: It is important for a common citizen to take time off and actually look into the thought process, the work and beliefs of such 'leaders' or 'provocateurs'.

1) A label-representing leader would essentially believe that life is a continuous struggle where the strong overpower the weak and that it is natural that people are struggling. (The inherent belief is that resources are scarce and that people must compete to get a bigger slice of the pie.)

2) Such a person would also believe that in such 'natural struggles' which happen between the other group and his own, his own group should get due justice. Then, when it is a pie that has to be divided among many families, he would believe that his family should get a good piece. And when in the family, he would think that he himself should get the lion's share. (The inherent belief is that being self-centered is natural for humans.)

3) For such a person, it is necessary to be in places of power if he wants justice for himself and for those he represents. (The inherent belief is that seeking power for a selfish cause is part of human nature.)

4) All this indicates that they lack inherent faith in fellow humans. And this, in turn, arises from a very low image they have of themselves and humans in general. (The inherent belief is that we cannot trust other people with our welfare—humans are all basically animals.)

5) But such leaders also have a positive quality. For such a label-representing leader, good leadership is about being honest in a scenario where everyone else is being 'naturally' selfish. As a leader, he thinks he must make sacrifices 'against his own nature' for the sake of others in the group. Such 'sacrifice' gives him qualities that, in turn, give him greater abilities than people in his group for whom he is fighting. But hanging in the balance between the selfishness of his group and his own limited selflessness, this representative has a hypocritical or a confused existence. In this, he does more harm than good. He thinks man is definitely an animal, that people need culturing and that he has been lucky to advance ahead of others. (The inherent belief is that we can't trust others. If anyway one has to be a representative, it better be me.)

These leaders/provocateurs actually believe these things. They are convinced that this is true about human beings. This is because they have experienced this as the truth in everyday life. This is what they have read in the literature at their disposal. There may be no bad intentions; they may be acting out of genuine belief that man is selfish by nature and that man is an animal. And they operate honestly from that belief/perspective.

They may even be fair-minded and just. But this fairness is about the belief that 'the one with the gun takes it all'. In Hindi, the saying is: 'his is the cow who wields the stick.' They will try to get hold of the gun/stick; and if someone else has the gun/stick, they will resign themselves to that fate that the cow will go to the other person. These people think of hardened hearts as being the real nature of man. For them, being agitated in the mind, disturbed in the heart and struggling against other groups is supposed to be the 'normal' thing.

In conclusion, we can say that this fourth enemy, mind poisons, is, by far, the most dangerous of enemies because though the enemy affects the very soul of a nation, there is great difficulty in recognizing that it is an enemy for one entrapped by this enemy. This enemy usually comes in the disguise of being a friend. It says to a selected group of citizens, 'I am concerned about you.' Then, it victimizes them.

Mind poisons eventually weaken individuals. They convert communities into smaller clusters of aggressive and weak people fighting with each other. And this affects their team output severely.

Fighting the fourth enemy: To win victory over the mind poisons, one must focus on what is good, and act with calm and solid internal strength/conviction. Easily said than done, one may say.

The provocateurs may be stating truths to substantiate their designs, that so-and-so incident took place where people from 'our' group were hurt by people from the 'other' group and that too when 'we' did 'nothing' to 'them'. They may try to imply that the 'natural' reaction to such data is anger. And if you are not angry about it, they claim it means that you are not patriotic or that you are not loyal.

But one must realize that there is a choice hidden in this. The response, when one gets to know of such facts, and the quality of that response is not automatic.

The response can be determined by the approach of the listener. One can react in two ways if he decides to act:

a) React aggressively

b) Act assertively

The benchmark to go by is to check whether calmness has been compromised. If one allows hate or anger to come in and capture him, then he has been blinded by the fourth enemy. In such cases, there is an aggressive reaction.

In contrast, if one remains calm even when adverse facts are presented to him, then his mind is free to sift through the material presented. It is also free to choose a firm and assertive response—at excellence.

A great help in this direction is the mere awareness that the fourth enemy is truly an enemy. Once the impact of their work is known, one can easily avoid getting too influenced by such thoughts lest he is tricked into losing something. Therefore, one needs to be very cautious of 'friends' who do things to steal away the higher consciousness one may be in. These are not friends, however genuine their protestations and arguments may be. Do I fall for the trick of focusing on the third person who they are complaining against, or do I continue to keep my awareness fixed on the one who is playing games with my mind? It is not without reason that someone said, 'God protect me from my friends. I can save myself from my enemies.'

Aware that such a thing like the fourth enemy exists, the reader must look out for it in his daily life and in his teams, observe its effects, understand its mechanisms and build self and team capabilities toward neutralizing the fourth enemy efficiently.

Identifying that one's own mind-set has been compromised is half the work done: All action against the fourth enemy starts with the identification that the problem exists among us and that one is probably already its victim of it. Maybe not intentionally, but victim nonetheless… Following are some of the indices:

1) The existence of heartburn, anger and grudges targeted at someone indicates that one has been compromised. (It is the idealism of ancient Indian thought that Lord Krishna did not have anger toward Duryodhana nor did Lord Rama toward Ravana.

They operated at a higher level of consciousness which they seek to instill in us.)

2) If one has a tendency to segregate people as good or bad, *based on labels,* instead of deciding the merit of each individual on the basis of his *individual good and bad actions,* then it indicates compromise (a judgmental attitude). In the same way, the use of identities and labels to passionately recognize even strangers as friends or enemies, on the basis of the labels alone, indicates compromise (prejudice).

3) A victory over another group should ideally leave behind a feeling of magnanimity, calmness and peace. But instead, if victory over 'enemies' leaves behind a heavy heart along with mistrust, bitterness and discontent in one's own camp, then it means that the definition of the 'enemy' was based on a compromise. In such an instance, deep within oneself, one is constantly fighting a feeling of guilt.

4) Efficiency level of one's team drops, team spirit is weakened and there is general fear and suspicion in the immediate environment in which one exists—all this indicates the presence of mind poisons (strained relationships).

When such indices are seen, one can know for sure that one is already a victim of the fourth enemy. Awareness of this itself goes a long way in resolving such problems.

Choosing the right principles of action: It is not necessary to react or respond in all situations, but when persecution happens against a group, it is important that people get together to curb it. If there is violence against women, then action must be taken to stop it. But does this mean that women must get riled up against men? For example, if there is violence against people of one particular religious community, does it mean that these people should get all worked up and take up cudgels? That is not the response. If so, then that response would be weak, and no real gains can be made. The same issue must be tackled without the mind poison—and firmly too. And for doing this, it is important to resort to the higher principles.

Take the principle of nonviolence for instance. Is it just about avoiding anything that will bring physical pain to a person or draw blood out of him? Does it mean that even a doctor must not pick up a knife to do surgery? Does it also mean that a 'social doctor' must not pick up a sword and do surgery on society? What matters in nonviolence is the spiritual principle that lies within, not the physical aspect; it has to do with the mind and the heart not the body. Nonviolence is said to be properly executed *only when one does not hate the other*.

Hate not the British, not the bully, not the one doing injustice—no one. And yet, tell them, 'Sir, what you are doing is incorrect.' That is the heart of the principle of satyagraha. Therefore, nonviolence has two dimensions, the spiritual and the physical. Between the two, it is far more important to hold up the spiritual principle than the physical. The spiritual principle of 'love for all, regardless and unconditional' is the higher element. In that sense, even the actions taken by Lord Krishna in the context of the Kurukshetra War and by Mohammed the Prophet to stop persecution are valid as nonviolence as there was no hate.

Needless to say, to be able to bind oneself to the non-injury of others is a great sacrifice. That coupled with non-hatred of the other can make angels out of men. The principle therefore has this timeless value, but its perfection lies not in non-injury to the physical body but in the non-degeneration to hate. The principle of nonviolence has value only if it is devoid of mind poison.

Even more powerful is the principle of dharma (divine rule of law) as enshrined in the Ramayana. The only time when Lord Rama is said to have lost his cool was when he discovered that his wife was missing. He got the information of her abduction from an injured bird. At that instant, overcome by anger, he was about to hurl that terrible arrow into the ground, but he gathered himself back to calmness with the assistance of his brother Lakshmana, and he went about the rest of the Ramayana in complete internal control over himself. Until the very end, he continued to do what was ordained to him in dharma. He held no hate even against Ravana. In fact, when Ravana was on his deathbed, Lord Rama asked Lakshmana to go over to Ravana and learn from him. He never gave up doing his dharma even though he had to do it at the cost of living separated from his beloved wife whom he loved and trusted till the end.

Take yet another example. Arjun was fighting the war, among other things, because his wife had vowed that she would not tie her hair until her tormenter Duryodhana was punished. Arjuna kept that anger within him up to the time when Lord Krishna, in his masterpiece, *The Bhagavad Gita*, taught him to give it up and fight for dharma instead..

Dharma is the highest of principles, and it never comes out of hate, an agitated mind, fear, anger or worry. To be able to perform from a dharmic disposition is the highest one can achieve. (The watered-down version of this, which is in use in today's world, is to do one's duty according to the rule of law and uphold it without personalizing anything. No hate, no revenge… Just the application of law.)

Look for Gurus who can guide: There are people who are in a league of their own who can offer genuine help and succor in this regard. The list may be long, but the author can give a guarantee on some of them:

The renowned Gurus Sri Sri Ravishankarji of Art of Living fame, Achariya Goenkaji of Vipasshana (recently passed on) and the renowned Hugging Saint Amritanandmayidevi are all angels in their own right who offer powerful yogas to help break free from the clutches of hate and anger. But the one close to the author's heart is Sir Shree Tejparkhiji of Happy Thoughts fame. These Gurus who wield influence in this day and age can be trusted completely as far as assistance goes toward fighting the fourth enemy. The list is not exhaustive, and the reader must seriously take up the exercise of identifying others who fall in the same class.

Choose the right leaders: The task of choosing leaders must be done with great care. We have seen how label-representatives, in the process of wanting to be champions of various groups, end up spewing mind poison into society. Every group that wishes to prosper must ask itself this question: 'Is this the kind of person we must elevate to the status of a leader?'

True that if such a person happens to belong to 'our' label, he will do special things for us. But then, in the larger scheme of things, will his contribution to the group be positive or negative?

a) Will he not throw tidbits to his teammates and gobble the bulk? After all, he believes in self-exclusiveness.

Why should he do differently when it comes to differences between him and members of his team? If he believes in his 'own group', he will also believe in his 'own relatives' compared to his teammates and his 'own family' compared to his relatives and in his 'own self' compared to his family.

b) Is he capable of understanding the importance of 'we'? He will be called upon to take many decisions, as part of his duties he aspires to take on, that will decide important aspects of the lives of his followers and possibly others—far more important than the tidbits he may offer to his followers. Will he do justice to those decisions?

c) Can he truly be a father figure?

d) He is a 'taker' and not a 'giver'; is such a man right for a leadership position?

e) Label-representing leaders doubt the lessons given to us by the wise. They may give lip service to the things the wise people say, but deep in their minds, they know that it is not true. They entertain doubts about the integrity and humaneness of human beings and even question the possibility of existence of selfless work. ('All men are selfish,' is what they say.)

We have studied the beliefs that inspire the self-representatives. Let us contrast that with the beliefs of genuine leaders as indicated below:

Selfish-Label Representative	**Selfless-Universal Representative**
Resources are scarce, so people must compete to get a bigger slice of the pie.	There is enough love, money, health, resources and opportunities.
Being self-centered is natural for humans.	Being self-centered indicates ignorance in humans.
Seeking power for a selfish cause is part of one's nature.	All positions of authority have to be executed selflessly with a duty/dharma perspective.
We cannot trust other people with our welfare. Humans are all basically animals.	All humans are the same, and they are essentially spirit. We trust the spirit.
We can't trust others. If anyway one has to be a representative, it better be me.	Trust and faith must be reposed in the highest. The righteous must be the representatives.

The selfish-label representatives (*Jhund Babas*) should definitely be given a good balanced-minded hearing but only after filtering out the mind poison they pass on along with their arguments. They could make valid points, which have to be taken care of in the smooth running of a just nation. But people like them should never be put in places of authority and decision-making. The worst of all places they could be put in are places where they could have an impact on the design and structure of socio-political systems.

Fighting back the fourth enemy at the personal level: A *Mahaveer* wins victory over such ego-driven divisiveness in an irreversible manner. No amount of hate can provoke such a person. But that does not mean that self-realization is the only way to fight the fourth enemy, and it does not mean that mortals have no hope.

A *veer*—a man of courage—can still be victorious by being alert to such mechanizations. One can 'realize the hero in him' and can stay grounded and unaffected. Even the worst of the fourth enemies will be surmountable for an ordinary person. There is nothing new in this. Nothing great either… Some people do it naturally. They are the ones who are generally known as 'cool' guys. Some of them are charismatic. Of course, the disposition of the wise will also be similar.

This battle actually requires yoga. Personally, each person has to look for a technique (yoga) or generate one for himself which he finds most effective for the purpose. This yoga must be practiced and perfected. Following is a yoga that one can try to be insulated from the effect of mind poison.

A yoga to try: We have seen that if our response comes from hatred, the battle has been lost and the provocateur or divider has won. If on the other hand, the appropriate response arises from a calm mind, then the veer (hero) has asserted himself and one has been victorious. The calm mind alone has the potential to give the most sensible and potent response.

So, the following yoga may be tried when one feels that anger is rising within oneself and that it must be replaced by peace, firmness and excellence. The situation is that that one is listening to the divider. The divider is placing before you, very clearly, all the reasons why one ought to start getting angry. His reasoning and arguments are perfect. He can even pick quotes from the scriptures.

His passion, his diction and his 'facts' are convincing beyond a doubt—so much so that one should be angry. And one begins feeling anger inside. One is slipping into hate. The hate may be directed at some person, some other group or at the divider himself.

At such a time, one should close his eyes for a moment and imagine the divider standing just in front at arm's length distance. And lo! He has begun to shrink in size. Make a fist, and using it as a hammer, knock the divider on top of his head downwards. This is all being done in the mind. As one keeps knocking, the divider becomes smaller and smaller and smaller till he becomes as small as a harmless, toothless mouse (or a loveable kitten). At that time, having caught him by the ear, one ought to pat him on his cheeks using one's fingers like one would admonish a naughty mouse. A very tiny mouse who is trying to talk big things… Having done that to satisfaction, one ought to open his eyes, feel oneself smile and look around for others who have won. Happy is he who finds smiling faces around him.

After having won, being free from any 'obligation' or 'browbeating', without prejudice, one should objectively and clearly look at the facts one needs to know. Using that calm self and sharp mind, one can easily patronize the rule of law. One needs to identify one's duties and go about doing it to the best of his ability.

Think through your responses for various occasions and be ready: There are essentially three places where one may be called to put effort so that a suitable response can be given to the fourth enemy:

1) Taking action after a provocateur has already succeeded in provoking anger and hatred
2) Taking action when a provocateur is actually dishing out the mind poison (hot air)
3) Taking action pre-emptively when one is expecting a provocateur to do it

It should be left to the creativity of the individual as to how he decides to handle each of these stages. It is after all a game that the provocateur is playing. If one is forewarned, he can win this game. Ultimately, one may do exactly what the other person wants. However, to act with a calm mind, objectively, and to know that one is acting from a position of strength and that the mind poisons have not got the better of one's mind is valuable.

A village that looks forward: Any successful community in a village should be able to cut out the fourth enemy ruthlessly. Mind-poison games must be won with ease. It doesn't matter if those prejudices come from tradition, religion, polity, economy, social institutions or any other source. Nothing should make men lose their cool. And this victory has to be won by the villagers themselves. No one can do it for anybody else. In doing this successfully, we will be inheriting the best of the ideals of this ancient land.

All societies are definitely composite as defined by various parameters like age, gender, language, culture, relationships, friendships, ideologies, religion, education and profession. So, the challenge in any society and in any village is to continuously strive toward working from the depth of calmness regardless of composition. It is the essential requirement for tapping into both the innermost potentials of the individual members of the village and the highest potential of the village team itself. None of the differences between men should then matter. The differences should not draw up walls between hearts.

➢ Village communities must protect themselves from mind poisons of all kinds.
➢ They must endeavor to build their society and polity not on the basis of a belief that 'selfishness is the nature of humankind' but rather on the belief that 'man in his natural form is essentially selfless'.
➢ The systems they develop must be based on mutual trust and faith in one another.
➢ The institutions must reflect Gandhian values.

The political arrangement in today's 'representative' parliament unfortunately does not help this cause. The present political environment seems to be rewarding dividers and sending them into positions of authority. However, this was not how it was originally conceived when the nation came into existence. The thinking of the best of the leaders and saints of modern India is to come up with a socio-political environment that rewards 'universal representatives', the kind who think 'I represent everyone. My community is proud of sending a selfless son/daughter for service of the higher cause.' That is the honorable sentiment.

If this change has to come in the socio-political thinking of India, then the foundations have to be laid in the villages themselves. It is a revolution in thought which the villages of India must spearhead. 'In our village, we only select "universal representatives" as leaders.' That is a vital benchmark which a village team must attain if it is ready to soar.

The *Brahst-aastra*: The trump card of the divisive leaders lies in the fact that they do not allow clear reason to surface. This is their Brahst-aastra, their ultimate weapon for victory. It involves communicating as if there is no time to think and as if action must be immediately taken out of total faith in what they have to say. The idea is to raise a cacophony, a shouting match, a judgmental condemnation of one another and intolerant accusations. Usually accompanied by strong egoistical positions, there is a deep sense of self-righteousness. Such people usually have the battle lines drawn deep in their minds and see themselves in the middle of a war in which they would lose if they do not shout. They don't listen in a substantial measure. Their communication is one-way. This is referred to in the scriptures as 'barking dogs'.

People like them cannot be reasoned with. They just turn around and bite. The idea is not to get provoked by them and never let them lead (blind leading), lest we too become blind. Faith in leaders is necessary though. Often, we may have to act out of trust. But it is worthwhile to take note that such trust needs to be selectively placed on leaders who qualify for that trust based on the points below:

> ➤ The line separating the warring sides, as drawn by such leaders, separates the good and righteous from evil. They never divide on the basis of 'identity labels' or 'belief brands'.

> ➤ The leader allows for free thought, reasoned discussion and relief from mental burden.

> ➤ There is no browbeating or dogmatism.

> ➤ They only ask their devotees to act out of faith, and such faith is elicited out of free will. Most of all, such faith facilitates an upward spiritual journey.

In choosing this kind of leader, the fourth enemy is automatically defeated.

To summarize, we have dealt with four enemies that confront the villages of India and inhibit their capacity for self-rule. We have also dealt upon the possible solutions for each of them.

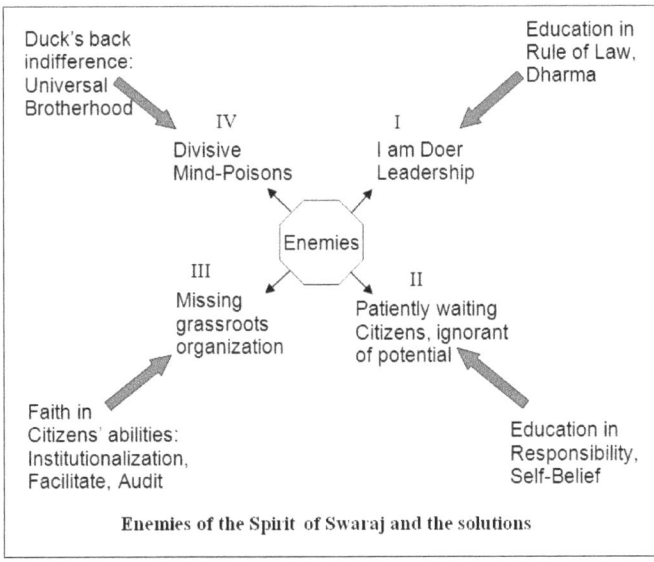

Enemies of the Spirit of Swaraj and the solutions

Enemies of the spirit of swaraj and the solutions: Though these four enemies are integral to life today in rural India, people fail to notice that these are enemies in most cases. Awareness goes a great way toward solving these problems. The first two enemies can be considerably weakened by changed attitudes, and this can be brought about by merely making known that the normal way for leaders and citizens to think today is truly an error in approach. Awareness also leads to constructive action against the enemies. In the case of the third enemy, lack of institutionalization, the realization of the merits of collective action through institutions will make the well-wishers and stakeholders focus their efforts on creating and sustaining meaningful institutions.

Awareness of the fourth enemy and its link to the Ultimate Freedom helps not only in avoiding great ills brought forth by dividers and provocateurs but also in setting priorities right with respect to living fulfilling lives.

It is usual that there are vested interests that prop these enemies up, but core human nature (man is a social/spiritual being) is such that these efforts cannot be sustained for long. The enemies can be defeated.

The villages surely have their task cut out for them. But the commitment to freedom must enlighten the approach to tackling these enemies, and therefore, the village must go the length to do all it takes. The idea is to weaken the four enemies in every initiative that arises from the village. It is a sustained effort that must become a habit in the village's public life. And the creative energies of the citizens, leaders and other well-wishers must be constantly applied to give befitting replies when these four enemies try to make an appearance.

Section V

Partnership with the Surrounding Environment

Every village has an organic interdependence with the surrounding society. This environment consists of many external agencies and institutions that have symbiotic relationships with the villages. Now, for a village to have sustained self-rule, even this interdependence needs to be carefully designed and nourished.

Of all the possibilities for the external interactions of the village, perhaps the interactions in the inter-village forum (among a group of neighboring villages as defined in the upcoming chapter) are the most vital with respect to triggering, nourishing and sustaining a grassroots-level freedom. This forum also has the potential to be central to the prosperity of the nation itself because great leadership can be fostered both for the villages and for the nation on this platform.

The village citizens and village institutions are direct stakeholders, and they will easily understand the value of freedom and be willing to work toward it. There are also individuals who, though living outside the villages, actually work for the welfare of villages. And surely, they are also well-wishers of village freedom. Then, there are external agencies and institutions too who act with the aim of welfare and prosperity for villages. All these agents must understand the significance of the inter-village forum and focus considerable energies on that forum in order to maximize the gains for the villages.

The inter-village forum is defined among a group of neighboring villages. This sphere of influence can be known as a community of villages. It is more or less the size of a mandala as defined in the Chola times. In administrative and utilitarian terms, it is equivalent to a city or town of optimum size, roughly of the same size as a PURA cluster.

In comparison to the national, state, district, taluka and village levels, this level is of prime importance as far as the second freedom is concerned. Various significant inputs which target the strengthening of team spirit in each village can be handled here. At this level, villages are compared. Ideals that display how villages may bring the best out of a team effort can be placed on a pedestal and exemplified. This is, in fact, the zone of 'public life' for the villages.

This level also becomes the place where villages offer mutual support, trash out ideas to tackle common problems, prepare plans for joint action and act in unison to tackle problems that cross village boundaries. Their successful interaction at this level will result in initiatives that can help in the dramatic emancipation of the participating villages.

This sphere of influence also has significance in the process of character building of individuals. At this level, people will be able to draw meaningful conclusions with regard to the efforts of the people behind successful village movements. While villages are areas where individuals can work upon their individualities and their abilities at teamwork, the inter-village level is the zone where these attributes are evaluated and exemplified. Naturally, through adequate interaction between villages at such a level, a competitive edge results, and it betters the physical, intellectual and spiritual health of the citizens of the concerned villages.

These benefits, which we have so far seen, accrue to individuals and communities at the grassroots level, and surely, more can be listed. But such benefit is not restricted only to the grassroots. The vitality of this level also stems from the fact that this is one zone in the entire national scheme that can serve as a foundation for building up the 'character' of the representative bodies in the country—starting from the panchayat and up to the parliament level. Keeping all this in mind, the tasks here must be handled with foresight.

The size: How many villages should the inter-village cluster contain? Its composition, with respect to the number of villages included, the population and the geographical spread, is to be defined using the following factors:

1) It should prove to be of use in catalyzing a thriving grassroots system in the participating villages.

2) The taluka and the block should be the next higher units of administration.

3) The definition of boundaries should be made on the basis of geographical, cultural and historic considerations, more or less on the basis of definitions already existing on the ground.

4) As in the PURA model, it should contain a minimum of 8 to 10 villages but not more than 25. Somewhere between ten in sparsely populated areas and twenty in densely populated areas seems appropriate. The actual figure can be decided through iteration.

5) It should have a zone of influence that can be defined on the basis of the distance an individual can physically reach. A distance that can be covered through one to two hours of quick walking could be the diameter of the defined zone.

6) It should be the area over which welfare workers and experts can give substantial and regular personalized service, as opposed to being constrained to give only guest appearances in bigger domains. It must be an area that is convenient for individuals from NGOs, government, religious institutions, political parties and commercial organizations to render their services by interacting on a person-to-person basis at the grassroots level.

7) This size must also ensure that public functions like fairs, sporting events, youth festivals and children's *melas* will have a sufficiently large target population for meaningful participation and interaction.

8) The police, revenue, judicial and development sub-units should also have domains that coincide with these boundary definitions.

An advantage of this size was brought out by P. V. Indiresan in his 116th article of the Vision 2020 series. While laying out arguments justifying the size of the PURA clusters, he said that the villages should form an agglomerate large enough to have the best of modern amenities with suitable connectivity (electronic, economic, physical, educational) at reasonable cost, efficiency and self-sufficiency. All this would therefore satisfy the economic and educational requirements of this domain in adequate measure.

The culture of win-win: As for this inter-village forum, even more important than the economic and administrative factors is the culture (or soft power) that is key. The four enemies of self-rule namely attitudes of leaders and common citizens, institutionalization and finally sweet poisons all need to be battled chiefly on this warzone. The opportunities to exemplify the correct attitudes are immense here. Here, the efficiency, merit and wisdom of public functionaries will have to stand the test of public scrutiny. Excellence in public life should set live examples before the youth. The forum must act as a school for the selection and training of candidates who are to be offered by the villages, as representatives, to higher representative bodies of the state. If the balance is struck correctly, then the best leadership will naturally emerge and move up the ladder of responsibility. The forum therefore forms a point at which the foundations are laid for merit-based selection and culturing for healthy parliaments and legislatures. The forum will also reflect, in its culture, that it wishes to be known for its excellent jurors, social integrity, sportsmen, intellectuals, economic achievements and ability to produce men of substance who go out to serve the nation and the world.

Another important feature of the cultural ambience of the cluster should be its undistorted view on austerity and joy. In the PURA model, economy and consumerism have been envisioned as chief drivers of activity. In contrast to this, a joyful attitude emanating from facilitating freedom and taking responsibility should be the chief driver in the community of villages.

There is no need that the activities in the pursuit of freedom should be conducted in the form of bitter pills that one is pained to swallow. Indeed, what is the use of participating in activities in which one does not find joy? It should be about the pursuit of joy. But as the wise say, if it is about a pursuit of joy, it can happen only when one is selfless and works independent of personal gain. This implies that interactions of all kinds in this level should pulsate with life rather than self-interest. 'Enlightened, universal self-interest' must instead be the mantra that drives public life at this level.

In discussing this point, we have already stepped into the spiritual. It has got to do with the 'state of being' of an individual, that is, enthusiasm or the lack of it and joy or the absence of it. These things are better understood through matters of faith and wisdom. However, we can satisfy ourselves with the idea that the right way to go about it is to be firm in the pursuit of universal humanism. It calls for well-wishers to get the necessary things done while at the same time sharing with the beneficiaries a world of joy, satisfaction and contentment in the very activities taken up—the journey being as fulfilling as the destination. It is about the results of genuine freedom, but it is also about a great journey. It must be a reflection for all that Gandhiji, Tagore and Swamy Vivekananda stood for.

The pursuit of freedom has elements of transcendence embedded in it. The significance of `irrelevance-of-materialism' for the joys of life should be sensed here in the very spirit of the surroundings, in the attitudes governing peoples' interactions and in the successes attained by people in self-government activity. A message on the rounds in social media puts it aptly, 'How wealthy a person is can be decided on the basis of the things he possesses which money can't buy.' Joy can be experienced only if the level of consciousness rises. The pursuit of panchayati swaraj must be embedded in the zone of self-actualization. Freedom and its pursuit are indeed a celebration of a higher state of being.

Where leaders and politicians can make a difference: When a grassroots-level leader wishes to make a difference, it is at the inter-village forum that he can deliver maximum impact. Activities of maximum productivity must be taken up in this small community of villages. He must facilitate team work through complete inclusion. He must participate in formal or informal teams to hammer out solutions for intra-village and inter-village challenges. He must use the forums of traditional India like fairs, competitions, tournaments and temple festivals to encourage interaction and excellence.

As such, the leader should be a connoisseur of the arts and sports. He should ensure patronage for these activities. In fact, he should promote patronage as a value in itself which needs to be cherished, encouraged and highlighted in the public life of the inter-village forum. And he needs to do all this knowing that the call to service here is more of an obligation than a choice. This obligation is not compelled by ideologies or other cognitive processes but by virtues of the heart—freedom being an expression of the highest in man. If the leader wishes to really strengthen the nation, both at the grassroots level and at the highest level, it is in this zone of the inter-village forum that he has to put in his efforts. An efficient administrator and statesman will focus his energies in a big way at this forum.

The best way of offering external assistance to a village in its efforts at self-emancipation is to assist 'capacity-building for freedom'. A village will require various strengths for enhancing its freedom, and helpful external agencies should assist the village in developing those strengths. We shall look at a list of those areas where such strengths need to be nourished. (Refer to the diagram at the end of this chapter for a comprehensive picture.)

Knowledge: This is the most vital of inputs that needs to go into a village if its capacity for freedom is to be increased. Every good work starts with a good thought. Every manmade creation first needs to appear as an idea in the mind of the one that creates it (referred to in *The Monk Who Sold His Ferrari* by Robin Sharma and other similar books). It is through infusing knowledge in a target population that such good thoughts can be sown in the minds of the people of a village. Once the seeds are sown, the citizens of the village themselves can go about creating those things in the world around them. Therefore, there is a special need for organizations to cater knowledge inputs to rural communities. It is useful to classify them as formal (general and specific) and informal (skills and wisdom) education.

Formal education (general): This primarily consists of the formal education system as we know it. Ensuring that there is no illiteracy, that every child is educated and that there are openings for higher studies for those desirous is the need under this heading. The usual institutions, schools, colleges and training institutions, will be expected to think innovatively to meet this aim of establishing institutions of merit in rural areas. To meet the immediate challenge though, there is a need for extra-village organizations to depute expertise for this specific task into the villages. One way of doing this can be by arranging comfortable village retirement homes for retired experts—especially for retired educationists. Such persons can then move into the rural setting through a symbiotic arrangement. The spirit of this particular effort by retired persons should have an element of voluntary service. The villagers should also go out of their way to make them comfortable in the rural setting.

Formal education (specific): The primary aim under this heading is to pump knowledge that is particularly relevant to the enriching of life in that village into it. It should encompass everything practical that can make life in the villages better. This will include (and not be limited to) subjects like machine maintenance, vermiculture, alternate energy, water management, judiciary basics, police support, village bookkeeping, health work, computer data management and basic health. This is one area that will see a revolution of sorts. All the relevant transferable knowledge needs to be collected and separated into these subjects. For each subject, a complete syllabus needs to be built up. And the syllabus for each subject should be covered in three or four grades of certificate courses. The basics of these levels/grades should not even require that the students should be educated/literate. It can be an entirely practical course at the end of which a participant can receive a certificate. That should qualify him to apply for the next grade and so on till he is an expert in that area. Through this, we can create experts in a whole lot of subjects.

If a village has managed to notch up fifty or sixty odd certificates, then it means that so much knowledge has been pumped into the village. The spectrum of such certificates will be a good way of ensuring that diverse and relevant knowledge is being transferred to and held in a particular village.

In fact, this is one method by which catalysis for growth can be affected by external agencies. Bare minimum requirements can be imposed on a village community. For example, a village panchayat can be said to be officially recognized only when there is a net total of fifty certificates in the village on at least ten different subjects (or more severe or diluted variations of this depending on the need).

A lot of special efforts are needed in this direction. Building up a database of knowledge and information is the first step. Then, there is a need to organize that knowledge, work on its delivery mechanisms, have a testing system to assess how well the students have done and finally implement a feedback mechanism both to reinforce the source of the knowledge and to refresh the student in due course of time. This, of course, needs extensive planning and effort by the government, possibly in partnership with agencies.

Informal education (skills): There is a special need to ensure that skills, especially those that are required for making a living in a city-based setting, are transferred to the members of a village. Such skills are vital components of survival and success in a world that runs on capitalistic principles. These can be taken care of by commercial organizations, which will automatically come to rural areas if there is a culture of patronage for the same in the villages, that is, if rural people are willing to spend money to do the courses. Schools can also take initiative for training students in the requisite skills. Such an upgrade will create greater confidence in the rural folk. This will also shift some commercial activity toward the villages, which will indirectly help in building up the rural economy.

Informal education (wisdom): This is one of the most controversial yet vital components among the ingredients that need to go into a village. The problem is that when there is a basic debate in the scientific world over the authority of the wise, institutionalizing wisdom does not come easy. Consequently, there is no question of there being any 'modern' institutions that cater to this need. But there are a host of traditional institutions that focus on wisdom which need patronage.

As of now, in order to meet this need, a lot of faith needs to be placed in the learning that is transferred within families. Further, there is a need to revive many folk and classical arts which acted as vehicles for transferring the wisdom of the ancients.

Then, there are the temples. They have an important role to play. The mandate of a temple is complete only when there is deep awareness in the devotees of the stories relating to these deities that have been recorded in the ancient texts. This naturally means that the temples need to patronize institutions and artists who have to go back among the masses and popularize these ancient tales of wisdom, valor and sacrifice. There's a tremendous amount of wisdom that can be transferred in this method, and until alternatives to the scriptures are developed by the wise of this age, there is a need to refresh the minds of the masses with the substance in the scriptures in this manner. As of now, there are more powerful mass communication tools in comparison to the times when these ancient stories or histories were generated; this means that presently, there is a need for great creativity to repackage this ancient wisdom in order to deliver it at the grassroots level.

The word 'temple' in the above paragraph, of course, is generalized for all religions. Every religion has an essential dimension of spirituality at its core in which there is great wisdom. Each religion should therefore creatively repackage that wisdom so that at least the wisdom in it gets across into a secular setting without the dogmas surrounding the faith creating hurdles.

It might even take a few decades before wisdom becomes an integral part of schooling. However, one never knows. There are good chances that it will not take that long. But till such a time that the scientific world accepts the objectivity of the truths reflected in spirituality, there is a need to carry on focusing efforts in the area of spiritual uplift and wisdom as is admissible in the best of religions.

Team discipline: Every external agency that has anything to do with a village has a particular manner in which it deals with a village, and it also has designed certain expectations from a village. In all such dealings and expectations, it is extremely important, from the standpoint of patronizing freedom in villages, to force the village to act as a team. Unfortunately, this is one area in which political parties, NGOs, socio-religious organizations and even some wings of the government have been acting in a manner that is opposed to team-building.

A strategy adopted by the Maharashtra Electricity Board is an excellent example of facilitating the teams in villages. Those villages which worked as a team to manage their power consumption according to a pre-determined format were rewarded with 24-hour electricity supply.

Those villages that failed to do this experienced periodic power cuts.

There are two criteria under this heading which can be pointed out for special attention, which the external agencies and all agents working for the uplift of a village should focus on.

Unity: One cannot overstate the importance of this vital ingredient required for a village's move toward freedom. If the village is together, it has great capacity for freedom. This is one area in which one should never tolerate dilution. We may once again note here that in the vision for the nation, the makers of the Indian constitution thought of a scheme where even the municipality elections were not to be fought along party lines. And that implies the same in villages too. The reason for this thought process was that there should be no cause added into the socio-political arrangement of a local community that would end up dividing people. This means that even the founding fathers saw this as a necessary ingredient of a prosperous nation. Needless to say, the nation can move things decisively forward only when the villages act united. We can even take an extreme stand and say that anyone or anything that divides a village, even for selective good, is in fact an enemy of the people of that village (Refer to Chapter 3.7 of this Part 2 of the book).

Unity definitely produces a quantum leap in strength. For one dwelling in a village, there is nothing more benevolent than a unified team that is focused on the emancipation of all its citizens. If any external agency attempting emancipation acts in a manner that compromises the village's unity, then it rather not come in.

Dynamism: There is no fun in being united if nothing is done on the basis of that unity. The village team should be dynamic. There are many responsibilities/challenges which the village team has to shoulder. With whatever resources it has at its command, with a commonly held vision guiding it and with a zest for life, it should plan and execute the necessary activities.

Therefore, all external agencies interacting with the village should nurture this dynamism in the villages. It should be taken for granted that there is infinite energy in a village and that any productive activity will be met by more than halfway by the citizens of that village. A lot of activities should be planned so that the productive energies of the members of the village are expressed. These need not be breadwinning efforts. It could even just be work done at hobbies or work taken up on the basis of social obligation. It is important though that whatever be the nature of the activities, the commitment to contribute should be total in that limited time when the effort is on.

Finances: Let us accept at the outset that if a group, whichever it is, does not have spending power, then its capacity for action in the commercial environment is heavily restricted. It is inappropriate to say that one wants to strengthen villages and, at the same time, give them no financial authority. The main actor in rectifying this is definitely the government which needs to allow greater financial authority in the hands of village councils. If the state is not capable of putting money directly in their hands, it should at least allow the villages some scope for taxation. This is the first aspect related to finances. One should help a community in enhancing its *spending power*.

The other aspect is *village income*. Organizations interested in the emancipation of the villages should help the villages develop abilities to generate higher profits in the present commercial setup. There is also a need to encourage the flow of investment capital into rural settings.

The governments need to play an important role here. Enforcing their targets of PURA will mostly suffice. If the skill sets of the rural folk are enhanced, it will be more profitable for production or service-based commercial organizations to shift base into rural settings.

But one needs to mention that in all this, the role of the local leaders cannot be overstated. Success of endeavors like PURA depend as much on 'supply' by the government as on 'demand' by the people. And as economists put it, 'desire' is not 'demand' if it is not backed by money. The people need to commit themselves to the cause and invest in team-building, goal-setting and shouldering some of the burden. Hence, the people themselves should come up with projects that can improve the earning capacity of the rural populations. This means that they should bet their money on it.

Political institutions: There is also a need to set up village institutions that are dedicated to carry out specific administrative tasks. We have seen earlier that committees need to be set up in order to look into various aspects of life in a village. There is a need for a judicial element to be present in a village. There is also a need for a local cell which has privileged access to the concerned police station. Organizing committees for festivals and other events which the village may take on are also required. An information cell is required as well. While some of these can be ad-hoc committees, there is a specific need for some institutions to be established on a permanent basis.

With respect to such institutions, there are two important tasks which need to be taken up by external agencies and individuals who seek the welfare of the village. We have looked upon them as the cardinal principles (Chapter 3.4 of this Part 2). The first aspect is building institutions and giving them due recognition. The second aspect is that these institutions should function within the boundaries laid down by the constitution. This means that these institutions need to be constantly or periodically audited as the need arises. Therefore, this leads us to the next important aspect of political institutions, which is external audit. A wing of the government should have this as its task exclusively. In a way, this will shift the responsibility of the government from actually doing something to monitoring what is being done and applying corrective measures wherever required. With such an arrangement, the chances of effectively implementing the needs of the constitution are radically enhanced.

To summarize, setting up political institutions within a village community enhances its capacity for freedom, but completeness can be achieved only if it is constructively audited by a mechanism that is faithful to the constitution. Only by these two aspects happening together can the capacity for freedom truly be improved.

Technology upgrade: The ability to thrive in the present socio-economic context requires good connectivity in terms of both transport and communication. This upgrade is vital for the success of villages in a capitalistic setup. The same also applies to the complete spectrum of commercial and wellbeing technologies. Whether the technology has something to do with farming, primary processing, data processing, preservation or marketing, getting suitably upgraded may make a difference between the persistence of a livelihood source and the end of it due to becoming obsolete.

Therefore, the external organizations which occupy themselves in this service of disseminating technology will be adding a vital ingredient toward enhancing the capacity for freedom in the villages. The challenges to these external agencies will be threefold: developing technologies, adapting them for use in the target area and effectively transferring them into the concerned villages.

The vital: It is probably the most important component that decides the capacity for freedom. There are connotations to this (inherent in the word dharma), which are not easily comprehended through modern terminology and have to be set aside for a future date and a different context. However, for the moment, we can focus on the important aspects which are easily understood. Of importance is the sense of duty (or farz, as it is known in Urdu). This is an attitude or habit that has to be ingrained in every individual—from childhood—since it is beneficial to both the society and the individual.

Now, is the ingraining of a sense of duty in an individual a hoodwinking or a way of cheating an individual so that he becomes a useful component of society? An analysis of the matter, which need not be gone into here, proves that it is not so. When the duty is defined on the basis of a benevolent law designed by wise men, it is in the best interest of even the one who is doing the duty. Unfortunately, it is hard to convince one easily about this. Lucky ones have teachers to guide them. Sometimes, it is the culture which a person holds that teaches them to nourish better things—like the sense of duty, for instance. Anyway, all external agencies dealing with a village need to be sensitized so that they constantly seek to instill a sense of duty in the minds of citizens.

The best possible contribution for this can come from the creative media. Surprisingly, whenever the sentiment of dutifulness has been portrayed correctly by a performance, it has spelled success for that creative endeavor. The best stories, whether in a successful film or a TV show, have more often than not honored that sense of dutifulness. But these are not the only possible ways of doing it. There are other channels for communication like art forms, sports and all kinds of teacher-student situations which have great potential as well. Every well-meaning individual should take up every opportunity he gets to help get the message about doing one's duty across.

Very closely related to the sense of duty is the rule of law. This is another component of the 'vital'. It is important that a village relishes the sense of rule of law. It is the rule of law which should be seen as the greatest benefactor of individuals. In this, the constitution of India becomes supreme, and everybody works toward upholding it. By effectively translating the rule of the constitution onto society, the highest good can be done to the people of the nation. But, of course, as we have just seen, the constitution itself should be tuned for the highest and the best, which definitely was the sentiment and effort of the founding fathers.

This upholding of the law has to be nurtured through all possible forums, activities and interactions of the members of the village. Unfortunately, some of the biggest defaulters for this are the modern-day movies where the concept of the rule of law is lost to what is termed as the 'angry young man syndrome'. Societies cannot be built that way. Where the rule of law is supreme, the Divine is accorded the highest place and peace, and prosperity invariably follows.

Summary: The following diagram is a summary of the considerations we have made above.

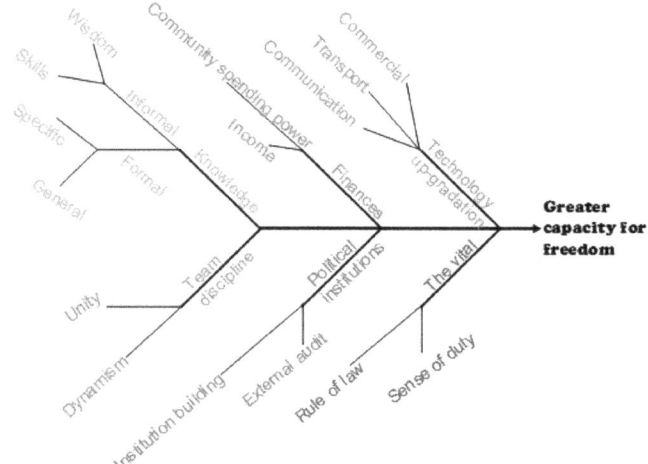

The Support Perspective For Panchayati Swaraj

The image shows the entire scope for external support. The way to look at these details is that if any of these inputs are strengthened, the capacity for freedom increases. Conversely, if any of these imports are weakened, the capacity for freedom of that village community diminishes.

This means that when a well-meaning agency (or person) takes up responsibility for the village and tries to initiate and promote freedom in local communities, the agency will actually be setting up institutions and opportunities that can provide for these inputs, as listed in the diagram.

In order to achieve completeness, there is a need to ensure that all the points listed above are covered through the institutions and activities. The totality of the spectrum is important. Further, there is no need for a one-to-one correlation between institutions and requirements to be met. A single need can be supported and backed up by more than one external institution, and one institution or activity can take care of many of these needs simultaneously. But the necessary way forward is to ensure that all these aspects are covered as best as possible.

If these inputs are efficiently delivered to the villages, one can rest assured that the village communities will grow in strength and eventually contribute to the strength of these external agencies that first came in their support. It is in the completion of that cycle that the nation will find its prosperity.

Given the stark realities of today's villages, doubts surely arise. Is this pursuit of freedom feasible? Can the 'dung heaps' truly be converted into Gandhiji's 'gardens of Eden'? Can the uneducated and wretched majority of village dwellers play any constructive role in transforming the villages? Can the rampant poverty, bitter casteism and human rights abuses allow any reform or revolution in the Indian hinterland? Will the vested interests cooperate?

Should we not be skeptical about the possibility of reform or revolution then?

The odds surely seem stacked against the possibility of constructive change, but a closer look does reveal that there are possibilities that still remain unexplored. For one thing, 'leader action' has its limits but 'people action' has incredible potential. The same wretched kind of people once stood behind Gandhiji in droves and shook the very foundations of the colonial rule in India—and that too more than a century ago. Why should we conclude that such energies do not exist today? Besides, due to the massive leap forward in communication technology, the task of mobilizing the people may in fact be easier today.

Let us for the moment focus on the possibilities. Let's say that reform is actually possible. Let us say that this change will happen. And if this is to happen, where will all the action come from?

Taking the process forward along the lines of the vision of the Mahatma surely requires innovation and ingenuity. It will also need committed people who will be the torch-bearers of freedom. Despite all this, the greatest work will happen when the average citizen uses the little opportunity that he has to better the chances of the village's success—those little drops of water will make the mighty ocean.

There will be opposing forces, mostly on account of bad attitudes and vested interests. But then, who can stand up to people who are on a roll when they have tasted freedom? When the average Indian rises up and stands tall to the fullness of his being, taking full responsibility

and experiencing freedom, then it would only make sense for those in opposition to quietly toe the line.

A leader of such citizens must be one who sincerely seeks welfare for all. Not just for his tribe, his family, his group… For all! True freedom does not lie in being locked in individual identities. Rather, it lies in rising above them. If the citizens are going to rise to freedom, then that leader must ensure that he is facilitating it rather than opposing it. For when citizens identify the sweet-speaking fourth enemies for what they truly are, that will be the end of that 'narrow representative'. People who have realized the value of freedom will then only look out for 'righteous universal representatives'. The sooner the aspirants for leadership fall in line, the better it is for them.

There are innumerable stories in India of villages that have achieved various aspects of freedom. In Manikant Desai's Urli Kanchan near Pune, the sarpanch takes pride in saying that every individual in the village, irrespective of caste, sits and dines together. Illango in Kuthambakkam has evolved a process of financing village endeavors using trusts, and his village has declared 100% freedom from hunger. Many other panchayat presidents continue to learn from him. Baba Amte's village is a green oasis in the midst of surrounding dry lands. Anna Hazare's Ralegaon Siddhi is an outstanding example for environment protection and planned infrastructure development in a village which stands heads and shoulders above other villages in the vicinity. Shivaji's village Kattanbhavi is green and has a high water table while the immediate next village is dry and has a low water table. Farmer leader Nalkhande declares that in his village in Vidarbha, there won't be any suicides. Such stories can be replicated in every village of the nation if the village teams are inspired to take the best from these examples and adapt the solutions into their own settings.

A bureaucracy plotting for welfare: In the present Indian scenario, the bureaucracy can create a great impact. Each functionary—whatever his status—has a sphere of influence within which he is the king. It is about pushing for freedom in that domain. If Lord Krishna could bend laws to ensure dharma, why can bureaucrats not bend laws to ensure freedom?

The colonial idea of a bureaucrat being the giver and the villager being the receiver needs the door. When a nation has decided to rise up to freedom, the bureaucrat must be the facilitator and the auditor; he must realize that his success in his duty lies in believing that the village dweller can rise to freedom, rather than in hypnotizing the villager into the belief that he cannot. Yes, he can! Yes, that poor illiterate person can take care of his own government!

Before independence, there was a design to keep the Indian commoner in check or, at least, to keep him at arm's length, which the bureaucracy had to enforce. There is no need of enforcing that design today. Instead, if each functionary tips the scales in the direction of empowering the villages, in his little zone of influence, there will result a deluge toward making the villages self-reliant and strong. That strength can do wonders to our society and nation. However powerful the resistance, however mighty the lethargy in the power structure and however widespread corruption may be, none of these will stand a chance against that deluge. Great amounts of work need to be done to fine-tune the administration to cater to freedom rather than a colonial rule. But all that work will be reduced to no work at all when each person plays even a small part in the little domain in which he is king—and it will be a delight too.

There is a district magistrate for each district; there is an officer in each block. How many such people do we have in the entire nation? Is it possible that none of them in the entire nation will device ingenious ways of getting things done so that the village is strengthened? Naturally, there will be vested interests that have to be countered. But if a breakthrough is achieved in one place, then can it not be adapted ingeniously elsewhere to suit the new setting? Or at least, can it not be duplicated all over?

And why restrict it to just these few functionaries of the administrative services? It applies to all classes and groups in the executive, the judiciary and the legislature. They too have their role to play for the freedom of their nation.

The nation will definitely look for prudent, pragmatic and effective leadership from such functionaries.

Every sector will help: In every sector of life, a visionary effort is needed. For example, an arrangement for a low-cost medical facility should not be attempted through sending unwilling MBBS greenhorns to villages who are to learn by trial and error. It indicates utter disrespect for human life in villages. The medical fraternity and the ministry and departments concerned with medicine need to think innovatively out of the box. The box that is being mentioned here is the belief that one needs to be an MBBS graduate to even think of taking on medical responsibilities, that nurses cannot be gradually upgraded through certification over the years to take on increasing responsibility and eventually attain MBBS degrees when they have learned enough to qualify for the exams, that allopathic medicine is the only legal way forward, that medical support can only come for money and that traditional forms of medicine cannot be institutionalized. Ingenuity has to be displayed in order to break open this boxed-up thinking. And definitely, in a nation of a billion people, a lot of that ingenuity will already be present.

A team of doctors should probably design a course structure wherein a person picks up a new kind of medical degree in the course of many years interspaced with breaks so that he will have attained a higher grade after each break, which will authorize him to take up a bigger responsibility every time he upgrades. Where is the need to stick to a pattern that has been designed keeping in mind a society that is not the same as the one we have in India?

Medicine has been quoted just as an example, and even these are random suggestions that representatives of the medical fraternity may think of before coming up with a solution. What is important is the spirit of innovating in order to serve a freedom. Efforts at such innovation need to be taken up in the police force, the judiciary, education, training, sports, arts, temple management, the organization of fairs, political parties, the giving out of contracts, the assessment of contract works, etc.

Giving due respect to the goodness present in oriental, occidental and indigenous systems, the best solutions have to be worked out in the present context. That is what the nation asks of us today: design each system to suit freedom.

India has what it takes: The mighty British power in India stood shaken when the common Indian offered his little hand of support toward civil disobedience and swadeshi. But the scene is different now. The average citizen on the street is joined by many in the heart of the Indian government establishment. There are lakhs of government executives who will conspire to support the resurgence of the villages. The task, therefore, is that much easier. Once the villages get going, the opposition is likely to get crushed along the way.

Farsightedness mandates that leaders must invest heavily in freedom if leadership is what they truly wish to offer. Fence sitters won't count; only he can light up a path to freedom who believes that freedom is the way to be. If the civilizational indicators of the Sindhu-land are right, then the nation is destined to rise to its second freedom, and nothing can stop it. Chauvinism on the basis of gender, caste, language, ideology, religion, status, education, wealth etc. will not thrive. Leaders will surely rise from among the thousand million Indians who will overthrow 'narrow representation' and take up 'open universal representation'. Whether we will pick up that baton in this generation itself is the question. We must resolve soon whether we wish to perpetuate slavery or thrive in freedom.

What finally matters is the inner call. It has to do with whether people learn to enjoy the hero within and find contentment in living that life of detachment and fun and benefiting from the Tagore-Gandhi vision. If the impact of selfless servants and exalted martyrs is felt in a company of average citizens, we can rest assured that the goal is as good as reached for productive work is at hand. The joy of life must be experienced in living that immortal spirit, in creatively adapting solutions to suit one's locality and in hitting the right notes when enemies and challenges make an appearance.

The reality that will unfold the next moment is hidden from everyone. What challenges or opportunities lie ahead, only time will tell... But that is immaterial. All it takes is the resolve that we need no less than freedom, and even problems will turn into opportunities. Our villages must and will transit to freedom.

Appendix

A: THE SIX FREEDOMS IN DETAIL

This appendix elaborates on the rationale behind the various freedoms discussed in Section II of this Part 2 of the book. It is to be read in tandem with the corresponding freedom from that section (Chapters 2.2 to 2.7) if one seeks to find out why each freedom is important.

APPENDIX A.1 – REVENUE ACCOUNTING FREEDOM

Accounting Freedom 1: Land Records:

Relevance: It has been found that when knowledge about land ownership is hidden away in the books in the tahsildar's offices, it gives great scope for cheating and fraud. A lot of litigation can be avoided if there is clarity on who owns what, and there is no reason why the people of a village should not know who owns which piece of land. A great burden will be lifted off the social life of the village if this transparency can be realized in villages.

Detailed rationale: Through this, the village body is aware as to in what manner the land is changing hands. With the community being aware of this, disputes can be anticipated, and necessary preventive measures can be taken by the village community. Eventually, in an India that has risen to second freedom, every village will have a nyay panchayat (grassroots-level court). In such a situation, the presence of these land records will go a long way in solving disputes instead of relying on the extra-village judicial mechanisms. Even in the present situation, arbitration processes can be legally initiated; such records will be a great help. Even in the case when such disputes are taken out of the bounds of the village, the higher authorities in the executive and judiciary will have direct evidence from the village and find it easier to arrive at decisions on the advice of the village representatives.

It is a known fact that a huge percentage of cases now pending in the courts are based on land disputes.

Further, there is also evidence that this is one of the prime reasons for crime in the villages. Once people are ensnared in the courts on land issues, it is a journey of ego clashes, heartburn, misery and impoverishment. A great burden will be lifted off the backs of village dwellers if they are not subjected to this, and it can be achieved by stimulating compromises at the grassroots level through credible arbitration processes. For such a system of arbitration to exist, it is important to ensure transparency in land records.

Accounting Freedom 2: Taxes (a record of taxation and expenses):

Relevance: This freedom is a great help to achieve and sustain transparency—it has a role in reducing corruption. It helps in the analysis of trends, and this helps better planning. It gives great insight when a village takes up initiatives on its own; it therefore prepares the ground for authority being shouldered effectively by the village itself. It provides a reference point for the state to be able to monitor the health of a village community.

Detailed rationale: A system that supports freedom needs to ensure freedom for the villages to take up their own initiatives and effective auditing by the next higher level of government. Maintaining records of transactions made by the village in a systematic manner helps in both aspects. A team that is clear in its accounts finds it easy to take up new initiatives and pursue its activities smoothly. If accounts are maintained in a manner such that external audit is easy, then it reflects greater credibility in the village team. The higher authorities and other donors can then trust the village team with financial and other resources; they will be assured that there will be minimal misuse.

Making a start at maintaining such records will lay the foundations for great work ahead; it will instill seriousness in common citizens regarding the use and management of funds.

Accounting Freedom 3: Scheme List

Relevance: If a village has an up-to-date list of the schemes of the government, it will help the village plan well and ensure that the members of the village are benefited. It must also keep an open record of all those who have received such benefits so that everyone is aware. This will ensure fairness in the distribution of such benefits. It will also reduce corruption.

Detailed rationale: The prime minister of India once said that only seventeen paisa of a rupee actually reaches the beneficiaries. The other money is siphoned off. Very often, this benefit that reaches the villages also goes only to the party workers who are in power and not to the needy. Therefore, instead of providing welfare to the people, this actually helps in the continuation of a political system that is based on corruption. For such a system to give success to politicians, the people must continue to remain dependent. The result is that the system is not very happy to genuinely develop/improve people. This needs to change. When there is transparency and fairness, such benefits will not be on the basis of political loyalties but on the basis of need. People will not become 'dependent' on politicians. Rather, they will become 'independent' and pursue the highest good. They can vote freely for the best people to lead them. When there is honesty and sincerity in those chosen to rule, it is best for everyone. It is also good for the nation. Such honesty is better for the sake of building our own strengths, our village and our nation. Building on the basis of honesty and sincerity alone can we attain the highest potential. This a necessary condition for the way to true freedom.

Accounting Freedom 4: Census

Relevance: This data is important from the point of view of development planning, both from the level of grassroots organizations and from the higher levels of government. Proper statistics also plays an important role in the effective transfer of benefits at the time of compensation during acquisition. Targeted benefits can be better given if this data is correctly available. It is also important from the point of view of setting goals for the villages and deciding on the nature and quantity of benefits that must be given to a village.

Detailed rationale: Much of the time, when sincere and efficient officers of the administration wish to decide on giving benefits to a particular region or a particular group of people, they fall short of data to make the right decisions. A caution is that such information can be misused, but it can also be gainfully used to provide benefits or to target persons and groups. Such data in the hands of miscreants is dangerous; but the same information can also be used for their protection. But, in all, it is important from an administration point of view so that well-wishers can see where the village currently stands and what changes may be required for further development.

APPENDIX A.2 – ECONOMIC FREEDOM

Economic Freedom 1: Adaptation and Integration

Relevance: If a village cannot stand on its feet in the present economic scenario, it will lose out in many ways. It will not be able to beat poverty. Members of the village will have to travel outside in order to succeed. It will be a perpetual sink of welfare measures. It will hamper social stability. It will not be able to develop on the other freedoms that are vital for it becoming a panchayati swaraj. It must shape its processes in such a way that it will be able to create its own space in the nation's economy while retaining its value systems and indigenous processes. The questions it needs to ask are these. Does it understand what it means to shift from developing to developed status? If so, is it playing accordingly? Is it developing those parameters in the village which will enable its members to compete successfully in the new economic environment? How well does it cooperate with the surrounding villages to ensure that productivity and commerce are enhanced through partnership?

Detailed rationale: After the coming of the changes of 1991, there has been a shift in the focus of the Indian economy. Many erstwhile protections have been removed, and all the players have to find their own ways to survive in the competitive environment of the marketplace. Once the implications of this are understood, it naturally follows that a village community must plan and move in such a way that it will fit comfortably into the new economic system.

At this point, it does not make sense to withdraw into a shell and say that we do not want the new system. The system is inevitably upon us. Even nations like China that were working on an alternate model have had to withdraw and accept the pursuit of a market-based system. This cannot be avoided. Once this inevitability is understood, then it remains for the village to find out ways by which it can compete in the market place so that the economic needs of the village can be adequately met.

This freedom is more of a measurement parameter. The faster it develops a model for thriving in the present trade and commerce arrangements, the better. Of course, there will be a need for assistance from outside the village. It will help if external agencies work on making knowledge that will increase this awareness available in capsule form so that villages can easily swallow them. But ultimately, it will be upon the village itself to understand the dynamic needs of the ever-changing economic world and develop the nimbleness to thrive in any situation.

Economic Freedom 2: Employment

Relevance: A free nation and a free village cannot be based on an economy that keeps people perpetually poor and squeezes cheap labor out of them. It is important for the village to target a goal in which everyone is gainfully employed to a level such that the person and his family can pursue their highest destinies. This also requires the family to be able to participate fully in the cultural setting of the village and the modern economy.

Detailed rationale: It is similar to how a nation strives to ensure that all its employable citizens have productive jobs. The same responsibility also needs to be shouldered by the village team. Lack of employment opportunities usually sends the villagers to look for employment elsewhere, especially in the cities. This is usually coupled with a drastic fall in the self-respect and status of these migrants. Lack of job security in villages also leads to ills like human trafficking and suicides. These can be stopped through the primary efforts of the local community alone. The modern means of communication and the existence of a host of service industries can ensure that jobs are made available at remote locations in the nation's hinterland. The need is to raise the skill and knowledge levels of the village while, at the same time, creating job opportunities through the setting up of industries.

There are many advantages to doing this. Businesses in remote locations can be profitable on account of low-cost labor, accessible raw materials and low-cost overheads. It calls for the presence of the fourfold connectivity of the PURA model. But this cannot be done by merely pushing from above (government). The village communities must realize the importance of these things and ensure that there is a pull for them at the village end. It all begins when the village team steps up and holds itself responsible for employing its employable citizens.

It is important for the villages to focus on their competitive advantages here. Initially, they can focus on industries that are available, but eventually, they must specialize into areas that allow them to compete comfortably in the international market.

Economic Freedom 3: Financial

Relevance: In an economic environment that demands monetary capital for various needs, the cost of capital must be low. This means that the interest that one must pay should be reasonable, which can be achieved by making the entire process efficient. The system in the village must stand on its feet and at the same time be able to help the members of the village community. It must be a win-win situation. Too much burden on the givers of loans may kill the industry that is supposed to help. And too much of power in the hands of money lenders, besides being unethical, is also detrimental to the wellbeing of the villagers.

Detailed rationale: Through the pursuit of best practices, the Indian leadership has adopted the present capitalist system. In this system, a person holding capital has some advantages. (Other similar traits that offer advantages in this setup are holding knowledge, skills and degrees.) Even agriculture has now become capital-intensive; earlier, all the farmer had to do was keep some of his produce for seed. He had fertilizer and pesticides from natural sources in his village. Now, he needs to buy everything, seeds to plant, diesel to run certain equipment and even electricity (if the government does not offer it for free). If he does not invest, he is not competitive enough and may find it difficult to make ends meet. The fishermen too have to invest in nets, boats and diesel/petrol. These traditional professions are therefore encountering drastically increased possibility of losses in a way that is probably unprecedented in history. Besides this, the social dynamics ensure that families spend on marriages, dowries, various traditional festivals and sacraments, gaining prestige, buying costly utilities, buying new luxuries, etc. Moreover, families' fragmentation leads to greater pressure on family finances that are replenished by only a single earning member. Under such circumstances, the pressure to borrow is high.

In such a situation, the pressure on individuals and families can be mitigated if the village environment ensures that a healthy financial system is operational and facilitates better living. A healthy financial system also includes a healthy culture of repayment, of taking loans that are within means and of living within means. This calls for action in villages both from a commercial point of view and a cultural point of view.

Economic Freedom 4: Technological

Relevance: It is nice that city-dwelling citizens of India may adopt principles of khadi and *swagrami* and buy products made in village—though they may be of low quality—in order to help village producers. But this must not be taken for granted. Such special support is good for a kick-start, but eventually, the processes in the villages must become globally competitive. The products should soon develop and become of such quality that a 'demand' for these manufactured products emerges. This is only possible if there is continuous innovation, if the best practices are adapted and if the best technologies around the world are absorbed in the village processes.

In the internet age, with fast communication capabilities, this is definitely not a difficult thing to achieve. There are numerous agencies working in that direction, and village teams should go to them for these new technologies. The village must strive continuously to produce quality goods and improve upon what they have.

Detailed rationale: The nation has adopted a free market economy. In such a system, it is not appropriate for villages to remain attached to old technologies (unless there are very valid reasons). If a new technology gives better holistic results, then it must be adopted. For example, organic farming technologies are of far more value than chemicals-based farming. The former is holistic while the latter gives a short spell of success and is damaging in the long run. It is important that what is 'best' must be pursued. In areas of food processing and manufacturing, the best technologies will give the village and its produce a competitive edge in the market. The adoption of new, clean and efficient technologies also indicates that a village is focused on progress and that it is alive to innovation.

A very important advantage of the use of better technology is that it saves time and effort. As a nation becomes free, it must apply its energies to the higher things in life and not merely spend its man hours on survival. The village must be able to encourage art, education, culture, literature, etc., which are indices of high thinking and dwelling in actualization. If too much time and effort of the people of a village is taken up for mere survival, then it leaves lesser time for the finer things in life. Therefore, technology is important; eventually, as new technology leads to improvement, the village will start patronizing village sports teams, cultural teams, educationists, artists, etc. With the work of efficient administrators and wise leaders, society will change. The roles of people will be less focused on economic activities aimed at survival; there will be a culture of sufficiency, and a lot of time will be spent in pursuing these higher things in life. For example, if ten-year-olds and twelve-year-olds are being made to work so that their families can survive, then with improved technology, their work will not be required to help a family survive. They can then be sent for education while the parents can do all the work needed for the family's survival. This will bring greater success to the 'family' as an institution.

It is evident that technology must be pursued by villages at all cost. However, to begin with, this quest can be compromised in pursuit of the principles of khadi and swagrami till self-reliance starts kicking in.

Economic Freedom 5: Resource Economization

Relevance: What nature gives is truly unlimited. But that can be realized and utilized only if it is used efficiently with an attitude of plenty. What is there has to be replenished for the future generations. In all economic and other activities, there is a need to ensure that this principle is followed very religiously. For example, a proper attitude to conservation can ensure the perpetuation of clean and perennial water supply, rich ecosystems in forests, plentiful underwater animal and plant life in fishing zones, clean air, less diseases and lesser damage to crops and cattle. This needs to be an integral part of all good cultures.

Detailed rationale: To be able to plan in such a way that all kinds of resources are constructively utilized should be a responsibility of the village. Masked unemployment meaning underutilization of human resources, rotting produce meaning inappropriate marketing or non-adoption of food processing technologies, low water tables meaning improper ecological and water management are examples of concerns which a village has to address. The important themes in this are stated below:

a) Earth has to grapple with the crisis of degradation of the environment, and if every village in the world does not do its bit, then the chances of recovery are small. It is therefore important to handle resources efficiently in every village.

b) Next, in order to be competitive in a modern-day economic order, the village team needs to learn to use all its resources efficiently—every small measure counts.

c) The third aspect is about the question of recycling waste. An efficient system for this will ensure hygiene, manure and conservation. Efficiency in this gives many side benefits, all of which has great immeasurable value.

d) Most of all, the perpetuation of life in a village and the needs of the future generation need to be ensured, and for that, conservation and replenishment methods are a must.

APPENDIX A.3 – CULTURAL FREEDOM

The vision of Rabindranath Tagore aptly describes what the environment in a village has to really be.

Where the mind is without fear and the head is held high
Where knowledge is free
Where the world has not been broken up into fragments
By narrow domestic walls
Where words come out from the depth of truth
Where tireless striving stretches its arms towards perfection
Where the clear stream of reason has not lost its way
Into the dreary desert sand of dead habit
Where the mind is led forward by thee
Into ever-widening thought and action
Into that heaven of freedom, my Father, let my
country awake.

Cultural Freedom 1: Education

Relevance: This freedom is important because, through this, the citizens of the village can pursue the best of available education opportunities available anywhere and adequately empower themselves to participate and thrive in the modern economy. Modern systems are designed in a way such that the key to progress and prosperity is education. (Therefore, in the modern world, people seek to ensure fairness and justice by ensuring that every child is educated.) If a village cannot ensure this to its citizens, it is making them handicapped in a world that is driven by the power of education.

Detailed rationale: In the villages of today, traditional professional knowledge is indeed transferred from parents to children. But this knowledge is meant to meet the requirements of a different time and a different economic situation—for the economic system of the past. Relying on these alone to help children gain economic survival/success in the present economic scenario is a bad idea. Children in the villages, while still being good at what their traditional occupation requires, must also gain a foothold in the competitive contemporary world. Experts agree that this can be achieved by education. It is therefore the basic minimum that a person needs so that he is set on a course to explore the best he has to offer to the world. It is a take-off platform, and therefore, basic education must be ensured to all children at all costs.

It is true that there are certain negative influences that come in through modern education, which traditional people do not desire for their children. But that needs to be corrected in other ways. It is better to pursue a goal of collecting good from everywhere (including modern education) rather than protecting children from what is seen as harmful and consequently making them ill-equipped to participate in the modern economy. Ultimately, the system must take the best from all worlds. Sound knowledge in the arts and sciences from the scientific world, skills for earning a basic livelihood in the present economic environment and the best of values from personality development and spirituality must all be added into the syllabus. The elders in a village and parents must ensure that the education of children is holistic in a true sense. And yet, they must not interfere with the performance of teachers. Ultimately, it is what they patronize (support) that will gain strength in their village. They should support the right thing.

Cultural Freedom 2: Skill Sets

Relevance: Seen from an individual angle, when individuals have skill sets that are relevant to participation in various manufacturing units or services, they can be confident that they can make themselves useful to society and earn their livelihood easily without depending on doles. From the village community standpoint, the ability of a village to run systems within the village depends on the spectrum of skills available among its members. The greater availability of such skill sets in a village directly means the existence of better services for the members of a village.

Detailed rationale: A productive and prosperous society is one which makes available, to its people, various goods and services that improve the quality of living. At the community level, this includes a wide array of skills not restricted to 'job' skills. A lot of it consists of those services that are rendered for free in families, in friends' circles, in village festivals, in inter-village competitions, etc. Some of these are included in calculating the GDP of a nation while others are not. However, even those which are not counted serve a similar purpose—of increasing the levels of prosperity of a nation. The same applies to a village too. The availability of these skills is therefore a holistic estimate of how prosperous a village truly is. Skills are

required to run the political, executive and judicial system and economy-based systems. Better skills result in better productivity, improved marketing, better services, efficient processing of farm produce, improved health care and so on. All these skills have more than one dimension. Many appear as skills of the hand, but they go in coordination with skills of the mind. Very often, they need to be accompanied with skills in interpersonal interactions.

Therefore, a village may be considered free only if its members possess a minimum spectrum of skills required for services in the village and in the present socio-political-economic environment.

Cultural Freedom 3: Traditions

Relevance: In our rich, intellectual past, there have been outstanding philosophers whom Indian intellectuals fail to recognize today. Their inputs into the traditions of India are invaluable and need to be preserved and studied.

Those things that enrich life are usually converted into elements of tradition and culture and are transferred down from one generation to the next. They usually serve in improving the quality of life. They induce better skills in the 'art of living'. They improve human interaction, and they aid in holistic education.

By cutting off the negative traditions that are in violation of the constitution of India, the rest need to be preserved and encouraged so that Indian-ness can be lived and experienced in its complete wholeness. Therefore, being aware of the pitfalls, the villages must do their best to uphold their traditions the best they can.

Detailed rationale: In the Indian subcontinent, there is a rich diversity of traditions from time immemorial. These traditions hold in them the wisdom of the ages. These traditions serve to complete the 'education' of even the illiterate. These are therefore an integral part of the soul of a nation. Many times, it is difficult to point out the reasons for certain traditions being transferred down, but even in such cases, the one who experiences the tradition knows its value and therefore wishes to transfer it to the next generations. Elements of tradition and culture also define the modes of interaction which a community develops, and they help in smoothing out the relationships which members of a community share with each other.

If a particular group/community has survived for a long time, then it can be taken for granted that there are very sound elements of culture within that group/community. In such a case, every effort must be made to support the culture.

There is a need for caution though. There is always the possibility of certain practices accidently or deliberately being passed down as traditions but which have their origins in diabolic intentions. It is also possible that traditions that were started with very noble intentions got degraded in due course of time. Therefore, one must not take everything as being perfectly correct. It is a difficult balance, but it can be handled. It has to be resolved with great thought and deliberation.

For resolving this, human rights can be taken as a benchmark. If there are traditions which are not in conflict with human rights, then they can be preserved. If, however, there are some others which conflict with human rights principles, then there is a need to resolve them. In these instances, taking the stand that human rights are correct may also be as wrong as taking a stand that the traditions are correct. For example, we have seen how eastern traditions encourage people to *do their duty*; almost opposite to this, human rights traditions ask people to *fight for their rights*. It is known to Indian civilization that when a community is duty-based, that community prospers. Any community that is rights-based ends up with selfishness at a mass scale; such communities are weak. This issue has not been resolved at the global level as of yet, and so, conflict can be expected. However, keeping the wellbeing of one another above everything else, these conflicts can duly be resolved.

Cultural Freedom 4: Freedom in the Arts

Relevance: The arts play an important role in producing well-groomed personalities and fruitful societies. Those who care for and hope to build fruitful societies should ensure that the members of their community are gifted with the benefits of the arts to the greatest extent possible. Gandhiji too has particularly specified art in his vision for villages. The vision of Tagore puts art at the heart of human progress. Indeed, the best cultures are connoisseurs of the arts.

This is especially relevant in order to balance out life in a society that has come to worship consumerism. While consumerism tends to postpone happiness to the next thing to be consumed, it is in living in the present moment that one can experience happiness. In exploring this paradox, one understands that art helps a person's ability to live in the present moment; it is then that his creative juices flow and he can experience the bliss of the little (and huge) things around him. The pursuit of art is therefore the pursuit of living in the present moment and finding the highest joy.

Detailed rationale: There has rarely been a civilization—or even any long-lasting community—that does not have an art form that is special to it. Even tribes have their own forms of dance, music and traditions of storytelling. Art, therefore, cannot be considered as either incidental or individual pursuits; the village community has to take up art as one of its central themes to work upon.

Some of the greatest experiences in human expression are in the arts. Most arts have both a physical and a spiritual dimension to it besides the social. A thriving culture always uses arts as a means for experiencing what Maslow calls self-actualization.

It is argued in some circles that humans are actually spirits having a physical experience (not physical beings having a spiritual experience). It is therefore deducted that genuine self-expression is not of the body but of the spirit; highest self-expression is therefore not about possessions but about expression of creativity and the highest freedom. These traits of creativity and highest freedom are seen and experienced when an artist hits his 'zone'. Some call it a state of bliss. Others call it a connection with the Divine. Some say, 'I enjoy it.' Some have called it the power of music while others call it the bliss of dance. People well-versed in meditation techniques speak of art in terms of dynamic meditation—the mind is totally absorbed into excellence, it is at peace and the Self expresses itself.

If we wish to avoid mention of the spirit and return to things that we can observe directly, we can still see that absorption into the arts produces better concentration, more peaceful people, greater fun, passionate personalities, meditative individuals, etc. The best of kings always encouraged great art. It is a sign of class. It induces a certain discipline in people, and many of the distinguished personalities we know have claimed that it contains the highest experience a man can have. So, art must definitely be encouraged.

Cultural Freedom 5: Spiritual

Relevance: The village communities need to be aware that the clash of religions is still an unresolved issue in the present global intellectual world, but this is not the case in Indian spiritualism. Of course, there have been politicians, religious heads, kings, chieftains and all kinds of so-called leaders in India too who have tried to use religion to play power games. And such attempts will always be made in politics. But that is a battle every society must fight and a victory every society must win in order to thrive—to rise above differences and call the bluff on all those who try to divide. A community that successfully puts the Supreme Power within each human at a higher pedestal than the differences of mind and body (ideology and practices) will overcome any such divisive attempts. This defines the extent of freedom the village has attained with regard to the final frontier.

Detailed rationale: The 'opium of the masses' surely lessens the burdens which people unnecessarily carry through life because of inferior thought processes. Genuine spiritualism tunes them into a calm mind and enables the tapping of their highest potential. It is about short-circuiting the hierarchy of wants (Maslow) and making self-actualization the centerpiece of life—starting not from 'needs and wants' but rather from 'inspiration and self-actualization'.

Spiritualism caters to individuals, and to that extent, it is considered a personal affair. However, there are social dimensions to it which are centerpieces of life in highly spiritual societies like India. Mutual relationships flower brilliantly in communities, societies, groups, etc. where the spiritual quotient is genuinely high (independent of religion).

There is one dangerous word that is often used in the context of peace between religions: tolerance. Though it intends to do something positive, it has a substratum that is contrary to spiritualism. People think that they are doing a great thing by 'tolerating' other people. However, they still consider them as 'other' people. This is a half-righteous stand to take as it also displays a lack of wisdom. Such people give greater importance to the 'difference' in men than to the 'sameness'. In other words, to them, God is not overwhelmingly important in a way that individuality and labels become insignificant. They act as brand ambassadors for their religions but are not success stories of their religions. Such people have not achieved the crucial task for which religions are designed in the first place—transcending the individual and achieving total surrender to God.

The solution is not 'I will not change. You will not change. Let us tolerate each other'. The solution is 'How come I am not so well-versed in my own religion that I cannot understand that other person's sincere prayer and appreciate his selfless work'. To see universal goodness is the challenge. An inability to see it is the handicap that needs to be overcome.

APPENDIX A.4 – HEALTH FREEDOM

Health Freedom 1: Sports

Relevance: Sports activities sit on the borderline between health and culture. Besides the physical and social dimensions, there is a spiritual dimension to it too. The totality of it ensures a ready personality in a sportsman and dynamism in a society. It is also one of the best ways in which a community builds and exhibits its capacity for teamwork. Good sportsmanship is an index of the quality of the people of a village.

When an excellent sporting culture becomes a hallmark of a village, it is proof in itself that the village has raised itself into prosperity and that it is not a dung heap any more. It is proof that its orientation is sound and that it has gained a thirst for higher things in life.

Detailed rationale: The indigenous system that existed before the advent of the European influence used several institutions that existed in the field of sports as pillars for sustaining civilization. For example, let us imagine that there is one particular coach of a particular game—say, kho kho—who has spent his life pursuing it. Having been with the sport long enough and especially if he were a person who gave focused thought to its multifarious dimensions, there is no doubt that he would have gathered a wealth of knowledge on proper nutrition, attitude and health. He could use the same to give primary advice to his wards and to the members of his village. And if he were part of the tradition of transferring knowledge to the next generation in the village, then he would radiate the learning that happened in the many generations before him. This coach would then be a small walking encyclopedia of health and nutrition—especially with reference to that particular region to which he belongs. Thus, in all such rural games that are taken seriously in a village community, a great amount of knowledge regarding health and nutrition is preserved and transferred down the line through sportspersons and sports Gurus. They automatically become sources of help for the villagers on matters of health, nutrition, hygiene, etc.

This is just one of the examples. Developing a better attitude, better team work, improved team spirit, a culture of fine health, a greater appreciation for work and wisdom are some of the other benefits that accrue. It also remains one of the best tools to bridge gaps between diverse sections of society.

Health Freedom 2: Health Care and Wellness

Relevance: Life in a healthy body is anytime better. The health of a nation is not measured by the number of hospitals in it; rather, it is measured by the number and quality of institutions that are directly responsible for maintaining the health and fitness of its citizens.

Detailed rationale: Overlapping with the other responsibilities related to sports, arts, culture, spirituality, hygiene, medicine and nutrition, this aspect of freedom will also make itself manifest in certain initiatives centered on wellness and pro-active healthcare.

The inclusion of spiritualism in the list of related subjects given above is deliberate. It has been established that the health of the person is deeply related to the state of his mind, which has deep connections with spirituality. If relevant spiritual activities and disciplines are stripped off their religious color and applied in the daily life of the village. They will stimulate nicer attitudes, calmer dispositions and higher efficiencies. Such activities should be induced into the life blood of a village with great deliberation.

Health Freedom 3: Hygiene

Relevance: A lot of hygiene-related issues can be handled at the community level alone. Success at this has a lot to do with the control of diseases and promotion of healthier living. There is an important spinoff though; products made in villages and food served in its eateries must be made according to the best, practical cleanliness standards that can rival those used in the sanctum sanctorum of temples. This has the potential to better the economic success of the commercial ventures emanating from the villages.

Detailed rationale: Hygiene will squarely be the responsibility of the village community. External agencies, including the government, will only set standards, facilitate and audit. True freedom in hygiene arises when the community takes upon itself the responsibility to improve hygiene in its surroundings. A village can be declared free on this count when certain minimum standards are met as specified by higher authorities. Public hygiene implementation can be vigorously pursued on the basis of the village legislature's decisions.

As for personal hygiene, though the village community can interfere only to a very limited extent, efforts to promote the same must happen very vigorously. Citizens can definitely be encouraged to do the needful through a variety of creative ways—including direct advice by physicians, health camps and personal mentoring.

There are international hygiene standards defined for production spaces. These relevant standards must be understood and implemented in adequate measure in the production facilities in the villages. The hygiene standards need to be attained and sustained a safe distance above the benchmark so that products from the villages cannot be faulted on this count. The villager must carry this reputation as he visits the city and travels elsewhere.

Health Freedom 4: Nutrition

Relevance: Proper nutrition is one of the foundations of great health and prosperity. While minimum standards are to be fulfilled, there is also a need to expand the scope of that knowledge so that nutrition type and levels required for sportsmen, soldiers, blue-collar workmen, farmers, fishermen, etc. are taken care of. Olympic-level fitness requires an all-pervading basic foundation which needs to be set up in all the villages of the nation. Nutrition required for Olympic standards can be built on that foundation. Finally, cooking as an 'art' must have 'science' as the support.

Detailed rationale: It is generally perceived that nutrition for individuals is a concern for the corresponding family. However, in a village that has arrived, a large burden of that concern should be on the shoulders of the village itself. Ensuring that growing children are well fed is a village problem. The village must address that concern by ensuring adequate income for the families and through social support, if necessary, in critical cases.

When a village possesses a great culture of sports and arts, nutrition automatically receives a great boost. In the traditions of excellent sportsmanship, tremendous amount of knowledge regarding nutrition is also passed down. And this wealth of information can enrich a village.

Health Freedom 5: Medical Care

Relevance: A medical system is an inevitable part of a system's health arrangements and is definitely not all of it. But even among medical systems, not all are effective for all illnesses or affordable to all sections of society. This poses a challenge and an opportunity. While saving traditional forms of medicine that are integral to the vast riches the various cultures possess, we can balance it with the goods that come from modern Allopathy. The present system is monopolized by Allopathy and is individually effective, but collectively, it is not affordable to a vast majority. Moreover, Allopathy is not culturally well-integrated with the Indian traditional system. Alterations are in order, but more than that a revolutionary departure in thinking is required if the agenda of freedom is to be met in all its dimensions.

Detailed rationale: There should be an arrangement to achieve a smooth link that can transfer critical patients from the villages to specialists at a hospital at the PURA or mandala level. The idea is that this higher-level hospital should be of such standard that even serious cases need not go any further. Every neighboring village must contribute to the building and maintenance of this central hospital.

The village should diligently work toward getting a medi-care policy for the entire village with the specific goal of targeting those illnesses that end up draining the resources of families with such patients. The fine print for such deals should be negotiated with the concerned insurance company, and this should be a village effort.

The village should also have a set policy to sponsor its health workers for value addition through higher studies. They should regularly be sent for higher courses. Such further education should not be burdened on the health worker's personal finances.

The village should also achieve a quick response coordination with all health care initiatives of the government. It should be tuned for quick responses during times of epidemics and medical emergencies. An arrangement to fight diseases is a necessary component of a village community. Freedom in this sphere consists of having an arrangement for taking care of the ill health of every member of the village if and when a sickness occurs.

People will definitely fall sick, and they also need support for the physiological changes that happen to humans from when they are born to when they die. Hospitals, therefore, are inevitable. However, recognizing that medicine is a universal need for both, the poor and the rich, arrangements must be made such that no individual is left out of the net.

Though a systematic amalgamation has not happened between the various systems of medicine at the national level and a proper coordinated system has not been established, the village teams are not to feel constrained by this. They can show the way by promoting various options/solutions within their own jurisdiction. Only time and situation will decide the best solution for each village team. The primary responsibility for making medical facilities available to the members of a village must lie squarely on the village itself and not on any other external agency, including the government. However, that will not absolve the government of its responsibility of ensuring that the needful happens. It must actively facilitate this move.

APPENDIX A.5 – GOVERNMENT FREEDOM

Governance Freedom 1: Legislative

Relevance: Notionally, this freedom is already granted through the Panchayati Raj amendments to the constitution. But there is a need of some change in both the way it is conceptualized at the center and the way the state governments are implementing it through their regulations. The entire body of eligible voters in the village has the right to sit together and decide upon laws pertaining to the village; however, this freedom has been rendered meaningless owing to various other factors. These need to be reviewed by lawmakers at the state and national levels.

Detailed rationale: Retaining a 'village policy and rules' document at the tahsildar's office is important because it serves as a reference for all those who need to deal with the village. Such a document can be used to audit the functioning of a village. Besides, it will act as a facilitator in arbitration processes.

Villages that have satisfied the audit requirements of the government should have a greater degree of legislative freedom. The fine details regarding what powers they would get when the village is granted the freedom to legislate can be decided on the ground by the appropriate authority in the Indian democracy. This picture is bound to evolve and emerge as time goes by, provided the need for the village to be a republic is recognized at the outset.

Governance Freedom 2: Executive

Relevance: The question may arise as to how highly educated people like a doctor or a teacher can serve under the executive control of a bunch of villagers. Such a question is possible now because of the reality we experience in our villages today. We say that because they are illiterate and incompetent, they cannot be made so powerful. The counterpoint to this is again that old adage from mind science, 'Everything that is created is created twice. First in the mind and then in the real world…' This is a law of human nature. Hence, if we never conceive that a villager will be able to have a stature such that he will be able to direct a doctor or a teacher, then we are planning for a perpetuation of today's miserable 'dung heap' state of affairs. When we start planning and executing for Gandhiji's 'Garden of Eden' we must start by 'believing' that this is possible and that this is the way it ought to be. Only then will it be so.

If this freedom is given, it will reflect the state's sensitivity, concern and due respect for local cultures and recognition for the third-generation human rights of the citizens. But in the same breath, it must be tagged that the villagers must earn this through their adherence to the constitutional aims and necessities.

Detailed rationale: Once we start establishing institutions with the final goal of a liberated village in mind, then one will find in due course that the village executives more than meet the requirements. The aim should not be to keep the professionals of mainstream society as superstructures on the village; rather, leadership in a village should be shown the need to rise to such heights that they can direct the efforts of even professionals. The implication then is that the inhabitants are not yet up to the mark and that there is much to attain. There is a lot of growing that needs to happen, and it will happen.

The structure of the village executive needs to be reviewed too. The administrative setup convenient for a village of fishermen will be different from that for a village of farmers or for a tribal society. The amendments to the constitution in pursuit of panchayati raj and the relevant enactments of the respective states need to be reviewed so that there is flexibility for the villages to design systems for themselves that are suitable for their respective villages.

Contract-giving power is a very special aspect of executive power in a village. For public projects to be executed within the village, the powers for handing out contracts should lie in the hands of the village executives themselves.

There are many gains in this. First of all, it will compel the members of the village to get updated and empowered to handle that responsibility. Next, when users become the givers of contract, the quality of the projects can be improved drastically. Contractors who deliver quality will naturally be rewarded with more contracts. This will be a good selection process for the 'survival of the fittest contractor'. The village dwellers can put in a condition that their own work force should be used for the work, which will improve the quality of labor and, better still, the quantity of it since there will be an element of voluntary work in it. Transparency will increase, and corruption in the government—at least as far as public development works concerning the villages are concerned—can be checked. Initiatives, plans and project reports should be originated by the village itself; the projects can be put up as proposals to the donor agencies—even the government. Once the project is sanctioned, the work can be contracted out by the villagers themselves.

It is better that the contractors run circles around the village executives rather than government offices. Obviously, one can expect hesitation on the part of the current administration to move in that direction, but in the long run, it is better to get the village executives to gain control for the contractors will be under the constant gaze of the users (villagers) themselves. If the process of documentation, mandatory in each village, is clear and transparent, corruption can be minimized and quality maximized across the board.

There is a need to develop a complete system around this core idea that the decision-makers should be the village executives. They can consider the aid and advice of the administrative and technical experts of the bureaucracy but have to make their own decisions. Such a thing will have repercussions on the political landscape, but the impact will be positive if the rule of 'user decides' is applied. This will promote political change in that political parties will push for a system in which political activists are paid over the table for their services. This, in turn, will eventually facilitate a cleaner political system. It will improve the quality of life of the nation in a variety of ways. The system has to be creatively worked out into an effective arrangement by planners who work on public administration (statesmen, bureaucrats and academics).

Governance Freedom 3: Judicial

Relevance: This is one of the most crucial of freedoms which the village needs to be granted. The underlying principle is that the village should have a limited right to be able to conduct its judicial activities on the basis of its tradition and culture. Potential for such activity should not get restricted by the insistence that one must apply the rigors of the thousands and thousands of laws drafted at the national and state levels (some international ones too). The need to refer to the rigors of law as mentioned in the law books must be avoided where possible. This arrangement of scanning the books for everything comes from the present arrangement of courts established on the modern ideal of rigor of law. In contrast, rights and responsibilities of the nyay panchayats must be based on rigors of tradition and rigors of practice which are the next two lower reference points that can be a surrogate for law. Incidentally, in the Indian parlance, dharma is known to be the highest surrogate—even higher than law. But this effectively comes into play when the legislature seeks to improve upon the law and uses the voice of the majority to determine what is humanely (divinely) the best possible law. However, for the nyay panchayat of the village to function, the village must be conscious of traditions and practices that have been reconciled with modern law as emanating from the constitution of India.

Taking this approach has many advantages. It is capable of giving some disciplining authority in the hands of the village. It will therefore strengthen the village community. Low-cost remedies for seeking justice will automatically be in place. If due respect is paid to the opinions of the five elders of the established judiciary, then much of the cases that are pending in courts for years can be resolved quickly at the lower levels in due course of time in an environment which is more customized to one's traditions and where the primary focus is on arbitration rather than contest.

Detailed rationale: If someone has been appointed nyay panch, then they will not be allowed to take any positions in the executive and legislative sections of the village until at least two years after their term in the nyay panchayat. There should be procedures laid down to make the impeachment of an erring official possible. At the same time, it should not be so simple that throwing out people seems to be a matter of whim or simple majority.

They will sit in benches of not less than three for any issue concerning their village. All proceedings will be recorded and documented. A copy of the same will be sent to the taluka level court periodically. The decisions of the nyay panchayats will be subject to review by a higher people's court (Higher Nyay Panchayat) that will be constituted at an inter-village level after which a review can be done by a nyay panchayat at the district level. The same case may also be taken to the taluka level magistrates. In those cases, there will be a caveat by which any one of the members of the nyay panchayat that gave the decision will be requested to depose before the magistrate or taluka court at government cost. Or as a minimum, the reports of the happenings of that particular case in the nyay panchayat will be looked into by the court before a decision is given. The alternative is the creation of a jury at the taluka magistrate level.

When appeals from these local courts (or panchayat courts) move to higher courts, if due regard is given by the judges to the customs and traditions of local populations while upholding the principles enshrined in the constitution, a lot of strength can be delivered to local communities. In so strengthening the hands of the grassroots-level judiciary, the possibility of delivering low-cost and time-bound justice increases phenomenally. Though it may require a radical shift from western arrangements of judicial systems, a careful look at the traditional systems like the one currently existing in Britain and that which existed in our own ancient past shows that, if handled systematically, much good can come out of it.

In all likelihood, this arrangement of the judiciary will end up being a panel of five elders. It should be left to the villages as to what the nature of the composition may be. These persons will have both the acceptability of the village and a suitable certification by the government. At the next level, the PURA level, there will be another bench of five members who are distinguished jurors from the concerned region. Similarly, another bench will be present at the district level. At the higher levels, the team can also consist of a representative of the present formal judiciary whose duty will be to take notes and give advice but give decisions in equal weight as a nyay panch.

It has been demonstrated in other judicial arrangements that it is possible to define the limits of the sphere of power for a local judicial arrangement which can adjudicate on the basis of local laws. The limits can be defined through centralized processes at the state or national level. The local laws can be set up by the locals themselves within the limits defined. Such local laws can be given a chance once they have been scrutinized by the government for compliance with the constitution of India.

Governance Freedom 4: Integration

Relevance: This is important for the smooth running of the government both at the local and higher levels. The dynamics of freedom can be sustained well if the interactions between the governments at the local and higher levels are harmonious. While it is easy to see that an excellent higher-level government can facilitate freedom through the local government, the reverse is not all that obvious—but true nonetheless. If villages are driven by the motives of freedom, then they can come together to pressurize political parties, the media, members of legislatures, government executives and the higher judiciary to move in the direction that is favorable to freedom. The obvious instrument is the vote, but other means of communicating with these authorities are also available in the institution of the village government, and all such interactions must be used effectively.

Detailed rationale: The village will be called upon to participate in all kinds of activities beneficial to the region in which it exists. It will be expected to contribute to the betterment of the nation, wellbeing of the citizens, general upkeep of law and order and the like. The free village will be a willing spoke in such activities; in fact, it should take it upon itself to shoulder initiatives on behalf of the other neighboring communities too.

Without being divided within itself, a village must play a productive role in the election of MPs and MLAs. It must arrange for these persons to be heard at public forums in the villages set up by the villages themselves.

The village must coordinate with development agencies at all levels (center-district and state-taluka) so that the development process designed for them is understood, advantage is taken of the opportunity, the officials are facilitated in the process of delivery and proper feedback is given to the concerned authorities.

The inter-village zone, where various villages come together for some collective good, is where great patronage needs to be offered for all kinds of welfare activities. It is in this zone that great initiatives for the betterment of the region and society need to be taken up. When such initiatives are taken up, the free village will come forward more than halfway to cooperate and help take any constructive project to its logical conclusion. In fact, this is the general area wherein all well-wishers will need to exert their best efforts. (This aspect has been taken up in Section V of this part of the book and it is of vital importance.)

A special mention may be made here of knowledge and skill upgrading. There will be many initiatives from outside the village to transfer knowledge, skills and technologies to the members of the village. These initiatives may be focused on economic benefits or benefits in any of the other spheres of life. Such training may be directed at the educated or those who are not literate. In all such activities, greater merit in the process of integration will mean enthusiastic participation so that the level of general good of the people, community and nation can be raised.

APPENDIX A.6 – VISION FREEDOM

Vision Freedom 1: Environmental

Relevance: Global climate change cannot be tackled by the nations and the companies that have already done huge damage to the world. The effort must come from local communities all over the world. If every community has a vision for taking care of its environment, the cumulative effect will achieve much more than what national leaders can even dream of. Every community must play its role in undoing what the human race has done so far.

Nonetheless, the benefits of environment protection are directly realizable by the village itself. Protection of the environment eventually leads to health, wellness, sustenance of the community and even enduring commercial success. It takes foresight and long-term commitment, but the benefits are certain. Moreover, it is a good example to set for the next generations. Raising the environment in priority is an obvious sign of the advancement of that village.

Detailed rationale: Such environmental aims will differ in content for forest villages, desert villages, archaeological villages, snowbound villages, swamp villages, tourist villages, seashore villages, etc. However, the inherent principle will be the same. The village will have a vision about the environment and develop a clear plan on how best to fulfill the vision.

The commitment will be initially measured in the goals when set; but as time goes by, it will be on the basis of commitment to the goals and the practical achievements in that direction.

Vision Freedom 2: Developmental

Relevance: This is a vision about how prosperous the village is—how it will have most if not all the required amenities that are needed for the wholesome development and living of individuals of that village. This should help make everyone in the team look at one particular horizon. It will give much needed focus for the village's aspirations, and it will serve as a strong reminder to external agencies that the indigenous people have their own aspirations and goals.

But then, though the general direction may be fixed, it should be interpreted into a dynamic plan. At reasonable intervals of time, the existing Gram Sabha should take it up and improve upon it and make it responsive to the challenges facing the village.

Detailed rationale: In developing such a vision, imitation is never the best solution. The development vision has to be unique to the needs of the village. Guidance/inspiration can definitely be taken from others, even from other towns and cities. But to have a vision that is tailor-made for the indigenous culture and geographical setting of that village is important.

This will require the elders of a village to be given a good ear even if they're not literate. The traditions of a village have much wisdom passed down, which are sometimes beyond the grasp of modern thinking. After excluding those practices which violate the constraints of the constitution, it is important to make every attempt to retain the rest. Therefore, the developmental vision has to be rooted firmly in tradition, look forward into the modern and be uniquely designed according to the need of the particular village. Their own Vision 2020, if we may use the phrase given to us by Dr. Kalam… A two-year plan that is in pursuit of a five- or ten-year development vision would be in order. In fact, this will probably be the place where the efforts toward the second freedom of that village will commence. And sustaining, fine-tuning and diligently executing that vision would be the expression of its highest aspiration.

Vision Freedom 3: Contributory

Relevance: When a free community looks ahead, it will think of 'giving' to the nation more than 'asking' from it. It will want to achieve a position of such self-sufficiency that it can produce and contribute men and resources needed for building a great nation.

Detailed rationale: One of the greatest indices of free individuals or free societies is that they give to others out of a sense of abundance. That, of course, does not mean that everyone who gives is wise, or even that someone who is wise will definitely give you whatever and whenever you ask of him. But one thing is sure. Around such a person, there is always a feeling of plenty. There is enough. The free community, likewise, needs to have a feeling of plenty/ abundance in its disposition.

A great contributory vision can pour great energy into the life of a village—when a village seeks to give, it automatically assumes that it has grown and dwells in that excellence and prosperity. A great contributory track record is one of the best indices that can be used to determine the depth of a village's freedom.

Transition to Real Freedom: Through Institutions Built on Righteousness

Part 3

This part deals with how the various aspects of public life in the nation, the polity, the economy, the police force, the judiciary, social services, education, etc., must accommodate for a free nation… a nation of free people where even the citizens from rural India, educated or not, can live with dignity and to the complete tallness of their being.

Dedicated To
All Those
Who Strive
To
Uphold Dharma

Prelude

After re-visiting the merits of deep decentralization and ancient Indian thought relating to transcendence, we can see that there are huge opportunities that can be tapped into for the betterment of the nation. In both instances, there are solutions offered. In the case of panchayati swaraj, even action plans are provided for the stakeholders so that they can improve the efficiency and effectiveness of the efforts they put in. But there are other dimensions to life in India as well. And each dimension must fine-tune itself to facilitate freedom at the grassroots level.

This part of the book can therefore be seen to be as further elucidation of the idea of inspired living the way our ancients would have wanted us to live. One more step in the direction of what must be achieved in the practical world today… Central to this is the concept of dharma. This book explores how the nation must consider restoring its various processes to dharma.

Do revisit the first part of the book for a detailed exposition on the fundamentals of dharma—the way we must consider it in the India of the early 21st century.

Foreword

Mahatma Gandhi has inspired the likes of Martin Luther King, Nelson Mandela and Obama—not without reason. He is also the mascot for the *Swatch Bharat Abhiyan*. However, cleaning up the streets is only a token of the possibilities of Gandhiji's vision. Mahatma Gandhi is more relevant to cleaning minds. I firmly hold that free India has underutilized the Gandhian vision, and the persuasive arguments made by Nixon clearly show that we have indeed not done justice to him. Mahatma Gandhi had a vision for India, but the turmoil in the decade of Indian independence did not allow for the fruition of that vision. Gandhi wanted every Indian to have control over his own destiny, and that is far from the reality of today. And Nixon has taken up the laborious task of trying to interpret for us what that vision would mean in this time and age of Industrial Revolution by Disruptive Technology. I would say that his twenty-five years of research have indeed come up with compelling findings.

I have known Nixon for the last six years ever since he joined Great Lakes to help the mercurial Mr. T. N. Seshan with some research work. From there, he was sidestepped into a junior faculty position at Great Lakes, and in the meantime, he was on the job of writing his analysis of the way forward for India. He comes across as an earnest individual who goes about his work in the best way he can. He was one of the outstanding students of his batch when he completed the PGPM Flex program (equivalent to an executive MBA) at Great Lakes. He can play some good picnic songs on the guitar and sing along, but what has impressed me most about him is his deep understanding of the *Bhagavad Gita*. Along with the legendary T. N. Seshan, the three of us have authored a book on leadership called *Yogyathwa: Simple access to powerful relationship* which is a unique book that deals with transformational leadership as analyzed from first principles. It is heartening to see that Nixon has dedicated his talents towards this particular project instead of pursuing a career as a NET-qualified physicist. And this research related to visions, strategies and plans has produced something that must take up the thinking Indian's serious attention.

When setting up the Great Lakes Institute of Management, I had no doubts in my mind that the way to go for an outstanding Indian school was a 'Global Mind-set and Indian Roots', and that is the tag line for the school now. I have great instinctive belief in the deep wisdom of this land which talks of the whole world as one family. Yogyathwa was based on that principle, and this book by Nixon manifests that same faith in another valuable context.

This part of the book entitled *Transition to Real Freedom: Through Institutions Built on Righteousness* is a follow up on the Parts 1 and 2. In this part, he attempts to build a national narrative based on the principles that he has explored in the earlier parts. In the first two parts of the book, he has dealt with some very tricky questions that have tormented Indian and western intellects for a long time now. For example, from Part 1 of this book, it is evident that there is a baby sitting in the caste bathwater and that it is not all muck as it is usually made out to be; it cannot be dismissed in a flourish. He is showing a way to separate chaff from grain in this debate. He argues that it is only misunderstanding that has led to the ills of the system. This new perspective can transform the way we deal with caste and communal problems. We can truly put these issues aside and focus on the nation's development.

Part 2 of the book deals with something close to my heart—the self-empowering of the villages of India. In the experiential leadership training course called Karma Yoga initiative, our students at the Great Lakes in Chennai have adopted twenty-seven villages in the vicinity of the campus where they interact with the local population and participate in their development. While Karma Yoga trains the students in leadership, it gets them accustomed to the realities of the villages. The course has a transformative effect and helps the students pepper their passion with compassion and shows them the importance of 'Transformational Service Leadership' through 'Experiential Learning'.

An important point that is conveyed in the Karma Yoga initiative is for the students to empower the villagers so that the villagers rise on the strength of their own wings, and this is exactly the approach that Nixon has taken in this work. I vouch for the fact that there is immense talent in the villages that only needs nourishing and channelizing. I come from a poor village in the Pudukkottai district, but look at what my brothers and I have achieved in our lifetime! With the right values, guidance and teamwork, I am sure every village can rise which, in turn, will transform the nation.

Two sections in this book relate directly to the work I do; one on the management of economic goals and the other on education. I am in total agreement with Nixon that the purpose of the economy is to serve the people and not to mount misery on the poor of a nation. The idea of encouraging entrepreneurship in the rural areas is sound. But the challenge is huge because of severe bottlenecks, and I am sure the people of India will surmount them. We may have missed the manufacturing revolution, but I am sure at least services can be rendered to one another in the villages so that everybody gains. For a young India with more than 50% of the population below the age of twenty-five, the challenges may be great, but the opportunities are even greater. Small businesses spread out in the villages is the way ahead, and therefore, the surrounding environment must be enabling towards that.

As for education, I have always held that my third-grade-pass mother was a university to me and my brothers. And when Nixon defines education in its all-encompassing form as it being a phenomenon linking one generation with the next, I completely agree. True that even an illiterate man can be educated, and a Ph.D graduate may be ignorant. It all depends on what you give value to in education. What was the need of instituting the Karma Yoga project, of having the students themselves run the committees in Great Lakes, of ensuring experiential methods for teaching or of ensuring that the campus gets a good rating with Leeds? It is so that the students pick up much more than just knowledge as they go out. But I assure you: even that is not complete. A child starts learning from the womb, and I bless all those mothers and families that live high values and inspire their offspring to develop into better human beings.

I commend the use of the magic word 'dharma' in this book. We have explained in the book on Yogyathwa as to how it does not mean religion in the sense that it is used today. It is about being inspired by the Ultimate CEO Lord Ganesha (or Allah-U-Akbar if you are a Muslim or Jesus Christ if you are a Christian) and doing what is good for humanity without giving consideration to caste or creed or sex or religion. If the goal of a person's life is to do the will of the Ultimate CEO, it will bring great blessings upon him and those around him. Making dharma a part of everything they do—be it politics, economics, education, policing or administration, anything—is how Indians are expected to live. It makes them excel. In the parlance of Yogyathwa, it makes them true leaders. Let us find out what our dharma is in this present India and world and do it to the best of our abilities. I am sure that in the pursuit of dharma, we will not only get pleasure along the way but also joy and fulfillment of life.

As a baby I was placed on the lap of Gandhiji, the father of the nation, for some time, and I have considered it a blessing and an inspiration to do my work for the nation. And it delights me that when we are in the eve of the 150th year of the politician-saint's birthday, I am forwarding this book that attempts to address his concerns for the poorest of the poor among the Indians. Gandhiji had great faith in the common man. You give them the opportunity, and they will rise to the fullness of their being. It is time the people know what Gandhiji wants from them and what is possible. The directions Nixon has shown will go a long way towards understanding what that Gandhian vision is. I strongly recommend any Indian who feels frustrated that there is no way ahead for India to read it. Do not be too disturbed by references to dharma and the spiritual texts. Nixon's methods of drawing secular but spiritual wisdom from the works of the wise is sure to benefit serious thinkers and light up the path ahead a little more.

You, the Youth of the Nation, Must Act. I am delighted to place before you this compelling argument asking us to go back and understand what Gandhiji wanted for India. And the youth of this nation must act and act now. We have a task to do in the world, to rise up to great heights and to show how great peace is possible within and amongst religions of this world. It is all hidden in the wisdom of our ancient sages. You must draw from that wisdom and realize freedom for your fellowmen.

The work required is great, and if you must take the lead, then you must take unconventional decisions. I always tell my friends if there is a conflict between your interests and beliefs and the nation's interests and beliefs, then you take the backseat and the nation and the leadership chair should take the front seat.

Dr. Jaswant Singh of BJP is a friend of mine and the former home and finance minister in the BJP government. You may recall the incident where an Indian airplane was hijacked by a few terrorists from Pakistan. During the negotiations with the terrorists, Jaswant Singh as the then-home Minister had to decide between whether to send *his own son* as a hostage to the terrorists so that the remaining hostages could be released or stall and probably get hostages killed one at a time. Obviously, his personal interest and the family's recommendation was to not send the son, but he decided to do so in the interest of India. He agreed to send him. Of course, our brave commandos helped, and the folks also left to Kandahar. Who says India has no leaders? We have, but we have to find them. I have seen too many non-leaders flinch from this responsibility.

Even as you consider what you wish to do with your talents, *prepare to be lonely, and take a bold decision that may not be popular*.

Be proud of what *you want to be*. But be the *best*. The key is *you* need to *enjoy* your life. The day you wake up and feel frustrated that you need to go to work clearly tells you that you do it for someone else. There is a nice book called *Control Your Destiny; Or Someone Else Will* (on Jack Welsh) by Nel Tichy and another author from Fortune Magazine. If you have some doubts, pray to your mom wherever you are and ask her to guide you mentally. You will be blessed and will choose the right decision. Analyze with your brains and experience, but *decide by your heart*.

Many of us often wonder what lies in our future without ever noticing what is in front of us. The future relies on speculation and uncertainties, but the *present* (which is God's present to you) gives you the facts. No matter how harsh or sweet the present is, accept it, grow with it, enjoy it and be grateful for it. Start to be happy even among adversities *now* rather than waiting for what the future may hold. Everything is in your *attitude*; your attitude decides the altitude you reach. You are an eagle with energy and excitement. You soar to the highest altitude. Of course, don't hang around with chicken. Why? Chicken can't fly, and on top of it, you will get chicken flu.

Any time is the right time to ponder, think and plan. Who you should be is the great question you should ask yourself, and you should take inputs from your Gurus, parents, and good friends. But ultimately, you need to decide based on a SWOT analysis of yourself and the soul-searching question of what really turns you on. But as I always say, make sure that you are propelled with intellect and steered by values, and the answer will be there.

The way ahead for India may be tough, but note that whatever your heart combined with your brains can conceive and believe, you can certainly achieve. Of course, a lot of dough requires a lot of plowing. Impossible is not a fact; it is just an opinion. A smile is a curve that sets things straight. A Can-Do and Will-Do attitude will take you a long way. Play with passion, with a tinge of compassion.

Dare to dream with cream of will. Go for glory and become a great story for your future, for your family and for the nation…

God bless you all.

Jai Hind!

Prof. Bala V. Balachandran
Founder and Dean, Great Lakes Institute of Management, Chennai, India
J. L. Kellogg Distinguished Professor (Emeritus in service) of Accounting and Information Management
Northwestern University, Illinois, USA
Executive Professor and Strategy Advisor to the Dean, Bauer College, University of Houston, Texas, USA

Section I

India at the Crossroads: The Need to Move and the Direction to Take

Indians enjoy a great degree of freedom in comparison to so many other people in the world. An Indian can pursue his highest interests in relative peace, provided he is financially and educationally empowered because chauvinistic impositions have not had a free run in India (for the time being, at least). But this does not give the nation the right to rest on its laurels. That the nation is doing better than others on this score is not a valid standard to measure itself by. The nation which once attracted invaders and traders from lands afar because of its prosperity and wealth has been reduced to rank among the bottom 25% of the nations of the world on a variety of significant development indices. The economy is growing rapidly and pretty well by world standards, but disparity too is growing. There is a great deal of wretchedness and poverty still, and many social issues of highly adverse nature continue unabated.

Is this the best we can do as a nation? Though we need not indulge in questioning the sincerity of effort, we can surely question the validity of the methods used. There are higher time-tested ideals that have not been pursued with the necessary insight and conviction. The nation can work for universal justice and trusteeship in much better ways. And therefore, much remains to be done.

How free is India? The quality of freedom that the nation enjoys can be called to question. Do all Indians walk with their heads held high? Let alone *all* Indians, can even a majority of Indians walk with their heads held high? Think of a lost child having to fend entirely for himself in the hard, unforgiving cities of this nation. Think of one's own children, dirty and in rags, put into the hut of a very poor, wretched person; what if one's

child had to live that life accidentally? The average Indian would dread that. What does this say about the state of affairs of the nation? Who is to address the woes of the countryside and the slums—their rights, livelihood, education and self-respect? In extreme cases, people are starving to death. Is this the freedom one would want the nation to have seventy years after it was born?

A lost opportunity: Some required corrections did not happen when the nation got its independence. What happened at independence was more of a hurried reformation by a completely occupied and hard-pressed leadership rather than a revolutionary transformation. There was a need to convert an attitude of subjugation into one of genuine freedom, but that opportunity could not be taken up satisfactorily. The nation played it safe by perpetrating the erstwhile order in a diluted form; in a very significant way, the nation has retained an approach to public life that enfeebles the Indian. And the reason for this is not hard to find in the context of the time when India achieved independence.

The leaders of that time had a lot on their plates already. They were preoccupied with the socio-political turmoil of the time. They were wrestling with the immediate challenges of development that compelled attention and non-delayed action. And most of all, they were inspired by the ideas of progress and successful nationhood which were considered the global ideals of that time. The choices they made arose from those constraints. Seventy years on, the constraints have changed, and therefore, in a changed scenario today, there is enough justification for the present generation to revisit the decisions of the past and see if alternate routes are there for the nation to take today.

Maybe something more Gandhian or something with a little more indigenous content…

Which direction to take? East or West? One would have observed from practical reality that the Indian public opinion has a confused outlook which neither appreciates the depths of the Indian culture nor absorbs the western ways in its entirety. For instance, very few schools of today's India make a committed effort to instill western notions of nobility into their wards. Nobility is considered an important virtue in the western world. Similarly, neither is the concept of dharma taught to children with adequate conviction, which is central to the Indian ethos. The system of education therefore ambles on undecided as to which way to decisively go. With the coming of Indian self-rule and the nation deciding to persist with many major institutions of the pre-independence times, it maintained the status quo with regard to Indian culture. This has resulted in an uncertain no man's land between the two cultures. And the nation's confused existence in this no man's land has deprived it of that vital focus of peoples' energies; it has deprived the nation of the use of its indigenous culture, which can impart great strength to its endeavors.

And no one need be blamed for it. The fundamentals of Indian culture/thought have not been harmonized with western methods/thought through intellectual inquiry; this means that one is forced to choose one or the other, and the nation has chosen 'modern' thought. And even though this is the preferred choice for institution-building in India, most Indians are committed to their indigenous culture with unshakable life-and-death bonds.

The problem is further compounded by the fact that many political opportunists and dubious Gurus have usurped the role of representing the Indian ethos. In the resulting melee, the Indian citizen has not been able to decisively conclude as to whether it was Mohandas Karamchand Gandhi or Nathuram Godse who actually represented Indian Hinduism. Those who have taken to talking vociferously about Hinduism in the political arena seem to be those who are playing by Samuel Huntington's belief in the clash of civilizations theory. These narrow representatives claim to protect their own in their battle with irrational fundamentalists of Islam and other faiths, but at the same time, this does not manifest the indigenous culture's splendor. Irrational fundamentalists here in India are as good as they are anywhere: they take people further away from the best which spirituality offers. The net result is that, as of today, Indian culture does not receive adequate or true justice.

Thus, through the years, owing to the fact that the West-East debate has not been resolved adequately, there is an atmosphere of general stagnation and indecisiveness on the question of values, motivation methods and excellence. When there is a general degradation, no one is sure about how to arrest it. And unless the Americans finally discover how great Indian learning is, scholars in India do not seem inclined to take their ancient riches seriously. And there is a conscious attempt to refrain from using its merits to try and improve their lot. The net result is that the nation does not draw its inspiration for constructive action from the strength of its indigenous culture.

India must evolve its own solution: The nation's approach to issues in public life needs a re-orientation, and such re-orientation needs to be addressed at the level of civilizations. For example, we see that the nation has taken up believing in the Huntington idea of clash of civilizations (civilizations based on religions will constantly fight). That is the present political discourse. The nation needs to change and re-dedicate itself to the Hindu concept of 'commonality of civilizations', which alternatively suggests that great civilizations are born only when they get in tune with the one and only Highest Spirit.

When India gained independence, the elements of the Indian culture originally designed around kingship as the political method were not used as the mobilizing force. Rather, the dynamics of democracy, the parliamentary system and a mixed economy were adopted. And the nation has been counting on these to power its path to progress and prosperity. A twist was added with the coming of economic liberalization. Economic liberalization hopes to widen the gates for a free market system. It is an attempt at increasing commitment to the use of economic competition, consumer sovereignty, investor profits, etc. Through these free market initiatives, one hopes to pull the nation into progressive activity and consumer freedom.

But will the totality of this approach deliver to the nation the success it seeks?

Doubts arise because real success (even in the economic field) can come to a nation only when the motivation for an individual citizen's action (in all forms of economic and support activities) runs parallel with the ethics of action of that particular nation's indigenous culture. In this case, it is seen that since the practical manifestation of the free-running capitalist system does not cater to a Dharma Bhoomi (which, in turn, is supposed to be a holistic system where an individual, whoever he is, naturally ought to get his right to justice), it stands a very low chance of real success, especially in India. Rather, if these modern methods (especially capitalism) were to be used without proper cautions, it could end up doing much harm.

Obviously, at this juncture, India must organize a 'getting- into-terms' between the West and the East and avoid the alternative of intolerant and wild mutual condemnation. Proper harmonization is possible only if each civilization tries to understand the other. Those taught to look through western eyes need to study the East. They need to look at both the scope and limitations of what the East can deliver. And as for those scholars who are deeply committed to indigenous cultures and the various inherited religions, they should make an even-minded inquiry into the fundamentals of the western way of life, study its origins, look into its priorities, spot the values hidden within it (which make western civilization tick) and discuss, devoid of prejudices, as to how the best of values can help the best of nations shine. Currently however, because of the intolerant shouting and condemnation that prevails, destructive opportunism finds a free pasture. Division politics finds itself a feast, and the nation tends to border on hopelessness.

The current generation has the right: It is important to realize that the decision-makers of today do have the scope to mend social surroundings in accordance with what is best. Even at the lowest level of administration, the community level, there is great scope for people to control their destinies.

Let us take the education system, for instance. Should one take the line of complaining about it or doing something about it? Why complain about it when the present generation does indeed have the authority to re-orient it for the better? The purpose during the system's inception was to produce a new class of people with westernized tastes—for so many reasons—and from it, the system evolved. But, of course, the nation can change it! Today, the nation can re-orient it in a manner such that it will teach every child to live his life well through 'giving' and not 'asking'. It may be possible to inculcate the fruits of param vidya in some secular way, having seen that it can do some good to individuals and society!

Similarly, why should the remains of the zamindari system continue to strangle the countryside? Historians tell us that many of its features were introduced at some point or the other in our colonial history. Can this generation then not 'introduce' other finer points into it so that it contributes to a universal growth process?

There are many others. For instance, won't the policemen themselves be a more effective and happier lot if the entire force was more friendly? So also the judiciary… Can the nation not expand the reach of its structured judiciary to include what a layman, with a little training, can easily handle in his neighborhood? Would that not help the judiciary deliver time-bound and less costly justice?

As one probes into past realities as we have done in Part 1 and Part 2 of this book, it increasingly becomes certain that what is presented to the nation today is not a divinely-gifted, un-changeable problem but rather a standing challenge. The potential exists; things can be changed.

The responsibility is mine: The responsibility of taking the nation where it is supposed to finally go must squarely rest on the shoulder of each and every Indian, not the prime minister alone. If the ancient Indian civilization was worth anything and if dharma was worth anything at all, then it is this feeling (of all citizens being responsible) that is at the heart of what it is worth. Ancient Indian wise men never perceived the state as anything other than a projection of themselves and their people. Each one in his position was responsible for the proper running of the nation. This is the essential feeling in dharma.

Initially, in the Vedic age, the tasks that men were to perform were decided on the basis of aptitude and merit. Then for a long period of time, it was decided on the basis of birth. And now, in the modern era, it gets decided on the basis of education and appointment to various responsibilities in society. Irrespective of what method was (or is) used, if the citizens of a nation collectively take responsibility for themselves and if this sharing of responsibility is idealized in each citizen, then the nation can truly stand up to match the 'tryst of the ancients'.

Liberated beings are essentially trustees: And finally, strongly embedded in the indigenous culture is a sense of equal rights. All Indians have equal right to the resources of this land—this is guaranteed by an implicit Indian version of the charter of freedom. But, for practical reasons, the nation divides the resources and the responsibilities unequally by means of whatever system that has been adopted (democracy, capitalism, etc.). Each individual is given resources in accordance to the task he is to perform, and he is expected to give back in proportion to the resources he commands. Those who are given better resources would shoulder appropriate responsibility even if that position of eminence was achieved by the hard work of one's parents, teammates or one's own self. Therefore, if the system has given anyone a lot, then that person must give back to the nation proportionally—this is the way Indians are supposed to live. All this is at the heart of the sense of trusteeship that Gandhiji propounded.

What more does trusteeship say? There must be dignity of labor. Owing to the fact that the selfless worker sustains the system through his sacrifices, the nation, being obliged and grateful needs to pay back in good measure. These workers are considered as selfless even if they happen to be poor because there are many (and in India, most) among them who are pledged to poverty by choice as is ordained by their dharma in society (for example, the traditional dharma of most women is especially designed around handling limited monetary resources). The nation shall give due appreciation to the commitment of those—even among the poor—whose actions stem from trusteeship motivations (which incidentally are not motivations driven by selfishness or the want to survive). Trusteeship mandates that the nation shall perceive society with spiritual depth and not material shallowness, for such an attitude impacts its citizens, its social environment and the relationships among its citizens and delivers great good. Among the highest of these sacrificing poor are definitely the uncelebrated soldiers of India who put everything on the line. In vain does he live who does not understand and experience the beauty and nobility of their lives.

The consequences of the trusteeship culture are indeed surprising. It tells him who strives to practice trusteeship to 'strive to progress in society, in the competition environment, in order that one may shoulder even more responsibility'! That surely doesn't sound like a great motivating force, and the paradox is that it is! (Thanks again to ancient Indian learning—and to wisdom from across the globe—which shows how.) As human nature has it, and as the seers say, in the long run, a person's hindsight will reveal that the awareness of having shouldered his responsibilities with heart and conviction carries more weight, joy, contentment and satisfaction than all the self-aggrandizing milestones of life put together. All citizens are gifted with talents and opportunities to work for others and for dharma. Working on these opportunities—in the right spirit—is taught to Indians as both the means and the end of happiness and fulfillment. It is the success of having come up with the correct response/action that brings joy and satisfaction; the result does not matter.

> *"Let us not be slaves to the fruit of our actions. Let action itself be the fruit for us. Living this way is a life of true freedom."*
>
> *– Sirshree Tejparkhi*
> *Tej Gyan Foundation*

The same guidance, as from this contemporary saint, comes from this ancient marvel, the *Bhagavad Gita*:

> *Being steadfast in Yoga, O Dhananjaya. Perform actions, abandoning attachment, remaining unconcerned as regards success and failure. This evenness of mind (in regard to success and failure) is known as Yoga.*
>
> *Work (with desire) I verily far inferior to that performed with the mind unperturbed by thoughts of results. O Dhananjaya, seek refuge in this evenness of mind. Wretched are they who act for results.*
>
> *Bhagavad Gita: 2:47-48*
> *(Translated by Swami Swaroopananda)*

Therefore, trusteeship concerns demand that much work needs to be done to re-orient goals and priorities. The social systems need to be re-tuned to suit the beliefs of the ancient wise men. True liberation needs to be obtained by the masses and the grassroots communities in terms of changing attitudes. Only then will the nation stand up to the glorious ancient tryst which the ancient sages promised for its citizens.

Each sub-system that the nation is composed of must be revisited and studied as to how it can be made to reflect these essential values that come from the wisdom of the sages—how each sub-system must relate to dharma. And in the subsequent chapters, an effort will be made at describing some of this. It will be a littering of principles and ideals as well as thoughts and ideas for direct implementation, which will hopefully capture for the actors what that alternative perspective of the nation, coming from ancient India, might be.

Section II

A Polity That Nurtures Gandhian Freedom at the Grassroots

"…this nation, under God, shall have a new birth of freedom -- and that government of the people, by the people, for the people, shall not perish from the earth."

Abraham Lincoln, Gettysburg, Pennsylvania
November 19, 1863

While this quote from the remarkable address by Abraham Lincoln has inspired democracies across the world, a small addition in its paraphrasing could have brought to light an important aspect of government that can bring great freedom even under a prudent kingship. Democracy for Lincoln and the Americans was not only about the nature of the central rule that America aspired for, it was also in the grassroots-level freedom in which the local mayor-level governments offered scope for locals to express themselves as free individuals. Another remarkable example of that expression of common citizens comes from Netherlands. A great, successful and sustained team keeps the sea from inundating nearly 26% of the nation's landmass which, in turn, lies below sea level. That success emerges from the action taken under the *waterschap* of the local bodies of Netherlands. Waterschap, in turn, are a reflection of every citizen's sentiment of wanting to keep the waters away from the borders of the nation. Likewise, the grassroots-level system of Uttaramerur fame talks about a community of self-governing citizens who take charge of their own government. Whether it is the mayor in the US, the waterschap in the Netherlands or the village republics of Uttaramerur, they represent political expressions that are driven not from the king to the citizen but rather from the citizen to the king. These are self-expressions of citizens. And the government of a nation, whether it is a democracy or a kingship, must govern ensuring that this participation is nurtured at the grassroots level. It must not be a rule; it must be a self-rule—a rule WITH the people.

The governments in India at the center and the state must realize that while being a government OF, BY and FOR the people makes India a democracy, the true expression of freedom becomes a reality only when it is also a government WITH the people. They must realize that this freedom is contained in the decentralized vision that Gandjiji propounded. How this can be realized within the scope of the polity that has been set up through the constitution of India is the challenge.

With the shift from monarchy to democracy, India enters a new phase. It implies India's clean break away from the possibility of the four varna system because there will be no kings any more. With the coming of the Indian republic, a new smriti (similar to Manu Smriti and others) becomes operational in India, and the constitution of India is the foundation for the new dynamics. However, a new system is not considered to have attained the status of dharma if it is not all-embracing and does not cater to the happiness of every individual who lives in that society. Dharma is all about the highest spirit having its way in the processes of a nation. It is about taking every one along.

In a society that keeps dharma as its guiding principle, the belief is that the best that a man can attain is something beyond the material—beyond the limitations of the mind. In spite of the existence of material goods, amidst pleasures of the senses and pains, there is the possibility of a delightful state of being/existence which is considered the highest ideal a man can pursue. Societies that see this as the goal are known to have great levels of contentment, peace and excellence. Therefore, dharma is about every citizen having the promise of getting that which is considered the highest that is known to the Indian civilization. (Part 1)

Now, when people pursue this principle, when they are detached from material goods and when they can be flippant about material goods rather than be chained in thoughts about them, they are loosely constrained by needs alone. They have no 'wants'. The society shares what it possesses among its people according to the assigned responsibilities, and it nurses a culture of abundance. 'There is enough!' is the slogan.

Contrast this with today's world. This is not the idealism of the cosmopolitan culture. The modern thought process thrives in the opposite idea, that 'there is not enough' for everyone. It talks about competition for scarce resources. There is a constant yearning for more and a deep feeling of humans being 'incomplete' beings.

The pursuit of this alternate idealism unfortunately implies that the principle of dharma does not find its true manifestation in today's society. Let us call to focus certain aspects of the varna system that we referred to in the beginning of this chapter. Notorious as it is made out to be, that notoriety was never the intention at the time of its creation. Consider this story.

That special group: People were divided into groups of four, and each group was asked to work as a team. Each four-membered group was to handle responsibilities for work, defense and entrepreneurship in an effort to attain prosperity and happiness for itself.

Each team made its own typical arrangements. In one case, the members of that team did all the work equally. In another team, the members worked on each task in batches and so on. And the groups attained various degrees of success.

In one of the teams, there was an individual who was held in high esteem, respect and admiration by the other three. During their consultations, he suggested to the other three that equality did not necessarily mean that each one should do all the jobs. He said they could specialize. He took on the task of motivation and spiritual welfare. Each of the others could take up one or the other of the other responsibilities.

This person who was admired had charisma, was at peace with himself and had a disposition that said there was nothing that he really wanted. He did not find it important to hold possessions or pleasurable objects in order to be happy and contented; He was cool with the idea of pledging himself to poverty and lived on what he got as alms from the others. Incidentally, this team of four had great success in the inter-team competitions that happened.

In this story, the person who guided was known as a self-realized soul, and what he set up among the four was what was known as dharma. It is important to note here that he enjoyed a status in his group that was higher than the others, and the others conceded it to him on account of his charisma, peace, contentment, wisdom and ability to guide; and yet, he chose for himself a material status that was the lowest.

Thus, in this group, the loop was closed. The poorest man was catered for. In a pyramid that represents society, it was as if there was a short circuit from the top to the bottom.

In the other teams unfortunately, the best took the plum posts. They sat at the top of material hierarchies, and the bottom lot had to fend for themselves. In such cases, one can see that the loop is not closed. The last man does not have assured care. He has to fend for himself in a struggle to survive. Such a system does mimic some aspects of dharma, but it is not a dharmic arrangement when the system leaves some of its members to a miserable fate.

Science and technology at the time of the origin of the Vedas was such that the form of government had to be a monarchy. Practical experience proved that if they tried democracy or other system, the nations/tribes were not able to develop the requisite strength to fight off invaders and looters who ransacked and plundered neighboring nations/tribes at will. The simple-living and high-thinking spirituality of the Vedic people, in conjunction with the inevitability of monarchy, finally resulted in the creation of the four-classes based system. This, in turn, gave Indian monarchy a special flavor.

Indeed, history is proof for the fact that this learning and arrangement produced great strength in the Vedic civilization. But history is also proof of the fact that these concepts have been misunderstood and misused by many of the generations that followed down the line. The present generation too has inherited the knowledge of these concepts that has been transferred down from the sages of yore, and it too is challenged with the same question. Is this generation up to the task of making the best out of its ancient heritage?

And if this generation is going to succeed at this, how? The celebrated books and legends in Indian mythology are also opportunities for education. All that was needed was for a play of *Ramayana* or *Mahabharata* to be staged in a village, and great lessons got transferred to the general population even if it consisted of illiterate citizens. And yes, it also took the efforts of wise men to draw wisdom from these legendary works and teach people as to how exalted lives could be lived. Those families, societies, nations and generations, which were fortunate to come under the influence of the wise men capable of this, flourished.

And the popular stories told were usually about the warriors. Though the warrior clan formed only a small fraction of the entire population, it is not surprising that storytellers chose warrior's life-stories to communicate messages related to high living and dharma. Many (if not most) stories and legends have warriors as the main characters. For instance, the *Bhagavad Gita* is a great lesson on spirituality and dharma, and it presented to the reader in the context of the duties of a warrior. All others in society had duties too, but the communication of the principles seems to be more absorbing while having these 'king stories' as the backdrop. As for the listeners and viewers, taking heed of the advice given to the warrior, they could extrapolate and decode the messages that were meant for them.

And one must not underestimate the power of this communication. The principle of dharma, which is the hallmark of the *Ramayana* and *Mahabharata*, has been communicated with a lot of passion down the centuries—so much so that it is now deeply ingrained in the psyche of the nation. Dharma continues to assist Hindus (people who live in the land where the Sindhu flows) in making decisions based on higher principles, whether it pertains to the mundane day-to-day things or major decisions in life. It is deeply embedded in the thought process of the faithful (and the non-faithful) in India, and it holds out with significant strength against consumerism. It continues to make the faithful stand out in their work, relationships, intellect and drive. It prods them on toward the benefits of spirituality which the sages promised.

However, there is a problem in today's society. In the present context, the roles of all individuals have not been integrated into a dharmic whole; and this has resulted in a system that is not delivering effectively to create what is otherwise known to Indians as the 'Golden Bird' (*Sone ki Chidiya*). This failure to deliver can be on account of any or all three of the reasons stated below:

1) The design of the present arrangement in the nation state is inadequate.
2) Information regarding the roles people have to play has not been disseminated correctly.

3) The character of the Indian has fallen so much that he does not want to do his dharma anymore.

The last of the three is open to judgment, and it is improper to bracket everyone into one category. One gets a spectrum of people. There are outstanding individuals too who do their duty, and one hopes that this blessed tribe will increase exponentially. The nation must surely work toward that. As for the other two fronts, a lot of innovation is required.

Proper design of the overall democratic system and peoples' awareness of their role in it: In this time and age, democracy is considered the best of the available political systems by most of the free world. It is described as a rule *by* the people, *of* the people and *for* the people. It can be seen as a kingship with the grace being offered to the citizen to choose his king. True to this definition, either directly or indirectly, the citizens of today's democracies do put governments into place and therefore have a say in determining who will rule over them. These democracies are composed of various institutions (legs/wings), each having their respective role to play in order to create a complete system.

If those who hold office—all those who man the legislature, executive and judiciary—subscribe consciously or instinctively to the Vedic ethos of the land, they are expected to be dharmic in their disposition. This means that those occupying these positions must perform their duty without expectations and find their highest fulfillment in the Supreme Self.

Similarly, parallels can also be drawn for adharma. If the government under the king and the king himself turned out to be corrupt in an erstwhile kingdom, then it was said that adharma prevailed in that kingdom. Under such conditions, the various wings of the government would not deliver properly, and it would lead to suffering for the people. For example, consider the policeman. Taking a leaf out of his political masters, he resorts to taking bribes; bribe-taking becomes an important activity for him, and he tends to remain occupied in it. Being so, he has lesser enthusiasm for doing his designated work. If he does not do his designated work, the thieves and rapists in that kingdom will have a field day. Referring to the same concept in today's context, it can be said that corruption is a sign of adharma, irrespective of whether it is practiced at the highest or lowest levels.

The example of the policeman and crime is only incidental. One must note that every branch of the executive, legislature or judiciary must have officials focused on shouldering the system's responsibilities rather than on their self-aggrandizement through corruption. Else, the entire system tends to fail. Farmers committing suicide for systemic reasons and people starving to death in certain pockets are indicators of such failure.

Therefore, the question arises as to whether it is proper for a citizen to elect a person who tries to bribe him to get his vote. How is it possible that a citizen votes for such a person and still expects the systems in the government to deliver? How can that citizen expect that there will be dharma in society—that the rule of law will be religiously upheld in that society? If such corrupt practices are rewarded with victory at the elections, it means that the polity is not designed properly.

In a democratic context, dharma also enjoins a duty on the citizen: The citizen's prime duty is to choose a good leader. He is expected to take to dharma while making this democratic choice. Rising up in his consciousness, he must vote free from ego, keeping the nation and the welfare of all in mind. A failure of the citizen in this regard is therefore condemnable as adharma in accordance with ancient Indian thought. It is adharma when the voter, provoked by the speeches of dividers, chooses to vote for someone that seems to satisfy the needs of his agitated ego rather than overall goodness.

Besides this primary task of voting, the modern democratic systems also call on citizens to participate in various ways so as to assist the executive, judiciary and legislature. Some tasks are considered mandatory and others optional, and the law on this varies from nation to nation. Indians are called to assist the police as specified in the Criminal Procedure Code; the judiciary may also call upon them to testify in the course of delivering justice. Sometimes, views are invited from citizens so that the laws framed are of high quality. All this signifies a part of the dharmic role of an average citizen.

Leading lights must sensitize citizens on their dharmic duties in a democracy: Citizens are failing in their duties, and therefore, it is common today to see many leading lights lamenting that citizens are voting out of ignorance and that they are incorrigible. The truth is that these leading lights complain because they do not see the significance and potential of dharma. It is important to understand the psyche of the Indian masses. If citizens realize that voting is part of dharma, which, in turn, impacts their relationship with the Divine, then there are many ways and means by which the citizen can indeed be addressed and sensitized. If the entertainment industry were to transmit the message that people need to uphold today's dharma, if it is taught in schools to children that voting has to be done on the basis of selflessness and not selfishness and if this is the lesson that goes to the faithful whether they attend service at mosques, temples or churches, then great results are possible.

All this is admissible in the system even as it exists today.

But democracy as a system itself can be raised higher to embrace dharmic content further. The central message of this book is that the nation must learn to shift to the second freedom—to self-rule. In order to realize this, even the perception regarding democracy needs an important and substantial shift.

Democracy must be a self-rule, not just a rule. And it has to happen along with the people, involving them, not as if something (government) is thrown at them. Expanding Lincoln's famous definition of democracy further, we therefore say (as discussed in the start of this section):

'Democracy is a *self-rule*, *of* the people, *by* the people, *for* the people and *with* the people.'

Participation and leadership in community self-rule: In this democratic self-rule, one expects participation from the citizen at a far deeper level than in a mere democratic rule. In democratic self-rule, an individual is expected to participate actively in his community. The community must have the feel of a republic in which people have taken responsibility for their lives. The dimensions of the local government including legislature, the executive, the judiciary, development, culture, health, spirituality, etc. need to be taken charge of by the local people themselves, leaving little for the 'king' to do from outside.

If a village team does not take charge of its own emancipation, it is said to dwell in slavery. It is an index of the failure of the members of that village team in doing their duty or dharma in society.

The community leaders must take charge and ensure that every member of the village is taken care of, that there are effective partnerships built with neighboring villages and that the community exudes proper harmonization with righteous national aims.

Not just a king-maker but also a king when required: In a self-rule, the citizens must understand that democracy not only makes them king-makers, it also calls on them to be kings. Those that rise up to take responsibilities in polity are also merely citizens. Participating in polity is work. This is the duty of handling power. This is the taking up of the responsibility of the nation. This is the responsibility of having a say in polices drafted for the nation by influencing decisions in political party forums. Everyone who is a citizen of a democratic nation is expected to play his role in the political process—each according to the talents he possesses.

Seeking to occupy important positions in the political hierarchy can be power-mongering for the few who take to adharma and are focused on self-gratification. But to Lord Rama, it was a duty that he had to perform even though it meant separation from his dear wife who he trusted and loved. In whatever capacity one sees his talents relevant to society and wherever the need exists, he must play his part.

When the responsibility is on the king's shoulder, the duty of the average citizen at that time is just to feed his family—this happens in a rule. But in a self-rule democracy, the citizen must shell out time, effort and resources in service of the nation besides attending to his professional and family responsibilities. A democracy can thus be kept clean. The failure of the citizen to perform this dharma leads to the weakening of the nation.

The fourfold dharma of a citizen of a democracy: Summarizing, we can say that in a free democracy, a citizen has a fourfold dharma to perform in the political arena as follows:

a) Vote, keeping his attention focused on the highest

b) Assist the executive, legislature and judiciary according to the need of the law selflessly

c) Contribute to the systemic processes in the community in which he lives with welfare of all in mind

d) Effectively participate in the political process with a prayer of establishing peace and stability

If the citizen does not rise up to these needs, a democracy cannot rise to dharma. And yet, it is not about individuals. The hero is not the one who bashes up the villains single-handedly. Rather, he is one who gives up his ego and does the bidding of the Divine, who puts his fellowmen first or who is dedicated to the welfare of humanity even at all costs to himself. It is not about a lord or a hero coming over and being benevolent. Rather, it is about holding up a dharmic system by performing dharma and the whole system delivering in return.

Anyone who adheres to dharma creates a little heaven around him wherever he goes. So if the prime minister of a nation is dharmic, then that heaven can have a wide influence. But to see hope in a single person coming to the top and making a difference is not the right way to think in dharma. The system is important, not individuals; the system must deliver the goods that will emancipate. With a dharmic system in place and people at all levels being called to do their dharma, the best can be achieved. Dharma must be fashionable once again. The nation must rise to living in pursuit of the Highest Inspiration as the ancient sages taught—individuals must find glory and admiration in the contentment of that high living once again, and in that, the nation will be well on its way to claim its destiny.

Sportsmen should fall in love with the finesse of sports and not get lost in the pain of victory-defeat. The artist must ensure the full and unblemished expression of his joyous inner self. The scholar must transcend into humility. Action must come out of complete dispassion and highest excellence. Social interactions must revel in absolute equity of spiritual oneness. The Sadhus, *Sadhavis* and *Bhikus* must once again be dedicated to complete poverty and still find all the resources given to them to pursue the highest and render spiritual services without any hassle.

The modern setup has a ladder. On its top are perched the educated, the rich and the powerful. At the bottom are the poor, the illiterate and the powerless. Those at the bottom are hard-pressed even to live hand to mouth. The loop is not complete. This will not happen in a dharmic arrangement.

The decision-makers of the nation are expected to emerge from the political class. The wise of this age have not yet defined the profiles of those who have to play this role in a democratic setup (for example, the role of a Kshatriya in the erstwhile dharmic system was defined). Till such a time, it is incumbent on those that are endowed and in a position to search into their hearts to see what the 'Veda' (the Word, the Divine, Humanity) calls upon them to do at a given moment.

The dharma of a politician will emerge nonetheless. Once answers are found to the various issues facing Indian democracy, one hopes that it will qualify for being classed as a dharmic arrangement. Such an arrangement will also have a well-defined and ideal life-profile of a righteous and successful politician—a realistic profile which can be pursued by suitably talented youngsters for achieving great success in politics. It can then be said that the dharma of a politician has been discovered. So also the dharma of political parties…

No new class will be created because kingship duties are enjoined on everyone in democracy. It is the citizen himself who is the politician who has to perform the four roles we discussed earlier. Offering himself for election is also one of his dharmic duties as a politician, which he may have to take up at some or the other time in his life.

The actionable points that arise from this are that the citizen of India must be told that 'democracy dharma' expects more from him. Just as the ancients were called to perform duties without expectation in a 'kingship dharma', the citizens of this era too must play their roles in a holistic political system without expectation. That holistic system must be one that will deliver wholesomely to all the members. All citizens must therefore perform the four duties in polity to the extent admissible in the light of the other professional and societal roles entrusted to him and in harmony with the responsibilities there.

The citizen must be taught that the Highest Inspiration is the goal. To vote, assist in governance, contribute to polity and take up positions in the overall dharma is the duty expected of a citizen. Each of them must be pursued with his heart set on the Highest Promise of ancient India—this and only this will help him complete his role in democracy dharma.

Democracy in India will further evolve. The balance shifts each time the parliament passes new laws, when the election commission fine-tunes the election process or when the courts pass judgments which become precedents. Change in the Indian democracy is certain. The important part is whether the change is positive and. more importantly, whether it is guided by an ideal that is inspired by the highest.

The many ideas of freedom – Where does India stand? Notions of freedom can differ. For example, in his *Tryst With Destiny* speech, Pandit Nehru himself identified that independence did give freedom, but more was possible. Let us pick four such definitions that have been used at some time or the other in our historical past.

1) The first idea of freedom is that a nation is sovereign, free from foreign rule. Those that rule the nation call this nation itself as their home.

2) The second idea of freedom refers to a position in which the citizen knows fully well that the persons who now govern do so with the highest interest of all the citizens in mind, since he and his likeminded fellow citizens have put this particular person into the position of authority.

3) The third idea of freedom is that each citizen can pursue his own interests to the fullest as long as it does not interfere with others' rights and liberties; one is also empowered to control his destiny in that he has the freedom to grow to the fullness of his manhood and can exert his influence on the factors that affect him and his near and dear ones.

4) The last idea of freedom is spiritual where one breaks open his human limitations and reaches an inspired zone of his highest potential, where he is like a lotus leaf in water. Though immersed in the world, he is unaffected by it. He is at peace with himself and with those around him.

Now, what is the freedom that political India must target?

The first freedom happened for Indians when the colonial masters transferred power over to indigenous hands. The second freedom is the freedom that the citizens express in their vote. It is the freedom to pick and choose from the sample of political parties and candidates offered so that the best of that lot can rule them. The nation has managed to sweep governments in and out successfully. And it is something the Indian citizen has been experiencing happily for nearly seven decades now through the unbroken run of the constitution of India.

The third freedom, however, is that which allows every citizen to freely pursue the fourth freedom. The third freedom is the dream of Rabrindranath Tagore for the nation; it is the comprehensive freedom that Gandhiji was talking about. So, the question arises. Do Indians enjoy this third freedom? And the answer is no! Not all Indians… Not even a majority of Indians enjoy this third freedom!

And this does call for introspection. Two young, enterprising, foreign-returned, educated Indians made a study by deciding to live the life of the average poor for a month. They calculated the average Indian income and decided to spend a month surviving on that income. Surprisingly, they found that it restricted their motorized travel to less than five kilometers a day. It restricted access to doctors, medicine, hotels, film theaters and a host of other facilities, even nutritious food. And within those restrictions, God forbid if the poor man landed up as a victim to various kinds of evil.

This is, in fact, the state of affairs of the person who earns less than the average Indian income—that includes the 75% of the population of the nation. The people under the poverty line have it much worse. They must give up all idea of justice and live on the pity and graciousness of those that fortunately have resources. When the two youngsters again experimented with the village-level poverty lines (Rs. 26/- per day in 2012) set up officially by the Planning Commission of India, it made them live in a way that they could barely survive. Food had to be gruel. They had to walk for everything. And there was no question of getting any medicine or service of any kind. They gave up this part of the experiment before completing it. This is the plight of around 15 to 20% of the Indian population. If that is the state of the nation, does it not call for introspection and corrective action? This is surely not the freedom the freedom fighters dreamed of.

Does one need to look beyond democracy and capitalism in India? Human experience over the past few centuries indicate that the three major forces of democracy, socialism and capitalism are handy and relevant choices for running nations. The free world today acknowledges that the best possible system will extract the best from these three and ensure strong inbuilt defense mechanisms against their ills.

The present levels of technology, especially those related to travel and communication, make democracy a viable alternative (though it has its faults). Socialism contributes the idea of a safety net that aims at reducing the number of deprived people in a nation to zero; however, its application in communist states has resulted in systems that propagate much evil. Capitalism seems to be an efficient tool to raise the standards of living. However, it leads to disparity, wretchedness and consumerism.

In India, a middle path seems to have been struck among these three, and the shift toward capitalism has been accentuated since liberalization in 1991. Considerations do show that democracy is more viable than the alternative systems in as far as polity goes, since there is the possibility of the removal of bad rule if rulers cross the limits. And the best of the world powers are indeed democracies. But the level of peoples' participation presently, especially in India, seems inadequate. This partially springs from an absurd view that the righteous must not offer themselves for elections and that they are not righteous [sic] if they do. Capitalism does facilitate a merit-based system, and this will probably continue to be part of the system that one can conceive for India. And yet, a great part of the population of India seems to be at a loss when it comes to participating in it. A lot more checks are needed for this system to be effectively used in India. The idealism of a safety net in socialism is brilliant,

but a corrected concept of equality needs to be applied to raise it from a grossly materialistic perspective. In areas like justice and medicine, absolute capitalism would be a disaster. Justice must never come for a price. If the rich man is more likely to win court battles, then the judiciary and the overall system have failed miserably. All these indicate that balance is lacking. Somewhere, the nation also seems to be missing out on the nurturing of value systems and is messing up big time on account of it.

The question arises as to whether democracy, socialism and capitalism can be worked out into some other kind of balance so that their deficiencies can be covered. Can the poor be protected though a different kind of arrangement in the nation?

An answer seems to emerge in one of the perspectives that is often used in the present: Bharat vs. India. If the entire nation is seen to actually be two-nations-in-one—the first nation (Indian North or India) mostly consisting of the educated in the cities and the second nation (Indian South or Bharat) consisting of the illiterate persons from rural India—a solution does present itself. Reckoning the nation as two-nations-in-one, if the balancing of the three forces of democracy, capitalism and socialism can be altered to suit the needs of each of these sub-nations separately, some excellent results may be expected. And at the outset, let us say that it need not be India vs. Bharat. Instead, it can be India and Bharat.

Two-nations-in-one India – the challenge and the opportunity

Challenge: There is a nation within the Indian nation which is poverty stricken and oppressed. This second nation, which is basically concentrated in the villages, also extends into the slums of the cities. While the members of this second nation may enjoy great self-dignity and pride within their domain, they are looked down upon by those from the first nation. They are at a disadvantage in their capacity to profit from the system, from the system's benevolence, from rule of law and from dispensation of justice.

Vastly deprived of the fruits of the present education system, their chances of rising in the hierarchy, into the first nation, are very meager. Hence, they are at a disadvantage. And their case is considered a little above hopeless!

India can therefore be seen to consist of two nodes—one centered in the cities and the other centered in the villages. (According to the 2001 census, 72% of the Indian population live in villages.) The node that is centered in the cities draws its inspiration and strength from the learning in the scientific civilization, the benefits of cosmopolitan society, the English language, accumulated wealth, hegemonic dominance and using rural India and tribal India as a modern-day soft variant of a colony.

The rural node is characterized by greater degree of traditionalism, unorganized workforce, remains of caste-based atrocities, better community living, simple living, alternate visions of life and prosperity, vulnerability to inclement weather, higher mortality rates, healthy living (wherever food is not a problem), greater contentment, lower literacy rates, greater practical wisdom, local dialects, politically unorganized, lack of firm direction, etc.

A question arises as to whether both nodes need to be handled on the same footing. Or, looking at it the other way, what are the opportunities available in this two-node system that can spur India on to tapping into its highest potentials?

Opportunity: The nation that is comprised of the educated elite is significantly large in absolute terms and can produce spectacular economic results for India. Therefore, there is no need to look for similar economic results from rural India in order for the nation to achieve overall economic success. The second nation could be rather a beneficiary of the Gandhian vision; let it be a playground for the fruits of ancient Indian culture.

Then, what is wrong if the second nation has the right to survive and thrive on its own terms? As long as it is not going to interfere much with the primary aims of modern civilization, there is no great reason why rural India should not have its freedom! All that is needed is an acknowledgment by the members of the first nation that the simpleton in the village may have alternate visions and priorities, different from the mad chase for material wealth which appears to be the best way forward to the West-inspired Indian.

Why should it not be visualized in such a manner that it will be the prosperity of the rural background and splendor of its human touch which will start contributing to the joys in the cities? If the claim of ancient Indian learning is correct, the liberated second nation will be the one that provides India with the men it needs to man its great institutions—economic, political, scientific, etc.

Keeping this alternate perspective in mind, the best way out is to acknowledge the existence of these two nations and use it to advantage. Indian society may therefore represent a mixed economy with a difference. Rural India must lean toward socialism while the urban and industrialized parts may maintain a capitalistic leaning. In contrast to the hustle and bustle of city life, life in the villages can be visualized as relatively laidback in economic terms and yet pulsating with life. The rural socialism (different from communistic socialism) should provide a vital insulation from the rigors of the capitalistic structure, and at the same time, it must give scope for community living, free and liberated human spirit and universal learning.

From the economics point of view, it could be a capitalistic free market in industrialized areas and a protected, cooperative, socialistic and barter-inclined Indian social structure in the rural areas. The outcome of this arrangement will be that India will have two poles in society; rural, socialistic and traditional on the one hand and urban, capitalistic and cosmopolitan on the other. Together, they will constitute a strong foundation for the nation.

Is this two-nation conceptualization necessary? Many modern visionaries talk about the future consisting of a nation that has huge cities. The perception is that the current trend is likely to continue, and it is expected that people will simply move out of the villages and that the cities will grow bigger and unmanageable. But even by a small stretch of imagination, one can see that it cannot be a sound strategy for a prosperous nation. The environment will not sustain. We will have to continue living with the existing large quantities of wretchedness for a long time. Even decades down the line, we will be left with a section of people who will continue to be wretched. Another downside is that we will not be able to tap into our indigenous learning. We will be resigned to aping the West and its institutions. Moreover, we will probably continue designing our lives on the basis of two instead of four Purusharths—artha and kama alone—while ignoring dharma and moksha.

The nation must actively apply itself to this issue. It must plan in such a way that a sustainable alternate arrangement can be had and then facilitate the movement of the nation toward such an alternate arrangement. And if the right mix of stimulus, development and patronage is struck, the migration trend can be reversed. It may become fashionable for people to return to the villages because villages enjoy a different kind of prosperity that is inspired by the rich traditional past of India. The point being made here is that if the current trend is to be reversed, a start must be made by first conceptualizing as to how the alternative could possibly be and then explore what practical steps may be needed to affect such change.

For this to succeed, faith must be placed in the abilities of the people of rural India. A person from the first nation might simply say that the other nation is uneducated and that one should just forget about placing any responsibilities on them. The way out of this is the second nation rising up and proving its worth. And it surely can if there is a clear vision on how it can unite its communities and take charge. There are great examples of village communities across India that have successfully done this; and if it is possible in one village, it is possible elsewhere too. The village dwellers must look around and understand other success stories. They will then know what to do. City dwellers must help. The governments must fine-tune their establishments and stop putting hurdles in the way of the villages, which make them struggle to express themselves.

The need, therefore, is to attempt to conceptualize this journey and make a start. Loopholes can be fixed along the way. Once the second nation teams up, there will be no stopping India.

The expected advantages: Some of the possible gains can be listed as follows.

➤ The minimum needs of the people have a better chance of being met. This is because through decentralization, the shouldering of social welfare responsibilities will be shifted out of the hands of bureaucrats and into the community itself.

➤ If the communities are strong, they will be the first line of defense for the poor. The poor will have some effective insulation from the irregularities and cycles of modern capitalistic economies—the main strength of socialism.

➤ A choice between the materialistic and consumer-oriented western ideal and the spiritual simple living and high thinking of the East will be available options for all citizens, with reasonable restrictions and appropriate respective costs.

➤ The industrial sector can provide the base for higher needs and luxuries, and the rural sector can work more on the direction of necessities. These will complement each other in an integrated nation.

➤ Prosperity will definitely produce a better market in rural India (though, of course, a sober one). A great market in the second nation which the first nation can sell to… All it needs to do is give that nation the freedom to express its traditional best and facilitate the process as Bharat grows up sufficiently on its own strength.

➤ The shifting of the base of industries and production units toward villages may become inevitable because successful industries may find it easier to get cheap labor in the rural areas. Besides, if the traditions of India thrive in the villages, then the chances are that the quality of labor will also be better. (The Indian military is already finding that it is getting its best men from the rural and semi-urban areas rather than from the cities.)

Benevolence in the rural sector is bound to affect changes in the cities. Cities will eventually learn to strike a healthy balance between the West and the East. It may again be asserted that, in all probability, the spirit of Indianness will add splendor to what the West has achieved.

From the considerations above, the important points to note are stated here:

1) Rural India must have the right to have its own vision of prosperity and contentment, and it should not be clubbed with the aims of urban India.

2) Indians must see that the two Indias have their own strength, and it is important that the Indian South be given the opportunity to rise through its own

initiative, responsibility and strength. This must be facilitated at all levels.

3) India must stop photocopying West-based solutions and innovatively think of a unique path for India, keeping in mind the views of the best this land has produced as well as all the good the West has to offer.

4) India deserves its indigenous culture to be nurtured. Giving freedom and responsibility to rural India to manage its own affairs gives the nation an opportunity to express that traditional strength, and the opportunity must be taken.

In the previous chapter, we contemplated upon the macroscopic picture with respect to the need for decentralization. That India must look at the Indian Economic South and give it the freedom to operate as per its own aspirations. The same thing can also be looked at through the microscopic perspective. This has been taken up at length in the Panchayati Swaraj part. Here, however, we will summarize the same in the context of a national shift toward dharma and freedom.

The goal: Citizens must be in control of their own destinies. If this is the ultimate aim to be fulfilled, then people must have a say in defining the laws that apply in their immediate neighborhood. They must be able to act as executives in a manner such that the state, as it manifests in their immediate vicinity, is effectively under their control. They must be able to express their sense of justice and fair play while participating in public events within their local communities. And all this is not going to be possible if there are no meaningful local institutions. This should be the goal: the setting up and running of meaningful local institutions.

The present arrangement has a character of imposition: There is no denying the fact that the general intelligentsia in India more or less looks up to the achievements of Europe and the USA with awe—and one is quite justified in doing so. There are defects in the western systems too, but by far, the western world seems to be far ahead and is seen as the example which one may wish to emulate. Therefore, with the scale calibrated as such (West up and East down), those groomed in the present education system stake claim to greater awareness of the meaning and purpose of life than their rural, illiterate counterparts. The definition of the term 'prosperity' is also more or less decided in reference to the same West-inspired culture. This view has a tendency to manifest/assert itself when the elite create institutions in rural India. But this is a hegemonic view; it overlooks/slights indigenous content.

Care must be taken to ensure that the local bodies that are put into place do not become a medium to assert this perception. For example, the present arrangement amounts to saying that the West-educated thinker knows much more about life and about taking care of village women than those who live in the villages. Therefore, in order to empower women, randomly chosen villages are forced to select their leader from among the women—not the person who they feel is most suited among them for the job (maybe even a woman). In other words, irrespective of what the local culture is or says, the concept of 'liberated women', as the West perceives liberated women, is now being forced on to the villages. This is just one example. There are others too. For example, villagers are not credited with the awareness of what is good for a fulfilling life. They are not credited with the awareness of how to groom children, etc.

Another example is that the village leadership is not trusted with the welfare of lower castes. Churchill, a prime minister of the United Kingdom, believed that the Indians would kill each other if the British left for England and that they would live in perpetual hell. Similarly, the educated Indian likes to believe that great atrocities on the lower castes in the villages of India will happen if the villages are given a free rope. Therefore, out of fear that the villagers will commit atrocities on each other, the powers that be in India, in the infancy of its existence, ensured that the villages remained powerless.

Seventy years down the line, should the villages accept this position, or should they respond to the Indian elite saying: 'Please leave us to our means. We can take care of each other.'?

The village body is powerless: A simple analysis of the power dynamics at the grassroots level will show that power does not rest with the people. For example:

a)   Effectively, almost no financial power is given to the village panchayats.

b) The state-planted executives in the village who render 'government' services are not answerable to the village panchayats, and most of the time, they talk down to the villagers.

These features show that there has been a deliberate attempt to keep the villages weak, and surprisingly, this emerges from the constitution of India itself. There was originally a deliberate silence on the part of the constitution on the matter of village bodies. And the reason can probably be traced back to the leadership which felt that if villages were given power, the old system of untouchability would re-assert itself and there would be great atrocities committed on the lower castes.

Further, it is known that the efforts at decentralization that were brought into force—starting from Prime Minister Nehru's time to Prime Minister Narasimha Rao's time—have not effectively transferred power.

Nearly seven decades after the constitution came into force, the nation has neither been able to produce self-reliant villages (except a handful) nor has it effectively solved the problems concerning the lower castes, gender disparity, abject poverty and infant mortality.

The question remains as to whether the true emancipation of the poor, the women and the lower castes can really be affected without following the direction indicated by Gandhiji regarding village self-reliance or village empowerment.

Change is imminent, and it calls for a shift out of the 'I know better' colonial mind-set: At the core of the required change is for the state to shift from the position of 'doer' to that of a 'facilitator cum auditor'.

The two cardinal principles, that we saw in Part 2 of this book, which need to be effectively implemented are stated below:

a) Set up grassroots-level institutions and give them optimum authority to operate.

b) Set up an effective audit mechanism manned by the government so that the lower formations can be watched over as to whether they stay within their limits when they do their development works or when they take on other grassroots-level functions relating to the executive, legislature or judiciary.

Effective decentralization can bring in its wake much good to the nation: In genuine village republics based on magnanimous ancient wisdom, there is a better chance of the delivery of constitutional promises.

➢ When people see functioning political institutions up close, it is likely that they will give more importance to their participation in it either directly or during elections. They will be more careful about selecting their representatives. There are chances that a culture of selecting meritorious persons will be initiated.

➢ When the institutions within their reach produce tangible results, there will be greater enthusiasm to participate.

➢ It is a great human resources idea that can result in a great number of people taking up responsibilities.

➢ As such, these grassroots-level institutions are also likely to prove to be a training ground for throwing up future leaders.

➢ The vital ingredient in close-knit communities is the interpersonal bonds that exist among its citizens on account of their proximity and frequent interactions. In it, there is energy, a unique dynamics and an understanding which cannot be replicated in a relationship between people who do not live in proximity of one other. Exertion of power/authority and responsibility upon a community is best borne by the community itself because a community that lives in physical proximity understands each other's needs more than anyone from the outside. They will tend to dispute with each other, but they will also know how to do justice to one another and stand up for one another when the time comes. Effective decentralization will be able to capitalize on this unique strength. And it must be tapped into all over the country. It will be a human resources masterstroke.

➢ Another major argument in favor of decentralization is that the indigenous culture finds nourishment in successful village republics. It has been said of the arrangements in pre-modern India that villages remained insulated from uncertainties that happened at the level of chieftains or kings (higher level of administration). Villages were supposed to have enjoyed great stability. Historical analyses also show that this institution degraded over time. The trend needs to be reversed—keeping in mind the aspirations of the Indian constitution. Local communities know how to help themselves. All that is required is to ensure that they do not cross certain well-defined limits. A great amount of good can result from this move.

➤ Finally, it is evident from our consideration of the issue of two-Indias-in-one that the nation needs to allow the assertion of traditional wisdom, belief and rural simplicity in the second India. This can best be achieved by effectively transferring responsibility and initiative into the hands of the village dwellers themselves. The village republics are likely to move in a direction that may defy the usual definitions of prosperity and fulfillment driving cosmopolitan society and achieve completeness in spite of it. Chances are that given their freedom, they are likely to realize better indices with respect to literacy, education, nutrition, infant mortality, life expectancy, Human Development Index, etc.

In conclusion, it can be said that decentralization must be pursued with the following in mind:

a) Belief that rural India has the capacity

b) Knowledge that it will be a human resources masterstroke

c) Awareness that colonial maladministration needs to be reversed

d) Awareness that the present levels of technology and the present political and economic systems facilitate merit and that caste problems are improbable

e) Awareness that the nation can rise to prosperity only by freeing this huge population and that they can take responsibility for themselves

f) Awareness that it is the recommendation of the best of the Indian leaders (Gandhiji) that this is the success formula that many successful kingdoms of the past used, that this is the success formula which many of today's successful nation states use, that it is resonant with the free human spirit, that it offers an opportunity for indigenous culture to assert itself and that India will then legitimately be called a free nation as most if its population will have the means to influence their destinies.

2.4 RIGHTS-SEEKING VS. RIGHTS-GIVING: WHICH IS BETTER TO BUILD A NATIONAL ETHOS?

In dharma, or its variant *dhamam*, which the Buddhists are familiar with, the focus is on doing one's ordained duties with diligence. By doing so, a person is expected to attain the highest good that an individual can aspire for. Merely doing his ordained duty is considered to result in the meeting of life goals—contentment and ultimate self-satisfaction—even as he is doing his duty.

With this concept being central to the Indian civilization, society was sought to be built around the idea that there is no point in hankering for things. Instead, it was the wellness of the system itself that delivered to all its citizens. Seen from an individual standpoint, it can be said that one delivers to the system, and it is the system that takes care of him. The focus in dharma is therefore on duties.

When a society that is built on this foundation of duties comes up against the idea of human rights and when that idea is placed as a central principle to the running of the government of that nation, there is a tendency for the thinking in the nation to shift from a 'what-is-my-duty?' approach to a 'this-is-my-right!' approach. (This is different from having self-dignity.)

When the people and its culture have a 'what-is-my-duty?' approach and when the institutions of the state demand a 'give-me-my-rights' approach, it can lead to confusion. This is a major problem of the Indian nation; this makes the nation stand in a no man's land between the West and the East.

One must understand that the rights perspective goes against the ethos of dharma at different levels:

a) The system of wisdom that promotes dharma believes that when people become self-seeking, they are on a sure road to misery—there is no happiness on that road or at the end of it. When a person is made to ask for his rights, the system is actually teaching that person to be miserable.

b) The Indian seers do not conceive of a society where people are at odds to grab, seek, try to possess and then arrive at an equilibrium of the self-seeking forces. Rather, they think of a society where everyone does his part and everyone is taken care of. There is, therefore, a clash in thinking (or a clash of civilizations, if you may) at this point. Dharmic systems will have institutions that will deliver justice automatically. On the other hand, systems that believe that it is all about balancing power dynamics will contain institutions that will expect the individual citizen to fight for and seek justice. It will not be easy to fit one kind of institution into the traditions of the other.

c) This clash in the thought process manifests in society as a zone of uncertainty, or confusion, for the citizens; for instance, it leads to huge confusion when children are groomed in present-day schools. What should the teachers teach them? That they should be seen fighting for their rights or that they should be making sacrifices?

How then does today's society resolve this impasse? It must be understood that rights can be had only if they are given. At the heart of peace and justice in society is sacrifice, which is what makes those rights possible.

Consider a tribe living in a jungle full of wild animals. The wild animals keep attacking at every given opportunity and eat up the people they can get hold of. In such an instance, what is the right-to-life of a member of the tribe? It is nothing if there is no one standing on the border and fighting off the animals. Similarly, a farmer can have the rights over the tomatoes growing in his garden only if someone stops the thief from coming and taking it away; the thieves could be animals or people from another tribe. Therefore, it is evident that rights come into existence when there is someone working to protect those rights. It means there is a team in operation. There is someone working for that team, making sacrifices for it. And then, down the line, other teammates are able to 'enjoy' the rights given by the team.

If there is no sacrifice, there is no team. And if there is no team, there is no question of rights.

Looking at it from the point of view that people must be happy: The first condition for people to be happy is that they must not be self-seeking. This comes to us from the wisdom of the ancients. The second condition is that evil must not be committed on them (this is rather easily understood). And for people to be free from the ravages of evil, teams must be formed. The team must assure that its members will be treated in a proper manner. The team will set its standards by saying that anyone that is part of our team, or comes into our area, will be treated in so-and-so manner and will have these privileges.

Putting the two together, it is clear that the best way to look at human rights is that it is all about giving and not taking. Human rights are for giving, not seeking. No one is born with human rights. If he is born into a great team, he is definitely born with it, but that also enjoins on him the duty to keep the team strong and alive, which, in turn, calls for sacrifices from him.

The sum total of this argument is that rights-givers are sacrificers, and sacrificers are the light of society. But then again, they who take to making sacrifices as if it is their second nature are also supposed to be in the state of bliss which the ancient masters of India have spoken about in great length.

On the contrary, the promotion of self-seeking of human rights can lead to accentuate a self-seeking mentality, and this will lead to the inability of society finding sacrificial individuals, which will further lead to the inability of holding up human rights and the death of a team/nation.

Seeking to deliver human rights, through one's duties, leads to a selfless mentality. It leads to society having people who are sacrificial in their attitude. It leads to better values in children and members of society and to people giving up their own human rights for the sake of others. (It leads to happier people. See Appendix A.)

In conclusion, when the nation attempts to sensitize its citizens on human rights, these are two distinct ways which the nation may choose to present it. The choice which a nation makes has a great impact on what will eventually be the outcome in society.

Human rights are for giving, not asking. It defines the character of individuals and, ultimately, the strength of a society/nation. In India, which thrives on the ethos of dharma, human rights must be treated as the object of dharma. Indian dharma must deliver human rights to all. And the Indian citizen must merely seek to do his duty without expectations.

The founding fathers of the United States of America were skeptical about parties playing a role in public life. They hoped that it would be talented people pooled together in the two houses of the Congress who will take the nation forward. To this effect, they set up a presidential system which caters to a president who is almost a king for four years; the tenure of the president is quite firm unless he does something stupid—almost with an intention of wanting to throw it all away. In contrast, the parliamentary system, which India adopted, conceives of a prime minister who needs to have the support of the majority in the lower house if he wishes to continue to be the prime minister. He, therefore, needs to have a team with him. He cannot be a lone ranger member of the parliament (though, of course, we had the rare case of an independent member becoming the chief minister of a state); a prime minister needs a party. And so, a parliamentary system cannot be thought of without a party system in place.

Despite this basic difference between the two systems, both forms of democracy have moved into the direction of functioning with political parties—political parties have become a reality of the democratic system.

A careful look at this background indicates that attention may not have been paid to designing and fine-tuning the systems concerning political parties. As for the American founding fathers, they admittedly did not pay attention to defining the significance or role of political parties. The British rely on tradition, so they don't define it anyway (the system which has evolved, though, is at peace with the indigenous culture of Britain).

As for the Indian case, the Congress dominated proceedings completely for around eighteen or twenty years after independence. And for the most of three decades after that, it has been the only major political force. Therefore, much attention has not been paid to talking about how the party system may be standardized in India too. The intelligence or understanding about how political parties are to be set up and run is a result of

gradual evolution; in various countries around the world, people have worked upon it in a piecemeal manner and have come up with a spectrum of solutions.

Looking at it from this perspective, it is clear that the political parties continue to operate in a hazy, undefined and under-regulated zone. There remains much to be done in order to ensure that political parties, as an institution, play a constructive role in a democratic dharma. In this chapter, effort will be made to highlight certain issues connected with political parties that need to be addressed so that democracy may be strengthened and so that political parties play a constructive role in it.

Issue 1 – Decisions need to be taken on the amount of money required for political activities in a democracy: Presently, sustaining the armed forces takes up to about 11 to 12% of the Indian government's budget. Some 2 to 3% goes into education and so on. Now, if looked at this way, given that political parties are an important component of the democratic process, how much money can be spent on/by political parties?

As of today, almost nothing is spent officially on political parties by the state. But political parties need money for their day-to-day activities. They need money to support their establishment and personnel. They also need to fund special initiatives aimed at generating opinion in society, for or against issues that need to be taken up from time to time. Most of all, money is needed in order to fight elections. The question arises as to how they are going to get the money to fund all these initiatives.

Those elected into office (from the parliament to the panchayat) get a salary enough to cater for one family (and not even that at the lower levels). Perks and privileges do contribute to the maintenance of a small office. Even this is not available to those who do not get elected. And this legislator's salary is the only money political parties get in the form of 'payment' from the state. So then, how are political parties expected to support their people, organization and activities?

And since getting elected is uncertain, this little bit of official income is also not certain for politicians. The political parties need to survive. There has to be some source of income. What is that source?

1) One alternative is for the political party to collect funds from its 'members' in the form of membership fees. This implies that a citizen should join a party and fund it regularly so that its leaders will have the resources for their activities. But does India have a culture of generosity toward political parties? Is there a culture of selfless support for political initiatives? Does anybody consider it his duty to pay money to a political party? So, can relying on membership fees give parties the funds they require? The current political ethos in India is selfish, and any support to be rendered to the political parties is expected to be a quid-pro-quo for benefits in return. That drags the Indian polity down into the realms of selfishness. The hard truth is that in today's polity, the membership fees are nominal. Reverse payment is made by parties to election activists and to the general public sometimes so as to bribe for votes.

2) Still another way of getting funds is for parties to become stooges of those that have financial strength. Parties then manage to get money for political survival and for their political activities. In the bargain, they are compelled to protect the interests of their sponsors in the political sphere.

3) And finally, there is corruption. Having been elected into position, one is in a position to do favors to many people. The discretion available can be used as a bargaining chip for financial support. And in the present situation, there are many who are willing to pay under the table even if they are not forced to do so. This leads to accumulation of funds that are stashed away for further use in perpetuating a political party.

These last two options are the mainstay of politics in India. The distinguished and undistinguished personalities in politics, academics and the fourth estate know that this is the reality. The people at the higher levels may be sophisticated and cover their tracks well. But everyone knows. It is an open secret. That's how the present polity runs, so much so that it is considered as the normal thing to do in politics. They do it in hiding and keep a straight face in public. Exceptions are rare, but even though the exceptions keep themselves clean, they must turn a Nelson's eye to the filth in the murky system.

The two direct lessons that come out of it are stated below:

Lesson 1 – The common citizen must pay if he needs to be the beneficiary: The person who sponsors the candidate wins the loyalty of that elected legislator. If that is true, then if the average Indian citizen wants his interests protected, he must go out of his way and act in the political sphere (not limited to casting votes). This will also mean that he must contribute to the parties that he thinks are desirable.

Lesson 2 – If there is no financial patronage, there is no possibility of honesty in politics: If there is no over the board income for the politician—something that will give him at least bread if not butter—and if he is not going to be given the resources that are required for him to perform his duties, then it is a recipe for disaster. No individual who idealizes honesty will ever pledge himself to this service because it would mean that serving in the setup is close to impossible without dishonesty!

Indeed, what should an honest individual do if he needs to successfully serve in this political setup? The ideal that is presented is almost too fantastic. A politician in the tradition of a bhiku will collect funds from house to house, and he will have such a magnetic personality that even if he interacts with only a few people, all the people in the constituency will come to know who he is and will vote for him. (If he gets out of his house too much, there is a danger of overspending because he may not have the money that is needed and the election limits are ridiculous, so low that he cannot possibly send one postcard to each of the voters in his constituency.) That should be the profile of a clean political leader who can succeed.

And if all he does is this business of politics, what will he do for a living? The answer is that politics is only meant for a person with adequate means.

The question one can ask is why honesty is such a huge barrier for entry into the parliament. And the honest person is to compete against those who have no scruples in taking money in return for favors. He has to walk to reach all the members of his constituency. (One village a day means nearly three years to visit all villages without repeating even one.) In contrast, the unscrupulous and the men of means will go around in huge swanky cars. The honest person is authorized to send, at the most, one postcard per voter while the other person may give bribes to many of them so as to buy their votes.

The systemic logic is inconsistent. If a citizen wants the Kshatriyas led by Lord Rama to fight a battle on his behalf, he needs to ensure that the weapons required to fight are provided for. It is the height of stupidity-in-idealism if the enemy empowers the opposite army with swords and guns while one's own army is expected to fight back with sticks and stones. Why make the rules such that it is difficult for the honest to win elections?

The answer is with the citizens: The citizen must ensure that the honest and talented person, who is willing to make sacrifices for his country, has the resources he needs to do his duties. These resources must be given to him legally. These resources must be sufficient for him to fight on a level playing field. The citizen must assure him that there is a way of winning representation into the parliament without resorting to corruption, black money or underhanded dealings.

In broad lines, one can lay down that just as the judiciary, the executive, education, the police, the armed forces and the election commission have a certain budget fixed for them, politics must also have a budget. Political parties are to propose candidates who will occupy the one great forum meant to collect the wise elders of India. If this proposal is to be clean and if there is to be no hanky-panky, it is important that the costs to be incurred are properly covered by the system available in the nation. And one way of doing it is by intellectually defining that it is legitimate for any nation to spend as much as X% of its GDP toward the upkeep and functioning of a political process, including political parties. What this X will be needs to be worked out. But for the system of political parties to function effectively in society, the value of X needs to be fixed at a pragmatic amount. More importantly, provision must be made for parties legally obtaining the amount and spending it according to clear and transparent rules. (Refer to Appendix B for a possible solution to this problem.)

Issue 2 – Internal democracy in choosing leaders and internal communication for sharing ideas and venting emotions: In India, dissent is not tolerated in parties, and it results in multitudes of tiny parties as parties keep breaking up into factions. If parties have a proper democratic internal structure, then dissent will have a let-off vent. The members of the party will have the opportunity to debate upon issues and force voting; thus, there will be a way to legally challenge leadership. This will also lead to improved quality of leadership without breaking parties up into miniscule groups. This must be demanded as a minimum requirement to be met by a political party if it is to get legal financial support from the state according to well-defined rules.

Issue 3 – In dharma, there is transparency; honesty is the characteristic of a person who can lead a nation in dharma: We have seen that Dharma is central to the rising of a nation. Dharma, in turn, calls for rigorous adherence to the Highest Ideal. Can leaders or parties that do not show honesty and integrity truly sustain dharma and herald the rising of a nation? The people who practice evasion, who won't correct the system and who won't reset it in ways such that money that change hands in politics can be tracked do not have the honesty it takes to be true leaders in dharma. Those individuals (or parties) that do not open their palms to the nation and those who do not come clean on all aspects of their political activities (including funding) can never take India to its ancient glorious destiny. Prosperity in a nation cannot be achieved by handing over the reins of power to those who do not uphold dharma, who are not tuned to the Highest and who do not hold on to the basic values of honesty and integrity.

There must be strict audit of party accounts just like accounts of companies are strictly regulated through rules. If there is fudging, somebody needs to be held accountable. Defaulters must be duly punished. Laws must be framed in this regard, and a clear criterion must be fixed by which a defaulting party, if the mistake is grave enough, may even be disallowed from contesting in elections. No anonymous funding of political parties or of politicians should be allowed.

To summarize, as far as money goes, there are three basic necessities if political parties are to cater to dharma.

1) Provision must be made for political parties to have legitimate funds for their activities.

2) Political parties must have internal democracy and robust internal communications to ensure that they remain integrated and the leadership is not paralyzed.

3) There is a need for financial transparency. A party should have a leadership that cherishes the highest value systems attuned to dharma if it is to lead the nation into dharma and prosperity.

In democracy, elections are like a long-drawn festival. Like the great Indian festivals which celebrate the divine in many forms and ways, elections too must be a celebration of the upkeep of dharma. The voter must play his part as if he were distributing sweets, over that period of one month, for the success of his nation.

If people wake up to the requirement of dharma, any party that wishes to present itself for taking responsibility of steering the nation will definitely play ball or else lose out.

Dharma is built on the rock foundation that all men are equal. The highest self-experience which the ancient masters have talked about is independent of race, religion, sex, physique, intellect, thought process, belief system, etc. There is therefore no discrimination on the basis of any of these criteria. When this is the case, a democracy based on dharma must also reflect the same in the institutions it is composed of.

Therefore, a dharmic legislature must also in no way distinguish each member that is present in the house of the parliament. The same must be the case for any other law-making body in the nation too. This, of course, is not the case in India because these houses are publicly conceived to mean something else altogether—not by design, but surely by default...

Today, there is a beeline for ensuring 33% reservation for women in the parliament. Reservations for women have already been made in local bodies, and this new call seems to be a next step in a natural flow of the liberation theology propagated by many of the mainstream thinkers. It takes inspiration from the idea that reservation of constituencies was required for the lower castes. It is an extension of the idea that justice is delivered to the Anglo-Indian community through the nomination of two representatives of the community into the Lok Sabha. The idea is further strengthened by the fact that the governments try their best to accommodate as many communities or groups as possible when allotting ministries and forming cabinets.

This idea of representation of various groups seems like the perfectly normal thing to do; it is so deeply ingrained that it may appear to be the foundation stone on which the Indian polity is based. In truth, this is one of the most degrading features of a democracy.

All reservation ideas are open admissions that there is a lack of faith in the people who are to be voted into parliament or that there is a lack of mutual trust: How? The thinking is that if there are no women in the parliament, there won't be justice for women. If there are no seats reserved for the special categories, there won't be justice for the lower castes. If there is no reservation for Anglo-Indians in the Lok Sabha, they will get a raw deal and so on.

Note that the parliament is one of the highest bodies in Indian society. Does this go to say that its members, some of the best people in the land, will be incapable of doing justice to people other than their 'own'? If that is the case in the best of the land, then what hope can the nation have in the character of people at lower levels? Is the nation not starting off with the premise that people are, and will be, selfish? 'People-can-behave-selfish-at-times' is alright. But 'people-are-always-selfish'?

If that is the premise on which the parliament itself is established, then are all institutions in society based on the same idea? Mind science brings out an alarming fact from this.

If this idea has been induced at the highest level in a nation, is the same idea being subconsciously driven into all impressionable minds in society? Indeed, it is. It is like a constant psyching or brainwashing of the people of a nation. It comes down to sowing seeds into the minds of husbands and wives that they cannot take care of each other or of their children owing to their selfish natures.

It is said that a limited man becomes what he thinks. So, if the best among us express that selfishness is the nature of man, are we reinforcing that into the thought process of society? Yes! Indeed, this is happening.

This idea is not the foundation of society: Unfortunately, no society that ever believes that people are self-centered has ever prospered. All great social institutions, achievements and civilizations have been built on the impression that man is capable of sacrifice; in fact, it revels in sacrifice. All great achievements in human history have been achieved when the impersonal has been exalted. Check out Appendix A.

The edifice of Indian democracy stands not because of proper balancing of selfish interests but because there are exemplary individuals among Indians that are selfless. Within each of us humans, there is that element that impels us to do good. That is why the Indian democracy stands.

Would this nation stand without the sacrifice of the soldiers, the daring of the whistle-blowers, those who are ready to face consequences for standing up for what is right, housewives who dedicate themselves to their homes, family heads who take full responsibility for the care of each member of their families, parents who make sacrifices for their children and farmers toiling in the fields or workmen at their little jobs with a sense of giving? In Islam, sacrifice is even celebrated as a festival—Id ul Adha. If people do not make sacrifices to Allah, Yahweh, God the Father, Krishna Consciousness or even just to humanity, nothing can be achieved in society.

It is inconsistent for one to dream that India will attain superpower status or even great prosperity for that matter when one simultaneously believes that man is selfish. Let alone prosperity, it remains in doubt as to whether even natural justice will be done to everyone if this is the belief in the premier forum of the country.

The nation's present arrangement of having a parliament is as if the nation has built a temple and idealizes or perceives or proposes the likeness of the devil in the sanctum sanctorum.

(NB: There is one exception though. Checks and balances are required as there is always a fear of unscrupulous elements occupying such positions of responsibility. And to that extent, maybe representation is a necessary answer. But it cannot be all checks and balances and no hope for dharma.)

A parliament of selfish representatives: The problem is that the nation has run into a cyclic idea that starts with the representation psyche. There are representatives in the Lok Sabha to take care of the citizens' interests. The representatives typically represent selfish positions. (They are selfless in that they are fighting for others—but for others in their 'own' category.) So, during elections too, they appeal on the same lines. Both the candidates and the voters resonate with the idea. As such, each individual is expected to vote not for the nation, not for the welfare of all and not for the welfare of society, but for one of the labels that describes himself (caste, religion, language, status…). His vote is expected to be selfish. He votes people who vociferously take self-positions, and ultimately, the nation ends up with a parliament composed of members who are interested in their own groups.

Selfish leaders: This has been analyzed in some depth while reckoning the enemies of freedom in Part 2 of this book. These people, who express confidence in representing selfish interests, they represent their own interest when it comes to a competition among the members of their groups, so much so that they think it is their basic human nature to protect their personal interests in preference to those of others in their families. It is a culture they practice at all levels for they essentially believe that man is selfish.

The biggest catch is in the self-preservation of the politician. When it is a question of the politician vs. the rest of the citizens, the politician who believes in the 'group representation' ideology will, keeping to the belief that man is selfish, protect the interest of the politician. He, after all, wishes to perpetuate his own continuance (and his kith and kin). No wonder these politicians tend to perpetuate conditions that keep the meritorious outsiders out of the power dynamics. In this, politicians of all hues band up together.

If India seeks prosperity, the parliament cannot represent selfishness: The parliament must represent high inspiration! It should stand for a sacrificing ethos! It must stand for what is best in Indian society. In the parliament, there should be the highest of values which the nation wishes to exemplify in society. It should exemplify the values on which a thriving nation can be built.

As discussed above, making it a representative body and thereby making it the chief forum of mistrust eats at the very foundation of the nation. The existing cycle needs to be broken. Following are three ways this can be achieved.

1. Change mind-set: There is a need of a cultural war with the idea of what the parliament represents in the minds of the common citizen and the elected representatives.

2. Change parliamentary procedures: There is a need to fine-tune procedures in the parliament so that the members may represent general interests as a rule and never the interests of their own groups. This will require a lot of innovative thinking. For one thing, the speaker may call non-member specialists/representatives to speak to the parliament on crucial issues and answer questions posed to them by the parliamentarians to ensure that the perspective is known in the parliament. This task of speaking for certain groups should not be done by a member of the house. It may be something on the lines of 'testifying before the Congress' in the United States—anything that will allow specialists speak before parliamentarians.

3. Selfish representatives are non-leaders: There is a need for the absolute distrust of all those who vouch for group representation. The vengeance with which a person seeks representation must be an index of how much he believes that man is selfish. He believes that man is selfish because he feels that is his own essential nature. His thoughts make him that way. He thinks man is selfish, and he becomes selfish. This disqualifies him from leadership positions. He is incapable of, or unfit for, leadership positions.

It is in this context that the intentions of Mahatma Gandhi at the time of independence can be understood. He suggested that the Congress must split into two formations, one under Pandit Nehru and the other under Sardar Patel, and fight elections against one another.

Obviously, the Congress did not think it practical. They had this one Congress that consisted of the leaders of the freedom struggle who worked as a team, delivering many good things to the nation. But where they wrong in not accepting what the Mahatma had to say?

In order to understand this strange request from Gandhiji, one must understand the scenario that existed at that time. Before independence, there were many individuals who wished to join the freedom struggle. Those that felt India was one nation joined either the Congress or a more radical group like the Indian National Army. The other groups that existed at that time were those that saw the nation and society in terms of 'they' and 'we', whether it was the casteists, communists, linguists, racists or the communalists. Therefore, at independence, there was one party (other than the INA) which thought of the nation as consisting of one people while all other groups saw a fractured nation/society.

Gandhiji realized that an alternative to the Congress must arise, and when it does, it must arise out of one of the other groups/ideologies. And if and when such a thing happened, then the political debate would have a uniting force on the one hand and a dividing force on the other. God forbid, but if an Indian who saw all Indians as one were to find the Congress unfit because of misadministration or corruption, then he would be constrained to choose from any of the alternative ideologies which were built on basic principles of mistrust between Indians.

It turns out that the Mahatma indeed had tremendous foresight. It took about seventeen years for an alternative ideology to make an appearance in the states (communists then linguists) and about half century before an alternative (communal) came into place at the center. And indeed, these ideologies did play out as expected. In fact, politics has been reduced into a battlefield with chaos being created by one group having a one-nation ideology and a whole lot of groups with split-nation ideologies. The political dialog has been reduced into a hotchpotch representation matrix in which every other leader is a representative of some or the other group. It is so bad that politics itself is now being treated as a pariah. It is now fashionable to say, 'I won't stand for elections because I am righteous.' Well, it is not said verbally, but the implication is there nonetheless.

It can easily be argued that there is nothing wrong with this. That this is the way things are supposed to be. That ideologies don't matter and that this is the way it was meant to be. However, this is not true.

An ideology is an important component for the togetherness of any group. For instance, when a group is confronted with a big challenge and there is uncertainty about the direction to take, the group invariably refers back to the ideology that brought it together in the first place. That ideology directs the further moves of its members. If there is divergence, then a new ideology takes birth.

The manner in which an ideology plays its role can be seen in comparing the riots of 1984 and 2002. In

1984, when all hell broke loose and there was uncertainty everywhere, the agitated stakeholders referred to 'ideology' and found Gandhiji there. So, the cream of the leadership put its foot down, and the matter shut down in three days. (It is another matter that the team did not go the whole length which the Mahatma would have expected of it.) In comparison, in 2002, when the stakeholders referred back to their ideology it did not instruct them to withdraw. It made them continue for months. One must not be under the mistaken belief that the long-drawn persecution of the 'others' is what Hinduism seeks. Rather, it is what Hindutva seeks. Lord Rama would never have spoken of the citizens of his nation as 'they' and 'we'.

But the then prime minister himself, known to be a moderate face and a well-known statesman of modern India, spoke of a section of his citizens as 'they'—the unfortunate face of Hindutva. This does not represent true Hinduism. If the reference to ideology went back to Lord Rama, the mayhem would have stopped immediately. Therefore, if the right wing has to find a way out, it must in some way offload the chauvinistic right-wing ideologies of the mid-20th century and go back to the purity of Lord Rama and Lord Krishna. For this, they have better hope in going through Mahatma Gandhi than through the thought process that precipitated what Godse did.

Have no doubt that ideology does matter. And that alternative to the Congress, which will have an ideology that will take the nation forward as one team, is yet to emerge (many have tried but have not risen in stature). Every next election is an opportune time to yet again come up with something that may emerge as the alternative.

For the time being, discourage the narrow representative: Besides looking for that alternative team to emerge from the nation, it will do good to the nation if it can facilitate in the nation the creation of a culture which looks down upon narrow representatives.

Narrow representatives are those with a strong sense of selfishness, who have strong belief in taking care of their own interests and who may have the ability to represent a group as a vociferous son but never as an all-embracing benevolent father. The narrow representative will create enemies in a group of people on the basis of labels (he is this jati, that religion, this language, etc.) and not on the basis of righteous actions (whether you are my brother or not; if you have done injustice, you will pay). Narrow representatives promote adharma.

A parliament built on the principles of faith, belief in people, belief in essential selflessness and belief in the sacrifice of the selfless is the foundation of a great, prosperous nation. A person who represents in such a parliament will be an open representative. An open representative, therefore, upholds dharma.

It is important that the voter be sensitized against the narrow representative. He must patronize and vote for open representatives. He must understand that this is what dharma seeks.

Section III

The Spirit of Freedom Calls for a Modified Economic Praxis

The economy of our nation has the potential to do more. But it needs to break away from some fundamental concepts and start reflecting the highest that this land hopes to deliver to its citizens—that which will convert this economics into an integral part of a dharmic system. Let us explore by looking at various aspects of the economy that can be re-reckoned under the dharma perspective. But let us take a look at a few things before we get to that:

Economy-wise, we are doing our best by global standards: The nation is fortunate that the prime minister of two terms in the turn of the century was an outstanding scholar in economics. And a person of such high learning has had the privilege of guiding the economy for nearly two decades at the turn of the century. In fact, the team around him had many stalwarts who are acknowledged for their capacities in the field of economics. One can therefore be sure that the nation has been put into an economic orbit that is based on the best of principles known to the best of global modern scholars of economics. The new team that has displaced Mr. Manmohan Singh has tried some innovations, but the basic thrust still remains, and for all practical purposes, India continues to show promise and growth almost on par with the best in the world. Though this is the case, doubts still remain.

Economy first or life first? A straightforward question to ask is whether it is economic principles that should drive the modern world or whether economics must play a subservient role in a sphere where the primary purpose is life itself.

Can economic affairs of the nation be left to the vagaries of destiny, where certain overt and covert forces influence the dynamics in such a way that it is beyond the control of the Indian statesmen? Should the leadership be controlling the economy subject to the principle that freedom should thrive in all individuals in the nation or should the nation and its leadership be held hostage by an economic system that wrecks mayhem in the lives of many of its citizens?

The goal need not be doubted. If an economy is operating in full swing, then there is less unemployment, taxes collected are plentiful, the government gets the resources to take on welfare measures, there is greater trickledown effect, the nation has a bigger voice at international forums and the nation is able to build up its military strength too. When such is the case, why will the leader of a nation not want his economy to thrive? But if the primary purpose of living itself is compromised in an attempt to make the economy thrive, then it does not make sense.

There are very fundamental issues that need to be addressed to ensure that the economic system becomes part of the platform that upholds freedom. On the contrary, if it makes the earth a pleasure-sty for the rich and wicked and a perpetual hell for the poor, then that is undesirable. The economy must operate in a manner such that it can be supportive of a holistic dharma. The economy must create an environment where everyone has the liberty and enough means to pursue the highest, with the basic Herzberg's hygiene (motivation) factors taken care of. And this calls for sensitivity to several issues that are of great importance to the free Human Spirit or the Highest Self. The first question to ask is about the environment.

Can the nation slight the environmental challenge and romp ahead regardless of global consequences? Apart from being responsive to life and freedom, economics must also cater to the global environment. This is a matter of great urgency for the planet; the globe has finite material resources. A BBC report tells us that there are credible calculations which show that attaining the average material standards of the US for the entire population of the world will require 4.1 times the resources that are available in the world. India constitutes nearly a seventh of the population of the globe. Would the earth still remain a great place when all of India attains the level of prosperity the US has achieved? The degree of industrialization that will be needed, the degree of messing up that will be involved… We are never going to get there until we start mining other planets. (And even if the prosperity levels of the US are attained in India, there will still be a lot of poor people to be taken care of.)

How much can the planet take…? On the one hand, it is possible that the planet has a far greater ability for sustenance than scientists give it credit for. And hopefully, humankind can invent better technologies so that Mother Nature may be spared. But on the other, there might be an impending disaster in the making. There are reasons to fear a possible catastrophe after a particular unknown threshold is crossed. Something that will trigger great destructive energies which are otherwise locked up in the favorable conditions of today—something like a sudden meltdown of the fragile environment. Humankind cannot persist with the current rate of destruction of the environment. This further implies that it cannot persist with the current set of aims and goals, unless one has resigned himself to recklessly risking disaster. There is a need to look for and facilitate alternative goals and aspirations that will not make it necessary to destroy the planet.

And just in case, after everything, if the nation and the world still persist with the modern notions of prosperity and cannot give up the mad materialistic race, then the bare minimum that is obligatory on the present generation is to strive vigorously for solutions within the constraints imposed by these notions of prosperity. There is a need to look for solutions in the form of new technologies that are less damaging. Either that or resort to government-sponsored forced austerity measures. Having done that, humanity may hope like mad that nothing will go wrong. The present leaders seem to have chosen this path of action.

The sad part is that the measures that have so far resulted from the efforts of global leaders lack the missionary zeal that is required to stem the rot. As for forced austerity measures, which governments can take on, they seem to be a difficult pill to swallow. Governments are unlikely to resort to it unless nature forces it on humanity, and the impact will first be visible on the poor of the world. Everyone seems to be waiting for the TINA (There Is No Alternative) factor. When that happens, they will be forced into austerity as there will be no other alternative. That is a huge risk to take indeed.

Must India participate in this risk? Or should its economic policies zealously reflect concern for both the poor and the environment? Does this mean that India must follow a policy of abstinence whether the other nations follow suit or not? What if the others continue to play the prosperity game? This much is for certain. The present course is reckless, and the world must scratch its head to come up with some solution—and fast. But does it really have to be a compromise?

Should the nation plan for a society that cherishes material aggrandizement or one that cherishes detachment? Today, it is generally taught to an individual in society that he should passionately accumulate (or at least earn) as much as possible all his life if his aim is to court prosperity and happiness. But the wise refer to this as equivalent to chasing a red herring. They say that there is no happiness worth its name either on that journey or at the end of it.

Is this escapism? Are we going against selfish human instinct? Are we 'indulging' in ascetic principles? Are we 'deviating' from a human's basic desire for happiness? Are we demotivating dedicated workers by removing the sense of purpose required in the capitalist order? Indeed, is all this true? May be, may be not… But let's not conclude without properly investigating whether these accusations are fair.

Conclusions cannot easily be drawn one way or the other. This is again a step into the uncertain, for there are still many unresolved questions in this field. But we can look at the overall picture. Let us investigate the consequences.

Consider the path of self-aggrandization: The truth is that even a single such mind which chases desires cannot attain satisfaction, not even if that one mind were to be given possessions bit-by-bit over all the resources of the world. Can anyone really become blissful on this path of acquisition? Would a study of the law of diminishing returns finally bring forward the proof that the source of joy and satisfaction is not in the material plane at all?

What then does our human instinct say? Is it just possible that there is more happiness and fulfillment in life in the absence of endless wants? Is it true that the necessary condition for happiness is a pulsating life rather than the mere gratification of the senses through consumerism?

If this alternative is true, then there is great hope for humanity and the environment. All those resources which one thought was necessary to satisfy all of humanity may not be needed after all. That will mean that between the pursuit of happiness and the environment, humankind ends up with a win-win situation—nothing like the win-lose situation that the world seems to have resigned itself to as of today.

Capitalism is not a sacred cow; it too is an ideal – Practical capitalism must balance out the ideal's negatives: Capitalism as currently in operation and the ideal of capitalism are two different things. An analysis of the capitalistic utopia, as a system by itself, gives evidence that free-running absolute capitalism is ridiculous or senseless. Allowing capitalism to have a free run is counterproductive.

The stupidity of the idea becomes clear even to a die-hard fan of capitalism only when the idea is pushed to its idealistic extreme. For instance, centralized production is one of the characteristics of capitalism. Through economies of scale, it can raise production efficiencies and bring forward better quality products with lesser time and effort.

Now, can this principle be taken to the extreme idealistic limits? Can this idea be implemented on a system without absolutely any check whatsoever? Can we allow each individual the right to produce whatever he wants and as much as he wants, sell where he wants and gather any amount of money he can? Of course, no one will use violence or break laws. But even so, what if it so happens that there is one guy who finally outsmarts every other manufacturer through cutting costs, maximizing efficiency and with focus on quality? Can such an individual be allowed to become the sole owner and producer though he has done nothing illegal?

We can take it still one step further. This one big owner has developed this one incredible robot (a capitalist's delight) such that it can collect resources most economically (more economically than any other method), innovate to improve on any product that is present in the market, produce material goods with the latest techniques in a most aesthetically pleasing manner and then sell the products anywhere in the world, cheaper than any other similar product, and make a profit. And if it can do this for everything you can think of, which you can buy and sell and work as an agent for, then will any other person in the world have a job? Think of it. Who produces the food? The capitalist's delight. Who manufactures things? The capitalist's delight. Who puts things in the market and sells them? The capitalist's delight. Who provides the cheapest personal services? Robots of the capitalist's delight. And so on…

How do the others earn then? And how do they buy anything if they have no income? Of course, the only capitalist would pay tax, and the government will dole out funds in the form of social security on the basis of the safety net ideals. But everything turns out to be ridiculous. The economic system will have reduced every other individual into a non-consequential—a beggar, if one may. Is this not the situation into which many individuals and communities in the present world have been pushed into? We call them below-poverty-line people. Hence, when absolute capitalism happens (a single capitalist owning the capitalist's delight), we will have one capitalist and seven billion BPL people. Except for government servants… (Moreover, if even this government service can be outsourced to private part(y)ies, then those tasks that a robot can do will again be taken up to the capitalist's delight.)

Definitely, such cannot be the goal of togetherness. Rather, what is needed is a proper balance between idealism and practicality. The pursuit of the capitalist ideal must satisfy an even more fundamental goal of a fulfilling togetherness among humans. This means that capitalism, the ideal, is not fundamental. It is only a method. Rather, the final goal of a fulfilling togetherness in a nation should be the underlining root agenda.

Material prosperity is required, and therefore, capitalism is required. But worshiping capitalism as if it were a divine touch-me-not is a bad idea. Capitalism must serve the wellbeing of societies and subjugate itself to the concern of the wellbeing of even the very last individual.

It is true that there are tendencies in capitalism that cause a widening gap between the rich and the poor. Even this is not the problem in itself. The problem lies in the extent of adversity wrought by that economic disparity on the personal liberty of disadvantaged individuals. For example, just because someone does not have money, he does not get justice in the courts. That is not correct. Therefore, if a widening economic gap is going to be a natural consequence of using capitalism as an ideal, then that system needs to cater for certain arrangements so that the purchasing power of money cannot decide the quality of vital services. Indeed, justice must not be dependent on the income of a person. This is a practical defense mechanism that must be propped up in a capitalist order so that the overall system can deliver holistically. Another example is that the government must step in and create laws that limit monopolies. The government must artificially prop up low-technology-based production systems if that is able to give citizens a dignified/earned meal. (For example, if the government of pre-independence India had the interests of the poor in mind, it would have come out with a law that forbade the use of high technology for cloth production so that khadi could thrive at least till a time when the poorest man could stand on his feet.)

This means that the people who manage the Indian economy and also intervene to design economic systems for India must ensure the following vital benchmark: The primary purpose of the economic system is not the system itself but the people. On the one hand, the nation must continue to exist so that it can give with great benevolence to the citizens, and this calls for a robust economy. But on the other hand, every citizen must have access to a dignified opportunity to earn his living during his working years—something that is adequate to meet the basic needs of his family. The economic system (capitalism) must serve to balance these two aims if it is to contribute to a dharmic arrangement.

Shed the belief that this is a dog-eat-dog world; there is competition in dharma, but there is also great compassion: An analysis of capitalism reveals that it fosters a certain 'fear' in its competition mechanism; it's a 'fear psychosis' of a different kind. In the original fear psychosis that is associated with communism and fascism, people are cowed down into submission since they are afraid for their lives out of criminal intimidation; but in this alternate fear psychosis of capitalism, people live in fear of hunger and adversity.

The modern world believes that the wants of man are endless. Those who are part of the modern world eventually believe in it too; most of us do. (Except a few, of course, who are often clubbed along with the escapists; and the interesting part is that these special escapists are the ones who are most efficient in the system. Further, most of such persons emanate charisma.) Those who are so instilled with the belief that human nature is driven by endless wants are convinced about it. They have the energy to attempt to climb up the ladder of success in which higher levels signify increased possessions.

Further, when it is claimed that the material prosperity of the West is impossible for a nation like India, it is seen as nothing but the obvious—mostly owing to the belief that resources are scarce.

And knowing this, when planners persist with the use of the system of competition, it automatically implies that they are aware of, and give approval for, a mad dog-eat-dog competition that occurs within the economy; it is believed that one needs to be paddling hard or else one will be left behind. Questions of survival may even arise.

When the die-hard fan of the capitalist ideal sees suffering around him, he says:

➢ Why don't you join the competition and slog like us? Why do you wish to sit outside and laze around? If you are left behind, then you are dead. So, you better work.

- You are suffering? Oh! That's because you are not adjusting to the system. In any case, you can avail of social security sops.
- As for me, well, I'm busy surviving here. How can I do anything for you? And then, how do you think I will indulge in entertainment and pleasure if I keep thinking of you?
- About the globe and the sustainability of its environment? God alone knows! We should try to do something; let's make more laws. And let's appoint somebody and pay him a salary to take care of these things.
- Any barrier erected in the way of the freedom of the capitalist structure is a restriction on liberty! All laws have to be designed to nurture freedom.

One thought leads to the other, and it seems perfectly logical and resonant with the pursuit of liberty. So then, what is liberty? Stopping capitalism, giving it freedom or allowing it a free run? When either of the latter two choices that are favorable to capitalism are made, it is an accepted fact that there is going to be suffering in the process.

For example, it is often said, 'X% of people are currently under the poverty line. If everything goes all right, then the percentage should reduce by 10% within Y years.' That would be the opinion of a normal, honest, straightforward individual operating in the capitalistic system.

The net result is that people are made to entertain a fear that they may land up in the bottom of the heap with not enough to go around for everyone; and the antidote for that fear is to work for survival! And therefore, out of fear of losing out, he works! Is this not fear psychosis? For someone who is not so informed of the economic order, it is more direct. No work today means no food for his family and him today. So, he is out there to struggle.

In contrast, the environment in a dharmic arrangement is not fear psychosis but a delightful togetherness. The whole idea of putting everyone under a threat is not pleasing to the Supreme Self. The dharmic environment revels in the giving up of the idea of scarcity in resources by saying, 'There is enough for everyone.' (Refer to the works of Sirshree Tejparkhiji.) It delights in sharing a feeling of oneness with every member of society and expressing great compassion for all. Everyone is out there doing their duty, and their basic concerns are taken care of.

As such, in a dharma-based system, it is important that the design caters responsibilities for everyone and provisions for the satisfaction of everyone's needs. The government-based 'safety net' is a centralized system trying to offer some relief for the needs of the dropouts. But it is riddled with practical difficulties. Rather, dharma calls for a system that caters to a strong augmentation of the efforts of the government with the efforts of individuals, families, institutions and communities down at the grassroots level so that the human-to-human interactions deliver the safety net out of compassion.

- No reason other than one's own desire or one's utter laziness must be the cause of a person starving. Society must innovate solutions by which every individual has the means to earn the basic that is required for his family to propel itself into the competitive environment of the capitalist order.
- Swadeshi and Khadi were the solutions that were apt for the pre-independence era. Solutions such as these need to be innovated for this generation. Perhaps some modified versions of the same…

The economic order does not throw up the right kind of leadership that is free of the blinders of capitalism: 'How can I help it if you are poor and not able to catch on? This is a mad dog-eat-dog world of capitalism. I am busy running my race in order to survive. Please run yours too.' Is this attitude responsible? Is this a matured bearing? Can such an attitude govern nations? Is it not escapist with respect to the question of responsibility for fellowmen and future generations? But this is what the present planners have in mind when they are busy discussing poverty-line statistics and figures related to the extent of inefficiency of the welfare schemes while ignoring the fact that this very evening, a significant percentage of the Indian population is probably going to bed without a meal.

The attitude borders on brutality. It also reveals the helplessness of those running these systems. It turns out that the merits of capitalism are emphasized to shut the mind's eye to these uncomfortable thoughts. The merits of capitalism are used as an excuse to banish from the mind thoughts about the existence of feelings like fear, dog-eat-dog survival and satisfaction of greed in members of society at various levels.

The opposite is an enlightened approach to problem-solving, where the primary objective is the achievement of a caring togetherness. There is a necessity for reasonable checks on the capitalistic structure in the form of safety nets or guarding walls. These checks have to be an expression of the liberty of an empowered people and not sympathy for the downtrodden. This requires a paradigm shift in the thinking process.

At the root of the problem is the fact that the present systems are driven by capitalists (businessmen) who are essentially in control, and they operate through wage-earning administrators (political or bureaucratic). Those that excel in capitalism and succeed in it have the disposition of merchants and not kings. A merchant's concern and functional spectrum is severely restricted by his focus on the growth of his money-earning facility. The horizons of a wage earing administrator are even more restricted as he is concerned at the most with excellence in his job, his salary and his family. When the important functions related to the running of nation states are placed in the hands of people like them, the ideals of good government are lost in alternate priorities.

There is no denying the fact that the Indian civilization aims to ensure that all citizens of an enlightened society must be high-thinking and simple-living folk. They are supposed to be yogis and heroes who idealize the equality of humans, who are inspired to live and act in the present moment, who are not driven by relative gain and who are not limited in a purpose that confines them to worrying about their own homes. And they are trained to act selflessly. But besides the pursuit of this ideal, the pursuit of gyan yoga by those who are to guide society calls for an understanding and level of learning that is truly specialized and deep. And there is a need for another set of individuals who, by profession, put their lives on the line and who idealize standing up for the last individual unconcerned about that other person's financial status.

Simply put, the nation must be governed by Kshatriyas and Brahmins and not by Vaishyas and Shudras as is the case now. People working for salaries and for their businesses, even if selflessly, will lack the depth that is required to manage systems where the focus is altogether something else—self-realization for everyone and effective justice for everyone, irrespective of any demographical categorization.

A need to strengthen traditions that have spiritual sanction and purpose so that the adverse impact of capitalism is softened: What will be the consequence if it is indeed the truth that man's needs are *not* endless? Impossible, one might say. But that's what Indian culture is all about. The scriptures talk about the Self that is peaceful and capable of happiness by itself as the one that cannot be ornamented by pleasure and glory nor injured by pain or disdain. Now, who knows whether this is what one might observe if he took a closer look at himself?

This, of course, leads to a major debate, and there are committed people who agree with this and there are others who don't. If one's observation through life has confirmed an individual's faith in either of the ideas (selfless and selfish), then neither the individual who thinks that asceticism is escapism or that asceticism is the essence of existence can be accused of any hypocrisy.

The way out, therefore, is to let each to himself. Each individual can pursue the truth and work out for himself as to what is right. And as the ancients roughly put it, the four proofs to be used to make that study are observation/ experience, inference, scriptures (a record of experiences and inferences) and authority (an innate disposition that comes to the wise). And that study should be objective— without any bias—for the best results. As for the debate, it will perpetually be on. Even so, in the meanwhile, the bare minimum will be to allow for both perspectives, the consumerists and the spiritualists, to find expression.

Making provision for both alternatives: How do we let both possibilities exist side by side? How do we let both points of view prevail and let there be sufficient breathing space, in capitalism, even for those that believe in simplicity?

If all that the simpletons want is merely enough to go on with their lives, that is, simple living and high thinking coupled with sufficient liberty, then so be it. Why force on them the other view that life is an endless rat race after desires? Let this group of simpletons also have a playfield of their own. Let this opinion too thrive. Let the two options thrive in their respective zones, and let each not disturb the other. This will require that the nation to work toward the solution where the strengths of strong economy (with the liberty of the competitors) and the strengths of strong communities (with the liberty of the ascetics) are both available in a way such that they can thrive independently. So, on the one hand, there will be the nuances of capitalism, its ideal, its beliefs and its methods, which the modern world is familiar with. And on the other hand, there will be the principles that sustain a lifestyle that is more laidback in terms of economics but thriving with life of an alternate kind. This one can be called a community-centered life, which may be unfamiliar to the mainstream thought process and sometimes even contradicting the mainstream beliefs.

This alternative expounds that a better material standard of living is not necessarily the ultimate goal of living. It is not essentially true that people who are richer are happier. Happiness is in spite of one's material possessions. The simplicity of village life has enough in it for a complete life with regard to the dimensions that are really worth considering.

Putting it briefly, the goods of village life need not be conceived on the basis of aspirations of happiness-in-what-one-owns. So why not think and plan differently?

A different way: The services rendered outside the ambit of commercial exchanges could be substantial. These priceless services held in esteem by people, though such services may not be obtained by payment of high wages, are valued highly because excellence in such services can be obtained only by high idealism, inspiration, missionary zeal, feeling of collective good, ascetic wisdom or dharma. That, and only that, can lift a nation to its true potentials.

As a bare minimum, rural society must promote the Islamic concept of the rich annually giving away a small percentage of their wealth toward the wellbeing of the poor. If not directly, the society must promote at least some contribution toward causes and projects that eliminate poverty.

Another important spiritual solution that can be highlighted or set as a benchmark is the profound bhiku

tradition of the Buddhists or the ideal of the Brahmin in Hinduism. In these, the highest people in society are expected to nurture the ideal of resorting to alms for their food. (This is not begging.) If one looks at the impact of this on society, it counteracts the existence of desperation to survive in the citizens of a nation. The best in society are not desperate even when they have to depend on others for alms! This ensures a closing of the loop in dharma. In this, the highest in society (spiritually and intellectually) live the economic plight of the lowest wage-earners. The circle is closed because justice (legal protection and of life and liberty) that is dealt to the highest in society has a strong tendency to reach even the lowest of the wage-earners.

The villages of India are an opportunity to counterbalance tradition and capitalistic rigor; the economic solution is that rural produce must be patronized: There is a need to promote rural industries. Though the rural dimension of the two-nations-in-one solution needs to have a traditional mind-set, it does not mean that there will be no modern goods and services produced there. The Indian economy is predominantly agrarian because India is, to a large extent, still a nation of villages. And most villages rely on agriculture. But could there be adequate production in the rural areas such that all the people living in the agro-based hinterland can independently sustain themselves at least?

The freedom struggle had the important component of swadeshi. This was basically a humanitarian principle because it took birth in the background of a harsh goods-for-money system. If a man is not given something to eat because he has no money and if he is also not given an opportunity for a job which will allow him to earn that money with which he can eat, then that is ridiculous. The swadeshi movement drew its strength from this inherent consideration for the poor (Indian). Swadeshi asked for the rejection of produce that came from abroad and patronage of goods produced by Indians. Swadeshi came as a solution on behalf of the jobless, starving poor of India (who had paid rather dearly during periods of drought).

In a more refined form, this principle manifested in the economic aspect of the khadi movement. People were encouraged to spin cotton yarn by hand and make clothes out of them. This was to be in fashion and not the machine-made goods from the looms in Manchester. It was the manifestation of humanism. It was the nationalist's answer for a 'safety net'. It symbolized considerateness and universal justice—a right to livelihood. It is clear then why, though Indian ancient learning had nothing against the workers of Manchester, martial prosperity or science and technology, there was opposition to the use of modern machines in the preaching and practice of satyagraha, swadeshi and khadi.

An idealist of the capitalist system will see that these are against the principles of free market. The freedom to produce and open competition are so integral to capitalism. From the capitalist's point of view, it is a stupid idea to hinder mechanization. But seen from the practical point of view, as might be seen by a king or a wise man or a statesman, it does make a lot of sense. It has direct relevance to the ground realities; it offers relief to multitudes of people and brings peace to society. Toward these very aims, the activities in rural India today need to be organized. Due regard must be given to this high idealism that is a great gift from the freedom struggle.

Village industries need initial patronage and protection: India is all set to becoming a developed capitalist economy. One must be aware that in developed economies, even as little as 3% of the people alone are sufficient for taking care of agriculture in order to meet the needs of the rest. And in today's India, anywhere between 50 to 65% of people are dependent on agriculture. So, in the process of moving from a developing to a developed country, the nation may expect 40 to 50% of the population of the country to learn to depend on things other than agriculture for their living. If plans are not put into action for catering to this change in demographic, the nation is asking for a lot of future unrest and trouble.

A holistic regeneration is due, but before the nation gets there, there is a need for artificial protection being accorded to agriculture and agro-based industries, at least in the initial phase. So, as long as rural India has not adapted sufficiently to survive the transition of India from developing to developed status, a labor-intensive method needs to be adopted by the government at the village level. Initially, labor-intensive means of production may need

to be artificially propped up, but gradually, such means of production must learn to survive on their own without any special support. Within the shortest possible time, the products of these industries should be able to hold their own in the free market.

The five-point solution:
1) Deep decentralization
2) Shifting responsibilities to villages
3) Promoting labor-intensive industries in rural areas
4) Checking the free run of capitalism in the hinterland
5) Adhering to the spirit of khadi

This is the five-point package the nation must adopt today. This will call for many changes in strategy. The following ideas are suggested to break the boxed-up thinking in the search for solutions:

➢ Extension of a part of Article 370 to rural areas all over the country may be required so that outsiders cannot purchase land in rural and forested areas.

➢ No private use of high-tech farm implements till at least 95% employment rates are reached. High technology must be used only by cooperatives and complete village units on behalf of all citizens of the village.

➢ A ceiling on land-holding in these areas at the higher end and a simultaneous promotion of joint farming at the lower end of land-holding so that there is neither concentration in a single hand nor a drop in production due to a high degree of sub-division.

The spirit is important. Once the spirit of the package of five ideas is understood, unique solutions will definitely be innovated.

Tapping into the advantages of close-knit communities: One may even initially consider 'closed' communities at the village level (though, of course, cooperation with neighboring villages will produce the best effect). Without looking for economic indices out of individual villages, they can be encouraged to produce services and goods using local resources to meet local consumption. The value of money will be relatively low here. A system aiming at self-sufficiency through diversification and barter should be ideal in order to touch sustenance-levels. Surplus produce should facilitate outside trade. Villages specializing in certain products and services can be targeted at this level of surplus.

All this cannot be rigidly fixed through rules, but these must act as pointers for local leaders so that they can facilitate temporary fixes for their respective villages to get things going—so that villages will eventually do their own thing.

Making provisions for closed village economies may turn out to be unproductive in terms of economic indices. However, within each community, the people will have solved the fundamental problems in society. A whole spectrum of issues covering topics like education, health, civic sense, population control, woman's rights, caste problems, migration to cities, culture and sports can easily be tackled through self-help within communities. All it will take is a well-directed and strong stimulus in the sphere of human resources.

Self-sufficiency in village communities can also set them on the path of becoming potential markets— definitely so at the level of necessities. When constant demands are made on the better performance of villages in a spectrum of relevant fields, the standard of living in these villages should gradually improve. With it, the demand for products and services will also go up. What more does a national economy want? Demand, production, economic activity and near universal employment… Indeed, the promised fruits are many.

All the changes discussed above can be summarized as follows:

1) India must explore the possibility of valid and acceptable solutions that arise from the ancient Indian sages' ideal, which is that the highest in society are inherently content, independent of external needs being satisfied.

2) India must explore the possibility that simple living and high thinking can be the foundation on which a thriving society/nation can be built in the future.

3) The overall Indian solution must have a sustainable industrial base, a wise reining in of capitalism aimed at limiting its tendencies of absolute free run and an effective and indispensable safety net which exists more to sustain the splendor of life rather than to show pity or mercy.

4) Swagrami: The citizens of the nation need to patronize rural art and rural culture and bring into fashion products of rural industries by wantonly digressing from the path of idealistic consumerism. People must buy directly from villages in the spirit of khadi, and one must choose the village product over a 'company' product in the spirit of swadeshi. This new thrust that targeted bringing freedom to the villages can be described as swagrami. It must encompass the same feelings of compassion and action that were enshrined in khadi and swadeshi. The citizens may take up swagrami just for the heck of it or for the sake of nationalistic fervor through adherence to the spirit of swadeshi and khadi. However, ultimately, along the path of development, the goods and services produced in the villages must generate the strength to thrive independently in the free market. Without the existence of this promise to eventually become independent economically by participating competitively in the economy, the arrangements will not be adequate for a genuine transition to freedom. The villages must come up with products that have the three values of 'Clean, Quality and Necessary'.

5) Villages must be encouraged to initially take to mutual services using even barter if required, but they must plan as a team to ensure that members of their team are trained in diverse services that would be of use to the village.

6) In case the economic system allows for concentration of wealth/resources in a single hand, then it should be coupled with the placing of specified responsibilities in that hand. Land holders and resource holders must be obligated to patronize social activities in proportion to their holdings. Prosperity is implied responsibility.

Section IV

Revolutionary Augmentation of the Judicial Leg of Indian Democracy

The Indian judicial system has an inclination for long delays. It is overloaded with cases. It has been calculated that as of this day, if the courts of India stop taking on any more cases, then the judges would take 300 years just to clear the backlog. (In 2010, Justice V. V. Rao of the Andhra Pradesh high court said it would take 320 years.) Somewhere, all this contributes toward adding injustice in society. And worse, justice comes with a price tag, placed as it is in the context of the current socio-economic system!

Individuals can always be blamed for the shortcomings in systemic processes as much as they can be praised for the good in it. But beyond the human error factor, there are shortcomings of the judicial system itself, and these, in turn, call for an overhaul and pepping up of the system.

If the inabilities of the total system lead to callousness toward law and justice, if it leaves poor litigants in a limbo for their lifetimes and if the bumblebees break through the web of law, which adds to the burdens of the common man, then there is a need to go back to the drawing board and review the entire system of delivering justice in the nation.

Is the present judicial system dharmic? The judicial system, as ordained in a democratic state, in conjunction with capitalism, is hinged on several inbuilt ideals. These ideals are important because they aim at making the system whole. Or as the Indian ancients would say, 'The aspiration is to make the system dharmic.' The reality though is that the ideal itself can be called to question, and the practical manifestation is downright frustrating. All in all, the present system does not succeed in being holistic. Let us consider some of the issues that thus hamper the present system.

Today, money can buy better justice: It is common knowledge that the ability of a lawyer also plays an important role in the process of delivering justice in the present context, and all lawyers do not come with equal performance abilities! In the commercial setup, such talented lawyers charge more, and hence, their services are available only to the rich. With better services going to those who can pay more, the poor are naturally at a disadvantage. Those individuals serving the nation through low-paying livelihoods get a raw deal.

If better justice is purchasable by money, then the basic concept of justice is itself compromised. Maybe that was not what the ideal was and that was not how it was designed, but that is the way it has practically turned out to be. This is now more or less considered an integral part of the system, a 'given' which has to be accepted as is.

In a judicial system, the existence of such a disparity translates directly into one of the main scourges of poverty. This is not a problem that is specific to India; democracies across the world that follow capitalism have some or the other version of this problem.

A possible thrust for a solution: Given the fact that more than 70% of Indian citizens have severe limitations on their purse strings even at the level of needs, let alone luxuries, they need to have something more affordable. There is a need for a judicial process that can cater to the health of societies formed among those who are financially not well-off. Such alternatives should come as added features that may be integrated into the system that is now in force. We shall see more of this presently.

Dharma of a lawyer is decided by the larger cause: It is common knowledge that the advocate's duty is to protect the interest of their clients. On the other hand, being part of the system that delivers justice in society, it becomes their duty to ensure that the judiciary plays this role as an effective pillar of the state and useful wing of society. This means that punishment that is true and just must happen in accordance with and in proportion to the transgressions of the law. However, situations often arise in which lawyers find these two aims—aims of their clients and overall aims of justice—at cross purposes. And at such instances, many of them quote spirituality to say that it is their 'duty' to protect the client; and they go to great lengths to bring relief to their clients at all costs—whether it is deserved or not.

A possible thrust for a solution: Ancient Indian wisdom asks for such testing decisions to be taken by reckoning the following hierarchy. When practice/convention fails to resolve an issue, refer to tradition. If the issue still remains unresolved, look at the law. If the issue still remains unresolved even after this, refer to dharma. This means that this highest principle of dharma needs to be referred to in order to finally resolve such a conflict of interest. So, what does dharma have to say in this context?

Dharma is not about individuals. It is about the commonness in man. It is about the Divine in man. It is that which makes men equal in the eyes of God. It is about treating others as we would have others treat us. Thus, the ancients mean to say that a lawyer is bound to discharge his duties in a manner such that all are considered equal. In being fair to everyone, he must not fail the overall system or the judicial system—in the judicial system's purpose of being an effective pillar of a democratic state.

When lawyers work so as to defeat the legitimate processes in the courts in the interests of their clients, claiming that it their 'duty' to protect their clients. Truly, it is a sheepskin to cover the wolf's aim of making money at any cost. The loyalty is to money and not to the highest spirit. It is a conveniently interpreted sense of duty where making money is the priority and not a duty as ordained in dharma. It is a consumerist ideal in a reckless capitalist system and not in accordance with the ideal according to which the system was designed in the first place.

Duty is thus not fixed through a limited worldview of a client getting away using the debating skills of a pricy lawyer. Dharma encompasses everything. It is about

upholding law and order in society and must be seen from the highest perspective. A lawyer who does not thus work for the highest is indulging in adharma and must be recognized as such. Any other argument in favor of what he otherwise does is just that—an argument…

The divide is not a modern-ancient one. Do check up on why lawyers have a pocket stitched on the back of their coats/overalls near the shoulder. (We shall see that in detail presently.) Once this is understood, the true idealism of the modern system of justice that stretches its hands toward dharma reveals itself. The European civilization exerted itself in the early modern age through such idealism. It is definitely not subservient to a capitalist ideal. This ideal ensures that the judiciary rises above the considerations of the capitalist ideal. The best of our lawyers too are expected to target that.

Justice needs to have a public fervor: The system of law that is followed in the courts is often not comprehensible to the average citizen. Therefore, the feeling of justice does not have a popular base among the citizens. Indigenous tradition and culture do nurture that feeling, and it was ingrained through its governance, social and spiritual institutions. That has no parallel today. There is no effective judicial system in operation at the grassroots level, which can help the locals express and nurture their sense of justice. Popular culture is not sufficiently entertained in the courts, and there is no direct or indirect educative process that will help the average citizen understand and make sense of judicial processes. Some good films do make a difference though. And others further confuse the citizens.

A possible thrust for a solution: A sense of due and proper justice should be adequately supported and nurtured in the sphere of interaction between individuals at all levels. There must be enough knowledge and understanding of the law in the common citizen. Given a situation in a court and the outcome of the contest being known, he must instinctively know whether justice has been done or not. By developing this critical ability, the average citizen must also be able to recognize and appreciate individuals who are meritorious in delivering justice.

There is a need to stimulate this in the common citizen, and this can be achieved by setting up grassroots-level courts (we shall presently see how this can be done). The aim will be to draw from the strength possessed by communities, which, in turn, arises from the neighborhood bonds shared by a community's citizens. The system can be made operational by making the community itself run this court and allowing a judicial mechanism from the established court mechanism to periodically audit the processes that are happening there.

To summarize, the judicial system of the nation must have its edifice built equally on the law established by the constitution and on the 'sense of justice' of the people. The energy that drives the judiciary at the lowest level must emanate from the drive that one experiences while attempting to solve a problem in the neighborhood. And most of all, that sense of justice should be untouched by the presence or absence of wealth. Such a grassroots court has one more advantage. Given the geographical and cultural diversity of the nation, there is a need to look for a flexible system of justice adaptable to diverse local cultures. It must operate at the level of traditions and practices. This customization is possible to some extent in such courts.

Long-winding and cumbersome processes don't facilitate effective justice: Adding to the ills of the justice delivery system is the fact that superhuman efforts are demanded from laymen when they come out to help in the procedures related to law and order. The final picture is that the process in the judiciary and the related prosecution and police departments turn out to be lengthy, cumbersome, tedious and burdensome to most participants. This results in discouragement, and that slackens the effectiveness of the delivery of justice (a duty-conscious individual is unaffected though).

There is a basic difference between the people of the law and order mechanism and the average layman. Members of the mechanism are connected in such processes through their livelihood duties. However, the others are there because of citizenship duties. The question arises as to whether it is proper to consume the time and effort of the ones performing citizenship duties without proper compensation for their contribution and efforts.

On the contrary, the piling up of troubles on them is a great discouragement toward their performance of duties.

A possible thrust for a solution: This can be tackled in two ways. The first is that the citizens must be made aware that democracy and its efficient functioning comes at a cost, and it is important for citizens to bear that cost by taking up responsibilities in the related judicial functions so that they may continue to enjoy that democracy. As such, these activities must not be considered a burden. Rather, they must represent a call to duty which citizens must answer to the best of their abilities. The second is that the system itself should ensure that it does not load itself heavily on those citizens who are called out to help in the processes. The participants in the judicial process need to be properly compensated for their time and effort. If functionaries in the judiciary are operating at the level of dharma, then they will understand that lay persons too are operating in the same dharma at their respective roles in society. As such, their roles in society too must be duly respected. For example, a judge must honor and respect the fact that a soldier also has a dharma to perform and that the excellence of the soldier at soldiering must be duly respected. This is only a refined notion of the dignity of labor. There is inherent equality in dharma irrespective of where in society one is performing his duties, and one that holds authority in a court of law must acknowledge this. While being called to perform duties in courts of law, it does not make sense if the lawyers, judges and court officials get compensated while the average citizen who is pulled out from his dharmic duties and asked to perform duties in court does not. The average citizen must therefore be treated with due dignity and be adequately compensated for his participation in the judicial process. Such sensitivity on the part of judges will encourage the average citizen to participate more enthusiastically in judicial processes.

Should increase in lawlessness give more bread and butter to men of law? One more important parameter the reformers of the judicial system must consider is the need for effectively changing the success criterion in the courts. If, for instance, the quick completion of a case by a lawyer is rewarded with an ad-hoc payment and if the dragging of the same case ensures a permanent salary, then the lawyers will find a lot of reasons to explain why the particular case they are handling is taking a lot of time. This happens in other fields as well. For example, should a doctor be happy if people are healthy or if they are sick? A close look at the financial reward system will indicate how the existing system motivates a strong tendency to work along those lines which will give financial reward—meaning that lawyers and doctors prosper if there is crime and sickness, respectively. The present judicial system rewards its members in various ways for delays. With a huge bunch of people waiting outside the courts for justice and with little justice to get, the price for justice naturally goes up. Indeed, the demand for judges goes up, but they don't get any financial benefit out of it (unless taken under the table). The corruption opportunities for the personnel in the courts and the fee-demanding power of the lawyers go up substantially. Naturally, the system as a whole will tend to encourage or rather prosper in delaying justice. The basic arrangement that exists now is therefore flawed in its conception.

A possible thrust for a solution: In modern corporate literature, this issue is studied under risk management. For example, the purchase system of a company that wishes to maintain good quality and minimum pilferage will ensure that the person who places the order for a purchase, the one who pays the money and the one who receives the goods are three different people. This minimizes corruption. Similarly, the modern democratic systems use separation of powers. The person who catches and prosecutes the offender, the person who orders the quantum of punishment and the person who actually executes the punishment are three different people. If one person enjoys all these three powers, then there is a very high probability of miscarriage of justice.

In a similar manner, taking to risk management, the system must creatively come up with or encourage those solutions that will reward quick and efficient delivery of justice. Those working in the judicial system must find themselves rewarded financially or otherwise for successful completion of cases rather than for dragging them on for years. The system must induct new sets of lawyer-functionaries whose prosperity will depend on cases getting over quickly in the courts.

The existing system is basically reactive: Justice as delivered by the judicial system is reactive in the sense that it is supposed to reply to litigation. It has to sort out issues that are presented to it in the form of occurrences in society which need decisions on fixing blame and punishment. It is therefore a medicine in society. That is, a lawyer's profession contributes to the 'medication' or 'autopsy' aspect of an adverse event in society. As such, a lawman's income should be proportional to the amount of crime or conflict in society.

A possible thrust for a solution: Can more lawyers be hired to ensure that crime does not happen in society or that it is nipped in the bud? The nation must explore the possibility of developing judicial services that flourish even when there is no conflict in society so that it pre-empts flash points and solves problems by pre-reading the situation. This can also include tasks such as the following:

> One job is of training the people at the grassroots level on matters concerning justice and on the fundamentals of law. The training should be to the extent that even if these grassroots-level judges are illiterate, they should be able to operate effectively within set limits in their communities (we shall see more of this presently).

> Another job is to provide lawyers with authority that can enable them to facilitate and ink compromises without the contesting parties having to go through the rigors of the court (arbitration processes). Of course, the approval of a magistrate will be needed. Lawyers may be accorded recognition and financial reward for maximizing such compromises, even with existing filed cases.

> The lawyers can also have pro-active responsibilities toward ensuring law and order with respect to sustaining a judicial mechanism at the grassroots level. For example, they can be drafted into the processes that are required in order to have the activities of the grassroots courts audited by the higher judicial mechanism.

The question remains open though. Could there be lawyer-based services in society that will prosper when there is good in society and not when there are ills? Politics, perhaps…

THE IDEALISM OF THE EXISTING JUDICIARY

When a far-sighted statesman (wise man) sets up a system in due consideration of what inspires dharma, he comes up with ideals related to how the sub-systems need to work. Now, this statesman need not be an individual. It can be a group of people or an outcome of a process in evolution. But in order to meet the aims of that sub-system (here, we consider the judiciary), clear ideals are evolved so that proper and due justice is delivered to the people in general. Two such ideals need to be recalled and assessed in the present context of judicial system. Does following these ideals complete the system of true justice? Are these ideals being followed today? If the judiciary continues to function without accepting these ideals which complete the system, is it doing right?

Ideal judiciary – Two important traditions that gave completeness: When the judicial system was operational in the British monarchy in the middle of the last millennium, it had within it certain traditions which ensured that healthy justice was delivered in that nation. Aware that there would be poor people in society too, who would knock at the doors of the courts seeking justice, the judiciary incorporated within itself certain traditions that gave completeness to the arrangements. These have probably now disappeared. However, it is instructive to take a look at them to understand how the sense of justice in governance was contained in the principles. Such inspiration must get into the Indian system in some altered form so that true and universal justice can be delivered.

The tradition of isolation of judges: It was a tradition in the British system for incumbent judges to, as far as possible; isolate themselves from the government and public life. The judicial system was so designed that it would function at its best only when the judge took a call on the basis of the evidence presented to him at the court and without any prejudices. Therefore, judges were to avoid, as far as possible, all kinds of public interaction. If the Indian judiciary must deliver well, observance of this high idealism is required. This isolation is a required component of the system that we have adopted, and the pursuit of this ideal is required to deliver universal justice to all citizens.

Unfortunately, this is not followed in India. Judges access newspapers and other news sources. They mingle in society and sometimes, tragically, lawyers and judges live in the same home. (This is something Justice Venkatachallaiah tried to stem in his attempt at infusing values in the Supreme Court). All this compromises on the idealism. Further, with respect to court activism, judges seem to be calling for cases suo-motu. This takes the system away from the ideal in a significant way. This deviation from the ideal is a deviation from the completeness that is supposed to exist in today's overall system. What are the re-adjustments that need to be done in today's ideal judiciary to address this deviation? Justice Venkatachalliah's idea was not taken up. Maybe it should be; maybe even better ideas can emerge…

The pocket in the lawyer's back: In Britain's past, advocates had a small pocket sewn on their coats behind the right shoulder. Once the case was over, the advocates showed their backs to their clients, and the clients placed what they thought to be appropriate and what they could afford into that pocket. This mean that lawyers were not paid. They were patronized. Now, why this tradition?

The principle behind it is sound. It meant that every citizen had the right to use that advocate's talents for his defense, irrespective of the citizen's monetary status. And he could pay what he thought was fit in his case and what he could afford. If this were the practice today, then one could expect a reasonably level playing field in court. If lawyers can live to that idealism, then the overall system can deliver effectively. In the absence of such idealism on the part of the lawyer fraternity, alternate measures are necessary to ensure that the poor get proper justice.

Action needed to compensate for the loss of idealism: It calls for legislators, with the help of the judiciary, to get back to the drawing board and come up with robust, all-encompassing plans to ensure that correct, affordable and quick justice is delivered. There is a need for a new ideal that will define the dharma of the judge, lawyer, citizen and judiciary as a whole.

GIVING POWER BACK TO THE PEOPLE THROUGH THE RE-INTRODUCTION OF GRASSROOTS-LEVEL COURTS IN A MODERN SETUP

The present judicial system has evolved over the centuries ever since it was introduced by the British during colonial rule. Being a modern system based on what was functional in the advanced democracies and accepted with suitable modifications made at the time of Indian independence through the constitution; this system has come to stay. As far as the courts at the national, state and district levels are concerned, we have considered what changes may be required. However, at the grassroots level, a complete rethink and overhaul is required—probably inevitable.

There is no novelty in the idea here. One must know that in the present British system, which was originally used as an inspiration for our system, the actual trained judges form only 5% of the total judge population. The rest, approximately 95%, are magistrates who are not officially trained in law.

Comparing that to the traditional Indian system, these magistrates are equivalent to the panches of the Indian nyay panchayats (grassroots courts) of centuries gone by. Imagine if such a system of lay lawmen/magistrates/panches were to be instituted in India. Then, the number of judges would go up twenty times the present number. The smaller cases would then be disposed of at the level of neighborhoods itself. This would bring great relief to the judicial process—revolutionize it, for sure.

All that is to be done is to conceive of this alternative with well-defined rules based on successful precedents and adapt it for the present times. These grassroots courts must be so structured that they are auditable from above and yet are customizable and representative of a vibrant local community.

The grassroots-level structure needs to be defined at two levels, one at the community level within villages and another at the inter-village level (amidst a group of 10 to 50 villages). The judicial arrangements at these two levels will have similar thrusts, in that the aim in both cases will be to deliver justice at a cost which is reasonable to the economic status of the lowest of the low in rural India. And both the levels will aid each other in catering to that

aim. Let us hope that with the institution of such a system, the average Indian will gain better control over his destiny, get low-cost justice and develop a proper sense of justice and fairness in his bearing. We will make an attempt to visualize the main contours of such courts.

Village courts: Following are the required characteristics for the village courts.

1) The rigors of the higher courts must not be applied here. It must be more rigorous on justice rather than on law. It must display the flexibility to use wisdom while maintaining the sanctity of laws.

2) It must be an expression of the popular sense of justice, a sense that exists within individuals and manifests in factors like the bonds of community living, components and expressions of local culture and beliefs of general prosperity.

3) These courts must be subject to scrutiny from authorities at district and higher levels for compliance with constitutional standards.

4) Such courts must form a popular public forum so that the feeling of justice shared by the people at the community level has ample scope to thrive through debate and free expression.

5) It must be defined in such a way that it suits both the formality of the national judicial system and the informality of community living.

6) The persons elected to hold positions of responsibility must have authorization from the government (judicial mechanism) to hold their offices, apart from having the confidence of the villages (as being people suited for delivering justice).

7) The state (judicial administrative wing) must ensure that the hopeful-to-office are aware of the very basic necessities of constitutional awareness and issue a certificate of eligibility to that effect (training and certification).

8) This must be included as a qualification required for the village to attain the status of a free village / village republic / panchayati swaraj. (For example, at least five trained people should be present in the village as far as the judiciary is concerned.)

9) In the light of requirement of compliance with the constitution, routine reports from each village needs to be sent to a central focus which is at a higher level

(block or taluka). These reports must have sufficient depth and also brevity to keep the happenings open for scrutiny as required and to make the system open for public comment. Proper records of the same are to be maintained.

The next higher level: At the inter-village level, the following must be ensured.

1) The court must be a troubleshooting ad-hoc mechanism.
2) The court must consist of one legal expert as a member of the team.
3) The team itself must consist of noted panchayat justices from the local area and be headed by a panchayat justice who is held in high esteem by the people in the field of doing justice.
4) Such a team should be initiated at a suitable level as and when the need arises.
5) The modalities of how the team is to be made up may be worked out by keeping the following in mind:
    a) It must express an area's sense of justice.
    b) It must strengthen the judicial system both at the lower and higher levels.
    c) It must increase peoples' confidence in the judicial system.
    d) It must create an environment where men of justice will be honored.
    e) It must be participatory, accessible and open to all.
6) The role of the government official (judicial administration) will be that of a legal expert who will contribute equally to the process as the others and carry one vote as a judge—the same as the other, even uneducated, justices on a panel. He should not act in the capacity of a supervisor or overseer. He will be responsible for making reports of the happenings in proper format as records for further use at the taluka and district offices and courts of appeal.
7) Such a court will deal with inter-village disputes and disputes that come in the form of an appeal from the village-level judicial mechanism.

Protecting the authority of panchayat courts:

1) The limits to which the local courts can go must be well-defined. That is, the type of cases they can look into and the limits of the punishment they can dish out must be well-defined (the experience of Britain to be explored).
2) The balance of power must be worked out in a manner such that the village courts do carry weight (importance) by virtue of the inalienable rights and authority vested in them. In balance, the higher courts must also be able to prevent any miscarriage of justice by exerting their authority over the local courts which they routinely audit and through the transfer of cases to themselves if needed.
3) Decisions made by lower courts through due process will carry certain sanctity in law that is well-defined.
4) There should be inbuilt defenses to ensure that appellants will find it difficult to take the system for a ride.
5) Similarly, the courts at the district and higher levels must have powers to call cases from these courts for review. And such a process can, in line with the traditions of the judiciary, be triggered by appeals and other means. But this process of taking cases upwards should be well-defined so that the decisions and value of the lower courts are not undermined.
6) Ultimately, the old golden rule still remains. 'It is preferable to solve problems mutually rather than go to third parties.' This should be the first attempt to solve local problems. The local judicial authorities should be authorized to certify and apply the seal of approval to agreements and settlements made outside of courts.

The possibilities of such a system are stupendous. If something can be done about the 300-years-worth of cases, this is probably it. At the community level, people know the facts. Chances are that much of the litigation at the higher levels can be avoided by solving them credibly at the community level itself.

Finally, in consonance with the initiation of grassroots-level processes and owing to the fact that a whole lot of judges (panches/magistrates) will come into play and that a popular sense of justice will gradually develop, the jury system can become a definite possibility in India.

Section V

The Peoples' Police Force: Conspicuous Arm of a Dharmic Executive

In a list of ironies about India, one specific one is this: when we go near a policeman in India, we feel nervous rather than reassured. Is something wrong?

In a self-rule, the relationship between the government authority and the citizen is not defined as ruler-ruled but rather as governor-governed. Further, elitism and heroism in a self-rule is not decided on the basis of material wealth, scholarship or temporal status but on the basis of yogic abilities and wisdom. Therefore, when a nation shifts from being an imposition to a self-rule, the shift of attitude will be perceptible. Conversely, when individuals or communities revel in a positive attitude and in being yogic and cherish wisdom, they become deserving of self-rule.

This transition from rule to self-rule will be most visible in the police force compared to other branches of the government machinery. The police force, like any other executive, must operate within the framework of the laws. Laws are bound to evolve in a democracy, but the change that is spoken about here is not about the change in laws. The change spoken about has to do with the spirit. This is about the character, attitude and personality of the ruler.

To make it simple, let us imagine that a person has committed a crime against the state, and the police are bound by law to arrest that person. Will they behave the same way if they were sent by Stalin/Hitler as they would if they were sent by Mahatma Gandhi? There will be a world of difference, and that is vital in deciding if a particular government sustains a self-rule. The police force will reflect the character of the ruler.

A colonial character is today's norm: It is true that in 1947, the police force was transferred to a new leadership.

Indeed, this new leadership consisted of Indians who were the torch-bearers of the freedom struggle. It seems apparent that the police would have undergone a transformation. However, this is not true. The essential character of the colonial enforcement has been retained in a substantial way.

That the police was now following the orders of a new leadership was apparently not enough to radically change the approach of policing. The police regiments and formations had to rewrite their operation codes and formation charters. They had to change their training contents and patterns to reflect a new manner of policing. However, all this was not done. They were not reborn when they transited into operating in a free country. Even new formations were patterned on old ones. The old colors resurface even today when a ruthless leadership sends the forces out to 'suppress' the enemies of the state.

We have seen elsewhere that no one in history need be blamed for not affecting this change. The challenges of the late 40s and early 50s of the last century did not allow for effective transition. Perhaps the nation was not ready then either. But if freedom is to be realized, then that shift must happen at some time or the other. We can expect the nation to have the required stability to transit to that freedom seventy years after independence.

So, what is that shift supposed to be?

In colonial India, freedom of the natives was not the primary purpose for the system. Rather, the natives were the object of concern against whom the forces functioned as a defense mechanism. The authority which the police possessed and the actions that sprung out of the powers invested in it bore the seal of approval of colonist culture.

The police force was the enforcing arm of the rulers. Being a tool molded into shape by the rulers, in accordance with their motives (which were both good and notorious in parts), it developed a characteristic orientation, an appropriate attitude and a set of methods/procedures unique to its foreign nature. 'Law and order' was, of course, the reason for its existence, but law and order was based on the following characteristics of that colonial rule:

➤ It was suspicious. Naturally, since virtually anyone could be an enemy of the state.

➤ It was suppressive because the nation was held together basically by force, not benevolence.

➤ It had a tinge of isolation, since the masters did not actually identify themselves with the masses and, as such, were 'rulers' and not 'governors'.

➤ It was elitist too. Since racial feelings were behind the setup, since the 'government' came from the elite and since elitism was believed necessary for the submission of the Indian nation, it was so.

All this got written into the rules of conduct of the police formations. Any benevolent consideration toward the people was secondary to this. Instead, the raj was keen on a 'law and order' mechanism that would preserve its exclusivist agenda and remove all traces of threat to its existence from the conquered population. At its best, the executives of the system could give a humanizing touch to its otherwise fundamentally repressive and careless nature.

As such, did the police force take up the usual law and order duties like arresting thieves, intervening in a bashup and managing conflicts over land? Yes, it did all of this. Did its members attempt to help society function in a way that reflected the best of British methodology? Surely, there were outstanding exponents who were 'British' in their approach in order to reflect high culture. But over and above this, it still remained a colonial force driven by the motive to survive in an alien land.

Contrast such a force with a group of people who have of late discovered that someone among them is stealing stuff from others. So, they appoint two people to give up all their other jobs and pay attention only to investigate as to who that thief is.

In such a situation, one will understand that the policemen who are thus appointed will not deal with people as if they have been implanted from the outside. They will not come swinging a stick and knock people around to fish out as to who the thief is. In fact, these people will consider themselves part of the group like how the members of the group will consider the two to be part of them. They will be respectful to all others and also to the person who they think is the thief.

Is that not why policemen in the United States are supposed to read out the rights of the people they arrest when they arrest them? You have the right to remain silent. Anything you say can be used against you in a court of law. You have the right to an attorney.'

An external implant is distinctly different from a one-among-us. It is the attitude that is important. An external agent can, in fact, come and behave like a one-among-us. In contrast, in today's India, the village *patil* who gets appointed as a police representative of the village and who is one among the members of the village is expected to adopt the attitude of an 'external implant'. This speaks volumes of what the true nature of the regime is.

One telling characteristic of an imposition is in its propensity to use fear to intimidate. The authorities will believe in terrorizing the people who are doing wrong so that they will be intimidated into doing right.

Another important characteristic of such a rule is that it will be personality-centric and not system-centric. Egos will be involved. Individuals will try to benefit. And the complexion of the force will vary with the characteristic of the ruler.

The dharma perspective on policing: The paradigm shift that is necessary can be best construed on the basis of the eternal principle of dharma that is endemic to India. Dharma offers scope for both the sensibility for tackling issues with sensitivity and concern and the physical and moral force/power that is required to tackle errors with incredible strength and righteousness.

According to Adi Shankaracharya, dharma is the most beneficial of beneficial things. You want to do good? Then, abide by what is dharmic. Or in other words, uphold dharma.

It is a citizens' system: In a mechanism that runs on an ethos of swaraj. The people are the owners of the system; it is their system. The system should emanate from the people themselves, and as such, it should be a projection of them. Each individual must have a sense of identification with the work that the police do. Then, society will be awakened to the need of law and order and be made up of individuals who are, in a way, policemen themselves. That is, the citizens should know the significance of the existence of a sound law and order mechanism. In the spiritual plane, it can be said that the Universal Spirit in each individual will compel each one from within that there must be order in society. It will therefore prod them to be part of a holistic process that brings peace through such an executive force.

In such a setting, citizens will, by themselves, attempt to tackle the problems that arise around them with:

> ➢ The scope of informality accorded to them in small communities
> ➢ The powers bestowed upon them by the constitution through citizenship
> ➢ The help of some of their own people who are given formal duties—the police

Thus, based on the ideas of fair play, justice and rule of law (which are themselves components of a sense of dharma present in every individual), this formal structure of the police force needs to take shape. Therefore, the policeman will be one among them and not a component of the suppressive arm of the regime.

When the police take to dharma: The concept of dharma inspires policemen with great principles to live by. It calls for a sense of duty without expectation. It calls for an anger-less and worriless approach to problem-solving. It evokes the divine strength that is available in the togetherness of man. It revels in righteousness. It gives great contentment and satisfaction. The pursuit of dharma also brings out excellence in performance. If executed in the right spirit, it promises the highest that spirituality has to offer, the benefit of nirvana itself.

Needless to say, the outstanding people in the executive branches of the government, inclusive of the police, have been those who have stood by their dharma, regardless.

This must become the formal code of inspiration for men in office—the Indian way. When people stand up for dharma, it is difficult to run a system that can affect evil. Dharma is at home with an ethos of self-government or self-rule.

What can be worse for a free nation than using individual fear or mortal terror to keep together and run a system instead of using the sense of dharma? The police must function with the spirit and strength of friendship instead of the terror of brute force. (One should hear them say to the lawbreakers, 'I'm sorry! That's the way the law is!') The prime concerns should be to deliver 'natural justice' or 'consequences of wrong action' instead of enforcing the 'revenge' of society. The motive should be the 'preservation of self-rule' and not 'implementing a ruthless system'.

In dharma, there is a general movement away from individual responsibility and toward collective effort in the police force. It is not only the officer who has in him the will, dharma (so to say), impulse and sensitivity to establish a responsive system for law and order. This is an elitist attitude and a colonial one. Every individual of the force, owing to his sense of dharma, should be an equal in the system by virtue of his desire that there should be law and order in society. Even the smallest official is capable, in spirit, of representing the police force in the totality of its responsibility. In fact, even an average citizen is capable of thus representing the police force in its responsibility. Only, his sphere of activity will be defined by the authority and responsibility invested in the position he holds, whether it is as a low-level, 'non-officer' cadre of the force or just an average citizen.

Even a common citizen must see himself as an actor in policing. The police force should hence act as a team inclusive of the citizen. Crime should find the system, inclusive of citizens, coming down on it. It should not be confronted merely by certain individuals from the police force as if it is in the interests of the officers alone (that's colonial in its attitude).

Community participation in policing; guarded from the inside and monitored from the outside: At the level of communities, a major responsibility of the members is to understand the need for staying within the confines of the law on their own. The need for external interference is an index of the inability of communities to sort out problems by themselves. As such, the localities will become (and be) responsible for the maintenance of internal law and order. And they will check the anti-social behavior of their inhabitants in outside places as well. This will be a kind of collective responsibility of the locality itself. And this power to 'enforce' within the communities will be supported, among other factors, by the response of the police force to the needs/requests of such localities.

As for the police force, its basic duty will lie in monitoring as to what is happening in the area under its care. All groups composed of people have their ups and downs. In any zone of activity, aberrations are only human. There is bound to be some conflict or the other. As a result, a major responsibility of the police force will lie in estimating the content and depth of trouble that is brewing and then take appropriate action. That is, a major part of its responsibilities will be pro-active and not reactive. It will spot potential trouble spots and bring it to the notice of formal or informal organizations/institutions which can solve the problems. The thrust, rather than being on solving cases that comes to its door, must be on seeing that nothing is going wrong. And that will also include the task of inculcating in the citizens, among other things, a sense of responsibility toward law and order in the domain of their authority.

A self-policing panchayat: The aim of the training is to sensitize the general population to its responsibilities connected with policing. Besides, in order to inculcate the relevant attitudes, there is a necessity for changes in the organizational structure and in the thrust at the peripheral levels of the police force. How will these appear? Let us try to capture the spirit by sketching broad outlines.

In tune with panchayati swaraj, the village will be in contact with the police station of the concerned area through a team of village dwellers. This team will act as a channel of contact between the police force and the locality. They will have a certain set of goals laid down before them and certain responsibilities to shoulder. They will facilitate communication and ensure that adequate interaction is maintained between the community and the police force. This channel of communication will be several things at once—a routine feedback mechanism, a channel for sensitizing, confidence-building, a channel for socializing and a channel for information dissemination. Selection for being part of this team must be on the basis of election by the villagers using whatever method they have adopted for themselves. A pool of individuals who have a certificate of merit issued by the government on the basis of their individual competence and relevant learning will be eligible for the election.

Naturally, the basic principles of self-rule will be reflected here. That is, the villagers will be given a fair degree of autonomy in that they must be allowed to tackle their own law and order problems. The police system will be called upon to restrict itself to overseeing and aiding the village in the villagers' own pursuit of enhancing harmony.

An image of this new alternative situation can be conjectured as follows: Under the confines of the Indian constitution, the villages will be a law unto themselves, and the police will only act according to the modalities worked out in the grassroots-centered system. That is, the police force will interfere with 'force' in such a community only when the regulating forces within the village are at a loss to control a situation or when a crime has occurred in that village which is more severe than that which the village team is authorized to handle. Even here, the procedure followed by the force in the process will be in accordance with what is laid down earlier in well-defined terms as a 'village emergency.'

The police force will, however, be very active in the inter-village level and above. Apart from tackling lawbreakers who have a wider reach than a village, it should also tackle inter-village problems. Therefore, the police stations will be nerve centers for processing data coming from villages and information coming from higher levels.

Citizens' policing must also happen in cities: In the cities, the flexibility of city life will induce its own characteristics on the police force. The fluidity of city life, which is important in terms of a modern economy, will imply the requirement of a different approach. The mohalla communities and their committees (as brought out in the next paragraph) should get better definition and have their responsibilities well marked out. A well-planned, centrally-coordinated system (at police stations) must be in place. Having divided areas under each police station into relevant zones, appropriate routines and proactive and reactive mechanisms must be set into action. In any case, the cities can look for solutions that are available in 'modern' cities the world over. But objectivity is required, and there should be no fear of wanting to innovate.

Novel efforts must get the system's patronage: Incidentally, individuals and teams of the present police force do come out time and again with constructive solutions that belong to this class. However, the problem is that the nation does not have a broad-based system to back up such efforts and standardize it into a norm. Such efforts need to get a feeling that they are flowing with the tide rather than against it. (For example, check out Mr. Suresh Khopade's police reforms with respect to the mohalla committees in Bhiwandi, Maharashtra. Though of course, this needs some correction in terms of the colonial approach of the benevolent policeman.)

Section VI

Organize the Social Service Sector to Bring Completeness in Governance

The modern approach to work has some features that do not easily harmonize with the fundamentals of Indian civilization. One of these is the division of a person's life into phases of work and leisure. We have seen that in dharma, work is done without expectation of results and benefits. Therefore, in dharma, work in itself has fullness leading to complete satisfaction. So, both work and leisure activities are complete within themselves independently. One is not meant to compensate for or complete the other. However, in total contrast to this, modern life is designed a lot around struggling with 'work' and earning money so as to spend in 'leisure'.

Another one of these concepts of modern-day work that does not harmonize with the dharmic perspective is the concept of social work. Social work is construed as welfare-related work that is taken up without the rigor of making profits and with an intention of service. It is mostly sustained through donations. Again, in this too, work at one's job may be seen as the bitter pill to be swallowed in order to get a salary and command resources. Work in a social service setup may be seen as something giving inner satisfaction. In the dharma perspective, both normal and social work must be independently complete and fulfilling in themselves.

This experience, related to work and service, within each individual has two important aspects to it. The first is related to attitude. When an individual goes about his role without attachment to the result of his action, he experiences wholeness in all he does. People who work with attachment to results carry their own misery. The second is related to how one's work connects to the completeness of the entire system. If one sees that his work and the organization that he stands for is not contributing positively to humanity as a whole and if the wise of his age express dissatisfaction with the total arrangements within that system, then an individual also experiences incompleteness in the work he does.

As dealt in Part 1 of this book, dharma can be perceived as complete only when the overall system is designed by the wise, which would mean that all individuals in society are catered for and there is fairness in dealing with all members of society. So then, is a capitalist system truly complete as expected in a dharmic arrangement? No, not just by itself. Therefore, individuals in a pure capitalist order, whether they believe in pursuing dharma or not and whether they are self-seeking or selfless, will feel a sense of hollowness when they work at their responsibilities in a capitalistic society; even if they did it diligently. Those who have learned to be selfless will seek ways by which those that are left out will be somehow taken care of. As for those who are self-seeking, even unaware to themselves, they will find an emptiness which will trouble them from within. In a democratic-capitalistic system therefore, social work emerges as a solution that brings in wholeness.

Social work completes dharmic arrangements: Social work has an important role to play in the context of a democratic system like the present one that uses capitalism for handling its economy and where government action is inadequate in its efforts at tackling poverty. Social work is necessary to complete the dharmic arrangement when the primary system is built out of capitalism and democracy. Let us see how this can be brought about in the present scheme of things in India so that the overall system can be harmonized to be closer to a dharmic arrangement.

The aim is to enable the overall system to deliver with great empathy to all citizens.

In fact, social work has an important role in raising values and the level of consciousness in a democratic nation. Social workers have an important role to play in keeping the sanity of society. Let us explore this further.

Social service results from doing justice to an inner drive: Let us revert to looking at the issue from an individual's perspective. Man is a social/spiritual being. Somewhere deep down, every individual we see around us has a wish in him that he should be of use to those around him, at least in some small way. He finds peace, fulfillment and moments of great joy in little acts of giving. This kind of giving needs no motivation through name, fame or fortune. Such work is seen as beyond the scope of one's duties and has something to do with one's soul, perception of work, level of commitment in life and the manner of usefully spending time.

Typically, in a dharmic arrangement, one experiences this satisfaction when he performs his designated duties itself. But as we have seen, a dharmic arrangement needs to be all-embracing (with the loop/circle closed; Part 3, Section II, Chapter 2.1 That Special Group; Part 3, Section III A different way). If this is not true about society, then one does not find fulfillment in the normal work that one does. He knows that the arrangements do not suffice in society to cater for all. And as a result, he finds that a new additional category of work called 'service' is needed fill in the gaps.

Therefore, in the current system, people tend to distinguish between work done for livelihood and work done as service. They find immense satisfaction in doing some 'other' work in addition to their 'jobs' for the sake of 'service'. And we have just seen how this is connected to 'completeness' in a dharmic arrangement.

Now, each individual experiences, understands and expresses/acts on it, in his own way. In his mind, he is conscious of a certain level of commitment toward the service which he thinks is the most suitable or practical to his conditions. He observes the needs around him and plays his part according to the scope available to him and the abilities and resources at his disposal. Eventually, what he comes up with is unique to him, and it satisfies an internal thirst and gives him solace and spiritual comfort.

Organizing social work is a challenge, but it has great rewards: Since motivation levels and commitment levels to do social work varies from person to person. In a sample of social workers or, for that matter, in a sample of citizens, one can see a complete spectrum of possible approaches. In one end of that spectrum, there are those who live and breathe the motto of becoming useful, and on the other, there are those who do some small good when they incidentally get a chance or when it is urgently needed.

At the level of society, this adds up to a massive total, and it implies that there is tremendous potential for welfare activity. The problem on the ground is that all such work done is done in patches, and there is unwanted overlap. Often, the efforts are misdirected, and many times, there are people willing to do something good but cannot find a way to help out. Also, everyone knows that it makes no sense when people work at cross purposes, especially when they may be selfless in their respective beliefs/approaches. For example, someone who works for bonhomie within a village community finds that people focused on the uplift of a certain sub-community are forcing the expression of a divisive identity, which counteracts efforts at integration. These well-meant initiatives leading to unnecessary conflicts need to be dovetailed so that they do not act at cross purposes.

If all that effort can be channelized through a broad-based plan and if there is even minimal focus, the overall results produced can be significant. Indeed, such an attempt at organization will make ample sense to an individual when he sees that the results produced are better with merely better coordination and even without raising the intensity of his efforts.

Therefore, with an aim to tap into the social work potential available, there is a need for working toward coordination. This work of coordination will be social work too, and it must be directed toward the specific task of streamlining and focusing individual contributions into collective effort—all for the sake of mutual help, shared happiness and optimized output.

What we are reckoning is social work that aids social workers to do coordinated social work. And the social workers who do social work aimed at assisting social workers to do coordinated social work must get together and form an organization. Such an organization consisting of coordination social workers is what we will try to conceptualize.

How that organization will shape up: In such an organization consisting of coordination social workers, one can neither use principles of hierarchy used in military organizations nor Maslow's need-sequence type of motivation. A Social Service Coordination organization needs to have a structure that is based on ideals, methods, motivation profile and command structure suitable to the temperament of social work.

And whatever it is, it should be as if the workers seem to say, 'Let's get together, and work on an agreeable strategy for welfare. Let's maximize harmony and join hands at every opportunity. This will ensure that our efforts will give a better output.'

One must realize that such an organization must achieve two important goals in society.

➤ Looking at the way this organization functions, the other organizations in society, though meant for business, must learn to imbibe a dharmic perspective in their functioning. Thus, profit-based organizations and their workers must be inspired to function more with the aim of enhancing the welfare of society though they are in the business of making profits.

➤ The second is the purpose which Gandhiji sought to instill in the nation. It is known that Gandhiji wanted for the nation examples of selfless workers who would provide leadership through their service-oriented actions. This institution, which coordinates the work of social workers, must serve to highlight leaders who stand for service above the 'self'.

To push the system toward dharmic wholeness, social service must cater to some basic grassroots-level goals: A few important goals can be highlighted as follows:

1) *No one goes hungry:* There is a need to ensure that, in any given geographical region of reckoning, no one is scheduled to go hungry at the next meal by default.

A provision for midday meals through any institution in the concerned area should be in place as a final measure or a last resort for someone who has no alternatives. This could be a religious option (like the Sikhs have), a secular, government-based one (as in the scheme for midday meals in education) or like the Amma Canteens in Tamil Nadu and its equivalents now being replicated up in other states.

2) *A small job to earn:* To meet minimum needs, small responsibilities must be reserved for the needy so that they can still labor for what they get till such a time when a sound means of livelihood and placement in society is found for them. This will be, in some reincarnated form, the spirit of khadi.

3) *Beggar rehabilitation:* Beggary must be minimized as close as possible to zero. Instead, there must be that centrally-organized focus in every community which persons can approach with hopes of rehabilitation. Obviously, at these points, there should be a concentration of beneficial and constructive efforts too so that people, who come for survival, leave the institution with purpose and strength to give something back to society. There must exist a special and continuous effort to prevent the concentration of exploitation and indignity meted out at such places the way it generally happens now—places where they may lose even what is left with them. Those availing such a facility themselves are a workforce, and with their added help, there is a possibility of more than mere self-sustenance in such an institution.

4) *Proper targeting of donations:* There is also a requirement for assisting those who wish to make donations so that finances reach the right spots. Instead of being a channel for money, the coordinating forces of this structure should act as a contact-maker or contact-facilitator so that the beneficiaries receive aid directly from the donors.

5) *Research for development of a specific target area:* Another major responsibility will be in the collecting and processing of information (technological, consumer-based, social etc.) that is available in all forms of media and forums worldwide which will come of use to the target population. Here, reference

is being made to information of the kind that will be an aid in the practical day-to-day lives of the people in the target area, be it methods of farming, environment preservation, better fuels, better communication means, better economy for work, markets, etc.

6) *Help in citizens' interactions with the state:* There is also a need for organized effort in connection with the common man's interactions with the state mechanism.

   a) Offering suggestions to government authorities

   b) Helping the government in locating people for sponsored social service agencies

   c) Helping the government in locating areas for help

   d) Ensuring that relevant information about the government schemes are available to the people

   e) Helping the illiterate and the deprived receive their dues from the system

   f) Helping out in ombudsmen

   g) Giving feedback on government mechanisms

7) *Active dissemination of development information/data:* There is a need for undertaking responsibilities of *prachar* or, in other words, communicating ideas to the public in general. These, of course, come under the purview of informal education, but a specialized structure is necessary to take up the initiative. There is a need for a well-established network (enlightened and self-discriminatory at all levels) which will ensure that every last man is within reach of the messages meant for him.

8) *Life-stimulating activity:* There is a need to direct adequate resources of all kinds toward stimulating freshness and zest into the human spirit in that area. Be it through sports, arts, culture or sheer civil, selfless action, it should sustain an enthusiastic people. It should, in that spirit, actively contribute to all pro-active and reactive collective initiatives required in that area.

9) *Facilitating the six freedoms:* There is a need to facilitate the six freedoms of panchayati swaraj in the various villages, especially in those that do not have the ability to kick-start the process. The final aim of the effort is to ensure that the villages become masters of their own prosperity. For this, support must also be sought from village success stories of adjacent or even faraway areas.

10) *Research to improve the efficiency of social work effort in a given area:* And finally, there is the task of facilitating economy of effort in social work. This consists of first, identifying places in need of work in a particular locality. Second, identifying, tapping into and enhancing the social work potential of that area. And third, helping out the various independent grassroots-level institutions with the knowledge of where effort is needed, how much it might cost, how best things can be done and where one can get resources. Even such a coordinating work should be done as a social service and be offered as suggestions which the workers on the ground may or may not accept.

With these broad aims, one must look for a possible organized structure among the social workers.

INTER-PERSONNEL RELATIONSHIPS IN SOCIAL WORKERS' ORGANIZATIONS NEED SERVICE SPIRIT

No rigid command structure and yet cooperative: An organization comprising of social workers does not need the gravity of a rigid command structure as is otherwise required in a military organization. As it is dharmic for military personnel to stick to their duties in the light of the purpose of collective effort, it is also dharmic for social workers to work to a plan that synchronizes the efforts of a lot of other people since it is in the better interests of overall wellness. The basis of this lies in the belief that social work, in all goodness, is effective, fruitful and fulfilling if and only if the contribution is part of a broader, all-embracing outlook which hopes to solve all problems in totality. In any case, for social servants, this acceptance of coordinating guidelines must be voluntary.

Teaming-up and mutual respect: For a group of people, individual efforts at best add up to each other and cancel each other out many times. But when they are a team, the efforts produce results amounting to much more than the sum of individual efforts. That is how nature is. It will hence be better, any time, to work as a fruitful team and contribute in a team effort. This will require trust in each other, in seniors and the wise.

Loose federation – Enlightened anarchy: Now, while an organization structure is required, it can still represent a loose federation which manages to retain its focus. In fact, this is an excellent opportunity to use Gandhiji's idea of an enlightened anarchy.

There is no duty: Each individual, content and whole in himself, must accept to do a little bit of work because he himself wishes it were that way and experience within himself a sense of purpose in the collective effort. He has no qualms about taking ideas from a coordinating authority. He is independent and free because he is doing what he wants (note that there is no question of him doing any duty here), and he is free even while taking instructions from the coordinating authority because that is what he himself wills. That is what his soul wants—the will of Vasudeva, the will of The Father. In fact, structure or no structure, one should still be able to do well without hassles and strive, at all times, toward a constructive togetherness. Therefore, the attempt here should be to minimize any concrete organizational structure while at the same time make it easy for coordination.

Adequate defense against vested interests: Finally, the coordination system must have a good defense mechanism within it so that it is not overrun by zealots, political forces, crime or skeptics. This caution owes its existence to the knowledge that it is part of human nature to be prone to errors and that evil will always exist in the hustle and bustle of daily life. In this connection, it can be emphasized that it is necessary to have a well-defined but loosely-knit organizational structure anchored more in the spirit than in the material possessions of the organization.

A coordinating agency promoting a 'flat' structure: To an individual, the coordinating agency will come through as described below:

➢ Valuable since team effort gives better results (coordination/planning)

➢ Unique command structure as applicable to social workers

➢ There will be no 'orders'; coordinators will only 'help' those on the field in the effectiveness of their functioning, and 'the biggest of them will be the greatest servant of them all'

➢ Looking up to those that are distinguished in service

➢ Each one in the team being a willing spoke for the wheel of change

➢ Feeling complete in oneself; doing what one knows best and yet part of an inter-regional combined effort by doing one's bit

Practical constitution of social workers' councils: Councils of social workers must be formed at the district and the taluka levels. The councils will have members who are elected to represent the social workers of the next lower administrative units.

People working at the village level will elect members from among them into the taluka councils, and from those elected into the taluka councils, some will be elected to the district councils. That should give a membership of around 40-50 at the taluka level and about 100 at the district level.

A small body of coordinators will be elected within each such council, and they will have the basic function of coordination and of convening meetings. A small executive/clerical branch, of at the most three individuals, will be employed for tasks like correspondence, bookkeeping and other secretarial work for each council. They will work under the directions of the coordinators.

Minimal secretarial infrastructure: It is very important that the secretariat/executive be very small and that the bank balance be enough to attend to stationery, the salaries of one or two (or three) workers, the other daily costs of running an office and minor travel expenses. Funds will bypass the councils. Money will be short-circuited from the source to the destination by bypassing the coordination center. There will be focus on information accumulation and not resource gathering. Minimizing this centralization has its payoffs in that the union can be a loose federation, more voluntary and relatively corruption-proof.

Fine structure of councils – customized and flexible: The fine structure of the councils must be decided by the members of the council itself, and it should preferably be a structure that, in their opinion, will most effectively handle the tasks in the concerned region. The ground realities will also decide on the duration of the term of the office bearers (two to three years, in rotation). A pre-determined fraction of members should be replaced each year as they complete their tenures. Most tasks, other than routine maintenance work for the organization as mentioned above, must be taken up on a task force basis.

Setting up task forces using volunteers: The councils will maintain records of social workers in their particular domain and of all volunteers who have offered to help if there is a need. Task forces will be based on such voluntary workers teamed up to address particular issues as and when the need arises. The coordinators/council members must shoulder the responsibility of constituting task forces and suggest representatives for task forces initiated at higher levels.

Maximizing output through planned teamwork and cooperation: These councils must meet from time to time as required and monitor the team aspects of the social work going on in the concerned area. They must aim at bringing out the best from the joint effort and celebrate the value system that compels them to work together. In that togetherness, they must attempt to cater to all the tasks that are usually in the domain of social workers in that particular geographical area.

They must have awareness of the importance of having inter-regional cooperation. They must feel compelled to 'work' toward that goal if the processes at the grassroots level have to be strengthened. Hence, through these units of togetherness, they must also contribute to processes taking place at higher levels such that the efforts at the grassroots and higher levels will complement and mutually support each other.

Setting benchmarks for society by proper profiling of candidates for the councils: As far as possible, only full-time social workers must be elected into the councils. Within each council, the chief coordinator/convener must be elected on the basis of all-can-vote-anyone-from-the-group type of secret ballot. A similar method may be again adopted for completing the coordinating body.

In fact, the election process in the councils must be, in many ways, an actual demonstration of the spirit of a good selection procedure that may come of use in elections (as applicable in the political process). The person must be selected on the basis of his excellence in service. Once he is selected, he must execute these duties in the spirit of doing his dharma—in the interest of collective efforts in social work.

While electing: An ideal coordinator should have the best of the following traits.

1) He may or may not have religious convictions, but he must give due respect to others' individuality, even if they belong to other affiliations, on the basis of the work they do.

2) He must preferably be a person who can be totally dedicated to social work (monks, priests, retired personnel, etc.) or someone who does not have any other pressing commitments.

3) He must have the basic abilities for coordination and leadership.

4) He must possess skill for administrative work or, at least, the inclination to learn it quickly.

5) He must possess the best of values found in a Gandhian satyagrahi. That is, he must have

   a) Belief in an open-minded pursuit of truth

   b) Awareness of the shortcomings and ignorance in men and the ability to remain un-prejudiced and non-judging under such circumstances while earnestly attempting to stimulate reform

   c) Preference for non-violent, non-militant methods as against non-violent, militant ones

   d) Belief that in the absence of the availability/possibility of non-violent, non-militant methods, non-violent, militant methods are the best option and the courage for the same

   e) Awareness that evil always exists and courage to tackle evil without fear of adverse consequences to himself

   f) The ability to do his duty or his role in dharma, rather than do favors for others

   g) Strength in humility

All in all, the questions to be addressed during elections are: Who will be the best among us to represent the true spirit of service of our district? Who among us will be the best-suited person to help coordinate our efforts and inspire a constructive togetherness?

He must never end up as a narrow representative or, in other words, a lobbyist. Rather, he should represent like how a normal, wise father does in a family—an open representative, if one may. He must be a good example for the service capacity of the workers in a district—like an icon. He must be somebody from whom ordinary mortals can draw their inspiration, someone whom all those taking up social service responsibilities in the concerned area will easily identify themselves with.

The council must be non-political and one of its kind for an area:

(1) Political non-interference: The social work councils must contain only those individuals or organizations that do not have any political leanings. That is, these members and member organizations must not be components of political parties. The participants of the social council members in the political process should restrict themselves to the concern of the universal empowerment of people. They must contest no elections for civic offices. Those that are interested in contesting elections should leave the organization. If needed, there could be a parallel setup which consists of members who profess a political leaning. But such an organization is an altogether different issue, and between the two, for matters related to social service, the non-political types will be the seniors.

Such segregation is important in a parliamentary democracy for the following reasons:

1) Social service organization must serve to raise the bar in public life. This is the best way to set standards in society. For example,
   a) It will help to create a benchmark to measure the worthiness of election contestants in other spheres of life.
   b) It will serve as an inspiration for an alternate vision of a serving polity rather than a self-seeking one that is currently the norm.(a Gandhian goal).
2) The negative traits contained in power-mongering must be kept away from the core of social service itself.
3) This will help to keep the abstemious away from the hassles of politicking.

But this does not mean that politicians must be a selfish lot. It still remains that both political and apolitical persons must play important roles in dharma. Both are important. Each one must excel in the duty he has to perform, whether in office or otherwise. Temporal power needs to be handled, after all, and it has to be handled effectively with the best of attitudes. This will require people who do act in the day-to-day world but with their hearts and minds immersed in austerity. To get people of this quality, it is essential that both forms of service should flourish in society but with separate identities. The duty of the two should be hence perceived separately in a participant's perception of dharma. Therefore, the principle of keeping the social service network exclusive to non-political persons is important. In any case, those with political leanings can definitely volunteer in task forces set up by the social workers and vice versa.

(2) Singularity of social work coordination organizations: This is the second important concern with respect to social work coordination. There are questions raised as to whether it is natural to club together a group of do-gooders into a harmonious unit because of the presence of human ego. The fear is that there will be as many points of view as there are individuals. Therefore, it might take mammoth tasks to put such people together. This is however contested by the perspective which accepts as truth the existence of the universal self (we are all one inside). This perspective claims that it is inherent human nature to come together in fruitful togetherness and contribute to the combined effort.

In the instance of the multiplicity of such groups, it will be easy for sincere well-wishers and the lay public to identify, with ease, that group of workers who genuinely form the union of social workers. A true worker will know the value of combined effort. In fact, if a set of social workers cannot forge togetherness, then they are definitely not worth their salt. That is, what wisdom do such people possess which they intend on giving to those they supposedly serve?

And in the interest of social service and team effort, the unity of social workers will keep gate-crashers out of the picture. This can be achieved very easily when there is very little hardware or fixed resources in the coordinating effort and a loose organizational structure. In fact, a formal structure need not exist at all except in the form of a spirit which will go something like this: 'Some friends get together at the taluka level or the district level, keep each other informed, help each other plan together, build up resources commonly and enliven each other's spirits.'

For this, in principle, they must accept that each locality needs a broad, multi-pronged approach and that keeping in touch with each other will give a hoard of added strength. In the same spirit, they should also support processes going on at an inter-regional level by giving a due position of honor to the wise and the true spirit of social service. And finally, there is no question of embarrassment in excluding someone who does not fit into the circle when such exclusion is dharmic.

The instinct to participate comes from within an individual. Every individual who participates in this process understands what the team is doing and has a holistic view. He experiences a certain fullness and satisfaction through his being aware of the mission and purpose of his team and its work, even though he takes up only a small responsibility.

Every leader in this sphere is truly followed out of the follower's individual free will.

A Holistic Healthcare System Must Cater to Every Indian: Thinking Beyond the Boxes of Allopathy and Capitalism

A radical solution is imminent for healthcare: The Indian resistance wished to wrestle freedom out of the hands of the British using khadi as a tool. And the idealism in khadi was this: 'If the poor have no way to earn, how can they be asked to pay? Create work first; technology and prosperity can come later.' The same yardstick must be applied today too. If the Indian economy has failed to give adequate income, enough to avail basic necessities for the average citizen and his family, then the government must ensure that either the income is raised or arrangements are made to provide for the citizen within the given income, however low that income may be. Otherwise, the Indian system has failed the idealism of the freedom struggle.

Consider that the nation has an average income per person of around Rs. 100 per day (this is a figure from 2012). And consider that more than 70% of the Indian population earns below this level. Moreover, a significant percentage, around 10%, lives on less than Rs. 32 per day. This means that the nation must provide decent food, health, security, education and housing within this amount if it has to meet the goals which the freedom fighters of the nation set for the British rule prior to freedom. Clearly, the cost of food, education and medicine is way above what can be obtained within this income. Medicine is definitely way outside the reach of this goal. The present arrangement is therefore woefully inadequate.

This is alarming. If the nation does not think in revolutionary terms, even the basic goals of the freedom struggle can never be met. Capitalism does not have the answer for this. The immediate solution that has been found is to tax the rich and feed the poor—but the idea of creating a nation of beggars (70%) is not healthy. Changes need to be made in the way the nation plans; commercialization of health services must not accentuate deprivation. And radical solutions are in order if that is the only way out.

Fortunately, there are certain areas to explore which can shift the scenario closer to the freedom-struggle ideal. Let us understand the system as it exists first and then look at the scope that is available.

The present medical institution is a limb of the capitalist system: Like most services available in the capitalistic world today, the medical service too has evolved in the environment of modern science and technology coupled with capitalistic value systems. While science and technology continuously expand the frontiers of the cures available within the service sector, the economic aspect is organized around capitalism.

In capitalism, the price of a commodity gets fixed on the basis of demand and supply. Prominent among the factors that decide the price of medical services are the nature of the illness, the cost of medicines, the scarcity of doctors, the reputation of the doctor, the cost of the hardware the doctor uses, the doctor's saleability, the gravity of the certificates the doctor holds, the 'practice' of the doctor, the eagerness of a patient to get cured, the prevalence (or absence) of alternatives and the patient's monetary status. Therefore, it is within this framework of 'service (commercial)' that medical attention is given to patients. Medical insurance and state welfare act as breathers that soften the impact of harsh hard-core capitalism.

There are also renegades to totalitarian capitalism. These are the 'service-minded' doctors/personnel who charge their patients using principles that go contrary to those of the capitalist ideal. But for such exceptions, the medical costs are prohibitive, and the best of services are available only to those who can afford it. The costlier treatments are available only to a select percentage of the overall population.

Also, being a part of the capitalist system, there is one other characteristic that comes to the system of medicine naturally. In capitalism, the survival or continuance of any service depends on the saleability of the service. One does not hear of loss-making companies lasting very long unless it is artificially propped up by a concerned government or through donations from NGOs, corporates or generous patrons. So is the case with the medical services; they cannot flourish if there are no rich patrons. And India is a country with a lot of poor people. This means that doctors find it commercially unviable to set up shop in a major portion of the Indian hinterland. Apparently, they are also not enthused enough by the government doles offered at present to make them move to those areas and practice.

The current system is predominantly cure-based and reactive: Another characteristic of the present set of medical services is that it is predominantly reactive. There are huge institutions (private and public) which, even when they function at their best, are only concerned with fighting illnesses, fighting causes that created illnesses or fighting epidemics. It is mostly about correcting the situation once an ailment has happened and not so much about preventing ailments from happening.

1) Health services rendered at health centers are supposed to take care of other major issues in a human life cycle like pregnancy, childbirth, death, etc.

2) Pro-active responsibilities are effectively restricted to 'preaching' about things like health and hygiene, good nutrition, contraceptives, dangerous diseases and the like.

3) Vaccines are exceptions and are targeted at protection against diseases.

Despite the existence of these, it is clear that the overall system has an attitude that goes somewhat like this: 'You are ill? Come, I'll cure you.'

Government support dilutes the impact of hard-core capitalism: Taking the specific case of government hospitals, one can say that they are milder on ideal capitalism since they are part of the welfare services rendered by the government. However, they too have a basic reactive mechanism in that they are dedicated to curing illnesses. In relation to the private hospitals though, they perform more pro-active functions.

Need for an alternative approach: Having taken note of these characteristics and having seen the basic challenge a statesman faces in his attempt to cater to the ideals of the freedom struggle, let us proceed to visualize alternatives so that a sense of what has to be achieved in society can be had. What needs to be done so that it can be made possible for a lot more people to avail medical aid?

Solutions by virtue of dealing with the dynamics of demand and supply of medical services: How does one cater to a vast population of more than a billion? How does one plan in such a way that all are covered? When the cost of treatment is prohibitive in a country where a large percentage of the people find it difficult to find their next meal, how can medical treatment be arranged for all? Should the nation carry forward this pyramid-like system where costlier treatments are available only to increasingly smaller number of people high up in the pyramid and close to nothing is available to those at the bottom? Is life then a mad chase to climb up the money pyramid?

Ask an economist, and he will say that one way to bring down prices is to reduce the demand and increase the supply. This looks like a convenient platform from which one can consider various possible solutions. With the addition of another principle of adding counter services, there should be four or five areas to work upon so that this cost is brought down.

Needless to say, it must gel with the principle of self-rule, and the solution must come more from the people than through artificial plug-ins by the higher authorities. Of the suggested solutions, the first will be difficult for the rational world to digest. But let's take it up first anyway. There are valid reasons behind it.

Decreasing demand (1) – A people that is free from the misery of longevity will cherish self-rule: This perspective is based on an understanding of the 'self'. It is controversial in the sense that the beliefs are scientifically un-tested. It is not a matter that has been decisively dealt with one way or the other in modern intellectual circles, but while the debate is on, it is only appropriate that one also looks at the other perspective that comes from spiritualism. It is a matter concerning life and death.

Many cultures teach that one should grow beyond the fear of death. In fact, one should even embrace death if duty calls for it. Such an attitude is, of course, far from palatable for a consumerism-based society. Therefore, it is left to individuals to choose their own point of view. But the rider to it is that each individual is supposed to bear the consequences of the belief he holds. One that has the ability to look beyond death is supposed to be making the most of this world, and one that cannot is supposed to have a miserable existence. This perspective has the following things to say:

a) One is supposed to work for better health not because he will be spending less on medicines or because he won't die fast then, but because it is his duty to keep his physiological system healthy. Else, he will be interfering with nature out of a 'demonic' resolve if he does not ensure the proper maintenance of his own body. In this alternate point of view, one keeps healthy because he wants to be fit and fine to go about his tasks to the best of his ability.

b) When people revel in this alternate perspective, the demand for medical services emanating from the fear of one's life will come down considerably, and people will not be that desperate to live longer lives. People will focus on quality rather than quantity.

c) Also, it can be inferred that the 'fear' of death and fear of disease are no means to discourage addiction to things like smoking, drugs or alcohol because that leads to the opposite effect on people. People will smoke simply to defy fear, and that gives an individual a certain release from bondage. That liberation is enjoyable; and this pursuit of liberty through such habits is, on the contrary, something good. Fear does not work with the brave. There is therefore no point

in trying to 'scare away' individuals from the so-called harmful things; merely informing them about the side-effects will more than suffice.

Rather, having reckoned this factor, it becomes clear that indifference is the best attitude toward vices. And the best way to help an addict out of such an ailment is by focusing on good health and freedom from mental weakness and dependence, rather than provoking any fear of death or ruin. This alternate method of threatening with the fatal possibility of death, in a sense, tends to destroy an individual's character by getting him confused.

It must be seen that such an alternate point of view is integral to the ethos of self-rule since it is in sync with the highest freedom known to man, often referred to as the freedom of the Supreme Self, freedom of the immortals or Ultimate Freedom. Medicine can manifest into an adequate support mechanism for swaraj only if it accepts and builds upon the ethic of fearlessness even in death. If the medical service continues being money-centered, thriving upon the foundation of mortal fear as it does today, the chances that it will serve a self-rule are not good.

It will interest one to take note, at this point, that the erstwhile Ayurveda doctor also played a spiritual role in the community and in the lives of the patients. A system that is consonant with the spiritual dimension may be the need of a nation like ours.

So, the sum total of this argument is that if this perspective of being free in mind and spirit is accepted, amplified and nourished in society, commercial demand will drop considerably while the spiritual dimension will grow. This makes for a better society while providing greater satisfaction to both doctor and patient. This is the promise from the spiritual perspective.

Decreasing demand (2) – Creation of a healthy society; that is, putting greater effort on prevention rather than cure: It amounts to focus on upping the health of individuals so that no one falls sick and, therefore, there is no need of going to medical centers. The strategy needs to be integrated into the culture of the people, and this should be one of the primary concerns of grassroots-level freedom.

More institutions than merely the medical fraternity have to be involved in keeping a watch on the health of individuals. These initiatives must include efforts at enhancing the health, hygiene and nutrition among the members of a community. It has to include those activities too which aim at keeping individuals at the peak of their health (sports, performing arts, etc.). Medical services too must gravitate more toward pro-active responsibilities.

Besides re-defining the basic aims of the healthcare system, a more sympathetic approach to traditional systems of food, health and medicine is also in order. It will not be sensible to ignore the delicate balance that has lasted for centuries. In fact, the methods currently used in the mainstream should actually come as a complement and complete traditional systems rather than supplant them.

By the end of the twentieth century, it has been more or less conclusively established that the mind has a direct influence on the health of an individual. Meditation and other techniques are found to improve health and wellness. In fact, many practices related to spiritualism give great dividends to health. Mind science itself has established that all cures need not be in terms of medicines that are applied, ingested or injected. Simple techniques of positive thinking release productive juices in our body and improve health. Simultaneously, it is a known fact that the converse is also true. Many illnesses are due to the inability of individuals to remove negative influences from their minds. This calls for the promotion of a culture of wellness. Yoga, meditation, *reiki*, laughter clubs, aerobics, *vipassna*, *sudarshan kriya*, etc. need to be encouraged. The *rajyoga* method is secular, does not need a spiritual belief system and has a meditation and a physical dimension. The results are tangible, and hence, it is one of the best solutions to pursue.

Creation of positive service – A health service which prospers in health rather than in sickness: Why should doctors provide service only to the sick? Should they not serve healthy individuals?

 ➤ Why should illnesses be the means of earning for doctors and not health?
 ➤ Why can there not be a system that is concerned with the health of each individual rather than a system which makes each individual take care of his own health?

 ➤ Why can the system not function in a manner such that one takes care of his friend's health?

This will require renewed impetus on the concept of family doctor but with a positive twist to it. We shall see it presently.

Increasing supply (1) – Thinking outside the allopathic box: It is true that Allopathy is the way the world is going. It is based on modern science and consists of a systematic approach to understanding the machine that the human body is and how damaged machines (human bodies) can be repaired and maintained. Therefore, following the modern world and the best it has to offer necessarily means following Allopathy as a solution. Rather, it means building a solution for the nation with it as the basis.

The forces of macro-economics rely on allopathic medicine and talk in terms of the percentage of population covered. They rely on projections into the future when prosperity will have trickled down to the lowest levels. But this is not a good approach for the present. The various strategies adopted by the government to entice or force doctors to practice in rural areas do not seem to be bearing great results. The allopathic system coupled with the capitalistic arrangement, as set up in India, has not given and is not likely to give the all-inclusive solution that one desires in a dharmic arrangement.

Is there a way out? Why this needless stress on Allopathic medicine?

What about the other branches of medicine that were known to man since time immemorial? Sidda, Ayurveda, Unani? It is true that modern science may be able to punch holes into the basic literature of these forms of medicine, and these alternatives are not complete solutions either, but in practical terms, these alternatives do represent an accumulation of human experience over centuries and even millennia in certain cases. It must be remembered that, owing to the integrated nature of traditional medicine into a lifestyle that has evolved through the centuries, it will not be wise to wipe out these methods and replace them by modern ones. To ignore the treasure troves that these represent is not a sensible approach.

Each system of medicine has its own characteristic features. They are the best options in the areas that are unique to each. Traditional methods and medicine are best for home-use, and allopathic medicine is good for high-tech cures. For serious illnesses, traditional medicines are basically low-cost options, whereas the best of modern methods, though radical and quick, come with huge price tags. Most traditional methods are not invasive and offer simple solutions to the relatively complicated processes of the allopathic system.

This offers a great opportunity. If a vision can be built around including doctors of traditional systems into the overall plan of governance of the nation, then the number of medical practitioners can be increased several-fold. This will result in an increase of the supply. The vision should be able to indicate how the various systems are to relate to each other and how they must mutually cooperate to effectively cover 100% of the population.

The state must develop such a vision. All systems must be involved, and a balance must be struck. The statesmen must plan in such a way that legitimate alternatives from the various streams of medicine are available to citizens. They should be permitted to choose from among those.

But there are difficulties. In truth, there are numerous dimensions to medicine and cure. We have already seen that the state of mind of a person is directly linked to his physical health. (In fact, it is a question of whether the chicken or egg came first. Does a defective mind lead to a defective body, or does a defective body lead to a defective mind?) Beyond such an observation which looks at least slightly logical, there are other spiritual ones which seem to defy logic. Recent studies have concluded that prayers affect cures. Moreover, the amount of faith an individual has in his doctor and in the doctor's medicines is also found to play a role in the process of cure.

Owing to such factors that defy scientific definition, it becomes rather difficult to mark out boundaries for individuals or for systems of medicine in a manner such that practitioners may be constrained to readily stay within their areas of function.

But this should not induce a hands-off or 'I-can't-interfere' approach from the government. Instead, there must be a broad plan of action so that some reasonable degree of coordination is achieved. Necessity is the mother of invention; something can be worked out.

It will also not make any sense to make laws that may end up restricting the potential and effectiveness of any of the systems to any extent whatsoever. Ultimately, a vision needs to be projected to the common citizen so that he is not confused about the options and that he has something to look forward to. The various systems of medicine must exist side by side in such a manner that a family doctor should be able to prescribe solutions from any of the available branches. And in case of illnesses, the doctor should have the option of sending those under his care to a specialist of any system depending on the preferences, traditions and economic status of the family.

Such an integrated vision must be built with the last man in the village as the starting point and by ensuring that it makes available to him a spectrum of choices. He must have a system before him which assures the best humane attention and care with several technical options (systems).

Family doctors, traditional physicians, *dhais*, health workers, doctors and specialists should be neatly fitted into the system so that their excellence, ability, skill and knowledge are put to effective use in a way such that they complement the overall system. There must be a commonly held agreement on when specialist help is required and when functionaries at the lower levels should pass on their cases to the invasive and high-priced modern methods.

Beginning with a pilot plan, a system should be developed over the years till there is something suitable to cover the entire population. In fact, a benchmark can be set. Each Indian citizen should have access to a minimum of two systems of medicine from which he can choose based on his own prioritization (including finances).

Finally, it is the patient himself who must decide what he wants. It will be up to him to trust or not trust an individual doctor or a system of medicine. And it will be up to the doctor, of whichever stream, to establish a practice for himself. But local communities will assist. And state and central governments will facilitate the establishment of national coordination, governing and promotional agencies for each of the systems of medicine. Besides this, schools and apprentice-based systems must be promoted in good measure so that a robust system evolves quickly.

Increasing supply (2) – Thinking outside the MBBS box: Again, there is no need to insist that only an MBBS certificate holder should be prescribing medicines for others.

a) One example is the nurses. Nurses have tremendous practical experience. Their minds dwell on aspects of medicine for at least eight hours a day each day of their working life. This amounts to a lot. If it is supplemented with focused theoretical study taken in steps, gradually, over a period of ten or fifteen years, they can graduate to completing an MBBS degree. In fact, each step in the process of transition can give them increasing powers to 'practice'. These powers may be well-classified/categorized and regulated in terms of the positions they are allowed to hold in a hospital and in society.

b) The necessity of certification and standardization arises in a capitalist system with the view that a service can be purchased at will at commercial centers and from any 'certified' source. The medical council, by giving the MBBS certificate to a doctoral candidate, says that XYZ person carries their seal of approval to practice (since the graduate has been trained accordingly and has passed his exams). Now, if people of a community go to a doctor (quack) out of their own free will because it suits their pocket and because it is a solution for them, why should the state be hassled by it as long as it is clearly displayed in that doctor's hospital that he is not an MBBS degree holder? The important point is that instead of snubbing him, attempts should be made to bring such persons into the system so that the flaws in his service are minimized and there is one more medical worker on the ground.

c) One set of alternatives to the MBBS doctors we have considered so far consists of the medical practitioners of other systems of medicine. This also means that there will be regulatory authorities for other systems of medicine as well as is the case for MBBS doctors. Red, blue and green crosses are already in use. Other colors of crosses, easily distinguishable from the above three, can be used to indicate the other systems of medicine.

Now, if, there are practitioners who enjoy the confidence of a community apart from even these, there must be some kind of informal training provided which will target such practitioners toward one or the other well-defined notch in a hierarchy of any of the main systems, which will, in turn, ensure that his work contributes to the overall system. As always, such a physician will be responsible for his own actions in that he will have to answer to community law as laid down by the local community. This, in turn, will be based on the recommendations regarding Dos and Don'ts by the medical fraternity. Therefore, the authority to grant or refuse permission for such people to operate will entirely depend on the local community.

This will also mean that within the allopathic system, there is a need for a hierarchy among health workers, beginning with the dhais and ending with the MDs. All such health workers must belong to a well-regulated system with a proper hierarchical structure and well-defined domains of service. The process of certification and regulation will need strengthening; there needs to be clear cut limits to the authority a student may gain through such certification.

And in the absence of such a certification, it will entirely be a matter between the quack and those who trust him. After all, he is their doctor, their best option. Why should the state interfere, especially if it cannot help the citizen otherwise?

Now, can the medical fraternity, from all the systems put together, sit with the government and develop a sound plan of action? If they can do that while keeping in mind the spirit of grassroots freedom and ensuring a people-centric agenda, it will be a great boon to the nation.

Facilitating other institutions for holistic health and medicine: While taking a holistic view of health services, it must not be burdened on the medical fraternity alone. Following is a list of institutions involved, and these must be integrated into the overall plan.

The family: It is the most important of the available institutions for healthcare. The specialty of the family lies in the closeness of ties. The awareness of another person's health is highest here, and here lies the potential for the kind of personal attention and nursing so gravely required during illnesses. Most of all, it is here that awareness about nutrition, home medicines, tonics, sanitation, food preparation, etc. can make a vital difference to individuals' health and, hence, their individual output. It is therefore necessary that in the traditions transferred down in families, the system of health should be a major area of focus. In fact, this is the way it is with most cultures. Unfortunately, this is part of the baby that is being thrown out with the bathwater when people decry casteism in India.

Now, that is another issue altogether, and only time will tell how the caste-consciousness will evolve. But one way or the other, the truth remains that in order for the family to be an effective instrument of health, the family traditions have to constantly receive inputs from outside agencies like formal education, community health programs, government or other initiatives, art forms, games, yoga and meditation techniques, and, most of all, traditions of rural sports and traditional medicine. Apart from this, the modern systems of health and nutrition should give inputs so that the gaps left by the other means are filled up appropriately. Only then will the arrangements in each individual family be wholesome.

The community: Where it is left off at the family level, there it should be picked up at the level of the community. Knowledge gathered by elders through their experience should be used to sort out as much as possible within the periphery of community services. This is also a level at which resources can be held in common. Therefore, at this level, there should be a complete vision which has to deal with the availability of emergency services, availability of home medicines, nutritional inputs, routine check-ups, vaccines and other such things related to the health and hygiene of each and every individual in that community. The community is burdened with the primary role. This is at the heart of panchayati swaraj—communities should express themselves fully here.

Sports and dance forms: These constitute a set of activities which have to be encouraged and sponsored by communities with the ultimate aim of improving physical health standards (apart from spiritual and mental ones).

Sports and games tend to create springs of tremendous awareness of health, nutrition and medicine in those who are involved, namely sportsmen, sport Gurus and sports institutions. The final result is that the knowledge passed down the generations within families and communities gets reinforced by the efforts of these people, and the output of the nation progresses to meet its true potential—even in the Olympic arena. We shall see more of this separately.

The family doctor: This is a dying institution which needs to be revived. This set of doctors must be paid when individuals enjoy good health. Family culture should include routine checks from doctors of their choice. Such doctors must have well-honed skills in diagnosis, home medicine, sanitation and nutrition balancing within families' characteristic food habits. They need to also have an awareness of the relevant culture and the specialties of the region in which they operate. They must maintain records of the history of the health of individuals, update it regularly and advise the family on whether to go for specialists' help during illnesses—and if so, to whom.

Such a service should border on interactions like the ones priests have with families. It should be bound by bonds of friendship and duty, and payment should be an amount set by mutual agreement according to a set social standard. The payment can be a fixed amount paid on a monthly basis or, better still, a percentage of the family income with an upper and lower ceiling. The size of the population which a doctor may be expected to serve can be estimated centrally by public authorities on a round figure basis. A statistical average may be given as a guideline.

It will also prove beneficial to the system to change doctors once in about three years or so. The doctors may also be given a break once in a while with the intention of giving them an opportunity to pursue higher studies.

Medical research institutions with the duty of monitoring society: So that adequate health standards are achieved, there is a need for analysis and creative inputs on health factors. This will require research institutions that have a distinct `application' dimension capable of issuing warnings about impending problems pro-actively. They also need to provide solutions for rare problems occurring over a region.

These research institutions can also help in designing and upgrading a course curriculum that touches all aspects of a community health program so that formal certificates can be issued to persons who study and qualify with the requisite standards. This is according to the requirements of local self-government.

Government and private hospitals: These will continue to function as they do for the time being but will also gradually adjust to the requirements of a holistic solution. New initiatives for research and rural health support may need to be added to civil hospitals. A special branch for sports medicine is also likely to be required. There will be a focus toward specialization since routine medicine will increasingly be handled at the lower levels. Insurance companies will probably come into the picture in a big way if the 'health services' and not merely the 'illness services' grow in strength. We have seen in Part 2 of this book how Dr. Shetty's efforts and Aravind Eye Care hospitals have thrown up tangible solutions that cater to the poor in society. Perhaps, these models can be multiplied and even cross-fertilized for better impact.

Self-rule is destiny; all planning for systems must be done with that in mind: To some, many of the suggestions offered here will seem radical. They may not be new, but radical nonetheless. And a question will arise as to how practical these will be.

The answer is that slavery cannot perpetuate forever. Sometime in the future, the nation will step up to dharma and move toward self-rule. Such a system will run on alternate principles. Such a system will be focused on *every* individual. Such a system will not be rigorous on money. Such a system will have decentralized active agents taking a lot of initiative. If that is the destiny of the nation, then every sub-system will have to fall in line—the medical sub-system too.

If the nation wishes to target itself toward a self-rule, then, with the right inputs from the government and the associated individuals, the system should gravitate toward something that is more caring and all-embracing. In fact, as we have seen, that vision of self-rule in ancient India incorporated an Ayurveda doctor who doubled up as a priest or a counselor to the families he served. There is great benevolence in that system, and it is not entirely based on the dry service-for-money exchange which is characteristic of an ideal capitalistic order.

If the choice offered to the modern world is between a friendly and complete system oozing contentment and a system based on the 'endless wants' mentality of consumerism, then the choice of the former is already made in the desire for self-rule.

At the cost of sounding repetitive, one needs to add that the world does not have the other option. The situation of a decentralized self-rule is critical from the environment point of view. The world environment dictates the terms. The path of endless wants is the sure road to the extinction of the human race since the globe cannot possibly take it anymore. A more austere system must be the way ahead. It must gain the support of the common man who is enthused by the vision of self-rule. The medical fraternity and the statesmen in the government must keep these parameters in mind when they plan ahead and attempt to provide medical services as part of a system that caters to a free nation consisting of village republics. And though this be the compulsion, the resonance with a fulfilling life may be more with the compelled model.

Section VIII

Sports and Art Forms: Foundation Stone of Life and Civilization

What do sports mean to people? There are individuals who are serious about sports and arts for the sake of human interaction, recreation, exercise and adventure. But by far, most people consider these as entertainment (for these are known sources of pleasure and excitement), and a few persons consider these as means of livelihood and status (in related activities and in the support structure). Several institutions also look upon games and sports as a source of glory at competitions. A miniscule minority of the population take it as a prayer, a method for concentration, a trigger for alertness, etc. Most artists and sportsmen consider arts and sports as that which brings the best out of them. Therefore, these are the basic motivating ideas which, as of today, spur institutions, governments and individuals to action in the field of sports and arts.

Each nation has its own take on what sports is all about. In as far as India is concerned, there are campaigns being run for 'marks for sports' and most recently for 'fitness'. And these are making an attempt to change mind-sets. However, the old perception lingers on, and as such, the focus of the intellectual mainstream is on the spoils of victory—the medals at the Olympics, the trophies at the world games, the money for winners and the glory for the triumphant. The idea of sports being a promoter of team spirit, health and other virtues is something of an afterthought.

Therefore, an Indian, having grown up in a cultural environment that holds this view, will not readily agree with sayings like 'the important part of sports is not winning but playing well'. Most will wonder whether there is any sense in it. There are, of course, many who will be able to quote such sayings but will lack the conviction to translate that awareness into related activities in life.

There is a valuable spiritual dimension to sports and arts: For the good of sports and society, these opinions must change in a very fundamental manner. The overall status of sports and art forms should be elevated from their present status of being a source of mere entertainment, relaxation and profession to being a necessary part of an individual's personal life. They must become an integral part of life in a community too. As the actress and dancer Mallika Sarabhai points out, 'Arts are generally perceived to be the cherry on the cake; it should be rather thought of as the yeast.'

Obviously, this point of view is acceptable only if due regard is given to the wisdom of seers. That is, there is a need to take into reckoning the view that the best in man, in terms of potential for action and happiness, is brought out by the best of sports and arts. Or, as we have it in the *Bhagavad Gita*, 'The path of knowledge and the path of action lead to the same goal.'

That goal is, as indicated by the wise, the best that man can be in his lifetime. One need not go that far into the unknown too. With a little bit of analyzing, by focusing on the attitudes of the majority of the best of artists and sportspersons, by paying heed to the latest concept of 'the zone' now taking shape in the West (it's about the state of mind in which top players peak during performances; the study is in the context of basketball) or the 'tunneling effect' as athletes put it and by falling back a little onto the works of Rabindranath Tagore, Swami Vivekananda and others like them, it is easy to come to a similar conclusion. Abraham Maslow has also extensively studied this under the concept of 'peak experiences' and 'plateau experiences'.

A group's approach to sports and arts must therefore reflect connoisseurship: Understanding sports and arts in its higher dimensions will result in a change in view about a lot of other things related to sports and arts. All sporting and art activities should be firmly grounded in health-consciousness, personality development, character building and spirituality rather than in victories, profession, prestige and entertainment. New institutions will have to be set up and old ones readjusted to suit this extended framework of utility.

In the light of grassroots freedom, the change in fundamentals will manifest itself onto the beliefs and initiatives of the neighborhood community. It will create a new set of aims in communities and produce additional sources of motivation to patronize the arts. And if this approach turns out to be right, it will find perfect resonance with indigenous arts and sports forms available in every locality/community.

From a national perspective, such activities will be taken up with a more enthusiastic outlook. It will be looked on as a means to ensure that there is productive activity in the villages. It will be seen as a source for team spirit. It will be counted upon to provide a good reference point for physical and spiritual health standards. And of course, it will also be seen as a means for release, entertainment and prosperity.

Looking at it from individuals' point of view, such activities will stimulate in each citizen the need to inculcate a certain sense of self-discipline and strength of character (viz. freedom from weakness at crunch moments). It will help individuals develop the ability to focus on the 'now' and rely on the 'power of now'. It will prod individuals to relish being in the action-world and down to earth. It will encourage them to give their all to their performances while being in the 'zone'. Excellence will be their watchword. As Rajnikant, the South Indian matinee idol puts it, 'Irrespective of how great your past achievements are, each time you need to get back to scratch, down to the floor, to the bottom and work upwards from there.' He relates to it as a cause for humility and success. Consequently, the arts and sports provide a proper working space so that participants may learn more about themselves. Such activities help sensitize individuals in the appreciation of true merit, hard work and excellence.

Institutional reforms to cater to a sporting and artful nation: When the purpose, motivation and reason for the arts and sports in a nation are readjusted to the higher goals that inspire the best of sportsmen and sporting communities, the institutions that cater to these activities also need to be readjusted to suit the altered goals.

Among the institutions concerned with sports, there are two broad categories. One consists of the kind of organizations or institutions that are associated with the top-down initiatives that exist today. Such organizations and initiatives will be concerned with the various sports that have popularity and standardization at the global level. At the national level, these organizations include the ministry of sports, the bodies that come under it, the various autonomous bodies concerned with the various sports, the federations answerable to international federations, the organizing committees of various sporting events, etc.

The other kind of organizations will be those that concern themselves with indigenous sports that are popular in particular localized regions anywhere. These organizations must be basically built from the ground up, based on the popular will of the people. These organizations must have the strength and enough executive power to keep the said games fruitful to the cause of society.

As for the former up-to-down category, addition of new institutions may not be required. However, there is a need for work toward molding the existing institutions in such a manner that they are as democratic, transparent, involving and accessible as possible.

As for the latter group of down-to-up initiatives, there is a need for a lot of work. New institutions need to be created in virtually every village of the country. Traditional institutions need to be rejuvenated, and new methods of patronization need to be found. The character and purpose of the possible institutions can be roughly described in the following examples.

Akhadas **(and sports/art Gurus) and their funding:** These will be learning centers working at the grassroots level, focused on a particular game/art but disseminating much more than mere techniques and skill connected with it. The akhadas will also form a nerve center or storehouse for a lot of information. These are to be built on traditional lines. They will have to be built around acharyas and Gurus—coaches who are friends, philosophers and guides to the students. These teachers will be human institutions constituting treasures of knowledge held within a community. These persons who run akhadas must be trendsetters, icons and inspirers carrying on their work through their unique missionary zeal. They should very much be an integral part of life in any particular community.

The important difference today will be that these traditional akhadas will now have a new system of patronage in a democratic self-rule environment; it is needed for their survival. It will not be all that easy to have the students take up professional specialization in such games; rather, the focus should be on part-time training without compromise on the aim of excellence.

Patronage for such institutions was earlier arranged through the support of kings, rich persons, local zamindars, etc. The reason for this patronage was partly because sports were also a form of identifying talent for intake into armies and higher office. But that was not all. Kings prided themselves on the availability of 'gems' in their courts. Men of learning and the arts were patronized since the kings were taught to be connoisseurs—a sign of great prosperity of nations. Now with the absence of such arrangements under kingship, there is a need for new methods of patronage.

CSR-supported initiatives and advertisement budgets and local government supported initiatives seem to be the most attractive options for patronage besides patronage by the rich. This will be facilitated if there is widespread awareness among the people that sports and arts are an integral part of a good life.

To sum up, the local communities, government officials and individuals (from within or outside each sport) must go out of their way to ensure that akhadas develop around inspirational sports teachers and that they find support and sustenance without any compromise on quality or self-dignity of the institution.

Elected bodies for managing sports/art forms: A federation concerned with the management of every individual traditional game/art form needs to be constituted while keeping in mind the extent of the population over which that particular game/art is popular. Such elected bodies must ultimately represent the popular will of those who participate either directly or indirectly in that sport. That is, it should be an autonomous body dedicated to a concerned sport; and as such, it should have domain over the area determined by the popularity of the sport. The elected members will represent a popular body authorized to handle issues pertaining to that sport.

Therefore, the actual organizational structure itself will depend on factors like the geographical extent of the game's popularity, the nature of the game itself, the game's special requirements and the finances required. Or in brief, the realities on the ground will specify the nature of each organization. These organizations need to be as objective as possible, in the sense that they should be independent of personalities. The duty guidelines should be well-defined so that the sport/art form gets sustenance from the system rather than individuals.

It will be interesting to see what kind of solutions emerge. But an outline is attempted here nonetheless:

- They should be institutions by whose efforts the sport/ art form finds nourishment at the grassroots level.
- Such organizations should have the ability to lift up exemplary leadership in that sport into positions of authority.
- Such popular organizations must be guarded from direct political, bureaucratic or other interference so that the sport gets to be led by the best of men dedicated to the sport/art. Their authority in the relevant matters, in turn, must ensure that the service is useful and effective.

Among the responsibilities of such institutions will be the following:

- Establishment of a proper relationship with other similar organizations
- Working out timetables for major programs in order to optimize participation
- Directing the functioning of an optimum-sized executive which will directly deal with administration of the sport/game
- Helping make arrangements for centers of training, research or medicine and helping the dissemination of knowledge for improvement of techniques

> Helping knit the useful benefits of the game into the general life of the communities and the local institutions

> Playing an important role in ensuring excellence in the spiritual and physical health of individuals and of communities

Regional sports centers: They will be a factor in the top-down process. They must primarily offer services of various kinds related to health and sports for a particular region. Even the local or traditional sports must be able to gain from this source as follows:

1) Each center will manifest as a resource center servicing the complete spectrum of games. Very similar to a library, but it will be much more. It will have a full repository providing information on training methods, sports medicine, coaching techniques, game skills etc., which should be easily available to those who need it. A person going to the center looking for information about any game, be it pertaining to basic rules, advanced skills or the constructing of infrastructure, should be able to find it.

2) The center can also help in working out year-round programs so that there is good coordination between different games in the particular region.

3) Such regional centers must be supported by other research organizations undertaking application research in subjects like nutrition and medicine. Taking up unsolved queries and passing them on to research institutions will also be part of the responsibilities of such a regional center.

4) The center must take up pro-active projects like the stimulation of sports through training camps, initiating meeting processes, routine technology-transfer initiatives, refresher courses, etc.

5) One wing of such an institution should be dedicated to the provision of infrastructure for sports training which are too costly for small clubs. Such facilities are to be made available on a well-formulated basis. Preference must be given to the current and upcoming sportspersons of the region who have distinguished themselves and who have the potential to do well at the higher levels of the relevant game.

In brief, it can be described as a support base for coaches and sport Gurus in that they are given the best and latest available for their work. It should be a facilitator for coordination and a channel for technology transfer.

Though it is a top-down process in that the basic financing and intellectual resources come from government funding, it will still be run by directors elected from the region. The committee in charge may consist of members elected into office by sports organizations in the region, officials appointed by the state/central governments and functionaries of the institution itself. The proportion of popularly elected members should be greater than the appointed ones. The affiliated sportsmen, officials and teachers/coaches must form the electorate.

Apart from these, the usual institutions should continue to operate viz. educational institutions, sports schools, academies for particular games, clubs, leagues, sports institutions, associations, etc. Hopefully, they will be more imaginative and aware of the fact that sports and art forms form an integral part of the lifeblood of any society that believes in civilized living.

Similar solutions for art forms: Traditional art forms will receive similar impetus. The arts will be cherished for the very same values that sports are. Some of them, especially dance forms, will be cherished for physical health reasons too. Institutions similar to those meant for managing sports will be required. However, the tasks involved will be slightly different. The Guru-based institutions, elected bodies for particular arts, centers of culture, etc., which are prevalent today, will continue to exist and hopefully flourish too. These institutions will have to concentrate on encouraging live performances because the audience is part of such a performance. They must also encourage every individual in society to have minimum proficiency in a few of the art forms while simultaneously aiming for excellence in one or the other of them.

Traditional arts will hence be cherished for many reasons as follows:

> For individuals' development
> For the sake of a neighborhood community
> As religious work
> As communities' expression
> As a nation's identity

They will receive much more reverence at homes and at educational institutions than is usual today. Blessed are those that are already practicing this. Aestheticism and excellence will even be an integral part of the various tasks of normal human life like cooking, housework or office work.

The arts will also form a vehicle for *gnyan* (wisdom) in that 'performances' based on religious themes will be taken up with the idea to educate both performers and viewers. The contributions to temples (donations/offerings) will be partly used to patronize traditional learning, classical arts and folk arts for the sake of both better spiritual awareness/knowledge and spiritual health.

At the community level, initiatives must be taken up for keeping the neighborhood alive through group performances of various arts during events like festival celebrations, home functions, temple celebrations, get-togethers, etc. And at the national level, the arts must be taken up as food and nourishment for the nation. No nation is worth its name if a strong culture of patronage of the arts is missing.

Patronage for the arts and sports – Celebration of life and service to society: Advertisements have been one of the most important sources for financing sports and arts in the present society. Besides this, there are initiatives arising from nationalistic fervor and some support from individual patronage too.

Hopefully, in the new scenario, the following will take place:

➤ Individual patronage will see greater heights.

➤ Initiatives of nationalism will hopefully be replaced by initiatives for a better civilization.

➤ In addition to the motive of advertisement, companies will give patronage with the intention of 'boosting their workers' morale'. (It is soothing for an individual to know that he not only works for profit but also for prosperity. He is happy that there is a direct benefit to society and culture due to the existence of the company. That makes his service, job and life more fulfilling for him. This is an essential component of CSR.)

➤ One can also hope that there will be far greater inflow of money due to cultural activities in the form of fees, tickets and individual patronage because of changes in priority.

➤ Even temples will play their role in the patronage of sports and arts.

➤ Government initiatives at the higher levels of administration, and at the local level, should have a broader vision and widen their scope of support.

➤ Also, occasions like fairs, festivals and other similar meets must ensure the allocation of enough resources to support inter-village competitions in arts and sports. The patronage showered on these activities will be owing to the realization of their importance to life at the inter-community level. The financing will, of course, come from the usual sources sought from on such occasions.

Finally, it is important to remember that no system of taxation must be used to garner resources for sports and arts. Shelling out money for support must not be compelled because these are matters pertaining to the spirit which cannot be forced. Any force will be counterproductive. A nominal fee from those concerned should be admissible. This should be fixed at a minimum which will be necessary to run the basic services of grassroots-level organizations. Above that minimum, it should be left to free will—no mortal or moral coercive forces must be used. In any case, when it is understood that sports is something more than entertainment, a lot of funds can flow into it. For example, there is a huge industry charging exorbitant money for children's books, toys, dresses... Why will some of that money not get channelized into sports once its importance is understood?

It is a subtle issue of participation in a life process, which an individual should cherish and support from his heart. If it is sincere, it is an index of class or connoisseurship. Society must ensure that its younger generations pick up these values. Training institutions must orient individuals in such a manner that they target the highest goal. Planning and coordination forces should integrate this supreme idea in their plans. And finally, the rewarding and honoring initiatives pertaining to both fields should exemplify the highest that man can achieve in both body and in spirit. Sports and arts are apt playfields for secular spirituality.

Education Must Address Civilizational Needs and Not Just Economic Needs

Modern education tends to provide an exalted status to the fortunate few who get educated. As it turns out, the benevolent of these 'educated' take interest in solving the problems of the less fortunate. Though such intentions are good, this solution is inappropriate for a nation that seeks second freedom. In a self-rule, people must be empowered to solve their own problems. The aim must not be to make a class dependent on another but to ensure that each group achieves self-reliance in the knowhow that is required for its day-to-day tasks.

What truly distinguishes a person? Elitism on the basis of education is rampant in society, and it can be experienced in the feeling of degradation that is conveyed in the use of the term 'village bumpkins' (or *gawar*) or in the way people are looked upon when they fit into the classification of 'illiterates'.

In principle, a judgmental disposition is always wrong, and therefore, the looking-down-upon attitude of those who interact with village dwellers must not be encouraged or patronized. However, the plight of these two categories of people—village dwellers and illiterates—does signify some deficiencies, and it is important to be objective about it. What deficiencies do these two classes of people truly signify?

For example, a certain brain is exposed to the intricacies of flying (driving) a plane. *Good.* The concerned person will earn relatively more money. *Yes, surely.* He will live in a big house. *Maybe.* He will be globetrotting. *That's part of the job.* The question is why should this particular brain be considered more exalted just because it has learned the intricacies of making a plane take off and land rather than having learned the intricacies of a lesser profession—making fantastic shoes, for instance. (Abraham Lincoln's father was an outstanding shoe maker.) The answer is that in today's capitalist economy, it is education and training which decide matters of prestige and authority. Ultimately, the level to which an employee is educated decides if he can or cannot generate cash or other equivalents for his employers. But if we allow for the fact that brains are different merely because they have been given a different set of inputs, it becomes evident that there is an inherent equality. A certain brain (pilot) has been trained to fit a certain role. That is the objective truth. That is, a 'village bumpkin' will have known as much as anybody else had he grown up in a town. His handicap is technical; it is just about insufficient information (or better still, insufficient data) being fed into his brain.

Similarly, the difference between literacy and illiteracy lies in people having or not having, respectively, an additional channel for communication and exchange of ideas. This naturally and unfortunately puts the illiterate at a relative disadvantage; it reduces the amount of knowledge exchanged by him with society (especially in the information world). It is detrimental to his welfare in the capitalist order.

In any case, is it appropriate to equate an illiterate to a 'zero'?

There are other dimensions of life in which the simpleton may be very highly educated; he may have high EQ and SQ. And it is very much possible that his brain may be doing extremely well with the things he needs to handle in his day-to-day life. He may be living in a hut, but he might be living a contented life. He may not know scratch about reading and writing, but he might possibly talk to a child with his eyes. In other words, scholarship and literacy are not the only means by which the worth of an individual may be measured; in fact, these may not necessarily be appropriate indices to estimate the worth of individuals. The ancients have known that the ability to live one's life to the fullest is a better indication of class. Instead of using 'scholarship'-based indices, one may use those based on wisdom—which have a lot to do with having the right spirit and attitude.

In fact, mannerisms and value systems can be one of the other indices on which people can be valued; these too are learned and not inborn, but they are more basic and universal. Value systems have a great impact on individuals' relationships and on their excellence at whatever they do. It will decide whether they will happily sail through life or grind through it. Therefore, 'which individual has a better value system in the sense that it reflects in his excellence in responding to situations' is a more valuable issue to focus upon—if at all there is a need to make a comparison.

This does not mean that there is no merit in high academic scholarship. What can be appreciated in a person of high learning (or scholarship) is the hard work that must have gone behind the efforts of grooming him—by himself or his caretakers. One can also appreciate the dedication the person might have had for the pursuit of knowledge. That is, the educated man is appreciated because he represents dogged effort and dedication, rather than merely because he is schooled in the three R's.

The sum total is that from the ancients' perspective, it is not important as to whether a certain mind is trained for this task or that task; it is more important to see whether the mind is trained to do tasks well. That is, it is important to check whether an individual has achieved excellence with reference to his 'own task', whatever that task may be.

As for people demanding status on account of knowing the English language, it may be considered an absurdity. Language is a means of communication. It is a plate on which one offers his interactions to others. Whether the plate is made of gold, silver or wood is not important. The more important questions are: 'What is on the plate that is being offered?' and 'Is the plate being offered in a cultured manner?'

Take an outstanding English-speaking TV anchor, for instance. When a person grows up in a family or an environment in which people speak English, the chances are that he will become an expert at that language. The person will be better able to convert thoughts into words and vice versa when communicating in that language. But it is not this that distinguishes him. It is important that the person be a yogi while performing—in the sense that he needs to be focused on the task at hand. He needs to be in the present, in the now. He needs to be alert. He needs to be prepared with the subject on hand. In fact, what is more important is whether the anchor has a detached disposition, humble mannerisms and enthusiasm and excellence for the task at hand. If these things are taken care of, then he turns out to be an excellent anchor. But all these things are not directly related to knowing or not knowing a particular language.

Summing it all up, as far as exalted self-perception owing to high scholarship is concerned, Ferely Taylor aptly points out, 'To be proud of learning is the greatest ignorance.'

This is a truth known to wise men from time immemorial. Completeness in education is achieved only when one experiences a humble disposition despite great achievements; and this, in turn, indicates that he is fit and ready (alert) for even more achievements.

Primacy of wisdom in an individual's pursuit of education: Giving preference to wisdom leads to a different perspective from the point of view of the student. Formal education is commonly linked to the idea of 'happiness through wealth, fame and fortune'. In the best of param vidya traditions however, education is supposed to be connected directly with happiness. Wealth, fame and fortune are additional consequences, a bonus. Instead of thinking that education is primarily meant to satisfy one's consumer priorities, the advice is that it must rather be thought of as the primary means to understand the importance of the values contained in the option of simple living and high thinking. It is supposed to reveal to the student how to delight even in austerity and sacrifice and to teach him to be happy in spite of plentiful material goods. It is supposed to teach him that life is not about surviving amidst scarcity where there is a constant urge to gulp more and possess more. Instead, he must know to live in the virtue of plenty, to life's best, by the moment and to the full.

Now, does that take away the motive that drives entrepreneurship and earning? If people are not driven to possess more, how will they participate in the capitalist order and excel? The answer is that an alternative motive will drive the system; it will be the motive of taking responsibility. It will be the motive of doing one's dharma and of the pursuit of excellence. And this is expected to result in an output of better quality.

Since playing a role in society effectively involves 'earning', education will surely cater to that too. But it will ensure that for a successful student, money may be the aim but never the preferred motive for he will be looking for satisfaction of life goals. In fact, earning will have the attached moral responsibility or dharma of proportionate re-investment and sponsorship of benevolent activities. That sense of responsibility is important.

Indian learning defines four motives for action in man: kama (satisfying the senses), artha (urge to material prosperity and status), dharma (seeking the rule of law, peace and justice) and moksha (seeking self-actualization, self-realization and everlasting life). Learning must lead the student to understand that human life does not achieve fulfillment in the exclusive pursuit of the former two motives alone. Rather, it is the pursuit of the latter two that leads to completeness in man; and this takes care of the objects of the former two motives as well.

The education system tuned to a higher purpose: Therefore, when it comes to designing education systems, planners must ensure that the core priority must be a fulfilling life—beyond material motives, beyond the minimum of having a sense of security and beyond physical contentment. In this, the students must be prodded to let go of their egos and their physical identities and encouraged to get a deeper understanding of their essential natures. In motivation-theory jargon, we may say that there is a need for the education system to focus students on to the 'motivating' factors instead of 'hygiene' factors—of Herzberg's theory. Or, we can alternatively say that the pursuit of self-actualization should be the

primary concern of society and education and not the pursuit of base needs—of Maslow's theory.

Education must not restrict itself to becoming merely an entry ticket or an eligibility criterion for jobs in the rigorous fashion that it does today. Education must be based on both param vidya, learning pertaining to the divine nature of man, and aparam vidya—the rest of it. As far as education related to personality development is concerned, param vidya must become an important and necessary component of it.

And while this new thrust is initiated, knowledge about the world surrounding humans must be transferred to students in the institutions of learning, as is usual today—in the pursuit of aparam vidya. The usual aims of education must all be in place. It must increase the proficiency level of the entire population. Basic skills have to be imparted to all members of society so that each individual has adequate confidence in his ability to easily find livelihood in the existing system. He must have enough inbuilt strength, entrepreneurship abilities and knowhow if he must pursue monetary success—if he finds that it is needed for him. Education must be made as universal as possible so that nobody is denied access to a livelihood on account of lack of education. But that apart, the true calling of education must be about lifting the consciousness of humanity.

Education must be a process that gravitates from merely producing human inputs for various institutions to acting as a process that lifts a civilization to contentment and happiness.

Expanding the definition of education to include all learning processes in human interaction: From the arguments above, it becomes clear that an important lacuna of modern education lies in the limitation of its very definition. For example, to the question, 'Who is responsible for education?', the answer which one generally gets to hear is 'Schools', 'Colleges', 'Government' or 'Universities'. Definitely, something along these lines… This limits the definition of education to something that is delivered by certain formal institutions set up by the state. The truth is that education is much more than that.

Education must be considered as a phenomenon linking two generations. Education ought to include even those interactions that may take place in helping a visitor with directions in a new city or giving an offhand suggestion when a little boy is struggling to tie his shoelaces. Looking at education in this way will also mean that each and every individual is responsible for education and is constantly at the giving or receiving end of education. It is a process that extends all through life.

On the surface, this idea may sound ridiculous or trifling, but the genius of the ancient Indian masters lies in tapping into the potential of this definition and using the scope it provides to convey important lessons that are relevant to the life of the average citizen. In fact, that holistic vision used by the ancient Indian seers continues to be relevant to this day.

In due course of this chapter, we will look into various aspects of this widened scope of education which the ancients used. But before we get to that, let us place on record the advantages of using the ideas of this alternate system. That vision held by the ancients happens to be a suitable reference point to make plans today because of the following reasons:

➤ The system is comprehensive and carefully designed.

➤ The elements of Indian indigenous culture find fulfillment in it alone.

➤ Its negative traits are not non-correctable.

➤ Its use does not contradict the use of modern methods in any substantial way. Rather, it improves on what the moderns have.

➤ The void of value education can be effectively filled by widening the definition.

In what follows, we will explore the possibility of using the wider definition of education as used by past masters of India.

Specialized institutions catering education: Many forums have roles to play. Every section of society is involved. However, broadly speaking, there will be specialization in education. Institutions built primarily for education will continue to find a prominent place in the setup. These can be categorized into five major groups.

1) *The formal schools:* Most of the existing institutions will continue. Among the formal ones, institutions like the education department of the state, universities and associated colleges (professional and non-professional), institutions and boards catering to primary education, institutes based on industrial training and training for commercial activities will continue to play an important role. However, they must adjust to suit the wisdom-based outlook.

2) *The informal arrangements:* Among the informal ones are apprenticeship, on-job training, public utilities like libraries, museums, planetariums etc., public interest messages, literacy campaigns, training camps and seminars organized by both government organs and NGOs and the fourth estate. There are several private institutions as well. Some of them are commercial, and others are non-profit, welfare-oriented ones dealing with the sciences or metaphysics even. The motivation for running these spring from a wide possible spectrum of interests ranging from the austere to the selfish. It is important that these institutions also need to factor in matters related to attitude wherever they can.

3) *Research-based institutions:* R&D potential within and outside the formal education process will continue to be tapped into so that learning through discoveries continues and so that there is constant upgrading of knowledge.

4) *Panchayati swaraj institutions:* With regard to panchayati swaraj, there are two important channels that need to grow in strength. One is the participatory method of learning where novices are trained in politics, administration, judiciary, etc. through their involvement in grassroots-level institutions. The average citizen, through close association with formal institutions and through closely watching the local political processes in the immediate vicinity, will also have his civic sense sharpened. The other channel related to panchayati swaraj is the method of certification. This emerges from an elaborate system of training and examination which is related to imparting skills that are required for running grassroots-level processes in villages. (Refer to the Panchayati Swaraj part for details; Part 2, Section 5.2.) In this, a formal structure for granting

eligibility for holding office at the grassroots level is to be introduced. Such an eligibility criterion is, of course, based on a requirement of practical knowledge so that they can handle day-to-day responsibilities in village-based institutions. (e.g., certified bio-gas mechanic, certified kho kho coach)

5) *Traditional arrangements:* Education can also be transmitted through the following means:

➢ Traditions used in families and communities

➢ Scripture-based institutions like epics, puranas and folk tales

➢ Religious/spiritual organizations having a wide spectrum of institutions that disseminate skills and techniques for a better life, along with knowledge about the human self

➢ Arts- and sports-based institutions

All these can carry education-based responsibilities both in substantial measure and to great effect too. It will all get integrated into a complete system that should meet the requirements of a sustained civilization.

How a broader definition of education will affect some institutions:

a. Formal education: Basic formal education today consists of starting off a child with an introduction to a wide spectrum of fundamentals in various subjects till he is around 15 years of age. It is then followed up in the higher levels by an initiation into one or the other specific branch of study, which caters to a chosen career. This factor will remain undisturbed, probably upgraded continuously and mellowed down a bit to make it easy for the children; but two other important dimensions of education will have greater stress laid on them in this process:

➢ The param vidya aspect (secular but spiritual)

➢ Education that has applicability and usefulness in day-to-day life

We have already seen the former in the beginning of the essay. The latter content refers to the information a student must imbibe in him regarding the various branches of the overall socio-political-economic system in which he lives. The knowledge will be something which we can call 'application-oriented, common-sensical, awareness-based, popular knowledge' as opposed to merely 'textbook knowledge'. The aim of such education should be to spread knowledge about techniques, methods, the system, technology and better living standards, all of which have a direct bearing on the student's economic, social and civic life.

Average institutions focus almost wholly on getting students to mug up for exams. The better ones are not exclusively rigorous on examinations; rather, they consider it their primary duty to be imparting learning on the three R's. But even this is inadequate. An institution must not find its exultation in merely producing results in the knowledge sphere.

Education must be a delightful pursuit of awareness of the ways of nature while simultaneously upholding the competitive edge that has to do with performance in exams. Institutions must lay increased stress on matters pertaining to students' attitudes. The learning in schools must stimulate allegiance to dharma. The schools may need to incorporate learning with respect to the yogas of karma and gnyan.

Speaking in more familiar terminology, today's educational institutions must strengthen constructive and essential outlooks of individuals like mathematical accuracy, scientific pursuit of truth, a balanced sense of historicity, good civic sense, awareness of the requirement of communication skills, giving importance to interpersonal relationships, developing a holistic world view, having non-caviling attitudes, developing an appreciation for wisdom, cultivating an aesthetic sense, having special and demonstrated regard for courage and bravery, reveling in the pursuit of excellence and having a high sense of sacrifice. The idea is to raise the level of education in an institution from merely giving information to realizing these facets in children so that they are better prepared to tackle life.

Needless to say, these matters lie predominantly in the domain of cultures and family traditions. But surely, institutions dealing with formal education can include important inputs in this regard too. In this area, the role of the teacher will gain great importance.

Syllabus: To date, at the primary and secondary levels, the content of the syllabus is reasonably well-defined but it needs scaling down in order to accommodate some subjects which are directly relevant to day-to-day life in the corresponding geographical locality. In addition, there must emerge a well-defined list of characteristics (aims or targets, if one may say so) in the domain of attitudes, derived by educationists and spiritual persons of repute, which will have to be groomed in students. We have just seen what this could be like in the last but one paragraph. The course should be so designed, and the teaching process so sensitized, that the teacher targets a positive attitude, diligent participation, ability for concentration and other such well-defined aims in the student instead of merely feeding the student with data and having him examined. In fact, the set of such attitudes aimed at will characterize a particular school.

The schools must have the ability to carry out a proper personality analysis of the students, and on that basis, it must be capable of giving inputs to the students to improve their attitudes, character and outlook. There is no doubt that such an approach will be tapping into the latest techniques in psychology and mind science. But to those conversant with the right combination of spirituality-based techniques and methods, these things should be a cakewalk. With proper appreciation of secular truths in religion, like the different methods of yoga (raj yoga, karma yoga, etc.) and the use of culture and sports, much can be achieved with sufficient support from parents and the community in general. Due honor to the wise must be ensured.

This, of course, calls for very high levels of awareness in teachers. The very soul of the teaching faculty should rise. The best people from society have to teach, and this is possible only in societies where simple living and high thinking is a way of life. Distinguished persons who have retired from active service life should take active part in the education process of the future generations. It can be remembered in this context that in one stage in ancient India, life was institutionalized into four stages or ashrams viz. childhood/youth, married life, forest dwelling and *sanyas* (renunciation). Of these, the last two had much to do with studies—spiritual and otherwise. Particularly so was *vanaprastha* ashram, which had a lot of exploration about 'the self' in it. One may not want to replicate it today exactly as it was, but we can definitely accept the approach that useful time can be spent on educational pursuits, especially of the spiritual kind. Both learning and teaching have to be engaged with in the later stages of one's life. This can lift the quality of education to higher levels.

Ultimately, a school needs to be evaluated against a scale so as to determine how well it performs in as far as these considerations go. Perhaps quantitative estimates cannot be readily made in metaphysical matters. But it can be left to time to see if the required indices for standards emerge. In any case, assessment in this field will be rather informal, and any form of assessment will be made by local communities, parents, guardians and teachers themselves out of their own civic sense and wisdom. This, in turn, is subject to finding out the actual definition of the term 'wise' and to paying due tribute to those specified in this category.

The parents are up to this task anyway, only that a little lesser stress needs be laid on pass percentage and score percentiles while a lot more thought must be given to the param vidya dimension of grooming that is happening in the school.

b. Families and communities: Both these categories have this element of close living. People meet each other day in and day out, and it becomes a major channel for exchange of information and learning. In both cases, attitudes get triggered or transferred involuntarily. Motivation levels and targets get defined here. Standards for achievement also get involuntarily defined. Therefore, it becomes necessary that both the forums receive proper attention from the members of these units themselves and from those who bear responsibilities in higher administration in the nation so that the quality of what transpires here is top class.

For a child, the learning within a family can be, to say the least, phenomenal. Even Manu, who is attributed with having laid the cornerstone for the caste structure in Indian society, claims that all men are born equal. He indirectly means that even the drastic differences in castes have their origin in the training that they receive as children. Indeed, it is now an established fact that a child learns in his mother's womb. And there is a lot he picks up in the early stages of his life too, even before he goes anywhere near a school. The quality of what goes in at these stages has a drastic impact on his abilities and in his bearing way later in life. Most psychological theorists confirm that the initial years decide, in large measure, the personality of a person.

Good families and good family traditions are bases for building up merit in individuals. Families should be crucibles of the best of ideals. Such idealism should be both enhanced and honored, and the other channels of education (wherever possible) should be well-tuned to fill up any voids left by families and communities. But primacy needs to be accorded to families and communities.

What cannot be done within a family should be taken up by institutions at the inter-family level. A peep into any traditional indigenous culture in any place will give ample evidence of factors that cater to such a kind of education at both the family and community levels. Interestingly, even the modern scientific community of the global village and communities of various important nations and regions in the modern world have their own ways and means of ensuring such strengths to the oncoming generations. One can consider, for instance, how an American parent teaches his child the ways of the world of money, be it profit and loss, savings, self-reliance, etc.

As for neighborhood communities, the local leadership must facilitate such activities which will give the requisite atmosphere for the proper all-round development of its members. The highest of ideals and tapping into the fullest of their potentials should be the primary goal in all their endeavors. Families and communities must fall back on the wise to guide them—this is important. It can be considered as seeking to build foundations on rock rather than sand.

c. Participatory political/civic forums need to be optimally designed: At each opportunity in life, when an individual gets to hold positions of responsibility, he learns the tricks of the trade—ways to get in, ways to hold on to power, how to handle money, responsibility, etc. Educated with such ideas, if he feels himself up to the task, he targets the ultimate political forum—the national or state cabinet. So, the output that is seen in the parliament is the end product of this process of education that exists at the bottom.

Now, if the quality of the parliament needs to be improved, then the inputs need to go in at the level of the local bodies down below where the necessary training of attitudes takes place. The forums down under need to be based on democratic empowerment as against democratic rule. There should be representative forums of various kinds at the village and taluka level, be it based on sports and arts, politics, the judiciary, the executive or even a task force looking into some specific problem or development project. These forums must have a down-up bearing with a facility for continuous assessment by the common man. These offices must be patterned roughly to mimic the methods used in government processes and systems at higher levels ending in the parliament.

These grassroots-level forums, with an aim to also be useful in training citizens, must be designed such that they lead to the following results:

➢ Education of the general public on the ways of the system so that they learn to identify the best possible candidates for a particular office.

➢ Inculcation of ability in the general public so that they can assess continuously the quality of functioning of the representatives and political parties.

If the so-designed training at this level stimulates the citizen to adhere to the truth, if it stresses on a high level of integrity and if the element of dharma is properly instilled in it, then it is imperative that personnel of high integrity will eventually rise up to take up positions of power at the highest levels. Therefore, seeing the importance to the nation, and when there is still scope for designing socio-political-economic systems at the lowest levels, the said institutions should be designed with great care.

Participation in such institutions also offers scope in improving an individual's personality. It helps in the process of self-discovery. The general impression today is that people contest elections to enjoy the perks of the position held. Indian ethics put it differently as follows:

➢ First of all it is said that a wise man knows that the pleasure of holding positions has nothing to do with happiness by itself.

➤ Second, his approach to work is one of keeping himself busy with activity just as those who work with the motive of attachment, else it will destabilize them (*Bhagavad Gita*).

➤ Third, he wants the 'beings' to live in peace— *shanti, shanti, shanti* (peace within, peace in society, peace in the elements).

One can easily see from the *Ramayana* that holding authority can even be looked upon as a burdensome responsibility at the cost of what is dear to oneself. (According to the constitution of his time, being the eldest son, he was obliged to rule, but occupying the king's position asked for him to distance himself from his wife; so, he lost the company of his trusted beloved in the line of duty.) In fact, there is a lot about this in the epics, legends, scriptures and folk tales, and these can be best understood only after one has a good grasp of the issues involved in the positions of office.

Therefore, participation in the political process must be encouraged not for the perks but for the sake of dharma—the fourfold duty that a citizen has toward society—and for bettering oneself in the pursuit of administrative excellence.

It is clear that these grassroots-level forums form a remarkably underused mode of education today. In fact, without proper attention to the education process involved here, society manages to achieve the opposite of what it seeks to achieve as far as effective administration goes.

d. Rural certification: This has something to do with according eligibility to citizens for holding posts at grassroots-level forums. The primary aim, though, is the dissemination of information, literacy, knowledge of an enhanced standard of living and empowerment, all of which will improve the standard of living in the rural areas.

In this regard, it is necessary to build up a knowledge base which is a repository of all inputs required for improving the quality of life in the villages. Having built up such a collection of information,

➤ The subjects must be such that all facets of life in a village, inclusive of those induced by its geographical constraints, are taken care of. For example, electricity maintenance, machine maintenance, judge eligibility, bio-gas, accounts, water management, environment management, livestock maintenance, waste management, fertilizers and pesticides, basic health, etc.

➤ The knowledge will be subjected to continuous upgrading in order to keep abreast with the latest developments.

➤ The totality of knowledge must be divided into syllabi of the various subjects with well-graded levels.

➤ Semi-formal education will be carried out from this database.

➤ The gradation must be such that there is a level right from literacy in that particular field up to the highest specialization.

➤ Examinations will be held, and certificates will be granted.

➤ Within maybe about ten years of its implementation, only those holding the requisite certificates will be eligible to hold positions of authority within villages.

➤ Further, each village will have to produce a requisite minimum of certificates in the various subjects to qualify as 'free villages'. (These last two points are pressure points to encourage the village communities to patronize learning and accelerate their development.)

It seems possible that universities or district-level bodies will take up the responsibilities of knowledge-base-building and certification. However, a better option seems to be in the establishment of an autonomous body under the U. P. S. C., S. P. S. C. or the panchayati raj ministry, which, in the manner of the usual entrance exams, will conduct exams and issue certificates.

➤ It will be left to individuals to learn out of their own initiative.

➤ Infrastructure for supplementing self-study will have to be built up.

➤ The entire process should preferably be regionalized in such a manner that the process of examination is conducted and certificates are given at each district headquarters.

➤ Only authorization, regulation and auditing should come from the higher levels.

➤ Novel methods based on computerization, new techniques and subject-specific techniques can be tried out in the examination process, and an ideal solution that will best meet self-rule goals can be worked out. (Maybe something to do with practicals, an examination of the approach rather than the answer, random computerized testing or instant certification…)

As years go by, the level of difficulty of the subjects will increase till such a time when the specialization is abreast with the latest awareness from around the world. Having attained this, hopefully, the issues confronting the villages will be effectively handled at the roots itself.

Finally, in this context, it is rather vital to revisit the idea that prejudices based on illiteracy can be very harmful. Education must be carried out with the view that one is dealing with potential geniuses, whether they are literate or not.

e. The government: Continuing in its present role, the government will naturally be a catalyst and support for much of the aparam vidya-based education and that too in the best of secular traditions. But it will also play an important role in stimulating activities connected with sports and culture, which will go a long way in building up the moral fiber of the nation. Hopefully, it should adopt a holistic view on education and provide enough leverage and space for the parallel process of education to continue unhindered, in spite of not being assisted by itself. Education, in its totality, will require inputs in terms of infrastructure required, which the government will have to provide at least to some extent when heavy investments are required.

f. Spiritual organizations and sports/arts forums: Both these have roles to play. As for the religious institutions, it has been dealt with in great detail in the Return to an Ancient and Glorious Tryst (Part 1). It will suffice to say here that they must all uphold the ideal of *vasudaivakutumbakam* (World is one family), and the rest will fall in place. As for the role of sports and arts forums, it has been dealt with in the previous chapter dealing with arts and sports.

Dare to stand by indigenous legacy – Formal education needs to be supplemented with indigenous inputs: While finally deciding a course of action to pursue, it is important to realize that ditto-copying of systems is impossible and futile. But sadly, this is continuously being attempted. A major feature of modern education is its attempt to standardize and universalize education into something that the modern world is very familiar with. The thrust is, in a way, well-placed because the system of education took root in Europe; it is the scientific civilization, born in Europe, which has proved its mettle in comparison with other local cultures. But this idea cannot be stretched too far.

One needs to remember that in local cultures, complete lifestyles have evolved over many centuries. These cultures are defined by geographical, ethnic, social, religious and other specifications. Each of these cultures has many elements that characterize it, and it is impossible that all the facets of the target population may be adequately addressed by a one-fit-for-all kind of education system. In fact, many facets of European culture will remain undefined or un-reckoned in the original education arrangement in Europe. Thus, even if the European system of education is perfectly replicated in another culture, the entire content of learning present in European society will not get transferred to the target population. We can understand this from the fact that education has a wider definition, as we have seen. In fact, if an education system has the ability to transfer the contents of one civilization to the other exactly as is, then the target population will become a clone of European society.

There is a need for giving primacy to the local cultures; local cultures need to be adequately guarded and protected. Local cultures which have stood the test of time (for millennia in the Indian case), in most likelihood, will eventually come into their own after benefiting from the scientific attitude.

Keeping this in mind, it will be prudent if planners allow indigenous cultures to coexist and flourish. In fact, modern education must help indigenous learning mold itself in a manner such that both will flourish.

Section X

Media Can Help Raise the Level of Consciousness

Challenging times for the fourth pillar of democracy: At the present moment, the media world is in great chaos. The technological progress made through computers, hand-held devices, artificial intelligence and digital communication is spurring on great change. All this is, in a way, democratizing the intellectual public space. It is making established insiders in the media reassess their strategies and approaches. Business models, distribution strategies, viewership assessment, readership enhancement, content management and a host of such things related to the industry are being looked into innovatively in revolutionary terms.

Another dimension of the challenge comes to media through the coupling of democracy and liberalized capitalism. Each media house has to survive as a commercial enterprise in a capitalist workspace. This would mean that a media house must have its share of advertisements, juicy stories, resources, unhindered distribution mechanism and the like to remain relevant and profitable. This naturally makes the media houses both dependent and vulnerable. Media houses and media persons face immense challenges in their attempts at preserving their idealism in the face of commercial and political forces who try to compel otherwise. And while there are teams and individuals who continue to struggle to maintain their credibility, there are others who have accepted compromises.

There are textbooks and courses in journalism that speak about the right approach for a journalist. There are lessons about presenting balanced views, conducting interviews, giving news without a biased view, giving views based on hard data and the like, which the members of the media are generally schooled in. Surely, there would be good references to values as well. Many lessons about maintaining credibility and playing a constructive role in society are even openly discussed in public forums. Besides this, the people from the media learn the tricks of the trade in the course of their service. The good lessons they learn, the conviction they develop in those lessons and the situations they encounter will, in totality, determine their course of action as they perform their respective roles in the media.

Dharma perspective on media values: What does the dharma perspective, which we have reckoned in the earlier part of the book, have to say in this context? What are the lessons to the media from ancient wisdom regarding the way media must function? What is the perspective of the inner spirit (or the Highest Ideal known to man) with regard to media?

The importance of media in the present context cannot be understated. Experts have called it the fourth pillar of democracy on par with the three wings of the government—legislature, executive and judiciary. In other words, the experts say that for a democracy to function, this pillar must be strong. If this pillar is compromised, democracy is certainly weakened. And if the damage to the pillar is severe, there is a possibility that democracy will fail.

Democracy is the choice of the Indian nation's founding elders. They chose democracy as the political arrangement for free India and encoded that into the constitution. As a result, democracy emerges as a necessary component of the present-day dharma. Therefore, if democracy is dharma and media is a vital pillar for its support, then it enjoins a duty/dharma to society to uphold that pillar in pristine shape. Any step taken toward adding strength to this pillar of democracy is dharma, and any movement in the opposite direction is adharma. This means that professionals in media must reach out for the highest journalistic idealism in their pursuit of performing their roles in society. Drawing a parallel from the *Mahabharata*, we can say that just as it was Arjuna's dharma to fight, it is the media person's dharma to write (or represent) in the pursuit of highest welfare to all humanity. Lord Krishna would therefore suggest to the personnel in the media that the path to their attaining the highest goal lies in their excelling at media work.

> *3:34 In respect of each of the senses, attachments and aversions to objects are fixed. One should not come under their sway, for they are impediments in one's way.*
>
> *3:35 Better is one's own duty, though defective, than another's duty well performed. Death in one's own duty is better; the duty of another is fraught with fear.*
>
> Bhagavad Gita
> *Translated by Swami Vireshvarananda*

The *Bhagavad Gita* therefore reveals that the call of dharma is to focus on one's own work and duty above all else—to do such media work that sustains a great democracy. It means that when material enrichments and personal welfare are placed in juxtaposition to his duty, it is not his rights that he should be bothered about, but his duties instead. He must be bothered about doing his work in media the way the best in media have done in the past and in accordance with what has been taught to him in the best of journalism schools. In the same light, compromises on his credibility as a media person 1) for the sake of favoring someone who is his friend, 2) for someone who has paid him money or 3) in fear of harm coming to him is adharma. Therefore, a media house that favors one group or the other while deviating from its primary role as a credible component of the fourth pillar of democracy reduces itself to a propaganda machine. In as far as it does, it ceases to be a dharmic media house anymore.

On the same lines, one can deal with the question of conducting debates. A debate conducted by a judge, a referee, a speaker of a house, a presiding officer or a presenter (of both sides) happens best when the said middle man does not participate in the debate and/or takes sides according to his own inclinations and sticks to his task. His primary role is to maintain the decorum of the forum. His excellence is measured in the manner in which he conducts the debate—that is his duty. If he does his job right, the higher purpose of the debate gets fulfilled. And therefore, his role as a facilitator in the debate calls on him not to participate. In some of the related forums, he does get to make presidential remarks at the end. In some others, he may be called to also give a decision at the end in which he can 1) give his own personal views on the subject, 2) declare which topic won the day in his view and 3) state who debated well. But participating in the debate even as it goes on is a violation of his role of a judge or a referee. Though one may be inclined to hold one point of view or the other as correct 'in all truth and wisdom' because he believes it, the net result is that his participation in the debate creates an unfair platform, and that destroys the value of the entire debate itself. This, we may see, is a microcosmic validation of the passage from the *Bhagavad Gita* that we just saw. Or in other words, all parts of a system must play their roles. Only then will the total system work. And since that total system, when in operation, is conducive to dharma, an individual playing a role must seek to excel in his work alone. Therefore, in principle, the overall dharma is served in each one doing his own duty to the best of his ability. The media too must adhere to its duties as is ordained and must find excellence in this alone.

Facilitating the media to be dharmic: The media must be an effective entity in the democratic scheme of things. For this to happen, it is also incumbent on statesmen and thinkers who vouch for democracy to ensure that the space created for the media must be conducive to free and fair journalism. Just as in education, medicine and law, here too, those with money presently get to control the idealism of the service. To counter this, it is important to build into the systemic framework certain defense mechanisms so that the idealism of the media services is protected and so that it does not become subservient to other forces. In the case of medicine and law, we saw how one way out is to create counter services. In media, one can crowdsource funds as in digital media. Another is the method used in the United States where a degree of autonomy is built up through public funds. The BBC model also offers autonomy (though, of course, the channel is itself not entirely free from prejudices). Yet another option is, of course, that of increasing subscription fees so that one does not have to be dependent on advertisements. Maybe, in addition to these solutions, some other innovative possibilities may arise. However, nothing can beat the alertness of the informed citizen who is aware as to which entity in the media world is 'compromised' and which one is 'dharmic'.

Raising the quality of debate in the various institutions of the nation: A task needs to be taken up in the nation which is vital for its prosperity, and the media has a huge role to play in it. Discussions and debates are fundamental in all human interactions at all levels. The interactions in the parliament, the universities and the media are highly visible ones, and the debates here have great impact. These debates must be peppered with wisdom, humor, cordiality, compassion, reason and must have certain nobility in it. If that happens, then the job gets done better in each case, and the overall environment becomes better for every citizen.

While these three forums are particularly visible, there are numerous other less visible ones like teacher-student interactions and interactions between friends, within families, between citizens and government offices and between strangers, which are all no less important. These form a continuum with the three we reckoned earlier. In their totality, all these interactions reflect the health of a nation, society and individuals—it reflects mutual wellbeing. To ensure that these interactions are of great quality, it is important to raise the level of consciousness in discussions and debates.

The media, which is the mainstay of public interaction/communication, has a very important role to play in raising the standard of human interaction. It can support an educative process, and the consciousness of a nation can rise as a result. To understand how this is possible, let us look at some fundamental points that have to do with attitude. We have dealt with this in another way in understanding the enemies of freedom in Part 2 of the book and in the introduction. We shall re-emphasize it in the context of media houses. These points may be considered as three important pitfalls that all humans must avoid in communication/interaction. A media house must be deeply educated and aware of these. This is because the ability to handle this has a direct bearing on its success.

The pitfalls (1) - Log in the eye syndrome: This has something to do with a 'judgmental' attitude which not only makes you judge others, but also judges you in return. In the Bible, Luke 6:42 and Matthew 7:1-5 refer to this idea.

Judge not, that you be not judged. 2 For with the judgment you pronounce you will be judged, and with the measure you use it will be measured to you. 3 Why do you see the speck that is in your brother's eye, but do not notice the log that is in your own eye? 4 Or how can you say to your brother, 'Let me take the speck out of your eye,' when there is the log in your own eye? 5 You hypocrite, first take the log out of your own eye, and then you will see clearly to take the speck out of your brother's eye.

Matthew 7:1-5
English Standard Version (ESV)

This is often interpreted very shallowly as saying that if we point fingers at someone saying that he has made so-and-so mistake, we forget that we have made so many other mistakes. It is not that. This passage is about having a negative attitude in one's head and not recognizing it. It is about a mind that seeks to sit on a chair of judgment and term some person as good and another person as bad. It is about sticking judgmental labels on one another.

The non-judgmental attitude, for instance, does not allow you to even call Hitler or Pol Pot as 'bad'. This lesson comes to us from the two great epics of India. In the *Mahabharata*, though the average reader and even most characters in the book itself look upon Duriodhan as the villain, there is a scene in which Lord Krishna (God Incarnate) treats both Duriodhan and Arjuna (a hero) on par. He gives them equal right to ask him support for their war efforts. In the *Ramayana*, while the villain is Ravan, when Ravan lies on his deathbed at the end of the war, Lord Rama (again, God Incarnate) directs his brother Lakshmana to go and learn from him since Ravan was a learned scholar. Just as Christ's last words, 'Forgive them, Father, for they know not what they do' about the people who were bleeding him to death, the message from the wise is not to harbor a judgmental attitude against any one.

"People are not 'bad'; they are helplessly driven by tendencies that compel them to act in particular ways. So help those who are helpless."

– Sirshree Tejparkhi

In the absence of such wisdom, when we think someone is bad and somebody else is good, when we find it in our heads that one person is an angel and the other is a devil and when we look at those who we label as evil, we might say, 'Why should we not condemn those "#$%@…&#$%" for what they have done?' Though it seems logical enough and justifiable, there are implications/consequences to this that one may not find desirable.

Let them alone: they be blind leaders of the blind. And if the blind lead the blind, both shall fall into the ditch.

Gospel of Matthew, 15:14
King James Version

Media houses and individuals in society often engage in this (very costly) indulgence of sitting in pulpits and calling names. It is a tendency that does not come to children, but it gets practiced as we get along in life. The result is a mentality and attitude that is not conducive to excellence and happiness. It limits a person; if a community or group adopts it, it keeps the said group away from excellence.

When a media person or a media house practices this, it impacts the attitudes of its audiences as well. Taking people away from their childlike joy and happiness riles them up. And though it may spur excitement and agitation for some time, it is the antithesis of peace-filled excellence.

When Person A shoots his judgmental attitude at B, it easily spills over to C and D and so on. The most important point is that it has already numbed the one who holds that attitude—the attitude is reflexive. If you don't forgive, you are not forgiven.

However, once you get the attitude right, solutions can be attempted with an even mind. That is, once the log, the judgmental attitude, is taken away, specks can be addressed as we saw in the quotation from Matthew 7:5 above.

The pitfalls (2) - Wild dogs:
Another attitude that one must be aware of is what Jesus Christ terms as 'wild dogs'.

"Do not give what is holy to dogs--they will only turn and attack you".

Matthew 7:6
Good News translation

It is evident that the approach of some people can be very negative and aggressive in a particular situation. In the Indian spiritual texts, this attitude may be described as acting with a 'rajasic' disposition along with a demonic resolve of not wanting to listen. To people bearing such an attitude, reasonable and holy arguments cannot be offered. There is no recourse to reason, and there is no willingness to giving space for listening. A wild dog may also be hearing but not listening. And the aim is to wait to pounce. One needs to be aware that it is pointless debating or reasoning with persons such as these.

The pitfalls (3) – Pigs:
This pitfall is almost in the same category as the previous one. Here too, the person bearing this attitude is not in a mood to listen or reason out. The difference is that the person is focused on indulgences.

"Do not throw your pearls in front of pigs--they will only trample them underfoot."

Matthew 7:6
Good News translation

The attitude is very similar to 'tamas' as described in the Indian spiritual texts. It also represents someone who is so drowned in desires that he is not able to look at reason or at what is holy. It is difficult to reason out with people who get into such a disposition because there will be no value for what is good, righteous or pious. Reason too will not work, and priorities are fixed differently.

The importance of the pitfalls in media consideration: A media house must understand these concepts in great depth. The media entity's long-time sustenance and likeability at an instinctive level by the audiences lies in getting its attitude right. Watching the news channels as of today, it looks as if the ones that are shouting the most are successful. Truth be told, successful anchors have the ability to remain 'cool' even if they have riled up everyone else. They can just laugh it off and depressurize in an instant, and this is what makes them attractive. It is somewhere hidden in the attitude of 'don't take it too serious, man'—though one may pretend to be dead serious about some topic in the 'show'.

To summarize: One must watch out for the pitfalls because

1) it improves the resonance of the concerned media with the inner nature of the audiences—unless the purpose of the media house is propaganda.

2) it is about spreading positivity and stemming negativity in the world.

3) conscious awareness of media houses of these three pitfalls helps in educating society about it.

4) public dialog is encouraged to move into the higher levels of consciousness and, hopefully, people in the parliament will get accustomed or inspired to up the level of interaction in the parliament (and universities).

5) it will also improve communications and relationships in the general public.

An excellent media can check great ills in society. It can make a democracy thrive. It can deliver great positivity and prosperity to a nation, provided it remains pristine to its dharmic role. One that does his duty regardless is the hero Indian civilization has always deeply respected.

Appendix

A: FOR THOSE WHO THINK THAT THE SPIRIT OF DHARMA IS A FANTASY

The following was circulated via e-mail. The original references are kept as they are. Hope Ha Minh Thanh will pardon the author for not taking his permission to add his letter into this book. I don't think he will. Do read on, and you will know why.

EDITOR'S note: THIS letter, written by Vietnamese immigrant Ha Minh Thanh working in Fukushima as a policeman to a friend in Vietnam, was posted on New America Media on March 19. It is a testimonial to the strength of the Japanese spirit, and an interesting slice of life near the epicenter of Japan's crisis at the Fukushima nuclear power plant. It was translated by NAM editor Andrew Lam, author of "East Eats West: Writing in Two Hemispheres." Shanghai Daily condensed it.

Brother,

How are you and your family? These last few days, everything was in chaos. When I close my eyes, I see dead bodies. When I open my eyes, I also see dead bodies.

Each one of us must work 20 hours a day, yet I wish there were 48 hours in the day, so that we could continue helping and rescuing folks.

We are without water and electricity, and food rations are near zero. We barely manage to move refugees before there are new orders to move them elsewhere.

I am currently in Fukushima, about 25 kilometers away from the nuclear power plant. I have so much to tell you that if I could write it all down, it would surely turn into a novel about human relationships and behaviors during times of crisis.

People here remain calm - their sense of dignity and proper behavior are very good - so things aren't as

bad as they could be. But given another week, I can't guarantee that things won't get to a point where we can no longer provide proper protection and order.

They are humans after all, and when hunger and thirst override dignity, well, they will do whatever they have to do. The government is trying to provide supplies by air, bringing in food and medicine, but it's like dropping a little salt into the ocean.

Brother, there was a really moving incident. It involves a little Japanese boy who taught an adult like me a lesson on how to behave like a human being.

Last night, I was sent to a little grammar school to help a charity organization distribute food to the refugees. It was a long line that snaked this way and that and I saw a little boy around 9 years old. He was wearing a T-shirt and a pair of shorts.

It was getting very cold and the boy was at the very end of the line. I was worried that by the time his turn came there wouldn't be any food left. So I spoke to him. He said he was at school when the earthquake happened. His father worked nearby and was driving to the school. The boy was on the third floor balcony when he saw the tsunami sweep his father's car away.

I asked him about his mother. He said his house is right by the beach and that his mother and little sister probably didn't make it. He turned his head and wiped his tears when I asked about his relatives.

The boy was shivering so I took off my police jacket and put it on him. That's when my bag of food ration fell out. I picked it up and gave it to him. "When it comes to your turn, they might run out of food. So here's my portion. I already ate. Why don't you eat it?"

The boy took my food and bowed. I thought he would eat it right away, but he didn't. He took the bag of food, went up to where the line ended and put it where all the food was waiting to be distributed.

I was shocked. I asked him why he didn't eat it and instead added it to the food pile. He answered: "Because I see a lot more people hungrier than I am. If I put it there, then they will distribute the food equally."

When I heard that I turned away so that people wouldn't see me cry.

A society that can produce a 9-year-old who understands the concept of sacrifice for the greater good must be a great society, a great people.

Well, a few lines to send you and your family my warm wishes. The hours of my shift have begun again.

Ha Minh Thanh

This is the stuff that heroism and legends are made of.

The wise teach us that what ultimately matters is how much one can do for others, and it is important to see as to whether this is what the culture of a nation teaches its citizens. Ha Minh Thanh testifies that this was indeed instilled in a nine-year-old in Japan. This, of course, comes from the system of values that is indigenous to Japanese culture.

But this is not the case just with the Japanese. Most successful civilizations cherish such ideals in their systems. The idealism of knighthood is a crowning glory of the British culture. In either case, it is not a question of *my* rights. It is a question of *others'* rights. It is a question of responsibilities and duties. It is a question of sacrifice.

This idealism is integral to the Indian indigenous system as well in its principles related to dharma. Even today, people live and die for this. Only if one makes the effort to notice that this is so…

No! They are not fools who live such lives. It is in giving and in sacrifices that a civilization raises. This was taught to the Indians. It is so much a part of the Indian system that it runs in the veins. It builds Indian families. It holds the nation together despite everything. The only problem is that this concept is not effectively integrated into the present public dialog.

May it be brought forth into the national life in both letter and spirit.

B: AS LITTLE AS 2.5% OF INCOME TAX CAN HELP RAISE THE QUALITY OF POLITY: A ROUGH CALCULATION

Let us check some basics first.

Q) Do political activists need resources to be effective in the political field?
A) Yes.

Q) Should politicians gain legitimacy to represent citizens in a democracy or should they be planted into positions of authority by some other means?
A) Surely, they should seek support from the average citizen in two ways:
1) By seeking their vote in order to become a representative
2) By seeking the resources which they need in order to play a political role, inclusive of fighting elections

Q) Has the idealism of political parties seeking material resources from society worked in the Indian context?
A) The result is mixed.
a) Indian idealism (as can be construed from the arrangements in the constitution and books of law) seeks leaders who will be so inspirational that the average citizen will step forward, shell out money and resources and patronize the political parties.
b) But the practical realities are that such inspirational figures are few and far between. Such resources were garnered in recent times in great quantities during the 1977 efforts of Jaiprakash Narayan and then during the early 90s on account of the Ramjanmabhoomi movement. For a brief period in 2014, the Aam Aadmi Party got funds in such a manner. The communists have a system of grassroots collection that is relatively voluntary. Apart from these, the support offered to political parties is either by force or with an intention of getting something in return.
c) There is definitely no culture of voluntary duty toward the polity in the average Indian citizen.
d) When money is hard to get through the front door, the present politicians have made it a virtue

to collect money from the back door; it is almost equal to misappropriating doles of the government and selling it in return for the resources they need to fight elections. Honesty lies in not taking any of that money for themselves and putting up that money for party activities. It has become a legitimate means by which a party survives. It has become such a habit for government freebies to be sold in return for votes too.

e) With no outstanding leaders, idealism has failed, and the present political arrangement is reduced to an unpleasant arrangement where corruption is the need to survive. But this has a catastrophic effect on society.

Q) Is there a need to temper idealism with practical props so that a working arrangement is arrived at?

A) This seems to be the best way to go. Money must be made available to politicians from the average citizen. Only then will the politician work for the average citizen. And this can be done by ensuring a culture of 'giving for politics'. Surely, no one will accept an added tax for paying politicians. Will they? But unfortunately, if the route of paying for political work is not taken, the politicians will remain as selfish as they are today. How?

Consider this. If the state does not pay for politics, the tendency is to subvert the system. So, when the state pays zero, then 50% of the development funds are used up in wrong channels. A little lesser than this from public works is taken up, and extra money (almost like tax) is collected from people who seek jobs, who want government certificates, who want government contracts… Society is made to pay through crime, corruption, general slacking of government services and incompetent leaders.

If, on the other hand, a small percentage (as much as is spent on education in India or a fraction of what is spent on the military or on the crude oil expenses of the nation) is legitimately given for politics, then the chances are that more honest persons will take up politics as a career. Hopefully, the 50% corruption (Rajiv Gandhi said 83% goes to the system) will come down to 25%. There is likely to be a general cleaning up. Politicians may not need to toe the line of huge corporate houses. People will have to pay lesser to get jobs and contracts. In other words,

chances are that the cost to society will drop to a great extent if some legitimate funds are given for politics.

All that is needed is to give up the idealism that politicians should only beg for their resources; let them beg for votes, and let them be 'given' some resources.

Q) Who decides how much is to be given to each political party?

A) Consensus will finally bring the nation around to a figure (likely to be between 0.5 and 1% of the union budget) to be spent on politics. But instead of leaving it to the state to decide who will get the money, it should be left to the taxpayer to decide to which party this amount will go. In the case where the taxpayer does not want to expose his affiliation by nominating a political party, let the money be sent to a common pool from which the election commission will shell out according to some fixed rules and past elections.

Can a system be developed around these ideas?

Check out the following calculations. They are very rough and meant to give only a sense of how it needs to work out; but the election commission can come out with precise figures and recommendations.

India has a total population is 121,00,00,000 and a total of 543 constituencies. This means it has, on an average, 22,28,360 persons per constituency. If about 65% of these people are registered voters, then it means that there are, on an average, 14,48,434 voters per Lok Sabha constituency. India has a total of 7,20,000 villages. Each constituency then has 1325 villages. 3,287,263 square kilometers is the total land area of India. This means every constituency occupies, on an average, 6053 square kilometers or a square with each side extending 78 kilometers. (These figures are large because of thinly populated regions in India, but we are just making a rough estimate.)

An average candidate must thus address a total of 14.5 lakh voters during elections. He needs to serve them too. This will include frequent visits to them, visits to the various offices of the local bodies, participating in their activities (activities of 1325 villages) and crisscross a land that extends 78 kilometers on each side.

Let us first consider the running costs. Let's presume that running an effective 'candidate' office will require a staff strength of five persons. On an average, they may be paid Rs. 20,000/- per head per month. Even if the candidate traveled to one village each day and did that for 15 days and participated in meetings of 5 days each, he will travel 78 kilometers in 20 days (from the middle, halfway up and halfway down). So, his total travel will be about 1500 kilometers per month or about Rs. 9000 at Rs. 6 per km.

Add to it some office expenses, it will amount to Rs. 1.5 lakh per potential leader per month. For someone working at the level of the assembly constituency, it will amount to one lakh rupees per month, Let us presume that there are a total of four serious candidates for each of the constituencies. Accommodating the Rajya Sabha candidates and members of legislative councils as well, we get the following figures:

1,50,000 × 4 × (543+238) = 46,86,00,000

So, for 12 months, their expenses will be Rs. 562,32,00,000.

For the assembly constituencies, the expenses will be calculated as follows: cost per constituency × number of potential candidates × average number of assembly constituencies (dividing overall population by average population of an assembly constituency which is around two lakhs)

1,00,000× 4 × 6500 × 12 = 3120,00,00,000

Adding the running expenses for the above two for the duration of one year, we arrive at a figure of approximately Rs. 3682 crores. This will be the total expenditure each year on financing four potential candidates in each constituency (parliamentary and assembly) for their running expenses.

During elections, let us consider the cost for one candidate in a parliamentary constituency.

50 volunteers for 3 months (three meals per day and transport) 10,000 × 50 × 3 = 15,00,000

5000 volunteers for 4 days (two days before elections, day of elections and one day after; three meals per day and transport) 300 × 4 × 5000 = 60,00,000

5 jeeps for 2 months at Rs. 1500 per day = 4,50,000

1 flag per 100 people, 1 pamphlet per 2 persons and 1 banner per 1000 people will amount to 14,000 flags, 7,00,000 pamphlets and 1400 banners.

At Rs. 25 per flag, Rs. 1 per pamphlet and Rs. 200 per banner, the cost will come to Rs. 3,50,000 for flags + Rs. 7,00,000 for pamphlets + Rs. 2,80,000 for banners.

Advertisements (audio, visual and video): Rs. 10,00,000

30 street corner meetings at Rs. 10,000 each = Rs. 3,00,000

5 major rallies at Rs. 10,00,000 each = Rs. 5,00,000

This adds up to approximately Rs. 83,00,000, which may be round off to Rs. 1,00,00,000.

Let us then consider the cost for one candidate in an assembly constituency. For 30 volunteers for 3 months (two meals per day and transport), 1500 volunteers for 4 days (three meals per day and transport), 3 jeeps for 2 months, flags, pamphlets, banners, advertisements (audio, visual and video) and 30 street corner meetings, it will approximately come up to Rs. 30,00,000.

Consider three serious parties in the fray. The total parliamentary election expenditure will be

453 × 1,00,00,000 × 3 = 1359 crores

Typically, an assembly constituency has about one seventh the population of a parliamentary constituency. If they will cost about a third of the expenses of a parliamentary constituency, we can fix the total expenses across the country to 7/3 times the total expenses for parliamentary expenses, or nearly double. So, we may fix the expenses for elections to assemblies at Rs. 2718 crores for the whole of India.

Therefore, the total expenses of the elections may be fixed at Rs. 4077 crores or approximately Rs. 5000 crores. Now, elections take place once in five years, and therefore, the cost per year will be 1000 crores. Therefore, for a political party, the overall charges for running in elections in each year will be 3682 + 1000= 4682 crores.

Let us consider some extra expenses—offering some help to certain deserving cases in their constituencies, support to well-wishers, expenses for modern means of communication, expenses for the travel of leaders across the country, etc. So, let us fix overall expenses on political activities per year at Rs. 10,000 crores.

Compare this with income tax (1,41,566 crores) and corporate tax (2,96,377 crores) which is a total of 4,37,943 crores. The political expenses will amount to just about 2.28% of these two taxes. Therefore, the political process, for which we have accounted above, will cost less than 2.5% of the revenues through income tax and corporate tax. Also, considering that the total revenue receipts for 2010–2011 was 11,97,396.76 crores, the political expenses will be about 0.83%. That is, the political expenses will be less than 1% of the total revenue. Note that all calculations are being made at the price levels of 2010–2011

So, what is the idea?

When an individual pays his income tax, he can also mention as to which party his political support funds should go to. So, of the taxes he pays, 2.5% will be given to that particular political party (this is not surcharge).

If he does not indicate any party, then that amount will be deposited to the election commission of India, which will calculate as to which party (based on past performance of the parties) the funds will be given.

If he says that he does not want to contribute to the political process, the money will go into the government coffers.

Similarly, 2.5% of the corporate taxes paid will be given to the party for which the investors of the factory will vote. If the corporate house does not decide the party, then it will be added into the election commission coffers for distribution to political parties according to fixed rules as in the above case. Else, it will go into the government coffers.

For a party to have eligibility to be nominated in income tax forms of individuals, it should have at least 1% of the votes cast in the previous general elections. For a party to have eligibility to receive funds from the election commission, it should be a national party, and funds will be allocated in accordance with voter percentage in the previous elections.

Justification:

1) More than this amount is being spent on politics anyway under the table.

2) When this is spent over the table, it offers an opportunity for the honest to have a fair shot at power.

3) All funds (party and elections) must be audited by independent auditors, and people must be held accountable to the law.

4) The corrupt will still be corrupt. They will use this money, make more money and use that under the table. True, but those that do not resort to corruption will have a fair shot at getting elected.

5) Election expenditure limit for candidates must be specified through a calculation that is done at each election. What should be fixed is the amount of material support that a candidate requires to be able to effectively function as a contestant for elections, and upper limits must be set by working backward. This calculation will be made by the election commission by strictly following the guidelines laid down by the parliament, and it will be declared between three and six months before each election or, alternatively, after the union budget each year, according to the current price levels.

***

Lightning Source UK Ltd.
Milton Keynes UK
UKHW051553210119
335934UK00008B/413/P